The Puerto Ricans:
An Annotated Bibliography

The Puerto Ricans:
An Annotated Bibliography

Edited by Paquita Vivó

Puerto Rican Research and Resources Center, Inc.

R.R. BOWKER COMPANY
New York & London, 1973
A Xerox Education Company

Published by R. R. Bowker Co. a Xerox Education Company
1180 Avenue of the Americas, New York, N.Y. 10036
Copyright © 1973 by Puerto Rican Research and Resources Center, Inc.
All rights reserved.
Printed and bound in the United States of America.

Library of Congress Cataloging in Publication Data
Puerto Rican Research and Resources Center.
The Puerto Ricans.
1. Puerto Rico—Bibliography. I. Vivó,
Paquita, ed. II. Title.
Z1551.P84   016.917295   73-8825
ISBN 0-8352-0663-7

Contents

Universidad Boricua—Puerto Rican Research and Resources Center, Inc., is a private, nonprofit, tax-exempt organization seeking to:

- identify, through research, the most pressing problems facing the Puerto Rican community in the United States;
- aid in the development of the resources necessary for their solution and to disseminate the gathered information to the affected population;
- establish a system of communication among Puerto Ricans and between Puerto Ricans and other minorities.

The Universidad Boricua is an institution specifically designed to provide a higher education to Puerto Ricans in the United States. It will provide access for Puerto Ricans to a greater number of professions and fields than are available to them now, and will develop curricula in new occupational fields. It will also develop and offer curricula on bilingual–bicultural education for teachers and administrators.

Preface

Four hundred and eighty years ago, in 1493, Spanish explorers came to an island, Borinquen, which was then inhabited by a people with a well-defined way of life, the Taíno Indians. Thus, Puerto Rico for more than 500 years has been accumulating a culture unique to the people of the island, expressed in their art and folkcraft, their music, their literature (written and folkloric), their history, their economic, social, educational, and political structure, their philosophical commentary, their religion. This unique culture has produced a new people of the New World. These new people, the Puerto Ricans, are the result of the commingling of three races and three cultures—the Taino Indians, the Africans brought in through the slave trade, and the Spaniards who came to colonize the island. This culture has a Spanish core and its members communicate in the Spanish language.

Puerto Ricans in the United States feel a hunger to know themselves which must be satiated, as the first step on the road toward finding the bond which unites all human beings and which is essential to a healthy group that can support and cushion its members. This bibliography can offer light to Puerto Ricans in search of their own roots and their cultural heritage. The bibliography will also serve as a resource to non-Puerto Ricans in the society who should and do want to know about their fellow citizens. Universities, colleges, research institutions, and other learned associations and individuals in the United States can find in it both a guide and an inspiration for further research.

It is the first time that an effort to present a complete bibliographic overview of Puerto Ricans has been completed and made available in English. We at the Puerto Rican Research and Resources Center, Inc., are very fortunate and would like to express well-deserved thanks to the staff team who made this bibliography a reality. For Paquita Vivó, the editor, and her chief assistant, Lourdes Miranda King, work on this bibliography was an act of love. Ms. Vivó's expectations of excellence and punctuality with deadlines extended to the entire team. Without the dedication and care of Dennis Schaefer and his perserverance and adeptness with the intricate machinery that is necessary to type a manuscript of this sort we could not have met our obligations. I know our Board of Directors, enjoying a moment of satisfaction over this accomplishment, joins me in thanking them as well as Gloria Jiménez, Luz Velasco, Julianne Hau, Suzanne McBride, and Marya Muñoz for their part in making this idea a reality.

A distinguished group of advisers made essential contributions to our work on this bibliography. The years of experience and the judgment of Dr. Ricardo Alegría, anthropologist, Director of the Institute of Puerto Rican Culture; Dr. Gordon Lewis, political scientist, professor at the College of Social Sciences, University of Puerto Rico; Dr. Arturo Morales Carrión, historian, Director, Centro de Investigaciones Históricas, University of Puerto Rico; and Dr. Luis Nieves Falcón, sociologist, previously Director of the Social Sciences Research Center of the University of Puerto Rico (now professor at Livingston College, Rutgers University), ensured that we neither ignored works whose merit demanded inclusion nor included amateurish or dangerously wanting pieces.

A special note of appreciation is included here to the National Endowment for the Humanities, the funding institution, for its support of the project. The findings and contents, however, do not necessarily represent the views of the Endowment. Dr. Herbert McArthur has a special place in our thoughts because of his encouragement and supportive role to the project.

To the readers and users of this bibliography, we at the Puerto Rican Research and Resources Center, Inc., hope that this bibliography will serve both as a source of enjoyment and as a useful tool. We will continue to bring it up-to-date with the record of our history as a people through our books, works of art, films, recordings, and any other communication technology that the future might bring.

Antonia Pantoja
Executive Director
Puerto Rican Research and
Resources Center, Inc.

Introduction

The initial selection of titles for this bibliography was based on a survey of library catalogs as well as numerous existing lists and partial bibliographies on Puerto Rico. Because of its accessibility to the bibliography staff in Washington, work commenced at the Library of Congress. The entire card catalog of the Library of Congress pertaining to Puerto Rico as well as numerous cross-references offered by the catalog were reviewed. Further searches were made under many other subject headings that are sometimes overlooked when searching materials on Puerto Rico, such as Spanish America, the Caribbean, and U.S. History—War of 1898. Also, after consulting the major dictionaries and standard reference works on the literature of the island, an extensive list of individual authors was drawn up. It was clear from this effort that a great amount of literature by Puerto Rican authors is never classified as Puerto Rican literature. Hopefully, then, librarians and researchers will find here references to many works often overlooked when the literature by or about the Puerto Ricans is being surveyed.

Besides the Library of Congress catalog, the Puerto Rican Collection at the University of Puerto Rico Library—which is undoubtedly the most complete collection on the subject of this bibliography—and the collections of the Ateneo Puertorriqueño, the Instituto de Cultura Puertorriqueña, the Centro de Investigaciones Históricas of the University of Puerto Rico, and the New York Public Library also were consulted. The selections, therefore, were compiled taking into consideration many of the existing major collections of Puerto Rican materials.

Since the bibliography was being compiled chiefly for use in the United States, the selection of titles gives preference to works in English and, when both English and Spanish versions of one work exist, it is entered under the English title with reference to the Spanish title in the entry or the annotation. But the fact that Spanish is the language most spoken and written by the Puerto Ricans is clearly evidenced by the vast number of works in this language. These include books and pamphlets on historical and cultural subjects not written about, or only superficially touched upon, in English works and, of course, literary works—criticism, essays, poetry, fiction, theatre—which are overwhelmingly written in Spanish.

It should also be pointed out that in the selection process, recent works were favored over older books on the same subject.

Careful search led to a bibliography that, although selected, is also retrospective, broad, and balanced. It is retrospective in the sense that the first known published works about Puerto Rico or by Puerto Rican authors were surveyed and included. It is also a broad bibliography, for it includes a diversity of aspects—history, culture, education, music, science, social conditions, and many others. In terms of time, it covers from the pre-Columbian era to contemporary political thought and economic development. It includes, too, the entire spectrum of thinking on Puerto Rican affairs, especially in the political field. Even works with a visible bias are included, for they help the reader to understand the various ideologies at work in the island.

The decision regarding inclusion in the bibliography, then, was chiefly governed by one condition: whether the work adds to the knowledge of Puerto Rico and the Puerto Ricans. Inclusion in the bibliography, however, does not imply recommendation of the material; it merely makes the knowledge available.

ORGANIZATION OF THE ENTRIES

To facilitate consultation, the entries have been divided into four sections. Part I includes books, pamphlets, and dissertations, divided thematically into 21 major subjects.

Part II lists government publications, subdivided into those issued by Puerto Rican government agencies and those issued by the United States federal government.

Part III includes a selected list of periodicals, plus a selection of articles from magazines and journals.

Part IV lists motion pictures and filmstrips.

INDEXES

The importance of consulting the subject index in using this bibliography cannot be overemphasized. For reasons of brevity and economy, works are entered only once. For example, a book dealing with the political development of the island, but which at the same time offers extensive information on social conditions and the present state of the economy, would be entered in the Government and Politics section, but in the index it would appear also under social conditions and economic conditions. To get a full picture of social or economic conditions, therefore, it is imperative to check those two classifications in the subject index, rather than consulting only the works listed in the Economy or Sociology sections.

For the convenience of users, title and author indexes are also included. In alphabetizing titles, the rule of disregarding the articles has been observed both in English and Spanish titles. *La Carreta*, therefore, is indexed under the letter "c". English-speaking users should also be aware that Spanish surnames are often composed of both the father's and mother's last names, e.g., Edwin Seda Bonilla. This name, therefore, appears in the index as Seda Bonilla Edwin, which is the correct Spanish form. For names with the particle "de," such as Eugenio M. de Hostos, the particle is not considered as part of the surname in indexing: Hostos, Eugenio M. de.

THE ANNOTATED ENTRIES

Books and pamphlets were inspected personally by the staff working on the bibliography in order to prepare a brief annotation stating the scope of the work and its central thesis, and whenever possible the authority or background of the author. In the case of some works, particularly those published in late 1972, it was impossible to locate copies for review before going to press. The indication "n.a." appears in those cases, in place of an annotation.

No efforts were made to assess the books and pamphlets critically, except to some extent in the case of juvenile literature. This exception is due to the fact that we feel that much of what is being offered in the United States as juvenile literature on Puerto Rico and the Puerto Ricans has little relation to the island and its people. But the children, and in some instances the teachers who receive and use the materials, often do not realize that those materials have little bearing on Puerto Rican reality. Therefore a conscious effort was made in the Juvenile Literature section to point out those instances when a book advanced misconceptions about Puerto Rico. In those cases where no Puerto Rican content was found, the book was eliminated altogether. It should be noted also that the Juvenile Literature section includes many works in Spanish that in Puerto Rico are considered juvenile literature but which in the United States might not correspond to the same grade level and could be more useful perhaps as supplementary readers for more advanced Spanish language courses, for adult education programs, or as resource materials for teachers in bilingual schools.

In the Literature section, only history and criticism, and essays include annotations. The subsections on fiction, poetry, and theatre were not annotated, although the contents of anthologies and collections are indicated in order to facilitate consultation. An annotation of a literary work written in Spanish would have involved a synopsis or a critical judgment of the work, neither of which we felt came within the scope of this bibliography. We invite users who can read Spanish to enjoy some of these Puerto Rican stories, novels, plays, and poetry themselves. An effort was made to include here not only the works of Puerto Rican writers whose literary production has been in their native Spanish, but also the works of second-generation Puerto Ricans born in the United States who write in English.

AVAILABILITY OF THE MATERIALS

In choosing works for inclusion in the bibliography, we bore in mind their availability. Availability was defined in terms of works currently in print or those that can be consulted easily through libraries in Puerto Rico and the United States. Consequently, few mimeographed or rare materials are included.

Although at first glance it would seem that many of the works included in the bibliography are not in print, a survey of current publishing activity in Puerto Rico reveals a quite different picture. A most vigorous effort toward publishing and reprinting out-of-print works has been going on in Puerto Rico for several years, a movement that has gone largely unnoticed in the library and book trade in the United States. A look at *Subject Guide to Books in Print* confirms this fact, for no works by Puerto Rican publishers are listed in this important reference work for bookstores and librarians. Besides the regular publishing efforts of the Editorial Universitaria, Editorial Cordillera, Editorial Edil, and many others, special publication programs aimed at making available out-of-print classics and works of historical value have been initiated by a number of publishers, notably Editorial Coquí and the Institute of

Puerto Rican Culture. This situation suggests the need for establishing some kind of cooperative program among Puerto Rican publishing institutions that would help disseminate and distribute such publications in the United States, rather than limiting them to the market in Puerto Rico. In the meantime, in order to help those libraries interested in increasing their holdings on Puerto Rico, a list of Puerto Rican publishers and some distributors who specialize or pay particular attention to the distribution of books in Spanish is appended. Many of them will send catalogs on request.

A special effort was made to include in this bibliography references to doctoral dissertations. Two works—*Doctoral Research on Puerto Rico and Puerto Ricans*, by Jesse J. Dossick, and *Theses on Pan American Topics Prepared by Candidates for Doctoral Degrees in Universities and Colleges in the United States and Canada*, by Frederick E. Kidder and Allen D. Bushong— survey the dissertation field from 1869 to 1966, and combined, they list more than 320 dissertations on Puerto Rico. As a result, it was decided to concentrate on dissertations submitted from 1966 until the end of 1972. Summaries of the dissertations listed can be consulted in *Dissertation Abstracts International* (prior to July 1969 known as *Dissertation Abstracts*), and microfilm or xerographic copy can be obtained, for a small fee, from University Microfilms in Ann Arbor, Michigan. The two compilations mentioned, and the dissertations included in this bibliography, together with Enid Baa's *Theses on Caribbean Topics*, will be useful in determining areas that are still wide open to researchers and investigators wishing to concentrate on Puerto Rico.

GOVERNMENT DOCUMENTS

References to Puerto Rican government publications included in this bibliography emphasize economic and social development and the basic laws and statutes of the Commonwealth of Puerto Rico. Locating and listing documents issued by the agencies of the government of the Commonwealth of Puerto Rico is a difficult task, for there is no periodical listing or catalog of such documents, nor has a complete bibliography of them ever been published. A step in the right direction is Ana R. de Alemañy's *Las publicaciones oficiales del Gobierno del Estado Libre Asociado de Puerto Rico: Bibliografía*, which to date has appeared only in a mimeographed version. We hope that the Biblioteca del Colegio Regional de Cayey continues its efforts in this direction and that an updated, even more complete bibliography along these lines will be published soon.

Regarding documents on Puerto Rico issued by the U.S. federal government, systematic investigation was limited to consulting the *Monthly Catalog, United States Government Publications* for the period from 1960 to 1972. But other important documents have been included regarding the island's relations with the United States since 1898. For a more complete analysis of United States–Puerto Rico relations from the U.S. government standpoint, researchers are advised to refer to other years of said *Catalog*, as well as to its predecessor, the *Catalogue of the Public Documents of the Congress and of all departments of the Government of the United States.*

PERIODICAL LITERATURE

Part II offers a selected list of periodicals currently published in or about Puerto Rico and some that, although no longer published, are a source of useful information. For a historic appraisal of journalism in the island, Antonio S. Pedreira's *El Periodismo en Puerto Rico* is recommended. For information on U.S. library holdings of Puerto Rican newspapers, a useful source is *Latin American Newspapers in United States Libraries: A Union List.*

The section on periodical literature also includes a selection of approximately 500 articles that have appeared in magazines and journals in Puerto Rico, the United States, and Latin America from 1960 to 1972. To compile them, the following indexes were consulted: *Reader's Guide to Periodical Literature; Social Sciences and Humanities Index; Index to Latin American Periodical Literature; Art Index;* and *Education Index.*

AUDIOVISUAL MATERIALS

Part IV includes references to motion pictures and filmstrips made in Puerto Rico and the United States touching on the island, its people, and its history. These audiovisual materials were not screened by the compilers of this bibliography, and the descriptions of the films and filmstrips are those provided in the catalogs of producers and distributors or in the Library of Congress catalog cards. The Puerto Rican Research and Resources Center expects in the future to screen and evaluate these materials in order to be able to issue, for teachers, associations, and other interested groups, a recommended list of those that can truly contribute to a better understanding of the Puerto Ricans.

It is worth mentioning that the Community Education Division of the Commonwealth Department of Education, which produced many of the Spanish films listed, is currently putting an English sound track on some of the films. Hopefully, a list of films available from them in English will be available later in 1973.

Like any effort involving selection, this first bibliography cannot expect to satisfy fully the needs of every single user. If the users want them, there will be revised editions or supplements in the future. We therefore urge them to send us their ideas and suggestions for improvement. They will be most welcome and careful consideration given to them.

This is a bibliography about one of the oldest communities in this hemisphere, a community that is relatively small in numbers if compared with other countries of the New World, but one with a rich cultural heritage of which its members are very proud. To students, librarians, writers, and others interested in learning more about Puerto Rico, we offer this evidence of that heritage.

Paquita Vivó
Editor

Abbreviations

bibl.	bibliography
bibl. refs.	bibliographical references or footnotes
c.	copyright
dept.	department
diagr(s).	diagram(s)
doc.	document
ed.	edition, editor, edición
engr(s).	engraving(s)
estab. tip.	establecimiento tipográfico
facsim(s).	facsimile(s)
Govt. Print. Off.	U.S. Government Printing Office
illus.	illustration, illustrated
impr.	imprenta, impressores
n.a.	not available
n.d.	no date (of publication)
n.p.	no place (of publication)
no.	number
núm.	número
p.	page, pages
pt(s).	part, parts
photo(s)	photograph(s)
port(s)	portrait(s)
pseud.	pseudonym
pub.	publishing
rev.	revised
ser.	series

t.	tome, tomo
tip.	tipografía, tipográfico
unp.	unpaged
v.	volume, volumen
1.	primera
2.	segunda
3.	tercera
1st	first
2d	second
3d	third
+	open entry
Jan.	January
Feb.	February
Mar.	March
Apr.	April
Aug.	August
Sept.	September
Oct.	October
Nov.	November
Dec.	December
en.	enero
feb.	febrero
mar.	marzo
abr.	abril
jun.	junio
jul.	julio
ag.	agosto
sept.	septiembre
oct.	octubre
nov.	noviembre
dic.	diciembre

Part I

Books, Pamphlets, and Dissertations (1–21)

1

BIBLIOGRAPHIES AND REFERENCE WORKS

1.1 Alemañy, Ana R. de, comp. Las Publicaciones Oficiales del Gobierno del Estado Libre Asociado de Puerto Rico: Bibliografía. Cayey, Universidad de Puerto Rico, Biblioteca del Colegio Regional de Cayey, 1968. 76 l. mimeographed.

Preliminary list of official publications of Puerto Rico, arranged by agencies. It was prepared from lists supplied by librarians of each agency and the staff of the library of the Colegio Regional. Dates of coverage and completeness of the bibliographic data vary widely from agency to agency.

1.2 Andic, Fuat, and Suphan Andic. "Special Article: An Annotated Bibliography of the Economy of Puerto Rico, 1954–1969." In HANDBOOK OF LATIN AMERICAN STUDIES, NO. 31. Gainesville, University of Florida Press, 1969. p. 574–587.

Bibliography preceded by a brief essay identifying some of the areas—inequity in income distribution, public finances, taxes and their impact on expenditures, budget in relation to economic development, etc.—that have not yet, in the authors' opinion, been the subject of systematic analysis.

1.3 ANUARIO ESTADISTICO. STATISTICAL YEARBOOK. San Juan, Junta de Planificación, Negociado de Economía y Estadística. annual.

A basic annual reference volume of economic and social statistics.

1.4 Archivo General de Puerto Rico. GUIA AL ARCHIVO GENERAL DE PUERTO RICO. San Juan, Instituto de Cultura Puertorriqueña, 1964. 167 p. illus. (Publicación, 1).

Description and survey of documentary sources at the General Archives of Puerto Rico, created by law in 1955. The records cover mostly the nineteenth and twentieth centuries.

1.5 Baa, Enid M., comp. THESES ON CA-RIBBEAN TOPICS 1778–1968. San Juan, Institute of Caribbean Studies and University of Puerto Rico Press, 1970. 146 p. (Caribbean Bibliographic Series, no. 1).

More than 1,200 entries, of which 230 concern Puerto Rico.

1.6 Bayitch, S.A. LATIN AMERICA AND THE CARIBBEAN: A BIBLIOGRAPHICAL GUIDE TO WORKS IN ENGLISH. Coral Gables, Fla., University of Miami Press, 1967. 943 p.

Includes an extensive list (p. 900–923) of books, pamphlets, and articles on Puerto Rico.

1.7 BIBLIOGRAFIA ACTUAL DEL CARIBE. CURRENT CARIBBEAN BIBLIOGRA-

PHY. v. 19. Compilada y editada por el personal de la Biblioteca Regional del Caribe. Introducción por María E.A. de Cardona. Hato Rey, P.R., Corporación de Desarrollo Económico del Caribe, Biblioteca Regional del Caribe, 1970. 259 p.

The first annual cumulative volume of this series processed by computer, a development which hopefully will mean quicker reference to comparatively current materials dealing with the entire Caribbean region. Part 1 includes classified entries; part 2 is an alphabetical index. A location code indicating the libraries known to have at least one copy of the item is a useful tool.

1.8 BIBLIOGRAFIA DE ASUNTOS JUVENILES EN PUERTO RICO. San Juan, Oficina del Gobernador, Coordinador de Asuntos Juveniles, 1966. 158 p.

Lists works published in and outside Puerto Rico between 1945 and 1965. It covers delinquency, education, the family, institutions, recreation, religion, health, and labor.

1.9 Bibliografía de Hacienda Pública. Bibliography of Public Finance. Prepared with the cooperation of Ana T. Dávila. Río Piedras, Universidad de Puerto Rico, Departamento de Economía, 1969. 110 l. mimeographed.

Lists books, pamphlets, dissertations, reports, and articles—in English and Spanish—to 1967, dealing with public finance. Many of the entries refer to Puerto Rico.

1.10 Bibliography on Puerto Rican Geology. Compiled by U. S. Geological Survey and Section of Minerology and Geology, Department of Industrial Research. [San Juan], Economic Development Administration, 1958. 14 l. mimeographed.

A useful list of books, pamphlets, reports, and articles on Puerto Rican geology, dated 1883 to 1957.

1.11 Bird, Augusto, ed. BIBLIOGRAFIA PUERTORRIQUEÑA DE FUENTES PARA INVESTIGACIONES SOCIALES, 1930–1945. Río Piedras, Centro de Investigaciones Sociales, Universidad de Puerto Rico, 1946–1947. 2 v. 547 p.

Unnumbered, unannotated bibliography of books, pamphlets, articles, and government documents. Volume 1 covers reference and general works, natural history, and health; volume 2 covers the economy, political and administrative history, culture, and history. The bibliography is presently being updated at the Social Science Research Center of the University of Puerto Rico.

1.12 Bravo, Enrique R., comp. AN ANNOTATED SELECTED PUERTO RICAN BIBLIOGRAPHY. BIBLIOGRAFIA PUERTORRIQUEÑA SELECTA Y ANOTADA. Translated by Marcial Cuevas. New York, Urban Center of Columbia University, 1972. 114 p.

An annotated, critical listing of 338 basic works, with references to some supplementary readings.

1.13 Bushong, Allen D., comp. DOCTORAL DISSERTATIONS ON PAN AMERICAN TOPICS ACCEPTED BY UNITED STATES AND CANADIAN COLLEGES AND UNIVERSITIES, 1961–1965: BIBLIOGRAPHY AND ANALYSIS. Austin, Texas, 1967. Published as a supplement to *Latin American Research Review*, v. 2, no. 2.

Sixty-one of the 950 dissertations listed in this volume pertain to Puerto Rico.

1.14 CATALOGO DE DOCUMENTOS DE LA SECCION NOVENA DEL ARCHIVO GENERAL DE INDIAS. v. 1. Prólogo de Cristóbal Bermúdez Plata. Sevilla, 1949. 822 p.

Documents of the Secretaría de Estado, which include 1,288 entries in nineteen *legajos* on Santo Domingo, Cuba, Puerto Rico, Louisiana, and Florida, dated from 1724 to 1834.

1.15 CATALOGO DE MATERIALES. Río Piedras, Universidad de Puerto Rico, Colegio de Pedagogía, Centro Audiovisual, 1971. 210 p.

Lists all the films, slides, records, and other materials, many of them on Puerto Rico, that can be found in the Audiovisual Center of the University of Puerto Rico. Materials are cataloged alphabetically by subject.

1.16 COMPENDIO DE LAS TESIS DE MAESTRIA PRESENTADAS ANTE LA

FACULTAD DEL DEPARTAMENTO DE ECONOMIA. Río Piedras, Universidad de Puerto Rico, Facultad de Ciencias Sociales, Departamento de Economía, 1970. 151 p.

Abstracts of theses presented by candidates for the degree of M.A. in economics at the University of Puerto Rico during the 1958–1969 period.

1.17 Cordasco, Francesco, Eugene Bucchioni, and Diego Castellanos. PUERTO RICANS ON THE UNITED STATES MAINLAND: A BIBLIOGRAPHY OF REPORTS, TEXTS, CRITICAL STUDIES, AND RELATED MATERIALS. Totowa, N.J., Rowman and Littlefield, 1972. 146 p.

A selected list of materials pertaining to Puerto Ricans in the United States. Particularly useful are the references to unpublished literature. A small selection of works on "the island experience" is also included.

1.18 Dávila Lanausse, José Nilo. BIBLIOTECA LEGUM PORTORICENSIS. COLLECTANEA JURIDICA; BIBLIOGRAFIA SELECTA DE PUERTO RICO, SIGLOS XIX–XX. Prólogo de Guaroa Velázquez. [San Juan], Colegio de Abogados de Puerto Rico, [1962?]. 505 p.

An excellent bibliographic source on legal matters in Puerto Rico from 1493 to 1958.

1.19 Dossick, Jesse J. DOCTORAL RESEARCH ON PUERTO RICO AND PUERTO RICANS. New York, New York University, School of Education, n.d. 34 p.

A list of 320 doctoral dissertations accepted at U. S. universities over a period of sixty-eight years to 1966, about half of them written by Puerto Ricans.

1.20 Fernández García, E., ed. EL LIBRO DE PUERTO RICO. THE BOOK OF PUERTO RICO. San Juan, El Libro Azul Pub. Co., 1923. 1,188 p. plates.

A basic source on conditions in Puerto Rico after twenty-five years of U.S. rule, plus background information on the island's history, culture, physical geography, etc.

1.21 Fernández Méndez, Eugenio. THE SOURCES ON PUERTO RICAN CULTURE HISTORY: A CRITICAL APPRAISAL. San Juan, Ediciones El Cemí, 1967. 55 p. ports., bibl.

This work is a critical, annotated inventory of basic documentary sources, the chronicles written by Europeans, and sources written by Puerto Rican historians and by foreigners "that bear a particularly intimate knowledge of the local situation." It formed part of the author's doctoral dissertation at Columbia University.

1.22 Géigel y Zenón, José, and Abelardo Morales Ferrer. BIBLIOGRAFIA PUERTORRIQUEÑA. Compilada en 1892–1894 y publicada por primera vez por Fernando J. Géigel y Sabat. Barcelona, Editorial Araluce, 1934. 453 p. ports., facsims.

Classified in three sections: books written and printed in Puerto Rico; books by Puerto Ricans; books by foreigners about Puerto Rico.

1.23 Gómez Canedo, Lino. LOS ARCHIVOS HISTORICOS DE PUERTO RICO, APUNTES DE UNA VISITA (ENERO–MAYO 1960). San Juan, Instituto de Cultura Puertorriqueña, Archivo general de Puerto Rico, 1964. 146 p. bibl. refs. (Publicación, 2).

A report on the status of the Puerto Rican archives by a member of the Academy of American Franciscan History.

1.24 Griffin, A.P.C., comp. A LIST OF BOOKS (WITH REFERENCES TO PERIODICALS) ON PUERTO RICO. Washington, Govt. Print. Off., 1901. 55 p.

Compilation by the chief of the Division of Bibliography of the Library of Congress which lists most of their holdings on Puerto Rico at the turn of the century, with a list of periodical articles, some Puerto Rican administrative documents, reports of local organizations, and similar documents.

1.25 GUIA DE FUENTES PARA LA HISTORIA DE IBERO-AMERICA CONSERVADAS EN ESPAÑA. Madrid, Dirección de Archivos y Bibliotecas, 1966–1969. 2 v.

Published under the sponsorship of

UNESCO and the International Council of Archives, these two volumes survey the documents pertaining to the history of Spanish America that are found in historical, military, ecclesiastical, and private archives in Spain, as well as in libraries and other cultural institutions. A large number of entries refer to Puerto Rico.

1.26 Harrison, John Parker. GUIDE TO MATERIALS ON LATIN AMERICA IN THE NATIONAL ARCHIVES. Washington, General Services Administration, National Archives and Records Service, 1961. 246 p. maps in pocket. (National Archives Publication no. 62-3).

Includes numerous references to diplomatic and consular materials pertaining to Puerto Rico.

1.27 Hooker, Marjorie. BIBLIOGRAPHY AND INDEX OF THE GEOLOGY OF PUERTO RICO AND VICINITY, 1866–1968. San Juan, Geological Society of Puerto Rico, 1969. 53 p.

Includes books, reports, articles, abstracts, and papers covering slightly more than one hundred years. Because of its location in an island-arc area, Puerto Rico is a focus for geologic study.

1.28 Hostos, Adolfo de. INDICE HEMERO-BIBLIOGRAFICO DE EUGENIO MARIA DE HOSTOS. San Juan, Comisión pro Celebración del Centenario del Natalicio de Hostos, 1940. 756 p.

The most complete bibliography and index of Hostos' writings, books, pamphlets, articles, notes, letters, etc. It includes also a listing of photographs and portraits of this Puerto Rican statesman.

1.29 El Imparcial. LIBRO DEL AÑO 1956–57. San Juan, Editorial El Imparcial, 1957. 480 p.

An almanac-type reference work published by one of the island's daily newspapers. It offers information on historical events, prominent people, government organization, laws, professional organizations, etc.

1.30 INDEX TO LATIN AMERICAN PERIODICAL LITERATURE, 1929–1960. Compiled in the Columbus Memorial Library of the Pan American Union. Boston, G.K. Hall, 1962.

Volume 7, pages 4653 to 4660, lists articles on Puerto Rico indexed by the Pan American Union Columbus Memorial Library. Periodicals indexed are, for the most part, of Latin American origin, and chiefly concern economic, political, governmental, social, and cultural fields.

1.31 INDICE GENERAL DE PUBLICACIONES PERIODICAS LATINOAMERICANAS: HUMANIDADES Y CIENCIAS SOCIALES. INDEX TO PERIODICALS: HUMANITIES AND SOCIAL SCIENCES. Prepared by the Columbus Memorial Library of the Organization of American States. v. 1+. Metuchen, N.J., Scarecrow Press, 1961+.

Published quarterly, the fourth issue of each year reprints those for the first three quarters and includes a cumulative author index. The index includes Puerto Rico.

1.32 Kidder, Frederick Elwyn, and Allen David Bushong. THESES ON PAN AMERICAN TOPICS PREPARED BY CANDIDATES FOR DOCTORAL DEGREES IN UNIVERSITIES AND COLLEGES IN THE UNITED STATES AND CANADA. Washington, Pan American Union, 1962. 124 p. (Columbus Memorial Library. Bibliographic Series, no. 5).

This list, which covers doctoral dissertations prepared between 1869 and 1960, includes approximately three hundred entries on Puerto Rico.

1.33 Kirschner, Madeline. PUERTO RICAN BIBLIOGRAPHY. Reprinted from RQ, Chicago, Fall 1969. p. 9–19.

A list of 240 Puerto Rican titles included in the Language and Literature Division of the Brooklyn Public Library.

1.34 Ledesma, Moisés. BIBLIOGRAFIA CULTURAL DE PUERTO RICO (ANOTADA). New York, Plus Ultra Educational Pub., 1970. 103 p.

A selective list of Puerto Rican poets, playwrights, musicians, and painters.

1.35 LATIN AMERICAN NEWSPAPERS IN UNITED STATES LIBRARIES: A UNION LIST. Compiled in the Serial Division, Library of Congress, by Steven M. Charno. Austin, University of Texas Press, 1968. 619 p. (Conference on Latin American History. Publication, 2).

Includes holdings of newspapers from Puerto Rico in seventy libraries in the U.S.

1.36 LIBROS PARLANTES. TALKING BOOKS. Washington, D.C., Division for the Blind and Physically Handicapped, Library of Congress, 1972. 10 p. English and Spanish.

Annotated list of Spanish-language titles and talking books for the blind and physically handicapped, including a few good selections on Puerto Rico. This division also publishes a list of titles available on records and in braille.

1.37 Lista de Tesis de la Escuela Graduada de Trabajo Social. Río Piedras, Universidad de Puerto Rico, 1971. 18 l. mimeographed.

Lists 163 theses accepted by the Graduate School of Social Work from 1945 to 1970.

1.38 MANUAL DE SERVICIO DE LAS AGENCIAS GUBERNAMENTALES. San Juan, Oficina del Gobernador, 1971. 346 p.

A guide to the services available from the various government agencies and programs, arranged alphabetically by agency. Each entry includes a brief description of the agency and its legal basis.

1.39 Mathews, Thomas. "Documentación sobre Puerto Rico en la Biblioteca del Congreso." In HISTORIA, v. 6, no. 2, October 1966, p. 89–142.

Surveys the materials related to Puerto Rican history contained in the Manuscript Division of the Library of Congress and some of the holdings of the Rare Book Division.

1.40 Morán Arce, Lucas, comp. ENCICLOPEDIA CLASICOS DE PUERTO RICO. [San Juan], Ediciones Latinoamericanas, 1971. 6 v. (477, 497, 568, 507, 496, 621 p.) illus., plates, ports., maps, bibl.

Contents: v. 1, Episodios históricos y descripciones de Puerto Rico. v. 2, Episodios históricos y descripciones de Puerto Rico; Relación cronológica de los sucesos de interés histórico para Puerto Rico. v. 3, Leyendas y cuentos; Los ensayos; La novela. v. 4, La novela. v. 5, El teatro; Poesías. v. 6, Poesías; Los municipios de Puerto Rico; Biografías de personajes históricos de Puerto Rico; Indice alfabético.

Reproduces many Puerto Rican classics in the fields of history and literature and includes five useful appendixes: a historical chronology, a summary of the history of each municipality, biographical sketches of prominent Puerto Ricans, a selected bibliography, and an alphabetical index covering all six volumes.

1.41 Morris, James O., and Efrén Córdova. BIBLIOGRAPHY OF INDUSTRIAL RELATIONS IN LATIN AMERICA. Ithaca, N.Y., New York State School of Industrial Relations, Cornell University, 1967. 290 p.

Includes books, pamphlets, dissertations, and articles on general labor matters, including labor economics and manpower, unions and the labor movement, labor–management relations, labor law, and social security. Puerto Rico is covered on pages 262–270.

1.42 New York Public Library. DICTIONARY CATALOG OF THE MAP DIVISION. Boston, G.K. Hall, 1971. v. 8.

Includes seventy-two maps of Puerto Rico, dated from 1696 to 1970.

1.43 New York Public Library. PUERTO RICO. Reprinted from Branch Library News, New York, October 1968. 11 p.

A brief sampling of books on Puerto Rico or by Puerto Ricans.

1.44 Parker, Franklin. PUERTO RICAN EDUCATION RESEARCH: ANNOTATED BIBLIOGRAPHY OF 66 UNITED STATES DOCTORAL DISSERTATIONS. Austin, Texas, 1964. 14 l. mimeographed.

Extracted from the author's Latin American Education Research: Annotated *Bibliography of 269 United States Doctoral Dissertations* (Austin, Institute of Latin American Studies, University of Texas, 1964). The dissertations on Puerto Rico are dated from 1923 to 1961.

1.45 Pedreira, Antonio S. BIBLIOGRAFIA PUERTORRIQUEÑA (1493–1930). Madrid, Imprenta de Hernando, 1932. 707 p. (Monografías de la Universidad de Puerto Rico, Ser. A, Estudios Hispánicos, 1).

A Puerto Rican classic. The most complete bibliography on Puerto Rico ever published.

1.46 THE PEOPLE OF PUERTO RICO: A BIBLIOGRAPHY. New York, Commonwealth of Puerto Rico, Department of Labor, Migration Division, n.d. 45 p.

Lists books, pamphlets, articles, and theses on Puerto Ricans in the United States.

1.47 REPORT ON SURVEYS, RESEARCH PROJECTS, INVESTIGATIONS AND OTHER ORGANIZED FACT-GATHERING ACTIVITIES OF THE GOVERNMENT OF PUERTO RICO: 1949–53. San Juan, Bureau of the Budget, Division of Statistics. 3 v. (58, 69, 89 p.).

Self-explanatory title.

1.48 Ribes Tovar, Federico. ENCICLO-PEDIA PUERTORRIQUEÑA ILUS-TRADA. THE PUERTO RICAN HERITAGE ENCYCLOPEDIA. San Juan, Plus Ultra Educational Pub., 1970. 3 v. (385, 431, 432 p.) illus., maps, ports.

Volume 1 covers history, including important historical figures, literature, arts, music, and government to the present. Volume 2 is devoted to Puerto Ricans in New York. Volume 3 discusses José Julio Henna, Pedro Albizu Campos, Puerto Rican women, the music and folklore of Puerto Rico, and its political geography.

1.49 Rivera, Guillermo. A TENTATIVE BIBLIOGRAPHY OF THE BELLES LETTRES OF PORTO RICO. Cambridge, Mass., Harvard University Press, 1931. 61 p.

Part 1 includes anthologies, bibliography, biography, art, criticism, drama, essays, history, legend, fiction,

oratory, poetry, folk tales. Part 2 includes unclassified works, writings incorporated in periodicals, and a special bibliography on Eugenio M. de Hostos.

1.50 Roca, Angelina S. de. Bibliography [About Bilingualism]. Río Piedras, University of Puerto Rico College of Social Sciences, n.d. 27 l. mimeographed.

An annotated bibliography of books and journal articles covering the period between January 1950 and June 1962.

1.51 Rodríguez Cruz, Juan. "Documentos sobre Puerto Rico que se Encuentran en los Archivos Nacionales de los Estados Unidos." *In* CARIBBEAN STUDIES, v. 5, no. 3, October 1965, p. 32–50.

Surveys Record Group 186 of the National Archives, known as the Records of the Spanish Governors of Puerto Rico, which include documents pertaining to the history of the island from the late eighteenth to the end of the nineteenth century.

1.52 Rodríguez Villafañe, Leonardo. CATALOGO DE MAPAS Y PLANOS DE PUERTO RICO EN EL ARCHIVO GENERAL DE INDIAS. San Juan, Municipio de San Juan, 1966. 134 p. illus.

An inventory and facsimile reproduction of 67 regional and local maps and architectural plans relating to Puerto Rico, dated 1519 to 1850, preserved at the Archivo General de Indias in Seville.

1.53 Sama, Manuel María. BIBLIOGRAFIA PUERTO-RIQUEÑA. Mayagüez, P.R., Tipografía Comercial-Marina, 1887. 159 p.

An annotated bibliography of 250 books published in Puerto Rico between 1831 and 1886, arranged chronologically.

1.54 SOCIAL SCIENCES AND HUMANITIES INDEX. v. 1+. New York, H.W. Wilson, 1907+.

"An author and subject index to periodicals in the fields of anthropology, archaeology, area studies, classical studies, economics, geography, history, language and literature, philosophy, political science, religion, sociology, and related subjects." Published quarterly with a bound annual cumulation. The index includes Puerto Rico.

1.55 THE SPANISH SPEAKING IN THE UNITED STATES: A GUIDE TO MATERIALS. Compiled by the Cabinet Committee on Opportunities for Spanish-Speaking People. Washington, Govt. Print. Off., 1971. 175 p.

An annotated listing of materials on Puerto Ricans, Mexican Americans, Cubans, and other Spanish-speaking groups in the United States.

1.56 TESAURO DE DATOS HISTORICOS. Preparado bajo la dirección de Adolfo de Hostos. San Juan, Departamento de Hacienda, 1951. 3 v. (154, 312, 308 p.) bibl.

An attempt to make available for general use many of the more than 300,000 historical entries prepared for the *General Historical Index of Puerto Rico*, based on private and public archives, books, and periodicals. The entries are arranged alphabetically by subject.

1.57 TESIS PRESENTADAS PARA EL GRADO DE MAESTRO EN ADMINISTRACION PUBLICA. Río Piedras, Universidad de Puerto Rico, Escuela de Administración Pública, 1971. 26 p.

A list of master's theses accepted by the School of Public Administration from its creation in 1945 to 1970.

1.58 Toro, Josefina del. GUIA DE BIBLIOTECAS DE PUERTO RICO. Rev. ed. San Juan, Sociedad de Bibliotecarios de Puerto Rico, 1971. 63 p.

An alphabetical listing of libraries by city, with basic information on each one.

1.59 Toro, Josefina del. "A Bibliography of the Collective Biography of Spanish America." *In* UNIVERSITY OF PUERTO RICO BULLETIN, v. 9, no. 1, Sept. 1938, p. 61–72.

Provides the names of persons included in collective biographies published during the early part of the twentieth century.

1.60 Toro Sugrañes, J.A. ALMANAQUE BORICUA. San Juan, Editorial Cordillera, 1972. 348 p.

A quick-reference almanac with statistics, significant dates, biographical sketches, and other similar information.

1.61 Tudela de la Orden, José. LOS MANUSCRITOS DE AMERICA EN LAS BIBLIOTECAS DE ESPAÑA. Madrid, Ediciones Cultura Hispánica, 1954. 586 p.

A description of manuscripts in the public libraries of Spain useful for the study of the history of the Americas, including Puerto Rico.

1.62 Ulibarri, George S. Preliminary Inventory of the Records of the Spanish Governors of Puerto Rico (Record Group 186). Washington, Office of Civil Archives, 1964. 22 l. mimeographed.

After a brief introduction explaining how these documents came into the possession of the National Archives, this document describes the records relating to political, civil, fiscal, military, naval, ecclesiastic, and administrative affairs from 1754 to 1898.

1.63 Velázquez, Gonzalo, comp. ANUARIO BIBLIOGRAFICO PUERTORRIQUEÑO: INDICE ALFABETICO DE LIBROS, FOLLETOS, REVISTAS, Y PERIODICOS PUBLICADOS EN PUERTO RICO DURANTE 1959–1960. San Juan, Departamento de Instrucción Pública, 1966.

Although cumbersome to use, this is a basic annual bibliographic source on Puerto Rico, published since 1948. It is plagued by long delays in its compilation and printing, with lags of from six to nine years between the dates of the entries and the actual date of publication of the bibliography.

1.64 Zirkel, Perry Alan, comp. A BIBLIOGRAPHY OF MATERIALS IN ENGLISH AND SPANISH RELATING TO PUERTO RICAN STUDENTS. Hartford, Conn., State Department of Education, Migratory Children's Program, 1971. 49 p.

A list "intended as a resource for teachers and other persons concerned with improving the educational opportunities of Puerto Rican pupils on the mainland as well as on the island."

2
ANTIQUITIES

2.1 Alegría, Ricardo, H.B. Nicholson, and Gordon R. Willey. THE ARCHAIC TRADITION IN PUERTO RICO. Reprinted from *American Antiquity*, v. 21, Oct. 1955: 114–141. bibl.

This paper describes excavations in a Puerto Rican cave site "which offers stratigraphic proof of a pre-ceramic, presumably non-agricultural complex underlying the pottery-bearing strata of the Igneri phase."

2.2 Coll y Toste, Cayetano. PREHISTORIA DE PUERTO RICO. Bilbao, Editorial Vasco Americana, [1967]. 261 p. illus., map, plates, port., bibl. refs. Reprint of 1907 edition.

A history of the Indians of Puerto Rico—their customs, religion, language, industries, etc.

2.3 Ekholm, Gordon F. "Puerto Rican Stone 'Collars' as Ballgame Belts." *In* Lothrop, Samuel K., and others. ESSAYS IN PRE-COLUMBIAN ART AND ARCHAEOLOGY. Cambridge, Mass., Harvard University Press, 1961. p. 342–355. illus.

Presents some new evidence to support the idea that the stone yokes of the pre-Columbian inhabitants of Puerto Rico were used as belts.

2.4 Fewkes, Jesse Walter. THE ABORIGINES OF PORTO RICO AND NEIGHBORING ISLANDS. New York, Johnson Reprint, 1970. 296 p. illus., plates, bibl. Reprint of 1907 edition.

This was one of two papers accompanying the twenty-fifth annual report of the U.S. Bureau of Ethnology to the Secretary of the Smithsonian Institution, 1903–1904. The paper was intended at the time to shed light on the inhabitants of an island that had recently come into the possession of the United States.

2.5 Fewkes, Jesse Walter. PORTO RICAN ELBOW-STONES IN THE HEYE MUSEUM, WITH DISCUSSION OF SIMILAR OBJECTS ELSEWHERE. Lancaster, Pa., New Era Printing Co., 1913. illus. (Contributions from the Heye Museum, no. 4). Reprinted from the *American Anthropologist*, v. 15, no. 3, July–Sept. 1913: 435–459.

Analyzes the characteristics of twelve specimens of elbow-stones, which the author believes were used for ceremonial purposes.

2.6 Fewkes, Jesse Walter. PORTO RICO STONE COLLARS AND TRIPOINTED IDOLS. Reprinted from *Smithsonian Miscellaneous Collection, Quarterly Issue*, v. 47, pt. 2, Oct. 10, 1904: 163–186. illus., plates (Smithsonian Institution, Publication no. 1480).

Describes the pre-Columbian tripointed stones and collars found in Puerto Rico and discusses the various theories regarding their use and meaning.

2.7 Fewkes, Jesse Walter. Prehistoric Porto Rico. *In* American Association for the Advancement of Science. PROCEEDINGS. v. 51. Washington, Gibson Bros., 1902. p. 487–512.

An overview of the pre-Columbian history of Puerto Rico, intended to draw the attention of U.S. anthropologists to the new U.S. possession.

2.8 Fewkes, Jesse Walter. PRELIMINARY REPORT ON AN ARCHAEOLOGICAL TRIP TO THE WEST INDIES. Reprinted from *Smithsonian Miscellaneous Collection, Quarterly Issue*, v. 45, 1904: 112–133. (Smithsonian Institution, Publication no. 1429).

An account of excavations in Puerto Rico and description of specimens from Puerto Rico and Santo Domingo.

2.9 Hostos, Adolfo de. ANTHROPOLOGI-CAL PAPERS. San Juan, Bureau of Supplies, Printing and Transportation, 1941. 211 p.

Includes an article on prehistoric Puerto Rican ceramics as well as chapters on other pre-Columbian objects from Puerto Rico and neighboring islands.

2.10 Hostos, Adolfo de. UNA COLECCION ARQUEOLOGICA ANTILLANA. San Juan, First Federal Savings and Loan Association of Puerto Rico, 1955. 106 p. illus.

Describes the author's interest in the archaeology of the West Indies and how his collection of artifacts was saved by a local women's club from being sold to Yale University and was donated instead to the University of Puerto Rico.

2.11 Joyce, Thomas Athal. CENTRAL AMERICAN AND WEST INDIAN ARCHAEOLOGY. New York, G.P. Putnam's, 1916. 270 p. illus., photos, maps, bibl. refs.

The second part of this book deals with the life and customs of the inhabitants of the West Indies before they came in contact with the white man. It touches on government, marriage and burial customs, war, religion, amusements, food and housing, dress, and artifacts.

2.12 Lovén, Sven. ORIGINS OF THE TAINAN CULTURE: WEST INDIES. Goteborg, Elanders boktryckeri aktiebolag, 1935. 696 p. map, bibl. refs.

Revised second edition of his German treatise on the subject, published in 1924. The work dwells in detail on Indian migration in the West Indies and on Tainan monuments, artifacts, houses and furniture, agriculture, religion, social conditions, musical instruments, and customs.

2.13 Mason, Otis Tufton. THE LATIMER COLLECTION OF ANTIQUITIES FROM PORTO RICO IN THE NATIONAL MUSEUM AT WASHINGTON, D.C. Reprinted from *The Smithsonian Report for 1876*. Washington, Govt. Print. Off., 1877. p. 371-393. illus.

A detailed description of the pottery and stone artifacts bequeathed to the Smithsonian Institution by George Latimer, the son of a Philadelphia merchant, who moved to Puerto Rico in 1874 and remained there until near the time of his death. According to sources cited by Mason, "the makers of these objects were a purely neolithic people . . . they were not savages, but were in the 'middle status of barbarism.' " Mason considers their implements of industry "the most beautiful in the world."

2.14 Morales Cabrera, Pablo, comp. PUERTO RICO INDIGENA: PREHISTORIA Y PROTOHISTORIA DE PUERTO RICO. San Juan, Imprenta Venezuela, [1932?]. 381 p. illus., plates, docs., bibl.

Documented history of the Indians of Puerto Rico, including a glossary of Indian words.

2.15 New York Academy of Sciences. SCIENTIFIC SURVEY OF PORTO RICO AND THE VIRGIN ISLANDS. v. 18, pts. 1–4. New York, The Academy, 1940–1952. 577 p. illus., maps, bibl.

Pt. 1, Porto Rican Archaeology, by Froelich G. Rainey (1940).

Pt. 2, A Large Archaeological Site at Capá, Utuado, with Notes on Other Puerto Rican Sites Visited in 1914–1915, by J. Alden Mason. Appendix: An Analysis of the Artifacts of the 1914–1915 Porto Rican Survey, by Irving Rouse (1941).

Pt. 3, Porto Rican Prehistory: Introduction; Excavations in the West and North, by Irving Rouse (1952).

Pt. 4, Porto Rican Prehistory: Excavations in the Interior, South and East; Chronological Implications, by Irving Rouse (1952).

2.16 Pichardo Moya, Felipe. LOS ABORIGENES DE LAS ANTILLAS. México, Fondo de Cultura Económica, 1956. 140 p. maps, tables, bibl.

A description of Indian life in the West Indies before the arrival of the European colonizers.

2.17 Rouse, Irving. "The Bailey Collection of Stone Artifacts from Puerto Rico." *In* Lothrop, Samuel K. and others. ESSAYS IN PRE-COLUMBIAN ART AND ARCHAEOLOGY. Cambridge, Mass.,

Harvard University Press, 1961. p. 342–355. illus.

Describes a collection of ground carved stone artifacts deposited recently in the John and Mabel Ringling Museum of Art in Sarasota, Florida. The collection is worthy of note, according to the author, because "it includes carvings of a different style from those ordinarily associated with the Tainan Indians in Puerto Rico and, second, because the provenience of the specimens is more precise than usual, so that it is possible to draw somewhat better conclusions concerning the cultural and chronological setting of the finds."

2.18   Smith, Hale Gilliam. ARCHAE-OLOGICAL EXCAVATION AT EL MORRO, SAN JUAN, PUERTO RICO. With historical background sections by Ricardo Torres Reyes. Tallahassee, Florida State University, Dept. of Anthropology and Archaeology, 1962. 97 p. illus., plates, diagrs., tables. (Notes in Anthropology, v. 6).

Reports the results of a two-fold study sponsored by the National Park Service, aimed at making available information for the restoration and interpretation of El Morro fort and determining the extent of archaeological research that might still be necessary at that site.

2.19   Stahl, Agustín. LOS INDIOS BORIN-QUEÑOS: ESTUDIOS ETNOGRA-FICOS. Puerto Rico, Imprenta de Acosta, 1889. 206 p. illus.

Description of the inhabitants of the island at the time of its discovery and of 740 Indian artifacts in the author's collection.

3
ARTS AND MUSIC

3.1   Arjona de Muñoz, Gloria, comp. FLOR DE VILLANCICOS. Prólogo de Federico de Onís; transcripciones musicales de Jesús Figueroa. 2. ed. aumentada. [San Juan] Editorial del Departamento de Instrucción Pública, 1964, c1963. 66 p. illus., music.

A selection of Spanish and Puerto Rican carols, with excerpts from writings about the Christmas season and a brief introduction on traditional Christmas music.

3.2   Angulo Iñiguez, Diego. PLANOS DE MONUMENTOS ARQUITECTONI-COS DE AMERICA Y FILIPINAS EN EL ARCHIVO DE INDIAS. Sevilla, Laboratorio del Arte, Universidad de Sevilla, 1933–1940. 5 v. unp. illus., plates.

A basic work for the study of colonial architecture in the New World. Volume 2 includes documents pertaining to several historic Puerto Rican buildings—Catedral (1801), Real Hacienda (1850), Aduana (1825) and Almacén de Pólvora (1788) in San Juan; and Aduana (1824) in Aguadilla.

An accompanying volume gives a brief description of these buildings.

3.3   Beattie, John Walter, and others, eds. THE PUERTO RICAN SINGER. New York, American Book Co., [1948]. 219 p. illus.

Includes the lyrics and music of game songs and traditional tunes from Puerto Rico and other Latin American countries, and some composed by Europeans.

3.4   Buschiazzo, Mario J. ESTUDIO SOBRE MONUMENTOS HISTORICOS DE PUERTO RICO. Santurce, Junta de Planificación de Puerto Rico, 1955. 74 p. map, diagrs.

A list of monuments and buildings dating before 1898, with a brief comment on their historical significance and thoughts on how their restoration could be accomplished.

3.5   Cadilla de Martínez, María. JUEGOS Y CANCIONES INFANTILES DE PUERTO RICO. San Juan, 1940. bibl.

A description of children's games

and songs—their structure, origin, value, and other aspects—with some melodies.

3.6   Callejo, Fernando. MUSICA Y MUSICOS PUERTORRIQUEÑOS. Prólogo de Amaury Veray Torregrosa. San Juan, Editorial Coquí, 1971. 283 p. ports. (Ediciones Borinquen).

A basic text on the musical scene in Puerto Rico up to the early part of the twentieth century, originally published in 1915. It includes historical notes, biographies of musicians and composers, a list of competitions and winners, and notes on the various types of Puerto Rican music.

3.7   Campos Parsi, Héctor. CUATRO CANTOS DE NAVIDAD. Diseño e ilustraciones de Carlos Marichal. San Juan, Instituto de Cultura Puertorriqueña, 1959. 14 p. illus., music.

Four pieces by this well-known contemporary Puerto Rican composer, two of them based on traditional Christmas melodies.

3.8   Canino Salgado, Marcelino J. LA CANCION DE CUNA EN LA TRADICION DE PUERTO RICO. Prólogo de Margot Arce de Vázquez. San Juan, Instituto de Cultura Puertorriqueña, 1970. 146 p. bibl.

A study on the lullaby in Puerto Rico and its ties to the same genre in Spain. It examines the themes and music and includes lullabies collected by the author from the island's oral tradition as well as some previously published in other works.

3.9   CANTARES NAVIDEÑOS, 1961. Anotados por Francisco López Cruz. Hato Rey, P.R., Programa de Educación Musical, Departamento de Instrucción Pública, 1960. 25 p. music.

Lyrics and music of the most popular Christmas songs on the island.

3.10   Chase, Gilbert. A GUIDE TO LATIN AMERICAN MUSIC. 2d rev. ed. Washington, Pan American Union, 1962. 411 p.

Includes references to articles on Puerto Rican music published in journals in Puerto Rico, the United States, and Latin America.

3.11   Coen, Augusto, comp. LA FIESTA DE CRUZ: MUSICA Y LETRA DEL "ROSARIO CANTAO." Noticia de Pablo Garrido. Ilustrado por Guillermo Sureda. San Juan, El Santo Rosario en el Aire, 1951. 44 p. For 2 voices.

Music and lyrics of a *Rosario Cantao*, or sung rosary, a religious observance that was traditionally held, especially in Ponce, on nine consecutive nights. The introduction includes notes on the origin of the feast and an analysis of the musical form.

3.12   COLECCION MARTINEZ: ALBUM DE ARTE. Introducción de María C. de Martínez. [Arecibo, P.R.], 1936. 19 p. plates.

Reproductions and descriptions of paintings by Pedro Tomás Martínez.

3.13   Curbelo de Díaz González, Irene. SANTOS DE PUERTO RICO. San Juan, Museo de Santos, 1970. 76 p. plates.

Examines the development of the traditional Puerto Rican form of wood carving known as *santería*, since its beginnings in the eighteenth century.

3.14   Delgado Mercado, Osiris. SINOPSIS HISTORICA DE LAS ARTES PLASTICAS EN PUERTO RICO. San Juan, Instituto de Cultura Puertorriqueña, 1957. 28 p. illus. (Ciclo de Conferencias sobre la Historia de Puerto Rico).

A brief survey of the arts in Puerto Rico, with text in English and Spanish.

3.15   Delgado Mercado, Osiris. PARET Y ALCAZAR. Prólogo de Diego Angulo Iñiguez. Madrid, Universidades de Puerto Rico y Madrid, Instituto Diego Velázquez, del C.S.I.C., 1957. 335 p. plates.

Biography of Luis Paret y Alcázar (1746–1799), a Spanish painter who lived in exile in Puerto Rico during 1775–1778. In Puerto Rico he was the teacher of José Campeche, Puerto Rico's first notable artist. A plate of Paret's self-portrait dressed as a Puerto Rican peasant carrying a bunch of bananas is included, as are drawings of a Puerto Rican peasant and a woman slave.

3.16   Deliz, Monserrate, comp. and arr. RENADIO DEL CANTAR FOLKLORICO

DE PUERTO RICO. 2. ed. corregida y aumentada. Madrid, Ediciones Espectáculos América, 1952. 303 p. For voice and piano.

An extensive selection of lullabies, game songs, and traditional songs is preceded by some brief notes on the special characteristics of Puerto Rican folkloric music.

3.17 Deliz, Monserrate. EL HIMNO DE PUERTO RICO: ESTUDIO CRITICO DE "LA BORINQUEÑA." Prólogo de A. Morales Carrión. Madrid, 1957. 176 p. illus., bibl.

Documented study on the origins of La Borinqueña, the official anthem.

3.18 Fernández, José Antonio. ARCHITECTURE IN PUERTO RICO. Introduction by Efraín Pérez Chanis. New York, Architectural Book Pub. Co., 1965. 267 p. illus., photos, plans.

Puerto Rican architecture from the colonial period to contemporary times, with strong emphasis on the latter. Covers housing, hotels, schools, churches, hospitals, and commercial and government buildings. Includes site plans and photographs.

3.19 Fernández, Wilfredo. LUIS HERNANDEZ CRUZ O EL TIEMPO ENEMISTADO. Fotografías de Oswaldo García. Río Piedras, Puerto Rico, Editorial Xaguey, 1972. 94 p. illus.

A study of the paintings of Luis Hernández Cruz.

3.20 Filardi, Carmelo. UNA EPOCA DE HISTORIA EN CARICATURAS POR FILARDI. Río Piedras, Editorial Universitaria, 1971.

A collection of caricatures by Filardi published in Puerto Rico between 1948 and 1963, in which the artist comments on personalities, issues, news, and politics of the period.

3.21 Fonfrías, Ernesto Juan. APUNTES SOBRE LA DANZA PUERTORRIQUEÑA. San Juan, Instituto de Cultura Puertorriqueña, 1967. 8 p. bibl.

Brief essay on the danza, with a discussion of the origin of La Borinqueña, now the official anthem, including the different lyrics used over the years.

3.22 Gaudier, Martín. LA BORINQUEÑA. 1. ed. aumentada. Barcelona, Ediciones Rumbos, 1959. 236 p. illus.

Documents, articles, poems, and speeches regarding the much-disputed origin of Puerto Rico's anthem.

3.23 Hernández Acevedo, Manuel, ed. PINTORES PUERTORRIQUEÑOS. San Juan, Ediciones Artísticas de Puerto Rico, 1968. 24 col. plates, 6 mounted. (Serie Pintores Puertorriqueños.)

Boxed edition of six portfolios on Puerto Rican painters Epifanio Irrizarry, Rafael Tufiño, Augusto Marín, Francisco Rodón, Manuel Hernández, and Luis Hernández Cruz. Each portfolio includes a brief note on the artist's life and career, selected reproductions of his work, and notes on the color plates. The portfolios are also available individually.

3.24 Homar, Lorenzo. AQUI EN LA LUCHA. Caricaturas de Lorenzo Homar. Introducción por J.A. Torres Martinó. Río Piedras, Cuadernos de La Escalera, 1970. unp.

A collection of political cartoons done between 1959 and 1970; an ascerbic commentary on the establishment.

3.25 INDUSTRIAL APPLICATIONS OF INDIAN DECORATIVE MOTIFS OF PUERTO RICO. APLICACIONES INDUSTRIALES DEL DISEÑO INDIGENA DE PUERTO RICO. Designs by Matilde Pérez de Silva; text and commentaries by Adolfo de Hostos; translated into English by Ida M. de Gallardo. Philadelphia, John C. Winston, c 1939. 55 p. illus., plates. English and Spanish on opposite pages.

Shows how some of the decorations found in pre-Columbian ceramic art, stone collars, and stone carvings can be adapted for use in modern ceramics, textiles, and architectural ornaments.

3.26 Instituto de Cultura Puertorriqueña. JOSE CAMPECHE, 1751–1809. Notas biográficas por Arturo V. Dávila. San Juan, Instituto de Cultura Puertorriqueña, 1971. 171 p. plates, bibl.

A brief biographical sketch of Puerto Rico's first painter of note, followed by black-and-white reproductions of his paintings. These are grouped under five categories: portraits, historical subjects, religious subjects, mysteries and the Blessed Virgin, and saints. It includes a detailed description of each work and information on its present location.

3.27 Kaiden, Nina N., Pedro Juan Soto, and Andrew Vladimir, eds. PUERTO RICO: LA NUEVA VIDA. THE NEW LIFE. Foreword by Ricardo E. Alegría. New York, Renaissance Editions, 1966. 1 v. unp. plates.

The works of some of Puerto Rico's most noted artists, accompanied by selections from well-known poets and writers. Translations into English are included, and a list of the plates (sixteen in color and fifteen in black and white), with sizes and media used, is appended.

3.28 Lee, Muna, ed. ART IN REVIEW: 1929–1938. Río Piedras, University of Puerto Rico, 1937. 196 p. illus., plates. (Bulletin. Ser. 8, no. 2, Dec. 1937).

Reviews and notes on the art exhibitions held at the University of Puerto Rico between 1929 and 1938, the first ones ever held on the island.

3.29 López Cruz, Francisco. EL AGUINALDO EN PUERTO RICO (SU EVOLUCION). San Juan, Instituto de Cultura Puertorriqueña, 1972. 46 p.

A study of the *aguinaldo*, or Puerto Rican Christmas carol. The author analyzes four aspects: lyrics, rhythm, melody, and harmony.

3.30 López Cruz, Francisco. EL AGUINALDO Y EL VILLANCICO EN EL FOLKLORE PUERTORRIQUEÑO. Ilustraciones de Rafael Ríos Rey. San Juan, Instituto de Cultura Puertorriqueña, 1956. 43 p. illus., music.

Music and text of traditional Puerto Rican Christmas carols.

3.31 López Cruz, Francisco. METODO PARA LA ENSEÑANZA DEL CUATRO PUERTORRIQUEÑO. San Juan, Instituto de Cultura Puertorriqueña, 1967. 184 p.

A manual for teaching the modern *cuatro*, a typically Puerto Rican instrument with five double strings.

3.32 López Cruz, Francisco. LA MUSICA FOLKLORICA DE PUERTO RICO. Prólogo de Walter Starkie. Ilustraciones de Antonio Martorell. Sharon, Conn., Troutman Press, 1967. 203 p. illus.

An analysis of Puerto Rican folkloric music, including the lyrics and music of approximately one hundred songs representative of the *plena, bomba, seis,* and other traditional forms.

3.33 Luce, Allena, ed. CANCIONES POPULARES. Boston, Silver, Burdett, c 1921. 138 p.

An extensive collection of traditional songs divided into four sections: Puerto Rican; Cuban, Spanish, and Mexican; patriotic and popular; and ancient and game songs, with brief comments in English and Spanish.

3.34 McCoy, James A. The *Bomba* and the *Aguinaldo* of Puerto Rico as They Have Evolved from Indigenous, African and European Cultures. Ph.D. dissertation, Florida State University, 1968. *In* DISSERTATION ABSTRACTS, v. 29, no. 7, p. 2294-A.

A study of two extant folk forms, the *bomba* and the *aguinaldo*, aimed at determining their evolutionary lineage, furthering the preservation of ethnic culture for future study, and investigating the discrepancies found in the historical literature.

3.35 Morel Campos, Juan. DANZAS DE JUAN MOREL CAMPOS. San Juan, Instituto de Cultura Puertorriqueña, 1958. 5 v. various pagings. music, ports.

The most complete collection of *danzas* by Morel Campos (1857–1896).

3.36 Morel Campos, Juan. OBRAS VARIAS. San Juan, Instituto de Cultura Puertorriqueña, 1958. 70 p.

Music and lyrics of other compositions by Morel Campos.

3.37 Muñoz Santaella, María Luisa, comp. CANCIONES DE NAVIDAD. San Juan, Departamento de Instrucción, 1950. unp. illus.

Lyrics and music of twenty traditional Christmas carols.

3.38 Muñoz Santaella, María Luisa. LA MUSICA EN PUERTO RICO: PANORAMA HISTORICO-CULTURAL. Dibujos de A. Torres-Martinó. Sharon, Conn., Troutman Press, 1966. 167 p. illus., music, bibl. (Puerto Rico: Realidad y Anhelo, 3).

Useful summary of the musical panorama of the nineteenth and twentieth centuries, with explanations of both the indigenous background and the Spanish and African influences. It is also available as a talking book for the blind and physically handicapped.

3.39 PABLO CASALS EN PUERTO RICO, 1955-1956. Text by Arturo Orzábal Quintana. San Juan, Departamento de Instrucción Pública, 1957. 86 p. photos, ports. (Ser. 3, núm. 106).

Records Casals' arrival in Puerto Rico, birthplace of his mother, and his activities during his first three-month visit. Includes the text of the governor's proclamation honoring Casals, statements, speeches, and newspaper articles.

3.40 Pedreira, José Enrique, comp. and arr. PUERTO RICO SINGS. English lyrics by Olga Paul. New York, Edward B. Marks, c 1957. unp.

An album of eleven representative songs, with lyrics in English and Spanish and a general introduction to Puerto Rican music.

3.41 PINTORES CONTEMPORANEOS PUERTORRIQUEÑOS. San Juan, Ediciones Artísticas de Puerto Rico, 1969. 224 p. plates. Text in English and Spanish.

A collection of reproductions of the works of thirteen contemporary Puerto Rican painters, preceded by a brief critical essay on the work of each. A useful summary of the historical background and the development of Puerto Rican painting in the twentieth century and biographical sketches of the artists represented complete the work.

3.42 REVISTA DEL INSTITUTO DE CULTURA PUERTORRIQUEÑA. núm. 51, abr.-jun. 1971. 55 p. plates, illus.

Special issue devoted to the Institute of Culture's museums and parks program. It describes the Indian Ceremonial Park in Utuado, the Museum of Military History, Porta Coeli Religious Art Museum, the Fine Arts Museum, and many others.

3.43 Sánchez Felipe, Alejandro. PUERTO RICO ARTISTICO, MONUMENTAL E HISTORICO: COLECCION DE DIBUJOS. San Juan, 1936. 22 p. illus.

A portfolio of drawings of historic buildings, including Palacio del Obispado, Catedral, El Morro, Capilla del Cristo, La Fortaleza, City Walls, Iglesia San José, and Convento de Porta Coeli.

3.44 Tobar, P. Emilio. LA IGLESIA DE SAN JOSE, TEMPLO Y MUSEO DEL PUEBLO PUERTORRIQUEÑO. SAN JOSE CHURCH. San Juan, Imprenta La Milagrosa, 1963. 254 p. illus., photos, plans, bibl. refs. English and Spanish texts.

A history of one of the oldest churches in Puerto Rico, whose plans date back to 1523.

3.45 Torres Torres, Modesto. DECIMARIO PUERTORRIQUEÑO. Río Piedras, P.R., Negrón, 1964. 104 p. illus., ports.

Brings together the aguinaldos, décimas, and other songs by Modesto Torres Torres, a peasant from the town of Orocovis.

3.46 Traba, Marta. LA REBELION DE LOS SANTOS. Fotos de Gabriel Suau. Apéndices de Irene Curbelo. Río Piedras, P.R., Ediciones Puerto, 1972. English and Spanish text.

A view of Puerto Rico's santos, or carved wood figures, by a South American critic. The appendixes, by a Puerto Rican authority, detail the various types of santos, the areas they come from, and their dates.

4
BIOGRAPHY

4.1 Abril, Mariano. ANTONIO VALERO: UN HEROE DE LA INDEPENDENCIA DE ESPAÑA Y AMERICA. San Juan, Real Hnos., 1929. 245 p. illus., ports.

Traces the life and political philosophy of Antonio Valero (1790–1863), a Puerto Rican who fought with the independence forces in Mexico, Peru, Colombia, and Venezuela. He was one of the first Puerto Ricans to voice a desire for the island's political independence.

4.2 Acosta Quintero, Angel. JOSE JULIAN ACOSTA Y SU TIEMPO. San Juan, Instituto de Cultura Puertorriqueña, 1965. 636 p. port.

Biography based on Acosta's papers and letters written to him by his son and grandsons. The first part was originally published in 1900. The book documents the life and times of this abolitionist leader (1825–1891) and proponent of assimilation with Spain.

4.3 Aitken, Thomas, Jr. POET IN THE FORTRESS: THE STORY OF LUIS MUÑOZ MARIN. New York, New American Library, 1965. 240 p. plates, bibl. (Signet Books).

A sympathetic biography of former Governor Luis Muñoz Marín, who, in the author's words, combines, "poetry and politics, toughness and tenderheartedness, idealism and practicality, the colossal energy of the doer and the contemplative nature of the thinker."

4.4 Alexander, Robert J. PROPHETS OF THE REVOLUTION: PROFILE OF LATIN AMERICAN LEADERS. New York, Macmillan, 1962. 322 p. bibl.

Essays on twelve Latin American leaders who the author believes have brought about "a revolution cut to the cloth of their particular nations." Among these he includes former Governor Luis Muñoz Marín.

4.5 Amadeo Gely, Teresa. BIOGRAFIA DE LUCAS AMADEO ANTOMARCHI, EN RELACION A LOS ASPECTOS SOCIALES, POLITICOS, Y ECONOMICOS DE PUERTO RICO. San Juan, Editorial Cordillera, 1964. 165 p. port., bibl.

A frankly laudatory biography of Amadeo (1845–1911), stressing his contributions to banking and to solving Puerto Rico's economic problems.

4.6 Arana Soto, Salvador. LUIS MUÑOZ RIVERA, SAVIA Y SANGRE DE PUERTO RICO. San Juan, 1968–1970. v. 1, 4, (207, 1640 p.) bibl.

An analysis of Muñoz Rivera's writings and speeches, and his political career.

4.7 Bonafoux, Luis. BETANCES. San Juan, Instituto de Cultura Puertorriqueña, 1970. 394 p. Reprint of 1901 edition. (Serie Biblioteca Popular).

This book draws heavily from and includes many texts of Betances' letters, speeches, and other documents. It portrays his life as revolutionary, writer, orator, physician, and head of his family.

4.8 Carreras, Carlos N. BETANCES, EL ANTILLANO PROSCRITO. San Juan, Editorial Club de la Prensa, 1961. 184 p. bibl. (Publicaciones de obras de autores puertorriqueños).

Biography of Ramón Emeterio Betances, patriot, and leader of the late nineteenth century.

4.9 Carreras, Carlos N. HOMBRES Y MUJERES DE PUERTO RICO. México, Editorial Orión, 1961. illus.

Short biographies of prominent Puerto Rican figures of the nineteenth and twentieth centuries, intended for use in the island's junior high schools.

4.10 Carreras, Carlos N. HOSTOS, APOSTOL DE LA LIBERTAD. Madrid, Impr. y

Litografía Juan Bravo, 1950. 214 p. port., bibl.

A biography of Hostos concentrating on his political activities.

4.11 Carreras, Juan. SANTIAGO IGLESIAS PANTIN. SU VIDA, SU OBRA, SU PENSAMIENTO: DATOS BIOGRAFICOS, EPOCA 1896-1940. 2. ed. San Juan, Editorial Club de la Prensa, 1970. 242 p. illus., bibl.

Born in Spain, Santiago Iglesias Pantín (1872-1939) lived in Cuba for several years and in 1896 moved to Puerto Rico, where he became the foremost leader of the labor movement. This biography analyzes his political and social philosophies, his work in favor of Puerto Rican workers, and his association with the American Federation of Labor and the Pan American Federation of Labor.

4.12 Ceide, Amelia. STAHL: ESTUDIO BIOGRAFICO. San Juan, Editorial Club de la Prensa, 1960. 137 p. illus.

Biography and anecdotes of Agustín Stahl (1842-1917), botanist, scientist, and ethnologist, who first began the classification of the flora and fauna of Puerto Rico.

4.13 Coll, Edna. CAYETANO COLL Y TOSTE: SINTESIS DE ESTIMULOS HUMANOS. San Juan, Editorial Universitaria, 1970. 147 p. ports., facsim., bibl.

A biography of the founder of the *Boletín Histórico de Puerto Rico*, touching on his work as thinker, historian, storyteller, and poet. Includes a useful bibliography of all his writings and a selected subject index to the *Boletín Histórico*.

4.14 Coll y Toste, Cayetano. PUERTORRIQUEÑOS ILUSTRES. Segunda selección. Recopilación de Isabel Cuchí Coll. Barcelona, Ediciones Rumbos, 1963. 357 p.

Brief biographical sketches of important figures in the history of Puerto Rico, from its first governor, Juan Ponce de León, to José de Diego, poet and politician of the turn of the century, culled from the *Boletín Histórico de Puerto Rico* edited by Coll y Toste.

4.15 Córdova, Lieban. SIETE AÑOS CON MUÑOZ MARIN, 1938-1945. San Juan, Editorial Esther, 1945. 197 p. plates, ports.

Personal reminiscences of the man who was secretary to Luis Muñoz Marín during the first years of his public participation in the political life of Puerto Rico.

4.16 Córdova Landrón, Arturo. SALVADOR BRAU, SU VIDA Y SU EPOCA. San Juan, Editorial Coquí, 1968. 152 p. photos, bibl. Reprint of 1949 edition. (Ediciones Borinquen).

Discusses the contributions made by Brau (1842-1912) as politician, dramatist, poet, historian, and journalist. Includes some poems written by him expressing dismay and disenchantment with Spain upon her turning Puerto Rico over to the United States in 1898.

4.17 Corretjer, Juan Antonio. ALBIZU CAMPOS. Montevideo, El Siglo Ilustrado, 1969. 121 p. (Colección Libros de Bolsillo).

Four essays on Pedro Albizu Campos—his career as politician and revolutionary, his role in the Ponce massacre, and his participation in the nationalist insurrection of 1950.

4.18 Cruz Monclova, Lidio. BALDORIOTY DE CASTRO (SU VIDA, SUS IDEAS). San Juan, Instituto de Cultura Puertorriqueña, 1966. 419 p. bibl. refs. (Serie Biblioteca Popular).

A biography of one of the leaders of Puerto Rico's abolitionist movement and a deputy to the Spanish Cortes. Román Baldorioty de Castro (1822-1889) founded the newspaper *El Derecho* and wrote in *La Crónica*. The book describes the campaign for Puerto Rican autonomy launched by Baldorioty in 1880 from the latter paper. He died in 1889, however, eight years before Puerto Rico finally achieved its charter of autonomy from Spain.

4.19 Cruz Monclova, Lidio. LUIS MUÑOZ RIVERA: DIEZ AÑOS DE SU VIDA POLITICA. Prólogo de Eugenio Fernández Méndez. San Juan, Instituto de Cultura Puertorriqueña, 1959. 707 p. bibl. refs.

A documented study of Muñoz Rivera's activities during the years 1887–1898, the period of the most intensive campaign for and the triumph of the autonomist movement in Puerto Rico.

4.20 Díaz Soler, Luis M. ROSENDO MATIENZO CINTRON: ORIENTADOR Y GUARDIAN DE UNA CULTURA. Río Piedras, Ediciones del Instituto de Literatura Puertorriqueña, Universidad de Puerto Rico, 1960. 2 v. (734, 521 p.) illus., bibl.

An exhaustive work on Rosendo Matienzo Cintrón (1855–1913), prominent politician and writer. Volume 1 includes his biography, with emphasis on his political activity within the autonomist movement and in the early years of U.S. rule. Volume 2 brings together the articles written by Matienzo between 1900 and 1912.

4.21 Fernández Juncos, Manuel. SEMBLANZAS PUERTORRIQUEÑAS. Puerto Rico, Tip. de J. González Font, 1888. 202 p.

Biographical essays on Manuel Alonso, José Julián Acosta, Alejandro Tapia, José Pablo Morales, Salvador Brau, and Manuel Corchado.

4.22 Fernández Méndez, Eugenio. SALVADOR BRAU Y SU TIEMPO. San Juan, Universidad de Puerto Rico, 1956. 120 p. illus., port., bibl., refs.

This study details Brau's love of liberty and of his country and considers his career within the context of the social and political situation in Spain and Puerto Rico during the nineteenth century.

4.23 Figueroa, Sotero. ENSAYO BIOGRAFICO DE LOS QUE MAS HAN CONTRIBUIDO AL PROGRESO DE PUERTO-RICO. Prólogo de José Julián Acosta y Calvo. Ponce, P.R., Est. Tip. "El Vapor," 1888. 356 p. (Biblioteca Puertorriqueña). Reprint. San Juan, Editorial Coquí, in press.

Biographical essays on thirty Puerto Rican figures of the eighteenth and nineteenth centuries.

4.24 Gautier Dapena, José A. BALDORIOTY, APOSTOL. San Juan, Instituto de Cultura Puertorriqueña, 1970. 180 p. (Serie Biblioteca Popular).

The life and work of one of the outstanding figures in the island's history, who was active in the political scene between 1853 and 1889.

4.25 Géigel Polanco, Vicente. VALORES DE PUERTO RICO. San Juan, Editorial Eugenio María de Hostos, 1943. 169 p.

Brief biographies of seventeen outstanding Puerto Ricans of the nineteenth and early twentieth centuries.

4.26 Gonzalez García, Sebastián. LA JUVENTUD DEL PADRE RUFO. San Juan, Universidad de Puerto Rico, 1963. 21 p. Reprinted from Revista Extramuros, no. 4.

Manuel M. Rufo Fernández (1790–1855) was born in Spain, and in 1832 he came to Puerto Rico, where he distinguished himself as an educator. This biographical essay focuses on Father Rufo's youth.

4.27 Gotay, Modesto. HOMBRES ILUSTRES DE PUERTO RICO. Barcelona, Ediciones Rumbos, 1960. 132 p. ports.

Illustrated biographical sketches of more than 200 outstanding men and 12 women, arranged alphabetically.

4.28 Hostos, Adolfo de. HOMBRES REPRESENTATIVOS DE PUERTO RICO. San Juan, Impr. Venezuela, 1961. 206 p.

Biographies of twenty–nine Puerto Ricans of the nineteenth century who excelled in diverse fields–how they became outstanding men, their contributions, and their relations with each other and with the times in which they lived. Includes a chronology of world events that influenced the development of liberalism in Puerto Rico.

4.29 Hostos, Adolfo de. TRAS LAS HUELLAS DE HOSTOS. Río Piedras, Editorial de la Universidad de Puerto Rico, 1966. 214 p. photos, illus.

The author, son of Eugenio María de Hostos, reminisces about life with his famous father—travel and residence in Chile, Haiti, and the Dominican Republic, his father's work, and the author's efforts at following in his father's footsteps.

4.30 Hostos, Eugenio Carlos de, ed. EU-GENIO MARIA DE HOSTOS, PRO-MOTER OF PAN AMERICANISM: A COLLECTION OF WRITINGS AND A BIBLIOGRAPHY. Madrid, Impr. J. Bravo, 1954. 311 p. port., bibl.

A collection of writings on de Hostos' ideal of a united hemisphere, among them José A. Balseiro's essay, "Eugenio María de Hostos, Hispanic America's Public Servant." It also includes some of Hostos' addresses and a bibliography of writings by and about him.

4.31 Hostos, Eugenio Carlos de, ed. HOS-TOS, PEREGRINO DEL IDEAL: IDEARIO Y TRABAJOS ACERCA DE EUGENIO MARIA DE HOSTOS Y APENDICE. París, Ediciones Literarias y Artísticas, 1954. 461 p. port., bibl.

Collection of essays by various authors revolving around de Hostos' philosophy, his literary works, his role as a citizen of the Americas, and his work in Puerto Rico, the Dominican Republic, and Cuba. Extensive biographical and bibliographic material is appended.

4.32 Lebrón Rodríguez, Ramón. LA VIDA DEL PROCER MUNOZ RIVERA. San Juan, Imprenta Soltero, 1954. 76 p.

Personal reminiscences of the author, who worked with Muñoz Rivera from 1890 to 1916.

4.33 Malaret, Augusto. MEDALLAS DE ORO. 3. ed. San Juan, Cantero Fernández, 1942. 163 p.

Originally published in 1909, this book offers some glimpses into the lives and works of Manuel Fernández Juncos, Salvador Brau, Román Baldorioty de Castro, José Gautier Benítez, and Pachín Marín.

4.34 Maldonado, Teófilo. ESTE FUE MI MAESTRO: DON JOSE COLL VIDAL. San Juan, Talleres de la Primavera, 1960. 215 p. photos, facsim.

Homage to the man who was director of El Mundo for many years and who served as the author's mentor in the newspaper field.

4.35 Maldonado, Teófilo. HOMBRES DE PRIMERA PLANA. San Juan, Editorial Campos, 1958. 435 p.

Journalistic accounts, previously published by the author as articles in the newspaper El Mundo, of prominent Puerto Rican political figures and important events since the 1920s.

4.36 Maldonado, Teófilo. LUIS A. FERRE: CIUDADANO. San Juan, Talleres de La Primavera, 1960. 209 p. photos.

Laudatory biography of a leader of the pro-statehood movement, with special emphasis on his work, philanthropies, and influences, to 1960, eight years before he became governor of Puerto Rico. Includes some of his addresses.

4.37 Maldonado Denis, Manuel. DON PEDRO ALBIZU CAMPOS (1891–1965), O EL SACRIFICIO DEL VALOR Y EL VALOR DEL SACRIFICIO. Reprint from Cuadernos Americanos, México, núm. 1, en./feb. 1966. 38 p.

A short biography of the late president of the Nationalist party of Puerto Rico.

4.38 Maldonado Denis, Manuel. PEDRO ALBIZU CAMPOS: SELECCIONES. México, Ediciones Veintiuno, 1972. n.a.

4.39 Mathews, Thomas G. LUIS MUÑOZ MARIN: A CONCISE BIOGRAPHY. New York, American R.D.M. Corp., 1967. 61 p. plates, bibl. (A Study Master Publication).

A brief, factual biography of the first elected governor of Puerto Rico (1948–1964), highlighting his political career.

4.40 Medina Ramirez, Ramón. PATRIO-TAS ILLUSTRES PUERTORRIQUEÑOS. Santurce, P.R., 1962. 169 p. ports.

A former president of the Nationalist party writes about eight patriots whose efforts in favor of independence he feels have not been adequately understood. They are: Antonio Valero (1790–1863); Román Baldorioty de Castro (1822–1889); Ramón Emeterio Betances (1827–1899); Segundo Ruiz Belvis (1829–1867); Eugenio María de Hostos (1839–1903); Rosendo Matienzo Cintrón (1855–1913); José de Diego Martínez (1867–1918); and Pedro Albizu Campos (1891–1965).

4.41 Melón de Díaz, Esther M. PUERTO RICO: FIGURAS DEL PRESENTE Y DEL PASADO Y APUNTES HISTORICOS. Río Piedras, P.R., Editorial Edil, 1972. 225 p. plates.

Biographical sketches of more than four hundred outstanding figures in Puerto Rico's history.

4.42 Meneses de Albizu Campos, Laura. ALBIZU CAMPOS Y LA INDEPENDENCIA DE PUERTO RiCO. Habana, Editorial Cultura, 1960. 90 p.

Contemporary history as seen through the eyes of the widow of Pedro Albizu Campos. She discusses the independence movement, how she met Albizu Campos, her life with him, and the Puerto Rican situation.

4.43 Mergal Llera, Angel M. FEDERICO DEGETAU, UN ORIENTADOR DE SU PUEBLO. New York, Hispanic Institute in the United States, 1944. 200 p. port., bibl.

This biography of Degetau (1865–1914), originally a doctoral dissertation at Columbia University, discusses the literary, pedagogical, and political aspects of his work.

4.44 Mirabal, Antonio. PROCERES DEL ARTE: JUAN MOREL CAMPOS. Ponce, P.R., Oficina Municipal de Historia, 1956. 40 p.

A short biography of Juan Morel Campos, perhaps the best known *danza* composer of Puerto Rico. The pamphlet lists nearly two hundred *danzas* and other compositions.

4.45 Morales Carrión, Arturo. THE LONELINESS OF LUIS MUÑOZ RIVERA. Washington, D.C., Office of the Commonwealth of Puerto Rico, 1965. 9 p. (Puerto Rico Booklet Series, no. 1).

Address on the occasion of Luis Muñoz Rivera's anniversary, focusing on his term as Puerto Rico's resident commissioner in Washington from 1910 to 1916.

4.46 Negrón Muñoz, Angela. MUJERES DE PUERTO RICO: DESDE EL PERIODO DE COLONIZACION HASTA EL PRIMER TERCIO DEL SIGLO XX. San Juan, Imprenta Venezuela, 1935. 266 p. illus.

Brief biographical sketches of prominent Puerto Rican women.

4.47 Neumann Gandía, Eduardo. BENEFACTORES Y HOMBRES NOTABLES DE PUERTO RICO. Ponce, P.R., Tip. La Libertad, 1896–1899. 2 v. Reprint. San Juan, Editorial Coquí, in press.

Short biographies of Puerto Ricans of the late nineteenth and early twentieth century.

4.48 Pedreira, Antonio S. UN HOMBRE DE PUEBLO; JOSE CELSO BARBOSA. 2. ed. San Juan, Instituto de Cultura Puertorriqueña, 1965. 230 p.

A biographical study of José Celso Barbosa (1857–1921), who rose from a poor, Negro family to become a noted physician and political leader. He was one of the founders of the Partido Republicano.

4.49 Pedreira, Antonio S. HOSTOS, CIUDADANO DE AMERICA. San Juan, Instituto de Cultura Puertorriqueña, 1964. 173 p. Reprint of 1932 edition. bibl. (Serie Biblioteca Popular).

A probing essay on Hostos' political, social, and educational thought. Pedreira places him on a par with Andrés Bello, Domingo Sarmiento, and José Martí as forgers of a hemispheric conscience.

4.50 THE REPRESENTATIVE MEN OF PORTO RICO. n.p., F.E. Jackson & Son, 1910. 340 p. illus.

Photographs and short biographical sketches of prominent Puerto Ricans and U.S. officials in Puerto Rico during the early years of the twentieth century.

4.51 Rexach Benítez, Roberto F. PEDRO ALBIZU CAMPOS: LEYENDA Y REALIDAD. San Juan, Editorial Coquí, 1961. 22 p. bibl. refs.

Documented essay in which the author presents contrasting views of Albizu—the more widely accepted one of an ardently anti-American revolutionary who discarded the democratic process in favor of violence and another of a liberal thinker who favored "a necessary relationship between Puerto Rico and the United States."

4.52 Ribes Tovar, Federico. ALBIZU CAMPOS, PUERTO RICAN REVOLUTIONARY. Translated by Anthony Rawlings. New York, Plus Ultra Educational Pub., 1971. 252 p. bibl. (Puerto Rico Heritage Series).

Translation of *Albizu Campos, El Revolucionario*. A subjective view of the life and ideology of Pedro Albizu Campos, highlighting events in his life and in the development of the Nationalist party. The last chapter gives a chronological list of independence parties in the history of Puerto Rico.

4.53 Rodríguez Aldave, Alfonso. LABRA, EL PRECURSOR. Habana, Cuba, Nuestra España, 1940. 20 p.

Brief biographical study of Rafael María Labra (1840–1918). Although he was born in Cuba, Labra adopted Puerto Rico as his home and became a Puerto Rican deputy to the Spanish Cortes, where he was a champion of the movement to abolish slavery in Puerto Rico and Cuba.

4.54 Rodríguez Vera, Andrés. BARCELO, CAPITAN DE SU PUEBLO. San Juan, Imprenta Venezuela, 1939. 229 p. port.

The life of Antonio R. Barceló, a prominent political figure of the late nineteenth and early twentieth centuries. He was president of the political party, Unión de Puerto Rico.

4.55 Rosa-Nieves, Cesáreo, and Esther M. Melón. BIOGRAFIAS PUERTORRIQUEÑAS: PERFIL HISTORICO DE UN PUEBLO. Sharon, Conn., Troutman Press, 1970. 487 p. bibl. (Serie Puerto Rico: Realidad y Anhelo, 12).

An alphabetically arranged collection of short biographies of some three hundred persons who have distinguished themselves—both in the past and in the present—in Puerto Rican politics, literature, arts, science, and other fields.

4.56 Senior, Clarence. SANTIAGO IGLESIAS: LABOR CRUSADER. Prologue by Herman Badillo. Hato Rey, P.R., Editorial de la Universidad Interamericana, 1972. illus.

Describes the life of Santiago Iglesias, a prominent labor organizer who died in 1939.

4.57 Suárez Díaz, Ada. EL DOCTOR RAMON EMETERIO BETANCES: SU VIDA Y SU OBRA. [San Juan, Ateneo Puertorriqueño?], 1970. 39 p.

Lecture presented before the Ateneo Puertorriqueño, in November 1965, on this nineteenth-century political leader. The author believes Betances is the only leader of that period who constantly focuses on the problem of Puerto Rico's "need to affirm its nationality."

4.58 Tapia y Rivera, Alejandro. VIDA DEL PINTOR PUERTORRIQUEÑO JOSE CAMPECHE [Y] NOTICIA HISTORICA DE RAMON POWER. San Juan, Imprenta Venezuela, 1946. 105 p. Reprint. Barcelona, Ediciones Rumbos, 1967.

Biographical essays on the painter José Campeche (1752–1809) and Ramón . Power (1775–1813), first Puerto Rican deputy to the Cortes in Spain. Power's speeches before the Cortes are appended.

4.59 Tió, Aurelio. DR. DIEGO ALVAREZ CHANCA (ESTUDIO BIOGRAFICO). San Juan, Instituto de Cultura Puertorriqueña, and Universidad Interamericana de Puerto Rico, 1966. 450 p. illus., maps, bibl. (Publicaciones de la Asociación Médica de Puerto Rico).

A biographical study of Diego Alvarez Chanca, a physician who accompanied Columbus on his second trip to the New World, during which he discovered Puerto Rico. An extensive description of the West Indies, in a letter by Alvarez Chanca, found 300 years after it was written and constituting the first document on the area's geography, flora, fauna, theogony, and ethnology, is reproduced in full.

4.60 Todd, Roberto H. DESFILE DE GOBERNADORES DE PUERTO RICO, 1898–1943. 2d rev. ed. Madrid, Ediciones Hispano-Americanas, 1966. 203 p. photos.

Fragmentary account of the American governors of Puerto Rico from 1898 to 1943.

4.61 Todd, Roberto H. JOSE JULIO HENNA, 1848–1924. San Juan, Cantero Fernández, 1930. 44 p. ports.

Account of the activities of Dr. José Julio Henna, a little-known but nonetheless important figure in the history of the island, who was president of the Puerto Rican Section of the Partido Revolucionario Cubano in New York.

4.62 Todd, Roberto H. PATRIOTAS PUERTORRIQUEÑOS: SILUETAS BIOGRAFICAS. Prólogo de Agustín E. Font. Madrid, Ediciones Iberoamericanas, 1965. 214 p. photos.

Gathers short biographical essays and articles on leading figures, many of whom were personal friends of the author—Hostos, Acosta, Muñoz Rivera, Barbosa, Zeno Gandía, and many others.

4.63 Torregrosa Liceaga, Angel M. JUAN B. SOTO, EDUCADOR Y ORIENTADOR DE JUVENTUDES. San Juan, Imprenta Venezuela, 1938. 196 p.

A biography of an educator and writer who was chancellor of the University of Puerto Rico from 1936 to 1941.

4.64 Vecilla de las Heras, Delfín. FRAY PABLO BENIGNO CARRION DE MALAGA, OBISPO DE PUERTO RICO: VIDA, OBRAS, Y ESCRITOS. Río Piedras, P.R., Editorial Plus Ultra, 1960. 2 v. (392, 276 p.) plates. (Publicaciones

de Historia Eclesiástica de Puerto Rico, Sección para Eruditos, 1).

This biography of Bishop Carrión is useful for the study of the Catholic church in Puerto Rico during the nineteenth century. It includes a list of his pastoral letters and other writings; many of them are printed here.

4.65 Villarini, Angel R., and Juan E. Hernández Cruz. PEDRO ALBIZU CAMPOS: VIDA Y PENSAMIENTO. [San Juan]. Editorial de Educación Política, Partido Independentista Puertorriqueño, [1970]. 59 p.

This pamphlet, first of what is expected to be a series of Albizu's collected writings, contains articles written and statements made in 1930 by the nationalist leader concerning his philosophy on the role of women, historical dates, nationalist policy, and imperialism. Includes a chronology of Albizu's life.

4.66 Zeno de Matos, Elena. MANUEL ZENO GANDIA: DOCUMENTOS BIOGRAFICOS Y CRITICOS. Prólogo del Dr. Francisco Manrique Cabrera. San Juan, 1955 [i.e.1956]. 219 p. ports., illus., bibl.

The novelist's daughter has collected biographical data, letters, and articles praising his work and exploits.

5
CIVILIZATION

5.1 Alegría, Ricardo E. EL INSTITUTO DE CULTURA PUERTORRIQUEÑA: LOS PRIMEROS 5 AÑOS, 1955–1960. San Juan, Instituto de Cultura Puertorriqueña, 1960. 99 p. illus.

A report on the first five years of operation of the Institute of Puerto Rican Culture, created in 1955 with the purpose of "contributing to preserve, promote, enrich and make known the cultural values of the people of Puerto Rico."

5.2 Arana Soto, Salvador. PUERTO RICO: ALMA Y PAISAJE. San Juan, 1970. 86 p.

Brief essays on the island—its natural beauty and its "soul."

5.3 Babín, María Teresa. PANORAMA DE LA CULTURA PUERTORRIQUEÑA. Prólogo por Andrés Iduarte. New York, Las Américas, 1958. 509 p. illus., maps, bibl. (Biblioteca puertorriqueña, 2).

Clear and well-written survey of Puerto Rican civilization in all its expressions: history, land, people, folklore, art, music, literature, national characteristics, customs, and everyday life in general. A basic source for the study of Puerto Rican culture.

5.4 Babín, María Teresa. THE PUERTO RICANS' SPIRIT: THEIR HISTORY, LIFE, AND CULTURE. Translated by Barry Luby. New York, Collier, 1971. 180 p. bibl. refs. Also published in Spanish: LA CULTURA DE PUERTO RICO. Ed. abreviada. San Juan, Instituto de Cultura Puertorriqueña, 1970.

Useful, brief, general survey of the cultural history of Puerto Rico showing how the roots of its cultural heritage, the geographical and physical nature of the island, its historical development, and its inhabitants are expressed through literature, folklore, art, and traditions. A chronology of important historical events is appended.

5.5 Buitrago Hermanet, Argelia María. Ethnic Identification of Puerto Rican Seventh Graders. Ph.D. dissertation, University of Massachusetts, 1971. In DISSERTATION ABSTRACTS INTERNATIONAL, v. 32, no. 8, p. 4350-A.

The identity crisis experienced by Puerto Rican seventh graders, both on the island and on the mainland, is treated in this study as a basis for studying the process of assimilation and ascertaining the students' degree of cultural solidarity.

5.6 Fernández Méndez, Eugenio. HISTORIA CULTURAL DE PUERTO RICO, 1493–1968. ed. rev. San Juan, Ediciones El Cemí, 1970. 351 p. illus., bibl. refs.

A cultural history of Puerto Rico, written by a Puerto Rican anthropologist. It covers the Iberian antecedents of Puerto Rican society and contains an extensive treatment of Salvador Brau and his time—the period in which the Puerto Rican nationality was formed. The author also discusses the cultural changes that have resulted from the encounter of two cultures in the island.

5.7 Fernández Méndez, Eugenio. LA IDENTIDAD Y LA CULTURA: CRITICAS Y VALORACIONES EN TORNO A LA HISTORIA SOCIAL DE PUERTO RICO. 2. ed. rev. y aumentada. San Juan, Instituto de Cultura Puertorriqueña, 1965, 249 p.

Addresses, essays, and articles collected around the central theme of identity and culture. They cover ideas on education, adolescents, students, national character, industrialization, the family, and minorities.

5.8 Hostos, Adolfo de. CARIBBEANS BORN AND BRED. New York, Vantage Press, 1968, c1969. 206 p.

Descriptions and reminiscences, with a historical undertone, of life in Puerto Rico, by the son of Eugenio María de Hostos.

5.9 Laguerre, Enrique A. PULSO DE PUERTO RICO, 1952–1954. San Juan, Biblioteca de Autores Puertorriqueños 1956. 416 p.

A selection of cultural information programs and literary criticism broadcast during the two years 1952–1954, which the author considers a transition period. He focuses on people active in the cultural life of Puerto Rico and includes studies on the press, history, tourism, education, arts and letters, folklore, and research.

5.10 Maldonado Denis, Manuel. PUERTO RICO: MITO Y REALIDAD. Barcelona, Ediciones Península, 1969. 269 p.

Collection of essays, speeches, and articles on the colonial status of Puerto Rico and the contrast, in 1968, between the struggles for liberation in other parts of the world and the perpetuation of colonialism there. The author, a strong advocate of independence for Puerto Rico, analyzes the historical and sociological factors of political and economic subordination, cultural assimilation, the role of the intellectual, and the independence movement both today and in the past.

5.11 Mañach, Jorge. TEORIA DE LA FRONTERA. Introducción de Concha Meléndez. Río Piedras, Editorial Universitaria, Universidad de Puerto Rico, 1970. 171 p.

A series of lectures published posthumously in which the author, a Cuban, deals with the theme of the frontier, "especially our (the Latin American) cultural frontier with the United States, seen not only within itself, but in what it holds for present and future relations between the two Americas." In a last chapter on Puerto Rico he explains why he considers the island the meeting point for the cultures of the hemisphere—not so much because of its geographical location, but because of its historical and cultural heritage.

5.12 Martín, José Luis. MEDITACIONES PUERTORRIQUEÑAS: UNA ZAMBULLIDA EN LA CONCIENCIA PUERTORRIQUEÑA. San Juan, Departamento de Instrucción Pública, 1959. 75 p. illus.

Reflections on various aspects of the Puerto Rican experience which have determined its essential nature. The Indian, Spanish, African, and North American elements are all discussed.

5.13 Mellado, Ramón. PUERTO RICO Y OCCIDENTE: ENSAYOS PEDAGOGICOS. San Juan, Editorial Edil, 1969. 185 p. bibl.

A compilation of four essays by a former secretary of education about Puerto Ricans and their society, their culture, and their education. Principal themes of the essays are: man and his mental processes, Puerto Rican society, and Puerto Rico and the Western world.

5.14 Orama Padilla, Carlos. POSTAL DE TIERRA ADENTRO: EL HOMBRE Y EL PAISAJE. Barcelona, Ediciones Rumbos, 1963. 212 p.

Collection of brief narratives on various types of Puerto Ricans, in particular the *jíbaro* or peasant.

5.15 Padín, José. AMERICAN CITIZENSHIP AND OTHER ADDRESSES. San Juan, Puerto Rico School Review, [1934]. 20 p.

Three important speeches by a commissioner of education who distinguished himself by his defense of the preservation and enrichment of the island's Hispanic culture.

5.16 Padín, José. PERSONAS SOBRE COSAS. San Juan, Biblioteca de Autores Puertorriqueños, 1951. 225 p.

A collection of speeches, lectures, and articles in which the author comments on different aspects of Puerto Rican life, with emphasis on everyday experience. He discusses the function of the school in the life of the island, the Americanization of Puerto Rico, democracy and public opinion, the duties of a citizen, and the educational function of the Church.

5.17 Pedreira, Antonio S. INSULARISMO: ENSAYOS DE INTERPRETACION PUERTORRIQUEÑA. Madrid, 1934. 237 p. Reprint. Río Piedras, P.R., Editorial Edil, 1969. 176 p. (*his* Obras Completas, v. 3).

This classic interpretation of the collective Puerto Rican spirit delves into the essence of what is Puerto Rico and the Puerto Rican by examining the history, ethnology, psychology, literature, and folk arts.

5.18 Rodríguez Pastor, José. LA IMPORTANCIA DE SER PUERTORRIQUEÑO. San Juan, Editorial Cordillera, 1971. 68 p. (Colección Picachos).

Eight articles and one poem in which the author rejects statehood for Puerto Rico and defends the present political status as the way to preserve language and identity while at the same time maintaining an "honorable association" with the United States.

5.19 Santullano, Luis. MIRADA AL CARIBE: FRICCION DE CULTURAS EN PUERTO RICO. México, El Colegio de México, Centro de Estudios Sociales, 1945. 85 p. (Jornadas, 54).

Although the author, a Spaniard, is deeply disturbed by and immensely critical of the acculturation he sees taking place in Puerto Rico, he concludes that "Puerto Ricans are Puerto Rican." The cultural tradition, language, and civilization inherited from Spain, together with native and other newly acquired elements, are producing, in his opinion, some very special manifestations and characteristics that define the Puerto Rican.

5.20 Vientós Gastón, Nilita. INDICE CULTURAL. Río Piedras, Ediciones de la Universidad de Puerto Rico, 1962–1971. 4 v. (290, 267, 182, 242 p.).

Contents: v. 1, 1948–55 and 1956. v. 2, 1957–1958. v. 3, 1959–1960. v. 4, 1961–1962.

Collection of columns written for the most part for *El Mundo*, under the title "Indice Cultural." In them, Ms. Vientós comments on the literary scene in Puerto Rico and abroad, as well as on contemporary local topics.

5.21 Wagenheim, Kal. PUERTO RICO: A PROFILE. Foreword by Piri Thomas. New York, Praeger, 1970. 286 p. illus., bibl. (Praeger Country Profile Series).

A good introductory text on Puerto Rico. After placing the island in its Caribbean context, the author, a long-time resident of Puerto Rico, looks into its cultural, historical, geo-demographic, economic, and social aspects. He discusses also, at some length, the island's politics and government.

6
COOKERY AND NUTRITION

6.1 Aboy de Valdejulli, Carmen. THE ART OF CARIBBEAN COOKERY. Garden City, N.Y., Doubleday, 1957. 254 p. illus.

Recipes for Puerto Rican and international dishes. (Also published in Spanish: *Cocina Criolla*. 12. ed., South Braintree, Mass., Alpine Press, 1967. 467 p.)

6.2 Blanco, Ana Teresa. Nutrition Studies in Puerto Rico. Río Piedras, Social Science Research Center, University of Puerto Rico, 1946. 96 l. tables, graphs, bibl. refs. mimeographed.

Discusses the various growth and dietary studies done in Puerto Rico and the incidence of deficiency diseases and recommends measures to improve nutrition.

6.3 Cabanillas, Berta. ORIGENES DE LOS HABITOS ALIMENTICIOS DEL PUEBLO DE PUERTO RICO. Madrid, Gráficas Bachende, 1955. 19 p.

Historical essay on agricultural production, nutritional patterns, and food imports and exports.

6.4 Cabanillas, Berta, and Carmen Ginorio. PUERTO RICAN DISHES. 2d ed. Río Piedras, P.R., 1966. 151 p. illus.

Traditional island recipes, with a glossary of Spanish terms used in local cookery. Ms. Cabanillas is the author of *Cocine a Gusto*, also available as a talking book for the blind and physically handicapped.

6.5 EL COCINERO PUERTORRIQUEÑO. San Juan, Editorial Coquí, 1971. 271 p. facsim.

New edition of the first known book of Puerto Rican cookery, first published in 1859.

6.6 Descartes, Sol Luis, S. Díaz Pacheco, and José R. Noguera. FOOD CONSUMPTION STUDIES IN PUERTO RICO. Río Piedras, P.R., Agricultural Experiment Station, 1941. 76 p. illus., tables, diagrs. (Bulletin no. 59).

A bulletin that integrates the results of five separate reports by the Agricultural Experiment Station on different aspects of food consumption in Puerto Rico. Each food is discussed from the standpoint of amounts available for consumption, consumption rates, factors affecting consumption, and sources of supply.

6.7 Díaz Pacheco, Santiago. CONSUMO DE ALIMENTOS EN LA ZONA RURAL DE PUERTO RICO. Río Piedras, P.R., Estación Experimental Agrícola, 1941. 23 p. tables, diagrs. (Boletín núm. 57). English summary.

Reports the results of a 1939 survey on food consumption among 439 rural families.

6.8 Díaz Pacheco, Santiago. CONSUMO DE ALIMENTOS EN LA ZONA URBANA DE PUERTO RICO. Río Piedras, P.R., Estación Experimental Agrícola,

[1940]. 29 p. tables, diagrs. (Boletín núm. 57) English summary.

Reports the results of a food consumption study comprising 1,900 families in twenty-two cities and towns in 1937. Together with the preceding report on the rural areas, it provides a picture, not only of food consumption patterns, but of general economic and social conditions at the time.

6.9 Dooley, Elizabeth B.K. PUERTO RICAN COOKBOOK. Introduction by Muna Lee. Richmond, Va., Dietz Press, 1948. 175 p. illus.

Provides recipes for native dishes plus many American, European, and West Indian recipes, adapted to the local produce.

6.10 Figueroa de Valentín, Edith. Attitudes towards Foods of Homemakers Living in Tras Talleres, San Juan, Puerto Rico. Ed.D. dissertation, Texas Tech. University, 1971. *In* DISSERTATION ABSTRACTS INTERNATIONAL, v. 32, no. 4, p. 1745-A.

A study aimed at determining factors that might affect food consumption. It discusses the attitudes of homemakers toward the adequacy of their diets and toward food as it relates to nutrition, health, cost, tradition, and other factors.

6.11 Hill, E.B., and J.R. Noguera. THE FOOD SUPPLY OF PUERTO RICO. Río Piedras, P.R., Agricultural Experiment Station, 1940. 32 p. bibl. (Bulletin no. 55). Spanish summary.

Analysis of how the island can attain greater self-sufficiency in food production. It summarizes the authors' findings on the amounts and kinds of food available there for human consumption.

6.12 PORTO RICAN COOK BOOK. Published by the Ladies Aid Society of the First Methodist Church of San Juan, Porto Rico. San Juan, M. Burillo, [1909?] 130 p.

A cookbook published some ten years after the U.S. invasion "to enable Americans in Porto Rico to make the best possible use of the good things on the island."

6.13 Roberts, Lydia Jane. THE DOÑA ELENA PROJECT: A BETTER LIVING PROGRAM IN AN ISOLATED RURAL COMMUNITY. Río Piedras, University of Puerto Rico, 1963. 113 p. illus., charts, tables.

Report on the first five years of an innovative pilot program to help families in a rural *barrio* of Comerío to improve their nutrition and the conditions of their home and community living.

6.14 Romano, Dora R. de. COCINE CONMIGO. San Juan, 1970. 406 p.

Includes recipes of traditional Puerto Rican dishes as well as international favorites.

6.15 Vincenty, Carlos. THE PRESENT STATUS OF YEAST IN HUMAN NUTRITION WITH PARTICULAR APPLICATION TO THE PUERTO RICAN RURAL DIET. San Juan, Economic Development Administration, Department of Industrial Research, 1950. tables, bibl. Reprinted from *El Crisol*, v. 6, no. 83, 1950: 83-94.

Reports the results of tests to develop an economical process for manufacturing yeast that might be utilized to supplement the Puerto Rican diet, and discusses various ways in which such yeast could be used.

6.16 Willsey, Elsie Mae. TROPICAL FOODS. San Juan, University of Puerto Rico, 1925–1927. 3 v. (Dept. of Home Economics, University of Puerto Rico. Bulletin nos. 1–3).

Contents: v. 1, Vegetables: Chayote, Yautía, Plantain, Banana. v. 2, Vegetables: Arracacha, Breadfruit, Casava, Lerén, Malanga. v. 3, Vegetables: Rice and the Legumes.

Booklets aimed at standardizing the traditional recipes of Puerto Rico and introducing new ways of serving tropical vegetables and fruits.

7
DESCRIPTION AND TRAVEL, AND GEOGRAPHY

7.1 Baggs, William C. PUERTO RICO: SHOWCASE OF DEVELOPMENT. Encyclopaedia Britannica, 1962. 38 p. illus., maps, bibl. Reprinted from 1962 *Britannica Book of the Year*.

A brief account of Puerto Rico's state of economic, social, educational, and political development in the early 1960s, with some information on the island's history and geography.

7.2 Bird, Esteban A. FISHING OFF PUERTO RICO. Foreword by Frank O'Brien. New York, A.S. Barnes, 1960. 111 p. plates, maps, tables.

A book on the development of deep-sea fishing as a sport in Puerto Rico.

7.3 Bowen, J. David. THE ISLAND OF PUERTO RICO. Philadelphia, Lippincott, 1968. 136 p. illus. (Portraits of the Nations Series).

A general introductory text to the island and its people.

7.4 Brown, Dwight Alan. Erosion and Morphometry of Small Drainage Basins in Eastern Puerto Rico. Ph.D. dissertation, University of Kansas, 1969. *In* DISSERTATION ABSTRACTS INTERNATIONAL, v. 30, no. 6, p. 2754-B.

This is a study of the relations of drainage basin form and process. The rainy tropical environment of eastern Puerto Rico provides an excellent location for examining form-process relations where fluvial processes strongly dominate the array of morphogenic energies.

7.5 Browne, George Waldo, and Nathan Haskell Dole. THE NEW AMERICA AND THE FAR EAST. Introduction by Edward S. Ellis. Boston, Marshall Jones, 1901–1910. 10 v. illus., plates, maps.

Volume 8 describes a journey through Cuba and Puerto Rico, which had recently become U.S. possessions.

It records how North Americans reacted at the turn of the century to these tropical islands and their inhabitants, who led "careless, indolent lives."

7.6 Bryan, William S., ed. OUR ISLANDS AND THEIR PEOPLE AS SEEN WITH CAMERA AND PENCIL. v. 2. Introduced by Major-General Joseph Wheeler, United States Army, with special descriptive matter and narratives by José de Olivares. St. Louis, N.D. Thompson Pub., 1899. 776 p.

Photographs and descriptions of "the people and the islands lately acquired from Spain," including Hawaii, the Philippines, and Puerto Rico. This book provides a valuable source for the study of the land, the people, and the way of life in 1898.

7.7 Chiesa de Pérez, Carmen. ENJOY PUERTO RICO: INTIMATE VIEWS AND TOURS. 1st ed. New York, Vantage Press, 1961. 316 p. illus., map.

As is the fate of most guide books, this one is outdated by the changes in roads, hotels, restaurants, places of entertainment, and telephone numbers. However, the second part of the book offers a useful survey, from early historical events to prominent Puerto Ricans of today.

7.8 Clark, Sydney, and Margaret Zellers. ALL THE BEST IN THE CARIBBEAN, INCLUDING PUERTO RICO AND THE VIRGIN ISLANDS. 7th ed. New York, Dodd, Mead, 1972. 420 p. illus.

Chapter 11 of this tourist guide is devoted to Puerto Rico. It briefly describes travel arrangements, sights, holiday side trips and tours, restaurants, and shopping.

7.9 Dewell, James D. DOWN IN PORTO RICO WITH A KODAK. New Haven,

Conn., Record Pub., 1898. 102 p. photos., illus., map.

A U.S. businessman records his trip to the island in January 1898.

7.10 Dinhofer, Alfred D. OUR MAN IN SAN JUAN. Design and illustrations by Ian. San Juan, Starpress, 1964. 128 p. illus., ports.

A collection of articles originally published in the *San Juan Star.*

7.11 Flinter, George Dawson. AN AC-COUNT OF THE PRESENT STATE OF THE ISLAND OF PUERTO RICO. London, Longman Rees, Orme, Brown, Green and Longman, 1834. 392 p. Reprint. San Juan, Editorial Coquí, 1971.

This book, a classic in its field, describes Puerto Rico as seen by an officer in the British Army who spent twenty-one years in the West Indies. It covers the climate and geography, social structure, government, commerce, agriculture, slavery, labor, and prison conditions. The author examines the colonial administration of Spain, compares it with that of France and England and makes recommendations on policy improvements. He offers an enlightened argument for the emancipation of slaves and the cessation of the slave trade. The author's analysis also dispels the often-repeated Spanish "black legend," by comparing the treatment of slaves by the three major colonial powers.

7.12 Gascó Contell, Emilio. MES Y MEDIO EN PUERTO RICO. Madrid, Afrodisio Aguado, 1964. 71 p.

A Spaniard records his impressions of a trip to Puerto Rico.

7.13 George, Marian M. A LITTLE JOURNEY TO CUBA AND PORTO RICO. Rev. ed. Chicago, A. Flanagan Co., 1930. 159 p. illus. (Library of Travel).

One of the many travel books on Puerto Rico written during the twenties and thirties, which gave rise to many of the misconceptions and stereotypes still prevalent today.

7.14 Gruber, Ruth. PUERTO RICO: IS-LAND OF PROMISE. New York, Hill and Wang, 1960. 216 p. illus.

Journalistic account and description of Puerto Rico in the late fifties and early sixties; covers political life, leaders, industrialization, labor, socioeconomic conditions, and migration.

7.15 Hancock, Ralph. PUERTO RICO: A TRAVELERS' GUIDE. Princeton, N.J., D. Van Nostrand, 1962. 304 p. map.

Alphabetically arranged compilation of facts and information, useful for both inexperienced and seasoned travelers.

7.16 Hannau, Hans W. PUERTO RICO. Munich, W. Andemann (Distributed by Doubleday, Garden City, N.Y.), 1967. 60 p. plates, map. (Panorama Books). English and Spanish captions.

This is a pictorial travel guide to Puerto Rico. Thirty color plates illustrate the descriptive text which gives a general view of history, geography, and the most important sights.

7.17 Huebener, Theodore. PUERTO RICO TODAY. New York, Holt, [1960]. 116 p. illus.

A brief survey of the geography, history, and government of Puerto Rico precedes an overview of its cities, economy, education, cultural life, and people. (Issued also in Spanish by the same publisher: *Así es Puerto Rico.*)

7.18 Jiménez de la Romera, Waldo. CUBA, PUERTO-RICO, Y FILIPINAS. Fotograbados de Joarizti y Mariescurrena. Dibujos de Passos y Riquero. Cromos de Xumetra. Barcelona, Est. Tip. Editorial de Daniel Corteza, 1887. 944 p. (*His* España: sus monumentos y artes; su naturaleza e historia, v. 11).

A nineteenth-century Spanish traveler offers a general description of these islands—their geography, indigenous culture, colonial history, the various foreign attacks and sieges, and their monuments.

7.19 Jones, Clarence F., and Rafael Picó, eds. SYMPOSIUM ON THE GEOGRAPHY OF PUERTO RICO. Río Piedras, University of Puerto Rico Press, 1955. 503 p. illus., maps, bibl. refs.

Compilation of essays on the characteristics of Puerto Rico's land use; an outgrowth of the work done in the Rural Land Classification Program between 1949 and 1951, including the results of research and field work. The writings cover the development of survey techniques, landform types, the limestone belt, the pineapple industry, and land utilization studies by regions.

7.20 La Orden Miracle, Ernesto. IMAGE OF PUERTO RICO. Madrid, Ediciones Cultura Hispánica, 1965. unp. photos, color plates, maps, bibl.

English version of *Estampas de Puerto Rico*, a collection of photographs and color plates on Puerto Rico, its people, the historical monuments, landscape, architecture, folk arts, and towns.

7.21 MAPAS DE CARRETERAS ESTATALES DE PUERTO RICO AL 1 DE ENERO DE 1971. San Juan, Autoridad de Carreteras, 1971. 63x85 cm; scale 1:220,000.

Shows existing, under construction, and planned primary, secondary, and local roads, with their numbering system and distances.

7.22 Monteagudo, Antonio M. ALBUM DE ORO DE PUERTO RICO. GOLDEN ALBUM OF PUERTO RICO. Havana, Artes Gráficas, 1939. 510 p. illus.

Pictorial account of the island in the 1930s. It includes several hundred photographs of public buildings, historical monuments, prominent persons, outstanding architecture, and scenery.

7.23 Morton, C. Manly. ISLE OF ENCHANTMENT: STORIES AND PEOPLE OF PUERTO RICO. St. Louis, Mo., Bethany Press, 1970. 93 p.

The author, who taught at the Evangelical Seminary for twenty-three years, has written these stories on the old Puerto Rico, vestiges of which still remain in the mountains, on the "simple way of life, and the simplicity of those who live it." The author's purpose is "to keep alive that which is invaluable in the understanding of the people of today." He feels that "those who forget or become ashamed of the struggles and privations of their ancestors soon become unworthy of the heritage they have received."

7.24 Mower, Roland Deloy. The Discrimination of Tropical Land Use in Puerto Rico: An Analysis Using Multispectral Imagery. Ph.D. dissertation, University of Kansas, 1971. *In* DISSERTATION ABSTRACTS INTERNATIONAL, v. 32, no. 10, p. 5863-B.

This study evaluated various types of multispectral remote sensor imagery to assess their usefulness for discriminating and mapping land use categories found in a tropical environment.

7.25 Page, Homer. PUERTO RICO: THE QUIET REVOLUTION. New York, Viking Press, 1963. 175 p. illus. (A Studio Book).

A balanced photographic essay covering all aspects of Puerto Rican life.

7.26 Picó, Rafael. THE GEOGRAPHIC REGIONS OF PUERTO RICO. Río Piedras, University of Puerto Rico Press, 1950. 256 p. illus., maps, bibl.

This book, based on the author's doctoral dissertation, covers the diversity of Puerto Rico's physical environment. It defines eleven regions and subdivisions based on physical and economic factors and describes each region and the aspects that give it a definite character: topography, climate, soils, vegetation, economic activities, and population.

7.27 Picó, Rafael. NUEVA GEOGRAFIA DE PUERTO RICO: FISICA, ECONOMICA, Y SOCIAL. Con la colaboración de Zayda Buitrago de Santiago y Héctor H. Berríos. San Juan, Editorial Universitaria, Universidad de Puerto Rico, 1969. 460 p. illus., tables, maps, bibl.

The most complete work on this topic, it covers many aspects of the geography of the island: the physical environment and its influence on life, topography, hydrology, minerals, oceanic resources, climate, vegetation, soils, population and land, economic structure, agriculture, manufacturing, tourism, commerce, transportation, economic prospects, and geographic regions.

7.28 PUERTO RICO. Barranquilla, Colombia, Editora Nacional, 1949. 420 p. illus., map, tables. (Colección América, t. 10).

A comprehensive survey of Puerto

Rico written by specialists in the subjects covered, including Emilio S. Belaval, Facundo Bueso, Ramón Lavandero, Arturo Morales Carrión, María Luisa Muñoz, and others. The book covers an excellent cross-section of the land, people, civilization, culture, and history, as well as information pertaining to the period in which it was written.

7.29 PUERTO RICO. Prepared with the cooperation of the American Geographical Society. Garden City, N.Y., Doubleday, 1968. 64 p. illus., maps. (Around the World Program).

This book briefly describes various aspects of the land, people, and history of Puerto Rico with emphasis on contemporary developments. Tipped in color plates illustrate the text.

7.30 PUERTO RICO; A GUIDE TO THE ISLAND OF BORINQUEN. New York, University Society, 1940. 409 p. maps, plates, bibl. (American Guide Series).

This book, compiled and written by the Puerto Rico Reconstruction Administration in cooperation with the Writer's Program of the Work Projects Administration, was one of the first comprehensive tourist guides to the island.

7.31 Ober, Frederick Albion. PUERTO RICO AND ITS RESOURCES. New York, D. Appleton, 1899. 282 p. plates, map.

A comprehensive work written for the most part as the result of the author's personal experience and observations. It includes coverage of many diverse aspects of the island, from an analysis of its strategic and commercial importance to its forms of entertainment, with references to many other aspects such as agricultural products, natural history, climate, and hurricanes.

7.32 PUERTO RICO FACHADA AL CIELO. Recopilación de interés urbanístico preparada y publicada mediante la colaboración del Instituto de Cultura Puertorriqueña y el Departamento de Obras Públicas. San Juan, 1967. 183 p. photos, map, diagr.

Collection of eighty-two aerial photographs, with street diagrams and brief historical and population summaries of all the cities and towns in Puerto Rico. Knowledge of traditional urban centers can help in understanding the lifestyle of the people they serve and in the planning of future communities.

7.33 Ramos Llompart, Arturo. DE ESTE SAN JUAN ROMANTICO: CANTIGA DE UNAS PIEDRAS Y UNOS HOMBRES. San Juan, Editorial Club de la Prensa, 1964. 206 p. illus.

Collection of articles published in the *Diario de Puerto Rico, El Mundo,* and *Bohemia* about the city of San Juan.

7.34 Ramsey, Ullman James, and Al Dinhofer. "Puerto Rico." *In their* CARIBBEAN HERE AND NOW: THE COMPLETE 1971–1972 GUIDE TO THE SUNNY ISLANDS AND VACATION LANDS. 3d ed. New York, Macmillan, 1970. p. 237–270. map.

This chapter is a compact visitors' guide to the island, including basic facts on travel, climate, clothes, food, geography, transportation, and places of interest and information on Vieques, Mona, and Culebra.

7.35 Rand McNally. PUERTO RICO: MAPA OFICIAL. Chicago, Ill., 1970. 33x82 cm. Scale ca. 1:230,000.

Prepared for Texaco, this road map includes a town index, a distance table, and useful information for the traveler.

7.36 Richardson, Lewis Cutler. PUERTO RICO, CARIBBEAN CROSSROADS. Produced under the sponsorship of the Board of Publications, University of Puerto Rico; photography by Charles E. Rotkin. New York, U.S. Camera Pub., 1947. 144 p. illus., maps.

Documentary study of Puerto Rico between 1944 and 1946. Both the text and the photographs give a balanced cross section of life in the island in the 1940s. The presentation is neither one of an idyllic tropical paradise, nor one of total squalor and social injustice.

7.37 Robinson, Albert Gardner. THE PORTO RICO OF TODAY; PEN PICTURES OF THE PEOPLE AND THE COUNTRY. New York, C. Scribner's, 1899. 240 p. plates, maps.

The author, a war correspondent, accompanied one of the first detachments of the U.S. army of invasion to Puerto Rico. From August to October 1898, he wrote for the New York *Evening Post* a series of letters about the people and the country he saw. This account is based on those articles.

7.38 Samiloff, Louise Cripps. DISCOVERING PUERTO RICO. Philadelphia, Whitmore Pub., 1969. 152 p.

This book is a sympathetic and readable description of life in Puerto Rico for visitors and for those who, like the author, decide to live there. It covers old San Juan, places with interesting scenery, the people, the economic and political situation, racial integration, and the cost of living.

7.39 Santana, Jorge, and Emilio Colón. SAN JUAN. Fotografías de Jorge Santana y texto en español e inglés por Emilio M. Colón. San Juan, Editorial Coquí, in press.

A pictorial history of the capital of Puerto Rico, including aerial photographs; interior and exterior shots of residential and public buildings and the people who live or work in them; maps; plans; etc.

7.40 Schwartz, Marvin W. PUERTO RICO. New York, Madison Square Press, 1969. unp. illus. Parallel text in English and Spanish.

This book is a photographic essay in black and white on Puerto Rico's people, art, nature, and historical monuments as seen by a sensitive photographer. A brief epilogue by Ricardo E. Alegría touches on the origins and traditions of the island.

7.41 Slater, Mary. "Puerto Rico: Island with Two Faces." *In her* THE CARIBBEAN ISLANDS. New York, Viking Press, 1968. p. 106–121. illus., map.

Besides the more usual tourist information such as places of interest, sights and tours, the chapter devoted to Puerto Rico offers information on its culture and history.

7.42 West, Robert C., and John P. Augelli. MIDDLE AMERICA: ITS LANDS AND PEOPLES. Englewood Cliffs, N.J., Prentice-Hall, 1966. 482 p. illus., maps, tables, bibl.

A comprehensive geography of the West Indies, Mexico, and Central America. Besides chapters on individual countries, including one on Cuba and Puerto Rico, the work also has general chapters on pre-European aboriginal, European colonial, and nineteenth- and twentieth-century human geography of the region.

7.43 Yurchenko, Henrietta. HABLAMOS: PUERTO RICANS SPEAK. New York, Praeger, 1971. 136 p. illus.

Transcripts of interviews with fifteen Puerto Ricans active in diverse fields: an octogenarian, an elderly *santero*, an herb doctor, a self-proclaimed witch, the leader of a cult, an artist, a former secretary of labor, a Brazilian dissident priest, an intellectual, and others. By selecting such atypical individuals, the author fails to meet her stated objective of helping the reader "understand the Puerto Ricans on the Island and therefore also the Puerto Ricans in their own communities in the States."

8
ECONOMY

8.1 Allen, Charles H. "Opportunities in Porto Rico." *In* Wood, Leonard, and others. OPPORTUNITIES IN THE COLONIES AND CUBA. New York, Lewis, Scribner, 1902. p. 275–369.

The first U.S.-appointed civil governor of Puerto Rico describes economic conditions and opportunities on the island at the beginning of the century.

8.2 Andersen (Arthur) and Co. TAX AND TRADE GUIDE: PUERTO RICO. 2d.

ed. Chicago, 1972. 179 p. map, bibl. (Tax and Trade Guide Series).

Intended for use by A. Andersen offices and their clients, this book offers basic information on the government, business organizations, taxes, industrial incentives, employment and labor legislation, and banking and finance.

8.3   Andic, Fuat M. DISTRIBUTION OF FAMILY INCOMES IN PUERTO RICO: A CASE STUDY OF THE IMPACT OF ECONOMIC DEVELOPMENT ON INCOME DISTRIBUTION. Foreword by Rafael Picó. Río Piedras, Institute of Caribbean Studies, University of Puerto Rico, 1964. 173 p. illus., tables. (Caribbean Monograph Series, no. 1)

Examines the hypothesis that economic development tends to reduce income inequality, using the evidence provided by Puerto Rico's economic development since the 1940s. Estimates changes in the degree of inequality in the distribution of income in Puerto Rico.

8.4   Arroyo, Rafael. STUDIES ON RUM. Río Piedras, Agricultural Experiment Station, University of Puerto Rico, 1945. 272 p. graphs, tables, bibl, refs. (Research Bulletin no. 5) Spanish summary.

This book publishes the results of an in-depth study conducted between 1936 and 1942 on rum manufacture, one of the first scientific inquiries into what was to become one of the island's leading industries. Research covered the fermentation process and related matters such as yeast selection, pretreatment of raw materials, and mashing operations.

8.5   Austin, Oscar Phelps. OUR TRADE WITH HAWAII AND PORTO RICO. Philadelphia, American Academy of Political and Social Science, 1902. p. 47–52. (Publications of the American Academy of Political and Social Sciences, no. 339).

This reprint of a brief article by the chief of the Federal Bureau of Statistics provides tables of U.S. commerce with Puerto Rico during the period 1892-1901.

8.6   Baer, Werner. THE PUERTO RICAN ECONOMY AND UNITED STATES ECONOMIC FLUCTUATIONS. Foreword by John Kenneth Galbraith. Río Piedras, Social Science Research Center, University of Puerto Rico, 1962. 155 p. tables, diagrs., bibl.

An analysis of past, present, and possible future effects of economic fluctuations in the United States on the Puerto Rican economy. It discusses the two U.S. recessions in the 1950s and concludes that their effect on the island was mild, but that reactions to those two recessions did not reveal the true sensitivity of Puerto Rico to the U.S. economic cycle.

8.7   Barela, Fred. THE PUERTO RICAN LABOR RELATIONS ACT: A STATE LABOR POLICY AND ITS APPLICATION. Río Piedras, Editorial Universitaria, Universidad de Puerto Rico, 1964. 241 p. bibl.

A study of the development and application of the law governing labor relations in Puerto Rico, based on an analysis of nearly six thousand cases brought before the State Labor Relations Board. Barela was director of the island's Office of Labor Relations from 1947 to 1962.

8.8   Barton, Hubert C. PUERTO RICO'S INDUSTRIAL DEVELOPMENT PROGRAM, 1942–1960. Cambridge, Mass., Center for International Affairs, Harvard University, 1959. 50 p. tables, graphs.

A historical survey of the policies, laws, and institutions governing the island's economic development program, by one of its chief advisers.

8.9   Bhatia, Mohinder S. REDISTRIBUTION OF INCOME THROUGH THE FISCAL SYSTEM OF PUERTO RICO. Foreword by Alvin Mayne. San Juan, Puerto Rico Planning Board, 1960. 49 p. tables.

Paper aimed at spelling out in quantitative terms the incidence of taxation and the effects of government expenditures on various income brackets, and at highlighting the overall effects of the fiscal system on spending-unit income brackets in Puerto Rico.

8.10 British National Export Council. PUERTO RICO: THE HIDDEN AMERICAN MARKET. London, B.N.E.C., 1968. 41 p. map.

A British analysis of the Puerto Rican market, arranged by product categories.

8.11 Caribbean Scholar's Conference, 2d, Mona, Jamaica, 1964. THE CARIBBEAN IN TRANSITION: PAPERS ON SOCIAL, POLITICAL AND ECONOMIC DEVELOPMENT. Edited by Fuat M. Andic and Thomas G. Mathews. Foreword by Thomas G. Mathews. Río Piedras, Institute of Caribbean Studies, University of Puerto Rico, 1965. 353 p. tables, map, bibl., refs.

Papers on Puerto Rico: "Changes in the income of the Puerto Rican Labor Force, 1949–1959," by F.M. Andic; "The Commonwealth Concept," by J.E. Arrarás; "Administrative Reform and Political Change in Puerto Rico," by C.T. Goodsell; "Apuntes preliminares sobre la 'intelligentsia' puertorriqueña y del Caribe hispánico," by M. Maldonado Denis; "Personalism as a Pattern of Political Interaction," by E. Seda Bonilla; "Foreign Sector Lessons of the Puerto Rican Development Experience," by A.P. Thorne.

8.12 Carroll, Henry K. REPORT ON THE ISLAND OF PORTO RICO. Washington, Govt. Print. Off., 1899. 813 p. tables. Reprint. San Juan, Editorial Coquí, in press.

Submitted to President McKinley by Commissioner Carroll after the war of 1898, this report was the result of his visits to the island to investigate its civil, financial, and social conditions. It contains an exhaustive appendix that reproduces testimony given at hearings held by him in Puerto Rico, statements and petitions presented to him, and statistical tables obtained from official sources.

8.13 Cestero, Belén H. BALANCE OF EXTERNAL PAYMENTS OF PUERTO RICO, FISCAL YEARS 1941–42 TO 1947–48. San Juan, Office of Governor, Bureau of the Budget, Division of Statistics, 1950. 58 p. tables. English and Spanish text.

Tables, plus a short analysis of the balance of payments situation in 1946–1947 and 1947–1948 compared with that of the previous five years.

8.14 Clapp & Mayne. A STRATEGY OF REGIONAL ECONOMIC DEVELOPMENT FOR THE CARIBBEAN: A REPORT TO THE CARIBBEAN ECONOMIC DEVELOPMENT CORPORATION. San Juan, Caribbean Economic Development Corp., 1968. 90 p. tables, charts, bibl.

A summary of problems related to the economic development of the Caribbean area as a whole, recommending steps that the Caribbean countries could consider jointly to raise family income and government revenues so as to increase purchasing power, stimulate the formation of domestic capital, reduce dependence on grants-in-aid, and increase the funds available for social services. There is a brief appendix entitled "Insights into Puerto Rico's Economic Development."

8.15 Clark, Victor Selden, and others. PORTO RICO AND ITS PROBLEMS. Washington, Brookings Institution, 1930. 707 p. plates, diagrs., tables, bibl., refs.

A landmark study conducted in 1928–1929 by the Brookings Institution with the purpose of determining the chief economic and political problems besetting the island at the time and making recommendations that might help solve them. It analyzes rural and urban conditions, government organizations, public finance, external trade, public works, and other areas.

8.16 Cochran, Thomas C. THE PUERTO RICAN BUSINESSMAN: A STUDY IN CULTURAL CHANGE. Philadelphia, University of Pennsylvania Press, 1959. 198 p. bibl. (A Social Science Research Center Study, College of Social Sciences, University of Puerto Rico).

Documented study of institutional and cultural change on the part of the Puerto Rican businessman under the impact of U.S. influence since 1898. It includes a brief survey of the island's business history from 1898 to the late 1950s. (Also published in Spanish: EL HOMBRE DE NEGOCIOS PUERTORRIQUEÑO, Río Piedras, P.R.,

Centro de Investigaciones Sociales, 1961. 209 p.)

8.17 Coley, Basil Glasford, A Comparative Analysis of Some Factors Affecting Economic Growth in Jamaica and Puerto Rico, 1957–1967. Ph.D. dissertation, University of Illinois, 1971. In DISSERTATION ABSTRACTS INTERNATIONAL, v.32, no.10, p. 5435-A.

The primary purpose of this study was to derive testable hypotheses concerning causative relationships in regional economic development and industry location.

8.18 Colón, Edmundo D. LA GESTION AGRICOLA DESPUES DE 1898. Editada por Jaime Bagué. Prólogo de F. A. López Domínguez. San Juan, Imprenta Venezuela, 1948. 700 p. bibl.

A documented survey of the island's agriculture from 1898 to 1944.

8.19 Colón de Zalduondo, Baltazara. The Saving and Consumption Variables in the Puerto Rican Economy. Ph.D. dissertation, Rutgers University, 1971. In DISSERTATION ABSTRACTS INTERNATIONAL, v.32, no.9, p. 4798-A.

The author contends that a high rate of consumption actually contributes to economic growth, given the specific features of Puerto Rico's industrial sector, and that a reduction in consumption, as advocated by the Planning Board, would threaten further development of those local industries which have specialized in products not in direct competition with those of nonlocal industries.

8.20 Commerce Clearing House. PUERTO RICO TAX REPORTER: ALL TAXES ... ALL TAXABLES. Chicago, c1964. Various pagings.

Analyzes the tax structure and provides information on income, property, business, license, motor vehicle registration, and excise taxes, and on court decisions and rulings regarding the tax structure.

8.21 COMMERCE WITH CUBA AND PUERTO RICO AND IMPORTS INTO THE HAWAIIAN ISLANDS. Washington, Treasury Department, Bureau of Statistics, [1898?]. p. 2019-2074. tables.

Reprinted from the Summary of Finance and Commerce for June 1898, this volume has very detailed statistics on U.S. trade with Puerto Rico from 1851 to 1897. Also includes information on Puerto Rico's trade with Great Britain, France, Germany, and Spain from 1889 to 1896. A separate document, Foreign Commerce of Cuba, Porto Rico, Hawaii, the Philippines, and Samoan Islands, published by the U.S. Treasury Department Bureau of Statistics, [1899?] updates the report to include trade during 1898.

8.22 Curtis, Thomas D. LAND REFORM, DEMOCRACY AND ECONOMIC INTEREST IN PUERTO RICO. Tucson, University of Arizona, College of Business and Public Administration, 1966. 64 p. bibl., tables.

Examines, from both the economic and the political viewpoints, land tenure on the island before and after the reform program of the 1940s, and the U.S. contribution to that reform. With a view to helping the U.S. and other nations grapple with policy alternatives regarding unavoidable reforms, the author points out that had the United States not given financial, legal, and political support to the reform program of the island's liberal leaders "it is probable that land reform would have been achieved by revolution."

8.23 Dana, Arnold Guyot. PORTO RICO'S CASE: OUTCOME OF AMERICAN SOVEREIGNTY, 1898–1924, 1925–1928. New Haven, Conn., Tuttle, Morehouse and Taylor, 1928. 64 p.

Written "to secure justice for a suffering people," this booklet summarizes a series of articles written on a visit to the island by Dana, a retired U.S. statistician, in which he described social and economic conditions.

8.24 DeBeers, John S. A STUDY OF PUERTO RICO'S BANKING SYSTEM. San Juan, Puerto Rico Finance Council, 1960. 160 p. charts, questionnaires, bibl., tables.

Reviews the facilities that the banking system of Puerto Rico provides for various sectors of the economy and recommends legislative, administrative, and policy actions that would improve them.

8.25   DiPaolo, Gordon Anthony. The Marketing Planning for Industrial Promotion of the Economic Development Administration of Puerto Rico. Ph.D. dissertation, New York University Graduate School of Business Administration, 1970. In DISSERTATION ABSTRACTS INTERNATIONAL, v.35, no.5, p. 1939-A.

Examines the problem of how to attract foreign investment to a relatively underdeveloped area.

8.26   Di Venuti, Biagio. MONEY AND BANKING IN PUERTO RICO. Río Piedras, University of Puerto Rico Press, 1950. 307 p. tables, bibl.

Presents an overall picture of the local monetary, credit, and banking set-up and explains the many interrelationships and economic variables that play an important part in the life of the island.

8.27   Di Venuti, Biagio. BANKING GROWTH IN PUERTO RICO. Baltimore, Waverly Press, 1955. 167 p. tables, bibl.

Reviews the status and policies of banking and finance in Puerto Rico in the early fifties, and suggests changes for strengthening the system.

8.28   Eastman, Samuel Ewer, and Daniel Marx, Jr. SHIPS AND SUGAR: AN EVALUATION OF PUERTO RICAN OFFSHORE SHIPPING. Río Piedras, University of Puerto Rico Press, 1953. 239 p. illus., maps, plates, bibl. refs.

Detailed study of Puerto Rico's external transportation, harbors, terminal facilities, and other port services. Rates and their impact on the island's industrialization program are also studied.

8.29   Echenique, Miguel. "The Foundation and Process of Industrial Development in Puerto Rico." In Winsemius, Albert, and John A. Pincus. METHODS OF INDUSTRIAL DEVELOPMENT. Paris, Organization for Economic Co-operation and Development, 1962. p. 115–125.

A brief discussion of some characteristics of the Puerto Rican economy and the active program to attract external industry.

8.30   Economic Associates. INDUSTRIAL SUPPLY AND DISTRIBUTION IN PUERTO RICO. Project Director, Amadeo I.D. Francis. Washington, D.C., 1963. 159 p. tables. (Small Business Study).

A study on the adequacy of the island's distribution facilities for supplying industry, agriculture, and government, prepared for the Economic Development Administration of the Commonwealth of Puerto Rico under the Small Business Administration Management Research Grant Program. It reviews requirements, existing facilities, operations, prices, and problems, and makes recommendations for improvement.

8.31   Economic Planning Seminar of the Commonwealth of Puerto Rico. San Juan, 1958. PROCEEDINGS. Mexico, Regional Technical Aids Center, International Cooperation Administration, 1960. 494 p. diagrs., tables.

Gathers twenty-four papers on industrial development, economic, social, and physical planning, human resources, population, agriculture, and public services.

8.32   Ellison, John Neil. The Impact of Tax Exemption and Minimum Wage Policy on Industry Structure in an Interregional Setting: The Case of Puerto Rico and the U.S. Mainland. Ph.D. dissertation, The George Washington University, 1969. In DISSERTATION ABSTRACTS INTERNATIONAL, v.30, no.2, p. 467-A.

This study tested the hypothesis that the tax exemption and minimum wage policy practiced in Puerto Rico, in an effort to promote economic development, should have resulted in a substantial concentration of development in industries having either greater capital or stronger labor-intensification trends than those found in comparable industries on the U.S. mainland. Findings of the study indicate that future success of industrial development efforts will ultimately depend on how well Puerto Rican products compete with similar products manufactured in low-wage areas of the United States.

8.33   Enamorado-Cuesta, José. PORTO RICO, PAST AND PRESENT: THE IS-

LAND AFTER THIRTY YEARS OF AMERICAN RULE: A BOOK OF IN-FORMATION. New York, Eureka Printing Co., 1929. 170 p.

Questioning the credibility and sincerity of the way the people of the United States acquire information about Puerto Rico, the author sets out to provide another point of view. He places emphasis on social and economic conditions, condemning the control of the bulk of the island's agricultural wealth by a very small number of people, largely for their own benefit, while the majority of the rural population owned no productive land and had to live on very low wages.

8.34 Freyre, Jorge F. EXTERNAL AND DO-MESTIC FINANCING IN THE ECO-NOMIC DEVELOPMENT OF PUERTO RICO. Río Piedras, University of Puerto Rico Press, 1969. 202 p. tables, bibl.

A systematic study of "the economic policy questions related to the sources of financing capital formation in Puerto Rico ... analyzed within the framework of a macroeconomic growth model." The work, originally presented as the author's thesis (Yale, 1966), analyzes the investment requirements for achieving growth targets, the role of domestic savings and external investment, and the scope of alternatives for achieving self-sufficiency in the financing of Puerto Rico's economic growth.

8.35 Friedlander, Stanley L. LABOR MI-GRATION AND ECONOMIC GROWTH: A CASE STUDY OF PUERTO RICO. Cambridge, Mass. Institute of Technology Press, [1965], 181 p. bibl. (M.I.T. Monographs in Economics).

Examines the effectiveness of migration as a tool for economic growth, with particular reference to Puerto Rico during 1946–1960.

8.36 Galbraith, John Kenneth, and Richard H. Holton. MARKETING EFFICIENCY IN PUERTO RICO. In collaboration with Robert E. Branson, Jean Ruth Robinson, and Carolyn Shaw Bell. Cambridge, Mass., Harvard University Press, 1955. 204 p. diagrs., tables.

A comprehensive study of the mar-keting of food and other products of everyday use in Puerto Rico. It offers a model marketing system that would be more efficient and less costly than the one in use.

8.37 Gayer, Arthur D., Paul T. Homan, and Earle K. James. THE SUGAR ECON-OMY OF PUERTO RICO. New York, Columbia University Press, 1938. 326 p. tables, bibl.

A study of the structure and operation of the sugar industry, which, when this book was written, was the most important in the island, and its relation to the general Puerto Rican economy.

8.38 González, Antonio J. ECONOMIA POLITICA DE PUERTO RICO. 3. ed. San Juan, Editorial Cordillera, 1971. 168 p. tables.

An analysis of the economy, within the framework of Puerto Rico's political relationship with the United States.

8.39 Hancock, Ralph. PUERTO RICO: A SUCCESS STORY. Princeton, N.J., Van Nostrand, 1960. 187 p.

Journalistic account of the development of the island. In the final chapter the author expresses doubt that the American people will "continue to accept a privileged situation in Puerto Rico which gives industries in the island an unfair competitive advantage" over those on the mainland.

8.40 Hanson, Earl Parker. PUERTO RICO, ALLY FOR PROGRESS. Princeton, N.J., Van Nostrand, 1962. 136 p. illus., tables. (Searchlight Book, 7).

The author surveys briefly the economic, political, and social panorama of Puerto Rico and suggests that a study of the island's experiences with aspects of socialism could be of assistance to poor countries emerging from colonialism.

8.41 Hanson, Earl Parker. PUERTO RICO, LAND OF WONDERS. New York, Alfred A. Knopf, 1960. 320 p. map.

Draws on a previous book by the same author about Puerto Rico, *Transformation: The Story of Modern Puerto Rico* (New York, Simon and Schuster, 1955). However, it updates much of the data and discusses the problems of an industrial nation now faced by the island.

8.42 Harrison, Kelly Max. Agricultural Market Coordination in the Economic Development of Puerto Rico. Ph.D. dissertation, Michigan State University, 1967. *In* DISSERTATION ABSTRACTS, v.28, no.3, p. 850-A.

In June 1965 an interdisciplinary team of researchers from Michigan State University began a two-and-one-half-year study to evaluate, in Puerto Rico and in northeast Brazil, the validity of Walt Rostow's national market concept and to determine the role that food marketing plays in economic growth. This thesis reports their findings in the agricultural marketing portion of the Puerto Rican study.

8.43 Hibben, Thomas, and Rafael Picó. INDUSTRIAL DEVELOPMENT OF PUERTO RICO AND THE VIRGIN ISLANDS OF THE UNITED STATES: REPORT OF THE UNITED STATES SECTION, CARIBBEAN COMMISSION. Port of Spain, Trinidad, 1948. 300 p. tables, bibl.

The first 268 pages of this report are devoted to "a technical survey of economic development in Puerto Rico from the beginning of the American Administration to the present time, with particular emphasis on the development of industry."

8.44 Hitchcock, Frank Harris. TRADE OF PUERTO RICO. Washington, D.C. Govt. Print. Office. 1898. 84 p. tables. (U.S. Department of Agriculture. Section of Foreign Markets. Bulletin 13).

An interesting review of the imports and exports of Puerto Rico during each calendar year from 1887 through 1896, arranged both by countries and by products.

8.45 Holmes, John MacDougal. The Impact of Nuclear Energy Centers on the Economy of Puerto Rico. Ph.D. dissertation, University of Tennessee, 1970. *In* DISSERTATIONS ABSTRACTS INTERNATIONAL, v.31, no.9, p. 5396-B.

An economic model was developed for determining the optimum combination of industrial activities for a nuclear energy center as a function of energy cost, and also the impact of this center on its economic region in terms of increases in gross product, employment, and capital demands.

8.46 Ingram, James C. REGIONAL PAYMENTS MECHANISMS: THE CASE OF PUERTO RICO. Chapel Hill, University of North Carolina Press, 1962. 152 p. tables, bibl. refs.

A study of the gross flow of funds to and from the Puerto Rican economy. It analyzes the impact of inflows of capital, the mechanism of adjustment in the balance of payments, and the interactions with income and prices.

8.47 Isard, Walter, Eugene W. Schooler, and Thomas Vietorisz. INDUSTRIAL COMPLEX ANALYSIS AND REGIONAL DEVELOPMENT: A CASE STUDY OF REFINERY-PETROCHEMICAL-SYNTHETIC FIBER COMPLEXES AND PUERTO RICO. Cambridge, Technology Press of M.I.T., c1959. 294 p. tables. bibl.

A study "addressed to the problem of (a) identifying some specific combinations of industrial activities for which Puerto Rico is likely to be an economically favorable location, and (b) estimating in dollars and cents terms the magnitude of the locational advantage of such combinations in Puerto Rico."

8.48 Jaffe, Abram J. PEOPLE, JOBS AND ECONOMIC DEVELOPMENT: A CASE HISTORY OF PUERTO RICO, SUPPLEMENTED BY RECENT MEXICAN EXPERIENCE. Foreword by Charles D. Stewart. Glencoe, Ill., Free Press, 1959. 381 p. tables, maps, bibl.

An attempt to extract from the Puerto Rican experience those "findings and information that could be relevant and helpful to other underdeveloped parts of the world which have embarked on programs of economic and social development."

8.49 Kemmerer, Edwin Walter. MODERN CURRENCY REFORMS: A HISTORY AND DISCUSSION OF RECENT CURRENCY REFORMS IN INDIA, PORTO RICO, PHILIPPINE ISLANDS, STRAITS SETTLEMENTS AND MEXICO. New

York, Macmillan, 1916. 564 p. tables, bibl.

Part two of this book discusses in detail the Puerto Rican currency reform of 1899–1900, with a useful overview of currency history in the island prior to American occupation.

8.50 Knowles, William H. "Manpower and Education in Puerto Rico." *In* Harbison, Frederick, and Charles A. Myers, eds. MANPOWER AND EDUCATION: COUNTRY STUDIES IN ECONOMIC DEVELOPMENT. New York, McGraw-Hill, 1965. p. 108–139. table, bibl., refs. (Series in International Development).

An essay in which the author, director of the Industrial Relations Study Center at Inter-American University of Puerto Rico, points out some of the problems of meeting the demand for highly trained, experienced manpower for the island's economy.

8.51 Koenig, Nathan. A COMPREHENSIVE AGRICULTURAL PROGRAM FOR PUERTO RICO. Washington, D.C. Govt. Print. Off., 1953. 299 p. plates, tables, map, bibl.

A study of agriculture in Puerto Rico against the background of the people and their land. It analyzes problems of soil erosion and land utilization, as well as use and control of water, marketing, and agricultural credit and finance.

8.52 Lange, Irene Lydia. Marketing Institutions in the Economic Development of Puerto Rico, 1950–1964. Ph.D. dissertation, University of Illinois, 1968. *In* DISSERTATION ABSTRACTS, v.29, no.3, p. 734-A.

The purpose of this study was to analyze the interdependence of marketing institutions and the supply systems (agriculture and manufacturing), the facilitating systems (transportation, communication, and finance), and the sociocultural environment in Puerto Rico.

8.53 Lastra, Carlos J. THE IMPACT OF MINIMUM WAGES ON A LABOR ORIENTED INDUSTRY. San Juan, Government Development Bank for Puerto Rico, 1964. 139 p. tables, diagrs., questionnaire, bibl. (A Social Science Research Center Study. Govbank Technical Paper, no. 1)

A study of the individual firm's active, direct responses to changes in the minimum wage rates. The effect of increases in minimum wages on such variables as employment, profits, sales, and the total wage bill is derived as a corollary.

8.54 Little (Arthur D.), Inc. REPORT ON TEN-YEAR INDUSTRIAL PLAN FOR PUERTO RICO TO THE PUERTO RICO ECONOMIC DEVELOPMENT ADMINISTRATION. Washington, International Cooperation Administration, Technical Aids Branch, Office of Industrial Resources, 1961. 100 p. tables. (Supplements to the Technical Digest Series).

A report prepared in 1951 presenting a program and recommendations for budgetary action to cover expanded industrialization. It was reproduced by the International Cooperation Administration in 1961, indicating that events in the preceding ten-year period had verified the validity of the plans suggested, and that perhaps some of the information might prove useful to countries going through a similar growth process.

8.55 Maccoby, Eleanor E., and Frances Fielder. SAVING AMONG UPPER-INCOME FAMILIES IN PUERTO RICO. Río Piedras, University of Puerto Rico Press, 1953. 165 p. tables, questionnaires. (A Social Science Research Center Study).

The major purpose of this study, based upon interviews with the heads of 630 families with incomes of $2,000 or more, was to determine the numbers who saved and the amounts they saved and to learn something about the potentialities for the accumulation of a local pool of capital.

8.56 Maldonado, Rita M. THE ROLE OF THE FINANCIAL SECTOR IN THE ECONOMIC DEVELOPMENT OF PUERTO RICO. [Washington, Federal Deposit Insurance Corporation, 1970]. 152 p. tables, graphs, bibl.

An evaluation of the role of financial institutions, both public and private, in the economic development of Puerto Rico, with emphasis on the significance of the savings-investment process that takes place through those intermediaries. It was the author's doctoral dissertation for the New York University Graduate School of Business in 1969.

8.57 Manheim, Uriel L. PUERTO RICO BUILDS: RECENT AND FUTURE HOUSING TRENDS. San Juan, Housing Investment Corp., 1968. 48 p. tables, graphs, photos, maps.

A survey of the island's residential construction industry, with an appraisal of present and future demand in the housing market.

8.58 Martin, Robert Grant, and O.C. Hester. MARKETING AND PRICING PUERTO RICAN RAW SUGAR. Washington, U.S. Dept. of Agriculture, Agricultural Marketing Service, Marketing Economics Research Division, 1960. 40 p. diagrs., tables, bibl. refs. (Marketing Research Report no. 394).

A study undertaken at the request of the Puerto Rican sugar industry to describe the market for Puerto Rican raw sugar and the economic forces which influence marketing and pricing practices. It analyzes price formation and factors influencing prices, examines alternative pricing methods, analyzes raw sugar price fluctuations, and compares market prices with those received by the island's raw sugar mills under various pricing methods.

8.59 Mayne, Alvin. DESIGNING AND ADMINISTERING A REGIONAL ECONOMIC DEVELOPMENT PLAN: WITH SPECIFIC REFERENCE TO PUERTO RICO. [Paris], Organization for Economic Cooperation and Development, 1961. 66 p. (Problems of Development).

The economic situation of Puerto Rico is used to exemplify the relationship between economic, social, and political factors and the way in which these elements influence planning and its implementation.

8.60 Mayne, Alvin. THE PROSPECTS FOR NUCLEAR ENERGY IN PUERTO RICO. Foreword by Philip Mullenbach. Washington, D.C., National Planning Association, c1958. 87 p. tables, maps, bibl., refs. (Reports on the Productive Uses of Nuclear Energy).

An analysis of the prospective role of competitive nuclear energy in a rapidly developing economy. It discusses the economic setting, fuel and power requirements and supplies, cost of production and delivery of energy, general effect on the economy, special economic effects of nuclear energy, and policy issues and alternative courses of action.

8.61 Mayne, Alvin, ed. PROCEEDINGS OF THE SEMINAR ON THE CONTRIBUTION OF PHYSICAL PLANNING TO SOCIAL AND ECONOMIC DEVELOPMENT IN A REGIONAL FRAMEWORK, MAY 23–27, 1960. [San Juan], Government Development Bank for Puerto Rico, 1965. 227 p. tables, maps, bibl., refs.

A "critical and clinical" evaluation of Puerto Rico's development program by planning experts from various countries. The major problem areas in physical planning taken up during the course of the seminar were the interrelation of agriculture and economic development with physical and social planning; the contribution of the internal transportation system; development planning for ports and its implication for development; housing programs and land use planning and their contribution to economic and social development.

8.62 Mayne, Alvin. "Progress, Planning, and Policy in Puerto Rico." In Nelson, Eastin, ed. ECONOMIC GROWTH: RATIONALE, PROBLEMS, CASES. Freeport, New York, Books for Libraries, 1971, c1960. p. 141–170. Discussion of paper, p. 256–263.

Paper presented at the Conference on Economic Development sponsored by the Institute of Latin American Studies at the University of Texas in 1958, in which the economic policies of Puerto Rico's government are discussed.

8.63 McAlpine, John D. AGRICULTURAL PRODUCTION AND TRADE OF PUERTO RICO. Washington, U.S. Department of Agriculture, Economic Research Service, Foreign Regional

Analysis Division, 1968. 27 p. tables, map, bibl.

An analysis of recent developments in Puerto Rico's economy and trends and prospects in the consumption, production, and trading of farm products.

8.64 McCann, Eugene C. EDUCATIONAL BACKGROUNDS OF TOP LEVEL BUSINESS MANAGERS IN PUERTO RICO. Baton Rouge, College of Business Administration, Louisiana State University, 1972. 42 p. tables, bibl., refs. (Division of Research. Occasional Papers no. 7).

Results of a study comparing the characteristics of U.S.-born and Puerto Rican-born managers.

8.65 McElheny, John Richard. Industrial Education in Puerto Rico 1948–1958: A Descriptive and Evaluative Report on the Program in "Operation Bootstrap" from 1948 to 1958. Ph.D. dissertation, Ohio State University, 1960. *In* DISSERTATION ABSTRACTS, v.21, no. 1, p. 135-A.

The major goal of this study was to investigate and evaluate the industrial education program in Puerto Rico and its contribution to economic development during the period 1948–1958.

8.66 Mejías, Félix. CONDICIONES DE VIDA DE LAS CLASES JORNALERAS DE PUERTO RICO. San Juan, Junta Editora de la Universidad de Puerto Rico, 1946. 215 p. tables, bibl. (Monografías de la U.P.R. Serie C: Ciencias Sociales, 2).

Based on the author's M.A. thesis at New York University, this study presents the historical background of the principal economic, political, and physical factors that have contributed to the living conditions of the workers and describes those conditions.

8.67 Miller, Kenton Riggel. Some Economic Problems of Outdoor Recreation Planning in Puerto Rico. Ph.D. dissertation, Syracuse University, 1968. *In* DISSERTATION ABSTRACTS, v.29, no.8, p. 2697-B.

This study provides a comprehensive review of outdoor recreation services in Puerto Rico, from early Spanish settlement to the early 1960s, with special attention to agencies and enterprises providing such services.

8.68 Mingo, John Jerald. Labor Mobility, Capital Importation and Economic Growth: The Case of Postwar Puerto Rico. Ph.D. dissertation, Brown University, 1970. *In* DISSERTATION ABSTRACTS INTERNATIONAL, v.32, no. 1, p. 78-A.

This study analyzes the interrelations between labor movements, capital flows, and growth in an open economy.

8.69 Moscoso, Teodoro. "Industrial Development in Puerto Rico." *In* Winsemius, Albert, and John A. Pincus. METHODS OF INDUSTRIAL DEVELOPMENT. Paris, Organisation for Economic Co-Operation and Development, 1962. p. 93–113.

The director of Puerto Rico's Economic Development Administration describes the island's development agencies and the industrial promotion program.

8.70 Packard, Walter Eugene. THE LAND AUTHORITY AND DEMOCRATIC PROCESSES IN PUERTO RICO. Río Piedras, Editorial Universitaria, Universidad de Puerto Rico, 1948. 49–101 p. Reprinted from *Inter-American Economic Affairs*, Summer, 1948.

A detailed analysis of Puerto Rico's Land Law, with a discussion of the land-tenure situation prior to its adoption and the policies and methods devised to implement it.

8.71 Perloff, Harvey S. PUERTO RICO'S ECONOMIC FUTURE: A STUDY IN PLANNED DEVELOPMENT. Chicago, Published for the University of Puerto Rico by the University of Chicago Press, 1950. 435 p. illus., bibl.

An in-depth study of the Puerto Rican economy—its historical background, characteristics, and trends, with emphasis on the rapid population growth. Useful for understanding the economic policies and programs of the island's government during the 1950s.

8.72 Picó, Rafael. PUERTO RICO: PLANIFICACION Y ACCION. San Juan,

Banco Gubernamental de Fomento para Puerto Rico, 1962. 312 p. plates, maps, diagrs., bibl.

Brings together a series of television lectures given by the author during 1960 to explain the planning process and its role as an instrument in the development of Puerto Rico. It gives some insights into the planning process as it affects, for example, urban affairs, housing, public works, and fiscal policy.

8.73   PORTORICO. Roma, Istituto Nazionale per il Commercio Estero, 1968. 156 p. plates, maps, tables.

A publication aimed at informing Italian exporters and investors of the market possibilities in Puerto Rico.

8.74   Quaglia, Jorge Alberto. EL PLAN DE FOMENTO EN EL ESTADO LIBRE ASOCIADO A EE.UU. DE PUERTO RICO. Buenos Aires, Banco Industrial de la República de Argentina, 1961. 80 p. tables, bibl. refs.

An Argentinian economist reports on his observations of the island's economic development programs and suggests that many of the incentives they offer could be applied under certain circumstances in Argentina.

8.75   Quintero Rivera, A.G. LUCHA OBRERA: ANTOLOGIA DE GRANDES DOCUMENTOS EN LA HISTORIA PUERTORRIQUEÑA. [San Juan ?], Centro de la Realidad Puertorriqueña, [1971 ?]. 165 p. illus., plates, bibl.

The author brings together a series of documents that he feels have been unjustly omitted from the historical record of Puerto Rico's labor movement: "La cuestión social y Puerto Rico" (1904), by R. del Romeral; "The Tyranny of the House of Delegates" (1913), by the Federación Libre de Trabajadores; "Páginas rojas" (1919), by Juan S. Marcano; "Empieza a quebrarse la FLT" (1934–1945); and "25 años de lucha" (1955), by Juan Sáez Corales.

8.76   Ramírez-Pérez, Miguel A. Functional Income Distribution in Puerto Rico, 1947–1966. Ph.D. dissertation, Rutgers University, 1970. In DISSERTATIONS

ABSTRACTS INTERNATIONAL, v. 31, no. 3. p. 887-A.

The study is primarily concerned with the methodological modification of the conventional approach to functional income distribution.

8.77   Reynolds, Lloyd G., and Peter Gregory. WAGES, PRODUCTIVITY AND INDUSTRIALIZATION IN PUERTO RICO. With the assistance of Luz M. Torruellas. Homewood, Illinois, Richard Irwin, 1965. 357 p. tables, bibl.

A joint publication of the Social Science Research Center of the University of Puerto Rico and the Economic Growth Center at Yale.

Part 1 of this book examines the development of the modern manufacturing sector against the background of the economy as a whole; part 2 focuses on the characteristics and policies of the new industrial managers in Puerto Rico; and part 3 analyzes the characteristics and behavior of the new factory labor force.

8.78   Ross, David F. THE LONG UPHILL PATH: A HISTORICAL STUDY OF PUERTO RICO'S PROGRAM OF ECONOMIC DEVELOPMENT. 2. ed. San Juan, Editorial Edil, 1969. 188 p. bibl.

On the whole a favorable and complimentary study of Operation Bootstrap. The author contends, however, that "most of the fundamental changes that have been made in Puerto Rico's development program have been made in response to unforeseen events" and that it is therefore difficult to forecast the road that the island's development will take in the future.

8.79   RURAL LIFE IN PUERTO RICO. San Juan, Department of Education, [1934 ?]. 86 p. tables, plates.

Offers a picture of rural life in the island during the early 1930s: economic aspects, food habits, housing, and activities of women and girl students.

8.80   Saldaña, Jorge E. EL CAFE EN PUERTO RICO. San Juan, Tip. Real Hermanos, 1935. 30 p.

A brief history of coffee since its introduction to the island in 1736, with recommendations regarding measures for rehabilitation of the coffee industry.

8.81 Sánchez Tarniella, Andrés. LA ECONOMIA DE PUERTO RICO: ETAPAS EN SU DESARROLLO. Madrid, Afrodisio Aguado, 1972. 251 p. tables, bibl.

This book is divided into three parts: a review of the historical-ideological background of Puerto Rico's economy; a review of the economic modernization that has occurred in Puerto Rico since 1940; and a discussion of some aspects of the island's economy—capital formation and national product, income distribution, institutional problems, and the challenge of future economic expansion. The author believes that an industrialization program with different emphases—less reliance on outside capital, greater participation of public agencies, and greater attention to industries that utilize local raw materials to make products for local consumption—should be the basis for the island's economy.

8.82 Seminar on Planning Techniques and Methods, San Juan, 1963. PLANNING FOR ECONOMIC DEVELOPMENT IN THE CARIBBEAN. Hato Rey, P.R., Central Secretariat, Caribbean Organization, [1965 ?]. 223 p. illus., tables, bibl.

A compilation of the lectures and discussion summaries of this seminar, designed for persons in the Caribbean region with responsibility for planning. Papers of special interest to Puerto Rico: Miguel A. Barasorda, "Tourism in Development Planning;" Miguel Echenique, "Economic and Industrial Planning;" and Carlos J. Lastra, "Planning for Commercial Development."

8.83 Servera, Joaquín. TRADING UNDER THE LAWS OF PORTO RICO. Washington, Govt. Print. Off., 1927. 44 p. (U.S. Bureau of Foreign and Domestic Commerce, Dept. of Commerce. Trade Promotion series, no. 58).

Presents information on the most important commercial laws in force in Puerto Rico in the 1920s with the purpose of calling the attention of U.S. businessmen to the market potential of the island.

8.84 Snoonian, Edward. A Comparison of Industrial Efficiency for Mexico, Puerto Rico, and the United States. Ph.D. dissertation, Michigan State University, 1971. In DISSERTATION ABSTRACTS INTERNATIONAL, v. 32, no. 6, p. 2864-A.

This study found that Mexican and Puerto Rican industries operating with capital levels equivalent to those of U.S. industries would not achieve the same labor productivity levels.

8.85 Stead, William H. FOMENTO: THE ECONOMIC DEVELOPMENT OF PUERTO RICO. Washington, National Planning Association, 1958. 151 p. maps, tables, bibl. (Planning Pamphlet, 103).

A look at Puerto Rico's economic development program, generally complimentary in tone. Although outdated, it offers useful information for those studying the early years of the program. Includes copies of the law creating the Puerto Rico Industrial Development Company and the organizational plan of the Economic Development Administration. (Also published in Spanish: El Desarollo Económico de Puerto Rico, México, Libreros Mexicanos Unidos, 1963.)

8.86 Strassman, W. Paul. TECHNOLOGICAL CHANGE AND ECONOMIC DEVELOPMENT: THE MANUFACTURING EXPERIENCE OF MEXICO AND PUERTO RICO. Ithaca, N.Y., Cornell University Press, c1968. 353 p. tables, questionnaire, bibl., refs.

Examines the technological advances in manufacturing made in Puerto Rico in the 1940–1965 period, and discusses the problems involved in the adoption of modern technology in the early stages of industrialization.

8.87 Taylor, Milton C. "What Happens When Exemptions End: Retrospect and Prospect in Puerto Rico." In Bird, Richard, and Oliver Oldman. READINGS ON TAXATION IN DEVELOPING COUNTRIES. Baltimore, Johns Hopkins Press, 1964. p. 245–256. bibl. refs.

Contends that Puerto Rico will not lose an appreciable number of firms upon the expiration of tax exemptions, because attractive profits will be possible even under a taxable status.

8.88 Taylor, Milton C. INDUSTRIAL TAX-EXEMPTION IN PUERTO RICO: A CASE STUDY IN THE USE OF TAX SUBSIDIES FOR INDUSTRIALIZING UNDERDEVELOPED AREAS. Madison, University of Wisconsin Press, 1957. 172 p. tables, bibl. refs.

Assesses the advantages and disadvantages of industrial tax exemption as subsidy in Puerto Rico and concludes that, although tax exemption has succeeded in attracting needed capital, its "indirect effects and disguised social costs" have been inordinately high.

8.89 Tirado, Irma G. LA ESLASTICIDAD-INGRESO DE LA CONTRIBUCION SOBRE INGRESOS EN PUERTO RICO Y JAMAICA, 1955-1963. Río Piedras, Universidad de Puerto Rico, Instituto de Estudios del Caribe, 1967. 147 p. tables, bibl. (Estudios Especiales, 4).

A comparative study of income tax elasticity in Puerto Rico and Jamaica. It concludes that elasticity is lower in Puerto Rico because of a less steeply progressive tax rate and the larger number of industries receiving tax exemptions.

8.90 Torres de Romero, Conchita. EL DESEMPLEO EN PUERTO RICO Y SUS PRINCIPALES CAMBIOS ESTRUCTU-RALES, 1950 A 1964. Río Piedras, Editorial Universitaria, Universidad de Puerto Rico, 1966. 132 p. tables, bibl. (Cuadernos de Cultura y Cultivo).

Analyzes the structural changes in the island's unemployment, and tries to explain why, despite considerable economic progress, it has remained very high.

8.91 Torruellas, Luz M. PUERTO RICO'S PRESENT AND PROSPECTIVE TECH-NICAL, SKILLED AND CLERICAL MANPOWER AND TRAINING NEEDS. Río Piedras, Centro de Investigaciones Sociales, Universidad de Puerto Rico, 1972. 387 p.

A research project by a senior professor in the Department of Economics at the University of Puerto Rico, under contract with the Commonwealth Department of Education. The book presents the results of an island-wide study of current and prospective employment and its occupational structure, with emphasis on the present state and future needs of clerical, craft, and subprofessional technical skills.

8.92 Vélez-Montes, Manuel A. PUBLIC POLICY FOR DEVELOPING MARKET ECONOMIES. Río Piedras, Editorial U.P.R., University of Puerto Rico, 1969. 119 p. graphs, bibl.

An examination of the relationship between the action of the state and economic development. The author seeks "to understand the mechanism underlying the economic transformation of societies which choose to develop while preserving free choice in economic conduct."

8.93 Vicente-Chandler, José, and others. INTENSIVE COFFEE CULTURE OF PUERTO RICO. Río Piedras, Agricultural Experiment Station, University of Puerto Rico, Mayaguez Campus, 1968. 84 p. illus., tables, bibl. (Bulletin, 121).

Describes the practices required to produce higher, more economical yields of coffee than those presently being obtained. Provides detailed information on varieties, production, harvesting, yields, costs, profits, etc.

8.94 White, Byron. Cuba and Puerto Rico: A Case Study in Comparative Economic Development Policy. Ph.D. dissertation, University of Texas, 1959. In DISSERTATION ABSTRACTS, v. 20, no. 6, p. 2092.

Examines the developmental policies resulting in the economic growth of Cuba and Puerto Rico from 1500 to May 1959, with emphasis on the period since 1939.

8.95 Wisdom, Harold Walter. Public Forestry Investment Criteria for Puerto Rico. Ph.D. dissertation, Syracuse University, 1967. In DISSERTATION ABSTRACTS, v. 28, no. 10, p. 3953-B.

This study develops an approach to forest planning within the context of a macroeconomic development program and under conditions of rapid social and technological change.

8.96 Wish, John Reed. Food Retailing in Economic Development: Puerto Rico, 1950–1965. Ph.D. dissertation, Michigan State University, 1967. *In* DISSERTATION ABSTRACTS, v. 28, no. 9, p. 3337-A.

The specific goals of the research were to describe accurately what happened in food retailing from 1950 to 1965, to investigate and explain the process by which change occurred in the Puerto Rican food retailing sector, and to understand better the variables correlated with innovativeness.

8.97 Wish, John R., and Kelly M. Harrison. MARKETING—ONE ANSWER TO POVERTY; FOOD MARKETING AND ECONOMIC DEVELOPMENT IN PUERTO RICO, 1950–65. Eugene, Ore., College of Business Administration, in cooperation with Center for International Business Studies, 1969. 191 p. illus., tables, bibl. (University of Oregon. Business Publications no. 3).

A study financed by the U.S. Agency for International Development. It describes and explains the changes in Puerto Rico's farming and food distribution system from 1950 to 1965.

9
EDUCATION

9.1 Benítez, Jaime. LA CASA DE ESTUDIOS SOBRE LA LIBERTAD Y EL ORDEN EN LA UNIVERSIDAD. Río Piedras, Universidad de Puerto Rico, 1963. 88 p.

A paper presented by the chancellor of the university at the time of the legislative hearings on university reform in 1963, and a major speech of his on the same subject also delivered that year.

9.2 Benítez, Jaime. EDUCATION FOR DEMOCRACY ON A CULTURAL FRONTIER: TWO ADDRESSES. Río Piedras, University of Puerto Rico, 1954. 26 p. (The University of Puerto Rico Bulletin. Ser. 11, no. 3).

Two speeches delivered in 1947 and 1954 in which the chancellor of the university describes the goals of the institution and the record of that seven-year period.

9.3 Benítez, Jaime. ETICA Y ESTILO DE LA UNIVERSIDAD. Madrid, Aguilar, 1964. 279 p. (Ensayistas Hispánicos).

Published in 1962 by the University of Puerto Rico as *Junto a la Torre: Jornadas de un Programa Universitario (1942-1962)*. Covers the role of the university as an institution of higher learning and as a part of the larger society; its responsibility to its students and to society; its values and ways of implementing them.

9.4 Benítez, Jaime. LA UNIVERSIDAD DEL FUTURO. Río Piedras, Universidad de Puerto Rico, 1964. 90 p. tables.

A report presented by the chancellor of the university to the Superior Educational Council in 1964, outlining growth targets for the next ten years.

9.5 Benner, Thomas Eliot. FIVE YEARS OF FOUNDATION BUILDING: THE UNIVERSITY OF PUERTO RICO, 1924–29. Prefaced by Jaime Benítez. Río Piedras, University of Puerto Rico, 1965. 157 p. illus.

Personal narrative by the University of Puerto Rico's first chancellor. It deals with the critical period of 1924 to 1929 when the basic shape of the institution as a center of higher learning was taking place.

9.6 Blauch, Lloyd E., ed. "Education in Puerto Rico." *In his* PUBLIC EDUCATION IN THE TERRITORIES AND OUTLYING POSSESSIONS. Washington, D.C., Govt. Print. Off., 1939. p. 89–132. (U.S. Advisory Committee on Education, Staff Study no. 16).

A summary of the state of education in the late thirties with some data on historical background.

9.7 Bragg, David Alwyn. The Teaching of Music Concepts in the Elementary Schools of Puerto Rico. Ph.D. dissertation, Florida State University,

1971. *In* DISSERTATION ABSTRACTS INTERNATIONAL, v. 32, no. 11, p. 6474-A.

The purpose of the study was to develop a guide for teaching music concepts in the elementary schools of Puerto Rico based on materials that are a part of the Puerto Rican culture.

9.8 Brameld, Theodore B.H. THE REMAKING OF A CULTURE: LIFE AND EDUCATION IN PUERTO RICO. With the assistance of Ona K. Brameld and Domingo Rosado. Foreword by Oscar E. Porrata. New York, Harper and Bros., 1959. 478 p. questionnaire, bibl.

This book presents the findings of a three-year study aimed at interpreting today's culture, with particular attention to education as a focal institution of Puerto Rican culture. The author analyzes the centralized system of Puerto Rican education and how it has performed during five decades of U.S. control. He also discusses and recommends new designs for curricula at all levels of education, including teacher training, and more democratic policies of organization and control.

9.9 Caselmann, Christian, Lamberto Borghi, and Morten Bredsdorff. THE EDUCATIONAL SYSTEM IN PUERTO RICO: RECOMMENDATIONS AND SUGGESTIONS. San Juan, Department of Education, 1960. 91 p.

At the request of Governor Luis Muñoz Marín, three European educators survey the educational system and make recommendations for improvements in all areas: teacher training; pre-elementary, elementary, and secondary education; teaching of languages; public and private schools; community and adult education; and administrative matters.

9.10 Claudio Tirado, Ramón. An Analysis of an Experimental High School in Puerto Rico. Ph.D. dissertation, Columbia University, 1971. *In* DISSERTATION ABSTRACTS INTERNATIONAL, v. 32, no. 2, p. 689-A.

This study examines the development of an experimental high school in Puerto Rico, based on the high school and college records of the experimental and control group students during three school years.

9.11 Coll y Toste, Cayetano. HISTORIA DE LA INSTRUCCION PUBLICA EN PUERTO RICO HASTA EL AÑO DE 1898. San Juan, 1910. 206 p.

A history of public education in Puerto Rico during the Spanish rule with emphasis on reforms introduced in the mid-nineteenth century.

9.12 Consejo Superior de Enseñanza. EL ANALFABETISMO EN PUERTO RICO. Río Piedras, 1945. 130 p. tables, bibl.

An analysis of the problem of illiteracy in Puerto Rico, which in 1940 affected 31.5 percent of the population, with suggestions for literacy programs and adult education campaigns.

9.13 Consejo Superior de Enseñanza. APUNTES SOBRE LA ENSEÑANZA DE LA LENGUA HABLADA Y ESCRITA EN LA ESCUELA ELEMENTAL. Río Piedras, Universidad de Puerto Rico, 1954. 303 p. bibl. (Publicaciones Pedagógicas, Ser. 2, no. 15).

Methodology for the teaching of languages and adaptation of the language curriculum to the students' needs. It includes specific examples and pilot classes applying the recommendations given.

9.14 Consejo Superior de Enseñanza. LA DESERCION DE ESTUDIANTES EN LA UNIVERSIDAD DE PUERTO RICO, RECINTOS DE RIO PIEDRAS Y MAYAGUEZ. Río Piedras, Universidad de Puerto Rico, 1966. 159 p. tables, bibl. (Publicaciones Pedagógicas, Ser. 2, no. 31).

A study of the drop-out problem at the university level.

9.15 Consejo Superior de Enseñanza. DOS DECADAS DE INVESTIGACIONES PEDAGOGICAS; OFICINA DE INVESTIGACIONES PEDAGOGICAS DEL CONSEJO SUPERIOR DE ENSEÑANZA. Río Piedras, Universidad de Puerto Rico, 1965. 318 p.

Summarizes the studies and analyses done by the Office of Educational Research of the Superior Education Council during a twenty-year period. Subjects include problems in the field of education; facilities available in the island; adult education and literacy programs; language arts; function of the institutions of higher learning;

human resources; and the use of radio.

9.16 Consejo Superior de Enseñanza. EDUCACION DE ADULTOS: ORIENTACIONES Y TECNICAS. Río Piedras, Universidad de Puerto Rico, 1952. 365 p. bibl. (Publicaciones Pedagógicas, Ser. 2, no. 13).

Presents the case for adult education programs and describes the programs carried out in Puerto Rico. It also offers philosophical, psychological, and methodological orientation for teachers of adults.

9.17 Consejo Superior de Enseñanza. ESTUDIO DEL SISTEMA EDUCATIVO. Río Piedras, Universidad de Puerto Rico, [1962]. 2 v. (1186, 1187–2500 p.) tables (Publicaciones Pedagógicas, Ser. 6, no. 1).

Report of the most comprehensive study done to date on the educational system of Puerto Rico. Prepared under the direction of Ismael Rodríguez Bou for the Committee on Education of the Puerto Rico House of Representatives, the four-year study covered every aspect—administrative, programmatic, organizational—of education at all levels.

9.18 Consejo Superior de Enseñanza. FACILIDADES EDUCATIVAS DEL ESTADO LIBRE ASOCIADO DE PUERTO RICO. Río Piedras, University of Puerto Rico, 1957. 390 p. tables, diagrs., bibl. (Publicaciones Pedagógicas, Ser. 2, no. 20).

Research study sponsored by the Superior Education Council under the direction of Puerto Rican educator, Ismael Rodríguez Bou. It aimed to determine the nature, quantity, and capacity of the existing educational institutions, both public and private, and analyze the organization of the educational system.

9.19 Consejo Superior de Enseñanza. PROBLEMAS DE LA EDUCACION EN PUERTO RICO. Río Piedras, Universidad de Puerto Rico, 1947. 287 p. tables, diagrs., bibl. (Publicaciones Pedagógicas, Ser. 2, no. 4).

An analysis of the educational picture with a detailed evaluation of text books in use at the time.

9.20 Corro, Alejandro del, comp. PUERTO RICO: REFORMA UNIVERSITARIA, 1963–65. Cuernavaca, México, Centro Intercultural de Documentación, 1966. 445 p. bibl. (Dossier, 6).

An extensive compilation of documents and articles resulting from the controversy surrounding university reform in the island.

9.21 Cuesta Mendoza, Antonio. HISTORIA DE LA EDUCACION EN EL PUERTO RICO COLONIAL. 2. ed. v. 1. México, Impr. Manuel L. Sánchez, 1946. v. 2. Ciudad Trujillo, R.D., Impr. Arte y Cine, 1948. 2 v. (434, 240 p.) bibl.

An extensive, documented history of education in Puerto Rico, which expands on the author's previously published doctoral dissertation (Historia de la Educación en Puerto Rico, 1512–1826. Washington, Catholic University of America, 1937). The first volume, which covers the years from 1508 to 1821, examines the development of education in three steps: its role as it related to the Indians; the establishment of the Cathedral and the Convent of Santo Tomás; and the founding of the Convent of San Francisco, which established the first institution of secondary education on the island. Volume 2 covers from 1821 to 1898 and discusses the evolution of education at the primary, secondary, and post-high school levels.

9.22 Dávila de Fuentes, Gladys. Problems in Teaching Disadvantaged Children in Puerto Rico: Recommendations for an Undergraduate Elementary School Teacher Preparation Program. Ph.D. dissertation, Columbia University, 1968. In DISSERTATION ABSTRACTS, v. 31, no. 1, p. 263-A.

This study was designed to explore what Puerto Rican elementary school teachers and supervisory personnel working in depressed areas—rural areas, slums, and public housing—consider to be their major problems in teaching disadvantaged children.

9.23 Epstein, Erwin H., comp. POLITICS AND EDUCATION IN PUERTO RICO: A DOCUMENTARY SURVEY OF THE LANGUAGE ISSUE. Metuchen, N.J., Scarecrow Press, 1970. 257 p. bibl. refs.

This book is a compilation of essays

and documents giving different points of view on the issue of language as the symbol of Puerto Rican culture and nationality. One part presents an overview of the school-language issue, another focuses on the use of English as the medium of instruction in many private schools, and the last section provides a cross-cultural perspective.

9.24 García de Serrano, Irma. THE PUERTO RICO TEACHERS' ASSOCIATION AND ITS RELATIONSHIP TO TEACHER PERSONNEL ADMINISTRATION. Río Piedras, University of Puerto Rico Press, 1971. 427 p. illus., graphs, tables, bibl.
The purpose of this study, which constituted the author's doctoral dissertation at New York University in 1966, was to analyze the program developed by the Teachers' Association with reference to selection, transfer, tenure, remuneration, and retirement of teachers and to examine the changes in personnel administration that developed from such programs from 1911 to 1962.

9.25 Géigel-Polanco, Vicente. EL PROBLEMA UNIVERSITARIO; UNA APROXIMACION CRITICA AL PROBLEMA DE LA UNIVERSIDAD. San Juan, Imprenta Venezuela, [1941]. 45 p.
Reproduces the text of a lecture by the author at the University of Puerto Rico in 1941, in which he points out that the success or failure of maintaining an autonomous university depends more on the attitude of students and professors than on a written law.

9.26 Gómez Tejera, Carmen, and David Cruz López. LA ESCUELA PUERTORRIQUEÑA. Sharon, Conn., Troutman Press, 1970. 262 p. ports., plates. (Puerto Rico: Realidad y Anhelo, 11).
A history of schooling in Puerto Rico from the time of its discovery to 1968, with a final chapter on future projections.

9.27 González, Mercedes Luisa. Development and Evaluation of a Programmed Procedure for Training Classroom Teachers to Make a Preliminary Identification of Children with

Certain Speech Disorders in Public Elementary Schools in Puerto Rico. Ph.D. dissertation, University of Michigan, 1969. In DISSERTATION ABSTRACTS INTERNATIONAL, v. 30, no. 9, p. 4410-B.
A study directed at developing and evaluating a programmed procedure for training teachers to screen and refer children with five types of speech defects, within the age range of five to eight years, in the public schools of Puerto Rico.

9.28 González de Guzmán, Julia A. An Investigation of the Vocabulary of Children When They Enter School in Three Areas of Puerto Rico. Ed.D. dissertation, Lehigh University, 1972. In DISSERTATION ABSTRACTS INTERNATIONAL, v. 33, no. 4, p. 1319-A.
The purpose of this study was to determine whether there are differences in the vocabulary understood by the children of the mountainous, coastal, and metropolitan areas of Puerto Rico.

9.29 Henríquez Ureña, Camila. LAS IDEAS PEDAGOGICAS DE HOSTOS. Santo Domingo, R. D., Talleres Tipográficos La Nación, 1932. 130 p. (Ediciones de la Revista de Educación).
An analysis of Hostos' educational and philosophical theories and the influential role he played in the history of Latin American education. The first part discusses Hostos' life and the rest is concerned with his works.

9.30 JOURNAL OF EDUCATION. Boston, v. 150. no. 2, Dec. 1967. Special issue titled: A Venture in Educational Anthropology: Puerto Rico as a Laboratory.
A brief introduction by Theodore Brameld on Puerto Rico as a laboratory in educational anthropology is followed by six articles: "The Culture Concept and its Relevance for Adult Education," by Francis L. Hurwitz; The Family in Puerto Rico as a Socio-Economic Unit," by Richard Avritch; "Religion and Education in the Puerto Rican Culture," by Joseph A. Keefe and Robert Nash; "Nativism in Puerto Rico: The Independence Movement," by Michael DiPaolo; "The Co-

operative Movement in Puerto Rico," by Maurice Mitchell; and "Music in Puerto Rican Culture," by Anne Streaty Wimberley.

9.31 Llabrés de Charneco, Amalia. The Effect of Two Shorthand Systems in Spanish on the Teaching of Shorthand in English to Bilingual Secretarial Students of Puerto Rico. Ph.D. dissertation, New York University, 1968. *In* DISSERTATION ABSTRACTS, v. 29, no. 2, p. 515-A.

The purpose of this investigation was to compare achievement and time taken to learn by students in English shorthand classes receiving simultaneous instructions in Spanish shorthand and using the Gregg system, with those of students receiving instructions in Spanish shorthand and using the Muñiz-O'Neill system.

9.32 López, R. Alfonso. The Principle of Separation of Church and State as Observed by the Public Schools of Puerto Rico from 1898 to 1952. Ph.D. dissertation, New York University, 1971. *In* DISSERTATION ABSTRACTS INTERNATIONAL, v. 32, no. 5, p. 2499-A.

This thesis surveys church-state relations and public education in Puerto Rico during the last decade of Spanish rule and attempts to determine whether the Americanization of the island during the period 1898–1940 involved changing the religious beliefs of Puerto Ricans through the public schools; whether there existed a relationship between emphasis on the island's Spanish culture from 1940 to 1952 and the observance of the principle of separation of church and state in the public schools; and whether U.S. Supreme Court decisions in this area were reflected in Puerto Rico's public schools.

9.33 Loubriel, Oscar. FINAL REPORT ON THE EFFECTIVENESS OF TWO UNIVERSITY TV COURSES. Río Piedras, Universidad de Puerto Rico, 1963. 104 p. tables, map.

A summary of a project to demonstrate the effectiveness of the use of television as a means to broaden the education of teachers in Puerto Rico. It includes a description of the courses transmitted, professors' and

coordinators' reactions to these courses, and the reactions of the students and persons not directly involved with the program. Comments and recommendations are also included.

9.34 Macho Moreno, Juan, comp. COMPILACION LEGISLATIVA DE PRIMERA ENSEÑANZA DE LA ISLA DE PUERTO RICO. Madrid, Tip. Viuda de Hernando, 1895. 1023 p.

A compilation of laws, regulations, and other information pertaining to primary education in the island during Spanish rule.

9.35 Mellado, Ramón. CULTURE AND EDUCATION IN PUERTO RICO. [Hato Rey], Bureau of Publications, Puerto Rico Teachers' Association, 1948. 140 p. bibl. (Educational Monograph no. 1).

This study, which was submitted as the author's doctoral dissertation at Teachers College, Columbia University, reviews the underpinnings of the educational philosophy in the early forties and makes suggestions for a reform of the school system.

9.36 Mir, Margarita María. Training of Paraprofessionals in a Teacher Education Program for Puerto Rico. Ed. D. dissertation, Columbia University, 1972. *In* DISSERTATION ABSTRACTS INTERNATIONAL, v. 33, no. 1, p. 214-A.

This study deals with two major trends in providing assistance to instructional staffs in schools: the training of paraprofessionals as auxiliary personnel in the classroom and the concept of new careers for the poor, especially in teaching.

9.37 Negrón de Montilla, Aida. AMERICANIZATION IN PUERTO RICO AND THE PUBLIC SCHOOL SYSTEM, 1900–1930. Río Piedras, P.R., Editorial Edil, 1970. 282 p. tables, bibl.

This study, which constituted the author's doctoral dissertation at New York University, is aimed at "finding out whether or not the Department of Education has been engaged in the process of Americanization of Puerto Rico, as revealed by the content of circular Letters issued by the commissioners of education from 1900 to 1930."

9.38 Nieves Falcón, Luis. RECRUITMENT TO HIGHER EDUCATION IN PUERTO RICO (1940–1960). Río Piedras, Editorial Universitaria, Universidad de Puerto Rico, 1965. 304 p. bibl., tables, questionnaire (Manuales y Tratados de Pedagogía).

A study aimed at defining "the social characteristics of those segments of the population which are availing themselves of the new and expanded education facilities offered at the University" and locating "the shift, if any, in the social status of the students."

9.39 Nieves Ortega, Luis A. Annual Reporting Practices of the Academic Deans and Department Heads at the Río Piedras Campus of the University of Puerto Rico. Ph.D. dissertation, Michigan State University, 1967. In DISSERTATION ABSTRACTS, v. 28, no. 3, p. 912-A.

The top administration of the University of Puerto Rico is not satisfied with the present operation of the administrative annual reporting system of the institution. Hence this study confronts the problem of how annual reporting practices of the academic deans and department heads within the Río Piedras campus can be made to serve best in the solution of the most important problems confronted by educational administrators.

9.40 Osuna, Juan José. A HISTORY OF EDUCATION IN PUERTO RICO. 2d rev. ed. Río Piedras, P.R., Editorial Universitaria, 1949. 657 p. map, bibl.

Based on the author's doctoral dissertation, this book views education on the island in three periods: under Spanish rule till 1898; under U.S. rule from 1898 to 1920, and from 1920 to 1945, a period that saw multiple changes in the policies and administration of the educational sector. Extensive coverage is given to the language issue.

9.41 Packard, Robert Lawrence. EDUCATION IN CUBA, PORTO RICO, AND THE PHILIPPINES. Washington, Govt. Print. Off., 1899. 909–983 p. Reprinted

from the Report of the Commissioner of Education for 1897-98, Chapter 20.

The new colonial power takes a look at the historical background and current state of education in its new possessions.

9.42 Porrata, Oscar. A SUGGESTED POLICY FOR THE ADMINISTRATION AND CONTROL OF PUBLIC EDUCATION IN PUERTO RICO. Río Piedras, Bureau of Publications, Puerto Rico Teachers' Association, 1949. 144 p. tables, bibl. (Educational Monograph no. 2).

A summary of the author's doctoral dissertation, the main purpose of which was to supply an analytical treatment of the powers granted by the Organic Act to the commissioner of education of Puerto Rico, and to the Insular Legislature to legislate on matters of educational policy.

9.43 PUBLIC EDUCATION AND THE FUTURE OF PUERTO RICO: A CURRICULUM SURVEY, 1948–1949. New York, Bureau of Publications, Teachers College, Columbia University, 1950. 614 p. tables.

An analysis of the educational system of Puerto Rico conducted by the Institute of Field Studies, Teachers College, Columbia University. It outlines the organizational framework of the educational system and discusses a series of specific curriculum problems such as language instruction and physical problems like buildings and equipment. It includes specific recommendations and identifies some of the governmental agencies that should take responsibility for their implementation.

9.44 Quintero, Ana Helvia, and Ada María Anglada. UN ESTUDIO SOBRE EL PROGRAMA EXPERIMENTAL DE PREPARACION DE MAESTROS. San Juan, Editorial del Departamento de Instrucción Pública, 1970. 294 p. tables, questionnaires, bibl.

A study of the experimental program on teacher education being carried out jointly by the University of Puerto Rico and the Commonwealth Department of Education, with financial assistance from the Ford Foundation.

9.45 Ramos, Lillian L. Expectations for the Role of the Principal as Perceived by Principals and Selected Teachers of the Public Senior High Schools of Puerto Rico. Ph.D. dissertation, Fordham University, 1971. *In* DISSERTATION ABSTRACTS INTERNATIONAL, v. 32, no. 4, p. 1807-A.

The general purpose and scope of this study is indicated in its title.

9.46 Reid, Charles F. "Education in Puerto Rico." *In his* EDUCATION IN THE TERRITORIES AND OUTLYING POSSESSIONS OF THE UNITED STATES. New York, Bureau of Publications, Teachers College, Columbia University, 1941. p. 210–293.

Reviews the conditions of the educational system in Puerto Rico and offers some specific recommendations.

9.47 Riestra, Miguel Angel. Puerto Rico: Culture and Education in a Transitional Era. Ph.D. dissertation, University of Illinois, 1962. *In* DISSERTATION ABSTRACTS, v. 23, no. 1, p. 127-A.

The writer proposes that the school can and should help allay Puerto Rico's cultural problems. Its role should not be limited to mere perpetuation and transmission of culture, but it should become a remaker of culture, by transforming itself into a center for discussing and analyzing selected conflicting issues, including cultural, political, religious, social, and economic problems, under a democratic method of problem solving.

9.48 Rivera Rivera, Pedro José. GENERAL STUDIES AS PREPARATION FOR COLLEGE WORK. San Juan, Department of Education, 1966. 102 p. tables, graphs, bibl.

This work, which constituted the author's doctoral dissertation at the University of Chicago, analyzes an experimental program in Puerto Rico aimed at transferring to the high school the responsibility of providing a liberal education for the youth of the island. The writer is now president of the University of Puerto Rico.

9.49 Rodríguez Bou, Ismael. LA LABOR DE INVESTIGACION QUE SOBRE LA ENSEÑANZA DE ESPAÑOL HA HECHO EL CONSEJO SUPERIOR DE ENSEÑANZA DE PUERTO RICO. Río Piedras, Universidad de Puerto Rico, 1962. 36 p. (Publicaciones Pedagógicas, Ser. 3, no. 8).

Booklet summarizing the research of the Superior Education Council in the fields of education, language arts, adult education and literacy, reading materials, and others. A previous, more complete report, *A Decade of Research at the Office of the Superior Council,* was published in English in 1956.

9.50 Rosado, Domingo. A Philosophical Study to Propose Objectives for Education in Puerto Rico. Ph.D. dissertation, New York University, 1959. *In* DISSERTATION ABSTRACTS, vol. 20, no. 10, p. 4054.

After a study based on a questionnaire and interviews with 296 school officials and lay leaders, the author concludes that education in the island is not geared toward the values of respect for freedom, human rights, and a fuller life, and offers some suggestions for redirection.

9.51 Rosado Díaz, Rev. Father Manuel. The Historical Development and Legal Status of the Public Schools of Puerto Rico. Ph.D. dissertation, University of Denver, 1967. *In* DISSERTATION ABSTRACTS, v. 28, no. 7, p. 2478-A.

A study of the historical development and the legal status of the public school system in Puerto Rico.

9.52 Sáez, Antonia. LA LECTURA, ARTE DEL LENGUAJE. 3. ed. Río Piedras, Ediciones de la Universidad de Puerto Rico, 1966. 401 p. illus., bibl.

Study and textbook on the teaching of reading as the basis of language arts in the elementary and secondary school curriculum. The text includes sample lessons, illustrations, exercises and themes for further study, and lists of supplementary readings.

9.53 Santos de Dávila, Luz M. Recruitment of Candidates for the Teaching Profession through Future Teachers' Clubs in Puerto Rico. Ph.D. dissertation, New York University, 1967. *In* DISSERTATION ABSTRACTS, v. 28, no. 4, p. 1230-A.

The purpose of this study was to determine the extent to which the activities of the Future Teachers' Clubs and cooperating agencies in Puerto Rico contribute to the recruitment of school teachers.

9.54 Sellés Solá, G. LECTURAS HISTORICAS DE LA EDUCACION EN PUERTO RICO. Primera Parte. Río Piedras, Universidad de Puerto Rico, 1943. 298 p. bibl.

A collection of documents dealing with Puerto Rican education from the early sixteenth century to 1850.

9.55 Silva de Bonilla, Ruth M., and Agneris Guzmán de Durán. OCCUPATIONAL PLANS AND ASPIRATIONS OF PUERTO RICAN AND AMERICAN HIGH SCHOOL SENIORS COMPARED. Río Piedras, University of Puerto Rico, Agricultural Experiment Station, 1955. bibl. (Bulletin 197).

Analyzes responses to a questionnaire obtained from 195 seniors in six high schools located throughout the island and compares the information with data available for U.S. students.

9.56 Soto, Juan B. LA UNIVERSIDAD Y LA ESCUELA EN EL DRAMA DE LA VIDA (ENSAYO DE CRITICA PEDAGOGICA). Río Piedras, Universidad de Puerto Rico, 1942. 245 p. (Monografías de la Universidad de Puerto Rico).

The author, who at the time of writing this book was chancellor of the University of Puerto Rico, outlines his idea of what the function of the university should be with regard to the principal problems of life itself.

9.57 Stahl, Mary Theresa. A Basis for Art Education in Puerto Rico. Ed.D. dissertation, Columbia University, 1971. In DISSERTATION ABSTRACTS INTERNATIONAL, v. 33, no. 5, p. 2246-A.

An interdisciplinary study aimed at establishing cultural and psychological foundations for art education programs. Part 1 describes and analyzes Puerto Rican art education as a social system, and part 2 examines the relationship between art education and the individual Puerto Rican, and that of the curriculum to both.

9.58 A SURVEY OF THE PUBLIC EDUCATIONAL SYSTEM OF PUERTO RICO. New York, Bureau of Publications, Teachers College, Columbia University, 1926. 453 p. maps, tables, diagrs.

A critical study by non-Puerto Ricans aimed at providing a better perspective of the educational system of the island. It includes the results of their analysis of existing conditions and constructive suggestions for further improvement.

9.59 Whitla, Dean K., and Janet P. Hanley. RESPONSIVENESS AND RECIPROCITY: THE ROLE OF THE COLLEGE BOARD IN PUERTO RICO. [Hato Rey], P.R., College Entrance Examination Board, 1971. 147 p. tables, graphs.

A report aimed at helping the College Board in Puerto Rico, created in the early 1960s, to define problems in education so as to be able to respond sensitively and productively to the needs of the island.

10
FOLKLORE AND TRADITIONS

10.1 Algería, José. RETABLOS DE LA ALDEA. San Juan, Biblioteca de Autores Puertorriqueños, 1949. 159 p.

Narrative inspired by the town's colorful characters—tailor, shoemaker, priest, mailman, midwife, photographer, and many others.

10.2 Alegría, Ricardo E. LA FIESTA DE SANTIAGO APOSTOL EN LOIZA ALDEA. Prólogo por Fernando Ortiz. San Juan, Colección de Estudios Puertorriqueños, 1954. 76 p. illus., bibl.

Study of the feast of St. James held yearly on July 25 at Loíza Aldea, a town in the northeastern part of Puerto Rico. The author describes and analyzes the festivities, inspired by devotion to the saint, that originated in ninth century Spain but which here are intermingled with the traditions and festivities of the African slaves. (An abbreviated English version appears in the *Journal of American Folklore*, v. 69, Apr. 1956, p. 123-134.)

10.3   Cadilla de Martínez, María. COSTUMBRES Y TRADICIONALISMOS DE MI TIERRA. San Juan, Imprenta Venezuela, 1938. 196 p.

Relates the origin of many traditions and customs pertaining to the music, dance, food, religion, superstitions, and other aspects of the Puerto Ricans.

10.4   Coll y Toste, Cayetano. LEYENDAS. Selección e Introducción por Ricardo E. Alegría. Ilustraciones de Rubén Moraira. San Juan, Instituto de Cultura Puertorriqueña, 1971. 87 p. illus.

A selection of Coll y Toste's *Leyendas Puertorriqueñas*, originally published in 1924-1925, for which he takes his inspiration from historical events and popular legends and draws pictures of an authentic national character.

10.5   Escabí, Pedro, ed. ESTUDIO ETNOGRAFICO DE LA CULTURA POPULAR DE PUERTO RICO; MOROVIS: VISTA PARCIAL DEL FOLKLORE DE PUERTO RICO. Prólogo de Ricardo E. Alegría; ilustraciones por Rafael Rivera Rosa. Río Piedras, Centro de Investigaciones Sociales, Universidad de Puerto Rico, 1970. 380 p. illus., maps, photos, phonodisc, bibl.

The first of what is expected to be a series about popular culture in different areas of the island. This volume covers lifestyles, feasts, sayings, games, music and songs, and crafts in the community of Morovis. A record is included in a cover pocket with four authentic folk songs of the area.

10.6   Fernández Juncos, Manuel. GALERIA PUERTORRIQUEÑA: TIPOS Y CARACTERES; COSTUMBRES Y TRADICIONES. Introducción de Concha Meléndez. Grabados de Carlos E.

Rivera. San Juan, Instituto de Cultura Puertorriqueña, 1958. 383 p. engrs.

Brings together two works originally published in 1882-1883, comprising a series of essays on Puerto Rican folklore, customs, traditions, culture, and society.

10.7   Garrido, Pablo. ESOTERIA Y FERVOR POPULARES DE PUERTO RICO. Madrid, Ediciones Cultura Hispánica, 1952. 250 p. illus., port., map, music.

A study of popular manifestations that are of a religious nature but outside the realm of religion itself, as for example, the tradition of not using a hammer or making loud noises during Holy Week, "so that Christ will not be offended." It also documents the beliefs and customs of the *espiritistas*.

10.8   Hansen, Terrence Leslie. THE TYPES OF THE FOLKTALE IN CUBA, PUERTO RICO, THE DOMINICAN REPUBLIC, AND SPANISH SOUTH AMERICA. Berkeley, University of California Press, 1957. 202 p. (University of California Publications. Folklore Studies, 8).

A work aimed at classifying the folktales of Hispanic America in a uniform and systematic way as an aid to comparative studies. Classifications include: animal, magic, religious, romantic, ogre, jokes and anecdotes, and formula tales.

10.9   Marrero de Figueroa, Carmen. TIERRA Y FOLKLORE. Prólogo de Antonia Sáez. San Juan, Editorial Cordillera, 1967. 193 p. illus.

Vignettes about the land and its people, with a section on legends and traditions relating to the feast of San Juan Bautista. The lyric book also contains a poem about the eve of San Juan, June 24.

10.10 Mason, John Alden. FOLKLORE PUERTORRIQUEÑO. I-ADIVINANZAS. San Juan, Instituto de Cultura Puertorriqueña, 1960. 227 p.

This collection of 800 riddles, first published in the *Journal of American Folklore* between 1916 and 1929, is considered one of the most important in Latin America. It represents the efforts of many school children who wrote them out for the compiler. Included are general riddles, humorous ones employing word play, others involving numerals, anecdotes, and riddles without an answer.

10.11   Ramírez de Arellano, Rafael W., comp. FOLKLORE PUERTORRI-QUEÑO: CUENTOS Y ADIVINANZAS RECOGIDOS DE LA TRADICION ORAL. Madrid, Tip. Avila, 1926. 290 p. (Archivo de Tradiciones Populares, 2).

A collection compiled, according to the author, in an effort to preserve Puerto Rico's heritage of stories, riddles, and other traditional literature in Spanish, in the face of a new ruling power that brought with it a new language.

10.12   Rosa-Nieves, Cesáreo. VOZ FOLK-LORICA DE PUERTO RICO. Prólogo de Walter F. Starkie. Sharon, Conn., Troutman Press, 1967. 128 p. bibl. (Serie Puerto Rico: Realidad y Anhelo, 6).

Study of the principal expressions of oral tradition in Puerto Rico including sayings, popular songs, legends, and Christmas carols. It discusses briefly their Indian, Spanish, African, and *criollo* origins.

11
GOVERNMENT AND POLITICS

11.1   Abril, Mariano. EL SOCIALISMO MODERNO. San Juan, Tip. La Primavera, 1911. 68 p.

Reproduces a series of articles on socialism and the problems of Puerto Rican workers published originally in the newspaper *La Democracia*. The author rejects the revolutionary socialism "that walks hand in hand with anarchism" and believes that "a strong and serious socialist party that can participate in and win elections will never be organized here unless intellectuals and professionals, and not just workers, help organize it, as has happened in Europe."

11.2   Albizu Campos, Pedro. INDEPEN-DENCIA ECONOMICA. [Río Piedras?], Publicaciones de Forum, Federación de Organizaciones Estudiantiles de la Universidad de Puerto Rico, 1970. 51 p. photo.

Brings together a series of nineteen articles published by Albizu Campos in 1930 dealing mostly with the island's economic situation.

11.3   American Academy of Political and Social Science, Philadelphia. PUERTO RICO: A STUDY IN DEMOCRATIC DEVELOPMENT. Edited by Millard Hansen and Henry Wells. Phila-delphia, 1953. 246 p. (*Its* Annals, v. 285).

This is a special issue of the *Annals* to coincide with the inauguration of the first governor elected under the Commonwealth Constitution. The essays and articles describe the events that led to it and their significance. Contributors include L. Muñoz Marín, A. Fernós-Isern, P. Muñoz Amato, J.K. Galbraith, T. Moscoso, J.H. Steward, C. Senior, and F. Ayala. Areas examined are political and economic development, fusion of culture, population, and future prospects.

11.4   Anderson, Robert W. PARTY POLI-TICS IN PUERTO RICO. Stanford, Calif., Stanford University Press, 1965. 269 p. bibl.

This book, based on the author's doctoral dissertation at the University of California, analyzes "the internal political dynamic that led to the public policies of the industrialization program and Commonwealth status." It studies and compares the workings of the political parties and "the political dimension of Puerto Rican development since 1940." The author concludes that there exists a party system based on a lack of consensus on the status problem, the issue at the center of party politics. An epilogue on the elections of 1964 is appended.

11.5 Andréu Iglesias, César. INDEPENDENCIA Y SOCIALISMO. San Juan, Librería Estrella Roja, 1951. 171 p.

A series of lectures and articles "aimed at clarifying some of the vital problems of the Movement of National liberation." It includes the author's testimony in 1950, as a representative of the Communist party of Puerto Rico, before a legislative committee that was considering a referendum on the island's political status.

11.6 Andréu Iglesias, César. LUIS MUÑOZ MARIN: UN HOMBRE ACORRALADO POR LA HISTORIA. [Río Piedras, P.R.], Editorial Claridad, 1964. 80 p.

The author, a separatist leader, reproduces some of the articles he published in *El Imparcial* during 1962. In them he bitterly criticizes Luis Muñoz Marín, whom he considers as archetype of the political, economic, social, and moral crisis in which the author feels the island is immersed.

11.7 Arana Soto, Salvador. MUÑOZ RIVERA—JOSE DE DIEGO: LA DISIDENCIA INDEPENDENTISTA. San Juan, 1970. 164 p. bibl. (His *Luís Muñoz Rivera: Savia y Sangre de Puerto Rico*, t. 4).

Traces the political thinking of L. Muñoz Rivera and J. de Diego during the late nineteenth and early twentieth centuries, focusing on the autonomist and separatist ideas that they espoused.

11.8 Arana Soto, Salvador. LA POLITICA EXTERIOR DE PUERTO RICO (EL PROBLEMA POLITICO DE PUERTO RICO). [Madrid?], 1967. 100 p.

An attempt to explain why the true autonomists in Puerto Rico are not fully satisfied with the political status formula as it now stands. The work was originally published as two articles in the *Revista de Politíca Internacional de Madrid*, Núms. 89 and 90, en./feb. and mar./abr. 1967.

11.9 Araquistain, Luis. LA AGONIA ANTILLANA: EL IMPERIALISMO YANQUI EN EL MAR CARIBE. Madrid, Espasa-Calpe, 1928. 296 p.

Narration of a visit by the author to Puerto Rico and other Antillean islands during 1926-1927, in which he indicts U.S. policies toward the Caribbean. The first chapter describes U.S. rule in Puerto Rico, with emphasis on economic and educational aspects.

11.10 Bagué y Ramírez, Jaime. LA ADMINISTRACION PUBLICA Y SUS RAICES HISTORICAS. San Juan, Imprenta Venezuela, 1960. 142 p.

A history of administrative organization in Puerto Rico from colonization to 1898. A detailed description of La Fortaleza, the governor's mansion, which dates from the mid-sixteenth century, is included.

11.11 Balbás Capó, Vicente. PUERTO RICO A LOS DIEZ AÑOS DE AMERICANIZACION. San Juan, Tipografía Heraldo Español, 1910. port.

The author, who was editor and publisher of the newspaper *Heraldo Español*, brings together more than one hundred of his articles, many of them dealing with the political scene in 1907.

11.12 Barbosa de Rosario, Pilar. LA OBRA DE JOSE CELSO BARBOSA. San Juan, Imprenta Venezuela, 1937-1957. 6 v. (173, 230, 191, 260, 367, 209 p.)

V. 1, *Un Hombre de Pueblo*. Biography of Barbosa (1857-1921), by Antonio S. Pedreira.

V. 2, *Post Umbra: Documentos para la Historia*. A collection of essays, reminiscences, and eulogies relating to Barbosa.

V. 3, *Problema de Razas*. A series of writings by this black patriot dealing with race problems in Puerto Rico and the United States.

V. 4, *Orientando al Pueblo, 1900-1921*. A collection of writings and speeches in which he advocates statehood for Puerto Rico.

V. 5, *De Baldorioty a Barbosa: Historia del Autonomismo Puertorriqueño, 1887-1896*. Documented history of the autonomist movement with emphasis on Barbosa's participation. The first part analyzes the ideological formation of Barbosa, and the second the struggle to achieve autonomy from Spain.

V. 6, *16 de Septiembre de 1896 al 12 de Febrero de 1897: La Comisión Autonomista de 1896.*

11.13   Barceló, Antonio R. FORMS OF GOVERNMENT OF PORTO RICO FROM 1898 TO 1923: CONSIDERATIONS OF THEIR SCOPE. San Juan, Tip. La Democracia, 1923. 21 p.

A brief look at the political development of the island during the first twenty-five years of U.S. rule. It reproduces excerpts from the platforms of the Unionist party presided over by Barceló, including that of 1922 declaring that "the creation of the Free Associated State of Porto Rico is from this day on the Program of the Party Unión de Puerto Rico." It includes also the joint resolution passed unanimously by the legislature of Porto Rico in 1923 creating a commission to go˙ to Washington "to promote reforms to the Organic Act of Porto Rico, as well as such matters as relate to the financial, political and social problems of Porto Rico."

11.14   Bayo, Armando. PUERTO RICO. Habana, Casa de las Américas, 1966. 56 p. illus., bibl. (Colección Nuestros Países).

A contemporary Cuban view of Puerto Rico, with heavy emphasis on U.S. control over the island, which the author calls a "Congressional Colony."

11.15   Bayrón Toro, Fernando. ANALISIS ELECTORAL DE PUERTO RICO (DIVISION Y REVISION DE LOS DISTRITOS). Introducción de Emilio M. Colón. San Juan, Editorial Coquí, 1970. 120 p. tables. (Ediciones Borinquen).

A study of the electoral districts of the island and the need to redistribute them in view of the constitution of the Commonwealth, which stipulates that senatorial and representative districts will be revised after each census. The book, which constituted the author's M.A. thesis at the University of Puerto Rico, includes information on the results of every election held in the island during this century.

11.16   Bhana, Surendra. The Development of Puerto Rican Autonomy under the Truman Administration, 1945–1952. Ph.D. dissertation, University of Kansas, 1971. *In* DISSERTATION ABSTRACTS INTERNATIONAL, v. 32, no. 10, p. 5700-A.

This study examines the development of the Commonwealth status as part of the policy of the United States after World War II to extend to Puerto Rico progressively larger measures of autonomy in its internal affairs.

11.17   Blanchard, Paul. DEMOCRACY AND EMPIRE IN THE CARIBBEAN: A CONTEMPORARY REVIEW. New York, Macmillan, 1947. 377 p.

A wide-ranging study of the Caribbean area written by an author who was a high official of the old Anglo-American Caribbean Commission from 1942 to 1946. It is divided into topical sections, as well as along lines of spheres of influence controlled by the various colonial powers. The book includes much material on Puerto Rico, especially on social and economic conditions and race relations.

11.18   Bothwell, Reece B. TRASFONDO CONSTITUCIONAL DE PUERTO RICO. PRIMERA PARTE 1887–1914. 2. ed. Río Piedras, Editorial Universitaria, 1969. 65 p. bibl. refs.

The first of what the author expects to be a series dealing with the political, historical, and juridical aspects of the development of the government of Puerto Rico. This volume emphasizes the years from the change of sovereignty in 1898 to 1914, the period of the adoption of a new Organic Charter for the island.

11.19   Bowie, Robert R., and Carl J. Friedrich. STUDIES IN FEDERALISM. Boston, Little, Brown, 1954. 887 p. bibl.

The purpose of these studies was to provide detailed comparative materials for the deliberations of the Mouvement Européen, headed by Paul-Henri Spaak, on a proposed European constitution. Study no. 14, on overseas territories, provides some background on the nature of the Puerto Rican Commonwealth formula.

11.20 Brown, Wenzell. ANGRY MEN, LAUGHING MEN: THE CARIBBEAN CALDRON. New York, Greenberg, 1947. 369 p. illus.

On the basis of his own visits, the author describes the policies of the governments in power in the various Caribbean islands. He places great emphasis on the social conditions of the places he visited.

11.21 Brown, Wenzell. DYNAMITE ON OUR DOORSTEP: PUERTO RICAN PARADOX. New York, Greenberg, 1945. 301 p. plates, map.

A personal account of an American who lived in Puerto Rico from 1936 to 1939, working as an English teacher, and his return there in 1945.

11.22 Buitrago Ortiz, Carlos. IDEOLOGIA Y CONSERVADURISMO EN EL PUERTO RICO DE HOY. Río Piedras, P.R., Ediciones Bayoán, 1972. 214 p. tables, bibl.

A study of conservatism in Puerto Rico aimed at identifying the principal trends and characteristics of the rightist elites in Puerto Rican society. The author is a professor at the University of Puerto Rico.

11.23 Calderón, Enrique. EL DOLOR DE UN PUEBLO ESCLAVO. New York, Azteca Press, 1950(?). 141 p.

This book takes both the United States and the Puerto Rican people to task for their perpetuation of a colonial system in Puerto Rico and asks that Puerto Rico be accepted as a full-fledged state of the union or that it be granted its freedom as a sovereign republic. Includes a chapter on Puerto Ricans in New York.

11.24 UNA CAMPAÑA PARLAMENTARIA. Madrid, Impr. de M.G. Hernández, 1873. 395 p.

A collection of proposals presented and speeches delivered by the Puerto Rican deputies—R.M. de Labra, J.M. Sanromá, J. F. Cintrón, J. Alvarez Peralta, and Luis Padial—before the Spanish Cortes in 1872-1873.

11.25 Capó Rodríguez, Pedro. SOME HISTORICAL AND POLITICAL ASPECTS OF THE GOVERNMENT OF PORTO RICO. Baltimore, 1919. Reprinted from the *Hispanic American Historical Review*, v. 2, no. 4, Nov. 1919. 543-585 p. bibl. refs.

Examines the principal features of the civil government established in Puerto Rico under the Foraker Act. It discusses also the Jones Act, which extended U.S. citizenship to the Puerto Ricans and provided for a reorganization of the government of the island.

11.26 Carrión, Benjamín. PUERTO RICO: UN PUEBLO 'MANOS A LA OBRA'. Quito, Ecuador, Edit. Casa de la Cultura Ecuatoriana, 1952. 35 p. illus.

A distinguished Ecuadorian writer describes the impressions he gathered of the island's political and cultural scene during a visit there on the occasion of the establishment of commonwealth status.

11.27 Castro, Paulino E. HISTORIA SINOPTICA DEL PARTIDO NACIONALISTA DE PUERTO RICO. San Juan, Impr. La Primavera, 1947. 72 p. ports., illus.

The secretary general of the Nationalist party writes the history of his party since its founding in 1922. It is preceded by the text of a letter written in 1892 by R.E. Betances to the director of the newspaper *El Porvenir*, published in New York, opposing Cuba's annexation to the United States and by a brief review of the pro-independence movements in the island prior to 1922.

11.28 Chiles, Paul Nelson. THE PUERTO RICAN PRESS REACTION TO THE UNITED STATES, 1888-1898. Philadelphia, 1944. 109 p. bibl.

An analysis of the newspapers of the 1888-1898 period. The study, which constituted the author's doctoral dissertation at the University of Pennsylvania, includes a brief survey of journalism in Puerto Rico, and reactions of the local press to the American press, U.S. politics, the Yankee peril, and economic factors. The author concludes that the most important U.S. influence was the economic and the least important was the cultural.

11.29 Coll y Cuchí, Cayetano. CUATRO MESES DE POLITICA. San Juan, Impresos Gil de Lamadrid, 1923. 209 p.

An analysis of the political situation in Puerto Rico based on personal experiences and on observation of his own Unionist party. He explains the party's opposition to the policies outlined by Governor E. Mont Reilly in his inauguration address.

11.30 Coll y Cuchí, Cayetano, comp. PRO PATRIA. San Juan, M. Burillo, 1909. 422 p. ports.

A compilation of documents pertaining to the activities undertaken by the Unionist party in 1909 against the Foraker Act. It includes a comparative analysis of the Autonomic Charter granted to the island by Spain in 1897 and the Foraker Act adopted by the U.S. Congress in 1900.

11.31 Coll y Cuchí, José. EL NACIONALISMO EN PUERTO RICO. San Juan, Gil de Lamadrid Hnos., 1923. plates, ports.

Explains the background of the creation of the Nationalist party in 1922. The book includes the texts of letters, addresses, newspaper articles, and other documents pertaining to the idea of independence, the creation of the party, and its first year.

11.32 Coll y Cuchí, José. UN PROBLEMA EN AMERICA. 2. ed. México, Editorial Jus, 1944. 234 p. ports.

The author, a leader of the Nationalist party, points out the injustice of the political system under which Puerto Rico is tied to the United States. He believes the United States has failed to "Americanize" the island and that it has been able to keep it under its rule only by military force.

11.33 Comité Cubano pro Libertad de Patriotas Puertorriqueños. POR LA INDEPENDENCIA DE PUERTO RICO, POR LA LIBERTAD DE SUS PATRIOTAS. Habana, 1939. 75 p. (Publicaciones, I).

Reproduces statements, resolutions, and other documents approved by the Cuban Committee for the Freedom of Puerto Rican Patriots and by other Cuban organizations in favor of independence for Puerto Rico.

11.34 Communist Party of Puerto Rico. THE CASE OF PUERTO RICO. Foreword by William Z. Foster. New York, New Century Pub., 1953. 15 p.

Memorandum submitted to the United Nations by the Communist Party of Puerto Rico in October 1953, opposing the resolution by which the United States would discontinue to submit information on Puerto Rico to the world body.

11.35 Córdova, Lieban. DE MI HOJA DE APUNTES. Barcelona, Editorial Rumbos. 1964. 354 p. ports.

Sketchy personal observations of the political events of the last four decades, emphasizing the activities of Luis Muñoz Marín, with whom the author worked for several years. He includes some personal anecdotes from his own experience.

11.36 Corretjer, Juan Antonio. CONTESTACION AL MIEDO. San Juan, 1954. 56 p.

An attempt to answer detractors of the independence movement by analyzing the often-heard reasons against a radical change in political status. The author says "the liberation of a people's spirit cannot be accomplished without defeating fear." His purpose is to allay such fears.

11.37 Corretjer, Juan Antonio. LA LUCHA POR LA INDEPENDENCIA DE PUERTO RICO. San Juan, Unión del Pueblo pro Constituyente. 1949. 149 p.

A view of the fight for independence for the island by one of its leading proponents.

11.38 Corominas, Enrique Ventura. PUERTO RICO LIBRE. Buenos Aires, "El Ateneo," 1950. 253 p.

A former chairman of the Council of the Organization of American States defends Puerto Rico's independence. The book deals mostly with the Interamerican Conference held in Bogotá, Colombia, in 1948 to study the means of erradicating colonialism in America, and with Puerto Rico's case and role in that conference.

11.39 Cruz Monclova, Lidio, and Antonio J. Colorado. NOTICIA ACERCA DEL PENSAMIENTO POLITICO DE PUERTO RICO, 1808-1952. México, Editorial Orión, 1955. 162 p.

The first part analyzes the six phases of liberalism in Puerto Rico during the nineteenth century. The initial phase occurred between 1808 and 1823, when Spain recognized Puerto Rico as an integral part of the Spanish crown. The movement culminated with the liberals' reorganization in 1886 as an autonomist force and the achievement in 1897 of autonomy for the island. The second part of the book is devoted to political movements from 1900 to 1952. The texts of the Autonomic Charter and the Constitution of the Commonwealth of Puerto Rico are appended.

11.40 CULEBRA: CONFRONTACION AL COLONIAJE. Río Piedras, P.R., 1971. 44 p.
A booklet on the fight by Puerto Rican groups to bring to an end U.S. naval operations on the island of Culebra, published by four radical groups: Movimiento Estudiantil Cristiano de Puerto Rico, Programa de Renovación e Investigación Social para Adiestramiento en la Misión, Comité Clérigos Pro-Rescate de Culebra, and Unión Latino Americana de Juventudes Evangélicas de Puerto Rico.

11.41 De Kadt, Emanuel, ed. PATTERNS OF FOREIGN INFLUENCE IN THE CARIBBEAN. New York, Oxford University Press, 1972. 188 p.
Contains material relevant to Puerto Rico.

11.42 Degetau, Federico. THE POLITICAL STATUS OF PUERTO RICO. Washington, Globe Printing, 1902. 16 p.
Lecture delivered at the School of Comparative Jurisprudence and Diplomacy of Columbia University on February 13, 1902 by the then resident commissioner from Puerto Rico to the United States, in which he states that the people of Puerto Rico aspire "to become an organized territory, with the certainty of soon being admitted as a state of the American union."

11.43 La Democracia. IN DEFENCE OF PUERTO RICO. San Juan, Tip. La Democracia, 1926. 89 p.
English compilation of twenty-six articles written in La Democracia be-tween February 27 and April 15, 1926, in reply to articles published in the Baltimore Sun indicating that the Puerto Rican legislature and other sectors of the island's administration were unfit to deal with the problem of constituting an honest and efficient government.

11.44 Diego, José de. NUEVAS CAMPAÑAS. Prólogo de Emilio S. Belaval. San Juan, Editorial Cordillera, 1966. 459 p.
The author brings together his political writings during the period from 1913 to 1916, all centered around the ideal of independence for Puerto Rico and of an Antillean federation.

11.45 Diego, José de. EL PLEBISCITO. Prólogo de Emilio S. Belaval. San Juan, Editorial Cordillera, 1966. 94 p. (Los Grandes Escritores de Puerto Rico).
Documents pertaining to the resolution presented by House Speaker de Diego in 1917 calling for a plebiscite in which the people of Puerto Rico would be able to determine their ultimate political status. The text of the resolution and de Diego's speeches are included.

11.46 Diego, José de. PORTO RICAN CITIZENSHIP: OPEN LETTER FROM SPEAKER JOSE DE DIEGO OF THE HOUSE OF DELEGATES OF PORTO RICO TO U.S. SENATOR MILES POINDEXTER. San Juan, Porto Rico Progress Pub. Co., 1913. 23 p. Spanish translation.
This open letter is of historical value since it revolves around the discussion of American citizenship for Puerto Ricans. It presents the various points of view and dispels the notion that U.S. citizenship was wanted by all Puerto Ricans.

11.47 Diffie, Bailey W., and Justin W. Diffie. PORTO RICO: A BROKEN PLEDGE. Introduction by Harry Elmer Barnes. New York, Vanguard Press, 1931. 252 p. bibl. (Studies in American Imperialism).
Analyzes the first thirty-two years of U.S. rule in the island and concludes that, although some progress was made, the United States failed to cope

with the island's economic, social, and political problems.

11.48 LOS DIPUTADOS AMERICANOS EN LAS CORTES ESPAÑOLAS; LOS DIPU-TADOS DE PUERTO RICO, 1872–1873. Madrid, Impr. de J. Alaria, 1880. 395 p.

A collection of speeches and other writings by Puerto Rico's deputies to the Spanish Cortes, bills they introduced, and a laudatory article on their work published in La América.

11.49 Enamorado Cuesta, José. EL IMPE-RIALISMO YANQUI Y LA REVOLU-CION EN EL CARIBE. San Juan, Editorial Puerto Rico Libre, 1966. 254 p. bibl.

The author calls for a revolution that would expel the United States from Puerto Rico. He believes that the objective of the United States is exploitation of the Puerto Ricans and offers as examples of U.S. imperialism its interventions in the Dominican Republic, Cuba, Panama, and Nicaragua.

11.50 Enamorado Cuesta, José. PUERTO RICO SE NACIONALIZA, NO SE "AMERICANIZA." San Juan, Editorial Puerto Rico Libre, 1970. 14 p.

Refutes Pablo García Kuenzli's El Proceso de Americanización en Puerto Rico. The author believes that Puerto Rico is increasingly nationalized and is moving towards complete political independence and liberation from the hold of North American imperialism.

11.51 Esté ano Pisani, Miguel A. d'. PUERTO RICO: ANALISIS DE UN PLE-BISCITO. Habana, Tricontinental, 1967. 126 p.

A Cuban professor of international public law denounces the 1967 plebiscite as unconstitutional, arbitrary, and farcical. He analyzes the colonial status from 1898, the Foraker Act of 1900, Public Law 600 of 1950, the status commission, and Resolution 1514 of the United Nations, which defined the concept of "free association."

11.52 Farr, Kenneth Raymond. The Problem of Institutionalization of a Political Party: The Case of the Partido Popular Democrático of Puerto Rico. Ph.D. dissertation, Tulane University, 1971.

In DISSERTATION ABSTRACTS IN-TERNATIONAL, v. 32, no. 4, p. 2152-A.

This study explores the problem of institutionalization of a political party founded upon and sustained by strong personal and charismatic leadership. The Partido Popular Democrático and its efforts to institutionalize, consciously begun in 1960, form the basis of the study.

11.53 Fernós Isern, Antonio. PUERTO RICO LIBRE Y FEDERADO. San Juan, Biblioteca de Autores Puertorriqueños, 1951. 229 p. illus.

The author, who was resident commissioner of Puerto Rico in Washington from 1948 to 1964, explains the actions and circumstances that led to Commonwealth status.

11.54 Ferré, Luis A. THE PLEA OF PUERTO RICO. [Ponce, P.R., Imprenta Fortuño], 1949. 24 p. English and Spanish.

Statement read at the public hearing held in Ponce, Puerto Rico on November 23, 1949, by a subcommittee of the Committee on Labor and Education of the U.S. House of Representatives, in which Mr. Ferré requests the "equal deal" of statehood for the island.

11.55 Fischman, Jerome I. The Rise and Development of the Political Party in Puerto Rico under Spanish and American Rule and the Historical Significance of the Subsequent Emergence and Growth of the Popular Party. Ph.D. dissertation, New York University, 1962. In DISSERTATION AB-STRACTS, v. 24, no. 10, p. 4270-A.

Traces the history of the emergence and development of political parties in Puerto Rico, from the latter half of the nineteenth century to the establishment of the Commonwealth in 1952.

11.56 Friedrich, Carl J. PUERTO RICO: MIDDLE ROAD TO FREEDOM. FUERO FUNDAMENTAL. New York, Rinehart, 1959. 86 p. bibl. Paperback.

A probing look into the nature of Commonwealth status by a professor at Harvard University. It identifies the novel features of this political formula and the principal shortcomings in the relations of Puerto Rico with the U.S. federal government. Friedrich also outlines the changes he feels must be made in those relations by 1975 if the commonwealth is to be placed on a "firm and permanent basis."

11.57 Fuster, Jaime B. LOS DERECHOS CIVILES RECONOCIDOS EN EL SISTEMA DE VIDA PUERTORRIQUEÑO. San Juan, Comisión de Derechos Civiles, 1969. 232 p. illus., bibl.
Basic information on civil rights in Puerto Rico, intended for the general public.

11.58 García Angulo, Efraín. PUERTO RICO: ESTADO FEDERAL O REPUBLICA AUTONOMA. New York, Las Américas, 1964. 247 p.
The author, an advocate of statehood for Puerto Rico, considers that the island's primary problem is economic. He analyzes the constitution and characteristics of the commonwealth status, its economy, political parties, education, and relations with the United States.

11.59 García de Serrano, Irma. LA SELECCION DE PERSONAL EN EL SERVICIO PUBLICO DE PUERTO RICO. [Río Piedras], Editorial Universitaria, Universidad de Puerto Rico, 1969. 312 p. tables, bibl.
A source of information on personnel administration in Puerto Rico from 1898 to 1967, with emphasis on the selection of personnel for public service. The work is based on the author's M.A. thesis at the University of Boston, 1959.

11.60 García Kuenzli, Pablo. EL PROCESO DE AMERICANIZACION EN PUERTO RICO: UN PROBLEMA ETICO. San Juan, Editorial Análisis, 1969. 16 p.
An essay analyzing the political and social situation since the arrival of U.S. troops in 1898. The author believes that Puerto Rico has already been "Americanized," but that such Americanization, by which he means the forging of a mature people, has prepared it for either independence or federated statehood.

11.61 García Passalacqua, Juan M. LA CRISIS POLITICA EN PUERTO RICO. San Juan, Ediciones Edil, 1970. 184 p.
Memoirs of the 1962–1966 period by an aide to Governors Luis Muñoz Marín and Roberto Sánchez Vilella. The author describes the ideological dissension within the Popular Democratic party between proponents of the status quo and younger members who were for renewal and reform, which led to a split in the PPD and its eventual defeat in the 1968 elections.

11.62 Géigel-Polanco, Vicente. EL DESPERTAR DE UN PUEBLO. San Juan, Biblioteca de Autores Puertorriqueños, 1942. 206 p.
A series of essays on the island's political situation to 1940, historical figures (Hostos, Betances), and education.

11.63 Géigel-Polanco, Vicente. LA FARSA DEL ESTADO LIBRE ASOCIADO. Río Piedras, Editorial Edil, 1972. 207 p. bibl.
The author analyzes the status of "Free Associated State" and expresses his belief that it is nothing more than a farce, for Puerto Rico is neither free nor a state, nor associated with anyone. He states that "the United States has maintained an iron shell over the colony with all its oppressive obstacles to the constitutional development of Puerto Rico, with the unmerciful exploitation of our market, with our impious commercial and cultural isolation from the free world, with the imposition of a scandalous cost of living. . . ."

11.64 Goodsell, Charles T. ADMINISTRATION OF A REVOLUTION: EXECUTIVE REFORMS IN PUERTO RICO UNDER GOVERNOR TUGWELL, 1941–1946. Cambridge, Mass., Harvard University Press, 1965. 254 p. illus., ports. bibl. refs. (Harvard Political Studies).
An analysis of Rexford G. Tugwell's governorship of the island, "an extraordinarily creative period of building and rebuilding the institutions of Puerto Rican governmental administration." These administrative reforms were of substantial help in the island's subsequent social and economic revolution.

11.65 GUIA PARA LAS ELECCIONES 1972: PROGRAMAS OFICIALES. San Juan, Banco Popular de Puerto Rico, 1972. 112 p.

The official platforms of the six political parties that appeared on the ballots in the elections of 1972. Includes an index that facilitates comparison of positions on the principal issues.

11.66 Gould, Lyman J. LA LEY FORAKER: RAICES DE LA POLITICA COLONIAL DE LOS ESTADOS UNIDOS. Río Piedras, Editorial Universitaria, Universidad de Puerto Rico, 1969. 186 p.

Detailed analysis of the first Organic Act approved by the U.S. Congress for Puerto Rico on April 12, 1900, establishing a civil government for the island. The author examines the historical, political, economic, and social conditions that led to its adoption. (The work is based on the author's doctoral dissertation, "The Foraker Act: The Roots of American Colonial Policy," summarized in *Dissertation Abstracts*, v. 19, no. 6, p. 1430).

11.67 Hayden, Sherman S., and Benjamin Rivlin. NON-SELF-GOVERNING TERRITORIES: STATUS OF PUERTO RICO. New York, Woodrow Wilson Foundation, 1954. 23 p. bibl.

Summarizes the issues considered by the eighth session of the U.N. General Assembly in 1953, when it decided that because Puerto Rico was no longer a nonself-governing territory, the United States would not have to continue transmitting information about it to the world body.

11.68 Holmes, Olive. PUERTO RICO: AN AMERICAN RESPONSIBILITY. New York, Foreign Policy Association, 1947. bibl. refs. Reprinted from *Foreign Policy Reports*, v. 22, no. 24, March 1, 1947, p. 282-292.

A general survey of the Puerto Rican situation based on a visit there. The author believes the island's troubles are compounded by "the absence of a clearly defined national policy for the eventual settlement of this 'unincorporated territory'" and asks that the United States submit the status question to the Puerto Ricans,

"with a pledge to be bound by the results."

11.69 Hunter, Robert J. The Historical Evolution of the Relationship between the United States and Puerto Rico: 1898-1963. Ph.D. dissertation, University of Pittsburgh, 1963. *In* DISSERTATION ABSTRACTS, vol. 25, no. 4, p. 2473-A.

This study traces the evolution of the relationship between the United States and Puerto Rico, culminating in the establishment of commonwealth status. The author points out that, despite the acceptance of the commonwealth principle by the majority of Puerto Ricans, many Puerto Ricans regard this status as transitory, with thousands continuing to agitate for statehood and many others for independence.

11.70 Iglesias Pantín, Santiago. LUCHAS EMANCIPADORAS (CRONICAS DE PUERTO RICO). Prólogo de Bolívar Pagán. 2. ed. San Juan, Imprenta Venezuela, 1958-1962. 2 v. (400, 301 p.).

Autobiography and memoirs of Santiago Iglesias Pantín, first labor leader and founder of the Socialist party, with a history of the labor and trade union movement in Puerto Rico from his arrival in 1896 to his appointment as the island's resident commissioner in Washington.

11.71 Jabulka, Jan. REPORT ON PUERTO RICAN COMMONWEALTH. Honolulu, Hawaii Statehood Commission, 1954. 20 p.

A series of ten articles written by the executive director of the Hawaii Statehood Commission after a visit to Puerto Rico in August 1954, with the purpose of looking into the political status of the island. He criticizes the Puerto Ricans' choice and defends statehood as the solution to Hawaii's status dilemma.

11.72 Kidder, Frederick E. The Political Concepts of Luis Muñoz Rivera (1859-1916) of Puerto Rico. Ph.D. dissertation, University of Florida, 1965. *In* DISSERTATION ABSTRACTS, v. 27, no. 1, p. 230-A.

An examination of the political philosophy of Luis Muñoz Rivera particularly as it concerned the political autonomy of Puerto Rico, showing the importance and viability of his ideas for recent political developments.

11.73 LeVeness, Frank Paul. The Commonwealth of Puerto Rico: Democracy Thrives in the Caribbean. Ph.D. dissertation, St. Johns University, 1968. *In* DISSERTATION ABSTRACTS INTERNATIONAL, v. 29, no. 2, p. 651-A.

This study examines the government of the Commonwealth from 1952 through 1964 to determine whether democracy truly existed there. The island is presented as an area of Latin America which, mainly through its own efforts, though with considerable aid from the United States, has overcome many of the difficulties currently existing in South and Central America.

11.74 Lewis, Gordon K. PUERTO RICO: FREEDOM AND POWER IN THE CARIBBEAN. New York, Monthly Review Press, 1963. 626 p. bibl. refs. (Also published in Spanish: PUERTO RICO: LIBERTAD Y PODER EN EL CARIBE, Río Piedras, Editorial Edil, 1969).

Well-documented analysis of the "general experience of Puerto Rican life . . . within the larger framework of the Pan-Caribbean world." The author bases his study on the "neo-colonial" character of Puerto Rican society and the relationship between the subordinate countryside and the dominant metropolis. He identifies the problem, examines the history, and analyzes the present conditions of society, government, and education.

11.75 Liebman, Arthur. THE POLITICS OF PUERTO RICAN UNIVERSITY STUDENTS. Austin, Texas, Institute of Latin American Studies, University of Texas Press, 1970. 205 p. tables, questionnaire, bibl. (Latin American Monographs, 20).

The author believes that there is little in the historical, cultural, economic, and political environment of Puerto Rican students "that would predispose them toward idealism and nationalism," although his findings showed students to be more politically active than voters in general. Noting in the epilogue the recent militant pro-independence demonstrations at the university, the author states that only a minority of students participated and that, if surveyed today, their political profile would not differ significantly from that of 1964, when he did his study. But he adds, "although these recent activists are a minority, I think that they are a growing minority, larger in size and more militant than student activists of a few years ago."

11.76 López Landrón, Rafael. CARTAS ABIERTAS PARA EL PUEBLO DE PUERTO RICO. Mayagüez, Impr. Unión Obrera, 1911. 166 p.

A series of open letters published in *El Aguila* in Ponce between 1910 and 1911, in which López Landrón, who had been a deputy to the Spanish Cortes, tries to dispel the notion that the Autonomic Charter granted by Spain to Puerto Rico toward the end of the century was better for the island than the Organic Act. In the letters he discusses in detail both laws, drawing parallels and pointing out differences. Although he concludes that U.S. rule over the island was superior to Spanish, he emphatically does not mean that "the present state of affairs which the U.S. imposes on us is even desirable for our people."

11.77 López Tamés, Román. EL ESTADO LIBRE ASOCIADO DE PUERTO RICO. Prólogo del Luis Sela y Sampil. Oviedo, España, Publicaciones del Instituto de Estudios Jurídicos, 1965. 284 p. bibl.

This book, which constituted the author's doctoral dissertation for the Universidad de Oviedo, Spain, 1964, is an analytic interpretation of the Estado Libre Asociado that differs from the official one. The author studies the difficult situation of maintaining the present trend of economic development together with political and cultural autonomy and foresees Puerto Rico as a future state of the Union.

11.78 Lugo Silva, Enrique. THE TUGWELL ADMINISTRATION IN PUERTO

RICO, 1941–1946. Río Piedras, P.R., 1955. 185 p. ports. bibl.

Analyzing the annual reports of Governor Rexford G. Tugwell to the president of the United States, his public papers, and his government reports, the author examines the period of 1941–1946. With the appointment of Governor Tugwell, Puerto Rico started on the road to economic reform. The book, based on a thesis presented at Ohio State University, includes the most important laws passed by the legislature of Puerto Rico and approved by the governor.

11.79   Mathews, Thomas G. PUERTO RICAN POLITICS AND THE NEW DEAL. Foreword by Rexford G. Tugwell. Gainesville, University of Florida Press, 1960. 345 p. bibl.

This book, which was the author's doctoral dissertation at Columbia University in 1957, studies and analyzes political activity in Puerto Rico during the period of the New Deal in the United States. The author covers from just prior to the election of 1932 to the close of 1938 and emphasizes the interaction between the administration in Washington and the U.S.-appointed government on the island. Mathews also analyzes the reasons for the failure of many New Deal programs in Puerto Rico. (A Spanish translation was published recently: La política puertorriqueña y el Nuevo Trato, Río Piedras, Editorial Universitaria, Universidad de Puerto Rico, 1970.)

11.80   Mathews, Thomas G., and Fuat M. Andic, eds. POLITICS AND ECONOMICS IN THE CARIBBEAN. Río Piedras, Institute of Caribbean Studies, University of Puerto Rico, 1971. 284 p. (Institute of Caribbean Studies. Special Study no. 8).

Contains several chapters on Puerto Rico.

11.81   McIntosh, William. The Development of Political Democracy in Puerto Rico. Ph.D. dissertation, University of Minnesota, 1953. In DISSERTATION ABSTRACTS, v. 12, no. 5, p. 859.

A study aimed at examining and evaluating the available information on the development of political democracy in Puerto Rico up to attainment of commonwealth status in 1952.

11.82   Medina Ramírez, Ramón. EL MOVIMIENTO LIBERTADOR EN LA HISTORIA DE PUERTO RICO. Prólogo de Francisco Matos Paoli. [San Juan, 1970]. 3 v. in 1 (695 p.).

The late acting president of the Nationalist party of Puerto Rico tells the history of the nationalist movement and its leaders.

11.83   Medina Ramírez, Ramón. VERBO ENCADENADO. San Juan, 1955. 96 p.

The author, a nationalist leader, brings together various speeches, articles, and other writings centered on the nationalists' struggle for independence and the repression of which he feels they have always been victims.

11.84   Miranda, Luis Antonio. LA JUSTICIA SOCIAL EN PUERTO RICO. San Juan, Talleres de la Correspondencia, 1943. 204 p.

Defense of the social and economic program of the Popular Democratic party prior to the 1944 elections. It elucidates the development of local political parties.

11.85   Morales Carrión, Arturo. "The historical roots and political significance of Puerto Rico." In Wilgus, A. Curtis, ed., THE CARIBBEAN: BRITISH, DUTCH, FRENCH, UNITED STATES. Gainesville, University of Florida Press, 1958. p. 139–169. bibl. refs.

Documented paper tracing the historical development of the idea of commonwealth status, both in Puerto Rico and the United States.

11.86   Morales Otero, Pablo. COMENTARIOS ALREDEDOR DEL DESARROLLO POLITICO DE PUERTO RICO. San Juan, Biblioteca de Autores Puertorriqueños, 1970. 294 p.

Summarizes and comments on political events in Puerto Rico from the nineteenth century to the plebiscite on its political status held in 1967.

11.87   Morales Yordán, Jorge. DESARROLLO POLITICO Y POBREZA. San Juan, Editorial Cordillera. 1971. 94 p., tables, bibl.

Three essays centered around the

themes "of the search for the contemporary Puerto Rican reality, its structural interpretation, and the need to change it." The author is a professor in the School of Public Administration of the University of Puerto Rico.

11.88 Movimiento Pro-Independencia. PRESENTE Y FUTURO DE PUERTO RICO: LA DOCTRINA DE LA NUEVA LUCHA DE INDEPENDENCIA. Río Piedras, P.R., Misión Nacional Albizu Campos del Movimiento Pro Independencia de Puerto Rico, 1969. 78 p.

Reproduces the document approved by the Pro-Independence Movement in 1968 expressing its positions on the economic, political, military, and cultural situation of the island and its program for national liberation.

11.89 Muñoz Marín, Luis. PUERTO RICO IN THE AREA OF DEMOCRACY [and] FOURTH OF JULY ADDRESS. Río Piedras, University of Puerto Rico, 1941. 36 p. (Bulletin. Ser. 12, no. 1) English and Spanish texts.

Two addresses by Muñoz shortly after he became president of the senate, in which he discusses concepts of civilization and democracy.

11.90 Muñoz Morales, Luis. EL STATUS POLITICO DE PUERTO RICO. Prólogo de Manuel Fernández Juncos. San Juan, Tip. El Compás, 1921. 171 p. port., bibl.

A distinguished lawyer looks at the political status of Puerto Rico under both Spanish and U.S. rule and offers some "orientations" for the future, analyzing what each of the status alternatives would entail. A series of important documents are appended, including the Autonomic Charter of 1898, the Foraker Act, and the Jones Act.

11.91 Muñoz Rivera, Luis. CAMPAÑAS POLITICAS. Seleccionadas y recopiladas por Luis Muñoz Marín. Madrid, Editorial Puerto Rico, 1925. 3 v. (309, 362, 341 p.) (*His* Obras Completas, v. 1-3).

A collection of articles and letters written by the noted autonomist leader between 1890 and 1916, and his notes for a book (1896-1900).

11.92 Munro, Dana G. INTERVENTION AND DOLLAR DIPLOMACY IN THE CARIBBEAN, 1900-1921. Princeton, N.J., Princeton University Press, 1964. 553 p. map, bibl. refs.

Written by a scholar who was once an aide in the U.S. State Department, the book does not discuss Puerto Rico specifically but analyzes the character of, and the driving forces behind, the new U.S. policies toward the Caribbean during the first twenty years of this century. The book is generally favorable to the U.S. point of view.

11.93 Nieves Falcón, Luis, Pablo García Rodríguez, and Félix Ojeda Reyes. PUERTO RICO: GRITO Y MORDAZA. Río Piedras, P.R., Ediciones Librería Internacional, 1971. 284 p. illus.

A detailed account from a radical viewpoint of the events of March 1971 at the University of Puerto Rico main campus, accompanied by numerous photographs, excerpts from the local press, and eye-witness accounts by individual students. It is in reality a narrative account of the growing politicization over the last few years of certain segments of the university student body linked with the various independence political movements.

11.94 Ocampo V., Tarsicio, comp. PUERTO RICO: PARTIDO ACCION CRISTIANA, 1960-62: DOCUMENTOS Y REACCIONES DE PRENSA. Cuernavaca, México, Centro Intercultural de Documentación, 1967. 457 p. (?) bibl., doc. (Dossier no. 11).

Thorough documentation in Spanish and English of the controversy brought about by the establishment of a church-backed political party, Partido Acción Cristiana, in 1960 after the defeat of a religious instruction bill.

11.95 Ordóñez, Eduardo. ESTADO LIBRE ASOCIADO DE PUERTO RICO. Prólogo de Enrique Recourt García. Monterrey, México, Impr. de la Universidad de Nuevo León, 1967. 67 p. bibl.

The author traces the development of the different forms of government during various historical periods in Puerto Rico. He analyzes with particular detail the establishment of commonwealth status, and points out that the political situation has remained basically the same after adoption of the commonwealth formula.

11.96   Pabón, Milton. LA CULTURA POLITICA PUERTORRIQUEÑA. Río Piedras, P.R. Editorial Xaguey, 1972. 314 p. tables.

This book was the author's second report to the Commonwealth Commission on Civil Rights, submitted in the mid-sixties. It expands on the information included in the first (*Los Derechos y los Partidos Políticos en la Sociedad Puertorriqueña*, Río Piedras, P.R., Editorial Edil, 1968), but it places greater emphasis on developing a theory about Puerto Rican political culture, rather than concentrating on the question of rights and institutions as such. The author is particularly interested in identifying "the patterns of intolerance and official practices of discrimination and persecution against minority political groups that defend independence for Puerto Rico."

11.97   Pabón, Milton, Robert W. Anderson, and Víctor J. Rivera Rodríguez. LOS DERECHOS Y LOS PARTIDOS POLITICOS EN LA SOCIEDAD PUERTORRIQUEÑA. Río Piedras, P.R., Editorial Edil, 1968. 172 p. tables.

The full text of a report submitted by three advisers to the Commission on Civil Rights of Puerto Rico in 1958 about major problems in the field of political rights in the island. The report considers juridical and technical aspects, as well as the sociological conditions that affect full employment of political rights.

11.98   Pacheco, Padró, Antonio. PUERTO RICO, NACION Y ESTADO. San Juan, Comité Nacional Puertorriqueño, 1955. 302 p. bibl. refs.

This book covers the period from 1930 to 1953—the political panorama, economic and social change, the status question, and the island's case before the United Nations. Various documents are appended.

11.99   Padilla Pérez, Carlos. PUERTO RICO AL RESCATE DE SU SOBERANIA. Buenos Aires, [A. Cafferatta], 1958. 178 p.

(Publicaciones del Partido Nacionalista de Puerto Rico).

A Puerto Rican nationalist leader who has lived for many years in Latin America writes about the struggle for independence for Puerto Rico.

11.100   Padín, José. CONSIDERACIONES EN TORNO AL REGIMEN COLONIAL. Río Piedras, Junta Editora de la Universidad de Puerto Rico, 1945. 33 p.

An address during commencement exercises at the University of Puerto Rico by the then commissioner of education in which he strongly urges the Puerto Rican people to break the shackles of political and economic colonialism.

11.101   Pagán, Bolívar. CRONICAS DE WASHINGTON. Prólogo de José Arnaldo Meyners. San Juan, Biblioteca de Autores Puertorriqueños, 1949. 293 p.

A series of articles written by Pagán while he was resident commissioner in Washington, in which he comments about the United States, its leaders, and contemporary issues.

11.102   Pagán, Bolívar. HISTORIA DE LOS PARTIDOS POLITICOS PUERTORRIQUEÑOS, (1898–1956). San Juan, Librería Campos, 1959. 2 v. (342, 399 p.) illus.

A documented history of Puerto Rico's political parties from the time of annexation to the United States to the initial years of commonwealth status.

11.103   Pagán, Bolívar. IDEALES EN MARCHA: DISCURSOS Y ARTICULOS. San Juan, Biblioteca de Autores Puertorriqueños, 1939. 306 p.

Speeches and articles by and about Bolívar Pagán during the 1930s, most of them dealing with his political and social ideals. Pagán, a leader of the island's socialist party, was later appointed resident commissioner of Puerto Rico in Washington.

11.104   Pagán, Bolívar. PROCERATO PUERTORRIQUEÑO DEL SIGLO XIX: HISTORIA DE LOS PARTIDOS POLITICOS PUERTORRIQUEÑOS, DESDE SUS ORIGENES HASTA 1898. San Juan, Editorial Campos, 1961. 587 p. bibl.

History of Puerto Rican political parties from their origins in the nineteenth century under Spanish rule to the change of sovereignty in 1898. It studies the ideology of the various political parties and their leaders in Puerto Rico against the background of the conditions existing in the Spanish government at the time. Biographical sketches of political figures of the century are included.

11.105 Parrilla Bonilla, Antulio. PUERTO RICO: SUPERVIVENCIA Y LIBERACION. Prólogo de Margot Arce de Vázquez. Río Piedras, P.R., Ediciones Librería Internacional, 1971. 358 p.

Reproduces some of the selections included in the author's Puerto Rico: Iglesia y Sociedad, 1967-1969, and adds some newer writings on religion, politics, and the cooperative movement. It covers most aspects of Puerto Rican life, as seen by a radical Catholic priest.

11.106 Partido de la Independencia de Puerto Rico. PROGRAMA ECONOMICO Y POLITICO. San Juan, Tip. Real Hnos., [1912]. 40 p.

Reproduces the document that created in 1912 the Partido de la Independencia de Puerto Rico and its program for economic and political development.

11.107 Partido Independentista Puertorriqueño. MEMORIAL. San Juan, 1953. 42 l. mimeographed.

Memorandum presented to the General Assembly of the United Nations in 1953 by the Independence Party of Puerto Rico (PIP) regarding the political status of the island. According to the PIP the island remains a colony, violating the spirit of the United Nations' commitment to self-government.

11.108 Partido Independentista Puertorriqueño. SUPPLEMENTARY MEMORANDUM OF THE PUERTO RICO INDEPENDENCE PARTY HOLDING THAT THE TERRITORY OF PUERTO RICO HAS NOT YET ATTAINED A COMPLETE MEASURE OF SELF-GOVERNMENT. New York, 1953. 22 l. mimeographed.

A supplementary memorandum to the preceding Memorial.

11.109 Partido Nacionalista de Puerto Rico. NACIONALISMO ENARBOLA LA BANDERA DE LA RAZA EN LARES. San Juan, 1971. 47 p.

Brings together several articles and letters, and a speech by Pedro Albizu Campos on the commemoration of the Día de la Raza, October 12, to mark the Hispanic heritage of the peoples of Spanish America.

11.110 Partido Nacionalista de Puerto Rico. PLANTAO EN LA REVOLUCION. San Juan, 1967. 19 p. (Ediciones Año Pre-Centenario de la Proclamación de la República).

Reproduces an interview with Pedro Angleró shortly before his death in 1931, in which he recalls his participation in the Lares Insurrection of 1868. Also included are various tributes to Angleró.

11.111 Partido Nacionalista de Puerto Rico. PUERTO RICO: PROBLEMA INTERNACIONAL. San Juan, 1949. 191 p. illus., ports.

Publication of the Foreign Affairs Ministry of the Nationalist party presenting its position on Puerto Rico's political situation. The Autonomic Charter of 1897, the Treaty of Paris, and other documents are appended.

11.112 Partido Popular Democrático. COMPILACION DE PROGRAMAS, 1940 A 1956. San Juan, 1958. 62 p.

Compilation of the Popular Democratic party's platforms from 1940 to 1956.

11.113 Petrullo, Vincenzo. PUERTO RICAN PARADOX. Philadelphia, University of Pennsylvania Press, 1947. 181 p.

Presents an overall picture of Puerto Rico and its people in the forties. The primary thrust is one of description of conditions in the island, its history, its culture, and the American impact, within the framework of a denial of self-government.

11.114 Porter, Kirk H., and Donald Bruce Johnson, comps. NATIONAL PARTY PLATFORMS, 1840–1968. Urbana, University of Illinois Press, 1970. 768 p.

A compilation of all the platforms of the major parties of the United States, and of the principal minor parties. It is an indispensable source for what U.S. political parties have or have not said and done in connection with Puerto Rico and the Puerto Ricans.

11.115 Preiswerk, Roy, ed. DOCUMENTS ON INTERNATIONAL RELATIONS IN THE CARIBBEAN. Río Piedras, Institute of Caribbean Studies, University of Puerto Rico, 1970. 853 p.

Contains documentary material on international aspects of the Puerto Rican government.

11.116 Quintero Rivera, Angel G. EL LIDE-RATO LOCAL DE LOS PARTIDOS Y EL ESTUDIO DE LA POLITICA PUER-TORRIQUEÑA. Prólogo de Milton Pabón. Río Piedras, Centro de In-vestigaciones Sociales, Facultad de Ciencias Sociales, Universidad de Puerto Rico, 1970. 163 p. tables, questionnaire, bibl.

A study of the internal operations and organization of the Popular Democratic party in San Juan, aimed at determining the validity of several hypotheses regarding relations within the party organization, the roles at various hierarchical levels, and the views of participants in party activities.

11.117 Ramos de Santiago, Carmen. EL GO-BIERNO DE PUERTO RICO. 2. ed. rev. San Juan, Editorial Universitaria, Universidad de Puerto Rico, 1970. 813 p. illus., tables, maps, bibl.

A comprehensive study of the government of Puerto Rico. The first part examines constitutional developments from the nineteenth century to the 1967 plebiscite. The second part deals with the electoral process and political parties and organizations. There are also sections devoted to the structure and functions of the Estado Libre Asociado and to municipal governments.

11.118 REPORT OF THE COMMISSION OF INQUIRY ON CIVIL RIGHTS IN PUERTO RICO. n.p., 1937. 70 p. plan, photos.

Report of the commission formed to investigate at the request of a non-partisan group of citizens of Ponce the events of March 21, 1937, known as the Ponce Massacre. The commission, headed by Arthur Garfield Hays of the American Civil Liberties Union, concluded that the civil liberties of Puerto Ricans were repeatedly denied by Governor Blanton Winship and that "the Ponce Massacre was due to the denial by the police of the civil rights of citizens to parade and assemble," a denial that "was ordered by the Governor of Puerto Rico."

11.119 Rexach Benítez, Roberto, and Celeste Benítez. PUERTO RICO, 1964: UN PUEBLO EN LA ENCRUCIJADA. San Juan, Ediciones Ateneo Puertorri-queño, 1964. 45 p. bibl. refs.

The authors, both members of the Popular Democratic party and supporters of commonwealth status, provide an interpretation of the economic, social, and political changes that the island has undergone since 1935.

11.120 Reynal, Vicente, and Roberto Lugo. MANUAL DEL GOBIERNO CIVIL DE PUERTO RICO (1493–1972). Río Piedras, P.R., Editorial Edil, 1972. 153 p. maps, tables, diagrs., bibl.

A manual of civil government in Puerto Rico. The book is divided into four parts: a survey of the constitutional evolution of the island; a review of the political process, with basic information on the principal political parties; the structure and operations of the Commonwealth government; and a brief explanation of municipal government.

11.121 Rigual, Néstor. EL PODER LEGISLA-TIVO DE PUERTO RICO. Río Piedras, Ediciones de la Universidad de Puerto Rico, 1961. 220 p. bibl.

A thorough description and analysis of the Puerto Rican legislative branch. The author discusses the basis of legislative power, election of members, the caucus, the legal historical framework, responsibilities of the legislators, parliamentary rules, and other aspects of the legislative process.

11.122 Rigual, Néstor. RESEÑA DE LOS MENSAJES DE LOS GOBERNADORES DE PUERTO RICO, 1900–1930. Río

Piedras, Editorial Universitaria, 1967. 256 p. ports.

Spanish abstracts of the annual "state of the island" reports delivered to the Puerto Rico legislature between 1900 and 1930 by the nine Washington-appointed governors.

11.123 Rivera Correa, Ricardo Romualdo. THE SHADOW OF DON PEDRO. New York, Vantage Press, 1970. 61 p. bibl. refs.

The author pays homage to the late Nationalist leader and reproduces excerpts from documents relating to his defense of Luis F. Velázquez. It was in the brief filed with the Supreme Court of the United States in connection with this defense that Albizu challenged the validity of the Treaty of Paris, a point he hoped would bring about Puerto Rican independence. The Supreme Court denied the petition for a writ of certiorari without considering the case on its merits, thus giving Albizu a victory in the criminal case and with it the liberty of Velázquez, but ensuring the loss of his political goal of independence for Puerto Rico.

11.124 Rodríguez Bou, Ismael. LAS NUEVAS GENERACIONES DE PUERTO RICO: ESBOZO DE UN TEMA. Prólogo por Enrique Laguerre. Barcelona, M. Pareja, 1965. 146 p. bibl.

An educator looks at the role of the younger generations in the life of the country. He pays particular attention to the clash of generations within the Popular Democratic party during the early 1960s.

11.125 Rodríguez Graciani, David. REBELION O PROTESTA: LA LUCHA ESTUDIANTIL EN PUERTO RICO. Río Piedras, P.R., Ediciones Puerto, 1972. 150 p. illus.

Describes, from a radical viewpoint, the growing movement of student unrest at the University of Puerto Rico, covering from 1964 to 1971, the year in which the Council on Higher Education dismissed Jaime Benítez as president of the university.

11.126 Roosevelt, Theodore. COLONIAL POLICIES OF THE UNITED STATES. With an introduction by Walter Lipp-man. New York, Arno Press, 1970, c1937. 204 p. bibl.

Colonel Roosevelt was Governor of Puerto Rico from 1929 to 1932. In this book, he candidly traces the development of U.S. colonialism and the course of events in Puerto Rico and the Philippine Islands. Roosevelt advocated the idea of Puerto Rico as a meeting place of the Spanish and Anglo cultures in the Western Hemisphere. He concludes that the 1898 imperialistic dream is unrealizable.

11.127 Root, Elihu. THE MILITARY AND CO-LONIAL POLICY OF THE UNITED STATES. New York, AMS Press, 1970. 502 p. Reprint of 1916 edition.

This volume of addresses and reports forms part of the collected papers of Root's career as secretary of war, secretary of state, and senator. The section on Puerto Rico (p. 161–184) and other sections help trace the origin of and the reason for the policy of the United States in Puerto Rico, Cuba, and the Philippines at the turn of the century.

11.128 Rowe, Leo S. THE UNITED STATES AND PORTO RICO; WITH SPECIAL REFERENCE TO THE PROBLEMS ARISING OUT OF OUR CONTACT WITH THE SPANISH-AMERICAN CIVILIZATION. New York, Longmans, Green, 1904. 271 p.

An analysis of the social, political, and legal problems stemming from U.S. contact with the Spanish-American civilization in Puerto Rico that arose from "the mere fact that extension of American sovereignty cannot, in and of itself, develop the qualities requisite for the successful working of free institutions, and any attempt to build on such a principle is certain to bring disaster." Rowe was a member of the commission to revise and compile the laws of Puerto Rico from 1900 to 1901 and chairman of the Porto Rican Code Commission from 1901 to 1902.

11.129 Sánchez Tarniella, Andrés. NUEVO ENFOQUE SOBRE EL DESARROLLO POLITICO DE PUERTO RICO CON UN APENDICE SOBRE LA IDEA DEL VOTO PRESIDENCIAL. Río Piedras, P.R., Editorial Edil, 1970. 161 p. bibl.

A study of Puerto Rico's political development during the last one hundred years, with emphasis on the development during the latter part of the nineteenth century of "an interesting tradition of liberalism, a fact that should perhaps be set apart as the most valued achievement of our history."

11.130   Sánchez Tarniella, Andrés. SIGNIFICADOS. Madrid, Afrodisio Aguado, 1972. 215 p.

A compilation of six essays by the author dealing with the political process, the Grito de Lares, the election process, democracy, and the nature and theoretical conception of the economic problem.

11.131   Sánchez Vilella, Roberto. DISCURSOS DE CAMPAÑA 1964. San Juan, Comité de Amigos de Roberto Sánchez Vilella, 1964. 80 p.

A collection of speeches delivered during the 1964 campaign by Roberto Sánchez Vilella of the Popular Democratic party, who was elected governor.

11.132   Seda Bonilla, Edwin. LOS DERECHOS CIVILES EN LA CULTURA PUERTORRIQUEÑA. Río Piedras, Editorial Universitaria, Universidad de Puerto Rico, 1963. 145 p. tables, questionnaires.

A research study based on interviews with 918 persons aimed at diagnosing the degree to which Puerto Ricans are knowledgeable about their civil rights and the extent to which they have favorable or negative concepts that have a bearing on the development of a genuinely democratic community.

11.133   Serrano Geyls, Raúl, and Roberto Rexach Benítez. UN SISTEMA DE ELECCIONES PRIMARIAS PARA PUERTO RICO. San Juan, Ediciones de la Universidad de Puerto Rico, 1955. 135 p. bibl.

With the purpose of making the election process in Puerto Rico more honestly democratic, the authors suggest a primary election system. To strengthen their case they evaluate the system of primaries in the United States and analyze the political circumstances that determined its adoption.

11.134   Silén, Juan A. WE, THE PUERTO RICAN PEOPLE: A STORY OF OPPRESSION AND RESISTANCE. Translated by Cedric Belfrage. New York, Monthly Review Press, 1971. 134 p. bibl. notes. (Also published in Spanish: HACIA UNA VISION POSITIVA DEL PUERTORRIQUEÑO, Río Piedras, P.R., Editorial Edil, 1970. 219 p. bibl. refs.)

This book is designed to explain the Puerto Rican people's fight for independence. The author describes the various separatist insurrections that took place in 1835 and 1868, the Nationalist revolt of 1950, the growth of pro-independence sentiment in more recent years, and the general economic, educational, and social panorama.

11.135   Smith, Carlos J. ESTRUCTURAS POLITICAS DE PUERTO RICO. Madrid, Afrodisio Aguado, 1971. 146p. (His Cuadernos de Ciencias Sociales, 1).
n.a.

11.136   Soltero Peralta, Juan Enrique. EL CAMINO DE LA LIBERTAD. Río Piedras, P.R., Editorial Libertad, 1946. 454 p. bibl.

Presents in a question and answer format the arguments in favor of independence from an economic point of view. The second part of the book deals with testimonies, the Tydings Bill, and other documents.

11.137   Soto, Juan Bautista. PUERTO RICO ANTE EL DERECHO DE GENTES. Prólogo por Antonio R. Barceló. [San Juan], Tip. La Democracia, 1928. 122 p.

A discussion of the political status of the island. The author supports an independent status with a republican constitution, and maintains that the United States should want for Puerto Rico the same rights it claimed from Great Britain and for which it fought for its independence.

11.138   SPEECHES DELIVERED ON THE OCCASION OF DEPOSITING THE SIGNED ORIGINAL OF THE CONSTITUTION OF THE COMMONWEALTH

OF PUERTO RICO. San Juan, Office of the Secretary of the House of Representatives, 1956. 48 p. ports.

Statements by A. Fernós Isern, E. Ramos Antonini, V. Gutiérrez Franqui, and L. Muñoz Marín on July 25, 1956. Appended are statements on Puerto Rico's political status by José Figueres, President of Costa Rica, and by members of the U.S. Congress.

11.139 Templin, Ralph T. SYMPOSIUM: IS PUERTO RICO FULLY SELF-GOVERNING? [Cedarville, Ohio, 1953?]. (Human Frontiers. People, Platforms and Projects). Reprinted from The Journal of Human Relations, v. 11, no. 1, Autumn 1953, p. 88-111.

Presents summaries of the government's position paper advocating that the United States cease to transmit information to the United Nations about Puerto Rico on the grounds that the island had achieved complete self-government, and also the statements of opponents to such a move on the basis that the island was still a colony.

11.140 Toro y Cuebas, Emilio del. PATRIA. San Juan, Biblioteca de Autores Puertorriqueños, 1950–1959. 3 v. (467, 166 p.)

A collection of del Toro's articles, speeches, reports, and essays written between 1894 and 1943 in which he expresses his desire for statehood for the island, comments on numerous other political issues, and discusses his career as a lawyer and judge. In 1909 he became an associate judge of the Supreme Court of Puerto Rico, over which he presided from 1922 until his retirement in 1943.

11.141 Tugwell, Rexford Guy. THE ART OF POLITICS AS PRACTICED BY THREE GREAT AMERICANS: FRANKLIN DELANO ROOSEVELT, LUIS MUÑOZ MARIN AND FIORELLO H. LA GUARDIA. Garden City, N.Y., Doubleday, 1958.

Tugwell, a New Dealer who was governor of Puerto Rico, describes the activities and styles of Roosevelt, Muñoz and La Guardia—all of whom he knew personally—in the political field. His alliance with Muñoz "began abruptly in 1941 and ended as abruptly in 1946." The book ends with an imaginary conversation among all three principal subjects.

11.142 Tugwell, Rexford Guy. CHANGING THE COLONIAL CLIMATE. Selection and explanatory comments by John Lear. New York, Arno Press and the New York Times, 1970. 265 p. (American Imperialism) Reprint of the 1942 edition. bibl. refs.

A collection of messages from Tugwell to the Puerto Rican people during his tenure as governor.

11.143 Tugwell, Rexford Guy. PUERTO RICAN PUBLIC PAPERS OF R.G. TUGWELL, GOVERNOR. San Juan, Service Office of the Government of Puerto Rico, Printing Division, 1945. 378 p.

Collection of the public papers of Rexford G. Tugwell. Included are his "Report on the Five-Hundred-Acre Law" and the Statement to the Chavez Sub-Committee of the Senate Committee of Territories and Insular Affairs.

11.144 Tugwell, Rexford Guy. THE STRICKEN LAND: THE STORY OF PUERTO RICO. New York, Greenwood Press, 1968, c1946. 704 p. bibl. refs.

The last American governor of Puerto Rico, 1941–1946, reports on his tenure. In a now classic book on this period of Puerto Rican political history he offers insights into colonial administration, the emerging Puerto Rican leaders, President Roosevelt's New Deal programs on the island, and the programs of the Popular Democratic party.

11.145 United States–Puerto Rico Commission on the Status of Puerto Rico. STATUS OF PUERTO RICO: HEARINGS. Washington, Govt. Print. Off., 1966. 3 v. (563, 560, 770 p.) (89th Cong., 2d sess. Senate. Doc. no. 108).

Contents: v. 1, Legal-Constitutional Factors in Relation to the Status of Puerto Rico. v. 2, Social-Cultural Factors in Relation to the Status of Puerto Rico. v. 3, Economic Factors in Relation to the Status of Puerto Rico.

In-depth hearings held between May and December 1965. There are testimonies by government officials, politicians, educators, writers, lawyers, and individual citizens. An indispensable source for the study of the political situation of the island.

11.146 United States–Puerto Rico Commission on the Status of Puerto Rico. STATUS OF PUERTO RICO: REPORT. Washington, 1966. 273 p. bibl.

A report to the president of the United States on the conclusions and recommendations of the United States–Puerto Rico Commission on the Status of Puerto Rico, after several months of hearings. It includes a summary of the legal-constitutional factors, economic factors, and sociocultural factors in relation to the status of Puerto Rico, the history and organization of the commission, and an excellent bibliography on the three major areas covered by its work.

11.147 United States–Puerto Rico Commission on the Status of Puerto Rico. STATUS OF PUERTO RICO: SELECTED BACKGROUND STUDIES PREPARED FOR THE UNITED STATES–PUERTO RICO COMMISSION ON THE STATUS OF PUERTO RICO. Washington, 1966. 973 p. bibls.

Contents: "The Puerto Rican Political Movement in the 19th Century," by L. Cruz Monclova; "Historical Survey of the Puerto Rico Status Question, 1898–1965," by R.J. Hunter; "Significant Factors in the Development of Education in Puerto Rico," by I. Rodríguez Bou; "Unionism and Politics in Puerto Rico," by W. Knowles; "Puerto Rico: An Essay in the Definition of a National Culture," by S.W. Mintz; "The United States and the Dilemmas of Political Control," by W.T. Perkins; "Selected Trends and Issues in Contemporary Federal and Regional Relations," by C.J. Friedrich; "The Netherlands, French, and British Areas of the Caribbean," by Institute of Caribbean Studies, University of Puerto Rico; "Toward a Balance Sheet of Puerto Rican Migration," by C. Senior and D.O. Watkins; "Inventory of Government Departments," by Department of Public Administration, University of Puerto Rico.

These studies, and their accompanying bibliographies, are an excellent source on the island's history,

culture, politics, and the economic and social situation.

11.148 Urrutia Aparicio, Carlos. PUERTO RICO, AMERICA, Y LAS NACIONES UNIDAS. México, D.F., 1954. 56 p. bibl. refs. Reprint from *Cuadernos Americanos*, no. 1, en./feb. 1954.

A Guatemalan discusses Latin America's perplexity at Puerto Rico's rejection of independence and criticizes the political formula adopted by the island in 1952. He analyzes the "Puerto Rican case" before the United Nations and concludes that the island lacks full self-government.

11.149 Vélez Aquino, Luis Antonio. Puerto Rican Press Reaction to the Shift from Spanish to United States Sovereignty, 1898–1917. Ed.D. dissertation, Columbia University, 1968. *In* DISSERTATION ABSTRACTS, v.29, no.7, p. 2103-A.

A study that begins with a description of the climate molded by the press in 1900 concerning the political situation of the island and ends with a summary of conditions in 1917. It evaluates the role played by the press in the intervening years in helping define Puerto Rican–American relations.

11.150 Vientós Gastón, Nilita. COMENTARIOS A UN ENSAYO SOBRE PUERTO RICO: "PUERTO RICO, 1964: UN PUEBLO EN LA ENCRUCIJADA" DE ROBERTO F. REXACH BENITEZ Y CELESTE BENITEZ. San Juan, Ediciones del Ateneo Puertorriqueño, 1964. 45 p.

A series of newspapers columns published between July 11 and September 5, 1964, in which the author criticizes what she considers the superficiality of "Puerto Rico, 1964: Un Pueblo en la Encrucijada," by R. Rexach Benítez and C. Benítez. According to her, their article shows a lack of historical awareness by stating that the true history of Puerto Rico starts with the generation of 1940. She believes also that the article suffers from an excessive reliance on economic indicators and material values.

11.151 Wells, Henry. GOVERNMENT FINANCING OF POLITICAL PARTIES IN PUERTO RICO. Foreword by William H. Vanderbilt. Princeton, N.J., Citizen's Research Foundation, 1961. 43 p. tables, bibl. refs. (Citizens' Research Foundation Study No. 4).

A study of the advantages and flaws of Puerto Rico's Election Fund Act, the text of which is appended, with some recommendations on how to improve it and a suggestion that U.S. political parties "could doubtless benefit from a judicious borrowing of Puerto Rican techniques in the field of party finance."

11.152 Wells, Henry. THE MODERNIZATION OF PUERTO RICO: A POLITICAL STUDY OF CHANGING VALUES AND INSTITUTIONS. Cambridge, Mass., Harvard University Press, 1969. 440 p. tables, map, bibl. refs. (Also published in Spanish, with an epilogue updating the subject: *La Modernización de Puerto Rico*, Río Piedras, P.R., Editorial Universitaria, 1971.)

This book is an analysis of the process of modernization with emphasis on the political sector, which originated the process of change. He examines Puerto Rico's value system and institutions, the effects of the change of sovereignty, culture conflicts, and "the Muñoz Era" (1941–1964).

11.153 White, Trumbull. PUERTO RICO AND ITS PEOPLE. New York, Frederick A. Stokes, 1938. 383 p. plates, maps.

A war correspondent who had been in Puerto Rico in 1898 returns and takes a probing look at the social, economic, and political situation of the island after forty years of U.S. rule.

11.154 Williams, Byron. PUERTO RICO: COMMONWEALTH, STATE OR NATION? New York, Parents Magazine, 1972. 249 p. bibl.

n.a.

12
HISTORY

12.1 Abad, José Ramón. PUERTO RICO EN LA FERIA EXPOSICION DE PONCE EN 1882. San Juan, Editorial Coquí, 1967. 351 p. port. Facsimile of 1885 edition.

A Dominican who adopted Puerto Rico as his home describes the great Ponce Fair of 1882 and its impact on the development of the island's agriculture, industry, and commerce. A brief biographical sketch of Abad, originally published in the *Puerto Rico Herald* in 1902, is included.

12.2 Abbad y Lasierra, Fray Iñigo. HISTORIA GEOGRAFICA, CIVIL Y NATURAL DE LA ISLA DE SAN JUAN BAUTISTA DE PUERTO RICO. Reconocimiento por Sebastián González García; notas por Luis M. Díaz Soler; estudio preliminar por Isabel Gutiérrez del Arroyo. San Juan, Ediciones de la Universidad de Puerto Rico, 1959. 320 p. illus., maps, bibl.

New edition of the first great classic in Puerto Rican historiography, originally published in Madrid in 1788. Al-

though the first half of the book presents a documented, almost chronological account of the island since its early colonization in 1508, the work's chief contribution is its description of Puerto Rico's socioeconomic development during the second half of the eighteenth century. It is an important source for the study of this period.

12.3 Alegría, Ricardo E. EL FUERTE DE SAN JERONIMO DE BOQUERON, MUSEO DE HISTORIA MILITAR DE PUERTO RICO. San Juan, Instituto de Cultura Puertorriqueña, 1969. 65 p. illus., ports., bibl.

A description of the San Jerónimo Fort, which now houses the museum of military history of Puerto Rico, with a brief historical account of various English and Dutch attacks from the sixteenth to the eighteenth century and the U.S. invasion in 1898.

12.4 Alzina, Ismael d'. GRAPHIC HISTORY OF PUERTO RICO: FIRST ERA. Translated by Justo Pastor Lozada. San Juan, Ediciones Limitadas Cemí, 1957. plates, ports. In portfolio.

As expressed by the title, this is a history told in pictures—eighty-one of them—covering the period up to the early nineteenth century. A description is given of each event that inspired a drawing.

12.5 Arana Soto, Salvador. CUBA Y PUERTO RICO NO SON; O LA ENFERMEDAD DE CUBA. San Juan, Luis D. Paret, 1963. 343 p. bibl.

The author criticizes those persons who today honor the Puerto Ricans of the late nineteenth century who wanted to tie their island's destiny to Cuba's. He points out the differences between the two islands and insists that Puerto Rico should not look to Cuba and its heroes for solutions to its own problems.

12.6 Arana Soto, Salvador. DEFENSA DE LOS CAPITANES GENERALES ESPAÑOLES, CON UNA NUEVA INTERPRETACION DEL S. XIX PUERTORRIQUEÑO. San Juan, 1968. 175 p. bibl.

The author brings together four diverse essays, the first of which deals with the defense of Puerto Rico by the Spanish captains-general against attempts by foreign powers to take it over. The second reinterprets Puerto Rican politics during the nineteenth century, and the third discusses the men he considers as the real visionaries of these political struggles. In the last essay he discusses the circumstances and results of the 1967 plebiscite on the political status of the island.

12.7 Arana Soto, Salvador. HISTORIA DE NUESTRAS CALAMIDADES. San Juan, 1968. 215 p. bibl.

A history of the hurricanes, earthquakes, epidemics, and armed invasions "which have warped our history for four centuries."

12.8 Arana Soto, Salvador. LOS MEDICOS EN EL DESCUBRIMIENTO DEL MUNDO NUEVO Y EL HOMENAJE AL DR. CHANCA. San Juan, 1967. 94 p. illus., ports.

The author, chairman of the Committee of History and Culture of the Medical Association of Puerto Rico, pays homage to the medical doctors who were involved in the discovery of the New World, especially to Dr. Diego Alvarez Chanca, who accompanied Christopher Columbus during his discovery of Puerto Rico.

12.9 Asenjo, Federico. LAS FIESTAS DE SAN JUAN. San Juan, Imprenta del Comercio, 1868. Reprint. San Juan, Editorial Coquí, in press.

A historical record of the celebration of the Fiestas Patronales (Patron Saint Feasts) of San Juan. The author describes "what they used to be and what they are today" and offers a detailed, "truthful account" of the celebrations in the year 1868. He includes information on the exhibit by the young artist Francisco Oller and provides a list of the forty-two works shown on that occasion.

12.10 Ballesteros Gaibrois, Manuel. LA IDEA COLONIAL DE PONCE DE LEON: UN ENSAYO DE INTERPRETACION. San Juan, Instituto de Cultura Puertorriqueña, 1960. 292 p. bibl.

An historical interpretation of Ponce de Leon's motivations in his governing of the island, within the context of the colonial era in which he lived.

12.11 Belmonte, Francisco. ANALISIS IDEOLOGICO DE LA PERSONALIDAD NACIONAL DE PUERTO RICO. Santurce, P.R., Imprenta Soltero, 1953. 192 p.

Discusses mainly the origin of the Puerto Rican flag and the flag of the Lares insurrection, as well as the activities of Puerto Rican revolutionary leaders of the latter part of the nineteenth century.

12.12 Berbusse, Edward J. THE UNITED STATES IN PUERTO RICO, 1898–1900. Chapel Hill, University of North Carolina Press, [1966]. 274 p. bibl.

The author seeks to emphasize the tensions and essential changes that occurred in Puerto Rico during the last years of Spain's hegemony and the initial years of U.S. rule. The author describes the conflict of ideas and the growth of political institutions in the island during the nineteenth century, reviews the operations of the U.S. military government from 1898 to 1900, and analyzes the pressures that led the U.S. Congress to draft a bill giving the island a civil government. A chapter is included on the religious and educational conflicts that arose during the first years of U.S. occupation.

12.13 Blanco, Enrique T. LA HUELLA DE ESPAÑA EN SAN JUAN DE PUERTO RICO. San Juan, Editorial Coquí, in press.

A history of the city of San Juan from 1508 to October 18, 1898. It discusses the founding of the capital, the construction of the most important buildings and fortifications, the introduction of improvements, and many other aspects.

12.14 Blanco, Enrique T. LOS TRES ATAQUES BRITANICOS A LA CIUDAD DE SAN JUAN BAUTISTA DE PUERTO RICO. 2. ed. San Juan, Editorial Coquí, 1968. 114 p.

Originally published in 1947, this book describes three British attacks on Puerto Rico—by Sir Francis Drake in 1595, by Lord Clifford, Earl of Cumberland, in 1598, and by Sir Ralph Abercrombie in 1797.

12.15 Blanco, Tomás. PRONTUARIO HISTORICO DE PUERTO RICO. 6. ed. San Juan, Instituto de Cultura Puertorriqueña, 1970. 140 p. bibl.

A useful synthesis of the history of the island around a central theme of the development of a Puerto Rican nationality.

12.16 Blanco Fernández, Antonio. ESPAÑA Y PUERTO RICO, 1820-1930. [San Juan], Tip. Cantero Fernández, 1930. 332 p. illus.

A study of the origin and development of Puerto Rico's commerce with Spain and of the economic activities and institutions of the island.

12.17 Blanco y Sosa, Julián E. VEINTE Y CINCO AÑOS ANTES; APUNTES PARA LA HISTORIA. Puerto Rico, Sucesión de J.J. Acosta, 1898. 250 p.

A collection of articles published by Blanco, a Puerto Rican deputy to the Spanish Cortes during the period 1871 to 1873 that marked intense activity against and the final abolition of slavery in Puerto Rico.

12.18 BOLETIN HISTORICO DE PUERTO RICO. San Juan, Imprenta Cantero Fernández, 1914-1927. Facsimile edition. New York, Kraus Reprint, 1968. 14 v.

Published bimonthly for fourteen years, this valuable collection of bulletins reproduces documents and other writings that are basic sources for the study of Puerto Rican history. The *Boletín* was founded and edited by Cayetano Coll y Toste.

12.19 Bonsal, Stephen. THE AMERICAN MEDITERRANEAN. New York, Moffatt, Yard, 1913. 488 p. illus., map, bibl.

A geographic description and historical account of each of the territories in the Caribbean area, including Puerto Rico. A statistical appendix is included.

12.20 Bothwell, Reece B., and Lidio Cruz Monclova. LOS DOCUMENTOS ... ¿QUE DICEN? San Juan, Universidad de Puerto Rico, 1960. 447 p. Also in English.

A compilation of some of the most important documents related to the history of Puerto Rico in the latter part of the nineteenth century. Each section of documents is preceded by a brief interpretive essay.

12.21 Brau, Salvador. LA COLONIZACION DE PUERTO RICO, DESDE EL DESCUBRIMIENTO DE LA ISLA HASTA LA REVERSION A LA COLONIA ESPAÑOLA DE LOS PRIVILEGIOS DE COLON. 3. ed. Anotada por Isabel Gutiérrez del Arroyo. San Juan, Instituto de Cultura Puertorriqueña, 1966. 639 p. port., bibl.

New edition of a classic in Puerto Rican history first published in 1907. It is a documented study of the first half-century (1493-1550), based on considerable research at the Archivo General de Indias in Seville.

12.22 Brau, Salvador. HISTORIA DE PUERTO RICO. Introducción, por Emilio M. Colón. San Juan, Editorial Coquí, 1966. 312 p. illus., maps. Reprint of 1904 edition.

Although outdated, this is still a useful, documented, well-written history of the island, by a Puerto Rican historian. It covers the period from the time of discovery to the years immediately following the Spanish American War.

12.23   Brau, Salvador. PUERTO RICO Y SU HISTORIA; INVESTIGACIONES CRITICAS. Nueva edición aumentada. Valencia, Imprenta de F. Vives Mora, 1894. 404 p.

A series of studies aimed at correcting some erroneous concepts about the prehistory and early history of Puerto Rico, such as the indigenous name of the island, the place where Columbus landed, and the original site of San Germán.

12.24   Buell, Charles E. INDUSTRIAL LIBERTY: OUR DUTY TO RESCUE THE PEOPLE OF CUBA, PORTO RICO AND THE PHILIPPINE ISLANDS FROM THAT GREATEST OF ALL EVILS—POVERTY. Plainfield, N.J., 1900. 116 p.

The author, who was secretary of the U.S. Special Commission to Puerto Rico, suggests that the U.S. government should send Americans in groups rather than individually to settle and utilize government lands in the possessions acquired from Spain. He expresses the opinion that such a policy would create new sources of employment for the American working man and suggests that the mixing of Americans with natives would tend to Americanize the islands with greater speed.

12.25   Cadilla de Martínez, María. REMEMORANDO EL PASADO HEROICO. San Juan, Imprenta Venezuela, 1946. 667 p. bibl.

A historical survey of Puerto Rico from its discovery to 1945.

12.26   Callcott, Wilfred Hardy. THE CARIBBEAN POLICY OF THE UNITED STATES, 1890–1920. New York, Octagon, 1966. 524 p. bibl. Reprint of 1942 ed. (Albert Shaw Lectures on Diplomatic History, 1942).

The author focuses his attention on what he feels was the central theme of the foreign policy of the United States for the years 1890 to 1920 in the Caribbean region. He argues that there was a very definite program to bring this region under the control of the United States for defense purposes and economic considerations.

12.27   Caro Costas, Aída R., comp. ANTOLOGIA DE LECTURAS DE HISTORIA DE PUERTO RICO (SIGLOS XV–XVIII). San Juan, 1971. 713 p. illus., bibl.

Chronologically arranged source book and anthology of documents, monographs, and chapters from books, dealing with the first four centuries of Puerto Rican history.

12.28   Caro de Delgado, Aída R. EL CABILDO O REGIMEN MUNICIPAL PUERTORRIQUEÑO EN EL SIGLO XVIII. San Juan, Municipio de San Juan, Instituto de Cultura Puertorriqueña, 1965. 229 p. illus., bibl.

A documented study of municipal organization and operation in Puerto Rico during the eighteenth century, as exemplified by the two municipal corporations then existing, the Cabildo of San Juan and the Cabildo of San Germán. The work is based on the author's doctoral dissertation at the Universidad Central de Madrid, 1954.

12.29   Caro de Delgado, Aída R. RAMON POWER Y GIRALT. San Juan, 1969. 229 p. bibl. refs.

Compilation of documents previously scattered in various publications relative to Ramón Power y Giralt's years, from 1810 to 1812, as Puerto Rican deputy to the Spanish Parliament of which he became first vice-president. It includes the minutes of the Cabildo of San Juan, the instructions given by the various municipalities, and letters, addresses, and writings of Ramón Power.

12.30   Caro de Delgado, Aída R. VILLA DE SAN GERMAN: SUS DERECHOS Y PRIVILEGIOS DURANTE LOS SIGLOS XVI, XVII y XVIII. San Juan, Instituto de Cultura Puertorriqueña, 1962. 235 p. facsim., bibl. refs.

A brief essay on the defense by the city of San German of its rights and privileges. It is followed by an extensive collection of Royal Decrees and other documents found in Spanish archives regarding specific actions taken by the residents of San Germán.

12.31 Castellanos, Juan de. ELEGIA A LA MUERTE DE JUAN PONCE DE LEON DONDE SE CUENTA LA CONQUISTA DE BORINQUEN. Estudio preliminar de María Teresa Babín, selección traducida al inglés por Muna Lee. San Juan, Instituto de Cultura Puertorriqueña, 1967. 113 p.

Reproduces Elegy VI of Castellano's *Elegías de Varones Ilustres de Indias*, whose first part was published in Madrid in 1589 and which narrates the Spanish conquest of Puerto Rico under Ponce de León. An English translation is included of those sections that describe the island's geography and Indians as well as Ponce de León's courage and exploits.

12.32 Celis Aguilera, José de. MI GRANO DE ARENA PARA LA HISTORIA POLITICA DE PUERTO RICO. San Juan, Impr. de Acosta, 1886. 113 p.

The political activity of 1869 to elect Puerto Rican deputies to the Spanish Cortes and the controversy within the Liberal party the following year regarding the ideologies of its leaders are narrated by a participant. Documents issued by the party during that period and a series of articles that appeared in the press are included.

12.33 Chadwick, French Ensor. THE RELATIONS OF THE UNITED STATES AND SPAIN: THE SPANISH-AMERICAN WAR. New York, Russell & Russell, 1968. 2 v. (412, 514 p.) maps, bibl. Reprint of the 1911 edition.

Documentary history of the Spanish-American War. The Puerto Rico expedition is described in volume 2.

12.34 Cifre de Loubriel, Estela. CATALOGO DE EXTRANJEROS RESIDENTES EN PUERTO RICO EN EL SIGLO XIX. Río Piedras, Ediciones de la Universidad de Puerto Rico, 1962. 252 p. maps.

A compilation of the names of 4,800 foreigners who resided in Puerto Rico during the nineteenth century, with a brief notation on each.

12.35 Cifre de Loubriel, Estela. LA INMIGRACION A PUERTO RICO DURANTE EL SIGLO XIX. San Juan, Instituto de Cultura Puertorriqueña, 1964. 441 p. bibl.

A study of Spanish immigration into Puerto Rico during the nineteenth century, with some background on immigration from the fifteenth to the eighteenth century. The reasons for the exodus from Spain as well as the numbers, origins, and professions of the immigrants are provided. The third and longest part of the book is an alphabetical listing of the immigrants.

12.36 Coll y Cuchí, Víctor. DESCUBRIMIENTO DE PUERTO RICO. Caguas, P.R., Tip. R. Morel Campos, 1934. 118 p. plates.

The author believes that Columbus disembarked in Aguada on the northern part of Puerto Rico's west coast, thus refuting Montalvo Guenard's theory.

12.37 Coll y Cuchí, Cayetano. HISTORIA DEL GRAN PARTIDO POLITICO PUERTORRIQUEÑO UNION DE PUERTO RICO. San Juan, Tip. La Democracia, 1930. 298 p.

A leader of the Unionist party reviews the political history of the island since the takeover by the United States, with emphasis on developments within his own party. He documents the controversy between the Republican and Federal parties, as well as Muñoz Rivera's abandonment of the Federal party to found the Unionist party.

12.38 Coll y Toste, Cayetano. HISTORIA DE LA ESCLAVITUD EN PUERTO RICO. 2. ed. Compilación y prefacio de Isabel Cuchí Coll. San Juan, Publicación de la Sociedad de Autores Puertorriqueños, 1972. 267 p.

A collection of documents on the history of slavery in Puerto Rico until its abolition in 1873.

12.39 Coll y Toste, Cayetano. RESEÑA DEL ESTADO SOCIAL, ECONOMICO E INDUSTRIAL DE LA ISLA DE PUERTO RICO AL TOMAR POSESION DE ELLA LOS ESTADOS UNIDOS. San Juan, Imprenta La Correspondencia, 1899. 485 p. tables.

This report, submitted by the secretary of the treasury on November 20, 1898, describes the economic conditions of the island upon its takeover by the United States. It gives details on the municipalities, including their population, industry, agricultural assets, commerce, and fiscal situation.

12.40 Colón, E.D. DATOS SOBRE LA HISTORIA DE LA AGRICULTURA DE PUERTO RICO ANTES DE 1898. San Juan, Cantero Fernández, 1930. 302 p.

The first two parts deal with the history of agriculture on the island from its beginning through the nineteenth century. The third deals with individual products.

12.41 Córdoba, Pedro Tomás. MEMORIAS GEOGRAFICAS, HISTORICAS, ECONOMICAS Y ESTADISTICAS DE LA ISLA DE PUERTO RICO. 2. ed. facsimilar. San Juan, Instituto de Cultura Puertorriqueña, 1968. 6 v. (264, 456, 498, 463, 422, 482 p.) Reprint of 1831–1833 edition.

These volumes are a compilation of information concerning geographic, historical, economic, and statistical aspects of Puerto Rico. The first volume reproduces the history of Puerto Rico as recorded by Fr. Iñigo Abbad. The second offers an exhaustive description of each town on the island. In the third volume the author comments on Abbad's history, offers a historical chronology, and lists the terms of the captains-general of the island from 1731 to 1822. The remaining three volumes concentrate exclusively on the period from 1822 to 1832, during which the author served in the Spanish colonial administration on the island.

12.42 Corretjer, Juan Antonio. LA HISTORIA QUE GRITO EN LARES. Guaynabo, P.R., Cooperativa de Artes Gráficas Romualdo Real, 1970. 103 p.

The secretary general of the Liga Socialista Puertorriqueña writes about the Lares insurrection and about several pro-independence and nationalist leaders—Antonio Valero, Pedro Albizu Campos, and others.

12.43 Cruz Monclova, Lidio. EL GRITO DE LARES. San Juan, Instituto de Cultura Puertorriqueña, 1968. 40 p. illus., plates. (Serie Libros del Pueblo).

This excerpt from Cruz Monclova's book *Historia de Puerto Rico del Siglo XIX* deals with the 1868 insurrection which proclaimed the first republic of Puerto Rico.

12.44 Cruz Monclova, Lidio. HISTORIA DE PUERTO RICO, SIGLO XIX. 6. ed. Río Piedras, Editorial Universitaria, Universidad de Puerto Rico, 1970. 3 v. in 6 (740, 410, 646, 484, 454, 538 p.) illus., ports., bibl. refs.

A documented political, social, and economic history of Puerto Rico against the background of events in Spain from 1808 to 1898.

12.45 Cruz Monclova, Lidio. HISTORIA DEL AÑO 1887. 3. ed. Río Piedras, Editorial Universitaria, Universidad de Puerto Rico, 1970. 385 p. bibl.

A documented historical account which traces the development of the Autonomist party in Puerto Rico during the second half of the nineteenth century, with emphasis on the repressive measures imposed by Governor General Romualdo Palacio against those who advocated separation from Spain. Much of the information is drawn from newspapers of that period.

12.46 Dávila, Arturo V. LAS ENCICLICAS SOBRE LA REVOLUCION HISPANOAMERICANA Y SU DIVULGACION EN PUERTO RICO. San Juan, Instituto de Cultura Puertorriqueña, 1965. 92 p. illus., facsims., bibl.

A brief documented essay on the dissemination in Puerto Rico of two Papal Encyclicals issued in 1816 and 1824 condemning seditions against the Spanish Crown. A collection of documents, including the texts of the letters, is appended.

12.47 Davis, Richard Harding. THE CUBAN AND PORTO RICAN CAMPAIGNS. New York, Books for Libraries, 1970. 360 p. illus., photos., maps. Reprint of 1898 edition.

A war correspondent offers his observations on the military campaigns of the U.S. forces in the war against

Spain. Chapter 8 covers the Puerto Rican campaign.

12.48 DIARIO ECONOMICO DE PUERTO RICO, 1814–1815. Ordenación y estudio por Luis E. González Vales. San Juan, Editorial Coquí [y] Asociación de Bancos de Puerto Rico, 1972. 2 v. various pagings. port.

Facsimile edition of the second newspaper published in Puerto Rico, 1814–1815, under the direction of Alejandro Ramírez, first *intendente* or treasurer of the island, who is considered the father of public finance in Puerto Rico. It is an indispensable source for the study of the island's economic history and also throws light on the early history of periodical literature in Puerto Rico. Published under the sponsorship of the Bankers Association of Puerto Rico, the volumes are preceded by an article on Ramírez and two useful indexes by title and subject.

12.49 Díaz Soler, Luis M. HISTORIA DE LA ESCLAVITUD NEGRA EN PUERTO RICO (1493–1890). 3. ed. San Juan, Editorial Universitaria, Universidad de Puerto Rico, 1969. 432 p. illus., bibl.

The most extensive study to date of slavery in Puerto Rico. The first part deals with the traffic of slaves until its abolition in 1873; the second studies their life and work; the third relates to their rebellions, and the last describes the abolition process. Nine appendixes reproducing original letters and manuscripts about the black slaves in Puerto Rico are included.

12.50 Enamorado Cuesta, José. PROTO-HISTORIA E HISTORIA DE PUERTO RICO. v. 1. Río Piedras, P.R., Editorial Edil, 1971, c1970. 1 v. (234 p.) bibl.

In this first volume, the author covers the period from the discovery to the first half of the sixteenth century.

12.51 ESCRITOS DESCONOCIDOS DE JOSE MARTI. Recopilación, prólogo y notas de Carlos Ripoll. New York, Eliseo Torres & Sons, 1971. 223 p. (Torres Library of Literary Studies, 1).

A compilation of 125 items published between 1892 and 1895 in the newspaper *Patria* and not included in Martí's collected works. The collection, compiled by a professor at Queens College in New York, includes references to the Puerto Rican section of the Cuban Revolutionary party and to some of the Puerto Ricans who were assisting the Cuban revolutionary effort.

12.52 Esteves Völckers, Guillermo. TARJETERO-HISTORICO. Madrid, 1960–1964. 2 v. (656, 431 p.) illus., maps, facsims., port., bibl.

A study of Columbus' second voyage, during which he discovered Puerto Rico, based on documents found in the Archivo de Indias in Seville.

12.53 Fernández Méndez, Eugenio. CRONICAS DE PUERTO RICO: DESDE LA CONQUISTA HASTA NUESTROS DIAS. 2. ed. Río Piedras, Editorial Universitaria, Universidad de Puerto Rico, 1969. 2 v. in 1 (694 p.) bibl. refs.

A compilation of some of the primary sources for the study of the cultural history of Puerto Rico, starting with the discovery of the island according to the Chronicles of Michoacán of 1493.

12.54 Fernández Méndez, Eugenio. LAS ENCOMIENDAS Y ESCLAVITUD DE LOS INDIOS DE PUERTO RICO, 1508–1550. Sevilla, Escuela de Estudios Hispanoamericanos, Consejo Superior de Investigaciones Científicas, 1966. 67 p. maps, bibl. refs.

A historical account based on primary and secondary sources of the *encomienda indiana*, or labor forced upon the native Indians. It covers the beginnings of Spanish colonization in 1508 to the abolition of the *encomienda* in the Spanish West Indies in 1542, and the measures taken locally to achieve its final suppression.

12.55 Fernández Méndez, Eugenio. PROCESO HISTORICO DE LA CONQUISTA DE PUERTO RICO, 1508–1640. San Juan, Instituto de Cultura Puertorriqueña, 1970. 92 p. illus., bibl. refs.

An analysis of two periods of the island's history: the years 1508–1535 which saw the conquest and colonization of Puerto Rico and the short duration of an economy based on mining; and the period 1535–1640, which saw the first cycle of a sugar-based economy.

12.56 HISTORY OF PUERTO RICO: FROM THE BEGINNING TO 1892. New York, Anaya Book Co., 1972. 474 p. illus., bibl. refs.

Part 1 gives a brief account of the geographical features of the island and its people and presents a history from the discovery and colonization through the nineteenth century. Part 2 deals with the development of a political conscience. The book includes several appendixes: a series of articles on the island's mining resources, the personal memoirs of Alejandro O'Reilly written in 1765, and four documents dealing with political events in the nineteenth century.

12.57 Fisher, Horace Newton. PRINCIPLES OF COLONIAL GOVERNMENT ADAPTED TO THE PRESENT NEEDS OF CUBA AND PORTO RICO, AND OF THE PHILIPPINES. Boston, L.C. Page, 1900. 56 p.

The author, pointing out the political incapacity of Cuba, Puerto Rico, and the Philippines, suggests reversion to a "Pueblo System" as the starting point for the political regeneration of these islands. This, he believes, would progressively develop their capacity for self-government and individual initiative.

12.58 Fonfrías, Ernesto Juan. PUERTO RICO EN LA DEFENSA DEL IMPERIO ESPAÑOL EN AMERICA: ENSAYO BREVE. Prólogo de Julio F. Guillén. San Juan, Editorial Club de la Prensa, 1968. 105 p. illus., plates, bibl.

Describes Puerto Rico's defenses against attacks by British, Dutch and French pirates during the sixteenth, seventeenth, and eighteenth centuries.

12.59 Freidel, Frank Burt. THE SPLENDID LITTLE WAR. Boston, Little, Brown, 1958. 314 p. illus.

A photographic account of the Spanish-American War, with a brief historical essay on the events that led to it.

12.60 Freire, Joaquín. PRESENCIA DE PUERTO RICO EN LA HISTORIA DE CUBA: UNA APORTACION AL ESTUDIO DE LA HISTORIA ANTILLANA. San Juan, Instituto de Cultura Puertorriqueña, 1966. 212 p. maps, plates, bibl.

A testimony by a Cuban writer to the many Puerto Ricans who helped the Cuban fight for independence. He points out also the contributions of Puerto Ricans to the Cuban economy, culture, and politics during the latter part of the nineteenth century and the earlier part of the twentieth.

12.61 Gautier Dapena, José A. TRAYECTORIA DEL PENSAMIENTO LIBERAL PUERTORRIQUEÑO EN EL SIGLO XIX. San Juan, Instituto de Cultura Puertorriqueña, 1963. 152 p.

Traces the development of liberalism during the nineteenth century in Spanish-ruled Puerto Rico. The author discusses its leaders, their ideologies and activities, and how the movement splintered into three political positions: assimilation, autonomy, and independence.

12.62 Géigel Sabat, Fernando J. BALDUINO ENRICO: ESTUDIO SOBRE EL GENERAL BALDUINO ENRICO Y EL ASEDIO DE LA CIUDAD DE SAN JUAN DE PUERTO RICO POR LA FLOTA HOLANDESA EN 1625. Barcelona, Editorial Araluce, 1934. 213 p. illus., maps.

A description of the attack on the city of San Juan by the Dutch under Boudewijn Henricksz, or Balduino Enrico. The sources are a book by Joannes de Laet published in Leyden in 1644 and never before translated into Spanish; the *Historia geográfica, civil y natural de la isla de San Juan Bautista de Puerto Rico*, by Fray Iñigo Abbad, and the contemporary narration of the event by Diego de Larrasa, lieutenant auditor of San Juan.

12.63 Géigel Sabat, Fernando J. CORSARIOS Y PIRATAS DE PUERTO RICO, 1819–1925. San Juan, Cantero Fernández, 1946. 262 p. tables, bibl.

A documented study showing the relations between the Spanish authorities of Cuba and Puerto Rico and the

Americans at the beginning of the nineteenth century when the United States was trying to clear the Caribbean of pirates. At first Spain did not collaborate with the U.S. Navy, although it did later. The author tells how Cofresí, the best known Puerto Rican pirate, was imprisoned and executed by the Spanish authorities in 1825.

12.64 Gómez Acevedo, Labor. ORGANIZACION Y REGLAMENTACION DEL TRABAJO EN EL PUERTO RICO DEL SIGLO XIX (PROPIETARIOS Y JORNALEROS). San Juan, Instituto de Cultura Puertorriqueña, 1970. 502 p. illus., ports., bibl.

In-depth study of labor laws and regulations between 1838 and 1877, with special emphasis on the *libreta* system, a form of compulsory labor.

12.65 Gómez Acevedo, Labor. SANZ, PROMOTOR DE LA CONCIENCIA SEPARATISTA EN PUERTO RICO. Prólogo de Manuel Ballesteros Gaibrois. San Juan, Ediciones de la Universidad de Puerto Rico, 1956. 293 p. port., bibl.

An analysis of the political situation in Puerto Rico between 1837 and 1875 that deals primarily with the two terms of Laureano Sanz as governor, 1868–1870 and 1874–1875. The author sets out to determine whether the unpopular and irresponsible conduct of this governor promoted a separatist conscience in the island.

12.66 González, Antonio J. APUNTES PARA LA HISTORIA DEL MOVIMIENTO SINDICAL DE PUERTO RICO 1869–1941. México, Editorial Cultura, 1957. Reprinted from *Revista de Ciencias Sociales*, v. 1, no. 3, Sept. 1957: 449–468.

A brief, documented article on the history of the labor movement in the island between 1896, when Santiago Iglesias Pantín arrived, until 1941, the last year of the existence of a labor party in Puerto Rico.

12.67 González Ginorio, José. EL DESCUBRIMIENTO DE PUERTO RICO; EXAMEN CRITICO DEL SEGUNDO VIAJE DE DON CRISTOBAL COLON Y DE LAS AUTORIDADES EN RELACION CON LA HISTORIA DEL MISMO (PRESENTACION DE DOS NUEVAS AUTORIDADES). San Juan, Imprenta Venezuela, 1936. 328 p. maps, facsims. Reprint. San Juan, Editorial Coquí, 1971. 328 p. bibl.

Based on writings by some of the persons who accompanied Columbus on his second voyage, during which he discovered Puerto Rico, the author provides a chronology and tries to reconstruct the trip and determine where exactly in Puerto Rico Columbus landed.

12.68 Gutiérrez del Arroyo, Isabel. HISTORIOGRAFIA PUERTORRIQUEÑA. San Juan, Instituto de Cultura Puertorriqueña, 1969, c1957. 26 p. bibl.

A useful, albeit brief, survey of trends in Puerto Rican historical writing from 1582 to 1927.

12.69 Gutiérrez del Arroyo, Isabel. EL REFORMISMO ILUSTRADO EN PUERTO RICO. México, Asomante, El Colegio de México, 1953. 259 p. bibl.

Taking as her starting point the *Memorias Geográficas, Históricas, Económicas y Estadísticas de la Isla*, by Pedro Tomás de Córdova, the author sets out to learn about and analyze the spirit of Puerto Rico in the first four decades of the nineteenth century within the framework of its historical circumstances, its institutions, and political thought. She discusses the influence of the "high-heeled despotism" in Puerto Rico, and the administrative, economic, social, and cultural reformist ideas and movements. A bibliography of Tomás de Córdova's works is appended.

12.70 Guzmán Rodríguez, M., ed. EPISTOLARIO DEL DR. BETANCES. Mayagüez, P.R., Tip. Comercial, 1943. 92 p.

A selection of Ramón Emeterio Betances' correspondence with Eugenio M. de Hostos, educator and politician, and Dr. Julio J. Henna, Chairman of the Puerto Rican Section of the Partido Revolucionario Cubano in New York.

12.71 Hall, Arthur D. PORTO RICO: ITS HISTORY, PRODUCTS, AND POSSI-

BILITIES. New York, Street & Smith, 1898. 171 p.

After a review of conditions in the island, the author expresses his wish that Puerto Rico may some day "become a bright star in the flag that brings protection and freedom to all!"

12.72 Halstead, Murat. OUR NEW POSSESSIONS: NATURAL RICHES, INDUSTRIAL RESOURCES ... OF CUBA, PORTO RICO, HAWAII, THE LADRONES AND THE PHILIPPINE ISLANDS, WITH EPISODES OF THEIR EARLY HISTORY. Chicago, Dominion, 1898. 400 p. illus., plates, port., map.

Descriptions based on personal observations and on interviews with leading figures. In chapter 25 the author analyzes the possibilities he foresees for the U.S. Caribbean possessions of Cuba and Puerto Rico.

12.73 Herrmann, Karl Stephen. A RECENT CAMPAIGN IN PUERTO RICO BY THE INDEPENDENT REGULAR BRIGADE UNDER THE COMMAND OF BRIG. GENERAL SCHWAN. Boston, E.H. Bacon, 1907. 109 p. plates.

Narrates General Schwan's campaign in the southwestern section of the island while commanding the third column of the U.S. Army invading Puerto Rico during the Spanish-American War. Special reference is made to the two engagements the forces had with the Alfonso XIII Regiment of Cazadores. A biographical sketch of Brigadier General Schwan is included.

12.74 A HISTORY OF THE HARBOR DEFENSES OF SAN JUAN, P.R., UNDER SPAIN, 1509–1898. San Juan, U.S. Army, Puerto Rico Coast Artillery Command, 1943, c1944. 168 p. illus., maps.

Documented study of the development of the fortifications of San Juan with emphasis on the English and Dutch attacks repelled between 1595 and 1625.

12.75 Hostos, Adolfo de. HISTORIA DE SAN JUAN, CIUDAD MURADA: ENSAYO ACERCA DEL PROCESO DE LA CIVILIZACION EN LA CIUDAD ESPAÑOLA DE SAN JUAN BAUTISTA DE PUERTO RICO, 1521-1898. San Juan, Instituto de Cultura Puertorriqueña, 1966. 590 p. illus., maps, bibl. refs.

Traces the historical development of the city of San Juan, from its founding in Caparra and transfer to the islet that is now the capital city of Puerto Rico until the American invasion. It examines various aspects of San Juan: its role as a military fortress, its economic development and government, religion, culture and education, institutions, and social mores.

12.76 Hostos, Adolfo de. INVESTIGACIONES HISTORICAS. San Juan, 1938. 188 p. illus., tables, maps, plans.

The first part of the book compiles and analyzes the information obtained from archaeological excavations performed by a team led by the author, official historian of Puerto Rico, with the purpose of locating the ruins of the town of Caparra. It describes their work in the field, analyzes the findings, and interprets their archaeological value. The second part deals with investigations aimed at determining Columbus' actual landing site.

12.77 Hostos, Eugenio María de. OBRAS COMPLETAS. 2. ed. (Facisimilar de la conmemorativa del centenario, 1939) San Juan, Instituto de Cultura Puertorriqueña, 1969. 20 v. port.

V. 1-2 (397, 438 p.), *Diario*. Memoirs, from birth in January 1839 to 1903, and a biographical sketch by Concha Meléndez.

V. 3 (398 p.), *Páginas Intimas*. Narrations, stories, and letters to or about his family.

V. 4 (287 p.), *Cartas*. Letters dated 1868 to 1902.

V. 5 (362 p.), *Madre Isla*. Political writings on Puerto Rico, 1898–1903.

V. 6 (442 p.), *Mi Viaje al Sur*. Essays in which he chronicles his travels in Colombia, Panama, Peru, Chile, Argentina, and Brazil.

V. 7 (451 p.), *Temas Sudamericanos*. Essays dealing with various aspects of South America. Includes "Tres Presidentes y Tres Repúblicas," his study on Chile which won a literary first prize in 1872, "Cartas Americanas," and others.

V. 8 (320 p.), *La Peregrinación de*

Bayoán. Allegorical novel written in 1863 in which Hostos denounces the Spanish rule of the Antilles.

V. 9 (494 p.), *Temas Cubanos.* Essays on Cuba.

V. 10 (442 p.), *La Cuna de América.* Writings on the discovery and the discoverer of America, observations on the Dominican Republic, and newspaper articles written in Santo Domingo.

V. 11 (307 p.), *Crítica en General.* Hostos' criticisms and reviews of art, music, theater, and literature, including his masterful essays on "Hamlet" and "Romeo and Juliet," as well as biographical sketches of writers of the times.

V. 12-13 (486, 386 p.), *Forjando el Porvenir Americano.* His writings on education and educational reform.

V. 14 (440 p.), *Hombres e Ideas.* Writings on various topics, including literary criticism, biographical sketches, and essays on economic policy.

V. 15 (441 p.), *Lecciones de Derecho Constitucional.* Treatise on political science and constitutional law.

V. 16 (464 p.), *Tratado de Moral.* Treatise on ethics.

V. 17 (249 p.), *Tratado de Sociología.* Synthesis of a sociology course that Hostos taught in 1901, as taken down by his students.

V. 18 (414 p.), *Ensayos Didácticos.* Essays which trace the history and development of education from prehistory to the nineteenth century. This volume also includes "Nociones de Derecho Penal" and "Nociones de Derecho Consitucional."

V. 19 (412 p.), *Ensayos Didácticos.* Treatise on Hebrew and Chinese logic, philology, and history.

V. 20 (370 p.), *Ensayos Didácticos.* Physical and cultural geography textbook. It follows the evolutionary, gradual or "concentric" principle of teaching, going from a child's intuitive knowledge to the inductive, deductive and scientific.

12.78   INAUGURATION OF THE FIRST CIVIL GOVERNOR OF PORTO RICO. May 1, 1900. Published by direction of the Commanding General, Department of Porto Rico. [San Juan?], 1900. 35 p. English and Spanish.

Describes the ceremonies of the arrival of Charles H. Allen and his inauguration as the first civil governor of the island.

12.79   INFORMACION SOBRE REFORMAS EN CUBA Y PUERTO RICO. New York, Impr. de Hallet y Breen, 1867. 2 v. in 1 (344, 330 p.)

Provides a record of the work accomplished by the Puerto Rican and Cuban commissioners designated in 1866 to submit proposals to the Spanish Cortes regarding economic and social changes for the two islands.

12.80   Jiménez Malaret, René. EPISTOLARIO HISTORICO DEL DR. FELIX TIO Y MALARET. San Juan, 1953. 189 p. port., facsims.

A collection of letters written to Félix Tió y Malaret by important political leaders at the turn of the century, with commentaries by the compiler.

12.81   Jones, Chester Lloyd. THE CARIBBEAN SINCE 1900. New York, Russell & Russell, 1970. 511 p. map, bibl. Reprint of 1936 edition.

An analysis of the economic and political relations of the United States with each of the countries of the Caribbean region during the first three decades of the twentieth century. Chapter 8 covers Puerto Rico's relations with the United States.

12.82   Labra, Rafael María de. LA ABOLICION DE LA ESCLAVITUD EN LAS ANTILLAS ESPAÑOLAS. Madrid, Impr. J.E. Morete, 1869. 118 p. tables.

Brings together a series of speeches by Labra regarding the proposed abolition of slavery in the Spanish West Indies. The appendix reproduces the drafts of the enactment abolishing slavery, as well as those for political and economic reforms that should accompany it.

12.83   Labra, Rafael María de. LA CUESTION COLONIAL, 1868-1869. Madrid, Tip. de Gregorio Estrada, 1869. 118 p.

Articles published by Labra in the newspaper *Las Cortes* about the colonial question in Cuba, Puerto Rico, and the Philippines.

12.84 Labra, Rafael María de. DISCURSOS POLITICOS, ACADEMICOS Y FORENSES. Madrid, Imp. M. Burgase, 1884–1886. 2 v.

Speeches delivered by Labra while he was a deputy to the Spanish Cortes. In them he comments about events in Cuba and Puerto Rico as well as on other political, economic, and social issues of the times.

12.85 Labra, Rafael María de. LA REFORMA POLITICA DE ULTRAMAR. Madrid, Tip. de A. Alonso, 1901. 1116 p.

A collection of speeches and other writings by Labra, dated 1868 to 1900, which deal mostly with the Spanish colonial administration of Cuba and Puerto Rico.

12.86 LECTURAS BASICAS SOBRE HISTORIA DE PUERTO RICO. San Juan, Editorial del Departamento de Instrucción Pública, 1970. 514 p. bibl.

A collection of essays, selections, and documents that constitutes an important source for the student of Puerto Rico's history. The book summarizes developments from the sixteenth through the eighteenth century; studies the constitutional development and struggle for rights of the eighteenth and nineteenth centuries; describes the social impact of economic development during the nineteenth and twentieth centuries, and surveys Puerto Rican society and culture in general.

12.87 Ledru, André Pierre. VIAGE A LA ISLA DE PUERTO-RICO EN EL AÑO 1797, EJECUTADO POR UNA COMISION DE SABIOS FRANCESES, DE ORDEN DE SU GOBIERNO Y BAJO LA DIRECCION DEL CAPITAN NICOLAS BAUDIN. Traducción de Julio Vizcarrondo. Prólogo de Eugenio Fernández Méndez. 5. ed. San Juan, Editorial Coquí, 1971. 178 p. Reprint of 1863 edition.

An account of the personal experiences of the author, a French naturalist, during his voyage to the Antilles in 1797. In it he describes the geographic position and gives a brief history of the island and its administration. Chapter 9 is of particular interest because it enumerates and describes the fauna and flora.

12.88 Lee, Albert E. AN ISLAND GROWS: MEMOIRS OF ALBERT E. LEE, 1873–1942. San Juan, A.E. Lee & Son, 1963. 169 p. illus.

Memoirs of a prominent Puerto Rican businessman.

12.89 Lodge, Henry Cabot. THE WAR WITH SPAIN. New York, Harper & Bros., 1899. 287 p. plates, ports., maps. Reprint. New York, Arno Press, 1970 (American Imperialism Series).

A history of the war of 1898, with a description of the campaign in Puerto Rico.

12.90 Maldonado-Denis, Manuel. PUERTO RICO: A SOCIO-HISTORIC INTERPRETATION. Translated by Elena Vialo. New York, Random House, 1972. 336 p. bibl. Translation of *Puerto Rico: Una Interpretación Histórico-Social.* México, Siglo Veintiuno, 1969.

The author, a professor at the University of Puerto Rico, discusses the history and present situation of Puerto Rico within the theme of struggle for national identity and independence.

12.91 Martí, José. NUESTRA AMERICA. Habana, Editorial Nacional de Cuba, 1963. 450 p. (*His* Obras Completas, v. 8).

The volume reproduces an article by Martí published in *El Federalista* of Mexico, in which he praises E.M. de Hostos' political philosophy, and two undated letters sent by Martí to R.E. Betances asking him to organize in Paris a "vigorous and active" group of supporters of the Cuban revolution.

12.92 Martí, José. MARTI Y PUERTO RICO. Prólogo, selección, y notas por Carlos Alberto Montaner. Río Piedras, P.R., Editorial San Juan, 1970. 192 p. bibl.

A professor at Inter-American University of Puerto Rico has brought together articles, letters, and statements by Jose Martí in which he touches on Puerto Rico. There are comments on Puerto Ricans such as Baldorioty, Betances, and Hostos, as well as on the Puerto Rican section of the Cuban Revolutionary party in New York.

12.93 Martínez, Julio Tomás. COLECCION MARTINEZ: CRONICAS INTIMAS.

Arecibo, P.R., [1946]. 84 p. illus., port., maps, facsims. Cover title: Colección Martínez: crónicas, notas de la guerra del 1898 en Puerto Rico, notas de arte.

Personal memoirs in which the author describes his home town, Utuado, and the role it played in the war of 1898. The second part of the book presents a graphic account of the military campaign, and provides a chronology of the most important events of the war.

12.94   Miller, Paul G. HISTORIA DE PUERTO RICO. Chicago, Rand McNally, 1939. 603 p. illus., bibl.

This book, written by a U.S.-appointed commissioner of education, was one of the first history texts used in the public schools of the island. It surveys chronologically events related to Puerto Rico's history.

12.95   Millis, Walter. THE MARTIAL SPIRIT: A STUDY OF OUR WAR WITH SPAIN. Boston, Houghton Mifflin, 1931. 427 p. plates, ports., maps, bibl.

A history of the Spanish-American War, starting with a discussion of the thinking on the part of President McKinley and other leaders in the United States just prior to the war. It covers the background, military campaigns, and settlement.

12.96   Mixer, Knowlton. PORTO RICO; HISTORY AND CONDITIONS: SOCIAL, ECONOMIC AND POLITICAL. New York, MacMillan, 1926. 329 p. illus., map, bibl.

Describes the geography, climate, and history of Puerto Rico from the pre-Columbian period until 1925. The author places emphasis on the economic and social conditions of the early part of the twentieth century, and includes a chapter on the *jíbaro*. A summary of the Organic Law and labor legislation then in effect is included in an appendix.

12.97   Miyares González, Fernando. NOTICIAS PARTICULARES DE LA ISLA Y PLAZA DE SAN JUAN BAUTISTA DE PUERTO RICO. 2. ed. Introducción por Eugenio Fernández Méndez. San Juan, Universidad de Puerto Rico,

1957. 146 p. bibl. refs. (Estudios Puertorriqueños).

The author, one of the two eighteenth century chroniclers of the island's history, served as secretary of the government during 1769–1779. In his *Noticias*, written in 1775, he describes the period from the colonization to 1775, based mostly on the now lost manuscripts of Fray Pablo Calderón de la Barca and on the official archives of San Juan.

12.98   Montalvo Guenard, Andrés. COMENTARIOS A HECHOS NEFANDOS EN LA HISTORIA DE PUERTO RICO. San Juan, 1946. 62 p. English and Spanish texts.

Relates the "abominable pages" in the history of the island.

12.99   Montalvo Guenard, J.L. RECTIFICACIONES HISTORICAS: EL DESCUBRIMIENTO DE BORINQUEN. Ponce, Editorial del Llano, 1933. 438 p. illus., bibl.

The author believes that Cabo Rojo, on the southern part of Puerto Rico's west coast, was the place where Columbus disembarked when he discovered the island in 1493.

12.100   Morales Carrión, Arturo. ALBORES HISTORICOS DEL CAPITALISMO EN PUERTO RICO. [Río Piedras], Editorial Universitaria, Universidad de Puerto Rico, 1972. 142 p. bibl. refs. (Colección UPREX. Ser. Humanidades).

The first part probes the sixteenth-century origins of capitalism in Puerto Rico. The second deals with the early relations of the island with the United States, from 1700 to 1815, based on Spanish, English, and U.S. sources.

12.101   Morales Carrión, Arturo. HISTORIA DEL PUEBLO DE PUERTO RICO (DESDE SUS ORIGENES HASTA EL SIGLO XVIII). San Juan, Editorial del Departamento de Instrucción Pública, 1968. 394 p. illus., maps, ports.

An analysis of the most important events of the first three centuries of the history of Puerto Rico, within a West Indian setting, written as a text book for the high schools of the island.

12.102 Morales Carrión, Arturo. PUERTO RICO AND THE NON-HISPANIC CARIBBEAN: A STUDY IN THE DECLINE OF SPANISH EXCLUSIVISM. 2. ed. Río Piedras, University of Puerto Rico, 1971. 160 p. bibl.

A documented study presented as the author's doctoral dissertation at Columbia University in which he traces the impact that the interisland contacts and communications in the Antillean area had on the history of Puerto Rico, prior to the final breakdown of Spanish power in the American continent. The study covers a broad span of time, but is concerned particularly with the eighteenth century. It makes use of British as well as Spanish sources.

12.103 Morales Muñoz, G.E. FUNDACION DEL PUEBLO DE LARES. San Juan, Imprenta Venezuela, 1946. 329 p. illus., facsims.

A documented study on the origin of this historic town.

12.104 Muñoz, Juan Bautista. PUERTO RICO EN LOS MANUSCRITOS DE DON JUAN BAUTISTA MUÑOZ. Estudio crítico por Vicente Murga Sanz. Río Piedras, Ediciones de la Universidad de Puerto Rico, 1960. 419 p. coat-of-arms, facsims., bibl. (Biblioteca Histórica de Puerto Rico, t. 1).

Reproduces the original notes on Puerto Rico that formed part of the famous manuscripts by Juan Bautista Muñoz on Spanish America, covering the period between 1505 and 1556.

12.105 Murga Sanz, Vicente. CEDULARIO PUERTORRIQUEÑO. Edición, estudio preliminar, notas e índices por Vicente Murga Sanz. Río Piedras, Ediciones de la Universidad de Puerto Rico, 1961–1964. 2 v. (456, 448 p.).

Volume 1 is a compilation and analysis of 464 Royal Decrees related to the island of Puerto Rico issued by the Spanish Crown between 1505 and 1517. The second volume covers the first phase, 1518–1525, of Charles V's reign over the Spanish West Indies.

12.106 Murga Sanz, Vicente. EL CONCEJO O CABILDO DE LA CIUDAD DE SAN JUAN DE PUERTO RICO (1527–1550).

Río Piedras, P.R., Editorial Plus Ultra, 1956. 449 p. illus. (*His* Historia Documental de Puerto Rico, v. 1).

A collection of documents pertaining to the *Cabildo* or municipal government of San Juan from 1527 to 1550, the period during which the foundations of Puerto Rican society were laid.

12.107 Murga Sanz, Vicente. JUAN PONCE DE LEON: FUNDADOR Y PRIMER GOBERNADOR DEL PUEBLO PUERTORRIQUEÑO, DESCUBRIDOR DE LA FLORIDA Y DEL ESTRECHO DE LAS BAHAMAS. 2. ed. Río Piedras, Editorial Universitaria, Universidad de Puerto Rico, 1971. 385 p. illus., bibl.

A well-documented study of Juan Ponce de León, stressing his activities as colonizer and first governor of Puerto Rico from 1508 to 1521. Ponce de León's remains rest in the San Juan Cathedral. A number of previously unpublished documents are appended.

12.108 Murga Sanz, Vicente. EL JUICIO DE RESIDENCIA, MODERADOR DEMOCRATICO. Santander, Aldus, 1957. 568 p. facsims., bibl. refs. (*His* Historia Documental de Puerto Rico, v. 2).

Documents, with an introductory essay, pertaining to the *juicio de residencia* or trial process of top government officials introduced in the island in the sixteenth century.

12.109 National Business Men's League. THE TREATY OF PEACE WITH SPAIN: MEMORIAL AND PETITION TO CONGRESS. Washington, 1899. 52 p.

A document prepared by Leonidas H. Hamilton, secretary of the National Business Men's League and endorsed by an extensive list of businessmen and corporations in Massachusetts, Rhode Island, and Missouri. In it they approve of the administration's conduct of the Spanish-American War and the terms of the Treaty of Peace, and recommend its prompt ratification.

12.110 New York Tribune. OUR NEW POSSESSIONS AND THE DIPLOMATIC PROCESSES BY WHICH THEY WERE OBTAINED. New York, 1899. 113 p.

illus., ports., maps. (Library of Tribune Extras, v. 11, no. 6).

A brief history of Cuba, Puerto Rico, and other islands acquired by the United States as a result of the Spanish-American War and of the negotiations at Paris that resulted in the Treaty of Peace with Spain. Biographical sketches of the peace commissioners, speeches and statements, and the full text of the treaty are included.

12.111 Padrón, Antonio E. EL "65" EN REVISTA: DATOS HISTORICOS, RELATOS Y ANECDOTAS, TIPOS Y CUENTOS DEL REGIMIENTO. New York, Las Américas, 1961. 389 p.

Narrations and anecdotes relating to the 65th Infantry Regiment, a unit of Puerto Rican volunteers organized by U.S. authorities shortly after the invasion of the island. The regiment played a noteworthy role in World War II and in the Korean War.

12.112 Partido Nacionalista de Puerto Rico. IMAGEN DE BETANCES. San Juan, 1967. 20 p. ports. (Ediciones Año Pre-Centenario de la Proclamación de la República).

Brings together an article by Betances about Msgr. Fernando Arturo de Meriño, who was president of the Dominican Republic and later archbishop of Santo Domingo, and a piece by Anténor Fermin about Haiti and the Federation of the Antilles in which he touches on Betances' role in developing the idea of the Antillean Federation.

12.113 Partido Revolucionario Cubano. Sección Puerto Rico. MEMORIA DE LOS TRABAJOS REALIZADOS POR LA SECCION PUERTO RICO DEL PARTIDO REVOLUCIONARIO CUBANO, 1895 A 1898. New York, Imprenta de A.W. Howes, 1898. 150 p. illus.

In 1895, led by J.J. Henna, a branch of the Cuban Revolutionary party known as the Puerto Rico Section was created with the purpose of breaking away from Spanish rule. This book explains very briefly how the movement came about. Letters related to the activities of the group, an official record of their sessions, and a complete financial report are appended.

12.114 Pedreira, Antonio S. EL AÑO TERRIBLE DEL 87: SUS ANTECEDENTES Y CONSECUENCIAS. 3. ed. San Juan, Editorial Biblioteca de Autores Puertorriqueños, 1948. 100 p. bibl.

A documented account of the period between 1865 and 1898. This period saw the creation of the first Puerto Rican political parties, the election of liberal reformist representatives to the Spanish Cortes, and the even more important growth of the autonomist movement in the island, all of which led the Spanish authorities to engage during 1887 in cruelly repressive actions against the *autonomistas*. The basic documents pertaining to the creation and development of the Autonomist party are appended.

12.115 Pedreira, Antonio S. EL PERIODISMO EN PUERTO RICO. Prólogo de Concha Meléndez. 2. ed. Río Piedras, Editorial Edil, 1969. 558 p. (*His* Obras Completas, v. 5).

Published posthumously in 1941, this book is a useful history of journalism in Puerto Rico to 1930. It includes statistical breakdowns of newspapers according to the year founded and number of papers in each town, a list of pseudonyms used by Puerto Rican writers, and an alphabetical listing of periodicals.

12.116 Peñaranda, Carlos. CARTAS PUERTO-RIQUEÑAS DIRIGIDAS AL CELEBRE POETA, DON VENTURA RUIZ AGUILERA, 1878–1880. Madrid, Sucesores de Rivadeneyra, 1885. 193 p. Reprint. San Juan, Editorial Cemí, 1967. 136 p.

A series of letters written by Peñaranda, a noted late nineteenth-century Spanish journalist, during an extended stay in Puerto Rico. They provide interesting information on life and customs, education, literature, administrative organization, and social and economic conditions in the island at the time.

12.117 Pérez Moris, José, and Luis Cueto y González Quijano. HISTORIA DE LA INSURRECCION DE LARES. Barcelona, Tip. de Narciso Ramírez, 1872. 342 p.

A description of the Lares insurrection of 1868 and of the events that led to it, written by Spanish officials. A useful collection of documents is appended.

12.118 Pratt, Julius W. AMERICA'S COLONIAL EXPERIMENT: HOW THE U.S. GAINED, GOVERNED AND IN PART GAVE AWAY A COLONIAL EMPIRE. New York, Prentice-Hall, 1950. 460 p. maps, bibl. refs. Reprint. Gloucester, Mass., Peter Smith, 1964.

A documented history "of the rise and decline of imperialist sentiment in the United States, of the acquisition of America's overseas possessions, their government, their economic development and problems, and their political aspirations." The author, professor of American history at the University of Buffalo, attempts to determine the motives, methods, achievements, and failures of the U.S. experiment in colonialism.

12.119 Pratt, Julius W. EXPANSIONISTS OF 1898: THE ACQUISITION OF HAWAII AND THE SPANISH ISLANDS. New York, P. Smith, 1951, c1936. 393 p. bibl. (Walter Hines Page School of International Relations. Albert Shaw Lectures on Diplomatic History, 1936).

Documented study tracing the rise and development in the United States of the movement for overseas expansion.

12.120 PUERTO RICO Y SU HISTORIA: LECTURAS ESCOGIDAS. 2. ed. rev. Selección e Introducciones por Arturo Santana y Eugenio Fernández Méndez. San Juan, División Editorial, Departamento de Instrucción Pública, 1971. 3 v. (308, 262, 280 p.).

These are the first three of what is expected to be a series of five volumes containing basic sources for the study of the history of Puerto Rico. The first volume covers the geography of the island, and its pre-Columbian and Iberian backgrounds, its discovery, and Spanish conquest and colonization. Volume 2 covers the attacks on the island by the English, French, and Dutch during the seventeenth and eighteenth centuries and the problem of illicit trade with those powers and ends with a description of social conditions at the time. Volume 3 deals

with the impact of the Enlightenment in America. It presents also a picture of the economic and social situation of the island in the eighteenth and nineteenth centuries.

12.121 Quiñones, Francisco Mariano. APUNTES PARA LA HISTORIA DE PUERTO RICO. 3. ed. rev. Río Piedras, P.R., Ediciones del Instituto de Literatura Puertorriqueña, 1957. 220 p.

The author, a victim of the political reprisals by General Romualdo Palacio against the Autonomist party in the latter part of the nineteenth century, offers his personal testimony of those events.

12.122 Rama, Carlos M. LA IDEA DE LA FEDERACION ANTILLANA EN LOS INDEPENDENTISTAS PUERTORRIQUEÑOS DEL SIGLO XIX. Río Piedras, P.R., Ediciones Librería Internacional, [1971]. Colección Diálogo, 1).

An essay on the idea of an Antillean federation that was advocated by Ramón Emeterio Betances and Eugenio M. de Hostos.

12.123 Ramírez de Arellano, Rafael W. LA CALLE MUSEO. Barcelona, Ediciones Rumbos, 1967. 50 p. illus., photos.

A history and description of the Calle del Cristo, perhaps the best-known and most-loved street in Old San Juan.

12.124 Randolph, Carman F. THE LAW AND POLICY OF ANNEXATION. New York, Longmans, Green, 1901. 226 p.

Although the annexation of the Philippines is the central theme of this book, it is at the same time a text for a general legal discussion of annexation as manifested in U.S. policies in 1898 regarding the incorporation of territories, and of the obligations, both moral and constitutional, that go with sovereignty. Appended documents include the U.S. Declaration of War against Spain of April 25, 1898, the Protocol of August 12, 1898, and the Treaty of Paris signed on December 10, 1898, and proclaimed on April 11, 1899.

12.125 Real Díaz, José J., comp. CATALOGO DE LAS CARTAS Y PETICIONES DEL CABILDO DE SAN JUAN BAUTISTA

DE PUERTO RICO EN EL ARCHIVO GENERAL DE INDIAS (SIGLOS XVI–XVII). San Juan, Municipio de San Juan e Instituto de Cultura Puertorriqueña, 1968. 311 p.

Catalog of letters and diverse petitions from the Cabildo of the capital of San Juan to the Spanish Crown from 1527 to 1800. Entries include date, sender, and gist of the communication.

12.126 RELACION DE LAS FIESTAS PUBLICAS DE 1831. San Juan, Editorial Coquí, 1971. 224 p. Facsimile of 1831 edition.

One of the earliest books with a Puerto Rican subject actually printed in the island. It describes the public festivals—including decorating with lights the homes and public buildings, dances, horse races, music, religious ceremonies, etc.—that were held in San Juan and other towns to celebrate the birth of the Infanta María Isabel in Spain.

12.127 Ribes Tovar, Federico. THE PUERTO RICAN WOMAN: HER LIFE AND EVOLUTION THROUGHOUT HISTORY. Translated from the Spanish by Anthony Rawlings. [New York], Plus Ultra Educational Pub., [1972]. 253 p. illus., bibl. (Puerto Rican Heritage Series. Plus Ultra Book, 4).

An uneven account of the nature of and changes in the activities of women throughout Puerto Rico's history.

12.128 Rivera, Antonio. ACERCANDONOS AL GRITO DE LARES. San Juan, Instituto de Cultura Puertorriqueña, 1958. 37 p. (Ciclo de Conferencias sobre la Historia de Puerto Rico).

A brief analysis of the political and social realities of the years preceding the Grito de Lares of 1868, when the short-lived republic of Puerto Rico was proclaimed.

12.129 Rivera, Antonio. EL LABORANTISMO, O LA LIQUIDACION DEL REGIMEN ESPAÑOL EN PUERTO RICO. México, Impr. Virginia, 1943. 185 p. bibl.

A study of *laborantismo* and *laborantes*, terms used in the second half of the nineteenth century to refer to those activists who favored independence from Spain. These activists used the press, public forums, and oral and written propaganda against the Spanish government.

12.130 Rivera, Antonio, and Arturo Morales Carrión. LA ENSEÑANZA DE LA HISTORIA EN PUERTO RICO. Ciudad México, Instituto Panamericano de Geografía e Historia, Comisión de Historia, 1953. 102 p. bibl. refs. (Memorias sobre la Enseñanza de la Historia, 9. Publicación núm. 161).

A review of the teaching of history in Puerto Rico at all levels—elementary, secondary, and university—in which the authors analyze the conflicting trends throughout the first half of the twentieth century regarding the role of history in the curriculum and the emergence of a school of Puerto Rican historians at the university.

12.131 Rivero Méndez, Angel. CRONICA DE LA GUERRA HISPANOAMERICANA EN PUERTO RICO. Madrid, Sucesores de Rivadeneyra, 1922. 688 p. illus., maps, plates, ports., facsims, tables.

A Puerto Rican commanding officer of San Cristóbal Fort reconstructs the history of the U.S. landing in Puerto Rico in 1898, in military as well as in political terms. The book is based on official documents, his diary, and eyewitness accounts.

12.132 Rodríquez Macías, Juana. EL CORREO EN PUERTO RICO. Sevilla, Escuela de Estudios Hispano-Americanos, 1958. 94 p. bibl.

A history of Puerto Rico's domestic and overseas mail system in the eighteenth and nineteenth centuries.

12.133 Ruíz Belvis, Segundo, José Julián Acosta, and Francisco Mariano Quiñones. PROYECTO PARA LA ABOLICION DE LA ESCLAVITUD EN PUERTO RICO. Introducción y notas por Luis M. Díaz Soler. San Juan, Instituto de Cultura Puertorriqueña, 1959. 103 p.

A new annotated edition of the liberal project for the abolition of slavery presented by the Puerto Rican delegates before the Spanish government in 1867.

12.134 Santana, Arturo F. PUERTO RICO Y LOS ESTADOS UNIDOS EN EL PERIODO REVOLUCIONARIO DE EUROPA Y AMERICA, 1789–1825. San Juan, Instituto de Cultura Puertorriqueña, 1957. 14 p. (Ciclo de Conferencias sobre la Historia de Puerto Rico).

A documented essay based on the author's doctoral dissertation. It analyzes the impact of the European and North American revolutions on Puerto Rico during 1789–1825, a period which marks also the start of economic and strategic-diplomatic relations of the island with the United States.

12.135 Santovenia, Emeterio S. BOLIVAR Y LAS ANTILLAS HISPANAS. Madrid, Espasa-Calpe, 1935. 276 p.

A Cuban historian examines Bolívar's writings and statements in order to determine the Liberator's policy towards Cuba and Puerto Rico.

12.136 Soto, Juan Bautista. CAUSAS Y CONSECUENCIAS, ANTECEDENTES DIPLOMATICOS Y EFECTOS DE LA GUERRA HISPANOAMERICANA. San Juan, La Correspondencia de Puerto Rico, 1922. 295 p.

Background of the Spanish-American War and an account of U.S. actions in the first years of its occupation of Puerto Rico.

12.137 SPANISH DIPLOMATIC CORRESPONDENCE AND DOCUMENTS 1896–1900. Presented to the Cortes by the Minister of State. Translation. Washington, Govt. Print. Off., 1905. 398 p.

English translation of Spanish documents dealing with general negotiations with the United States from April 10, 1896, until the signing of the Treaty of Paris on December 10, 1898.

12.138 Tapia y Rivera, Alejandro. BIBLIOTECA HISTORICA DE PUERTO RICO QUE CONTIENE VARIOS DOCUMENTOS DE LOS SIGLOS XV, XVI, XVII, Y XVIII. San Juan, Instituto de Cultura Puertorriqueña, 1970. 730 p. (His Obras Completas, v. 3).

Reproduces a collection of documents first published by Tapia in 1854, which are basic for the study of the island's history from its discovery to the latter part of the eighteenth century.

12.139 Tapia y Rivera, Alejandro. MIS MEMORIAS; O, PUERTO RICO COMO LO ENCONTRE Y COMO LO DEJO. Proemio de Cayetano Coll y Toste. Barcelona, Ediciones Rumbos, 1968. 252 p.

A new edition of Tapia's memoirs, published posthumously in 1927. The book is useful for the study of the first half of the nineteenth century.

12.140 Tapia y Rivera, Alejandro. NOTICIA HISTORICA DE DON RAMON POWER, PRIMER DIPUTADO DE PUERTO-RICO, CON UN APENDICE QUE CONTIENE ALGUNOS DE SUS ESCRITOS Y DISCURSOS. Puerto Rico, Estab. Tip. de González, 1873. 49 p.

A biographical essay on Power, accompanied by some of his works and speeches in the Cortes of Cádiz, where he acted as the first deputy representing Puerto Rico.

12.141 Tió, Aurelio. FUNDACION DE SAN GERMAN Y SU SIGNIFICACION EN EL DESARROLLO POLITICO, ECONOMICO, SOCIAL Y CULTURAL DE PUERTO RICO. Prólogo de Samuel R. Quiñones. San Juan, Biblioteca de Autores Puertorriqueños, 1956. 274 p. bibl.

The author sets out to prove that Columbus' actual landing place was near the mouth of the Guaorabo River, and that the first settlement on the island was San Germán, not Caparra. Documents, with comments, are appended.

12.142 Tió, Aurelio, ed. NUEVAS FUENTES PARA LA HISTORIA DE PUERTO RICO. San Germán, Ediciones de la Universidad Interamericana de Puerto Rico, 1961. 653 p. illus., maps, facsims., bibl.

Reproduces new documents to shed some light on controversial points in the island's history, including the exact place of Columbus' landing and the precise site and date of the first settlement.

12.143 Tirado, Modesto A. APUNTES DE UN CORRESPONSAL: GUERRA DE INDE-PENDENCIA. Prólogo de Enrique Gay Galbó. Habana, Molina y Compañía, 1942. v. 1. 242 p.

Personal observations of a Puerto Rican who went to Cuba in 1895 as a war correspondent for the newspapers of the Cuban revolutionaries. He offers information on the Puerto Ricans who were involved in the Cuban struggle for independence.

12.144 Todd, Roberto H. ESTAMPAS COLO-NIALES. San Juan, Biblioteca de Autores Puertorriqueños, 1946–1953. 2 v. (231, 171, p.)

The author writes about historical events he witnessed and about historical figures he met or worked with.

12.145 Todd, Roberto H. GENESIS DE LA BANDERA PUERTORRIQUEÑA: BE-TANCES, HENNA, ARRILLAGA. 2. ed. Madrid, Ediciones Iberoamericanas, 1967. 222 p.

A series of historical essays: one on the much disputed origin of the Puerto Rican flag, the others on three Puerto Ricans who distinguished themselves on the political scene in the latter part of the nineteenth century. The texts of many letters and other documents of historical significance are reproduced.

12.146 Torres Díaz, Luis. BREVE HISTORIA DE LA FARMACIA EN PUERTO RICO. Río Piedras, Editorial Universitaria, Universidad de Puerto Rico, 1951. 56 p. illus., facsims., bibl.

A brief history of pharmacy in Puerto Rico, written by the dean of the school of pharmacy at the university. It was done in collaboration with the American Institute of the History of Pharmacy's program to compile similar historical accounts for all the countries of Latin America.

12.147 Torres Mazzoranna, Rafael. LUIS MU-ÑOZ RIVERA Y EL PACTO CON SA-GASTA. Barcelona, Ediciones Rumbos, 1960. 30 p.

Brief analysis of the relations between Luis Muñoz Rivera, Puerto Rican autonomist leader, and Práxedes Mateo Sagasta, leader of the monarchical Liberal party in Spain. The pact reached by Muñoz Rivera and Sagasta was an influential factor in bringing Muñoz Rivera to power when autonomy was decreed by the Sagasta government in 1897.

12.148 Torres Ramírez, Bibiano. ALE-JANDRO O'REILLY EN LAS INDIAS. Sevilla, Consejo Superior de Investigaciones Científicas, 1969. 239 p. illus., maps, bibl. refs. (Publicaciones de la Escuela de Estudios Hispano-americanos de Sevilla, 187).

After a short biographical sketch of O'Reilly, the author concentrates on the missions assigned to O'Reilly by the Spanish Crown in the eighteenth century in Louisiana, Cuba, and Puerto Rico. His two-month stay in Puerto Rico in 1765 resulted in detailed reports on the island's physical and economic geography and on the military situation in the island.

12.149 Torres Ramírez, Bibiano. LA ISLA DE PUERTO RICO (1765–1800). Prólogo de José A. Calderón Quijano. San Juan, Instituto de Cultura Puertorriqueña, 1968. 344 p. illus., maps, ports., bibl.

A documented study of the social, economic, political, and military development of Puerto Rico during the latter part of the eighteenth century when, as a result of the British invasion of Havana in 1763, the Spanish Crown felt the need to strengthen the military, economic, and social position of Puerto Rico and other parts of the Spanish Antilles.

12.150 Turnbull, David. TRAVELS IN THE WEST: CUBA, WITH NOTICES OF PORTO RICO, AND THE SLAVE TRADE. London, Longman, Orme, Brown, Green and Longmans, 1840. 574 p. Reprint. New York, Negro Universities Press, 1969.

This book is an account of the author's tour through the West Indies between 1837 and 1839 and his observations regarding the slave trade. Chapter 25 discusses the situation in Puerto Rico and Martinique. He finds that "the slaves in Porto Rico form little more than a tenth part of the population," while in the other West Indies the white population was much less than the rest of the population which was composed of free coloured and slaves.

12.151 Valiente, Porfirio. REFORMES DANS LES ILES DE CUBA ET DE PORTO-RICO. Préface par Edouard Laboulaye. Paris, Impr. Centrale des Chemins de Fer, 1869. 412 p.

A study of the political, economic, and social reforms requested by the Puerto Rican and Cuban delegates at the Junta Informativa, or Advisory Board, called by the Spanish government in 1865. At the Junta, which met in 1866, the Puerto Rican delegates demanded the immediate abolition of slavery, with or without compensation.

12.152 Van Middeldyk, R.A. THE HISTORY OF PUERTO RICO: FROM THE SPANISH DISCOVERY TO THE AMERICAN OCCUPATION. New York, D. Appleton, 1903. 318 p. illus., bibl. (Expansion of the Republic Series).

The first history of Puerto Rico written in English. The author tries to portray to the American reader the salient characteristics of life in the island. The first part covers the historical events from the discovery to the Spanish-American War of 1898, and the second part deals with the people and institutions of the island.

12.153 Vivas, José Luis, and Gaetano Massa. THE HISTORY OF PUERTO RICO. New York, Las Americas, 1970. 103 p. illus., maps.

This introduction to Puerto Rican history is dedicated to the second generation of Puerto Rican-New Yorkers. (Also published in Spanish: Historia de Puerto Rico, 2. ed. rev. New York, Las Americas, 1962. The Spanish version is also available as a talking book for the blind and physically handicapped.)

12.154 White, Trumbull. OUR NEW POSSESSIONS ... FOUR BOOKS IN ONE. Chicago, Henry Pub., 1901. 676 p. photos, maps.

A descriptive account of the Philippine Islands, Puerto Rico, Cuba, and Hawaii by an enthusiastic advocate of U.S. expansion. It contains some interesting anecdotes and photographs

concerning the American military occupation of the island in 1898.

12.155 White, Trumbull. OUR WAR WITH SPAIN FOR CUBA'S FREEDOM.... Chicago, Monarch, 1898. 416 p. plates, ports., map.

Some of the background events leading to the Spanish-American War.

12.156 Whitney, Henry H. "Miles' Campaign in Puerto Rico." In THE AMERICAN-SPANISH WAR: A HISTORY BY THE WAR LEADERS. Norwich, Conn., C.C Haskell, 1899. p. 199–208. plates, maps, diagrs.

A description of the Puerto Rican campaign by a U.S. captain who did intelligence work in the island prior to the landing of U.S. troops in 1898.

12.157 Williams, Eric. FROM COLUMBUS TO CASTRO: THE HISTORY OF THE CARIBBEAN, 1492–1969. New York, Harper & Row, 1971, c1970. 576 p. illus., facsims., map, ports., bibl.

n.a.

12.158 Wilson, Herbert W. THE DOWNFALL OF SPAIN: NAVAL HISTORY OF THE SPANISH-AMERICAN WAR. London, Low, Marston, 1900. 451 p. plates, maps, ports., bibl.

An Englishman writes for the naval student the history of the Spanish-American War.

12.159 Zapatero, José Manuel. LA GUERRA DEL CARIBE EN EL SIGLO XVIII. San Juan, Instituto de Cultura Puertorriqueña, 1964. 623 p.

Naval and diplomatic history of the Caribbean during the eighteenth century. Analyzes the rivalry, background, and action of the British incursions against Spanish "strongholds" in the Caribbean area. Reproduces unpublished manuscripts from various Spanish archives.

12.160 Zeno, Francisco M. HISTORIA DE LA CAPITAL DE PUERTO RICO. San Juan, 1959. 2 v. (498, 240 p.) illus. (Publicación oficial del Gobierno de la capital).

The author, official historian of the city of San Juan, offers a multi-faceted and documented study of the city based on his research with the Libros de Actas del Cabildo de San Juan. It covers many aspects, among them the foundation of Caparra, the moving of the city to its present site, the contributions of Juan Ponce de León, the organization of the imperial and colonial administration, religious festivities, and public health.

12.161 Zeno, Francisco M., and Aída R. Caro. ACTAS DEL CABILDO DE SAN JUAN DE PUERTO RICO. San Juan, Municipio de San Juan, 1949–1970. 16 v.
Contents: v. 1, 1730–1750 (published 1949). v. 2, 1751–1760 (1950). v. 3, 1761–

1767 (1954). v. 4, 1767–1771 (1965). v. 5, 1774–1777 (1966). v. 6, 1777–1781 (1966). v. 7, 1781–1785 (1966). v. 8, 1785–1789 (1966). v. 9, 1790–1791. v. 10, 1792–1798 (1967). v. 11, 1798–1803 (1968). v. 12, 1803–1809 (1970). v. 13, 1809–1810 (1968). v. 14, 1811–1812. v. 15, 1812–1814 (1968). v. 16, 1815–1817 (1968).

A valuable edition of the proceedings of the cabildo or town council of San Juan from 1730 to 1817. It is a primary source for the study of life in the capital of Puerto Rico during the eighteenth and nineteenth centuries. The original language has been modernized to make consultation easier.

13
JUVENILE LITERATURE

13.1 Alegría, Ricardo E. HISTORIA DE NUESTROS INDIOS. Ilustrado por Carmen Pons de Alegría. Versión elemental, 4 ed. rev. Santurce, P.R., Editorial del Departamento de Instrucción Pública, 1969. 53 p. illus., bibl. Grades 6–9.
This simplified version presents the origins, daily life, customs, government, religion, and economy of the inhabitants of Puerto Rico as encountered at the time of discovery. Incredibly, the name of the Indians is never given in the text. Useful as a supplementary reader for the first years of junior high school.

13.2 Alegría, Ricardo E. DISCOVERY, CONQUEST, AND COLONIZATION OF PUERTO RICO, 1493–1599. San Juan, Colección de Estudios Puertorriqueños, 1971. 165 p. illus., bibl. Grades 6–9.
A survey of the first century of Puerto Rican history. The author's thesis is that by the end of the sixteenth century the foundations of Puerto Rican society were already established. The beautifully illustrated book is intended for Puerto Rican students in the United States. Unfortunately the English version is plagued with many grammatical errors, misspelled words, and literal translations.

(Also published in Spanish: *Descubrimiento, Conquista y Colonización de Puerto Rico*, San Juan, 1969.)

13.3 Alegría, Ricardo E., ed. THE THREE WISHES: A COLLECTION OF PUERTO RICAN FOLKTALES. Translated by Elizabeth Culbert. Illustrated by Lorenzo Homar. New York, Harcourt, 1969. 128 p. illus. Grades 4–6.
Presents a collection of twenty-three Puerto Rican folktales especially adapted for children, yet retaining the themes and details of the traditional versions. It is highly recommended. (Also published in Spanish: *Cuentos Folklóricos de Puerto Rico*, San Juan, Colección de Estudios Puertorriqueños, 1969.)

13.4 Allyn, Paul, pseud. THE PICTURE LIFE OF HERMAN BADILLO. New York, Franklin Watts, 1972. 48 p. photos. Grades 3–6.
A photographic essay on the childhood, education, and political life of Herman Badillo, born in Caguas and raised in New York, the first Puerto Rican elected to a voting seat in the Congress of the United States.

13.5 Barry, Robert E. THE MUSICAL PALM TREE: A STORY OF PUERTO RICO. Illustrated by the author. New York,

McGraw-Hill, 1965. 32 p. illus. Grades K–3.

This is the story of Pablito and how he earned enough money to buy his mother a *mantilla* as a present. The enterprising child showed tourists the marvels of San Juan, tailoring each sight to the visitor's interests. The musical palm tree was where he took a cellist to listen to the music of the *coquí*. Spanish words are used throughout the text and a pronunciation guide is included.

13.6 Barry, Robert E. A STORY OF PUERTO RICO: RAMON AND THE PIRATE GULL. Illustrated by the author. New York, McGraw-Hill, 1971. unp. illus. Grades 1–3.

Well-written and charmingly illustrated story of a young boy living near the beach in Ponce, Puerto Rico, and his adventure with a red gull that takes him to San Juan. Spanish words are interspersed throughout the text and illustrations. A guide to their pronunciation and meaning is included.

13.7 Barth, Edna. THE DAY LUIS WAS LOST. Illustrated by Lilian Obligado. Boston, Little, Brown, 1971. 62 p. illus. Grades 3–5.

Luis had been in the city for six weeks. Though he knows very little English, he decides that he can find his way to school by himself. His experiences upon being lost give an insight into how a Puerto Rican child perceives his surroundings and the people in them.

13.8 Beiler, Edna. TRES CASAS, TRES FAMILIAS. Illustrated by Ezra Jack Keats. New York, Friendship, 1964. 127 p. illus. Grades 4–6.

A Christian-oriented story about three families—Cuban, Puerto Rican, and Mexican—living in different areas of the United States. The church plays a role in the resolution of each story.

13.9 Belpré, Pura. DANCE OF THE ANIMALS. Illustrated by Paul Galdone. New York, Frederick Warne, 1972. n.a.

13.10 Belpré, Pura. OTE: A PUERTO RICAN FOLK TALE. Illustrated by Paul Galdone. New York, Random House,

1969. 32 p. illus. (Pantheon Books). Grades K–3.

An exciting tale based on Puerto Rican folklore in which a devil takes over a family after the father defies a superstition. The story is enhanced by lovely illustrations of the Puerto Rican landscape.

13.11 Belpré, Pura. JUAN BOBO AND THE QUEEN'S NECKLACE. Illustrated by Christine Price. New York, Frederick Warne, 1962. unp. Grades 2–4.

A picture book format of an amusing Puerto Rican folktale in which Juan, the innocent young hero, achieves the impossible through a combination of luck and ingenuity.

13.12 Belpré, Pura. PEREZ AND MARTINA. New ed. Illustrated by Carlos Sánchez M. New York, Frederick Warne, 1961. unp. col. illus. Grades K–3.

Popular Puerto Rican folktale written as it was handed down to the author by her grandmother. The delightful tale of the love between Pérez the mouse, and Martina, a vain cockroach, is enhanced by bright illustrations. Spanish edition and a recording in Spanish and English are also available.

13.13 Belpré, Pura. SANTIAGO. Illustrated by Symeon Shimin. New York, Frederick Warne, 1969. 31 p. illus. Grades K–5.

Full-page illustrations tell the story of Santiago, who misses the pet hen he left in Puerto Rico. A thoughtful teacher helps in solving the conflict with a visit to Santiago's home, which made it possible to understand "why Santiago lived in two places at once."

13.14 Belpré, Pura. THE TIGER AND THE RABBIT AND OTHER TALES. Illustrated by Tomie de Paola. Philadelphia, Lippincott, 1965. 127 p. illus. Grades 3–6.

A collection of eighteen folktales from Puerto Rico, some fantasy, others humorous, but almost always ending with a moral. Each story is illustrated with a pen sketch.

13.15 Berger, Josef. POPPO. New York, Simon & Schuster, 1962. 192 p.

Narrates the story of a Brooklyn family who befriend and take in a nine-year-old Puerto Rican boy.

13.16 Binzen, Bill. MIGUEL'S MOUNTAIN. New York, Coward-McCann, 1968. unp. illus. Grades K–3.
Miguel is a city boy who longed to climb a mountain. The photographs and text show how his wish came true when workmen piled dirt with their steamshovel.

13.17 Boehm, David Alfred. PUERTO RICO IN PICTURES. Rev. ed. Prepared by Robert V. Masters. New York, Sterling, 1969. 64 p. illus., map, ports. (Visual Geography Series). Grades 4–6.
Photographic essay accompanied by information on Puerto Rico's history, land, people, government, and economy.

13.18 Bouchard, Lois Kalb. THE BOY WHO WOULDN'T TALK. Illustrated by Ann Grifalconi. Garden City, N.Y., Doubleday, 1969. 74 p. illus.
Ten year old Carlos' confusion between Spanish and English in his new home in New York City causes him to refuse to talk.

13.19 Bourne, Miriam Anne. EMILIO'S SUMMER DAY. Pictures by Ben Schecter. New York, Harper & Row, 1966. 32 p. illus. Grades K–2.
This picture storybook tells graphically of a scorching day in the city. Inner-city children from Spanish-speaking neighborhoods can identify with Emilio and how he and his friends enjoy being sprayed with cold water by the sanitation street-washing truck.

13.20 Brau, María M. ISLAND IN THE CROSSROADS: THE HISTORY OF PUERTO RICO. Illustrated by Herbert Steinberg. Garden City, N.Y., Doubleday, 1968. 116 p. illus., map. (Zenith Paperback). Grades 6–9.
Readable survey of Puerto Rican history from its discovery to the adoption of its constitution in 1952.

13.21 Brenner, Barbara. BARTO TAKES THE SUBWAY. Photographs by Sy Katzoff. New York, Knopf, 1961. unp. illus. Grades K–3.

This story, illustrated with black and white photographs taken on a New York subway, captures the excitement of a Puerto Rican boy's first subway ride and all the new things he learns.

13.22 Buckley, Peter. I AM FROM PUERTO RICO. New York, Simon & Schuster, 1971. 127 p. photos. Grades 6 and up.
This is the story of Federico Ramírez, a twelve-year-old boy whose parents decide to return to Puerto Rico to a small fishing village, and his adaptation to the return migration. Realistic photographs illustrate the text. This book helps understand the differences between the lifestyles in a fishing village, in an urban slum in Puerto Rico, and in New York City.

13.23 Burchard, Peter. CHITO. Photographs by Katrina Thomas. New York, Coward-McCann, 1969. 48 p. unp. illus. Grades 1–4.
A young Puerto Rican boy living in New York City is homesick for the farm in Puerto Rico and his familiar surroundings. The picture book explores his feelings—doubts, fears, and final acceptance of a new environment.

13.24 Calitri, Princine M. COME ALONG TO PUERTO RICO. Minneapolis, T.S. Denison, 1971. 212 p. illus., map, ports. n.a.

13.25 Campion, Nardy R. CASA MEANS HOME. Illustrated by Rocco Negri. New York, Holt, 1970. 134 p. illus.
Lorenzo goes back to Puerto Rico for a visit. On his return to El Barrio in East Harlem, he compares the lifestyles and potential of both places.

13.26 Colorado, Antonio J. THE FIRST BOOK OF PUERTO RICO. New York, Franklin Watts, 1965. 74 p. illus., map. Revised edition, 1972. Grades 6–9.
Factual discussion on the geography, history, and way of life of Puerto Rico. The book is well illustrated with photographs and maps. A general reference work, it includes some Puerto Rican names for plants and objects.

13.27 Cepeda, Orlando, with Charles Einstein. MY UPS AND DOWNS IN BASEBALL. New York, Putnam, 1968. 191 p. Grades 6 and up.

In an autobiographical book the Puerto Rican who was baseball's most valuable player in 1967 talks candidly of his life in baseball, his having been a cripple, his triumphs, and his sorrows.

13.28 Christopher, Matt. BASEBALL FLY-HAWK. Illustrated by Foster Caddell. Boston, Little, Brown, 1963. 127 p. illus. Grades 2–4.
An uncomplicated baseball story about a Puerto Rican boy who proves himself.

13.29 Coll y Cuchí, Víctor. ESTAMPAS PUERTORRIQUEÑAS. San Juan, Editorial Departamento de Instrucción Pública, 1964. 155 p. illus. Grades 9 and up. Supplementary reading.
Published posthumously, these thirty-five brief narratives intended for Puerto Rican public school children are based on historic fact and traditional legends. The basic themes are the Indians, events in the history of the island, and historic figures.

13.30 Colman, Hila. THE GIRL FROM PUERTO RICO. New York, William Morrow, 1961. 222 p. (Morrow Junior books). Grades 6–9.
Melodramatic novel for girls centered on Felicidad, a Puerto Rican girl who moves to New York, and the problems she faces in the city.

13.31 Connors, Robert E., and Donald R. Haener. PUERTO RICO, AN ISLAND ON THE MOVE. Illustrated by Michael W. Connors and Robert E. Connors. Cooperstown, N.Y., Discovery Enterprises, 1972. 160 p. illus., maps.
Text and photographs introduce the geography, history, social structure, economy, culture, and modern achievements of Puerto Rico. A chapter is devoted to El Barrio and to mainland Puerto Ricans. The illustrations have captions in English and Spanish.
Useful as a social studies textbook and curriculum resource material, the book is part of a multimedia kit including study prints, filmstrip, transparencies, and spirit masters.

13.32 Cooper, Lee. THE PIRATE OF PUERTO RICO. Illustrated by David Stone. New York, Putnam, 1972. 78 p. illus. Grades 3–5.
Fictionalized story based on the life and exploits of Puerto Rican pirate Roberto Cofresí.

13.33 Crane, Caroline. DON'T LOOK AT ME THAT WAY. New York, Random House, 1970. 181 p.
A story of a Puerto Rican girl whose hopes to leave the squalor in which she lives are shattered when her mother dies, leaving her in charge of five brothers and sisters.

13.34 Dávila, Virgilio. PIPO. Hato Rey, P.R., Editorial Cordillera, 1968. 29 p. col. illus. (Colección La Chiringa). Grades 1–3.
A selection of poems in Spanish selected from a book written by Dávila for his grandchildren. The color illustrations are most attractive.

13.35 Departamento de Instrucción Pública. ALBORADA. Buenos Aires, Kapelusz, [1958]. 130 p. illus. Supplementary reading.
Anthology of childrens' poetry in Spanish—from Spain, Puerto Rico, and other Latin American countries—divided into four groups, nature and man, recreation and games, traditions, and legends.

13.36 Delaney, Eleanor Cecilia, and others. SPANISH GOLD. Illustrated by George M. Richards. New York, Macmillan, 1946. 426 p. illus., maps.
A book in which the authors introduce young readers to the Spanish heritage of Puerto Rico, Florida, Texas, New Mexico, and California and to the riches Spain brought to the United States, such as plants, tools, and animals, all of which they refer to as "Spanish Gold."

13.37 Dinhofer, Elisa and Al. CHICOS EN LA COCINA. KIDS IN THE KITCHEN. Diseñado e ilustrado por José Villavicencio. Santurce, P.R., Caribbean World Communications, 1971. 34 p. illus.
A colorful, bilingual cookbook designed for youngsters between the ages of 6 and 16. It is divided into three sections each with recipes of in-

creasing difficulty, most of which are for Puerto Rican dishes.

13.38 Dorvillier, William J. WORKSHOP, U.S.A.: THE CHALLENGE OF PUERTO RICO. New York, Coward-McCann, 1962. 121 p. illus., map. (Challenge Books: Eye witness Reports).

General summary of the progress achieved in Puerto Rico through Operation Bootstrap and what remains to be accomplished in the battle against poverty. The author believes that Puerto Rico "is one of the most convincing exhibits we have to contradict the communist charge that the U.S. is an 'imperialist' nation."

13.39 Edell, Celeste. A PRESENT FROM ROSITA. Illustrated by Elton Fax. New York, Julian Messner, 1952. 179 p. illus. Washington Square (Archway Paperback). Grades 4–6.

A widowed mother and her two children move to San Juan and later to New York from the imaginary town of Orcibo, driven away by the loss of their home in a hurricane. Not recommended.

13.40 Elisofon, Eliot. A WEEK IN LEONORA'S WORLD: PUERTO RICO. New York, Crowell, Collier and Macmillan, 1971. unp. photos.

A photographic essay on how an eight-year-old Puerto Rican girl spends her week in San Juan. Woven into her story are insights into the history and culture of Puerto Rico.

13.41 Feliciano Mendoza, Ester. CAJITA DE MUSICA: CUENTOS. San Juan, Editorial del Departamento de Instrucción Pública, Estado Libre Asociado de Puerto Rico, 1968. 74 p. illus. Grades 3–6. Supplementary reading.

A collection of delightful children's stories with literary value. Perucho Serrucho, el Grillo Cantor, Don Caracol Concol, Juan Coquí, and Perico Ricopé are some of the animals who inhabit this fantasy world.

13.42 Feliciano Mendoza, Ester. COQUI. 2. ed. San Juan, Editorial Campos, 1959. 68 p.

n.a.

13.43 Felt, Sue. ROSA-TOO-LITTLE. Illustrated by the author. Garden City, N.Y., Doubleday, 1950. unp. illus. Grades K–2.

This is the story of a little girl who more than anything else wants to learn to write her name so that she can get a library card and check out books. The book has no Puerto Rican content, except for the occasional use of a Spanish word and the dark skin of the people illustrated.

13.44 EVENTS IN THE HISTORY OF PUERTO RICO. Researched by Pablo Figueroa; illustrated by Samuel Morales; edited by Antonia Pantoja and Barbara Blourock. New York, Research for Urban Education, 1967. 56 p. illus., maps. Grades 7–12.

Clearly written and illustrated book covering historical episodes from the period preceding the island's discovery to the Spanish colonization.

13.45 Figueroa, John. ANTONIO'S WORLD. Illustrated by Sam Morales. New York, Hill & Wang, 1970. 60 p. illus. (A Challenger Book. La Raza Series). Grades 6 and up.

Two stories about Tony, a thirteen-year-old, sensitive Puerto Rican boy in New York City. In the first he gets a job with a junk man and quickly loses it, but he makes some friends and gains the respect of others in the process. In the second he fights to keep his status as champion kite flier against a boy from the next block.

13.46 Figueroa, Pablo. ENRIQUE. Illustrated by Bill Negrón. New York, Hill & Wang, 1970. 57 p. illus. Random-Singer, paperback. (Challenger Book, La Raza Series). Grades 6 and up.

Story of a fourteen-year-old Puerto Rican boy in El Barrio and his double, Indio, in New York City. It is sensitive to Puerto Rican culture and deals realistically with some of its aspects.

13.47 Forsee, Aylesa. PABLO CASALS, CELLIST FOR FREEDOM. New York, Thomas Y. Crowell, c1965. 229 p. bibl. Grades 6 and up.

A substantial part of this book is dedicated to Casals' years in Puerto Rico.

13.48 Garrastegui, Juan. LA ALTURA. Prólogo de Carmen Gómez Tejera. Buenos Aires, Imprenta López, 1970. 47 p. Grades 6-9.

This short novel, written especially for children, has been recommended by the department of education of Puerto Rico. Its descriptions of the mountains of the island and the way of life there add interest to the story of a young boy who spends some time with a wise uncle who teaches him to be generous with those less fortunate than he.

13.49 Gómez Tejera, Carmen, and Juan Asencio Alvarez-Torre, comps. POESIA PUERTORRIQUEÑA: ANTO-LOGIA PARA NIÑOS. Con unas palabras de Juan Ramón Jiménez. Habana, Cuba, Edición "Fiesta por la Poesía y el Niño de Puerto Rico," 1938. 411 p.

Anthology of poems appropriate for elementary school children written by Puerto Rican authors. The book follows a subject classification: nature, mother, country, love, childhood, religion, Spanish language, school, work,—in a combination of verse and sketches.

13.50 Greene, Roberta. TWO AND ME MAKES THREE. Illustrated by Paul Galdone. New York, Coward, 1970. 41 p.
n.a.

13.51 Hairston, William. THE WORLD OF CARLOS. Illustrated by George Ford. New York, G.P. Putnam's, 1967. 160 p. illus. Grades 6-9.

Carlos, a Puerto Rican boy, is spending the summer with his mother in New York City. Thinking he accidentally killed Juan in a fight, Carlos runs away in panic. On his day of flight he roams the city and encounters both kindness and hostility toward Puerto Ricans. The author shows an understanding of a Puerto Rican's culture and the problems that beset him in the United States. Unfortunately, many of the Spanish words used in the text are misspelled, and some Spanish phrases not commonly used by Puerto Ricans are included.

13.52 Hano, Arnold. ROBERTO CLEMENTE: BATTING KING. New York. G.P. Putnam's, 1968. 192 p. Grades 6 and up.

A biography of Roberto Clemente, well-known Puerto Rican baseball hero who died early in 1973 on a mercy mission to earthquake-stricken Managua, Nicaragua.

13.53 Heuman, William. CITY HIGH CHAMPIONS. New York, Dodd, Mead, 1969. 156 p. Grades 6-9.

A sports story about the quest for the city high schools basketball championship. Pedro Martínez is one of the boys in the team as is newcomer Tex Arnold; their tensions offer a lesson in human relations to young readers. Although the story does not have any Puerto Rican cultural content, it gives a glimpse into prejudice.

13.54 Heuman, William. CITY HIGH FIVE. New York, Dodd, Mead, 1964. 176 p. Grades 7-9.

First of the "City High" basketball stories in which the main character Mike Harrigan is introduced, as is his Puerto Rican friend, Pedro Martínez. The story touches upon the problems of a poor teenager who works after school.

13.55 Heuman, William. LITTLE LEAGUE HOTSHOTS. Illustrated by Harvey Kidder. New York, Dodd, Mead, 1972. 107 p. illus. Grades 4 6.

A baseball story about a Puerto Rican boy living with his uncle in a migrant workers' camp. He organizes a Little League team with other children of migrant workers.

13.56 Holbrook, Sabra. THE AMERICAN WEST INDIES: PUERTO RICO AND THE VIRGIN ISLANDS. New York, Meredith, 1969. 273 p. illus. Grades 10 and up.

Readable account of life in the Virgin Islands and Puerto Rico as viewed through the life of two families, the Kings of the Virgin Islands and the Vicarios from Puerto Rico. The book contains a chapter on Puerto Ricans on the mainland.

13.57 Holland, John, ed. THE WAY IT IS. Foreword by J. Anthony Lukas. New York, Harcourt, 1969. 87 p. illus. (Curriculum-Related Books). Grades 6 and up.

A collection of pictures and accompanying text giving a glimpse of what it is like to grow up in a big city slum. The photographs were taken and the text written by seventh- and eighth-grade boys from the Williamsburg section of Brooklyn.

13.58 Hull, Eleanor. MONCHO AND THE DUKES. Illustrated by Bernard Case. New York, Friendship Press, 1964. 143 p. illus. Paperback. Grades 6-9.

This is a story about Ramón (Moncho) Pagán living in East Harlem with his family. He is faced with the choice of joining the Dukes, a street gang, or the Admirals, a Protestant parish boys club. His decision shows a young boy's search for a meaningful life. A teacher's guide is available.

13.59 Johnson, James Ralph. PEPPER: A PUERTO RICAN MONGOOSE. Illustrated by the author. New York, McKay, 1967. 137 p. illus., bibl. Grades 5-9.

A wildlife story and introduction to Puerto Rican nature studies that describes the environment to young readers. The detailed and informative narrative follows Pepper, a mongoose, throughout the island of Vieques and describes his friendship with a kitten.

13.60 Keats, Ezra Jack, and Pat Cherr. MY DOG IS LOST! New York, Thomas Y. Crowell, 1960. unp. illus. Grades 1-3.

A readable story for young children, colorfully illustrated, about a young Puerto Rican boy who loses his Spanish-speaking dog and manages to find him in New York, although he speaks only Spanish.

13.61 Kesselman, Wendy. ANGELITA. Photographs by Norma Holt. New York, Hill & Wang, 1970. photos. Grades K-5.

Large book of excellent natural photographs telling the tender story of a little Puerto Rican girl whose family moves to New York, of her loneliness in the city, and her constant companion—a rag doll.

13.62 Kohan, Frances H., and Truda T. Weil. RAMON OF PUERTO RICO. Drawings by Herbert Townsend. New York, Noble and Noble, 1964. 280 p. illus. Grades 2-4.

This warmly told story of Ramón, a young Puerto Rican boy, and his low-income family takes the reader on a trip through Puerto Rico. The geography, history, customs, mores, and legends of the island are shown. It is enhanced by very good photographs, accurate descriptions, and study aids at the end of each chapter.

13.63 Kurtis, Arlene Harris. PUERTO RICANS: FROM ISLAND TO MAINLAND. New York, Julian Messner, 1969. 96 p. illus., map, ports. Grades 4-7.

Traces the history and development of Puerto Rico to the present, and discusses the problems and contributions of modern Puerto Ricans who move to the mainland. The book includes a pronunciation guide and glossary.

13.64 Lee, Muna. PIONEERS OF PUERTO RICO. Illustrated by Katherine Knight. Boston, D.C. Heath, 1944. 80 p. map.

Five short stories follow the fortunes of an imaginary Toro family through the generations from 1521 to 1940. Historical facts are interwoven throughout the tales. Outdated.

13.65 Lewiton, Mina. CANDITA'S CHOICE. Pictures by Howard Simon. New York, Harper & Row, 1959. 185 p. illus. Grades 4-7.

The story of an eleven-year-old girl who moves from Puerto Rico to New York. It gives a realistic picture of the fears and hopes of a Puerto Rican newcomer as well as a good understanding of Puerto Rican culture and family loyalties.

13.66 Lewiton, Mina. THAT BAD CARLOS. Pictures by Howard Simon. New York, Harper & Row, 1964, 175 p. illus. Grades 3-6.

A story about a mischievious ten-year-old boy who gets into trouble by borrowing things. It has little Puerto Rican cultural content.

13.67 Lexau, Joan M. JOSE'S CHRISTMAS SECRET. Illustrated by Don Bolognese.

New York, Dial, 1963. 59 p. illus. Grades 4-7.

A story about a young Puerto Rican boy's first Christmas in New York City and the problems that he encounters trying to earn the money to buy a Christmas gift for his mother. Illustrated in black & white, it touches on some cultural aspects.

13.68 Lexau, Joan M. MARIA. Illustrated by Ernest Crichlow. New York, Dial, 1964. unp. Grades 1-3.

Realistic story of how a treasure from a family's Latin heritage was sold to give a little girl a doll.

13.69 Mann, Peggy. THE CLUBHOUSE. Illustrated by Peter Burchard. New York, Coward, McCann, and Geoghegan, 1969. 71 p. illus. Grades 3-6.

A realistic and humorous story by the author of *The Street of the Flower Boxes*, whose hero, Carlos, is once more the principal character. A New York City block becomes a neighborly community when the Puerto Rican youngster loses his clubhouse and has to find a new one, only to realize that he has to share it with a rival gang.

13.70 Mann, Peggy. HOW JUAN GOT HOME. Illustrated by Richard Lebenson. New York, Coward, McCann, and Geoghegan, 1972. 94 p. Grades 3-6.

Juan reluctantly leaves his hometown of Barranquitas to join his uncle in New York. Isolated and lonely at first, he soon meets other children, plays with them, and turns out to be very good at stickball.

13.71 Mann, Peggy. THE STREET OF THE FLOWER BOXES. Illustrated by Peter Burchard. New York, Coward, McCann, and Geoghegan, 1966. 72 p. illus. (Archway Paperback). Grades 3-5.

The delightful story of how Carlos, a Puerto Rican, and his friends decorate their block and create community spirit with "Operation Transplant." Based on a true story, it was recently turned into a film special for NBC Children's Theater.

13.72 Mann, Peggy. WHEN CARLOS CLOSED THE STREET. Illustrated by Peter Burchard. New York, Coward,

McCann, and Geoghegan, 1969. 71 p. illus. Grades 3-6.

The setting and the characters are the same as those in *The Street of the Flower Boxes*. In this case, Carlos gets the help of a policeman and of the city government in order to plan adequately for the World Series of Ninety-fourth Street. Once more, Ms. Mann deals warmly with some of the problems faced by urban youth.

13.73 Manning, Jack. YOUNG PUERTO RICO: CHILDREN OF PUERTO RICO AT WORK AND AT PLAY. New York, Dodd, Mead, 1962. 64 p. illus. Grades 3-7.

This book briefly describes the background, historical framework, and progress in Puerto Rico, emphasizing education. The photographs and text tell of the diverse activities—educational and extracurricular—which occupy Puerto Rican children, including a first grade class, vocational courses, technical schools, games, music, clubs, and a travelling library. It is unfortunate that the excellent photographs are diminished by misspelling of several Spanish words in the text and by some factual errors.

13.74 Manrique Cabrera, Francisco. ANTOLOGIA DE POESIA INFANTIL. Santurce, P.R. Impr. Soltero, 1943. 130 p. (Biblioteca del Niño Puertorriqueño, 1).

Collection of poetry written by Puerto Rican children between the ages of five and sixteen.

13.75 McCabe, Inger. A WEEK IN HENRY'S WORLD: EL BARRIO. New York, Crowell Collier and Macmillan, 1971. unp. illus. (Face to Face Books). Paperback. Grades K-3.

This story narrates the week's events in the life of the Colón family with their five children in East Harlem, New York City. The text is illustrated with realistic photographs.

13.76 McFadden, Dorothy Loa. GROWING UP IN PUERTO RICO. Morristown, N.J., Silver Burdett, 1958. 144 p. illus. Grades 2-4.

A collection of stories about children growing up in Puerto Rico, what the changing times mean to them and their families, their interests, ambitions, and various ways of life. Some of the stories describe the Commonwealth government's development programs. A Spanish-English vocabulary is included.

13.77 McGuire, Edna. PUERTO RICO, BRIDGE TO FREEDOM. Foreword by Luis Muñoz Marín. New York, Crowell, Collier and Macmillan, 1963. 180 p. illus., ports., map.

This book presents a detailed, clear introduction to the history of Puerto Rico from 1493 to the present Commonwealth, with emphasis on the latter period. It also covers customs and cultural heritage. A pronunciation guide is appended.

13.78 Meléndez, Vera. AND THEIR NAMES LED THE REST: BIOGRAPHICAL VIGNETTES OF GREAT PUERTO RICAN LEADERS. n.p., c1968. 55 p. illus., bibl. Grades 5–7.

Very brief, superficial sketches of Puerto Rican patriots, writers, and statesmen.

13.79 Meléndez, Víctor, comp. ISLA DE PUERTO RICO (ANTOLOGIA): PROSA Y POESIA. San Juan, Editorial del Departamento de Instrucción Pública, Estado Libre Asociado de Puerto Rico, 1968. 135 p. Grades 9 and up.

Anthology of prose and poetry selections about Puerto Rico. Selections cover from the sixteenth century to the present and include the descriptions and impressions of distinguished Spanish visitors such as Tomás Navarro, Samuel Gili Gaya, and Pedro Salinas, as well as works by Puerto Rican writers.

13.80 Morgan, Carol McAfee. A NEW HOME FOR PABLO. Illustrated by Harvey Weiss. New York, Abelard-Schuman, 1955. 144 p. illus. Grades 6–9.

After surviving a hurricane in Puerto Rico, Pablo, his mother, sister, and grandmother decide to join his father in New York.

13.81 Muñiz de Barbosa, Carmen. DESDE LOS INDIOS DIAS. San Juan, Editorial del Departamento de Instrucción Pública, 1969. 96 p. illus., Supplementary reading.

A collection of stories. Some are based on legendary Indian *areytos* or folksongs, which tell how the Antilles islands were formed, what causes hurricanes, Borinquén, Niyuquén, etc; others are based on anecdotes about well-known Puerto Ricans.

13.82 Muñoz Santaella, María Luisa, and others, eds. CANTEMOS. New York, American Book, c1962. 169 p. illus.

A selection of childrens' songs, in English and Spanish, nine of them Puerto Rican.

13.83 Nash, Veronica. CARLITO'S WORLD: A BLOCK IN SPANISH HARLEM. Illustrated by David K. Stone. New York, McGraw-Hill, 1969. 32 p. col. illus. (Our Living Neighborhoods Series).

A Puerto Rican boy describes his family, home, school, friends, and amusements in the Spanish Harlem section of New York City.

13.84 Nelson, Natalie. DISCOVERING PUERTO RICO. New York, New Dimensions, 1970. 95 p. illus., maps. Grade 3.

Elementary social studies introduction to Puerto Rico in English and Spanish. The simplified text, in particular the Spanish translation, which has some grammatical errors, is inferior to the photographs. It is accompanied by a workbook.

13.85 Nelson, Natalie. PUERTO RICO. New York, New Dimensions, 1970. 79 p. illus., maps. Grades 4–5.

A more comprehensive introduction to Puerto Rico than *Discovering Puerto Rico* by the same author. This informative book covers geography, history, economic conditions, and customs. It includes a list of important historical events, a pronunciation guide, vocabulary, and recipes. A student workbook is available.

13.86 Nieves Falcón, Luis, ed. FABIAN. Fotografía por Angel Aponte. Texto de Wenceslao Serra Deliz. Diseño gráfico de Rafael Rivera Rosa. San Juan, Editorial Edil, 1968. 20 p. illus.

Book in Spanish about a small boy living in Puerto Rico's mountains. Illustrated with large black-and-white photographs, it shows Fabián at a rural school, at play, and at home.

13.87 Nieves Falcón, Luis, ed. POEMAS Y COLORES. Texto de Wenceslao Serra Deliz. Diseño Gráfico de Rafael Rivera Rosa. San Juan, Editorial Edil, 1968. 28 p. col. illus. Grades 1–3.

Beautiful illustrations done by children accompany fourteen poems. *Mi Música*, another book in this series, is in press.

13.88 NIÑOS Y ALAS: ANTOLOGIA DE POEMAS PARA NIÑOS. Bajo la dirección de Ismael Rodríguez Bou. Ilustraciones de Juan M. Sánchez. Río Piedras, Consejo Superior de Enseñanza, Universidad de Puerto Rico, 1958, c1957. 2 v. (567 p.), illus., bibl. (Publicaciones Pedagógicas, Ser. 2, núm. 19). Grades 1–6; Supplementary readings.

A collection of children's poetry written by Puerto Rican and other Hispanic poets, grouped by subjects.

13.89 Norris, Marianna. DOÑA FELISA: A BIOGRAPHY OF THE MAYOR OF SAN JUAN. New York, Dodd, Mead, 1969. 95 p. illus., ports.

The inspiring story of a remarkable, woman, Felisa Rincón de Gautier, who was mayor of San Juan for twenty years, and of her efforts to improve the life of the people there.

13.90 Norris, Marianna. FATHER AND SON FOR FREEDOM. New York, Dodd, Mead, 1968. 166 p. ports, illus.

The story of Luis Muñoz Rivera and Luis Muñoz Marín, two patriots whose courageous struggle for freedom and dignity for their people the author suggests as a possible source of inspiration to young people.

13.91 NUESTRA CARTILLA FONETICA. San Juan, Editorial Cultural, 1969. 40 p. illus. Grades K–1.

Beginning reader that employs the syllabic method for teaching reading. It does not present the vocabulary as isolated words, but combines them into complete sentences. The words are simple, many of them idiomatic everyday language in Puerto Rico.

13.92 Palma, Marigloria. TEATRO PARA NIÑOS. Barcelona, Ediciones Rumbos, 1968. 153 p.

Seven short one-act plays for children: five comedies—"El Conejito Infeliz;" "Las Lágrimas de Doña Toronja"—a delightful play in which the characters are named after tropical fruits of Puerto Rico—"Doña Carolita y Los Gigantones;" "Mamá Clocló;" "La Mosquita Tonta; a "theater fantasy," "La Mariposa y la Abeja", and one drama, "La Familia."

13.93 Pastor, Angeles. CAMPANILLITAS FOLKLORICAS. Ilustraciones por Jack Boyd, anotación melódica por María Luisa Mūnoz. River Forest, Ill., Laidlaw Bros., 1960. 128 p. col. illus., music. (Serie Puertas de la Luz).

This collection of traditional and well-known songs and games is divided into four sections: games and lullabies for infants, singing games for children from five to seven years old, riddles, and traditional children's ballads, accompanied by the corresponding musical tunes. The illustrations often reflect the gestures that go with the song or game and portray Puerto Rican children and parents in tropical surroundings.

13.94 Pastor, Angeles. ESTA ERA UNA VEZ BAJO LAS PALMERAS. River Forest, Ill., Laidlaw Bros., 1962. 128 p. col. illus. (Serie Puertas de la Luz). Grades 1–3.

Four short traditional stories: "El Pavo de la Abuela Zapatona," "Catilanguá Lantemue," "La Cucarachita Martina y el Ratoncito Pérez," and "Juan Bobo."

13.95 Pastor, Angeles. RONDA DE NIÑOS. Ilustraciones de Betty Alden. New York, American Book, 1949. 80 p. illus. Elementary grades.

Poems for children, inspired by their games.

13.96 Pérez Martínez, Aurelio. MI PUEBLO Y SU GENTE. [Puerto Rico], Cultural Puertorriqueña, 1960. 131 p.

Social studies text book for the fourth grade composed of five units: the community, foods, clothing, transportation and communications, and holiday readings for Labor Day, Columbus Day, Discovery of Puerto Rico,

Thanksgiving, Arbor Day, de Hostos' birthday, etc. Each unit is followed by an exercise and a testing lesson.

13.97 Ormsby, Virginia H. WHAT'S WRONG WITH JULIO? Philadelphia, J.B. Lippincott, 1965. 26 p. illus. Grades 1–2.

The other children talked among themselves in Spanish or in English, but Julio wouldn't talk at all, in this story of a Spanish-speaking boy who has trouble adjusting to his English-speaking class. The book uses some Spanish words and would be useful in classes where there are non-English-speaking children.

13.98 Plenn, Doris Troutman. THE GREEN SONG. Illustrated by Paul Galdone. New York, McKay, 1954. 128 p. illus. Grades 3 and up.

An entertaining fable of a Puerto Rican *coqui* and his adventurous trip to New York. (This book has been translated into Spanish by Antonio Colorado: *La Canción Verde*, Sharon, Conn., Troutman Press.)

13.99 Plenn, Doris Troutman. THE VIOLET TREE. Illustrated by Johannes Troyer. New York, Farrar, Strauss & Giroux, 1962. 128 p. illus. (Ariel Books). Grades 3–6.

A delightful tale about four animals, one of them Tico, a rooster, who find a new place to live in friendship and peace in the Puerto Rican countryside. (There is a Spanish version, *El Arbol de la Violeta*, Sharon, Conn., Troutman Press, 1964.)

13.100 Reit, Seymour. DEAR UNCLE CARLOS. Photography by Sheldon Brody. New York, McGraw-Hill, 1969. unp. col. illus. (My World Series, for Early Childhood). Grades K–2.

Picture story of a Puerto Rican girl who writes a birthday letter to her uncle in Puerto Rico. The colored photographs are very attractive, but the one Spanish word used in the text is misspelled.

13.101 Reynolds, Mack. PUERTO RICAN PATRIOT: THE LIFE OF LUIS MUÑOZ RIVERA. Illustrated by Arthur Skilstone, New York, Crowell-Collier Press, 1969. 101 p. illus.

Puerto Rican history from the dis-covery and colonization period through the nineteenth century serves as a background for this sim-plified biography of a prominent politician who gained autonomy for the island from Spain.

13.102 Rollins, Frances. GETTING TO KNOW PUERTO RICO. Illustrated by Haris Petie. New York, Conway, 1967. 60 p., illus., maps. (Getting to Know Series). Revised 1969. Grades 3–6.

After a brief survey of the history of Puerto Rico emphasizing the events from 1940 to the present, the reader visits a Puerto Rican family of nine and, with them, the island. The island tour acquaints the reader with economic conditions, customs, and the way of life. Appended are a pronunciation guide and a brief chronology of historical events.

13.103 Rosa-Nieves, Cesáreo. GIRASOL. 3. ed. Ilustraciones de Carlos Marichal. San Juan, Editorial del Depto. de Instrucción Pública, 1969. 51 p. col. illus. Grades 4–6. Supplementary reading.

Poems for children, many of them with Puerto Rican subjects—Coquí, Cajita de Yerba, La Chiringa, Mañanitas de San Juan, and others.

13.104 Rosario, Rubén del, Isabel Freire de Matos, and Antonio Martorell. ABC DE PUERTO RICO. Sharon, Conn., Troutman Press, 1968. unp. col. illus. (Puerto Rico: Realidad y Anhelo, núm. 8) Grades K–3.

A reading primer consisting of twenty-eight main words taken from Puerto Rican everyday language. Each main word is used in a brief poem and illustrated by Antonio Martorell. Besides these entries, each letter of the alphabet is illustrated with additional words. Some letters such as v and z have pronunciation notes. Helpful in teaching culture.

13.105 Sharoff, Victor, GARBAGE CAN CAT. Illustrated by Howard N. Watson. New York, Westminster Press, 1969. unp. col. illus. Grades 1–3.

Pablo, the young son of a Spanish-surnamed family—not identified as Puerto Rican—becomes very attached to a neighborhood alley cat. But when

Pablo's parents finally get a much-awaited apartment in the suburbs the question is whether the cat will prefer to move with them or whether he will prefer to stay with his fellow alley cats.

13.106 Schloat, G. Warren, Jr. MARIA and RAMON: A GIRL AND A BOY OF PUERTO RICO. New York, Alfred A. Knopf, 1966. unp. illus. (Borzoi Book). Grades 3–6.
A photographic essay depicting daily life in the Puerto Rican town of Quebradillas. Family life, customs, school, and social life are illustrated. There are a great many dated misconceptions.

13.107 Shotwell, Louisa Rossiter. MAGDALENA. Illustrated by Lilian Obligado. New York, Viking Press, 1971. 124 p. Grades 5–9.
Story about a sixth-grader who lives in Brooklyn with her old-fashioned grandmother. The character, understanding, and superstitiousness of this old woman are a reflection of Puerto Rican culture.

13.108 Shyer, Marlene Fanta. TINO. Illustrated by Janet Palmer. New York, Random House, 1969. 131 p. illus. Grades 4–8.
Tino had been homesick for the farm in Puerto Rico when his carefree Uncle Benedicto gave him an egg to hatch. The adventures and misfortunes brought about by trying to raise a chicken in a city apartment make entertaining reading.

13.109 Sloane, Irvin. THE SILVER CART. Illustrated by Irving Sloane. New York, Random House, 1971. unp. photos. Grades 3–5.
The story of Carlos and Eddy, two Puerto Rican boys living in New York City, who find a twenty-dollar bill. They use the money to go camping in the woods with a shopping cart for a knapsack. Realistic photographs illustrate the story.

13.110 Sonneborn, Ruth A. SEVEN IN A BED. Illustrated by Don Freeman. New York, Viking Press, 1968. unp. illus. Grades K–2.
Waiting to move into an apartment, a newly arrived family crowds into one room. This amusing picture book gives humorous treatment to an otherwise unfortunate situation.

13.111 Speevack, Yetta. THE SPIDER PLANT. Illustrated by Wendy Watson. New York, Atheneum, 1966. 154 p. illus. Grades 3–6.
A simply told story of a young Puerto Rican girl in New York City. Lonely and homesick, she made her love for growing things the key to new friendships and acceptance in a strange land.

13.112 Sterling, Philip, and Maria Brau. THE QUIET REBELS: FOUR PUERTO RICAN LEADERS. Illustrated by Tracy Sugarman. Garden City, N.Y., Doubleday, 1968. 118 p. map, ports. Paperback. (Zenith Books).
Presents in an interesting, accurate, and attractive way the lives of José C. Barbosa (1851–1921), Luis Muñoz Rivera (1859–1916), José de Diego (1866–1918), and Luis Muñoz Marín (1898–).

13.113 Stevens, Cecil E. BEFORE COLUMBUS. New York, Silver, Burdett, c1928. 191 p. illus. Grades 4–6.
Indian life in Puerto Rico before the colonization is woven into the story of Coa, a fifteen-year-old Indian boy. His son Yuhubo is told the folktales handed down from generation to generation. Some of the illustrations are of Indian stone objects and drawings.

13.114 Talbot, Charlene Joy. TOMAS TAKES CHARGE. Illustrated by Reisie Lonette. New York, Lothrop, Lee & Shepard, 1966. 191 p. illus. Grades 4–7.
A story of two deserted Puerto Rican children in New York City who hide out in an empty apartment to avoid the intervention of the welfare office. They make it, thanks to the self-reliance and cleverness of Tomás. The book has little cultural content. (Reissued under the title Children in Hiding. New York, Scholastic Book Services, 1971.)

13.115 Talbot, Toby. MY HOUSE IS YOUR HOUSE. Illustrated by Robert Weaver. New York, Cowles, 1970. 46 p. col. illus. Grades 4–6.

A ten-year-old Puerto Rican girl suffers the pains of the family's move from New York City to a new neighborhood in Long Island. The book gives rare insight into the culture and offers a realistic view of a child's resistance to change, the problems of urban life, and cultural differences.

13.116 Thomas, Dawn C. MIRA! MIRA! Illustrated by Harold L. James. Philadelphia, J.B. Lippincott, 1970. 47 p. illus. Grades 3–6.

Ramón, the son of a Puerto Rican family that moves to New York, is afraid to go into the elevator by himself, but the sight of his cousins outside playing in the snow is enough of an incentive to make him overcome his fear.

13.117 Tuck, Jay Nelson, and Norma Coolen Vergara. HEROES OF PUERTO RICO. In cooperation with Elsie E. González Paz. Foreword by Herman Badillo.

New York, Fleet Press, 1969. 141 p. illus., ports., bibl. Grades 6 and up.

Gives simplified biographical sketches of various Puerto Ricans who, from the eighteenth century to the present, contributed to the emancipation and development of their island. They are Ramón Power Giralt, Rafael Cordero y Molina, Román Baldorioty de Castro, Ramón Marín Solá, Eugenio María de Hostos, Luis Muñoz Rivera, José Celso Barbosa, José de Diego y Martínez, and Luis Muñoz Marín. Through them the reader can glimpse Puerto Rico's history, culture, and heritage. A teacher's handbook is available.

13.118 Weeks, Morris. HELLO, PUERTO RICO. New York, Grosset & Dunlap, 1972. 170 p. illus., bibl.

This book presents an overview of Puerto Rico's history, geography, economy, and customs, with emphasis on both the advantages and disadvantages of its association with the United States.

14
LANGUAGE

14.1 Alvarez Nazario, Manuel. EL ARCAISMO VULGAR EN EL ESPAÑOL DE PUERTO RICO. Mayagüez, P.R., 1957. 220 p. bibl.

Documented study which lists, analyzes, and compares forms and elements—phonetic, morphological, syntactic, and lexic—of the spoken language which are obsolete in standard Spanish but that have been preserved among the less educated people of Puerto Rico. Some of the expressions have their origin in old Spanish peninsular usage. Others come from the Indian and African languages incorporated into the island speech in the early stages of the colonization.

14.2 Alvarez Nazario, Manuel. EL ELEMENTO AFRO-NEGROIDE EN EL ESPAÑOL DE PUERTO RICO: CON-

TRIBUCION AL ESTUDIO DEL NEGRO EN AMERICA. San Juan, Instituto de Cultura Puertorriqueña, 1961. 453 p. maps, bibl.

An analysis of the African legacy in Puerto Rican Spanish. The author studies the geographic origins of the Africans who came to Puerto Rico, their speech in past centuries, the etymology and use of African words, and the Negro as a theme in present and past Puerto Rican expression.

14.3 Cebollero, Pedro A. A SCHOOL LANGUAGE POLICY FOR PUERTO RICO. San Juan, Impr. Baldrich, 1945. 133 p. tables, bibl. (University of Puerto Rico. Superior Educational Council Educational Publications, Ser. 2, no. 1).

A study of the policies involved in selecting a language for instruction in the public schools. It includes a brief history of the language problem in Puerto Rico, references to several pertinent studies made in Puerto Rico and elsewhere, and an analysis of the need for the English language in the island.

14.4 Colhoun, Edward R. Local and Non-local Frames of Reference in Puerto Rican Dialectology. Ph.D. dissertation, Cornell University, 1967. In DISSERTATION ABSTRACTS, v. 28, no. 1, p. 213-A.

This thesis considers two inter-related hypotheses. First, the linguistic systems of five Puerto Rican dialect areas are studied to test their correlation with standard Latin-American Spanish. Secondly the author deals with the problem of choosing a satisfactory model, in terms of a local or nonlocal frame of reference, for investigating dialect variations.

14.5 CONFERENCIA SOBRE LA ENSEÑANZA DE LENGUAS EN PUERTO RICO. San Juan, Editorial, Depto. de Instrucción Pública, 1965. 346 p.

Twenty-four papers—some in Spanish, others in English—presented at the 1961 conference by authorities such as Américo Castro, Mauricio Swadesh, Dell H. Hymes, Carmen R. Díaz de Olano, Edwin Figueroa Berríos, Wallace F. Lambert, Robert Lado, Rubén del Rosario, Federico de Onís, Uriel Weinreich, Angel Rosenblat, and others. This book is an excellent source for evaluating the teaching of Spanish and English in Puerto Rico.

14.6 Consejo Superior de Enseñanza. LA LENGUA HABLADA EN LA ESCUELA ELEMENTAL: TEMAS FAVORITOS Y ERRORES COMUNES DE SINTAXIS Y MORFOLOGIA. Río Piedras, Universidad de Puerto Rico, 1952. 96 p. tables, bibl. (Publicaciones Pedagógicas, Ser. 2, no. 14).

Study of a pedagogical nature to analyze and determine elementary school students' preferences in conversation topics and the most common syntactical and morphological mistakes they make in their use of the language.

14.7 Gili Gaya, Samuel. NUESTRA LENGUA MATERNA: OBSERVACIONES GRAMATICALES Y LEXICAS. San Juan, Instituto de Cultura Puertorriqueña, 1965. 140 p. bibl. (Serie Biblioteca Popular).

The distinguished Spanish linguist writes a normative grammar on standard Spanish for Puerto Ricans and other Latin Americans. Gili Gaya feels that the inferiority complex regarding the language spoken in Puerto Rico is more dangerous to Puerto Ricans than the influence of English.

14.8 Epstein, Erwin H. "Social Change and Learning English in Puerto Rico," and "A Truce between Two Cultures: Educational Transfer in the Americas." In Kazamias, Andreas M., and Erwin H. Epstein, eds. SCHOOLS IN TRANSITION: ESSAYS IN COMPARATIVE EDUCATION. Boston, Allyn and Bacon, 1968 p. 32–34, 356–369, tables.

In the first of these two essays Epstein argues that Puerto Rico is undergoing rapid changes and that knowledge of English is an important factor in becoming occupationally mobile. In the second he summarizes the attempts at Americanizing the island's schools and Puerto Rican reactions to them.

14.9 Fernández Vanga, Epifanio. EL IDIOMA DE PUERTO RICO Y EL IDIOMA ESCOLAR DE PUERTO RICO. San Juan, Editorial Cantero Fernández, 1931. 391 p.

A collection of articles in which the author strongly defends the use of Spanish as the medium of instruction in the island's schools if Puerto Ricans are to keep intact their identity and culture. For the same reason he also voices opposition to statehood for the island.

14.10 Fonfrías Ernesto Juan. DE LA LENGUA DE ISABEL LA CATOLICA A LA TAINA DEL CACIQUE AGUEYBANA (ORIGEN Y DESARROLLO DEL HABLA HISPANO-ANTILLANA): ENSAYO. Prólogo de Martín Alonso. San Juan, Editorial Club de la Prensa, 1969. 125 p. bibl.

Explores the origins of Spanish in Puerto Rico, which has its roots in the language of fifteenth-century Spain with influences from the *taíno* tongue. His approach is not that of a linguist but of a writer vitally interested in these topics.

14.11 Fonfrías, Ernesto Juan. RAZON DEL IDIOMA ESPAÑOL EN PUERTO RICO. San Juan, Editorial Universitaria, Universidad de Puerto Rico, 1966. 91 p.

Two essays defending the language of Puerto Rico: "Mística y realidad del lenguaje," and "Geografía, voz y espíritu de Puerto Rico en el idioma español."

14.12 Granda, Germán de. TRANS-CULTURACION E INTERFERENCIA LINGUISTICA EN EL PUERTO RICO CONTEMPORANEO, (1898–1968). 2. ed. Prólogo de Eladio Rodríguez Otero. San Juan, Ateneo Puertorriqueño, 1969. 226 p. bibl.

Structural analysis of cultural change and linguistic acculturation in Puerto Rico, applying the concepts of cultural anthropology to language and to the total Puerto Rican experience. This controversial book concludes that the influence of English in Puerto Rico together with the political, economic, and social patterns that it reflects, is endangering the Spanish language in the island.

14.13 Guasp, Ignacio. DICCIONARIO DE LA LENGUA MECHADA. Introducción de Washington Lloréns. San Juan, Editorial Campos, 1958. illus.

One of the island's leading satirists "defines" the vocabulary of Puerto Rican life and politics.

14.14 Hernández Aquino, Luis. DICCIONARIO DE VOCES INDIGENAS DE PUERTO RICO. Bilbao, Spain, Editorial Vasco Americana, 1969. 359 p., bibl.

Dictionary of taíno and taíno-derived words used in Puerto Rico in the fields of history, geography, fauna, flora, toponymy, and proper names. It includes excerpts from historical documents in which these words appear.

14.15 Jones, Morgan E. A Phonological Study of English as Spoken by Puerto Ricans Contrasted with Puerto Rican Spanish and American English. Ph.D. dissertation, University of Michigan, 1963. *In* DISSERTATION ABSTRACTS, v. 23, no. 6, p. 2127-A.

The major objective of this study was to describe the sounds and sound system of Puerto Rican Hybrid English, a second language or one spoken with a "foreign accent."

14.16 Leavitt, Ruby Rohrlich. A Comparative Study of Sociocultural Variables and Stuttering among Puerto Rican Elementary School Children in San Juan, Puerto Rico, and New York, New York. Ph.D. dissertation, New York University, 1969. *In* DISSERTATION ABSTRACTS INTERNATIONAL, v. 31, no. 3, p. 1586-B.

In order to test the theory that stuttering is a deviant language response to sociocultural stress the incidence of stuttering was investigated in a single ethnic group, Puerto Rican elementary public school children in San Juan and New York. The findings not only revealed no relationships between stuttering and bilingualism, but indicated that knowledge of English is a source of psychological gratification to Puerto Rican children in New York.

14.17 Lloréns, Washington. EL ESPAÑOL DE PUERTO RICO Y LA DECIMOCTAVA EDICION DEL DICCIONARIO DE LA REAL ACADEMIA ESPAÑOLA. San Juan, Editorial Club de la Prensa, 1957. 251 p. bibl.

This book is an alphabetical arrangement of some Puerto Rican words and meanings now included in the eighteenth edition of the *Diccionario de la Real Academia Española* and of others that were left out. The author comments on each and documents the usage with examples.

14.18 Lloréns, Washington. EL HABLA POPULAR DE PUERTO RICO. Preámbulo por Cesáreo Rosa Nieves. 2. ed. aumentada. Río Piedras, P.R., Editorial Edil, 1971. 159 p.

Contains the author's report to the fourth Congress of Academies of the Spanish Language, held in Buenos Aires in 1964, as well as excerpts from the bulletin of the Permanent Commission of the Association of Academies of the Spanish Language. Other articles are about the excessive use of the gerund in Puerto Rico, proverbs, a comparison between Spanish as used in Madrid, Bogotá, and San Juan, a criticism of Germán de Granda's book on the issue of language in Puerto Rico, and other related subjects.

14.19 Malaret, Augusto. DICCIONARIO DE AMERICANISMOS. 3. ed. Buenos Aires, Emecé Editores, 1946. 835 p. bibl.

First published in 1925, this book is the first general dictionary of Spanish-American vocabulary. Malaret gives the general usage, lexicology, geographic extension, and various meanings of each word. Other works by the same author include *Los Americanismos en la Copla Popular y en el Lenguaje Culto* (New York, S.F. Vanni, 1947), *Los Americanismos en el Lenguaje Literario* (Santiago, Chile, Editorial Universitaria, 1953), and *Diccionario de Provincialismos de Puerto Rico* (San Juan, Tip. Cantero Fernández, 1917).

14.20 Malaret, Augusto. LEXICON DE FAUNA Y FLORA. Madrid, Comisión Permanente de la Asociación de Academias de la Lengua Española, 1970. 569 p., bibl.

The book consists of some nine thousand words used in Latin America to identify the most important species of plants and animals. It includes both their popular and scientific names.

14.21 Malaret, Augusto. VOCABULARIO DE PUERTO RICO. 2. ed. New York, Las Américas, 1967. 293 p. bibl.

A brief survey of the history of Spanish in Puerto Rico followed by an alphabetically listed vocabulary. The vocabulary includes words used solely in Puerto Rico, Spanish archaic words still in use, Spanish words used with a different meaning, words derived from Indian languages, and neologisms. Each word has its geographic extension, social usage, examples from the earliest literary sources, and information on whether it has been accepted by Madrid's Royal Academy.

14.22 Muñiz Soufront, Luis. EL PROBLEMA DEL IDIOMA EN PUERTO RICO: ES- FUERZOS DE LA ASOCIACION DE MAESTROS DE PUERTO RICO PARA ALCANZAR LA SOLUCION DEL PROBLEMA. San Juan, Biblioteca de Autores Puertorriqueños, 1952. 298 p.

The author documents the efforts by the Teachers' Association to have Spanish recognized as the language of instruction in Puerto Rican schools.

14.23 Narváez Santos, Eliezer. LA INFLUENCIA TAINA EN EL VOCABULARIO INGLES. Barcelona, Ediciones Rumbos, 1960. 172 p. bibl.

Study on Tainan words that have become part of the English language, and the phonetic and semantic changes they have undergone. The author studies words such as barbecue, canoe, carey, cayo, papaw, and others.

14.24 Navarro Tomás, Tomás. EL ESPAÑOL EN PUERTO RICO: CONTRIBUCION A LA GEOGRAFIA LINGUISTICA HISPANOAMERICANA. 2. ed. San Juan, Editorial Universitaria, Universidad de Puerto Rico, 1948. 346 p. illus., maps, bibl.

This linguistic study, published in 1948, is the first synchronic study of the Spanish spoken in Puerto Rico and a fundamental source for anyone interested in this subject. The author, a Spanish philologist, analyzes morphology, phonology, and syntax and traces the linguistic atlas of the island. The author concludes that none of the phonetic changes peculiar to the colloquial language in Puerto Rico affect the phonological systems of standard Spanish.

14.25 Ocampo, Tarsicio. comp. PUERTO RICO: IDIOMA ESCOLAR, 1962–65: REACCIONES DE PRENSA. Cuernavaca, México, Centro Intercultural de Documentación, 1966. 260 p. bibl. (Dossier, 1).

Lists nearly eight hundred articles and reproduces many of them. The bulk constitute reactions to a 1962 pronouncement by Education Secretary Cándido Oliveras opposing English as the language of instruction in the island. It includes also some background items on the long-standing language controversy.

14.26 Perea, Juan Augusto, and Salvador Perea. GLOSARIO ETIMOLOGICO TAINO-ESPAÑOL, HISTORICO Y ETNOGRAFICO. Mayagüez, P.R., Tip. Mayagüez Printing, 1941. 127 p.

A collection of Spanish vocabulary with Tainan equivalents and a study of the indigenous etymology. It compares Tainan words with other indigenous American terms for the same object, and provides references to the historical sources where each term first appeared.

14.27 Pérez Sala, Paulino. ESTUDIO LINGUISTICO DE HUMACAO. Madrid, Ediciones Partenón, 1971. 110 p. illus., diagr., bibl.

A published thesis (M.A., University of Puerto Rico), the study contributes to dialectical knowledge of Puerto Rico by studying the town of Humacao as a linguistic area. It is based on a questionnaire and thirty informants.

14.28 Porras Cruz, Jorge Luis, Enrique A. Laguerre, Salvador Tió, and Carmen R. Díaz de Olano. RECOMENDACIONES PARA EL USO DEL IDIOMA ESPAÑOL EN PUERTO RICO. Hato Rey, P.R., Editorial, Depto. de Instrucción Pública, 1962. 185 p. bibl.

Observations and guidelines on correct Spanish usage, intended to serve as a manual for teachers. The book includes orientation on pronunciation, spelling and punctuation, syntax, and English loan words. Appended are glossaries for diverse fields of learning and a list of commonly misspelled words.

14.29 REPORT ON THE TEACHING OF ENGLISH IN THE HIGH SCHOOLS OF PUERTO RICO. Prepared by the Puerto Rico Commission on English of the College Entrance Examination Board. Hato Rey, P.R., 1969. 40 p.

Summary of the observations made by a commission appointed to study the teaching of English in Puerto Rico. Covers methodology, level of skills developed by the students, teacher training, and materials employed.

14.30 Rexach, María G. Improving Teaching Education for the Teaching of English as a Second Language in Puerto Rico. Ph.D. dissertation, New York University, 1961. In DISSERTATION ABSTRACTS, v. 22, no. 9, p. 3105-A.

Reaffirms the need for continuous improvement in the preservice education given to teachers of English as a second language in Puerto Rico. It proposes criteria for appraising and improving such education, examines the teacher-education programs offered in the island, and offers recommendations for their improvement.

14.31 Rodríguez Bou, Ismael. A STUDY OF THE PARALLELISM OF ENGLISH AND SPANISH VOCABULARIES. Río Piedras, Superior Educational Council of Puerto Rico, University of Puerto Rico, 1950. 313 p. bibl. (Publicaciones pedagógicas, ser. 2, no. 9).

This work, which constituted the author's Ph.D. dissertation at the University of Texas, is an evaluation of the parallelism of English and Spanish vocabularies in the Inter-American Tests. These tests were sponsored by the Committee on Modern Languages of the American Council of Education to provide measuring instruments that would yield comparable results in two languages and in different cultures.

14.32 Rodríguez Morales, Luis M. EL IDIOMA Y OTROS TEMAS. Barcelona, Ediciones Rumbos, 1968. 124 p.

Selection of speeches and writings, some of them previously unpublished, on the island's language, which the author considers the basis for the preservation of its culture.

14.33 Rosario, Rubén del. AMERICA: LENGUA Y CULTURA. Río Piedras, Ediciones de la Universidad de Puerto Rico, 1961. unp.

Booklet containing the author's speech in the Fiesta de la Lengua held in 1961. Its central theme is the Latin-American culture, a mixture with a Hispanic nucleus bound by a common language—Spanish—to which Puerto Rico's destiny is tied.

14.34 Rosario, Rubén del. EL ESPAÑOL DE AMERICA. Sharon, Conn., Troutman Press, 1970. 161 p. bibl.

Descriptive and comparative introduction to the study of the Spanish language as it is used in Latin America. It is intended for the general public and includes general considerations of phonetics, morphology, syntax, and the Spanish of the Antilles, Mexico, and Argentina.

14.35 Rosario, Rubén del. LA LENGUA DE PUERTO RICO: ENSAYOS. 7. ed. revisada y aumentada. Río Piedras, P.R., Editorial Cultural, 1971. 43 p.

A synthesis and summary of essays written by del Rosario since 1946 on the Spanish spoken in Puerto Rico. He stresses the uniqueness of Puerto Rican Spanish due to different historical experience. He makes a brief characterization of the phonology, morphology, and syntax, lists anglicisms, and discusses the symbolic role acquired by Puerto Rican Spanish as a political issue.

14.36 Rosario, Rubén del. "Uso y función del inglés en Puerto Rico." In Inter American Symposium on Linguistics and Language Teaching, II. EL SIMPOSIO DE BLOOMINGTON. Bogotá, Colombia, Instituto Caro y Cuervo, 1967. p. 69–77.

Reviews the history of the teaching of English in the island since the American occupation in 1898 and its influence on the Spanish spoken there.

14.37 Rosario, Rubén del. VOCABULARIO PUERTORRIQUEÑO. Sharon, Conn., Troutman Press, 1965. 118 p.

A dictionary of words used in Puerto Rico's everyday language. Its purpose is to identify those terms which are used strictly in the island, as opposed to peninsular, Latin American and Caribbean Spanish.

14.38 Sáez, Mercedes de los Angeles. Puerto Rican English Phonotactics. Ph.D. dissertation, University of Texas, 1962. In DISSERTATION ABSTRACTS, v. 23, no. 3, p. 1013-A.

The primary concern of this study is

to present the characteristics of the phonemes in English compared with Puerto Rican Spanish. Its findings are based on the spoken language of twenty-two subjects who were born, raised, and educated in Puerto Rico.

14.39 Salinas, Pedro. APRECIO Y DEFENSA DEL LENGUAJE. 5. ed. San Juan, Editorial Universitaria, Universidad de Puerto Rico, 1969. 72 p.

Address delivered by the eminent Spanish poet during commencement ceremonies at the University of Puerto Rico in 1944. The poet expresses joy at hearing Spanish again upon his arrival in Puerto Rico after several years in an English-speaking country, and strongly urges respect for, pride in, and dedication to the vernacular.

14.40 Shaffer, James Edward. The *Jíbaro* Dialect of Puerto Rico as Exemplified in Sections of "La Carreta" by René Marqués. Ph.D. dissertation, Louisiana State University and Agricultural and Mechanical College, 1971. In DISSERTATIONS ABSTRACTS INTERNATIONAL, v. 32, no. 7, p. 3982-A.

This study is an attempt to codify and demonstrate in English the differences between the *jíbaro's* language and that of other Spanish Americans.

14.41 Shiels, Marie Eileen. Dialects in Contact: A Sociolinguistic Analysis of Four Phonological Variables of Puerto Rican English and Black English in Harlem. Ph.D. dissertation, Georgetown University, 1972. In DISSERTATION ABSTRACTS INTERNATIONAL, v. 32, no. 12, p. 6959-A.

A study of the language contact between black and second-generation Puerto Ricans in Harlem. Tape recordings of informal interviews with forty-three adolescent boys form the basis for the study.

15
LAW

15.1 Amadeo, Santos, P. EL HABEAS COR-PUS EN PUERTO RICO (1899–1948). San Juan, 1948. 100 p. bibl.

A study of the application and operation of the process of habeas corpus in protecting personal liberty in Puerto Rico against illegal detention, covering the fifty years since its establishment in the island in 1898.

15.2 Amadeo, Santos P. EL PODER DE LOS TRIBUNALES EN PUERTO RICO PARA CASTIGAR POR DESACATO. Prólogo de Luis Blanco Lugo. Madrid, Editorial Revista de Derecho Privado, 1961. bibl.

A study of the power of the courts in Puerto Rico to indict for contempt of court, since the establishment of Anglo-American juridical institutions.

15.3 Beutel, Frederick Keating, and Tadeo Negrón-Medero. THE OPERATION OF THE BAD CHECK LAWS OF PUERTO RICO. Río Piedras, Editorial Universitaria, Universidad de Puerto Rico, 1967. 158 p. illus., maps, bibl. refs. (A Social Science Research Center Study).

A study of the application of the laws governing the issuance of bad checks in Puerto Rico, with a view towards perfecting them and incorporating methods used in the experimental theory of law.

15.4 Canals, José M. PROGRAMA DE ENTRENAMIENTO SOBRE DERECHOS CIVILES PARA LA POLICIA DE PUERTO RICO. San Juan, Estado Libre Asociado de Puerto Rico, Comisión de Derechos Civiles, 1970. 156 p. forms, bibl. refs. (CDC. Estudios y Monografías, 002E).

The author recommends to the Commonwealth's Civil Rights Commission a plan, including suggestions for specific training courses, aimed at instilling in the island's police force respect for the civil rights of the Puerto Rican citizenry.

15.5 Capó Rodríguez, Pedro. THE RELATIONS BETWEEN THE UNITED STATES AND PORTO RICO: JURIDICAL ASPECTS. Reprinted from the *American Journal of International Law*, v. 13, no. 3, July, 1919. 483–525. bibl. refs.

This is one of a series of articles published by the author in the *Journal* between 1915 and 1919. It discusses in depth the case of *Downes* v. *Bidwell*, an important judgment in the Insular Cases that helped develop the doctrine of nonincorporation. It analyzes also the civil and political rights of Puerto Ricans in the early twentieth century.

15.6 Casanova, Teobaldo. ESTUDIOS ESTADISTICOS DEL CRIMEN, CON ESPECIAL REFERENCIA A PUERTO RICO. San Juan, Casanova, 1967. 867 p. tables, diagrs., bibl.

A detailed analysis of crime statistics in Puerto Rico—incidence, extension, contributing factors—compared with crime in the United States and other parts of the world.

15.7 LAS CONSTITUCIONES DE PUERTO RICO. Historia y texto de las constituciones de Puerto Rico; recopilación y estudio preliminar de Manuel Fraga Iribarne. Madrid, Ediciones Cultura Hispánica, 1953. 553 p. bibl. (Las Constituciones Hispanoamericanas, 5).

An essay on the constitutional history of the island is followed by the texts of the island's constitutional documents from 1876 to 1952. Some of the documents are given both in English and Spanish.

15.8 Constitutional Convention, 1952. NOTES AND COMMENTS ON THE CONSTITUTION OF THE COMMONWEALTH OF PUERTO RICO. Foreword by Antonio Fernós Isern. Washington, 1952. 123 p.

The English text of the Constitution of the Commonwealth of Puerto Rico is preceded by its historical background and a review of the steps leading to its adoption.

15.9 Dávila Lanausse, José Nilo. LAS APORTACIONES DE DON LUIS MUÑOZ MORALES AL ESTUDIO DEL DERECHO PUERTORRIQUEÑO. Introducción Comprometida de Miguel Meléndez Muñoz. Prólogo de Manuel Rodríguez Ramos. [San Juan], Colegio de Abogados de Puerto Rico, 1960. 193 p.

This book is divided into three parts. The first is a biographical sketch of the eminent Puerto Rican jurist, Luis Muñoz Morales; the second comments on his numerous writings; the last is formed by several indexes to the bibliography by and about him.

15.10 Delgado Cintrón, Carmelo. LAS CONCESIONES PRIVADAS Y LAS ZONAS PUBLICAS DE TERRENOS EN LA ISLA DE CULEBRA; UN ANALISIS HISTORICO Y JURIDICO. San Juan, 1970. map. 87 p.

Examines from a historical-juridical viewpoint the process of colonization of the Puerto Rican offshore island, Culebra, and the problems arising in title-holding of private and public lands as a result of the change of sovereignty in 1898. The author questions the validity of some of the land claims by the U.S. Navy in Culebra and suggests that an independent commission be appointed to determine who actually owns each land title.

15.11 Delgado Cintrón, Carmelo. LAS ESCUELAS DE DERECHO DE PUERTO RICO, 1790–1916. Río Piedras, Asociación de Ex Alumnos, Instituto de Historia del Derecho Puertorriqueño, 1972. 110 p.

A history of the development of the teaching of law in Puerto Rico since 1790, when the first law lectures were proposed, until 1916, the year that saw the graduation of the first class from the law school of the University of Puerto Rico.

15.12 Delgado Cintrón, Carmelo. HISTORIA DEL DERECHO PUERTORRIQUEÑO (LAS INSTITUCIONES JUDICIALES DE PUERTO RICO), 1797–1952. Río Piedras, Escuela de Derecho, Universidad de Puerto Rico, 1971. various pagings. bibl.

Intended for students of a course on the history of Puerto Rican law, this volume divides administration of justice in the islands into three periods: 1797 to 1897; the years of the U.S. military regime, 1898–1900; and the first half of the twentieth century prior to the reforms introduced in the judiciary as a result of the adoption of the Constitution of the Commonwealth of Puerto Rico in 1952.

15.13 LOS ESTATUTOS LEGALES FUNDAMENTALES DE PUERTO RICO. Compilado por José María Bulnes y Héctor Estades. Río Piedras, P.R., Editorial Edil, 1970. 289 p.

A compilation of the texts of the basic constitutional documents of Puerto Rico from 1876 to 1952.

15.14 Estrella, Arturo. Antitrust Law in Puerto Rico: A Study on the Interplay of Federal and Local Legislation. Ph.D. dissertation, George Washington University, 1967. In DISSERTATION ABSTRACTS, v. 28, no. 9, p. 369-A.

This study traces the history of the Sherman Act in Puerto Rico to the comprehensive 1964 Anti Monopoly Act, which incorporates the basic provisions of the Sherman Act and the prohibitions against unfair methods of competition covered by the Federal Trade Commission Act. The comprehensive measures of the act provide the Commonwealth government with full-scale remedies against restraints of trade in the expanding Puerto Rican industrial economy.

15.15 Górritz Santiago, Carmelo J. REFLEXIONES SOBRE EL DERECHO CONSTITUCIONAL DE PUERTO RICO. San Juan, Editorial Campos, 1960. 611 p. illus., ports., facsims., bibl.

A documented constitutional and historical account of Puerto Rico's efforts to attain its legislative and constitutional rights, first from the government of Spain and then from the U.S. government. Numerous documents were studied to compare the island's association with Spain and the United States.

15.16 Hernández Colón, Rafael. MANUAL DE DERECHO PROCESAL CIVIL. Orford, N.H., Equity, 1969. 493 p. bibl. refs. (Estudios de Derecho).

A manual aimed at familiarizing law students with Puerto Rico's civil procedures. The book is based on the author's lectures as professor of civil procedure at the Catholic University of Puerto Rico.

15.17 López-Rey y Arrojo, Manuel. LA REFORMA PENAL EN PUERTO RICO. Río Piedras, Universidad de Puerto Rico, Facultad de Ciencias Sociales, Centro de Investigaciones Sociales, Programa de Criminología, 1967. 80 p. bibl. (Estudios de Criminología Puertorriqueña, 3).

An analysis of a draft penal code prepared by Dr. Francisco Pagán Rodríguez. The author examines the existing penal code and the problems involved in penal codification. The analysis was prepared at the request of the Commonwealth Department of Justice.

15.18 López-Rey y Arrojo, Manuel. EL TRATAMIENTO DE LOS RECLUSOS Y LOS DERECHOS HUMANOS EN PUERTO RICO. San Juan, Comisión de Derechos Civiles, 1970. 220 p. bibl. refs. (CDC. Estudios y Monografías, 004-E).

A report presented to the Puerto Rico Commission on Civil Rights dealing with the treatment of prisoners, particularly those arrested on drug charges. The author concludes that the penal system is antiquated and highly unjust as it relates to legal human rights, and he advances some suggestions for reforming the system.

15.19 Marín de Muñoz Amato, Nélida. PROBLEMAS ADMINISTRATIVOS EN EL PODER JUDICIAL DE PUERTO RICO. Río Piedras, Editorial Universitaria, University of Puerto Rico, 1964. 272 p. bibl.

A critical study of the administrative processes of the judicial branch of the Puerto Rican government, based on the author's doctoral dissertation. She summarizes the historical development of the judicial system and offers interpretation of its most important administrative aspects—

organization, programming, and personnel administration.

15.20 Mouchet, Carlos, and Miguel Sussini. DERECHO HISPANICO Y "COMMON LAW" ÉN PUERTO RICO. Buenos Aires, E. Perrot, 1953. 134 p. bibl. refs.

Two Argentine jurists study the meeting in Puerto Rico of Hispanic law and common law with the purpose of determining whether there is a true merger of both juridical systems or whether one dominates the other. They conclude that Anglo-American law has progressively advanced over traditional Hispanic law in the island and that the then newly-adopted constitution would not affect substantially the reasoning they used to reach that conclusion.

15.21 Muñoz Morales, Luis. COMPENDIO DE LEGISLACION PUERTORRIQUEÑA Y SUS PRECEDENTES. Río Piedras, Junta Editora de la Universidad de Puerto Rico, 1948. 314 p. (Trabajos de la Facultad de Derecho de la Universidad de Puerto Rico, 6).

A summary of the legislation in force in Puerto Rico to 1948, by the island's foremost legal authority. It lists chronologically all the decrees promulgated between 1898 and 1901, the first years of U.S. rule over the island, and the laws adopted by the Legislative Assembly between 1901 and 1948.

15.22 Muñoz Morales, Luis. LECCIONES DE DERECHO CONSTITUCIONAL. Río Piedras, Junta Editora de la Universidad de Puerto Rico, 1949. 2 v. (299, 344 p.)

A treatise on the fundamental principles, precedents, and historical development of constitutional law. The first volume deals with constitutional rights, the nature, importance, purpose, and powers of the state, and the different forms of government. In volume 2 the author discusses the U.S. constitution and its amendments and the organization and constitutional development of Puerto Rico up to the adoption of the Jones Act.

15.23 Muñoz Morales, Luis. RESEÑA HISTORICA Y ANOTACIONES AL CODIGO CIVIL DE PUERTO RICO. Río

Piedras, Junta Editora de la Universidad de Puerto Rico, 1948-1949. 2 v. (299, 344 p.) (Trabajos de la Facultad de Derecho de la Universidad de Puerto Rico, 5).

Part 1 describes the historical evolution of the Puerto Rican Civil Code. In part 2 the author annotates the 251 articles in Titles I through IX, which constitute the first book of the code and which deal with "the people."

15.24 Ochoteco, Félix, Jr. CODIGO CIVIL DE PUERTO RICO; Estudio Preliminar. Madrid, Instituto de Cultura Hispánica, 1960. 398 p. tables.

A brief study by Félix Ochoteco, in which he contends that the impact of two juridical systems and two cultures is forging a truly Puerto Rican law, is followed by the text of the island's civil code.

15.25 Paláu de López, Awilda. ESBOZO DE LA HISTORIA LEGAL DE LAS INSTITUCIONES Y TRIBUNALES DE MENORES DE PUERTO RICO. Río Piedras, Editorial Universitaria, Universidad de Puerto Rico, 1970. 119 p. bibl.

The author analyzes the Ley de Menores (Law on Juveniles) and data on juvenile delinquents provided by the police, the courts, and the public welfare records. She concludes that there is great legal confusion in the area of responsibility for regulatory policies in this field.

15.26 Puerto Rico. University. School of Public Administration. LA NUEVA CONSTITUCION DE PUERTO RICO: INFORMES A LA CONVENCION CONSTITUYENTE. Introducción de Carl J. Friedrich. [Río Piedras], Ediciones de la Universidad de Puerto Rico, 1954. 609 p. bibl.

A series of reports presented by the University of Puerto Rico School of Public Administration in 1951 to the Constitutional Convention. Many of their recommendations could still be useful as background for future constitutional amendments, legislation, and administrative reforms. In other aspects that coincide with some of the dispositions in the constitution the reports might be useful in clarifying their meaning.

15.27 Rodríguez Ramos, Manuel. CASOS Y NOTAS DE DERECHOS REALES. Rev. ed. Río Piedras, Editorial Universitaria, Universidad de Puerto Rico, 1963. 528 p.

A text by the dean emeritus of the law school at the University of Puerto Rico regarding the body of laws and court decisions on corporation taxes in Puerto Rico. More than forty cases out of a total of more than five hundred examined by the author are discussed.

15.28 Silving, Helen. CONSTITUENT ELEMENTS OF CRIME. Springfield, Ill., Charles C Thomas, 1967. 458 p. bibl. refs. (American Lecture Series).

The author, a professor of law at the University of Puerto Rico who has been advisor to the Legislative Penal Reform Commission of the Commonwealth of Puerto Rico, presents "(1) a project of a first Book of the General Part of a modern Penal Code, as well as an introductory part; and (2) an experiment in class instruction in criminal law conducted on a systematic, comparative and inter-disciplinary basis."

15.29 Torres-Peralta, Sarah Esther, and Ginoris Vizcarra. RELACIONES OBRERO-PATRONALES: DIGESTO DE DECISIONES. San Juan, Lawyers Publishers of Puerto Rico, 1960. 1 v.

An interpretive analysis of the judicial and administrative decisions promulgated by the courts and by the Labor Relations Board of Puerto Rico under Law 130 of 8 March 1945, as amended. Law 130 regulates the relations between workers and employers in those fields not covered by the Taft-Hartley Law, such as farm-related industries and all commercial operations conducted on the local level. A list of the judicial decisions of the Labor Relations Board is included.

15.30 Velázquez, Guaroa. DIRECTIVAS FUNDAMENTALES DEL DERECHO INTERNACIONAL PRIVADO PUERTORRIQUEÑO. Prólogo de Manuel Rodríguez Ramos. Río Piedras, Junta Editora de la Universidad de Puerto Rico, 1945. 105 p. bibl.

An analysis of one aspect of Puerto Rican law. The author is opposed to the acceptance and establishment of institutions of common law in Puerto Rico because they will interfere with the jurisdiction of preexisting Spanish civil law, used traditionally in the island. He condemns the fact that Anglo-American law is actually invading the legal jurisdiction of Puerto Rican private law.

15.31 Vázquez Bote, Eduardo. DERECHO CIVIL DE PUERTO RICO San Juan, Ediciones Jurídicas, 1972. 716 p.

First volume of a proposed series on civil law in Puerto Rico.

15.32 Villar Roces, Mario. PUERTO RICO Y SU REFORMA AGRARIA. Río Piedras, P.R., Editorial Edil, 1968. 196 p. tables, bibl.
A Cuban author analyzes Puerto Rico's agrarian reform law, which he considers quite strict and which he believes could serve as an example for other countries. The book, complimentary towards the island's efforts in this field, includes all the relevant statues and other basic documents.

16
LITERATURE
History and Criticism

16.1 Agraít, Gustavo. EL "BEATUS ILLE" EN LA POESIA LIRICA DEL SIGLO DE ORO. San Juan, Editorial Universitaria, Universidad de Puerto Rico, 1971. 212 p. bibl.
A study of the classical historical development of the theme *menosprecio de corte y alabanza de aldea* (admiration for the bucolic life) and its expression in the poetry of Spain's Golden Age.

16.2 AGUINALDO PUERTO-RIQUEÑO: COLECCION DE PRODUCCIONES ORIGINALES EN VERSO Y PROSA. Colaboradores: José Julián Acosta, Manuel Corchado, Ramón M. Calpegna, Manuel Alonso, Pablo Sáez, Juan Bautista Vidarte, Santiago Vidarte, Francisco Vasallo Cabrera. Puerto Rico, 1843. Facsimile edition: San Juan, Editorial Coquí, 1968. 170 p.
Published in 1843, this collection represents the first expression of a truly Puerto Rican literature. In spite of its title, it is not a regional, popular or folkloric work, but an attempt on the part of the authors to channel Puerto Rican literature along more universal lines by following the romantic school of the times. It was intended to be a gift volume for the Christmas season.

16.3 Arana Soto, Salvador. DICCIONARIO DE TEMAS REGIONALISTAS EN LA POESIA PUERTORRIQUEÑA. San Juan, Editorial Club de la Prensa, 1961, c1960. 265 p. bibl.
Encyclopedic arrangment of patriotic, national, and regionalist themes in the island's poetic output. Surveys some 656 works and 410 authors.

16.4 Arana Soto, Salvador. LAS POESIAS DEL DOCTOR CAYETANO COLL Y TOSTE. San Juan, 1970. 140 p. port., illus., bibl.
Although not a strict analysis of Coll y Toste's poetry, this book has interesting biographical and bibliographic data. It also includes an unpublished Spanish translation of Omar Khayam's *Rubaiyat*.
Arana-Soto is the author of *Los Médicos y la Medicina en la Literatura Puertorriqueña* (San Juan, 1969), on medicine as a literary theme and the presence of doctors in Puerto Rican literature.

16.5 Arana de Love, Francisca. LOS TEMAS FUNDAMENTALES DE LA NOVELA PUERTORRIQUEÑA DURANTE LA PRIMERA DECADA DE PUERTO RICO COMO ESTADO LIBRE ASOCIADO A LOS ESTADOS UNIDOS

(1952–1962). Washington, 1969. 93 p. bibl.

A study of themes in the fiction of six Puerto Rican writers during the first ten years of the commonwealth status: José A. Balseiro, Luis Hernández Aquino, Enrique A. Laguerre, César Andréu Iglesias, René Marqués, and Pedro Juan Soto.

16.6 Arce de Vázquez, Margot. GABRIELA MISTRAL: THE POET AND HER WORK. Translated by Helene Masslo Anderson. New York, New York University Press, 1964. 158 p. bibl.

English edition of the 1958 book *Gabriela Mistral: Poesía y Persona*, a biocritical study of the Chilean poet and her poetry. It includes a chapter on her use of Puerto Rico as a poetic theme.

16.7 Arce de Vázquez, Margot. GARCILASO DE LA VEGA: CONTRIBUCION AL ESTUDIO DE LA LIRICA ESPAÑOLA DEL SIGLO XVI. 3. ed. San Juan, Editorial Universitaria, Universidad de Puerto Rico, 1969. 142 p. bibl.

This book, first published in Madrid in 1930, analyzes the poetic works of Garcilaso de la Vega from a thematic and stylistic standpoint. It probes the poet's ideology and how it is framed within the ideals of the Renaissance. This study has been recognized as a cornerstone in Garcilaso's bibliography.

16.8 Arce de Vázquez, Margot. LA OBRA LITERARIA DE JOSE DE DIEGO. San Juan, Instituto de Cultura Puertorriqueña, 1967. 673 p. bibl.

De Diego's (1866–1918) political life has overshadowed de Diego the writer. This study examines his literary works, ideology, prose, poetry, and style. It also includes a chronology of the outstanding events in de Diego's life, and reveals the patriot's great cultural and human values.

16.9 Arriví, Francisco. AREYTO MAYOR. San Juan, Instituto de Cultura Puertorriqueña, 1966. 324 p. photos., bibl.

One of Puerto Rico's and Latin America's leading playwrights discusses the development of a national theater in Puerto Rico and its relationship with the Instituto de Cultura Puertorriqueña and its drama festivals.

16.10 Arriví, Francisco. CONCIENCIA PUERTORRIQUEÑA DEL TEATRO CONTEMPORANEO, 1937–1956. San Juan, Instituto de Cultura Puertorriqueña, 1967. 207 p. illus., facsims., ports.

An analysis of the renaissance enjoyed by the theater in Puerto Rico since 1930, the new generation of theater lovers, the foreign theater in Puerto Rico, and the attitudes of theatergoers to Puerto Rican and foreign drama.

16.11 ASOMANTE. San Juan. nos. 1 and 2, 1955.

Issues devoted to Puerto Rican literature.

16.12 EL AUTOR DRAMATICO: PRIMER SEMINARIO DE DRAMATURGIA. San Juan, Instituto de Cultura Puertorriqueña, 1963. 242 p. illus., ports., bibl.

Papers read during the seminar by Carlos Solórzano, Manuel Méndez Ballester, Alfredo de la Guardia, Nilda González, Francisco Arriví, Piri Fernández de Lewis, and Juan Guerrero Zamora.

16.13 Babín, María Teresa. JORNADAS LITERARIAS: TEMAS DE PUERTO RICO. Barcelona, Ediciones Rumbos, 1967. 351 p.

Collection of essays on literary criticism about Puerto Rican authors and their works. The book includes studies on Pachín Marín, José de Diego, Luis Palés Matos, Manuel Joglar Cacho, Miguel Meléndez Muñoz, and José A. Balseiro.

16.14 Balseiro, José Agustín. SEIS ESTUDIOS SOBRE RUBEN DARIO. Madrid, Editorial Gredos, 1967. 143 p. bibl. refs.

Study and analysis of certain poetic themes in the works of Ruben Darío: the presence of Wagner, Argentina, the English language, and the United States.

16.15 BOLETIN DE LA ACADEMIA DE ARTES Y CIENCIAS DE PUERTO RICO. San Juan. t. 3, núm. 3, jul./sept. 1967.

First part of this issue is devoted to Luis Lloréns Torres.

16.16 Braschi, Wilfredo. APUNTES SOBRE EL TEATRO PUERTORRIQUEÑO. San Juan, Editorial Coquí, 1970. 111 p. illus., ports. bibl. (Ediciones Borinquen).

A study of Puerto Rican drama from its beginnings to the 1950s, emphasizing the latter period. The book is based on the author's M.A. thesis for the University of Puerto Rico, 1952.

16.17 Cabrera, Yvette de Lourdes. LA DECIMA POPULAR EN PUERTO RICO: HISTORIA, VERSIFICACION, TEMATICA. México, Universidad Nacional Autónoma de México, 1960. 281 p. bibl.

Historical survey and analysis of the popular ten-line stanza composition the *décima*—its meter, survival, and selection of themes as an expression of the Puerto Rican spirit. The author's doctoral dissertation (Universidad Nacional Autónima de Mexico).

16.18 Cadilla de Martínez, María. LA POESIA POPULAR EN PUERTO RICO. Madrid, Imprenta Moderna, 1933. 366 p. bibl.

The author's doctoral thesis for the University of Madrid, this is a study of the origins, antecedents, and themes of the traditional poetry of Puerto Rico. The analysis includes chapters on music, the *décima, copla, romances,* and on children's game songs and rhymes.

16.19 EL CANCIONERO DE BORINQUEN: COMPOSICIONES ORIGINALES EN PROSA Y VERSO. San Juan, Editorial Coquí, 1968. 184 p. Facsimile of 1846 edition.

This collection, together with *Aguinaldo Puerto-Riqueño* and *Album Puertorriqueño,* forms the trilogy that marks the beginning of a local literature with Puerto Rico and Puerto Ricans as the central theme. Collaborators were Manuel A. Alonso, Ramón E. de Carpegna, Pablo Sáez, and Francisco Vassallo.

16.20 Canino Salgado, Marcelino. LA COPLA Y EL ROMANCE POPULARES EN LA TRADICION ORAL DE PUERTO RICO. San Juan, Instituto de Cultura Puertorriqueña, 1968. 176 p. music, bibl.

Shows how the two classical forms of Spanish popular folk poetry, the *copla* (four-verse stanza) and the *romance* (octosyllabic verses), have endured in Puerto Rico. The author compiled the material from subjects in thirty-four villages and towns. Includes a brief survey chapter on critical studies about folk poetry. Also, one on the music which usually accompanies the verses, the themes of folk poetry, and the linguistic resources employed in them.

16.21 Castro Pérez, Elsa. TAPIA: SEÑALADOR DE CAMINOS. San Juan, Editorial Coquí, 1964. 179 p. port., bibl.

Comprehensive study of Tapia's life (1826–1882), literary production, and the historical and literary period in which he lived. It provides a chronology of his works and an analysis of the various forms he cultivated.

16.22 Colberg Petrovich, Juan Enrique. CUATRO AUTORES CLASICOS CONTEMPORANEOS DE PUERTO RICO. San Juan, Editorial Cordillera, 1966. 261 p. bibl. refs.

A study of four contemporary writers—Concha Meléndez, Miguel Meléndez Muñoz, José A. Balseiro, and Cesáreo Rosa-Nieves.

16.23 CRITICA Y ANTOLOGIA DE LA POESIA PUERTORRIQUEÑA. Trabajos Presentados o Leídos en el Primer Congreso de Poesía Puertorriqueña Celebrado en Yauco, Puerto Rico, el 25 de agosto de 1957. San Juan, Instituto de Cultura Puertorriqueña, 1958. 178 p.

Papers presented at the first Congress of Puerto Rican poetry include works by Francisco Manrique Cabrera, Luis Hernández Aquino, Jorge Luis Morales, José A. Fránquiz, Francisco Lluch Mora, Ramón Zapata Acosta, and Félix Franco Oppenheimer. The second half of the book is an anthology of poems by Amelia Ceide, Juan Antonio Corretjer, Carmen Alicia Cadilla, Luis Palés Matos, Cesáreo Rosa-Nieves, Alfredo Margenat, Jorge Luis Morales, and M. Joglar Cacho.

16.24 Cuchí Coll, Isabel. DOS POETISAS DE AMERICA: CLARA LAIR, JULIA DE BURGOS. Barcelona, Talleres Gráficos de Manuel Pareja, 1970. 46 p.

Essay analyzing briefly the three men in Clara Lair's poetry and the figure of Julia de Burgos as a woman and poet. Includes excerpts from both writers.

16.25 EL CUENTO PUERTORRIQUEÑO EN EL SIGLO XX. Prólogo de Luis de Arrigoitía. Río Piedras, Editorial Universitaria, Universidad de Puerto Rico, 1963. 149 p. (Facultad de Humanidades. Seminario de Estudios Hispánicos).

Four studies of the short stories of Enrique A. Laguerre, Tomás Blanco, René Marqués, and José Luis Vivas Maldonado, written by college students as part of a course on literary criticism.

16.26 Cuevas, Carmen Leila. LOLA DE AMERICA. Hato Rey, P.R., Talleres Ramallo, 1969. 102p. illus., bibl. refs.

Study on the life and accomplishments of the poet, patriot and fighter for liberty, Lola Rodríguez de Tió (1843–1924).

16.27 Cuevas de Marcano, Concepción. MATIAS GONZALEZ GARCIA: VIDA Y OBRA. San Juan, Editorial Coquí, 1966. 96 p. bibl. (Ediciones Borinquen).

A brief critical study on the life of Matías González García (1866–1938) with an examination of his literary themes and style.

16.28 Curet de De Anda, Miriam. LA POESIA DE JOSE GAUTIER BENITEZ. San Juan, Editorial Coquí, in press.

16.29 Díaz de Olano, Carmen R. FELIX MATOS BERNIER: SU VIDA Y SU OBRA. San Juan, Biblioteca de Autores Puertorriqueños, 1955. 192 p. bibl.

This book studies the life and works of Félix Matos Bernier (1829-1937), journalist, writer, and political activist for independence.

16.30 Enguídanos, Miguel. LA POESIA DE LUIS PALES MATOS. Río Piedras, Ediciones de la Universidad de Puerto Rico, 1961. 89 p. bibl. refs.

Essays on the poetry of Luis Palés Matos, highlighting what is unique in his poetry. The author discusses the literary influences on Palés, and how his poetry affects the critic.

16.31 Espinosa Torres, Victoria. EL TEATRO DE RENE MARQUES Y LA ESCENIFICACION DE SU OBRA: LOS SOLES TRUNCOS. México, Universidad Nacional, Facultad de Filosofía y Letras, 1969. 579 p. illus., bibl.

Doctoral dissertation for the Universidad Nacional Autónoma de México by an experienced Puerto Rican director who has staged many of Marqués' works. The exhaustive study covers Marques' historical times and his entire literary production with emphasis on Los Soles Truncos. The book also includes a brief survey of the theater in Puerto Rico.

16.32 Feliciano de Mendoza, Ester. ANTONIO PEREZ PIERRET: VIDA Y OBRA. San Juan, Editorial Coquí, 1968. 178 p.

Originally submitted as an M.A. thesis, University of Puerto Rico, 1960, this work is a critical study of the life and poetry of Antonio Pérez Pierret (1885–1937).

16.33 Figueroa de Cifredo, Patria. APUNTES BIOGRAFICOS EN TORNO A LA VIDA Y OBRA DE CESAREO ROSA-NIEVES. San Juan, Editorial Cordillera, 1965. 319 p. facsims., port., bibl.

Criticism and analysis of Rosa-Nieves's writings from 1922 to 1962, touching on his versatility as an essayist, poet, short story writer, playwright and literary critic. Studies his poetic leitmotifs, style, and literary resources. Originally submitted as a thesis to the University of Madrid.

16.34 Figueroa de Cifredo, Patria. NUEVO ENCUENTRO CON LA ESTETICA DE ROSA-NIEVES. San Juan, 1969. 106 p.

Essays on landscape and stylistic forms and brief anthology of the poetry of Cesáreo Rosa-Nieves.

16.35 Figueroa de Cifredo, Patria. PACHIN MARIN, HEROE Y POETA (1863-1897). Prólogo de Cesáreo Rosa-

Nieves. San Juan, Instituto de Cultura Puertorriqueña, 1967. 220 p. illus., bibl. (Biblioteca Popular).

Although he was mainly known as a poet, Francisco Gonzalo (Pachín) Marín (1863–1897) also distinguished himself as a journalist and story writer. This biography of Pachín Marín is followed by analyses of the influences, subjects, and style of his poetry, his political ideals, and his work as a newspaperman and short story writer.

16.36 Fránquiz Ventura, José Antonio. LOS TIEMPOS POETICOS DE MANRIQUE CABRERA Y LA METAFISICA DEL TIEMPO EN SU POESIA. México, Ediciones Luminar, 1944. 31 p. bibl. refs. (Cuadernos de Filosofía de Luminar, 9).

Brief study of the themes of Manrique Cabrera's poetry.

16.37 Fonfrías, Ernesto Juan. PRESENCIA JIBARA DESDE MANUEL ALONSO HASTA DON FLORITO. Prólogo de Alberto María Carreño. San Juan, Editorial Club de la Prensa, 1957. 140 p. bibl. refs.

Using Manuel Alonso's *El Gíbaro* (1849) as a starting point, the author surveys the literature of the next 100 years to define the distinctive character of the *jíbaro*, or Puerto Rican peasant.

16.38 Franco-Oppenheimer, Félix. IMAGEN DE PUERTO RICO EN SU POESIA. México, Universidad Nacional Autónoma, 1964. 236 p. bibl. Reprint: San Juan, Editorial Universitaria, Universidad de Puerto Rico, in press.

Based on the author's doctoral dissertation, this book delves into how Puerto Rico's poets feel about their home. It discusses the development of the paradisiacal metaphor—at first the poets sing to nature, then to the people forged by it and lastly to the nation.

16.39 García Díaz, Manuel. ALEJANDRO TAPIA Y RIVERA, SU VIDA Y SU OBRA. San Juan, Editorial Coquí, 1964. 156 p. bibl., port. (Ediciones Borinquen).

Originally written as an M.A. thesis, University of Puerto Rico, 1933, this is

a critical study of the life and works of Alejandro Tapia y Rivera (1826–1882), who distinguished himself as dramatist, novelist, historian, poet, and orator.

16.40 Gardón Franceschi, Margarita. MANUEL ZENO GANDIA: VIDA Y POESIA. San Juan, Editorial Coquí, 1969. 176 p. bibl. refs.

A study on the life and poetic works of Manuel Zeno Gandía (1855–1930), based on the author's M.A. thesis at the University of Puerto Rico. This is the first comprehensive analysis of his poetry.

16.41 Gómez Tejera, Carmen. LA NOVELA EN PUERTO RICO: APUNTES PARA SU HISTORIA. Río Piedras, Junta Editora, Universidad de Puerto Rico, 1947. 138 p. bibl. (Departamento de Estudios Hispánicos, Cuadernos de la Universidad de Puerto Rico, 2).

The first analysis of Puerto Rico's fiction, originally written in 1929 as the author's M.A. thesis. She discusses the reasons why the genre did not develop prior to 1870 and examines literary efforts to 1929. Her study includes the philosophic, satiric, political, romantic, realist, naturalist and historical novels of Alejandro Tapia y Rivera, Manuel Corchado, Ramón E. Betances, Eugenio María de Hostos, Salvador Brau, Manuel Zeno Gandía, and others. It includes a chronological bibliography of both novels and authors.

16.42 González, Jose Emilio. LA POESIA CONTEMPORANEA DE PUERTO RICO, 1930–1960: San Juan, Instituto de Cultura Puertorriqueña, 1972.

A critical study of contemporary Puerto Rican poetry.

16.43 Hernández Aquino, Luis, comp. EL MODERNISMO EN PUERTO RICO: POESIA Y PROSA, San Juan, Ediciones de la Torre, Universidad de Puerto Rico, 1967. 216 p. bibl.

Anthology of poetry and prose by twenty-two authors influenced by the Hispanic modernist movement with an introductory study detailing its development in Puerto Rico. Each selection is preceded by a brief biographical sketch on the author and a list of his major works.

16.44 Hernández Aquino, Luis, comp. NUESTRA AVENTURA LITERARIA (LOS ISMOS EN LA POESIA PUERTORRIQUEÑA), 1913–1948. 2. ed. San Juan, Ediciones de la Torre, Universidad de Puerto Rico, 1966. 270 p. bibl.

Survey and analysis of the period 1913–1948 and the esthetic theories that were innovative in poetry: Lloréns Torres' *pancalismo* and *panedismo*; Palés Matos' *diepalismo, euforismo, noismo, atalayismo, integralismo,* and *trascendentalismo.* The book includes a collection of representative poems of the various movements, as well as their public statements.

16.45 Jesús Castro, Tomás de. ESBOZOS. Barcelona, Ediciones Rumbos, 1957. v. 2. 170p.

The author presents a collection of his essays, reviews and literary criticism, mostly on Puerto Rican writers. This volume discusses Samuel Lugo, Amelia Ceide, Luis Muñoz Marín, Carmen Gómez Tejera, Julia de Burgos and Cesáreo Rosa-Nieves, among others. A previous volume was published in 1945.

16.46 Jiménez de Báez, Yvette. LA DECIMA POPULAR EN PUERTO RICO. Xalapa, México, Universidad Veracruzana, 1964. 446 p. port. bibl. (Cuadernos de la Facultad de Filosofía, Letras y Ciencias, 21).

Analysis of the traditional and popular ten-verse stanza, usually improvised and danced in Puerto Rico. The author presents a historical survey of the *décima* in Spain and Latin America, traces its evolution and present state in the island, and examines its music, meter, and themes.

16.47 Jiménez de Báez, Yvette. JULIA DE BURGOS: VIDA Y POESIA. San Juan, Editorial Coquí, 1966. 210 p. bibl. (Ediciones Borinquen).

A study of the life and works of Julia de Burgos (1914–1953), lyric poet, focusing on her letters and autobiographical poems.

16.48 Jiménez de Báez, Yvette. LIRICA CORTESANA Y LIRICA POPULAR. México, El Colegio de México, 1969. 98 p. bibl. (Jornadas 64).

Study on the antecedents of Puerto Rico's present popular lyrical poetry, which the author traces to the courtesan poetry of the fifteenth and sixteenth centuries.

16.49 Laguerre, Enrique A., and Esther M. Melón. EL JIBARO DE PUERTO RICO: SIMBOLO Y FIGURA. Sharon, Conn., Troutman Press, 1968. 249 p. (Puerto Rico: Realidad y Anhelo, no. 7).

An anthology with an introductory study of the presence of the *jíbaro* or peasant in the literature of Puerto Rico. The book presents a comprehensive view of the *jibarista* literature and its historical development as seen in essays, poetry, fiction, and drama. Useful as a college textbook.

16.50 Laguerre, Enrique A. LA POESIA MODERNISTA EN PUERTO RICO. San Juan, Editorial Coquí, 1969. 217 p. port., bibl. (Ediciones Borinquen).

An updated version of the M.A. thesis of this well-known author in which he analyzes the development of the modernist movement in Puerto Rican poetry.

16.51 LITERATURA PUERTORRIQUEÑA: 21 CONFERENCIAS. San Juan, Instituto de Cultura Puertorriqueña, 1969. 616 p.

A collection of twenty-one lectures on Puerto Rican literature sponsored by the institute in 1957–1958. The series covers a broad spectrum of topics ranging from a chronological overview to the critical analysis of literary forms and schools.

16.52 Lloréns, Washington. LOS GRANDES AMORES DEL POETA LUIS LLORENS TORRES. San Juan, Campos, 1959. 47 p.

Address in which the author approaches his subject not as a literary critic, but as an admirer struck by the emotion in Lloréns Torres' poetry. He discusses the poet's love for God, beauty, family, country, and the Puerto Rican woman.

16.53 Lorand de Olazagasti, Adelaida. EL INDIO EN LA NARRATIVA GUATEMALTECA. San Juan, Editorial Universitaria, Universidad de Puerto Rico, 1968. 277 p. bibl.

Scholarly study on the influence of the Indian on Guatemalan fiction. The analysis gives the historical perspective, studies the *indigenista* movement with reference to Guatemala, and discusses the authors who have used the Indians as a literary theme, in particular Miguel Angel Asturias and Mario Monteforte Toledo.

16.54 Lugo de Marichal, Flavia. BELAVAL Y SUS CUENTOS PARA FOMENTAR EL TURISMO. Prólogo de Emilio M. Colón. San Juan, Editorial Coquí, 1972. 117 p. port., bibl. (Ediciones Borinquen).

Master's thesis, Universidad de Puerto Rico, 1972.

16.55 Lugo Guernelli, Adelaida. EUGENIO MARIA DE HOSTOS: ENSAYISTA Y CRITICO LITERARIO. San Juan, Instituto de Cultura Puertorriqueña, 1970. 207 p. bibl.

A study of Hostos' contribution as an essayist and literary critic. The author examines his ideas on literary criticism and style, with particular reference to the essays on *Romeo and Juliet* and *Hamlet*.

16.56 Manrique Cabrera, Francisco. HISTORIA DE LA LITERATURA PUERTORRIQUEÑA. 4. ed. Río Piedras, P.R., Editorial Cultural, 1971. 384 p. coat-of-arms, bibl. Paperback. (Biblioteca de Clásicos Puertorriqueños)

A survey of Puerto Rican literature which shows the development of representative Puerto Rican writers throughout various historical stages and literary movements. Each chapter includes an introduction and brief biographical sketch about each author.

16.57 Marrero de Figueroa, Carmen. LUIS LLORENS TORRES: VIDA Y OBRA (1876–1944). 2. ed. San Juan, Editorial Cordillera, 1968. 187 p. illus., bibl.

Biographical study and analysis of the poetry of Luis Lloréns Torres (1876–1944), considered one of Puerto Rico's greatest poets. Includes a brief anthology.

16.58 Martín, José Luis. ANALISIS ESTILISTICO DE LA SATANIADA DE TAPIA. Prólogo de Rubén del Rosario. San Juan, Instituto de Cultura Puertorriqueña, 1958. 198 p. port., diagr., facsims., bibl.

The author studies and analyzes the esthetic values in Alejandro Tapia y Rivera's epic poem and discovers its satiric and stylistic merits. Originally his M.A. thesis to the University of Puerto Rico, 1953.

16.59 Martín, José Luis. ARCO Y FLECHA (APUNTANDO A LA VIDA Y A LAS OBRAS): ESTUDIOS DE CRITICA LITERARIA. San Juan, Editorial Club de la Prensa, 1961. 291 p. bibl. (Publicaciones de obras de autores puertorriqueños).

Collection of essays, articles, and reviews of literary criticism divided into three parts: Puerto Rican, Latin American, and Spanish literatures. The Puerto Rican section includes criticism on Margot Arce, Alejandro Tapia, Cesáreo Rosa-Nieves, Félix F. Oppenheimer, Jorge Luis Morales, and Enrique Laguerre.

16.60 Martín, José Luis. LA POESIA DE JOSE EUSEBIO CARO: CONTRIBUCION ESTILISTICA AL ESTUDIO DEL ROMANTICISMO HISPANOAMERICANO. Bogotá, Instituto Caro y Cuervo, 1966. 510 p. illus., facsims., ports., bibl. (Publicaciones del Instituto Caro y Cuervo, 22).

A scholarly analysis of the style and contents of the poetry of the Colombian José Eusebio Caro, (1817–1853), and his life and times.

16.61 Martínez Masdeu, Edgar. JOAQUIN LOPEZ LOPEZ: SU VIDA Y SU OBRA. Introducción de Emilio M. Colón. San Juan, Editorial Coquí, 1972. 98 p. (Ediciones Borinquen).

First study of the Puerto Rican poet, Joaquin López López (1900–1942), author of *A Plena Lumbre* and *Romancero de la Luna*. The work was submitted as a thesis for the degree of Master of Arts, University of Puerto Rico, 1965.

16.62 Martínez Masdeu, Edgar, and Esther M. Melón. LITERATURA PUERTORRIQUEÑA: ANTOLOGIA GENE-

RAL. Río Piedras, P.R., Editorial Edil, 1970. 335 p. bibl.

A selection of works by the most important Puerto Rican authors of the nineteenth century. It begins with a poem written by Santiago Vidarte in 1843 and ends with the poetry written by José de Diego at the turn of the century.

16.63 Matos Bernier, Félix. ISLA DE ARTE. San Juan, Impr. La Primavera, 1907. 277 p.

Collection of essays on literary criticism, arts, and music by a leading critic calling for dedication to writing as a patriotic duty. The volume includes essays on Manuel Zeno Gandía, José de Diego, Frasquito Oller, Luis Muñoz Rivera, Mariano Abril and many others.

16.64 Meléndez, Concha. LITERATURA HISPANOAMERICANA. San Juan, Editorial Cordillera, 1967. 389 p. ports., bibl. refs. (Colección Hispanoamericana, 9).

This is a compilation of the lectures and classes on Latin-American literature given by this critic and writer at the Ateneo Puertorriqueño in 1939.

16.65 Meléndez, Concha. POETAS HISPANOAMERICANOS DIVERSOS. San Juan, Editorial Cordillera, 1971. 220 p. (Her Obras Completas, 11) (Colección Hispanoamericana).

This book presents twelve essays on poetry, including one on Rubén Darío published for the first time, and "Pablo Neruda en Su Extremo Imperio: Vida y Obra," recognized as one of the best studies on the Chilean poet. The other poets studied are Puerto Ricans: Luis Muñoz Rivera, Luis Palés Matos, Juan Martínez Capó, Obdulio Bauzá, Pedro Bernaola, and Carmen Marrero.

16.66 Meléndez Muñoz, Miguel. OBRAS COMPLETAS. Barcelona, Ediciones Rumbos, 1963. 3 v. (797, 842, 971 p.) bibl.

These volumes bring together the entire literary production of Miguel Melendez-Munoz, including some previously unpublished works. The first volume is preceded by a Master's

thesis by Josefina Lube Droz on Melendez Munoz' life and works.

16.67 Melón Portalatín, Esther. PABLO MORALES CABRERA, SU VIDA Y SU OBRA. San Juan, Editorial Coquí, 1966. 145 p. bibl.

A brief biography of Pablo Morales Cabrera (1866–1933), a distinguished short story writer and journalist. An analysis is made of the subjects and themes of Morales' writings, and of his literary style.

16.68 Morales, Angel Luis. DOS ENSAYOS RUBENDARIANOS. Río Piedras, Biblioteca de Extramuros, Universidad de Puerto Rico, n.d. 50 p. bibl.

Contents: "La Angustia metafísica en la poesía de Rubén Darío," "El Cristianismo en la poesía de Rubén Darío."

16.69 Morfi, Angelina. ENRIQUE A. LAGUERRE Y SU OBRA 'LA RESACA', CUMBRE EN SU ARTE DE NOVELAR. San Juan, Instituto de Cultura Puertorriqueña, 1964. 194 p. bibl.

Stylistic analysis of La Resaca which includes a survey of Enrique Laguerre's (1906–) literary production. The author's M.A. thesis for the University of Puerto Rico.

16.70 Morfi, Angelina. TEMAS DEL TEATRO. Santo Domingo, R.D., Editora del Caribe C. por A., 1969. 123 p.

Collection of essays and reviews which includes "Alejandro Tapia y La Cuarterona," "La resentida de Enrique A. Laguerre," "El apartamiento," "Nueva ruta en el teatro de René M. Marqués," Arriví's "Coctel de Don Nadie," and Piri Fernández' "Un grito en el tiempo." The book also deals with contemporary theater by Bertol Brecht, Eugene Ionesco, Emmanuel Roblés, J.B. Priestley, Tennessee Williams, and others.

16.71 Nolasco, Sócrates. ESCRITORES DE PUERTO RICO. Prólogo de Luis Muñoz Marín. Manzanillo, Cuba, Editorial El Arte, 1953. 232 p.

Contents: Nemesio R. Canales, Antonio Pérez Pierret, Miguel Guerra Mondragón, Luis Lloréns Torres.

The author was a friend of Nemesio Canales (1878–1923), and has written a study in which he explores Canales' relations with other writers of his times.

16.72 Onís, Federico de. LUIS PALES MATOS: VIDA Y OBRA, BIBLIOGRA-FIA, ANTOLOGIA. Santa Clara, Cuba, Instituto de Estudios Hispánicos, Universidad Central de las Villas, 1959. 85 p. illus., ports., bibl. (Autores Cubanos y del Caribe, 1).

Bio-critical essay of one of Puerto Rico's best-known poets. It includes an extensive bibliography of works by and about Palés, plus a selection of his poems.

16.73 Orama Padilla, Carlos. VIRGILIO DA-VILA, SU VIDA Y SU OBRA. 2. ed. San Juan, Editorial Cordillera, 1963, c1964. 179 p.

Biographical study of Virgilio Dávila (1869–1943), his life and his poetry, emphasizing Dávila's devotion to his land and countrymen.

16.74 Pasarell, Emilio Julio. ORIGENES Y DESARROLLO DE LA AFICION TEA-TRAL EN PUERTO RICO. Río Piedras, Editorial Universitaria, Universidad de Puerto Rico, 1951. 393 p. illus., facsims., ports., bibl.

This book describes theatrical companies, societies, playwrights, and personalities which contributed to the development of the Puerto Rican theater of the nineteenth century. The author includes the plays staged, the dates and casts, and criticism on them.

16.75 Pedreira, Antonio S. ACLARACIONES Y CRITICA. Río Piedras, P.R., Editorial Edil, 1969. 207 p. (*His* Obras Completas, v. 6).

Collection of articles and essays on literary criticism about authors and their works from 1930 to 1935.

16.76 PRIMICIAS DE LAS LETRAS PUER-TORRIQUEÑAS. San Juan, Instituto de Cultura Puertorriqueña, 1970. 516 p.

Brings together the trilogy of works that mark the beginnings of Puerto Rican literature: *Aguinaldo Puertorriqueño* (1843), *Album Puertorriqueño* (1844), and *El Cancionero de Borinquen* (1846). This new edition uses modern spelling.

16.77 Quiles de la Luz, Lillian. EL CUENTO EN LA LITERATURA PUERTORRI-QUEÑA. Río Piedras, Editorial Universidad de Puerto Rico, 1968. 293 p. bibl.

A study of Puerto Rican short stories since 1843, accompanied by an extensive bibliographic index by author and title.

16.78 Ramírez de Arellano, Diana. CA-MINOS DE LA CREACION POETICA EN PEDRO SALINAS. Madrid, Ediciones J. Romo Arreguí, 1956. 205 p. illus. (Biblioteca Aristarco de erudición y crítica).

Valuable study and analysis of the Spanish poet, author of *El Contemplado*, which was inspired by the Puerto Rican seas. The author examines the poem, *La voz a ti debida*, and the creative process as seen in the first manuscript version.

16.79 Ramos Mimoso, Adriana. VIDA Y POESIA DE JOSE ANTONIO DAVILA. Madrid, Ediciones Cultura Hispánica, 1958. 369 p. bibl.

Study on the poet José Antonio Dávila (1898-1941) in which the author analyzes his style, themes and poetic resources. A thesis submitted to the University of Madrid, 1953.

16.80 REVISTA DEL INSTITUTO DE CUL-TURA PUERTORRIQUEÑA. San Juan, v. 9, núm. 31, abr./jun. 1966.

Issue devoted to José de Diego on the centennial of his birth. Includes poetry and prose selections and articles by Concha Meléndez, Joaquín Freyre, Luis Hernández Aquino, José Emilio González, Evaristo Ribera Chevremont, Margot Arce de Vázquez, and Luis M. Rodríguez Morales.

16.81 Reyes García, Ismael. FRANCISCO MARIANO QUIÑONES: VIDA Y OBRA. San Juan, Editorial Coquí, 1963. 128 p. port., bibl.

Study on the times, life and works of Francisco Mariano Quiñones (1830–1908), author of essays and historical novels of the Romantic period. Thesis for the M.A. degree at the University of Puerto Rico.

16.82 Rivera, Modesto. MANUEL A. ALONSO: SU VIDA Y SU OBRA. San

Juan, Editorial Coquí, 1966. 144 p. bibl. (Ediciones Borinquen).

A biographical study of Manuel Alonso (1822–1889), who distinguished himself as a chronicler of Puerto Rico's traditions and the social scene in the island during the 19th century. Originally the author's M.A. thesis, University of Puerto Rico.

16.83 Rivera de Alvarez, Josefina. DICCIONARIO DE LITERATURA PUERTORRIQUEÑA. 2. ed. revisada y aumentada y puesta al día hasta 1967. San Juan, Instituto de Cultura Puertorriqueña, 1970. v. 1. 578 p.

The author presents a valuable historical survey of Puerto Rican literature from the sixteenth century to the present including authors, publications, movements, institutions, and activities related to literary endeavor. Biographical data, critical analysis, and bibliography are given for each author.

16.84 Rivera de Alvarez, Josefina. HISTORIA DE LA LITERATURA PUERTORRIQUEÑA. Santurce, P.R., Editorial del Departamento de Instrucción Pública, 1969. 2 v. (120, 198 p.) illus., bibl.

A comprehensive history of Puerto Rican literature written for use in the island's high schools. Volume one covers from the beginnings in the sixteenth century to the modernist period, 1911–1921. The second volume studies from the vanguard movement, 1920–1930, up to 1967.

16.85 Rivera Rivera, Eloísa. LA POESIA EN PUERTO RICO ANTES DE 1843. Prólogo de Concha Meléndez. San Juan, Instituto de Cultura Puertorriqueña, 1965. 316 p. bibl.

The bulk of this work is a study of Puerto Rican poetry during the first four decades of the nineteenth century. Also included are monographs on the literary expressions of the sixteenth through the eighteenth centuries.

16.86 Rodríguez Escudero, Néstor A. EL MAR EN LA LITERATURA PUERTORRIQUEÑA Y OTROS ENSAYOS. Barcelona, Ediciones Rumbos, 1967. 239 p. bibl.

The first part of this book is devoted to the sea as a literary theme in the works of about eighty Puerto Rican writers. The second and third parts consist of a collection of essays, articles, and book reviews on Puerto Rican and world literature.

16.87 Rodríguez Velázquez, Jaime Luis. LA POESIA DEL ROMANTICISMO AL MODERNISMO EN PUERTO RICO. México, Universidad Nacional Autónoma de México, 1965. 149 p. bibl.

The author's doctoral dissertation at the Universidad Nacional Autónoma de México, this is a comparative study of the romantic and the modernist movements in Puerto Rico's poetry in relation to the poetic trends in Latin America. The author refutes the thesis that these two literary movements reached the island belatedly.

16.88 Rosa-Nieves, Cesáreo. FRANCISCO DE AYERRA SANTA MARIA: POETA PUERTORRIQUEÑO, 1630–1708. San Juan, Editorial Universitaria, Universidad de Puerto Rico, 1963. 30 p. bibl. (Cuadernos de la Universidad de Puerto Rico, Departamento de Estudios Hispánicos, 3).

Monograph on a forgotten Puerto Rican priest, Francisco Ayerra de Santa María (1630–1708), who lived in Mexico during the seventeenth century. Some of his poems are included, as are an excerpt about Alonso Ramírez and relevant documents.

16.89 Rosa-Nieves, Cesáreo. HISTORIA PANORAMICA DE LA LITERATURA PUERTORRIQUEÑA (1589–1959). San Juan, Editorial Campos, 1963. 2 v. (754, 996 p.) ports., illus., bibl.

The first volume of this exhaustive history covers the period from 1589 to 1898, further subdivided into part one, 1589 to the advent of the printing press in Puerto Rico; part two, 1806 to 1898. Volume two covers from 1898 to 1959. The work is arranged chronologically according to esthetic movements or "generations." Each period is introduced by a study of that epoch so that the reader acquires not only a survey of Puerto Rico's literary development, but of its cultural history as well.

16.90   Rosa-Nieves, Cesáreo. PLUMAS ES-
TELARES EN LAS LETRAS DE PUERTO
RICO. San Juan, Ediciones de la Torre,
Universidad de Puerto Rico, 1967–
1971. 2 v. (632, 518 p.) photos., bibl.

Critical biographies of Puerto Rican
writers, with a bibliography of works
by and about each one. An introduction to volume 1, which covers
the nineteenth century, discusses the
origins of Puerto Rican literature and
the development of romanticism and
parnasianism. The introduction to volume 2 discusses modernism and post-
modernism.

16.91   Rosa-Nieves, Cesáreo. LA POESIA EN
PUERTO RICO: HISTORIA DE LOS
TEMAS POETICOS EN LA LITERA-
TURA PUERTORRIQUEÑA. 3. ed.
San Juan, Editorial Edil, 1969. 301 p.
bibl.

Survey of the origins and development of the various poetic generations in Puerto Rico, with an analysis
of their recurrent themes and excerpts from the works. The author ap-
pends an alphabetical list of pseudonyms used by Puerto Rican poets.

16.92   Rosario, Rubén del. EL ENDECASI-
LABO ESPAÑOL. San Juan, Junta Editora, Universidad de Puerto Rico,
1944. 116 p. bibl.

This book surveys the Spanish use
of the eleven-syllable verse, its development as a means of literary expression, and its meter, intonation,
and cadence.

16.93   Sáez, Antonia. EL TEATRO EN
PUERTO RICO (NOTAS PARA SU
HISTORIA). Río Piedras, Editorial Universitaria, Universidad de Puerto Rico,
1950. 185 p. bibl. (Cuadernos de la
Universidad de Puerto Rico, Departamento de Estudios Hispanicos, 5).

The author describes in what was
his M.A. thesis to the University of
Puerto Rico, 1930, the origins of
Puerto Rican theater in the last half of
the nineteenth century, starting with
the work of Alejandro Tapia y Rivera.
She traces its development as regional
drama with historical, political, and
social background. A brief appendix
covers the period 1930–1948.

16.94   Sales, María de. EL SENTIMIENTO
RELIGIOSO EN LA LIRICA PUER-
TORRIQUEÑA. Cuernavaca,
México, Centro Intercultural de
Documentación, 1966. 216 p. bibl.
(Sondeos, no. 15).

This study surveys the religious
themes and motifs in Puerto Rican poetry, offering examples of the presence of biblical references, allusions
to God, Christ, Mary, and the saints.
The author's M.A. thesis, University of
Puerto Rico, 1964.

16.95   Sánchez Boudy, José. LAS NOVELAS
DE CESAR ANDREU IGLESIAS Y LA
PROBLEMATICA PUERTORRIQUEÑA
ACTUAL. Barcelona, Bosch, Casa Edi-
torial, 1968. 97 p. bibl.

Brief study, with a distinct political
orientation, of the novels *Los derrotados, El derrumbe,* and *Una gota de
tiempo.* The emphasis is on the plot as
it relates to social theses and the island's political situation.

16.96   Siaca Rivera, Manuel. JOSE P.H. HER-
NANDEZ: VIDA Y OBRA. San Juan,
Editorial Coquí, 1965. 127 p. port., bibl.
(Ediciones Borinquen).

A comprehensive study, originally a
thesis for the author's M.A. at the University of Puerto Rico, 1951, of the life
and works of the poet José P.H.
Hernández (1892–1922), with emphasis on his style and main themes—
love, nature, and death.

16.97   Sierra Berdecía, Fernando. ANTONIO
S. PEDREIRA, BUCEADOR DE LA PER-
SONALIDAD PUERTORRIQUEÑA. 2.
ed. rev. San Juan, Biblioteca de Autores Puertorriqueños, 1942. 55 p.

An essay written shortly after Pedreira's (1899–1939) death stressing his
feelings for Puerto Rico, as expressed
in his literary works.

16.98   Silva, Ana Margarita. EL JIBARO EN LA
LITERATURA DE PUERTO RICO
(COMPARADO CON EL CAMPESINO
DE ESPAÑA E HISPANOAMERICA). 2.
ed. corregida y aumentada. Prólogo
de Miguel Meléndez Muñoz. San
Juan, Imprenta Venezuela, 1957. 165 p.
bibl.

The author examines the Puerto Rican *jíbaro*—his origins, language, culture, traditions—and compares him to

the Spanish and Latin-American peasant. The second part deals with the regional literature and its principal writers, in particular Virgilio Dávila.

16.99 Silva, Ana Margarita. MARIANO ABRIL Y OSTALO: SU VIDA Y SU OBRA, (1861–1935). San Juan, Editorial Club de la Prensa, 1966. 174 p. bibl.

A biography of Mariano Abril y Ostaló (1861–1935), a writer and patriot who staunchly defended the principles of liberty and sovereignty for his country. It quotes extensively from his writings.

16.100 Soto, Venus Lidia. EL ARTE DE NOVELAR EN 'GARDUÑA' DE MANUEL ZENO GANDIA. Prólogo por Margot Arce de Vázquez. San Juan, Editorial del Departamento de Instrucción Pública, 1967. 112 p. port., bibl.

Critical analysis of the realist-naturalist work, Garduña, first of the series Crónicas de un Mundo Enfermo. This book also gives historical and biographical data about Zeno Gandía and the social conditions around the 1890's. Originally an M.A. thesis, University of Puerto Rico.

16.101 EL TEMA DEL CAFE EN LA LITERATURA PUERTORRIQUEÑA. Introducción y selección por Ricardo E. Alegría. San Juan, Instituto de Cultura Puertorriqueña, 1965. 67 p. illus., bibl.

Deluxe edition illustrated by Carlos Marichal on the presence and praises of Puerto Rican coffee as a literary theme and traditional symbol. Includes works by Manuel Zeno Gandía, Ernesto Juan Fonfrías, Tomás Blanco, Juan Antonio Corretjer, Washington Lloréns, Virgilio Dávila, Ferdinand R. Cestero, Francisco Manrique Cabrera, José S. Alegría, Luis Lloréns Torres, Obdulio Bauzá, Trina Padilla de Sanz, Cesáreo Rosa-Nieves, Enrique Laguerre, Gustavo Palés Matos, José Julián Acosta, and Antonio Oliver Frau.

16.102 Tollinchi, Esteban. DEMONIO, ARTE Y CONCIENCIA: DOKTOR FAUSTUS DE THOMAS MANN. Montevideo, Uruguay, Arca, [1970]. 292 p. bibl. (Colección Ensayo y Testimonio).

A study on the German novelist's work, Doktor Faustus. The author, a Puerto Rican, includes his translation of key chapters, as well as his critical comments on them.

16.103 Vientós Gastón, Nilita. INTRODUCCION A HENRY JAMES. [Río Piedras], Ediciones de La Torre, Universidad de Puerto Rico, 1956. 98 p. bibl.

Study of Henry James' work, especially The Ambassadors. The analysis includes an interesting comparison of James and Ortega y Gasset.

Essays

16.104 Alonso, Manuel A. EL JIBARO: CUADRO DE COSTUMBRES DE LA ISLA DE PUERTO RICO. San Juan, Instituto de Cultura Puertorriqueña, 1970. illus. (Serie Biblioteca Popular).

First published as El Gibaro in Barcelona in 1849, this is the first book by a Puerto Rican author using Puerto Rico as its theme. This marks Alonso as the father of Puerto Rican literature. The work consists of a series of essays that describe the social life and customs, politics, and literary scene of the early part of the nineteenth century.

16.105 Arce de Vázquez, Margot. IMPRESIONES: NOTAS PUERTORRI-

QUEÑAS (ENSAYOS). Prólogo de Cesáreo Rosa-Nieves. San Juan, Editorial Yaurel, 1950. 148 p. (Colección Yaurel).

The author presents a group of essays on literature and literary figures. Among them are Eugenio María de Hostos, Antonio S. Pedreira, María Cadilla de Martínez, Luis Palés Matos, Luis Lloréns Torres, and Eugenio Rentas Lucas.

16.106 Arriví, Francisco. ENTRADA POR LAS RAICES: ENTRAÑAMIENTO EN PROSA. San Juan, 1964. 224 p. (Serie La Entraña).

Collection of articles and essays written between 1940 and 1961 on varied topics. The book's title is based on the essay on Enrique A. Laguerre's novel, *La Ceiba en el Tiesto*.

16.107 Babín, María Teresa. FANTASIA BO-RICUA: ESTAMPAS DE MI TIERRA. Decoraciones de Esteban Vicente. San Juan, Instituto de Cultura Puertorriqueña, 1966. 170 p. illus.

Nostalgic, lyric sketches elaborating on the author's memories and experiences in Puerto Rico as a child and a young woman.

16.108 Balseiro, José A. EL VIGIA: EN-SAYOS. Madrid, Editorial Mundo Latino, 1925–1942. 3 v. (301, 394, 138 p.).

Contents. v. 1, El Poeta y la Vida; "Don Juan Tenorio" y "Don Luis Mejía;" Ruben Darío y El Porvenir; Gautier Benítez y el Espíritu de su Epoca; Algo Acerca del Nacionalismo Musical Francés; Shakespeare y los Músicos; Juan Morel Campos y la Danza Portorriqueña. v. 2, Miguel de Unamuno, Novelista y "Nivolista"; Ramón Pérez de Ayala, Novelista; A. Hernández-Catá y el Sentido Trágico del Arte y de la Vida. v. 3, En Torno al Romanticismo; Notas Acerca de Gustavo Adolfo Becquer—Evocación de Emerson; Crítica y Estilo Literarios en De Hostos; Azorín (José Martínez Ruiz).

16.109 Balseiro, José Agustín. THE AMERI-CAS LOOK AT EACH OTHER. Translated by Muna Lee. Coral Gables, Fla., University of Miami Press, 1969. 256 p. bibl. refs. (University of Miami Hispanic-American Studies Series, no. 21).

Essays of literary criticism selected from two of the author's works: *Expresión de Hispanoamérica*, and *Seis estudios de Rubén Darío*. Contents: Lord Byron's South American Dream and the Greatness of Simón Bolivar; Rubén Darío and the United States; Some Political Trends in the Literature of Hispanic America; Eugenio María de Hostos, A Public Servant of the Americas; The Sense of Justice in José Martí; The Immortal Message of Andrés Bello; Luis Muñoz Rivera, Civil Poet of Puerto Rico; My Memories of Alfonso Reyes, Mexican Savant; Gabriela Mistral; Hector Villa-Lobos, the Man and His Music; The Pampa, the Horse and the Song.

16.110 Blanco, Tomás. LOS CINCO SEN-TIDOS: CUADERNO SUELTO DE UN INVENTARIO DE COSAS NUESTRAS. Con decoraciones de Irene Delano. 2. ed. San Juan, Instituto de Cultura Puertorriqueña, 1968. 77 p. illus. (Serie Biblioteca Popular).

As the title implies, *The Five Senses: A Looseleaf Inventory of Things that Are Ours*, are lyrical essays which capture images: the sight of the *guajana*, the song of the *coquí*, the aroma of freshly brewed coffee, the taste of Puerto Rican fruits, and the feel of the breeze.

16.111 Brau, Salvador. ECOS DE LA BATALLA. Prólogo-semblanza de Manuel Fernández Juncos. Puerto Rico, Impr. y Librería de J. González Font, 1886. 282 p.

A compilation of some of Brau's newspaper articles, grouped according to subject. Some of the articles are biographical; others are polemical; a few deal with the social and political history of the island as well as with the character of its people.

16.112 Canales, Nemesio. PALIQUES. 5. ed. San Juan, Editorial Coquí, 1968. 253 p.

This collection of satiric articles was first published in 1915. Reading them now reveals the timelessness of the issues.

16.113 Comisión pro celebración del centenario del natalicio de Eugenio María de Hostos. THE LIMA RESOLUTION, THE ESSAY ON HAMLET, AND OTHER PAPERS . . . . Cambridge, Mass., Harvard University Press, 1940. 117 p. front. (port.) (*Its* Bulletin no. 12).

At head of title: De Hostos Centenary Commission, San Juan, Puerto Rico.

Essay on *Hamlet* translated from the Spanish by Marietta Dodge Howland and Guillermo Rivera, p. 73–117.

16.114 Dávila, José Antonio. PROSA-ENSAYOS-ARTICULOS Y CARTAS LITERARIAS. Selección, notas, y prólogo de Vicente Géigel Polanco. San Juan, Sociedad de Autores Puertorriqueños, 1971. 286 p. port., bibl.

This collection of nonfiction prose of the poet José Antonio Dávila includes writings on literary criticism, civilization and culture, and stylistics.

16.115   Ferrer Canales, José. ACENTOS CI-VICOS: MARTI, PUERTO RICO Y OTROS TEMAS. Río Piedras, Editorial Edil, 1972. 350 p.

A collection of essays on Puerto Rico, Latin America, and the United States. Those pertaining to Puerto Rico include: Martí y Puerto Rico; Huellas de José de Diego; Margot Arce y Gabriela Mistral; El Ejemplo de Albizu Campos; Apunte sobre Concepción de Gracia; Por Nuestra Lengua y Nuestra Soberanía.

16.116   Fonfrías, Ernesto Juan. JUAN ES SU NOMBRE—ALGUNAS COSAS DEL ESPIRITU: ENSAYOS. San Juan, Editorial Club de la Prensa, 1969. 148 p. illus.

Seven historical essays, mostly on interpretation of the discovery of America, biblical passages, and Puerto Rican customs.

16.117   Fonfrías, Ernesto Juan. SEMENTERA: ENSAYOS BREVES Y BIOGRAFIAS MINIMAS. Prólogo de Francisco Guillén Salaya. San Juan, Editorial Club de la Prensa, 1962. 147 p. ports. (Publicaciones de Obras de Autores Puertorriqueños).

Collection of brief articles and essays on the arts, especially literature and authors. The book includes sketches of Ramón Emeterio Betances, Segundo Ruiz Belvis, Manuel Corchado y Juarbe, Luis Muñoz Rivera, Trina Padilla de Sanz, and Antonio R. Barceló.

16.118   Fonfrías, Ernesto Juan. TINTILLO BRAVO DEL QUEHACER PUERTORRIQUEÑO. San Juan, Editorial Club de la Prensa, 1968. 183 p. bibl. refs.

This book consists of essays and articles on a variety of topics—music, literature, language, history, and civilization. Among the sketches of prominent people are those of Rafael Hernández, Santiago Iglesias Pantín, and Rosendo Matienzo Cintrón.

16.119   Guevara Castañeira, Josefina. VOCES DE HISPANOAMERICA (ENSAYOS). Puerto Rico, 1969. 170 p.

Collection of essays on Latin America, some of them published in the author's previous works—Del Yunque a los Andes and Nuestra América—about Hispanic American literary criticism.

16.120   Lloréns Torres, Luis. "América; Estudios Históricos y Filológicos." In his OBRAS COMPLETAS. San Juan, Instituto de Cultura Puertorriqueña, 1967-1969. v. 2. 348 p. bibl.

Contents. Las Antillas; Descripción de la isla de Puerto Rico; Los héroes del descubrimiento; Primer viaje de Colón; Martín Alonso Pinzón y el descrubrimiento de Puerto Rico; Nombre indiano de esta isla; Estudios filológicos; Bibliografía.

See also, in Poetry section, his Obras Completas.

16.121   Lloréns Torres, Luis. "Artículos de Periódicos y Revistas." In his OBRAS COMPLETAS. San Juan, Instituto de Cultura Puertorriqueña, 1967–1969. v. 3. 620 p.

See, in Poetry section, his Obras Completas.

16.122   Lluch Mora, Francisco. MIRADERO: ENSAYOS DE CRITICA LITERARIA. San Juan, Editorial Cordillera, 1966. 260 p. (Colección Picachos).

A series of brief essays and reviews under two main headings—literary commentary and studies on poetry. It includes reviews on M. Alvarez Nazario's books, and comments on Eugenio María de Hostos, M. Zeno Gandía, Antonio S. Pedreira, and Abelardo Díaz Alfaro. The author examines the poetry of Evaristo Ribera Chevremont, Luis Palés Matos, Manuel Joglar Cacho, Ana Inés Bonnin Armstrong, Carmen Puigdollers, Ramón Zapata Acosta, Josemilio González, José C. Negroni and Cesáreo Rosa-Nieves.

16.123   Marqués, René. ENSAYOS, (1953–1966). 2. ed. revisada y aumentada. Río Piedras, P.R., Editorial Antillana, 1966. 243 p.

Collection of ten essays revolving

around the author's concern for the Puerto Rican people and his country's destiny in relation to the developments of the past three decades. The book includes, among others, Un personaje del folklore y un tema puertorriqueño de farsa; Pesimismo literario y optimismo político: su coexistencia en el Puerto Rico actual; El puertorriqueño dócil (literatura y realidad psicológica).

16.124   Marrero, Domingo. EL CENTAURO: PERSONA Y PENSAMIENTO DE ORTEGA Y GASSET. Santurce, P.R., Imprenta Soltero, 1951. 305 p. bibl.
This book consists of three essays on the life, personality, and philosophy of José Ortega y Gasset. The first essay, Ortega o El Centauro, studies aspects of his personality. Contorno del Centauro discusses his education and intellectual and cultural growth, and El Centauro Ante el Altar analyzes his religious thought.

16.125   Meléndez, Concha. PALABRAS PARA OYENTES. San Juan, Editorial Cordillera, 1971. 206 p.

16.126   Meléndez, Concha. OBRAS COMPLETAS. San Juan, Instituto de Cultura Puertorriqueña, 1970. 2 v. (596, 691 p.) bibl.
Contents. v. 1, Amado Nervo; La novela indianista en Hispanoamérica (1832–1889); Signos de Iberoamérica; Entrada en el Perú. v. 2. Asomante; La inquietud sosegada; Figuración de Puerto Rico; José de Diego en mi memoria.
Essays and studies of literary criticism on diverse topics written by an outstanding professor and critic.

16.127   Meléndez Muñoz, Miguel. ALGUNOS ENSAYOS. San Juan, Editorial Club de la Prensa, 1958. 214 p.
Contents. Jibaridad o afirmación puertorriqueña o bilingüismo; En torno del Rueda; En torno a nuestra lengua; El tiempo y la cultura; Por el fomento de nuestro gusto artístico; Un proceso de nuestra cultura; El jíbaro canta. El hogar y el niño campesinos; Artesanía, industrialización y maquinismo; Solidaridad social; La fuerza social política de las asociaciones; El sitio de los ingleses;

Apuntes sobre la criminalidad en Puerto Rico; Apuntes sobre los sucesivos descubrimientos de Puerto Rico.
Essays written in 1948 about diverse topics dealing with Puerto Rican culture and civilization.

16.128   Meléndez Muñoz, Miguel. LECTURAS PUERTORRIQUEÑAS. 4. ed. San Juan, Editorial Campos, 1959. 151 p.
Contents: Desde la revuelta de la guásima. Desde una orilla de nuestra vida; Añoranzas.
Lyrical essays on Puerto Rico, its landscape, typical objects, and people.

16.129   Morales Carrión, Arturo. OJEADA AL PROCESO HISTORICO Y OTROS ENSAYOS. San Juan, Editorial Cordillera, 1971. 189 p. bibl. refs. (Colección Cordillera).
A series of historical essays intended "to explain before my own conscience and my personal understanding of history, the sense of our evolution as a people." Besides the main essay from which the book's title is taken, other selections touch on historical figures—Manuel Elzaburu, Rosendo Matienzo Cintrón, and Luis Muñoz Rivera, literary criticism, language, and other subjects.

16.130   Muñoz Rivera, Luis. OBRAS COMPLETAS. Introducción, notas, y recopilación de Lidio Cruz Monclova. San Juan, Instituto de Cultura Puertorriqueña, 1968 + 8 v.
Contents. v. 1, Febrero–diciembre, 1889–1890. v. 2, Enero–diciembre, 1892. v. 3, Enero–diciembre, 1893. v. 4, Enero–diciembre, 1894. v. 5, Enero-agosto, 1895. v. 6, Septiembre-diciembre, 1895. v. 7, Enero-septiembre, 1896. v. 8, Febrero-diciembre, 1897.
A collection of this statesman's articles, essays and writings in prose.

16.131   Pasarell, Emilio J. ENSAYOS Y ARTICULOS. San Juan, Editorial Cordillera, 1968. 217 p.
The book is divided into two parts: essays on general topics and brief articles on the arts and literature.

16.132 Pedreira, Antonio S. ARISTAS: EN-SAYOS. Río Piedras, P.R., Editorial Edil, 1969. 175 p. (*His* Obras Completas, v. 1).

This collection is preceded by "Pedreira: Autorretrato en su Autocrítica," a study by Concha Meléndez of Pedreira's reflection on his prologues.

This collection of essays on diverse themes includes: La generación del 98; Ensayo cromático; Los amores de Don Quijote; En torno a Henrik Ibsen; De los nombres de Puerto Rico; ¿Portorriqueño o Puertorriqueño?

16.133 Pedreira, Antonio S. TRES ENSAYOS. Río Piedras, P.R., Editorial Edil, 1969. 107 p. bibl. refs. (*His* Obras Completas, v. 7).

Contents. La actualidad del Jíbaro; Curiosidades Literarias de Puerto Rico; De los Nombres de Puerto Rico.

Collection of essays written in the 1930s. One of them deals with the development of the *jíbaro* as a literary and scientific theme, another is based on little-known literary facts, and the third is a study on the various names given to the island.

16.134 Pedreira, Antonio Salvador. OBRAS COMPLETAS. San Juan, Instituto de Cultura Puertorriqueña, 1969. 2 v. (749, 718 p.).

Contents. v. 1, Insularismo; El Año Terrible del 87; Aristas; Aclaraciones y crítica; Tres ensayos. v. 2, El periodismo en Puerto Rico; Hostos, ciudadano de América.

16.135 Quiñones, Samuel R. TEMAS Y LETRAS. San Juan, Biblioteca de Autores Puertorriqueños, 1941. 213 p.

Book of fifteen short essays on literature, some of them devoted to Puerto Rican writers such as Manuel Zeno Gandía, Antonio S. Pedreira, Alfredo Collado Martell, Eugenio Astol, and Nemesio R. Canales.

16.136 Robles de Cardona, Mariana. BUSQUEDA Y PLASMACION DE NUESTRA PERSONALIDAD: ANTOLOGIA CRITICA DEL ENSAYO PUERTORRIQUEÑO DESDE SUS ORIGENES HASTA LA GENERACION DEL 30. San Juan, Editorial Club de la Prensa. 1958. 415 p. bibl.

Anthology of the essay in Puerto Rico from the mid-nineteenth century to the generation of the 1930s, useful for the study of Puerto Rican culture and character. Thirty writers are represented and each essay is preceded by a bio-critical sketch and a bibliography of its author.

16.137 Rodríguez, Rafael, and Iris Zavala, eds. LIBERTAD Y CRITICA: ANTOLOGIA DEL ENSAYO PUERTORRIQUEÑO. San Juan, Ediciones Librería Internacional, 1972.

n.a.

16.138 Rodríguez Morales, Luis M. ENSAYOS Y CONFERENCIAS. Barcelona, Ediciones Rumbos, 1962. 157 p.

Collection of lectures and essays by the Director of the General Archives of Puerto Rico. Many of those included deal with public documents or are based on them.

16.139 Rosa-Nieves, Cesáreo. ENSAYOS ESCOGIDOS (APUNTACIONES DE CRITICA LITERARIA SOBRE ALGUNOS TEMAS PUERTORRIQUEÑOS). San Juan, 1970. 176 p. bibl. refs. (Publicaciones de la Academia de Artes y Ciencias de Puerto Rico, Cuaderno núm. 5).

Collection of critical essays on a broad range of subjects, some of which have been discussed at more length in other books by the author. The following are among the topics discussed: romanticism in Puerto Rican literature, life and works of Francisco Alvarez Marrero, José Gautier Benítez, Lola Rodríguez de Tío, Matías González García, Miguel Meléndez Muñoz, and Luis Palés Matos.

16.140 Rosa-Nieves, Cesáreo. LA LAMPARA DEL FARO: VARIACIONES CRITICAS SOBRE TEMAS PUERTORRIQUEÑOS. San Juan, Editorial Club de la Prensa, 1957–1960. 2 v. (244, 223 p.).

Contents. v. 1, La Danza Azul de Tres Razas; Hombres, Corazones y Libros. Aurora en los Orígenes. v. 2, Rumbos del Discurrir Literario; Lucha de Fronteras Estéticas; La Alabanza, la Diatriba, y la Guachafita Isleña; Criterios sobre la Forma; Ocios de Sol en el Telar Isleño; Coquí; Del Perfil Histórico: Quehaceres del Pasado.

Collection of essays on varied topics, especially literary criticism, poetry, music, and history.

16.141 Rosa-Nieves, Cesáreo. TIERRA Y LAMENTO: RODEOS DE CONTORNO PARA UNA TELURICA INTERPRETACION POETICA DE LO PUERTORRIQUEÑO. San Juan, Editorial Club de la Prensa, 1958. 134 p.

Interpretative essays on Puerto Rico's identity and spirit. Included are the following: Exposición general del tema; Algunas características generales de la literatura Puertorriqueña; Pedro Isla del Mar Verde; Consuma lo que la tierra produce; Por las veredas de nuestros libros.

16.142 Sáez, Antonia. CAMINOS DEL RECUERDO. Prólogo de Concha Meléndez. San Juan, Instituto de Cultura Puertorriqueña, 1967. 228 p.

Book of memories and evocation written by an educator who devoted her life to teaching and writing. Among her reminiscences are the withdrawal of Spanish troops from Humacao in 1898, old-fashioned ways of life, and her travels.

16.143 Soto Ramos, Julio. CUMBRE Y REMANSO: ENSAYOS DE APRECIATION LITERARIA Y OTROS ARTI-CULOS. San Juan, Editorial Cordillera, 1963. 147 p.

A collection of book reviews and critical essays on Puerto Rican writers.

16.144 Soto Ramos, Julio. UNA PICA EN FLANDES (ENSAYOS Y OTROS ARTICULOS). San Juan, Editorial Club de la Prensa, 1959. 197 p.

Essays and articles of literary criticism, personalities in the arts, and book reviews.

16.145 Torres León, Armando, comp. ENSAYOS EN TORNO A PUERTO RICO. Prólogo de José A. Torres Morales. San Juan, Editorial Departamento de Instrucción Pública, Estado Libre Asociado de Puerto Rico, 1968. 111 p. bibl., refs.

This book is a selection of essays by outstanding writers about Puerto Rico, and the reevaluation of life and its meaning in the island. Some of the essayists are Antonio S. Pedreira, Mariana Robles de Cardona, Eugenio María de Hostos, Manuel Alonso, Nemesio R. Canales, Néstor Rodríguez Escudero, Rubén del Rosario, Salvador Tió, Antonio J. Colorado, Miguel Meléndez Muñoz, Abelardo Díaz Alfaro, Nilita Vientós Gastón, Enrique A. Laguerre, Concha Meléndez, and Eugenio Fernández Méndez.

Fiction

16.146 Agostini de del Río, Amelia. VIÑETAS DE PUERTO RICO. Madrid, Alfaguara, 1965. 212 p.

Sketches and short stories of a sentimental nature, set in Puerto Rico. Also available as a talking book for the blind or physically handicapped.

16.147 Andréu Iglesias, César. EL DERRUMBE. México, Club del Libro de Puerto Rico, 1960. 297 p.

Portrays contemporary life in a small town in Puerto Rico.

16.148 Andréu Iglesias, César. LOS DERROTADOS. 2. ed. Río Piedras, P.R., Editorial Edil, 1964. 209 p.

16.149 Andréu Iglesias, César. UNA GOTA DE TIEMPO. San Juan, Editorial Puertorriqueña, Publicaciones de la Revista Polémica, 1958. 147 p.

A day in the lives of nine people and how each one sees things and acts upon them serves as the vehicle for exploring contemporary Puerto Rican society.

16.150 ANTOLOGIA DE CUENTOS PUERTORRIQUEÑOS. Prólogo y selección por Enrique A. Laguerre. México, Editorial Orión, 1954. 175 p. (Colección Literaria Cervantes).

A collection of twenty stories in which the regional costumbrista element is emphasized. It includes short story writers from varying periods—from Manuel Fernández Juncos, Cayetano Coll y Toste, and Matías González García, to José Luis González and Abelardo Díaz Alfaro. The selection could be used as a high school reader.

16.151 Arana Soto, Salvador. LA CAMISA VOLANTONA, Y OTROS CUENTOS POLITICOS. San Juan, Editorial Edil, 1965. 101 p.
    Contents. La camisa volantona; Juan Perdío; Republicano malo; Los cipayos; Ya veo, o, El hombre de pocas palabras; La Prera; Severo y Carola; Mucho ruido; De infierno a infierno; El Cuatro de Julio.

16.152 Arce de Vázquez, Margot, and Mariana Robles de Cardona. LECTURAS PUERTORRIQUEÑAS: PROSA. Sharon, Conn., Troutman Press, 1966. 424 p. bibl. (Puerto Rico: realidad y anhelo, 2).

16.153 Balseiro, José Agustín. LA GRATITUD HUMANA. Miami, Fla., Mnemosyne, 1969. 196 p.

16.154 Bauzá, Guillermo. VIDAS INCONCLUSAS: NOVELA DE AMBIENTE UNIVERSITARIO. Barcelona, Ediciones Rumbos, 1963. 153 p. illus.

16.155 Belaval, Emilio S. LOS CUENTOS DE LA UNIVERSIDAD. San Juan, Biblioteca de autores puertorriqueños, 1935. 190 p.

16.156 Belaval, Emilio S. CUENTOS PARA FOMENTAR EL TURISMO. Barcelona, Ediciones Rumbos, 1967. 114 p.
    Contents. La viuda del manto prieto; La candelaria de Juan Candelario; Tormenta platanera; Capataz buena persona, montado en caballo blanco; El niño morado de Monsona Quintana; Santigua de santigüero; Mantengo; María Teresa monta en calesa; Conversión de la maestrita rural Isabelita Primpín.

16.157 Blanco, Tomás. LOS AGUINALDOS DEL INFANTE: GLOSA DE EPIFANIA. Con ornamentos musicales de Jack Delano e ilustraciones por Irene Delano. THE CHILD'S GIFTS: A TWELFTH NIGHT TALE. Translated by Harriet de Onís, with musical arrangements by Jack Delano and illustrations by Irene Delano. San Juan, Pava Prints, 1962. 33 p. mounted col. illus., music. English and Spanish.

16.158 Blanco, Tomás. CUENTOS SIN TON NI SON. Prólogo de Margot Arce de Vázquez. San Juan, Instituto de Cultura Puertorriqueña, 1970. 195 p. (Serie Biblioteca Popular).

16.159 Blanco, Tomás. LOS VATES: EMBELECO FANTASTICO PARA NIÑOS MAYORES DE EDAD. San Juan, Asomante, 1949. 135 p.

16.160 Braschi, Wilfredo. METROPOLI. Prólogo de Concha Meléndez. San Juan, Ediciones Juan Ponce de León, 1968. 197 p.

16.161 Caballero, Pepita. BAJO EL VUELO DE LOS ALCATRACES. Madrid, Ediciones Ensayos, 1956. 490 p.

16.162 Cadilla de Martínez, María. HITOS DE LA RAZA (CUENTOS TRADICIONALES Y FOLKLORICOS). San Juan, Imprenta Venezuela, 1945. 136 p.
    A series of eleven short stories inspired by historical facts or true characters, such as the town barber.

16.163 Carreras, Carlos N. LUNA VERDE, Y OTROS CUENTOS. 1. ed. Barcelona, Ediciones Rumbos, 1958. 176 p.

16.164 Castellanos Velasco, Francisco. CUANDO LA CAÑA ES AMARGA: NOVELA. México, Editorial Diana, 1966. 311 p.

16.165 Collado Martell, Alfredo. CUENTOS ABSURDOS. San Juan, Librería y Editorial Campos, 1931. 244 p. (Colección de novelistas, poetas y ensayistas de America).

16.166 Cordero, Ricardo. GUERRA CIVIL GONZALEZ. San Juan, 1970. 350 p.

16.167 Cotto Thorner, Guillermo. TROPICO EN MANHATTAN. 2. ed. Prólogo de Mariano Picón Salas. Editorial Cordillera, 1967. 186 p.

16.168 EL CUENTO. Selección y estudio por Concha Meléndez. Notas bio-bibliográficas por Josefina del Toro. San Juan, Ediciones del Gobierno, 1957. 332 p. (Antología de Autores Puertorriqueños, 3).

A representative selection of short stories by twenty-eight island writers, with bio-bibliographic sketches. Useful as a text since it traces the development of the genre.

16.169 CUENTOS PUERTORRIQUEÑOS DE HOY. 3. ed. Selección, prólogo, y notas de René Marqués. Río Piedras, P.R., Editorial Cultural, 1971. 287 p. bibl.

Anthology with an introductory essay on the "generation of the forties," with bio-critical notes by René Marqués, and autobiographies of the authors included. It includes stories by the eight most representative writers of the generation of 1940: Abelardo Díaz Alfaro, José Luis González, René Marqués, Pedro Juan Soto, Edwin Figueroa, José Luis Vivas, Emilio Díaz Valcárcel, and Salvador M. de Jesús.

16.170 Díaz Alfaro, Abelardo. TERRAZO. Prólogo de Mariano Picón Salas. San Juan, Instituto de Cultura Puertorriqueña, 1967. 128 p. illus. Reprint of 1947 edition. (Serie Biblioteca Popular).

A collection of short stories inspired by what is native to Puerto Rico and its countryside. Such stories as "El Josco," "Bagazo," "Santa Clo va a la Cuchilla," "Peyo Mercé enseña inglés," have earned the author recognition as one of the leading short story writers in Puerto Rico and Latin America.

16.171 Díaz Montero, Aníbal. LA BRISA MUEVE LAS GUAJANAS. San Juan, 1968. 157 p.

16.172 Díaz Montero, Aníbal. HABLANDO CON ELLOS: ENTREVISTAS. 3. ed. Barcelona, Ediciones Rumbos, 1967. 107 p. illus.

Contents. El último carrero de San Juan; El último coquero de Santurce; La Nueva Esperanza; El único herrero que le queda a Santurce; "Colorado" el boyero; Un Viejo Cuidacarros; El picapedrero de Vega Alta; "Ponce," cuadrero del ayer; Don Tele el pescador.

16.173 Díaz Montero, Aníbal. UNA MUJER Y UNA SOTA. 2. ed. rev. San Juan, 1970. 187 p.

16.174 Díaz Montero, Aníbal. VEREDAS DE LA FINCA. San Juan, 1968. 114 p.

16.175 Díaz Nadal, Roberto. CONTRASTES, CUENTOS, AGUAFUERTES, CRONICAS. Prólogo de Manuel del Toro. San Juan, Editorial Yaurel, 1965. 96 p.

16.176 Díaz Valcárcel, Emilio. EL HOMBRE QUE TRABAJO EL LUNES. 1. ed. México, Era, 1966. 143 p.

Contents. El Hombre que trabajó el lunes; La culpa; María; El alcalde; Sol negro.

16.177 Díaz Valcárcel, Emilio. MUERE SALCEDO. Río Piedras, P.R., Editorial Cultural, in press.

16.178 Díaz Valcárcel, Emilio. PANORAMA. Río Piedras, P.R., Editorial Cultural, 1971. 288 p.

16.179 Díaz Valcárcel, Emilio. PROCESO EN DICIEMBRE. Madrid, Taurus Ediciones, 1963. 148 p. (Narraciones, 10).

Contents. Proceso en diciembre; El soldado Damián Sánchez; El asalto; Andrés; La sangre inútil; La evasión; El hijo; Los héroes; El regreso.

16.180 Diego Padró, José de. EN BABIA (EL MANUSCRITO DE UN BRAQUICEFALO). 2. ed. corr. México, 1961. 641 p.

16.181 Diego Padró, José de. UN CENCERRO DE DOS BADAJOS. San Juan, Ediciones Juan Ponce de León, 1969. 453 p.

Other novels by the author include Ocho Epístolas Mostrencas, (Madrid, 1952) and El Tiempo Jugó Conmigo (Barcelona, Ediciones Rumbos, 1960).

16.182 Durán, Ana Luisa. PROMETEO Y EL ESTRENO. México, B. Costa-Amic, 1969. 114 p.

Two short stories by a Puerto Rican

writer living in California. Both are set in the United States.

16.183 Figueroa, Edwin. SOBRE ESTE SUELO: NUEVE CUENTOS Y UNA LEYENDA. 2. ed. Río Piedras, P.R., Editorial Cultural, 1971. 94 p.

16.184 Fonfrías, Ernesto Juan. CONVERSAO EN EL BATEY: HISTORIA DE UN JI-BARO BRAGAO. 2. ed. San Juan, Editorial Club de la Prensa, 1958. 301 p. illus.

Other books by the author of stories inspired by the Puerto Rican *jíbaro* are *Guásima* (San Juan, Editorial Club de la Prensa, 1957) and *Una Voz en la Montaña* (San Juan, Editorial Club de la Prensa, 1958).

16.185 Fonfrías, Ernesto Juan. RAIZ Y ESPIGA. 3. ed. San Juan, Editorial Club de la Prensa, 1970. 293 p.

16.186 González, José Luis. LA GALERIA Y OTROS CUENTOS. México, Biblioteca Era, 1972. 144 p.

16.187 González, José Luis. EL HOMBRE EN LA CALLE. n.p., Editorial Bohique, 1948. 75 p.

16.188 González, José Luis. EN ESTE LADO. México, Los Presentes, 1954. 180 p. (Los Presentes, 12).

Contents. En el fondo del caño hay un negrito; La galería; El enemigo; Una caja de plomo que no se podía abrir; Santa Claus visita a Pichirilo Sánchez; El arbusto en llamas; El pasaje; Esta noche no; Breve historia de una hacha; En este lado; Vocabulario regional puertorriqueño.

16.189 González, José Luis. EN LA SOMBRA. San Juan, 1943. 110 p.

16.190 González, José Luis. PAISA, UN RELATO DE LA EMIGRACION. México, Fondo de Cultura Popular, 1950. 71 p.

16.191 González García, Matías. CARMELA. 3. ed. San Juan, Editorial Coquí, 1966. 122 p.

16.192 Hernández Aquino, Luis. LA MUERTE ANDUVO POR EL GUASIO. 2. ed. Santo Domingo, R.D., Editorial del Caribe, 1968. 188 p.

Socio-historical novel in which the landscape, language, folklore, and people of the island are used to describe the last days of Spanish rule in 1898 and the invasion of Puerto Rico by the United States.

16.193 Hostos, Eugenio María de. LA PEREGRINACION DE BAYOAN. San Juan, Instituto de Cultura Puertorriqueña, 1970. 319 p. (Serie Biblioteca Popular).

Allegorical political novel first published in 1863, in which the author writes against Spanish rule and in favor of liberty. The three main characters, Marion, Bayoán, and Guarionex, stand for the three Antilles—Cuba, Puerto Rico, and Santo Domingo.

16.194 Juvenal Rosa, Pedro. LAS MASAS MANDAN. Barcelona, Araluce, 1936. 336 p.

16.195 Laguerre, Enrique A. CAUCE SIN RIO: DIARIO DE MI GENERACION. Madrid, Nuevas Editoriales Unidas, 1962. 229 p. (Grandes novelistas de nuestro tiempo). Reprint. Río Piedras, P.R., Editorial Cultural, 1968. 194 p.

16.196 Laguerre, Enrique A. EL FUEGO Y SU AIRE. Buenos Aires, Editorial Losada, 1970. 289 p. (Novelistas de Nuestra Epoca).

16.197 Laguerre, Enrique A. THE LABYRINTH. Translated from the Spanish by William Rose. New York, Las Américas, 1960. 275 p.

16.198 Laguerre, Enrique A. OBRAS COMPLETAS. San Juan, Instituto de Cultura Puertorriqueña, 1962–1964. 3 v. (690, 624, 568 p.).

Contents. v. 1, Semblanza; Prólogo; La llamarada; Solar Montoya; El 30 de febrero; Vocabulario. v. 2, La resaca; Los dedos de la mano; La ceiba en el tiesto. v. 3, El laberinto; La Resentida; Pulso de Puerto Rico; Palabras finales.

16.199 Lloréns, Washington. CATORCE PECADOS DE HUMOR Y UNA VIDA DESCABELLADA. San Juan, Editorial Club de la Prensa, 1959. 167 p.

Humorous short stories on Puerto Rican life which show the author's preoccupation with linguistic topics.

16.200 López Ramírez, Tomás. CORDIAL MAGIA ENEMIGA. Río Piedras, P.R., Editorial Antillana, 1971. 117 p.

16.201 López Vázquez, José. ESA MUERTE EN CARNE VIVA. Prólogo de Abelardo Díaz Alfaro. Río Piedras, P.R., Editorial Edil, 1971. 704 p.

16.202 Marqués, René. EN UNA CIUDAD LLAMADA SAN JUAN. 3. ed. ampliada. Río Piedras, P.R., Editorial Cultural, 1970. 207 p.
    Collection of fifteen short stories written between 1948 and 1966 with San Juan as the general theme. It includes Tres hombres junto al rio; Purificación en la Calle del Cristo; Otro día nuestro; La chiringa azul; El juramento; El miedo; and others.

16.203 Marqués, René. OTRO DIA NUESTRO. Prólogo por Concha Meléndez. San Juan, Instituto de Cultura Puertorriqueña, 1955. 129 p.

16.204 Marqués, René. LA VISPERA DEL HOMBRE. 2. ed. Río Piedras, P.R., Editorial Cultural, 1970. 287 p.
    Symbolic novel in which the protagonist's life from childhood and adolescence to manhood parallels the maturing of Puerto Rico.

16.205 Manrique, Manuel. UNA ISLA EN HARLEM. Madrid, Ediciones Alfaguara, 1965. 298 p.

16.206 Meléndez, Concha. EL ARTE DEL CUENTO EN PUERTO RICO. New York, Las Américas, 1961. 395 p. bibl. refs. (Biblioteca puertorriqueña, 4) Reprint. San Juan, Editorial Cordillera.
    Critical anthology of the short story written by members of the generation of 1930—authors born between 1900 and 1910 and the generation of 1940—those born between 1911 and 1929. Includes bio-bibliographic studies of the authors and analyses of their works.

16.207 Meléndez, Concha. LITERATURA DE FICCION EN PUERTO RICO: CUENTO Y NOVELA. San Juan, Editorial Cordillera, 1971. 195 p. (Her Obras Completas, 13) (Colección Hispanoamericana).

16.208 Meléndez, Julio. EL TELAR DE LAS SOMBRAS. Vega Baja, P.R., Editorial Guarico, 1970. 103 p.
    He has also written La Carne Indócil (1964), his first book of short stories.

16.209 Meléndez, Julio. EL BUITRE Y LA CARROÑA. Vega Baja, P.R., Editorial Cibuco, 1969. 219 p.

16.210 Méndez Ballester, Manuel. ISLA CERRERA: NOVELA BASADA EN LA CONQUISTA DE PUERTO RICO. Barcelona, Imp. M. Pareja, 1970. First published in 1938.

16.211 Morales Cabrera, Pablo. CUENTOS. Con un estudio biográfico-crítico de Esther Melón Portalatín. Ed. especial. San Juan, Instituto de Cultura Puertorriqueña, 1966. 441 p. bibl.
    Contents: "Pablo Morales Cabrera: Vida y obra," por E. Melón Portalatín. 3. ed. "Cuentos populares" por P. Morales Cabrera. 8. ed. "Cuentos criollos." 3. ed.

16.212 Morales Otero, Pablo. CUENTOS Y LEYENDAS DEL TOA. San Juan, Biblioteca de Autores Puertorriqueños, 1968. 120 p.

16.213 Muñoz, Manuel. GUARIONEX, LA HISTORIA DE UN INDIO REBELDE, SIMBOLO HEROICO DE UN PUEBLO Y DE UNA RAZA. San Juan, 1962. 222 p.
    A historical novel about Guarionex, the Indian chief or cacique who organized and led the 1511 rebellion against the Spaniards.

16.214 Nazario, Luis Adam. MI VIDA ESTUDIANTIL EN NUEVA ORLEANS (NOVELA AUTOBIOGRAFICA). Río Piedras, P.R., Editorial Edil, 1971. 215 p. illus.

16.215 Oliver Frau, Antonio. CUENTOS Y LEYENDAS DEL CAFETAL. 2. ed. Con un estudio biográfico-crítico de Margarita Vázquez de Rivera. San Juan, Instituto de Cultura Puertorriqueña, 1967. 332 p. port., bibl.
    Antonio Oliver Frau (1902–1945) collected his literary production in one book, Stories and Legends from the Coffee Lands. The short stories are his creation, the legends are from the

oral tradition. Margarita Vázquez de Rivera introduces the collection with a lengthy study on Oliver Frau's life and works.

16.216 Padró Humberto. DIEZ CUENTOS. San Juan, Imprenta Venezuela, 1929. 64 p.

16.217 Ramos Otero, Manuel. CONCIERTO DE METAL PARA UN RECUERDO Y OTRAS ORGIAS DE SOLEDAD. Río Piedras, P.R., Editorial Cultural, 1971. 132 p.

16.218 Ribera Chevremont, Evaristo. EL NIÑO DE ARCILLA. San Juan, Biblioteca de Autores Puertorriqueños, 1950. 145 p.

16.219 Rodríguez Escudero, Néstor A. CUENTOS DEL MAR, Y OTRAS PAGINAS. San Juan, Impr. Venezuela, 1959. 188 p.

16.220 Rodríguez Pastor, José. HONORABLE A MEDIAS. 2. ed. corregida. San Juan, Editorial Cordillera, 1968. 406 p. (Colección El Yunque).

16.221 Rodríguez Torres, Carmelo. VEINTE SIGLOS DESPUES. 2. ed. Río Piedras, Ediciones Puerto, 1972. 109 p.

16.222 Rosa-Nieves, Cesáreo, and Félix Franco Oppenheimer. ANTOLOGIA DEL CUENTO PUERTORRIQUEÑO. 2. ed. San Juan, Editorial Edil, 1970. 2 v. (415, 442 p.) bibl.
   Comprehensive anthology of Puerto Rican short stories in which forty authors are represented. Each story is preceded by a critical sketch of the author. This book is a basic reference source on the short stories of Puerto Rico.

16.223 Sánchez, Luis Rafael. EN CUERPO DE CAMISA. 2. ed. Río Piedras, P.R., Editorial Cultural, 1971. 102 p.

16.224 Sanz Muñoz, Manuel. LOS MIL OTOÑOS Y UNA PRIMAVERA. Hato Rey, P.R., Imprenta El Sol, 1971. 124 p.

16.225 Sierra Berdecía, Fernando. AGUAFUERTE. San Juan, Editorial Coquí, 1963. 21 p.

16.226 Silva, Margarita. LOS AVENTUREROS DE LOS SIETE MARES. San Juan, Editorial Cordillera, 1971. 238 p. (Colección El Yunque).

16.227 Silvestri, Reinaldo R. ALGARETE. Mayagüez, P.R., 1971. 62 p.

16.228 Soto, Pedro Juan. ARDIENTE SUELO, FRIA ESTACION. Xalapa, México, Universidad Veracruzana, 1961. 258 p.
   With characteristic sensitivity Soto explores the feelings of an eighteen-year-old high school student who migrates to New York and finds himself rejected both there and on his return to Puerto Rico.

16.229 Soto, Pedro Juan. EL FRANCOTIRADOR. México, Joaquín Mortiz, 1969. 297 p. (Nueva narrativa hispánica).
   Novel on Puerto Rico's university and political life. The situation of the Cuban exile living on the island is also presented.

16.230 Soto, Pedro Juan. LA PALMA DEL CACIQUE. México, Editorial Orión, 1962. 154 p.

16.231 Soto, Pedro Juan. SPIKS. Grabados de Lorenzo Homar, Carlos Raquel Rivera y Rafael Tufiño, impresos directamente del original. 3. ed. Río Piedras, P.R., Editorial Cultural, 1970. 78 p.
   A collection of short stories about Puerto Ricans in New York.

16.232 Soto, Pedro Juan. TEMPORADA DE DUENDES. México, Editorial Diógenes, 1970. 234 p. (Escritores de lengua española).
   Baldomero Linares, the protagonist of this work, embodies the ills of contemporary Puerto Rican society. An assiduous moviegoer, he escapes into the world of fantasy, avoiding the dullness of his empty life and the issues facing the island. A film company comes to the village of Barrizales and confronts the two cultures.

16.233 Soto, Pedro Juan. USMAIL (NOVELA). San Juan, Club del Libro de Puerto Rico, 1959. 346 p. Reprint. Río Piedras, P.R., Editorial Cultural, 1970. 316 p.

Now classic novel on life on the island of Vieques, and the influence of American troops upon it. The life of the main character, Usmail, parallels the fortunes of the island.

16.234 Tapia y Rivera, Alejandro. OBRAS COMPLETAS: NOVELA. San Juan, Instituto de Cultura Puertorriqueña, 1968. v. 1.

Contents. Cofresí; La antigua sirena; Póstumo el transmigrado.

16.235 Tapia y Rivera, Alejandro. ENARDO AND ROSAEL: AN ALLEGORICAL NOVELLA. Translated from the Spanish by Alejandro Tapia, Jr., and others. New York, Philosophical Library, 1952. 56 p. illus.

16.236 Vizcarrondo, Carmelina. MINUTERO EN SOMBRAS (CUENTOS). San Juan, Imprenta Venezuela, 1941. 155 p.

16.237 Zeno Gandía, Manuel. CUENTOS. New York, Las Américas, 1958. 117 p. port.

16.238 Zeno Gandía, Manuel. OBRAS COMPLETAS. Río Piedras, Ediciones del Instituto de Literatura Puertorriqueña, Universidad de Puerto Rico, 1955–1958. 3 v. (250, 189, 485 p.) illus. (Ediciones del centenario del nacimiento de don Manuel Zeno Grandía).

Contents. v. 1, La charca (crónicas de un mundo enfermo). v. 2, Garduña. v. 3, El negocio (crónicas de un mundo enfermo).

Poetry

16.239 Alvarez Marrero, Francisco. ANTOLOGIA. Selección, notas, y prólogo de Cesáreo Rosa-Nieves. San Juan, Ateneo Puertorriqueño, 1965. 103 p. (Cuaderno de Poesía, 19).

16.240 ANTHOLOGY OF PUERTO RICAN POETRY IN NEW YORK. New York, Monthly Review Press, in press.

16.241 ANTOLOGIA DE JOVENES POETAS. San Juan, Instituto de Cultura Puertorriqueña, 1965. 96 p.

Anthology of the works of ten Puerto Rican poets born around 1940, most of which emphasize the theme of painful awareness of the Puerto Rican reality. The young poets represented are: José Manuel Torres Santiago, Wenceslao Serra Deliz, Marcos Rodríguez Frese, Vicente Rodríguez Nietzsche, Antonio Cabán Vale, Andrés Castro Ríos, Angela María Dávila, Juan Sáez Burgos, Edgardo López Ferrer, and Antonio Emilio Ornes.

16.242 ANTOLOGIA DE LA POESIA PUERTORRIQUEÑA. Selección, introducción, y edición por Eugenio Fernández Méndez. San Juan, Ediciones El Cemí, 1968. 172 p.

Selections of eighty representative poets, giving a comprehensive view of Puerto Rico's poetic development.

Bio-bibliographic notes are appended.

16.243 ANTOLOGIA POETICA DE ASOMANTE, 1945–1959. Introducción por Concha Meléndez. Selección y notas por Juan Martínez Capó. San Juan, Ateneo Puertorriqueño, 1962. 139 p. (Cuadernos de poesía, 14).

Anthology of poems by thirty-six Puerto Rican writers published in Asomante between 1945 and 1959. Bio-bibliographic notes on the authors are appended.

16.244 Arce de Vázquez, Margot, Laura Gallego, and Luis de Arrigoitía. LECTURAS PUERTORRIQUEÑAS: POESIA. Sharon, Conn., Troutman Press, 1968. 445 p. bibl. (Puerto Rico: realidad y anhelo, 10).

Excellent selection of Puerto Rican poetry accompanied by critical analysis and bio-bibliographic sketches of the thirty-nine poets represented. The selection covers from Manuel A. Alonso (1822) to Jorge Luis Morales (1930). It is useful as a text book for college and adult courses.

16.245 Arriví, Francisco. ESCULTOR DE LA SOMBRA. San Juan, 1965. 172 p. illus.

Other books of poetry by the author are Ciclo de lo Ausente (San Juan, 1962) and Isla y Nada (San Juan, 1958).

16.246 Arroyo, Angel Manuel. SINFONIA EN COLORES. Prólogo por Vicente Géigel Polanco. New York, Sociedad Puertorriqueña de Escritores, Capítulo de Nueva York, 1969. 163 p.

The author also wrote Cenizas del alma (1949) and Láminas de mi infinito.

16.247 Avilés, Juan, Jr. CANTOS DE LA MAÑANA. New York, D.C. Diury, 1936. 90 p.

16.248 Babín, María Teresa. LAS VOCES DE TU VOZ: POEMAS. Santander, Spain, La Isla de los Ratones, 1962. 114 p.

16.249 Balseiro, José A. SAUDADES DE PUERTO RICO. Prólogo de Manuel García Blanco. LA POBREZA CAUTIVA. Prólogo de Alfonso Reyes. Madrid, Aguilar, 1957. 254 p. (Colección literaria; novelistas, dramaturgos, ensayistas, poetas).

Also by the same author is Vísperas de Sombra y Otros Poemas (México, Ediciones de Andre, 1959).

16.250 Bauzá, Obdulio. SELECTED POEMS. Texto original español con la versión inglesa de Helen Wohl Patterson. Prólogo de Concha Meléndez. Madrid, 1961. 133 p. Spanish and English on opposite pages.

16.251 Berio, Blanca. EL PASO. San Juan, 1971. 78 p.

Also by this poet is De 13 a 19 (San Juan, Ediciones Rumbos, 1969).

16.252 Blanco, Antonio Nicolás. ANTOLOGIA. Selección y prólogo de Luis Hernández Aquino. San Juan, Ateneo Puertorriqueño, 1959. 66 p. (Cuadernos de poesía, 9).

16.253 Blanco, Tomás. LETRAS PARA MUSICA. San Juan, Ateneo Puertorriqueño, 1964. 80 p.

16.254 Bonnin Armstrong, Ana Inés. FUGA, 1944–1948. Con un prólogo de Juan Estelrich y un retrato de la autora por Ramón de Capmany. Barcelona, Montaner y Simón, 1948. 145 p. port. (Colección Ariel, v. 3).

16.255 Burgos, Julia de. ANTOLOGIA POETICA. Prólogo por Yvette Jiménez de Báez. San Juan, Editorial Coquí, 1967. 133 p.

Another selection of Julia de Burgos' poetry is Poesías (San Juan, Instituto de Cultura Puertorriqueña, 1964. Cuadernos de poesía, 9).

16.256 Cabrera, J.F., ed. POETAS DE PUERTO RICO: POESIAS ESCOGIDAS SELECCIONADAS. México, Editorial Orbre, 1950. 188 p.

16.257 Cadilla de Ruibal, Carmen Alicia. TIERRAS DEL ALMA: POEMAS DE AMOR. San Juan, Ateneo Puertorriqueño, 1969. 123 p.

Also by the author is Antología Poética (San Juan, Imprenta Venezuela, 1941).

16.258 Cancel Negrón, Ramon, comp. ANTOLOGIA DE LA JOVEN POESIA UNIVERSITARIA DE PUERTO RICO. Selección, ordenación, y notas crítico-biográficas de Ramón Cancel Negrón, con la colaboración de Manuel Pareja Flamán. San Juan, Editorial Campos, 1959. 192 p.

16.259 Carrasquillo, Pedro. REQUINTO: POEMAS JIBAROS. Ilustraciones de Héctor H. Alvarez. New York, Las Américas, 1958. 122 p. illus.

16.260 Carreras, Carlos N. EL CABALLERO DEL SILENCIO. Prólogo de José A. Balseiro. San Juan, Biblioteca de Autores Puertorriqueños, 1940. 176 p.

16.261 Carrero, Jaime. AQUI LOS ANGELES. HERE THE ANGELS. Introducción y traducción de los poemas por Gilbert Neiman. Interpretación por Carmen Rodríguez. San Germán, P.R., Universidad Interamericana, 1960. 11 p. illus.

16.262 Ceide, Amelia. CUANDO EL CIELO SONRIE. San José, C.R., Editorial Borrasé, 1946. 181 p.

Also by the same author are Interior (San Juan, Imprenta Venezuela, 1936) and Puertas (San José, Costa Rica, Editorial Borrasé, 1946).

16.263 Claudio de la Torre, Josefina A. MI SINFONIA ROSA: POEMAS. México, B. Costa-Amic, 1969. 80 p.

16.264 Corretjer, Juan Antonio. YERBA BRUJA. Portada e ilustraciones de J.A. Torres Martinó. San Juan, Instituto de Cultura Puertorriqueña, 1970. 121 p. illus. (Serie Biblioteca Popular. Imagen de Borinquen, 4).

Other books by this prolific poet include *Alabanza de la torre de Ciales* (San Juan, 1965); *Agüeibana* (Ponce, Tip. del Llano, 1932), *Don Diego en el cariño* (San Juan, Editorial La Escrita, 1956); *El leñero* (New York, 1944); and *Tierra nativa* (San Juan, 1951).

16.265 Dávila, José Antonio. MOTIVOS DE TRISTAN: POEMAS, 1930-1934. San Juan, Ateneo Puertorriqueño, 1957. 63 p. (Cuadernos de poesía, 3).

16.266 Dávila, José Antonio. VENDIMIA: POEMAS, 1917-1939. 4. ed. Río Piedras, P.R., Editorial Cultural, 1967. 169 p.

Another book of poetry by Dávila has been published by Editorial Cordillera: *Poemas* (San Juan, 1964).

16.267 Dávila, Virgilio. OBRAS COMPLETAS. Prólogo de B. Martínez López. San Juan, Instituto de Cultura Puertorriqueña, 1964. 614 p. illus. Includes English translations of some of the poems.

Contents. Patria; Viviendo y amando; Un libro para mis nietos; Aromas del terruño.

A sixth edition of his *Pueblito de antes* was published recently (San Juan, Editorial Cordillera, 1972).

16.268 Delgado, Emilio R. TIEMPOS DEL AMOR BREVE. New York, Las Américas, 1958. 45 p.

16.269 Diego, José de. OBRAS COMPLETAS (POESIA). Prólogo de Concha Meléndez. San Juan, Instituto de Cultura Puertorriqueña, 1966. 550 p.

Contents. Poesía: Jovillos; Pomarrosas; Cantos de rebeldía; Cantos de pitirre.

Another anthology of de Diego's poetry is *José de Diego; Antología Poética* (San Juan, Ateneo Puertorriqueño, 1966).

16.270 Diego Padró, José I. de. ESCAPARATE ILUMINADO (AUTOBIO-

GRAFIA POETICA). Barcelona, Ediciones Rumbos, 1959. 229 p.

Another book by the same author is *La última lámpara de los dioses; temas de belleza y voluptuosidad* (2. ed. San Juan, Biblioteca de Autores Puertorriqueños, 1950. 244 p.)

16.271 Felices, Jorge. CANTARES DE BIAFARA: POEMAS. Madrid, Ediciones Castilla, 1970. 88 p.

16.272 Feliciano Mendoza, Esther. NANAS DE LA ADOLESCENCIA. San Juan, Editorial Yaurel, 1963. 98 p.

For other poetry by this author see her *Nanas de la Navidad* (San Juan, Editorial Campos, 1959) and *Voz de mi Tierra* (San Juan, Biblioteca de Autores Puertorriqueños, 1956).

16.273 Figueroa Chapel, Ramón. POESIA (1955-1958). Prólogo por Francisco Lluch Mora. Bilbao, Editorial Vasco Americana, 1969. 79 p.

16.274 Franco Oppenheimer, Félix. PROSAS SIN CLAVE. Ilustraciones por Juan Rosario. Prólogo por Evaristo Ribera Chevremont. San Juan, Editorial Yaurel, 1971. 86 p. illus.

Other poetry by Franco Oppenheimer includes *El hombre y su angustia, 1945-1950* (San Juan, Editorial Yaurel, 1950); *Del tiempo y su figura* (2. ed. Río Piedras, Editorial Edil); *Estas cosas asi fueron* (1956); and *Los lirios del testimonio* (San Juan, Editorial Yaurel, 1964).

16.275 Gallego, Laura. CELAJES. San Juan, Ateneo Puertorriqueño, 1959. 34 p. (Cuadernos de poesía, 8).

16.276 García Velasco, M., J.M. Fernández Nieto, and J.J. Cuadro Pérez. 3 POETAS: EBRIEDAD DE TRISTEZA, BUZON DE ALCANCE, CLARO FAVOR. San Juan, Editorial Club de la Prensa, 1966. 189 p.

16.277 Gardón Franceschi, Margarita. CON OJOS DE MOCHUELO ENLOQUECIDO: POESIAS. Río Piedras, P.R., Editorial Edil, 1970. 74 p. (Colección Poética Edil).

Also by Ms. Gardón is *La alondra se fue con la tarde; tres cánticos en la aurora* (San Juan, Ediciones Juan Ponce de León, 1966).

16.278   Garés, Tomás R. FRUTOS DE UNA NUEVA COSECHA. Prólogo de María Teresa Babín. New York, Sociedad Puertorriqueña de Escritores, 1970. 140 p.
Also author of *Agridulce* (1969).

16.279   Gautier Benítez, José. POESIAS. San Juan, Librería y Editorial Campos, 1955. 316 p. (Colección de novelistas, poetas y ensayistas de América).
A brief selection of Gautier Benítez' poetry was published at a later date: *José Gautier Benítez* (San Juan, Instituto de Cultura Puertorriqueña, 1960. Cuadernos de Poesía, 4). His *Obras Completas* are now in press (San Juan, Editorial Coquí).

16.280   Gaya de García, María Cristina. RAIZ Y CIELO: POEMARIO. Barcelona, Ediciones Rumbos, 1963. 121 p.

16.281   Géigel Polanco, Vicente. PALABRAS DE NUEVA ESPERANZA. San Juan, 1969. 114 p.
Also author of *Bajo el signo de Géminis; poemas de ayer y de hoy* (1963); *Canto de tierra adentro* (1965); and *Canto del amor infinito* (1962).

16.282   Gerena Bras, Gaspar. TRILOGIA LIRICA: ALJIBE, LOS SONETINOS DEL MAR, LAS CENIZAS TIENEN ALAS. San Juan, 1969. 246 p.

16.283   Gil de Rubio, Víctor M. POEMAS PUERTORRIQUEÑOS. PUERTO RICAN POEMS. Barcelona, Ediciones Rumbos, 1968. 157 p.
Includes English translations.

16.284   Gómez Costa, Arturo. SAN JUAN, CIUDAD FANTASTICA DE AMERICA: POEMAS, 1950–1956. Prólogo de Emilio S. Belaval. Barcelona, Ediciones Rumbos, 1957. 134 p.
Also author of *Las luces en éxtasis (Poemas del Viejo San Juan, Capital de Puerto Rico)*.

16.285   González, Josemilio. SOLEDAD ABSOLUTA. San Juan, Editorial Universitaria, in press.

16.286   González Alberty, Fernando. GRITO, POEMARIO DE VANGUARDIA. San Juan, Editorial Atalaya de los Dioses, 1931. 44 p.

16.287   González Concepción, Felipe. POEMAS DE LA VIDA Y DE LA MUERTE. Río Piedras, P.R., Editorial Edil, 1969. 98 p.

16.288   González Torres, Rafael A. UN HOMBRE SE HA PUESTO DE PIE. San Juan, Editorial Yaurel, 1967. 139 p.

16.289   Hernández, José P. H. OBRA POETICA. 2. ed. Con un estudio biográfico-crítico de Manuel Siaca Rivera. San Juan, Instituto de Cultura Puertorriqueña, 1966. 396 p. bibl.
Brings together Hernandez' three books of poetry—*Coplas de la vereda; El último combate;* and *Cantos de la sierra*—as well as poems published in newspapers and magazines and some previously unpublished ones. A bio-critical study is included.

16.290   Hernández Aquino, Luis. ENTRE LA ELEGIA Y EL REQUIEM; POEMAS. Río Piedras, P.R., Editorial Edil, 1968. 60 p.
Also author of *Isla para la angustia; poemas integrales* (San Juan, Ediciones Insula, 1943) and *Voz en el tiempo: antología poética; 1925–1952* (San Juan, Biblioteca de Autores Puertorriqueños, 1952).

16.291   Hernández Aquino, Luis, comp. CANTOS A PUERTO RICO. San Juan, Instituto de Cultura Puertorriqueña, 1967, 218 p. (Serie Biblioteca Popular).
A selection of poems in which the poets write about their homeland, a constant motif in the island's poetic tradition. The selections cover from the nineteenth century to the present.

16.292   Hernández Aquino, Luis, comp. POETAS DE LARES: ANTOLOGIA. San Juan, Instituto de Cultura Puertorriqueña, Centro Cultural de Lares, 1966. 123 p.
Includes bio-bibliographic sketches of the poets.

16.293   Hernández Cruz, Victor. SNAPS. New York, Random House, 1969. 135 p.

16.294 Hernández Vargas, Francisco. BRAZOS: POEMAS. San Juan, Imprenta Venezuela, 1939. 80 p.

16.295 Joglar Cacho, Manuel. POR LOS CAMINOS DEL DIA. 2. ed. Ilustraciones por J.A. Torres Martinó. Tipografía por Will Carter. San Juan, 1969. 24 p. col. illus.

Other works by Joglar Cacho include *Faena íntima* (San Juan, Imprenta Venezuela, 1955) and *La sed del agua* (Barcelona, Editorial Rumbos, 1965).

16.296 JOSE GAUTIER BENITEZ, VIDA Y OBRA POETICA. Introducción al texto por Cesáreo Rosa-Nieves. Río Piedras, P.R., Editorial Edil, 1970. 289 p. bibl. ref.

The collected poems of José Gautier Benítez (1851–1880) are accompanied by critical studies by Cesáreo Rosa-Nieves, Manuel Giménez, Manuel Elzaburu, and Alfredo Collado Martell.

16.297 Labarthe, Pedro Juan. INTERROGATORIO A LA MUERTE. México, Impresora Juan Pablos, 1961. 75 p.

Author of *Y me voy preguntando* (San Juan, Editorial Campos, 1959).

16.298 Lago, Jesús María. ANTOLOGIA. Selección y prólogo de Angel Luis Morales. San Juan, Ateneo Puertorriqueño, 1959. 107 p. bibl. (Cuadernos de poesía, 10).

16.299 Lergier, Clara Luz S. CON LOS OJOS DEL ALMA. Río Piedras, P.R., Editorial Edil, 1969. 80 p.

16.300 Licelott Delgado, Edna. Y CUANDO DIGO TODOS. Río Piedras, P.R., Editorial Edil, 1970. 56 p.

16.301 Lloréns Torres, Luis. OBRAS COMPLETAS. San Juan, Instituto de Cultura Puertorriqueña, 1967–1969. 3 v. (516, 348, 620 p.).

Contents. v. 1, Al Pie de la Alhambra; Sonetos sinfónicos; Voces de la campana mayor; Alturas de América. v. 2, América; El grito de Lares. v. 3, Artículos de periódicos y revistas.

Volume 1, which includes a foreword, biographical notes and an analysis by Carmen Marrero, covers his early romantic work, subsequent poems along modernist lines, and others that fall within his doctrine of *pancalismo*. Volume 2 includes an introduction by María Teresa Babín, and reproduces important works: *América*, first published in 1898 and an early attempt at what was to develop into the search for Puerto Rican identity in contemporary writers; and *El Grito de Lares*, a 1916 historical play. The third volume is a collection of articles published in numerous magazines and newspapers on a diverse range of subjects especially history, literature, politics, economy, and law.

16.302 Lluch Mora, Francisco. POEMAS SIN NOMBRE: CANCIONES. San Juan, Editorial Club de la Prensa, 1963. 69 p. illus.

His poetry also includes *El ruiseñor y el olvido* (Barcelona, Ediciones Rumbos, 1960); *Del asedio y la clausura* (San Juan, Editorial Yaurel, 1950); *Del barrio a Dios* (San Juan, Yaurel, 1954); and *Momentos de la alegría* (San Juan, Ediciones Yaurinquen, 1959).

16.303 López López, Joaquín. ROMANCERO DE LA LUNA. San Juan, Biblioteca de Autores Puertorriqueños, 1939. 155 p.

An anthology of his poetry, *Obra poética*, is in press (San Juan, Editorial Coquí).

16.304 López de Vega, Maximiliano. LAS CIEN MEJORES POESIAS DE PUERTO RICO (JOYAS POETICAS DEL ARTE BORICUA). Río Piedras, P.R., Editorial Edil, 1970. 309 p. bibl. (Colección Poética Edil).

Selection of one hundred poems encompassing the romantic, modernist, and postmodernist periods.

16.305 López de Victoria de Reus, María. SILABARIO DE ESPUMA, by Martha Lomar (pseud.). San Juan, Editorial Cordilla, 1963. 87 p.

Also by the author: *Vejez sonora* (San Juan, Editorial Cordillera, 1963).

16.306 López Suria, Violeta. ANTOLOGIA POETICA. Selección y prólogo por Juan Martínez Capó. Río Piedras,

Editorial Universitaria, Universidad de Puerto Rico, 1970. 262 p.

Among her other works are *Las nubes dejan sombras* (San Juan, Impr. Venezuela, 1965); *Obsesión de heliotropo* (Río Piedras, P.R., Editorial Edil, 1969); *La piel pegada al alma* (San Juan, Impr. Venezuela, 1962).

16.307 Lugo, Samuel. ANTOLOGIA POETICA. Prólogo de Luis Hernández Aquino. Río Piedras, P.R., Editorial Edil, 1971. 138 p.

Other books by Lugo are *Ronda de la llamada verde* (San Juan, 1949) and *Yumbra* (San Juan, Impr. Venezuela, 1943).

16.308 Manrique Cabrera, Francisco. DECIMAS DE MI TIERRA. San Juan, Editorial del Departamento de Instrucción Pública, 1967. 44 p.

The author has also written *Huella, sombra y cantar* (San Juan, Impr. Venezuela, 1943) and *Poemas de mi tierra tierra* (San Juan, Puerto Rico Progress, 1936).

16.309 Margenat, Hugo. INTEMPERIE: POEMAS. San Juan, 1955. 47 p.

16.310 Marín, Francisco Gonzalo (Pachín). ANTOLOGIA. Selección y prólogo de María Teresa Babín. San Juan, Ateneo Puertorriqueño, 1958. 99 p. (Cuadernos de poesía, 5).

16.311 Marrero, Carmen. SONETOS DE LA VERDAD. Introducción por Concha Meléndez. New York, Las Américas, 1964. port.

16.312 Martínez Capó, Juan. VIAJE. Prólogo de María Teresa Babín. San Juan, Ediciones Asomante, 1961. 129 p.

16.313 Martínez Sandín, Ramón F. ESPIGAS DE ENSUEÑOS. México, Talleres de la Editorial Estela, 1964. 79 p.

He is also author of *De mis naranjos en flor*.

16.314 Matilla, Alfredo, and Iván Silén, eds. THE PUERTO RICAN POETS: LOS POETAS PUERTORRIQUEÑOS. New York, Bantam, 1972. 238 p. bibl.

Bilingual anthology of twentieth-century Puerto Rican poetry, with emphasis on the post-1950 generation both in Puerto Rico and in New York.

16.315 Matos Paoli, Francisco. LA MAREA SUBE. San Juan, Ediciones Juan Ponce de León, 1971. 144 p.

His books of poetry include *Cancionero* (San Juan, Ediciones Juan Ponce de León, 1970); *Canto de la locura* (San Juan, Ediciones Juan Ponce de León, 1962); *Criatura del rocío (sonetos)* (San Juan, Ateneo Puertorriqueño, 1958); *Luz de los héroes* (San Juan, 1954); *Habitante del eco* (Santurce, P.R., Imprenta Soltero, 1944); and *Teoría del olvido* (Río Piedras, Universidad de Puerto Rico, 1944).

16.316 Miranda, Luis Antonio. EL ARBOL LLENO DE CANTOS. San Juan, Empresa Florete, 1946. 189 p.

16.317 Miranda Archilla, Graciany. EL ORO EN LA ESPIGA. San Juan, Imprenta Venezuela, 1941. 167 p.

16.318 Monteagudo, Joaquín. EL HOMBRE VERTICAL. Introducción de Francisco Lluch Mora. San Juan, Editorial Club de la Prensa, 1967. 92 p. bibl.

16.319 Molina, Francisco. CIUDAD ALLENDE EL ALBA. Puerto Rico, 1953. 112 p.

16.320 Morales, Jorge Luis. LOS RIOS REDIMIDOS. San Juan, Editorial Universitaria, Universidad de Puerto Rico, 1969. 54 p. illus.

The author has also published *Antologia Poética* (San Juan, Editorial Universitaria, Universidad de Puerto Rico, 1968).

16.321 Muñoz Igartua, Angel. VIBRACIONES: POEMAS. San Juan, 1960. 92 p.

16.322 Muñoz Marín, Luis. BORRONES. San Juan, Impr. La Democracia, 1917. 194 p.

16.323 Muñoz Rivera, Luis. LUIS MUÑOZ RIVERA: POESIAS. Ilustrado por Carlos Marichal. San Juan, Instituto de Cultura Puertorriqueña, 1961. 41 p. illus. (Cuadernos de poesía, 7).

Muñoz Rivera's *Tropicales* (New York, H.M. Call, 1902); *Retamas* (Ponce, P.R., Impr. El Vapor, 1891); and *Versos selectos* are included in his

Obras Completas (San Juan, Instituto de Cultura Puertorriqueña, 1968–   ).

16.324 Murillo, Antonio E. SONETINOS, MADRIGALES Y SONETOS. Prólogo por el Dr. Cesáreo Rosa-Nieves. Editorial Cordillera, 1963. 119 p. (Colección Silla de Guilarte)

16.325 Negrón Muñoz, Mercedes. TROPICO AMARGO, ARRAS DE CRISTAL, MAS ALLA DEL PONIENTE, by Clara Lair (pseud.). San Juan, Biblioteca de Autores Puertorriqueños, 1950. 132 p.

A selection of her poetry was published under the title *Clara Lair: Poesías* (San Juan, Instituto de Cultura Puertorriqueña, 1961).

16.326 Noriega Rodríguez, Carlos. BUSQUEDA Y ENCUENTRO. San Juan, Editorial Cordillera, 1968. 120 p. illus. (Colección Silla de Guilarte).

16.327 Novo de González, Mercedes. SENDEROS DE UNA MUJER: POEMAS. Barcelona, Carabela, 1970. 123 p.

16.328 O'Neill Rosa, Ismael. DE MI INTERIOR QUE SANGRA Y...OTROS POEMAS. San Juan, 1969. 123 p.

16.329 Orama Padilla, Carlos. SURCOS Y ESTRELLAS. San Juan, Editorial Club de la Prensa, 1959. 114 p.

16.330 Padilla, José Gualberto ("El Caribe"). EN EL COMBATE: POESIAS COMPLETAS. San Juan, Instituto de Cultura Puertorriqueña, 1969. 273 p. (Serie Biblioteca Popular).

Another anthology of El Caribe's poetry has been published under the title of *Antología* (San Juan, Ateneo Puertorriqueño, 1961. Cuadernos de poesía, 13).

16.331 Palés Matos, Luis. POESIA, 1915–1956. 3. ed. Introducción por Federico de Onís. San Juan, Ediciones de la Universidad de Puerto Rico, 1968. 305 p. bibl.

Among the best known of Palés poetry is *Tuntún de pasa y grifería* (Río Piedras, Ediciones de la Universidad de Puerto Rico, 1957). His first work, *Azaleas*, was published in 1915.

16.332 Palés Matos, Vicente. LA FUENTE DE JUAN PONCE DE LEON Y OTROS POEMAS. San Juan, Editorial Cordillera, 1967. 106 p.

16.333 Palma, Marigloria. ENTRE DOS AZULES: POEMAS. Barcelona, Ediciones Rumbos, 1965. 125 p.

Other poetry by the author includes *Agua Mansa, Agua Suelta* and *La razón del cuadrante.*

16.334 Pérez Marchand, Lillianne. TIERRA INDIANA. San Juan, Ediciones Asomante, 1962. 35 p.

16.335 Pérez Pierret, Antonio. BRONCES Y OTROS POEMAS. San Juan, Editorial Coquí, 1968. 107 p. facsim., port. (Ediciones Borinquen).

A previous collection of his poetry was published under the title *Antología* (San Juan, Ateneo Puertorriqueño, 1959).

16.336 POESIA PUERTORRIQUEÑA. Selección y prólogo de Luis Hernández Aquino. Río Piedras, Universidad de Puerto Rico, 1954. 129 p. (Cuadernos de la Universidad de Puerto Rico).

16.337 Puigdollers, Carmen. DOMINIO ENTRE ALAS. Prólogo de Josemilio González. New York, Las Américas, 1955. 62 p. (Colección Símbolo).

16.338 Quiñones Vizcarrondo, Samuel R. ¡VAMOS PLATERO! Prólogo de Evaristo Ribera Chevremont. San Juan, Biblioteca de Autores Puertorriqueños, 1966. 88 p.

16.339 Ramírez de Arellano, Diana. PRIVILEGIO. New York, Ateneo Puertorriqueño de Nueva York, 1965. 126 p.

Other books by Ms. Ramírez de Arellano include *Angeles de ceniza* (Madrid, Ediciones J. Romo Arreguí, 1958) and *Un vuelo casi humano* (Madrid, Ediciones J. Romo Arreguí, 1961).

16.340 Ramírez de Arellano de Nolla, Olga. DIARIO DE LA MONTAÑA, 1957–1960. San Juan, Ediciones Juan Ponce de León, 1967. 238 p. illus.

Other books of poetry by the author are *Cauce Hondo* (San Juan, 1947); *En mis ojos verás todos los mundos* (San Juan, 1968); *Dos veces retoño; nana* (San Juan, Ediciones Juan Ponce de León, 1965); and *Cada ola, y escucha mi alma un canto* (San Juan, Ediciones Juan Ponce de León, 1966).

16.341 Ramírez de Arellano, Haydeé. POEMAS. Santiago de Chile, Mar del sur, 1951. 58 p.

16.342 Rentas Lucas, Eugenio. SALMOS EN LA AURORA, AUTOBIOGRAFIA ESPIRITUAL: POEMAS. Prólogo de Monelisa Lina Pérez Marchand. San Juan, Editorial Yaurel, 1963. 84 p.

16.343 Reynal, Vicente. EN BUSCA DE MI MISMO: POESIAS 1970-71. Río Piedras, P.R., Editorial Edil, 1972. 179 p.

16.344 Ribera Chevremont, Evaristo. ANTOLOGIA POETICA (1929-1965). Introducción, selección, y notas por María Teresa Babín y Jaime Luis Rodríguez. San Juan, Editorial del Departamento de Instrucción Pública, Estado Libre Asociado de Puerto Rico, 1967. 105 p.

Other anthologies of Ribera Chevremont's poetry include *Evaristo Ribera Chevremont: Poesías* (San Juan, Instituto de Cultura Puertorriqueña, 1960); *Antología Poética* (Río Piedras, Editorial Universitaria, Universidad de Puerto Rico, 1957); *Nueva antología de Evaristo Ribera Chevremont* (San Juan, Editorial Cordillera, 1966); and *Antología Poética (1924-1950) y la Llama Pensativa (Sonetos inéditos)* (Madrid, Ediciones Cultura Hispánica, 1954).

16.345 Ribera Chevremont, Evaristo. CANTO DE MI TIERRA. Prólogo de Anita Arroyo. Río Piedras, Editorial Universitaria, Universidad de Puerto Rico, 1971. 96 p.

Among the other books by this eminent Puerto Rican poet are *Barandales del mundo* (San Juan, Biblioteca de Autores Puertorriqueños, 1944); *Color* (San Juan, Romero, 1938); *Desfile romántico* (San Juan, Real Hnos., 1914); *Principio de canto* (San Juan, Impr. Venezuela, 1965); *Punto final: poemas del sueño y de la muerte* (San Juan, 1963); *El semblante* (Río Piedras, Editorial Universitaria, Universidad de Puerto Rico, 1964); and *El*

templo de los alabastros (Madrid, Ambos Mundos, 1919).

16.346 Rodríguez de Tió, Lola. OBRAS COMPLETAS, POESIAS. San Juan, Instituto de Cultura Puertorriqueña, 1968. 455 p.

Contents. Prólogo, por A. Tió; Mis cantares; Claros y nieblas; Mi libro de Cuba; 10 de octubre.

16.347 Rosa-Nieves, Cesáreo, ed. AGUINALDO LIRICO DE LA POESIA PUERTORRIQUEÑA. 2. ed. rev. Río Piedras, P.R., Editorial Edil, 1971. 3 v. (550, 474, 518 p.).

Anthology of poetry from various aesthetic movements in Puerto Rico: romantic (1843-1880), parnassian (1880-1907), modernist (1907-1921), postmodernist (1921-1945), and vanguard (1945-1956). A brief bio-critical sketch of each writer is included.

16.348 Rosa-Nieves, Cesáreo. CALAMBREÑAS: DECIMARIO BORICUA. (MOTIVOS DE LA MONTAÑA Y LA CIUDAD). Ilustraciones de José R. Alicea. San Juan, Editorial Cordillera, 1964. 84 p. illus.

Collection of Puerto Rican poems reflecting popular feelings, in ten-verse stanzas.

16.349 Rosa-Nieves, Cesáreo. SIETE CAMINOS EN LUNA DE SUEÑOS: POEMAS. San Juan, Biblioteca de Autores Puertorriqueños, 1957. 121 p.

Contents. El jardín de la angustia en otoño (1930-1943); Pájaros de madrugada (1943-1955); Geografía de un corazón en crisálida (1938-1953).

Other poetry by the author includes *Diapasón negro* (San Juan, Editorial Campos, 1960); *Girasol* (San Juan, Editorial Campos, 1960); and *Los nísperos del alba maduraron* (San Juan, Editorial Campos, 1959).

16.350 Rosario Quiles, Luis Antonio. EL JUICIO DE VICTOR CAMPOLO: POEMA BIOGRAFICO. San Juan, Ediciones Bondo, 1970. 122 p.

16.351 Rosario Quiles, Luis Antonio, comp. POESIA NUEVA PUERTORRIQUEÑA; ANTOLOGIA. San Juan, Producciones Bondo, 1971. 323 p. bibl. ref.

16.352 Sáez Burgos, Juan. UN HOMBRE PARA EL LLANTO. Río Piedras, P.R., Editorial Edil, 1969. 77 p. illus. (Colección poética Edil).

16.353 Santos Tirado, Adrián. EL DECIR INFINITO: DECIMARIO LIRICO. Prólogo de Julio Meléndez. Vega Baja, P.R., Editorial Cibuco, 1968. 70 p.

16.354 Serra Deliz, Wenceslao. MEMORIA. Río Piedras, P.R., Editorial Edil, 1970. 55 p.

16.355 Silvestri, Reinaldo R. POEMAS DE UN SILENCIO AZUL. Sevilla, ECESA, 1969. 46 p.

16.356 Soto Vélez, Clemente. ARBOLES. New York, Las Américas, 1955. 23 p.

16.357 Tapia y Rivera, Alejandro. LA SATANIADA: GRANDIOSA EPOPEYA DEDICADA AL PRINCIPE DE LAS TINIEBLAS POR CRISOFILO SARDANAPALO (ALEJANDRO TAPIA Y RIVERA). 2. ed. San Juan, Impr. Venezuela, 1945. 340 p. illus.

16.358 Tejada, Juan. CLARIN SIN BROMA. Río Piedras, P.R., Editorial Edil, 1970. 164 p.

16.359 Torres, César G. POESIAS AROMAS DE LIMON. New York, Azteca Press, 1949. 76 p.

16.360 Torres, César G. RESOLANA: ANTOLOGIA POETICA. Prólogo de Odeón Betanzos Palacios. New York, 1970. 142 p. (Colección mensaje, no. 30).

16.361 Trías, Arturo. AUNQUE QUISE EL SILENCIO. Prólogo de Margot Arce de Vázquez. Sharon, Conn., Troutman Press, 1967. 64 p. (Nuevos escritores de Puerto Rico, núm. 1).

16.362 Trías, Arturo, and Hjalmar Flax. 144 [CIENTO CUARENTA Y CUATRO] POEMAS EN 2 LIBROS. San Juan, Editorial Ahora, 1969. 117 p.
       Contents.—44 poemas de Hjalmar Flax; 100 poemas de Arturo Trías.

16.363 Valbuena Briones, Angel, and Luis Hernández Aquino, eds. NUEVA POESIA DE PUERTO RICO. Madrid, Ediciones Cultura Hispánica, 1952. 388 p. (La encina y el mar).
       A prologue by Angel Valbuena Briones highlights and analyzes the works of thirty-four poets considered in this anthology. A bio-bibliographic note on each poet is included.

16.364 Vicéns, Nimia. CANCIONES AL MUNDO. San Juan, Ateneo Puertorriqueño, 1957. 64 p. (Cuadernos de poesía, 2).

16.365 Vidarte, Santiago. SANTIAGO VIDARTE: POESIAS. Ilustraciones de Carlos Marichal. San Juan, Instituto de Cultura Puertorriqueña, 1965. 40 p. illus. (Cuadernos de poesía, 10).
       A new collection of his poetry is in press: Obra Poética (San Juan, Editorial Coquí).

16.366 Vizcarrondo, Carmelina. POEMAS PARA MI NIÑO. San Juan, Imprenta Venezuela, 1938. 151 p. illus.
       Also the author of: Pregón en llamas (San Juan, Imprenta Venezuela, 1935).

16.367 Vizcarrondo, Fortunato. DINGA Y MANDINGA (POEMAS). 2. ed. San Juan, Editorial del Departamento de Instrucción Pública, 1968. 134 p.

16.368 Zeno Gandía, Manuel. POESIAS. Recopiladas y editadas por Margarita Gardón. San Juan, Editorial Coquí, 1969. 254 p. (Ediciones Borinquen).

Theatre

16.369 Arjona, Gloria. AUTO DE NAVIDAD. Ilustraciones de Carlos Marichal. San Juan, Editorial del Departamento de Instrucción Pública, 1969. 100 p.

16.370 Arriví, Francisco. "Cuento de hadas." In Solórzano, Carlos. TEATRO BREVE HISPANOAMERICANO. Madrid, Aguilar, 1970. 362 p.

16.371 Arriví, Francisco. MASCARA PUER-
TORRIQUEÑA. Río Piedras, P.R., Editorial Cultural, 1971. 366 p.

16.372 Arriví, Francisco. TRES PIEZAS DE TE-
ATRO PUERTORRIQUEÑO. San Juan,
Editorial del Departamento de Instrucción Pública, Estado Libre Asociado de Puerto Rico, 1968. 330 p.
illus., bibl.
   Contents. María Soledad; Vejigantes; Club de Solteros.

16.373 Bauzá, Guillermo. DON CRISTOBAL.
Barcelona, Ediciones Rumbos, 1963.
104 p.

16.374 Bauzá, Guillermo. LA GUERRA. San
Juan, 1969. 310 p.

16.375 Bauzá, Guillermo. LA LOBA. Barcelona, Ediciones Rumbos, 1954. 98 p.

16.376 Bonnin Armstrong, Ana Inés. EL
MENDIGO, Y OTROS DIALOGOS. 1.
ed. Barcelona, Ediciones Destino,
[1960]. 207 p. (Ancora y delfín, 186).

16.377 Brau, Salvador. OBRA TEATRAL. San
Juan, Editorial Coquí, in press. 2v.

16.378 Canales, Nemesio R. EL HEROE
GALOPANTE. 2. ed. San Juan, Editorial
Coquí, 1967. 61 p. First published in
1935.

16.379 Córdoba Chirino, J. LOS QUE
MURIERON EN LA HORCA. 2. ed. San
Juan, Editorial Cordillera, 1970. 234 p.

16.380 Cuchí Coll, Isabel. LA FAMILIA DE
JUSTO MALGENIO: PUERTORRI-
QUEÑOS EN NUEVA YORK. Barce-
lona, Ediciones Rumbos, 1963. 121 p.

16.381 Marqués, René. CARNAVAL
AFUERA, CARNAVAL ADENTRO. Río
Piedras, P.R., Editorial Antillana, 1971.
130 p.

16.382 Marqués, René. DAVID Y JONA-
TAN, TITO Y BERENICE: DOS DRA-
MAS DE AMOR, PODER Y DESA-
MOR. Río Piedras, P.R., Editorial An-
tillana, 1970. 101 p.

16.383 Marqués, René. JUAN BOBO Y LA
DAMA DE OCCIDENTE: PAN-
TOMIMA PUERTORRIQUEÑA PARA

UN BALLET OCCIDENTAL. 2. ed. Río
Piedras, P.R., Editorial Antillana, 1971.
48 p.

16.384 Marqués, René. LA MUERTE NO
ENTRARA EN PALACIO. Río Piedras,
P.R., Editorial Cultural, 1970. 147 p.

16.385 Marqués, René. THE OXCART.
Translated from the Spanish by
Charles Pilditch. New York, Scribner,
1969. 155 p. illus. (Scribner School Pa-
perbacks, SSP 25).
   The play in Spanish, La Carreta, is
now in its fifth edition.

16.386 Marqués, René. PURIFICACION EN
LA CALLE DEL CRISTO. Río Piedras,
P.R., Editorial Cultural, 1970. 21 p.

16.387 Marqués, René. SACRIFICIO EN EL
MONTE MORIAH. Drama en Catorce
Escenas Cinematográficas. Río Piedras, P.R., Editorial Antillana, 1969. 158
p. illus., ports., bibl.

16.388 Marqués, René. TEATRO: EL
HOMBRE Y SUS SUEÑOS; EL SOL Y
LOS MACDONALD. Río Piedras, P.R.,
Editorial Cultural, 1970. v. 2. 166 p.

16.389 Marqués, René. TEATRO: LA CASA
SIN RELOJ; EL APARTAMIENTO. Río
Piedras, P.R., Editorial Cultural, 1971.
v. 3. 212 p.
   El Apartamiento is also included in
Lamb, Ruth S., comp. and ed., Three
Contemporary Latin American Plays
(Waltham, Mass., Xerox College Pub.,
1971).

16.390 Marqués, René. VIA CRUCIS DEL
HOMBRE PUERTORRIQUEÑO. Río
Piedras, P.R., Editorial Antillana, 1971.
19 p.
   Based on the Catholic liturgy's elev-
enth station of the cross, when Jesus is
nailed to the cross, René Marqués
writes this brief work about the
Puerto Ricans' desire for liberty and
justice.

16.391 Marrero Núñez, Julio. EL HOMBRE
TERRIBLE DEL 87: VERSION LIBRE DE
UN EPISODIO HISTORICO EN TRES
ACTOS. Barcelona, Ediciones Rum-
bos, 1967. 72 p.

16.392 Méndez Ballester, Manuel. EL CLAMOR DE LOS SURCOS: DRAMA EN TRES ACTOS. San Juan, Talleres Tip. de la Casa Baldrich, 1940. 109 p.

16.393 Morfi, Angelina. ANTOLOGIA DE TEATRO PUERTORRIQUEÑO. t. 1. San Juan, Ediciones Juan Ponce de León, 1970. 235 p.
This first of three volumes is devoted to the most outstanding playwrights of the nineteenth century. It includes La Cuarterona, by Alejandro Tapia y Rivera; Héroe y Mártir, by Salvador Brau; Un Jíbaro, by Ramón Méndez Quiñones; and from the first part of the twentieth century, El Héroe Galopante, by Nemesio Canales. Useful as a college text.

16.394 Rosa-Nieves, Cesáreo. ROMAN BALDORIOTY DE CASTRO: (BIO-DRAMA EN TRES ACTOS Y EN VERSO). Santurce, Impr. Soltero, 1948. 111 p. (Teatro Puertorriqueño, t. 1).

16.395 Sánchez, Luis Rafael. LOS ANGELES SE HAN FATIGADO: FARSA DEL AMOR COMPADRIDO. Hato Rey, P.R., Ediciones Lugar, 1960. 131 p.

16.396 Sánchez, Luis Rafael. LA PASION SEGUN ANTIGONA PEREZ. Hato Rey, P.R., Ediciones Lugar, 1968. 132 p.
This work was presented in English by the Puerto Rican Traveling Theater in New York during 1972.

16.397 Sierra Berdecía, Fernando. LA ESCUELA DEL BUEN AMOR. San Juan, Editorial Coquí, 1963. 82 p.

16.398 Tapia y Rivera, Alejandro. "Teatro." In OBRAS COMPLETAS. San Juan, Instituto de Cultura Puertorriqueña, 1968–1970. v. 2.
Contents. Vasco Núñez de Balboa; La Parte del León; Roberto Devreu; Camöens; Hero; La Cuarterona.

16.399 TEATRO PUERTORRIQUEÑO: PRIMER FESTIVAL DE TEATRO. San Juan, Instituto de Cultura Puertorriqueña, 1959. 460 p. photos. Reprint. Río Piedras, P.R., Editorial Edil, 1960.
Contents. Manuel Méndez Ballester, Encrucijada; Emilio S. Belaval, La hacienda de los cuatro vientos; Francisco Arriví, Vejigantes; René Marqués, Los soles truncos.
Arriví's Vejigantes is also in Dauster, Frank N., ed., Teatro Hispanoamericano: Tres Piezas (New York, Harcourt, Brace & World, 1969. 272 p.).

16.400 TEATRO PUERTORRIQUEÑO: SEGUNDO FESTIVAL. San Juan, Instituto de Cultura Puertorriqueña, 1960. 403 p. photos. Reprint. Río Piedras, P.R., Editorial Edil, 1960.
Contents. Luis Rechani Agrait, Mi señoría; Enrique A. Laguerre, La resentida; Fernando Sierra Berdecía, Esta noche juega el joker.

16.401 TEATRO PUERTORRIQUEÑO: TERCER FESTIVAL DE TEATRO. San Juan, Instituto de Cultura Puertorriqueña, 1961. 610 p. photos.
Contents. René Marqués, Un niño azul para esa sombra; Piri Fernández, De tanto caminar; Myrna Casas, Cristal roto en el tiempo; Emilio S. Belaval, Cielo Caído; Gerald Paul Marín, En el principio la noche era serena.

16.402 TEATRO PUERTORRIQUEÑO: CUARTO FESTIVAL. San Juan, Instituto de Cultura Puertorriqueña, 1963. 802 p. photos.
Contents. Francisco Arriví, María Soledad; Salvador Brau, La vuelta al hogar; René Marqués, La carreta; Luis Rafael Sánchez, Sol 13, interior; Manuel Méndez Ballester, El milagro.

16.403 TEATRO PUERTORRIQUEÑO: QUINTO FESTIVAL. San Juan, Instituto de Cultura Puertorriqueña, 1964. 392 p. photos.
Contents. Manuel Méndez Ballester, Tiempo muerto; Emilio S. Belaval, Circe o el amor; César Andréu Iglesias, El inciso hache.

16.404 TEATRO PUERTORRIQUEÑO: SEXTO FESTIVAL. San Juan, Instituto de Cultura Puertorriqueña, 1964. 357 p. photos.
Contents. Manuel Méndez Ballester, La feria o el mono con la lata en el rabo; Edmundo Rivera Alvarez, El cielo se rindió al amanecer; Emilio S. Belaval, La vida.

16.405 TEATRO PUERTORRIQUEÑO: SEP-
TIMO FESTIVAL. San Juan, Instituto de
Cultura Puertorriqueña, 1965. 638 p.
photos.
    Contents. Luis Rechani Agrait,
Todos los ruiseñores cantan; René
Marqués, *El apartamiento;* Luis Ra-
fael Sánchez, . . . *O casi el alma;* Fran-
cisco Arriví, *Coctel de don Nadie.*

16.406 TEATRO PUERTORRIQUEÑO: OC-
TAVO FESTIVAL. San Juan, Instituto
de Cultura Puertorriqueña, 1966. 728
p. photos.
    Contents. Luis Rechani Agrait,

¿Cómo se llama esta flor? Manuel
Méndez Ballester, *Bienvenido, Don
Goyito;* Ana Inés Bonnin Armstrong,
La difícil esperanza; René Marqués,
Mariana o el alba.

16.407 TEATRO PUERTORRIQUEÑO: NO-
VENO FESTIVAL. San Juan, Instituto
de Cultura Puertorriqueña, 1968. 453
p. photos.
    Contents. René Marqués, *Los
soles truncos;* Luis Rechani Agrait, *Mi
señoría;* Francisco Arriví, *Vejigantes;*
Manuel Méndez Ballester, *Bienvenido, Don Goyito.*

17
MIGRATION

17.1 Abrams, Charles. "The Puerto Rican
Airlift." *In his* FORBIDDEN NEIGH-
BORS. New York, Harper and Row,
1955. p. 65–69.
    The Puerto Rican "problem" is
traced to the fact that Puerto Ricans
are forced to live under substandard
conditions and that this fact is not recognized by mainland Americans.

17.2 Abramson, Michael, and Young Lords
Party. PALANTE: YOUNG LORDS
PARTY. New York, McGraw-Hill, 1971.
160 p. illus.
    Some members of the Young Lords
Party talk about the history of their organization, their personal background, how each became involved
in the party, and their ideas. The second part of the book consists of a
photographic essay.

17.3 Agueros, Jack. THE SPANISH SPEAK-
ING COMMUNITY OF GREATER
CLEVELAND. Cleveland, Ohio, Institute for Soviet Studies, John Carroll
University, [1970?]. 56 p. tables, diagrs.,
maps.
    An initial attempt at defining the
numbers and characteristics of Spanish-surnamed persons in the Cleveland area.

17.4 Baglin, Roger F. The Mainland Experience in Selected Puerto Rican Literary

Works. Ph.D. dissertation, State University of New York at Buffalo, 1971. *In*
DISSERTATION ABSTRACTS INTER-
NATIONAL, v. 32, no. 6, p. 3290-A.
    This study examines the mainland
experience of Puerto Ricans as reflected in short story, novel, and theater.

17.5 Berle, Beatrice B. 80 PUERTO RICAN
FAMILIES IN NEW YORK CITY:
HEALTH AND DISEASE STUDIED IN
CONTEXT. New York, Columbia University Press, 1958. 331 p. illus., bibl.
    An intensive study of health and re-
lated problems of eighty Puerto Rican
families. Many of the problems were
related to anxiety and frustration due
to the fact that the "discrepancy between an individual's aspirations and
the limited employment opportunities open to him due to lack of
schooling or special skills cannot be
reconciled."

17.6 Boykin, Lorraine Smith. A Study of the
Food and Nutrient Intake of School-
Age Puerto Rican Children Living in
New York City and Attending a Nutrition Clinic. Ph.D. dissertation, Columbia University, 1970. *In* DISSERTA-
TION ABSTRACTS INTERNATIONAL,
v. 31, no. 4, p. 2082-B.
    This study was undertaken to pro-
vide more specific information on the

food and nutrition intake of six- to ten-year-old Puerto Rican children living in New York City.

17.7 Brand, Horst. POVERTY AREA PROFILES: THE NEW YORK PUERTO RICAN: PATTERNS OF WORK EXPERIENCE. New York, U.S. Bureau of Labor Statistics, Middle Atlantic Regional Office, [1971]. 62 p. illus., maps, bibl. refs. (Regional Reports, no. 19).

Presents the grim findings of the Urban Employment Survey on the labor market experience, economic status, and social characteristics of Puerto Ricans of working age who resided in Central and East Harlem, the South Bronx, and Bedford-Stuyvesant between July 1968 and June 1969. The document shows that "Puerto Rican workers were the most deprived of all workers residing in the city's major poverty neighborhoods."

17.8 Burma, John H. "Puerto Ricans in New York." In SPANISH-SPEAKING GROUPS IN THE UNITED STATES. Durham, N.C., Duke University Press, 1954. p. 156–187. maps, bibl. (Duke University Press Sociological Series, no. 9).

An overview of one of the groups that, in Burma's opinion, form a "unity of culture" because they speak the same language.

17.9 Caplowitz, David, and others. THE POOR PAY MORE. Glencoe, Ill., Free Press, 1963. 220 p.

Book based on a report on consumer behavior of residents of low-income public housing in New York City, which concluded that black and Puerto Rican families face more difficulties than other families studied. It documents the ways in which low-income families are exploited by merchants, salesmen, and loan sharks, and outlines a consumer education program for those families.

17.10 Chenault, Lawrence Royce. THE PUERTO RICAN MIGRANT IN NEW YORK. With a foreword by Francesco Cordasco. New York, Russell & Russell, 1970, c1938. 190 p. illus., tables, maps, diagrs., bibl.

A discussion of the early Puerto Rican migration to New York City,

based on the author's doctoral dissertation, Columbia University, 1938.

17.11 Cole, Mary. SUMMER IN THE CITY. Foreword by Msgr. Robert J. Fox. New York, P.J. Kenedy, 1968. 221 p. illus.

Narrative about the people and events in the Summer in the City Program, a city-wide antipoverty and community action program sponsored by the Catholic church in New York and their inspiring peace processions during the East Harlem riots of July 1967.

17.12 Coleman, Robert Martin. A History and Evaluation of the New York University Workshop—Field Study in Puerto Rican Education and Culture (1948–1967). Ph.D. dissertation, New York University, 1969. In DISSERTATION ABSTRACTS INTERNATIONAL, v. 30, no. 7, p. 2876-A.

The purpose of this study was to describe and analyze the objectives, programs and records of development of the New York University workshop.

17.13 Colón, Jesús. A PUERTO RICAN IN NEW YORK, AND OTHER SKETCHES. New York, Mainstream Publishers, 1961. 202 p.

Sketches and vignettes about the author's childhood memories, his life in New York in the early twenties, and his activities as a writer for a socialist newspaper. A revised edition, under the title of Puerto Ricans in New York, has been published by International Pub. Co., 1970.

17.14 Connecticut State Advisory Committee to the United States Commission on Civil Rights. El Boricua: The Puerto Rican in Connecticut. n.p., March 1972. unp. mimeographed.

A report that discusses Puerto Rican employment, health care, education, and housing in New Haven and Bridgeport. It is based on information received at public hearings and on investigations.

17.15 Cooper, Paulette, ed. GROWING UP PUERTO RICAN. Foreword by José Torres. New York, Arbor House, 1972. 216 p.

Seventeen Puerto Ricans living in

the United States open up to Ms. Cooper and tell her about a diversity of experiences: what it is like living in the ghetto, being a junkie and quitting, being a member of the Young Lords, and many other situations.

17.16 Cordasco, Francesco, and Eugene Bucchioni. Education Programs for Puerto Rican Students [Jersey City Public Schools]. Jersey City, Board of Education, 1971. 45 p. tables, bibl. refs. mimeographed.

Description and evaluation of the programs for Puerto Rican pupils in the public schools of Jersey City, followed by program recommendations for elementary and secondary levels.

17.17 Cordasco, Francesco, and Eugene Bucchioni, comps. THE PUERTO RICAN COMMUNITY AND ITS CHILDREN ON THE MAINLAND: A SOURCE BOOK FOR TEACHERS. Rev. ed. Metuchen, N.J., Scarecrow Press, 1972. 465 p. bibl.

First published in 1968 under title *Puerto Rican Children in Mainland Schools*, this is a collection of readings on the Puerto Rican family and its experience in the United States, and the experience of the Puerto Rican child in North American schools. A section on aspects of Puerto Rican culture is included.

17.18 Cruz, Nicky, and Jamie Buckingham. RUN BABY RUN. Introduction by Billy Graham. Foreword by Edward D. O'Connor. Plainfield, N.J., Logos International, 1968. 240 p.

Nicky Cruz, who at fifteen was sent by his father from Puerto Rico to New York, is now a Pentecostal preacher in California working with a church-sponsored program called Outreach for Youth. In this book he tells of the life of crime, addiction, and vice that he led for many years and how he became a worker for his fellow man.

17.19 Cunningham, Ineke. The Relationship between Modernity and Academic Performance in Students in a Puerto Rican High School, Their Parents and Peers. Ph.D. dissertation, Northwestern University, 1971. *In* DISSERTATION ABSTRACTS INTERNATIONAL, v. 32, no. 6, p. 3439-A.

This study found strongly positive correlations between student modernity and academic performance. It also found positive correlation between student modernity and peer modernity, although the correlation between student performance and peer academic performance was found to be even higher.

17.20 Dworkis, Martin. IMPACT OF PUERTO RICAN MIGRANTS ON GOVERNMENTAL SERVICES IN NEW YORK CITY. New York, New York University Press, 1957. 74 p. bibl., refs.

This study, conducted by graduate students in public administration from New York University under the direction of Professor Dworkis, assesses the impact of Puerto Rican migration on programs in the fields of education, employment, health and hospital services, crime and delinquency, housing, and welfare programs. The basic information is outdated but its warning that the impact of the Puerto Rican migration would be even greater in the decade to come and that the city would have to make special efforts to meet the language and cultural needs of the Puerto Ricans is still valid.

17.21 Eagle, Morris. "The Puerto Ricans in New York City," *In* Glazer, N., and D. McEntire. HOUSING AND MINORITY GROUPS. Berkeley, University of California Press, 1960. p. 144–177.

Field research which demonstrates that Puerto Ricans do not create slums but are forced, because of low incomes and discrimination, to move into existing slums or inadequate housing. Once their economic situation improves the Puerto Rican migrants tend to move into better housing which, interestingly, costs them less than housing in the slums.

17.22 THE EDUCATIONAL SETTING IN THE VIRGIN ISLANDS WITH PARTICULAR REFERENCE TO THE EDUCATION OF SPANISH-SPEAKING CHILDREN. Río Piedras, Social Sciences Research Center, University of Puerto Rico, n.d. 97 p.

A study conducted by a team of investigators sponsored by the Social Sciences Research Center, University of Puerto Rico, under contract with the Department of Education of the U.S. Virgin Islands. It examines the USVI educational system at junior and high school levels with reference to the teaching of Spanish-speaking Puerto Rican children, mainly in St. Croix. It constitutes a severe indictment of the almost total absence of any program to meet the problems of these children. It contrasts the old 'melting pot' concept with a new concept that would recognize the cultural plurality of the Virgin Islands, and recommends a new program based on the latter concept.

17.23 Ehle, John. SHEPHERD OF THE STREETS: THE STORY OF THE REVEREND JAMES A. GUSWELLER AND HIS CRUSADE ON THE NEW YORK WEST SIDE. Foreword by Harry Golden. New York, William Sloane Assoc., 1960. 239 p. illus.

The story of an Episcopal minister who takes over a church in a Puerto Rican neighborhood and involves himself in helping his parishioners.

17.24 Elsbery, James William. The Effect of Social Interaction with the Peers of the Wider Social System upon a Retardate Subculture: The Negro, Puerto Rican, and Caucasian Educable Retardate in the Job Market. Ph.D. dissertation, Columbia University, 1972. In DISSERTATION ABSTRACTS INTERNATIONAL, v. 33, no. 4, p. 1848-A.

A study designed to inquire into the influence of ethnicity, socioeconomic status, and interaction with nonretardates, upon a retardate's receiving employment through a formal school program geared to training for job readiness.

17.25 Ferree, William, Ivan Illich, and Joseph P. Fitzpatrick, eds. SPIRITUAL CARE OF PUERTO RICAN MIGRANTS: REPORT. Cuernavaca, México, Centro Intercultural de Documentación, 1970. various pagings. (Sondeos, no. 74).

Report of a conference on this subject held in San Juan, April 1955, with emphasis on the concern of the Catholic church for the migrants. Some of the papers touch on the cultural patterns of the migrants and the changes they undergo in the United States.

17.26 Fishman, Joshua, and others, eds. BILINGUALISM IN THE BARRIO. Bloomington, Indiana University, 1971. 696 p. questionnaire, tables, bibl. (Indiana University Publications. Language Science Monographs, v. 7).

A formidable two-year study of Puerto Rican bilingualism in the New York area.

17.27 Fitzpatrick, Joseph P. PUERTO RICAN AMERICANS: THE MEANING OF MIGRATION TO THE MAINLAND. Englewood Cliffs, N.J., Prentice-Hall, 1971. 192 p. tables, maps. (Ethnic Groups in American Life Series).

An attempt to examine the meaning of the Puerto Rican migration, focused on the Puerto Rican search for identity—to which he devotes about five chapters—and the experience of Puerto Ricans in New York. Much of the data is based on 1960 or earlier figures.

17.28 Freidel, Frank Burt. THE NEGRO AND PUERTO RICAN IN AMERICAN HISTORY. Boston, Heath, 1964. 27 p. illus., ports.

A look into the history of the two largest groups that migrated to New York between the beginning of World War I and the 1960s—Negroes from the South and Puerto Ricans—and their contributions to the United States. The Puerto Rican content is disappointingly superficial.

17.29 Furst, Philip W. PUERTO RICANS IN NEW YORK CITY. New York, Puerto Rican Social Services, 1963. 81 p. tables.

A compilation and interpretation of data in the areas of housing, education, health, delinquency, and employment.

17.30 García Olivero, Carmen. STUDY OF THE INITIAL INVOLVEMENT IN THE SOCIAL SERVICES BY THE PUERTO RICAN MIGRANTS IN PHILADELPHIA. New York, Vantage Press, 1971. 316 p. illus., bibl.

A doctoral dissertation which identifies and analyzes selected elements affecting the contact through which

Puerto Ricans and social workers seek to develop a viable relationship.

17.31   Glazer, Nathan, and Daniel P. Moynihan. BEYOND THE MELTING POT. Cambridge, Mass., M.I.T. Press and Harvard University, 1963. 360 p. map, tables, bibl. refs. (Joint Center for Urban Studies Series).

Puerto Ricans are compared and contrasted with other immigrant groups. The study discusses who the migrants are, their relationship to the island, employment opportunities, and the effect of migration on their culture.

17.32   Golub, Fred T. THE PUERTO RICAN WORKER IN PERTH AMBOY, NEW JERSEY. New Brunswick, N.J., 1956. 18 p. tables. bibl. refs. (Rutgers University, Institute of Management and Labor Relations. Occasional Studies, no. 2).

An analysis of the problems of adjustment faced by Puerto Rican unskilled workers in the industrial town of Perth Amboy. Although outdated, the work offers some glimpses into early patterns of employment and workers' conditions.

17.33   Gray, Lois S. Economic Incentives to Labor Mobility: the Puerto Rican Case. Ph.D. dissertation, Columbia University, 1967. In DISSERTATION ABSTRACTS, v. 27, no. 8, p. 2263-A.

Using the interchange between Puerto Rico and the mainland United States as a base for detailed analysis, the author seeks to explain long-term changes in the number, characteristics, and destination of migrants by examining the economic impact of movement on the occupational and income status of Puerto Ricans.

17.34   Halpern, Shelly. The Relationship between Ethnic Group Membership and Sex and Aspects of Vocational Choice of Pre-college Black and Puerto Rican Students. Ph.D. dissertation, Fordham University, 1972. In DISSERTATION ABSTRACTS INTERNATIONAL, v. 33, no. 1, p. 190-A.

This study was conducted among 255 tenth graders from three New York City high schools enrolled in a precollege program for poor and minority youth.

17.35   Handlin, Oscar. THE NEWCOMERS: NEGROES AND PUERTO RICANS IN A CHANGING METROPOLIS. 2d ed. Garden City, N.Y., Doubleday, 1962. 171 p. bibl. (New York Metropolitan Region Study).

Documented study on the problems and progress of Negroes and Puerto Ricans in New York City, compared with those of other immigrant groups. In spite of the graveness of their situation in terms of color prejudice, low income, unemployment, and lack of education, the author feels hopeful that the Puerto Ricans and the blacks can find adequate solutions to those problems "if the society of which these people have become a part allows them to act freely and as equals in it."

17.36   Hernández Alvarez, José. RETURN MIGRATION TO PUERTO RICO. Berkeley, Institute of International Studies, University of California, [1967]. 153 p. maps, tables, bibl. refs. (Population Monograph Series, no. 1).

An analysis of Puerto Rican migration based on a 25 percent sample of the 1960 census of Puerto Rico. It describes the history and significance of the island's migration as well as the characteristics of the migrants and those who return.

17.37   Hidalgo, Hilda. The Puerto Ricans in Newark, New Jersey (Aquí se Habla Español). [Newark?], Aspira of New Jersey, September 1970. unp. mimeographed.

A study by a group of students of Livingston College–Rutgers University, under the direction of Professor Hidalgo, with the purpose of gaining an "understanding of the situation of the Puerto Ricans residing in Newark, and based on such understanding recommend possible courses of action to begin solving the so called 'Puerto Rican Problem'."

17.38   Howard, John R., comp. AWAKENING MINORITIES: AMERICAN INDIANS, MEXICAN AMERICANS, PUERTO RICANS. Chicago, Aldine, 1970. 189 p. bibl. refs. (Trans-Action Books, TA-18).

A collection of articles published in *Trans-Action* magazine in which social problems are discussed and guidelines given toward their solution. Part three is about Puerto Ricans and includes "Puerto Ricans: The Making of a Minority Group," by John R. Howard; "Even the Saints Cry," by Oscar Lewis; "The Puerto Rican Independence Movement," by Arthur Liebman; and "The Death of Dolores," by Oscar Lewis.

17.39 INTERNATIONAL MIGRATION REVIEW. New York, Center for Migration Studies. v. 2, no. 2, Spring 1968.
Issue devoted entirely to Puerto Rican migration.

17.40 ISSUES OF CONCERN TO PUERTO RICANS IN BOSTON AND SPRINGFIELD. A report of the Massachusetts State Advisory Committee to the United States Commission on Civil Rights. [Washington, U.S. Commission on Civil Rights], February 1972. 104 p. tables.
A report on problems in education, housing, employment, and social services faced by Puerto Ricans in Boston and Springfield.

17.41 Jaffe, Abram J., ed. PUERTO RICAN POPULATION IN NEW YORK CITY. New York, Columbia University, 1954. 61 p.
Contents. A. J. Jaffe, "Demographic and Labor Force Characteristics;" Louis Weiner, "Vital Statistics;" Sophia Robinson, "Social and Welfare Statistics."
Well-documented papers delivered before the New York area chapter of the American Statistical Association, which unfortunately are now outdated.

17.42 Jones, Isham B. THE PUERTO RICAN IN NEW JERSEY: HIS PRESENT STATUS. Newark, New Jersey State Department of Education, Division Against Discrimination [now Division on Civil Rights], 1955. 48 p. tables.
This survey, based on 1950s data, discusses the location of Puerto Rican migrants in the state of New Jersey and some community reactions, both positive and antagonistic, towards them.

17.43 Kelly, Lenore Mary. Community Identification among Second Generation Puerto Ricans: Its Relation to Occupational Success. Ph.D. dissertation, Fordham University, 1971. *In* DISSERTATION ABSTRACTS INTERNATIONAL, v. 32, no. 4, p. 2223-A.
This study attempts to identify the factors related to varying degrees of occupational success that can serve as a guide to developing policy and programs, and which could assist both first- and second-generation Puerto Ricans in New York.

17.44 Klein, Woody, LET IN THE SUN. Foreword by John V. Lindsay. New York, Macmillan, 1964. 297 p.
A newspaper reporter takes the reader inside a tenement in New York's "worst block." He describes vividly the people within—many of them Puerto Ricans—the landlords, and the officials, and social workers who have dealt with the housing situation. The author feels "shocked and hurt by the neglect and callousness with which most people in New York react to the ugly fact that one million of their fellow citizens live in the slums."

17.45 Leach, John Nathaniel. Cultural Factors Affecting the Adjustment of Puerto Rican Children to Schooling in Hartford, Connecticut. Ph.D. dissertation, University of Connecticut, 1971. *In* DISSERTATION ABSTRACTS INTERNATIONAL, v. 32, no. 5, p. 2308-A.
Specifically, this study sought to compare Puerto Rican students in Hartford coming from the tobacco-growing hill areas and the coastal sugar plantations to identify differences in their language usage, social practices and conventions, attitudes toward legal authority, and attitudes toward literary pursuits.

17.46 Lewis, Gordon K. THE VIRGIN ISLANDS: A CARIBBEAN LILLIPUT. Northwestern University Press, 1972. 382 p.
Contains material on Puerto Ricans in the Virgin Islands, mainly St. Croix.

17.47 Lewis Oscar. A STUDY OF SLUM CULTURE: BACKGROUNDS FOR *LA*

VIDA. With the assistance of Douglas Butterworth. New York, Random House, 1968. 240 p. tables, bibl.

A study of one hundred low-income Puerto Rican families from four slums of the San Juan area, and their relatives who migrated to New York City. It is the product of exhaustive research into family case studies, and aims "to contribute to our understanding of urban slum life in San Juan" and "to examine the problems of adjustment and the changes in the family life of migrants to New York."

17.48 Lewis, Oscar. LA VIDA: A PUERTO RICAN FAMILY IN THE CULTURE OF POVERTY—SAN JUAN AND NEW YORK. New York, Random House, 1966. 669 p.

The author of the now classic, although still controversial study, tests the concept of a culture of poverty within the context of Puerto Rico. He lets the persons in the book speak for themselves through tape recorded interviews of a low-income Puerto Rican slum family, the Ríos, both in San Juan and New York. He tries "to give a voice to the people who are rarely heard, and to provide the reader with an inside view of a style of life which is common in many of the deprived and marginal groups in our society but which is largely unknown . . . to most middle-class readers."

17.49 Lockett, Edward B. THE PUERTO RICO PROBLEM. Foreword by George J. Oliver. New York, Exposition Press, 1964. 196 p. bibl.

A study of Puerto Rican migration to the United States. It appraises "the economic and social impact of island natives' movement to the mainland, its perils for mainland society and the economy, and explores prospects for reducing the migration volume and easing its mainland impact." It speaks of "certain foreign characteristics," of the "refusal, in a sense, to become 'American'," and other aspects.

17.50 Lucas, Isidro. PUERTO RICAN DROPOUTS IN CHICAGO: NUMBERS AND MOTIVATIONS. Washington, U.S. Office of Education, Bureau of Research, 1971. 100 p. tables, questionnaire, bibl. (Final Report, Project no. 0-E-108).

This study concluded that 71.2 percent of all Puerto Ricans who start classes in Chicago drop out before graduation. It found also that discrimination, lack of communication between parents and children, and lack of meaningful communication between the youths and the schools were the principal reasons for such a high dropout rate. The study ends with a series of recommendations aimed at reducing it.

17.51 Margolis, Richard. The Losers: A Report on Puerto Ricans and the Public Schools. New York, Aspira, 1968. 17 l. tables. mimeographed.

Based on visits to sixteen schools in seven cities, the author examines the predicament of Puerto Rican children in public schools in the United States—what they are, or are not learning, and what the schools are, or are not, doing to help them.

17.52 Mayerson, Charlotte Leon, ed. TWO BLOCKS APART: JUAN GONZALES AND PETER QUINN. New York, Holt, Rhinehart and Winston, c1965. 126p. illus.

Two seventeen-year-olds from the same New York City neighborhood—Juan, a poor Puerto Rican, and Peter, a white middle-class North American—talk to Mrs. Mayerson about their families, the neighborhood, the schools they attend, and politics.

17.53 McCauley, Margaret A. A Study of Social Class and Assimilation in Relation to Puerto Rican Family Patterns. Ph.D. dissertation, Fordham University, 1972. *In* DISSERTATION ABSTRACTS INTERNATIONAL, v. 33, no. 1, p. 428-A.

A study among Puerto Rican families living in New York City with the purpose of examining the association of Puerto Rican conjugal role relationships with socioeconomic status and degree of assimilation.

17.54 Méndez Santos, Carlos. LOS 'INMIGRANTES' PUERTORRIQUEÑOS EN LOS ESTADOS UNIDOS. Ponce, Universidad Católica de Puerto Rico, 1968. 20 p. port., bibl. refs. (Ciencias Sociales, Folleto no. 1).

A lecture delivered at the Catholic

University of America in Washington, D.C., analyzing the migration process of Puerto Ricans to the United States and their assimilation.

17.55 Mills, C. Wright, Clarence Senior, and Rose K. Goldsen. PUERTO RICAN JOURNEY: NEW YORK'S NEWEST MIGRANTS. New York, Harper and Bros., 1950. Reprint. New York, Russell & Russell, 1967. 238 p. illus., tables, bibl.

Field study conducted in two core areas in 1948 by a research team of the Bureau of Applied Social Research of Columbia University. Although the statistics are outdated, the book might still be useful for understanding some of the basic problems facing the migrants.

17.56 National Conference of Puerto Ricans, Mexican-Americans, and Educators on the Special Education Needs of Urban Youth, New York, 1968. HEMOS TRABAJADO BIEN: A REPORT. Edited by Nelson Aldrich. New York, Aspira, [1968?]. 74 p.

A summary of the discussions held May 14 and 15, 1968, on bilingualism, teacher and student attitudes, curriculum and textbooks, community involvement, and other issues affecting the education of the Puerto Rican students in the United States.

17.57 Naun, Robert John. Comparison of Group Counseling Approaches with Puerto Rican Boys in an Inner-City High School. Ph.D. dissertation, Fordham University, 1971. In DISSERTATION ABSTRACTS INTERNATIONAL, v. 32, no. 2, p. 742-A.

This study explores the possible differences in the effects of two different methods of group counseling on thirty-one ninth-and tenth-grade Puerto Rican boys living in a federally designated poverty area and attending an inner-city high school. Three groups were involved in the study, one receiving interventionist counseling, another receiving noninterventionist counseling, and a third group receiving no counseling at all.

17.58 NEW YORK MAGAZINE, v. 5, no. 32, Aug. 7, 1972.

Contents. The Big Mango; The Latin Diaspora; Nueva York; The Latin Elite;

The Man Who Took the IRT to San Juan; An Aficionado's Guide to the True Latin Style; La Situación; Geraldo the Proud; Art in the Barrio; The Machismo Mystique.

17.59 O'Neill, George C., and Nena O'Neill. VOCATIONAL REHABILITATION NEEDS OF DISABLED PUERTO RICANS IN NEW YORK CITY. New York, Puerto Rican Social Services, 1964. 118 p.

Results of a pilot research project designed "to derive hypotheses for further testing or to develop research strategy and priorities," which found a high degree of motivation among disabled Puerto Ricans. It stresses the fact that these people need bilingual personnel who will take a personal interest in the special problems encountered by Puerto Ricans during their rehabilitation.

17.60 Oxman, Wendy G. The Effects of Ethnic Identity of Experimenter, Language of Experimental Task, and Bilingual vs. Nonbilingual School Attendance on the Verbal Task Performance of Bilingual Children of Puerto Rican Background. Ph.D. dissertation, Fordham University, 1972. In DISSERTATION ABSTRACTS INTERNATIONAL, v. 33, no. 1, p. 195-A.

An investigation conducted among 256 fourth- and fifth-grade Puerto Ricans to determine whether bilingual minority group children showed evidence of alienation from school in a nonbilingual school environment, and whether attendance at a school with a bilingual program might have prevented or alleviated that alienation.

17.61 Padilla, Elena. UP FROM PUERTO RICO. New York, Columbia University Press, 1958. 317 p. illus.

Cultural anthropological study of a small group of Puerto Rican migrant families in a section of Manhattan, in which the author, with the assistance of a research team, explored "the social adaptations of Puerto Ricans to American slum life."

17.62 Pagán de Colón, Petroamérica. PROGRAMA DE COLOCACIONES DE TRABAJADORES AGRICOLAS

PUERTORRIQUEÑOS EN ESTADOS UNIDOS. San Juan, Departamento del Trabajo, n.d. 50 p.

A booklet written in the mid-fifties explaining the evolution of the migrant farm workers program from the first attempts by private employment agencies to hire and bring Puerto Ricans to work in homes, farms, and industrial plants in the United States, to the start by the Puerto Rican government in 1948 of an officially-supervised program to provide Puerto Rican laborers for farm work in the United States, with safeguards that would prevent their exploitation.

17.63 PAPERS ON PUERTO RICAN STUDIES. [Río Piedras], Puerto Rico Junior College Foundation and National Endowment for the Humanities, November, 1970. 139 p. bibls. mimeographed.

Contents. What is a Puerto Rican?, by A. Morales Carrión; Puerto Rico: su ambiente natural, by Z. Buitrago de Santiago; Política puertorriqueña y relaciones con los Estados Unidos, by T. Mathews; Puerto Rico's economic dilemma, by A.I.D. Francis; Boricuas; the Puerto Ricans in the United States, by A. Pantoja; Ethnic studies and cultural pluralism, by E. Seda-Bonilla; and El futuro de la realidad puertorriqueña, by J.M. García-Passalacqua.

Papers presented at a conference on Puerto Rican Studies held in San Juan, November 12–13, 1970, under the sponsorship of the Puerto Rico Junior College Foundation with the support of the National Endowment for the Humanities, with the purpose of establishing some initial ties among the various U.S. institutions already offering Puerto Rican studies programs, and between them and the various educational institutions in the island.

17.64 PHILADELPHIA'S PUERTO RICAN POPULATION WITH 1960 CENSUS DATA. Philadelphia, Commission of Human Relations, 1964.

A descriptive survey of the characteristics of the Puerto Rican population in Philadelphia, with comparisons with other white and nonwhite groups. It concludes that "Puerto Ricans residing outside the area of greatest Puerto Rican concen-

tration are on the average in a higher socioeconomic bracket ... following the pattern of many ethnic groups before them who scattered about the city as they were able to better themselves." The report identified some of the agencies providing services to Puerto Ricans.

17.65 Pollack, Erwin W., and Julius Menacker. SPANISH-SPEAKING STUDENTS AND GUIDANCE. New York, Houghton Mifflin, 1971. 86 p. bibl.

An attempt to interpret to teachers, school counselors, and others involved with students of Puerto Rican or Mexican-American background some of the historical, social, economic, and language differences that set them apart from other youths in the United States.

17.66 Protestant Council of the City of New York. Department of Church Planning and Research. A REPORT ON THE PROTESTANT SPANISH COMMUNITY IN NEW YORK CITY. New York, 1960. 138 p. maps, tables, bibl.

A survey of approaches to Puerto Rican and other Spanish-speaking groups taken by different Protestant denominations. Includes data on number of churches ministering to Puerto Ricans, size of church membership, types of programs they have developed, and names and addresses of the churches.

17.67 Puerto Rican Association for National Affairs (PANA). How Equitably are Bilingual-Bicultural Education Programs Servicing the Puerto Rican Students? [Washington, 1972]. 18 p. tables, bibl. refs. mimeographed.

An analysis, backed by ample statistics, which concludes that Puerto Ricans have been consistently ignored in the design and evaluation of bilingual education programs and that they have not received an equitable share of the benefits of such programs.

17.68 PUERTO RICAN PROFILES. New York City Board of Education, 1964. 96 p. tables. (Its Curriculum Bulletin no. 5, 1964–1965 ser.)

Intended as resource materials for teachers, this is a compilation of readings on Puerto Ricans, their background, and their experience in New York City.

17.69 Puerto Rican Research and Resources Center. Puerto Rican Migration—A Preliminary Report. [Washington], U.S. Commission on Civil Rights, 1972. 56 p. bibl. refs. mimeographed. Also published in Spanish.

A research paper prepared for the U.S. Commission on Civil Rights constituting an overall profile of the Puerto Rican community in the United States. It reviews their living conditions and the problems, particularly in employment, that they face.

17.70 THE PUERTO RICAN STUDY, 1953–1957: A REPORT ON THE EDUCATION AND ADJUSTMENT OF PUERTO RICAN PUPILS IN THE PUBLIC SCHOOLS OF THE CITY OF NEW YORK. J. Cayce Morrison, director. With an introductory essay by Francesco Cordasco. New York, Oriole Editions, 1972. 265 p. tables, bibl.

This report by the New York City Board of Education, originally published in 1958, summarized the findings of a four-year inquiry into the education and adjustment of Puerto Rican pupils in the public schools of New York City. The study analyzed the methods and materials for teaching and the socio-cultural adjustment of Puerto Rican pupils and parents. It also identified areas for action and improvement. Numerous other reports on specific aspects and curriculum materials were published by the board at the time as part of the Puerto Rican study.

17.71 Puerto Ricans in New York State (Puertorriqueños en el Estado de Nueva York) 1960–1969. New York, New York (State) Division of Human Rights, 1969. 67 p. bibl. refs. mimeographed.

Describes the numbers and characteristics of the Puerto Rican population of New York State, their housing conditions, the complaints charging discrimination against Puerto Ricans received by the State Division of Human Rights, and prospects for the future. A summary in Spanish is appended.

17.72 Rand, Christopher. THE PUERTO RICANS. New York, Oxford University Press, 1958. 178 p.

A journalistic account of the Puerto Rican migrants living in New York in the fifties—their origins, the barrio, and their lifestyle in the city.

17.73 Ribes Tovar, Federico. EL LIBRO PUERTORRIQUEÑO DE NUEVA YORK: HANDBOOK OF THE PUERTO RICAN COMMUNITY. New York, El Libro Puertorriqueño, 1968. 394 p. (Colección Grandes Emigraciones).

An attempt at collecting a record of Puerto Rican migration to New York. The author includes an overview of the Puerto Rican migration, data on "illustrious exiles," popular aspects of Puerto Rican life in New York, and information on some of the social, economic, and cultural problems encountered by the migrants.

17.74 Rogler, Lloyd H. MIGRANT IN THE CITY: THE LIFE OF A PUERTO RICAN ACTION GROUP. New York, Basic Books, 1972. 251 p. bibl. refs.

Study of a Puerto Rican citizens group in New Jersey, the Hispanic Confederation of Maplewood, conducted over a forty-four month period—from its inception to the point when they became an action group. The narrative gives insight into the problems, social change, viewpoints of the organizers, group dynamics, and methods involved in an action group and its study.

17.75 Rosner, Milton S. A Study of Contemporary Patterns of Aspirations and Achievements of the Puerto Ricans of Hell's Kitchen. Ph.D. dissertation, New York University, 1960. In DISSERTATION ABSTRACTS, v. 18, no. 5, p. 1886-A.

This study examines patterns of aspirations and achievements of one hundred Puerto Rican family units of Hell's Kitchen, New York City. More specifically, the objectives of the study are focused on determining the sociocultural variations related to gradations of achievement in the family units involved, and the relationship of these patterns of achievement with levels of aspirations in Puerto Rico and New York.

17.76 Rubinstein, Annette T., ed. SCHOOLS AGAINST CHILDREN: THE CASE FOR COMMUNITY CONTROL. New York, Monthly Review Press, 1970. 299 p. tables, bibl. ref.

This book is a compilation of readings on racial equality in education in New York City, and the alternate system of community control. It includes an essay by Doxey A. Wilkerson, "The Failure of Schools Serving the Black and Puerto Rican Poor," as well as references to Puerto Rican children in other essays.

17.77 Ruiz, Paquita. VOCATIONAL NEEDS OF PUERTO RICAN MIGRANTS. Río Piedras, Social Science Research Center, University of Puerto Rico, 1947. 84 p. bibl.

A study of the vocational, social, and educational needs of 3,024 male Puerto Ricans who had migrated to New York City during 1940–1944. It identifies some of the areas that could be given more attention prior to migration.

17.78 Schroeder, Richard C. SPANISH-AMERICANS: THE NEW MILITANTS. Washington, Editorial Research Reports, 1970: 709–729. (*Its* Reports, v. 11, no. 12).

A look at the recently emerged Spanish-American political activism which in the author's opinion is a direct result of the discrimination and exploitation of which the Spanish-Americans have been victims.

17.79 Senior, Clarence Ollson. The Puerto Rican Migrant in St. Croix. Río Piedras, Social Science Research Center, University of Puerto Rico, 1947. 42 l. tables, bibl. refs. mimeographed.

A study on the Puerto Rican migration to St. Croix: how, when, why, and how many Puerto Ricans came, the reaction to them, and how they fared. Although outdated, the study throws light on Puerto Rican emigration.

17.80 Senior, Clarence Ollson. Puerto Rican Migration. Río Piedras, Social Science Research Center, University of Puerto Rico, 1947. 166 l. tables, bibl. refs. mimeographed.

This publication is one of the first studies on the movement of Puerto

Ricans. It describes the process and extent of migrations from Puerto Rico to Hawaii, St. Croix, Arizona, South America, the Dominican Republic, and New York City.

17.81 Senior, Clarence Ollson. THE PUERTO RICANS: STRANGERS—THEN NEIGHBORS. Foreword by H. Humphrey. Chicago, Quadrangle, 1965. 128 p. illus., tables, map, bibl. Paperback.

Examines Puerto Rican migration against the background of earlier immigrations, the reaction of the dominant society to the Puerto Rican migrants, and the life of the migrant himself. The book was published in cooperation with the Anti-Defamation League of B'nai B'rith.

17.82 Sexton, Patricia Cayo. SPANISH HARLEM: AN ANATOMY OF POVERTY. New York, Harper and Row, 1965. 208 p. map, bibl. refs. Paperback.

A portrait of East Harlem "so that the reader can see more clearly what a 'slum' looks like." It describes the problems and conditions and offers solutions mostly to the need for community organization and for its development as a tool for social justice

17.83 Siegel, Arthur, Harold Orlans and Loyal Greer. PUERTO RICANS IN PHILADELPHIA: A STUDY OF THEIR DEMOGRAPHIC CHARACTERISTICS, PROBLEMS, AND ATTITUDES. Philadelphia, Commission on Human Relations, April 1954. 135 p. tables, bibl.

One of the first in-depth, scientific surveys of Puerto Rican migrants living outside of New York City.

17.84 Sierra Berdecía, Fernando. LA EMIGRACION PUERTORRIQUEÑA: REALIDAD Y POLITICA PUBLICA. San Juan, Editorial del Departamento de Instrucción Pública, 1956. 23 p.

This booklet contains an address by a former secretary of labor in Puerto Rico in which he gives a bird's-eye view of Puerto Rican migration from 1908 to 1956, and states the government's policy regarding migration.

17.85 Silverman, Stuart Harold. The Effects of Peer Group Membership on Puerto Rican English. Ph.D. dissertation, Yeshiva University, 1971. *In* DIS-

SERTATION ABSTRACTS INTER-NATIONAL, v. 32, no. 10, p. 5621-A.

This study investigated the importance of peer group influence on language development using three groups of junior high school students: Puerto Ricans with Negro friends, Puerto Ricans without Negro friends, and Negro youngsters.

17.86   Simmons, W. R. and Associates. THE SPANISH-SPEAKING SCENE: SILHOUETTE OF NEW YORK CITY TODAY. New York, El Diario-La Prensa, February 1963. 60 p. charts, graphs, table.

A market research study based on a sample of 1,039 Spanish-speaking persons. Offers information on numbers of Puerto Ricans, occupations, employment, buying habits, ownership of appliances, and other similar data.

17.87   Spanish-American Community Profiles: Bridgeport. New York, Puerto Rican Forum, August 1970. various pagings. tables. mimeographed.

A study prepared for the Spanish-American Development Agency which attempts to define the human resources and social setting, industrial and commercial base, manpower, income, and education of the Spanish-American community in Bridgeport, Connecticut.

17.88   A STUDY OF POVERTY CONDITIONS IN THE NEW YORK PUERTO RICAN COMMUNITY. 3d ed. New York, Puerto Rican Forum, 1970. 86 p. tables, chart.

A profile of the Puerto Rican New Yorker in the mid-1960s highlighting the problems that he confronts in income, education, employment, housing, and health. In a short synopsis of the situation since 1964, which is included in this new edition, the Puerto Rican Forum states that during the intervening years: "the overall situation of the Puerto Rican New Yorker cannot be said to have improved appreciably. In the areas of employment, income, housing and education, new statistics underscore a proportionate deterioration in comparison with the black and white populations." The most significant development during the period, it adds, is "the increasing

awareness of the need to engage in political action based on community participation."

17.89   Thomas, Piri. DOWN THESE MEAN STREETS. New York, Knopf, 1967. 333 p.

An autobiographical account by a Puerto Rican of life in East Harlem. It tells of his childhood in the slums, the violence, and his rebellion against it.

17.90   Thomas, Piri. SAVIOR, SAVIOR, HOLD MY HAND. Garden City, N.Y., Doubleday, 1972. 372 p.

After spending seven years in jail the author returns to the ghetto. This book chronicles in street talk his feelings as an ex-convict and his impressions of the world he finds around him.

17.91   Varo, Carlos. CONSIDERACIONES ANTROPOLOGICAS Y POLITICAS EN TORNO A LA ENSEÑANZA DEL 'SPANGLISH' EN NUEVA YORK. Río Piedras, P.R., Ediciones Librería Internacional, 1971. 121 p.

A discussion of linguistic penetration, bilingualism, and political and economic repression of Puerto Ricans, especially the younger generation of "Neo-Ricans." It discusses the nature and methodology of "Spanglish." The book is written from a radical viewpoint.

17.92   Wakefield, Dan. ISLAND IN THE CITY: THE WORLD OF SPANISH HARLEM. Boston, Houghton Mifflin, 1959. 278 p.

A reporter who lived in East Harlem for nearly six months chronicles the people, their lives, and their miserable living conditions.

17.93   Watson, Eloise Jean. The Employment Experience of Male Mental Retardates: A Study of the Relationship of Certain Cultural Factors to the Employment Experience of Negro and Puerto Rican Graduates of New York City CRMD Classes. Ph.D. dissertation, New York University, 1971. In DISSERTATION ABSTRACTS INTERNATIONAL, v. 32, no. 10, p. 5591-B.

This study was undertaken to determine whether two equally matched groups of Puerto Rican and Negro male retardates, all graduates of New

York City's public school CRMD classes, showed significant differences in their employment experience and, if they did, to examine these differences in relation to specific differences in the subcultures of the two groups.

17.94 Welfare Council of New York City. Committee on Puerto Ricans in New York City. PUERTO RICANS IN NEW YORK CITY: THE REPORT OF THE COMMITTEE. New York, 1948. 60 p.

Publication which describes the problems of Puerto Ricans in New York City and their needs in terms of "the local manifestation of a nationwide problem in which are involved on the one hand the overcrowding of cities . . ., and on the other hand, the unsolved economy of an island possession of the United States."

18
POPULATION

18.1 Bartlett, Frederic P., and Brandon Howell. THE POPULATION PROBLEM IN PUERTO RICO. Santurce, Puerto Rico Planning, Urbanizing, and Zoning Board, 1944. 117 p. tables, maps, diagrs., bibl. (Technical Paper, no. 2).

Part 1 is a study of the roots of the population problem as it affects Puerto Rico as a whole with some suggestions for possible solutions. Part 2 analyzes population characteristics and trends by regions and municipalities.

18.2 Calero, Reinaldo. ANALISIS DE ALGUNOS CAMBIOS RECIENTES EN LA POBLACION DE PUERTO RICO. Río Piedras, Universidad de Puerto Rico, 1964. 66 p. maps, tables, graphs. (Estación Experiemental Agrícola. Boletín, 183).

Analysis of the factors that determine the growth, size, and age-sex composition of the population in the sugar cane, coffee, and tobacco regions: birth and death rates and the rate of net migration. It presents also an analysis of the relationships between the fertility ratio and the net migration as dependent variables, and certain socioeconomic characteristics of the population as independent variables. English summary and conclusions.

18.3 Chaves, Antonio. LA DISTRIBUCION DE LA POBLACION EN PUERTO RICO. Río Piedras, Editorial Universi-

taria, Universidad de Puerto Rico, 1949. 46 p. maps, tables.

Analysis based on 1940 census figures of population distribution in the various regions of the island, which show a tendency toward concentration in the north and eastern areas.

18.4 Cofresí, Emilio. "Birth Control in Puerto Rico." In Conference on the Family in the Caribbean, 1, St. Thomas, V.I., 1968. PROCEEDINGS. Río Piedras, University of Puerto Rico Institute of Caribbean Studies, 1968. 147 p. tables.

A summary of birth control programs and related research.

18.5 Cofresí, Emilio. MALTUSIANISMO O NEOMALTUSIANISMO: NUESTRO GRAN DILEMA. Mexico, Editorial Cultura, 1968. 217 p. tables, graphs, bibl.

A professor at the University of Puerto Rico analyzes the island's population growth from discovery to 1966 and the composition of the population. He discusses the various forms of birth control, which he believes is the indispensable solution to the island's population problems.

18.6 Geisert, Harold L. THE CARIBBEAN: POPULATION AND RESOURCES. Washington, George Washington University, 1960. 48 p. tables, bibl. (Population Research Project).

An analysis of population growth, composition and distribution, and the relation of population to production in Puerto Rico and five other countries.

18.7 Hatt, Paul K. BACKGROUNDS OF HUMAN FERTILITY IN PUERTO RICO: A SOCIOLOGICAL SURVEY. Princeton, N.J., Princeton University Press, 1952. 512 p. tables, questionnaires.

Report of the findings of a field study sponsored jointly by the Social Science Research Center of the University of Puerto Rico and the Office of Population Research of Princeton University regarding basic attitude patterns and life conditions which affect fertility levels in Puerto Rico.

18.8 Hill, Reuben, J. Mayone Stycos, and Kurt W. Back. THE FAMILY AND POPULATION CONTROL: A PUERTO RICAN EXPERIMENT IN SOCIAL CHANGE. Chapel Hill, University of North Carolina Press, 1959. 481 p. tables, questionnaires, bibl.

This study, sponsored by the Social Science Research Center of the University of Puerto Rico, in cooperation with the Institute for Research in Social Science of the University of North Carolina, was aimed at depicting the workings of the family in fertility control and ascertaining why the equalization of birth rates and death rates has not occurred in the island even though "Puerto Rico's population is ripe for substantial declines in the birth rate both ideologically and technically."

18.9 Nerlove, Marc, and T. Paul Schultz. LOVE AND LIFE BETWEEN THE CENSUSES: A MODEL OF FAMILY DECISION-MAKING IN PUERTO RICO, 1950–1960. Santa Monica, Cal., Rand Corp., 1970. 105 p.

First of four "country studies" undertaken under the sponsorship of the Agency for International Development. It is intended as "a progress report on the feasibility and potential usefulness of comprehensive analysis of the system of family behavior that surrounds reproductive decisions." It develops a model of family decision making aimed at contrasting and evaluating "the dynamic repercussions of

alternative policy choices for the development of Puerto Rico."

18.10 Oser, Jacob. "Food and Population in Puerto Rico: A Case Study." *In his* MUST MEN STARVE? New York, Abelard-Schuman, 1957. p. 286–323.

The author discusses briefly Puerto Rico's population and food problems and the government's economic and agricultural policies, and concludes that such policies will have to be better directed if the food needs of the island are to be met adequately.

18.11 Presser, Harriet Betty Rubinoff. Sterilization and Fertility Decline in Puerto Rico. Ph.D. dissertation, University of California at Berkeley, 1969. *In* DISSERTATION ABSTRACTS INTERNATIONAL, v. 30, no. 7, p. 3108-A.

A study of the practice of voluntary female sterilization in Puerto Rico among women of reproductive age in the mid-1960s, based largely on data provided by the 1965 Master Sample Survey of Health and Welfare in Puerto Rico.

18.12 Proudfoot, Malcolm Jarvis. POPULATION MOVEMENTS IN THE CARIBBEAN. New York, Negro Universities Press, 1970. 187 p. tables, bibl. Reprint of the 1950 edition.

Survey sponsored by the Caribbean Commission with the purpose of analyzing evidence of population pressure in the area; past population increments that must be absorbed by migration or employment outside of agriculture; major migratory movements, and outlook for migration in the future.

18.13 Rico-Velasco, Jesús. Modernization and Fertility in an Ecological Analysis. Ph.D. dissertation, Ohio State University, 1972. *In* DISSERTATION ABSTRACTS INTERNATIONAL, v. 33, no. 2., p. 839-A.

An examination of the ecological correlates of community fertility levels of a society in the midst of economic development. Specifically, the research explored the effects of urbanization and industrialization, community socioeconomic status, and the participation of women in the labor force upon fertility ratios in a developing society.

18.14 Schmidt-Sánchez, Carlos. Changing Patterns of Population Fertility in Puerto Rico. Ph.D. dissertation, University of Illinois, 1967. *In* DISSERTATION ABSTRACTS, v. 28, no. 4, p. 1538-A.

This research deals with differential fertility in an industrializing country, Puerto Rico. In a broad sense it is a case study of society, attempting to describe the consequences of industrial growth on fertility behavior at a given point in time. The thesis provides detailed analysis of variation in fecundity, fertility values, and attitudes in relation to important demographic, social and, economic characteristics.

18.15 Stycos, J. Mayone. FAMILY AND FERTILITY IN PUERTO RICO: A STUDY OF THE LOWER INCOME GROUP. New York, Columbia University Press, 1955. 332 p. diagrs., tables, forms, bibl.

Sponsored by the Social Science Research Center of the University of Puerto Rico, this study concentrates on the sexual norms, character structure, fertility belief system, and birth control practices, as they affect and are affected by the family, and as they affect fertility. A final chapter synthesizes these various elements into a hypothetical model of lower-class fertility determinants. (Also published in Spanish: *Familia y Fecundidad en Puerto Rico: Estudio del Grupo de Ingresos Más Bajos*, Mexico City, Fondo de Cultura Economica, 1958.)

18.16 Thieme, Frederick P. THE PUERTO RICAN POPULATION: A STUDY IN HUMAN BIOLOGY. Ann Arbor, University of Michigan, 1959. 156 p. maps, diagrs., tables, forms, bibl. (Anthropological Papers, no. 13).

Summarizes the biological part of an anthropological field study of the Puerto Rican population carried out in 1948–1949 under the sponsorship of the Social Science Research Center of the University of Puerto Rico. It describes the biological characteristics of a selected sample of adult Puerto Ricans and the physical variability in the Puerto Rican population, in terms of differences in environmental or genetic background.

19
RELIGION AND PHILOSOPHY

19.1 Andino, Telesforo. EL ESPIRITISMO EN PUERTO RICO Y LA REFORMA. San Juan, Tip. San Juan, 1937. 226 p.

The author presents the concepts related to spiritism in a detailed manner. He believes the purpose of spiritism is to complement both philosophy and theosophy because the spirit is the cognitive and generative power of man, as well as the natural action of the soul.

19.2 Baselza, Edward M. Cultural Change and Protestantism in Puerto Rico. Ph.D. dissertation, New York University, 1971. *In* DISSERTATION ABSTRACTS INTERNATIONAL, v. 32, no. 4, p. 2205-A.

This study is concerned with the interaction of the sacred and profane within the cultural realm.

19.3 Campo Lacasa, Cristina. NOTAS GENERALES SOBRE LA HISTORIA ECLESIASTICA DE PUERTO RICO EN EL SIGLO XVIII. Sevilla, Escuela de Estudios Hispano-Americanos, 1963. 127 p. illus., facsims., maps, plans. (*Its* Publicaciones, 137).

Based on the documents of the Archivo General de Indias in Seville, the book summarizes the work done by the Catholic church in Puerto Rico during the eighteenth century. It explains how the church was organized, its architecture—especially that of the Cathedral of San Juan—its charities and educational work, and the relations between the civil government and the church.

19.4 Carreras, Carlos H. IDEARIO DE HOSTOS. San Juan, Editorial Cordillera, 1966. 250 p.

Selections demonstrating Hostos' ideology and philosophy, arranged in chronological order with references to his works.

19.5 Corro, Alejandro del, comp. PUERTO RICO: OBISPOS NATIVOS, 1962–65: DOCUMENTOS Y REACCIONES DE PRENSA. Cuernavaca, México, Centro Intercultural de Documentación, 1967. 358 p. (Dossier, 16).

Collection of documents, letters, and press coverage of the controversy over an autochthonous Puerto Rican clergy and episcopate which surfaced in 1962. It includes the historical background of the polemic.

19.6 Cuesta Mendoza, Antonio. HISTORIA ECLESIASTICA DEL PUERTO RICO COLONIAL, 1508–1700. Ciudad Trujillo, Imprenta Arte y Cine, 1948. 352 p.

Claims to be the first ecclesiastical history of Puerto Rico. The author interprets church events and organization since the arrival of the first bishop, Alonso Manso, in 1513. He also wrote *Los Dominicos en el Puerto Rico Colonial, 1521–1821* (México, Imprenta de Manuel León Sánchez, 1946) about the educational contribution made by the Dominican order in Puerto Rico until 1821, when they were forced to close the Colegio Santo Tomás de Aquino.

19.7 Custer, Watson S. A Decade of Church-State Relations in Puerto Rico 1952–1962. Ph.D. dissertation, Temple University, 1965. *In* DISSERTATION ABSTRACTS, v. 26, no. 7, p. 4098.

Examines the 1952–1962 period in which basic Roman Catholic and Protestant church-state issues were raised, considered, and decided upon by the people of Puerto Rico, including the attempt by the Catholic church in 1960 to use the church as an instrument of political action.

19.8 Díaz-Alonso, María Mercedes. An Approach to Church and State Relations in Puerto Rico. Ph.D. dissertation,

Catholic University of America, 1972. *In* DISSERTATION ABSTRACTS INTERNATIONAL, v. 33, no. 2, p. 692-A.

A study of Puerto Rico's approach to church and state relations during the years 1960–1962. It examines the problems that caused the rupture between the church authorities and the Commonwealth government in 1960; the position assumed by the church in Puerto Rico and in the United States; negotiations with the Apostolic Nuncio in Santo Domingo, and other aspects.

19.9 Dohen, Dorothy. TWO STUDIES OF PUERTO RICO: RELIGION DATA [AND] THE BACKGROUND OF CONSENSUAL UNION. Cuernavaca, México, Centro Intercultural de Documentatión, 1966. 246 p. maps, tables, graphs, bibl. (Sondeos, 3).

The first of these two analyses is a statistical study of the religious practices in Puerto Rico based on data compiled in 1958. The second work studies the relationship between the practice of consensual union and sociological conditions.

19.10 Fenton, Jerry. UNDERSTANDING THE RELIGIOUS BACKGROUND OF THE PUERTO RICAN. Cuernavaca, México, Centro Intercultural de Documentación, 1969. 72 p. bibl. (Sondeos, 52).

Discusses the practice of religion— Catholicism, Protestantism, Spiritism and Pentecostalism—by Puerto Ricans both in Puerto Rico and in New York. Concludes that in their religious rites Puerto Ricans are seeking "something that will give meaning" to the progress they have achieved, and that they do not want "a dead Christ, a schizophrenic Christ, a sectarian Christ, but .. a Christ who lives and acts and cares."

19.11 Fránquiz Ventura, José A. APRECIACION FILOSOFICA DE LA OBRA DEL DR. JUAN BAUTISTA SOTO. México, 1941. 42 p. bibl. (Cuadernos de filosofía de Luminar, 4).

A short, erudite, essay analyzing the philosophical content of the works of Juan Bautista Soto. The author compares his ethics with the ethical system of Eugenio María de Hostos which, although systematic, lacks metaphysical basis.

19.12 Fránquiz Ventura, José A. BORDEN PARKER BOWNE'S TREATMENT OF THE PROBLEM OF CHANGE AND IDENTITY. Río Piedras, University of Puerto Rico, 1942. 260 p. bibl. (University of Puerto Rico Bulletin, ser. 13, no. 1).

A doctoral dissertation on the relations of change and identity with reference to their treatment in the philosophical writings of Borden Parker Bowne.

19.13 Holsinger, Justus C. SERVING RURAL PUERTO RICO: A HISTORY OF EIGHT YEARS OF SERVICE BY THE MENNONITE CHURCH. Scottdale, Pa., Mennonite Publishing House, 1952. 231 p.

Describes the work carried out by members of the Civilian Public Service of the Brethren Service Commission in rural communities of Puerto Rico during the early 1940s. Activities were concentrated in Castañer, Zalduondo, and La Plata, sites of Puerto Rico Reconstruction Administration (PRRA) projects.

19.14 International Missionary Council. THE CHURCH IN PUERTO RICO'S DILEMMA: A STUDY OF THE ECONOMIC AND SOCIAL BASIS OF THE EVANGELICAL CHURCH IN PUERTO RICO. J. Merle Davis, Director. New York, Department of Social and Economic Research & Counsel, International Missionary Council, 1942. 80 p.

A survey of economic and social conditions of the island in the early 1940s, intended as a departure point for the work of the Evangelical church in Puerto Rico in the following decades.

19.15 López de Santa Anna, Antonio, S.J. LOS JESUITAS EN PUERTO RICO DE 1858 A 1886, CON OCASION DE CUMPLIRSE LOS CIEN AÑOS DE SU LLEGADA A LA ISLA, 1858–1958. Santander, Spain, Talleres de Artes Gráficas de los Hermanos Bedia, Publicación Privada, 1958. 190 p. illus., bibl.

Historic survey of the Jesuits' contri-

bution to education in Puerto Rico from 1858, when they arrived and opened the Seminario-Colegio de San Ildefonso, to 1886, when they left the island.

19.16 López-Melus, Rafael María. CINCUENTA AÑOS DEL CARMELO EN PUERTO RICO (1920–1970). Roma, Padres Carmelitas, 1970. 284 p.

A history of the activities of Carmelite monks and nuns in Puerto Rico during the last fifty years.

19.17 Mergal Llera, Angel Manuel. PUERTO RICO: ENIGMA Y PROMESA. San Juan, Editorial Club de la Prensa, 1960. 244 p. bibl.

Collection of philosophical essays elaborating on a theory about human relations and sociology that is based on a personal interpretation of christianity, philosophy, and theology. Chapter 3 is devoted to the dynamic structure of Puerto Rican culture divided according to three categories: somatic, psychic, and ethnic.

19.18 Moore, Donald T. PUERTO RICO PARA CRISTO: A HISTORY OF THE PROGRESS OF THE EVANGELICAL MISSIONS ON THE ISLAND OF PUERTO RICO. Cuernavaca, México, Centro Intercultural de Documentación, 1969. 332 p. bibl. (Sondeos, 43).

Traces "the development and expansion of evangelicalism as it occupied the various territories and populated areas of the island. It is concerned with both the occupation of territory by the evangelicals and the advance of the new churches toward indigeneity which involves three primary factors—the progress of insular self-support, the development of Puerto Rican leadership, and the achievement of local autonomy."

19.19 Odell, Edward A. IT CAME TO PASS. New York, Board of the National Missions, Presbyterian Church in the U.S.A., 1952. 174 p. illus.

A summary of the Presbyterian church's first fifty years of activity in Puerto Rico, Cuba, and the Dominican Republic. The section on Puerto Rico describes briefly the work of the first Presbyterian missionaries in the island; the period of development and extension; and the years between 1928 and 1952 when Presbyterian missionaries returned to the United States or began working under the direction of Puerto Ricans.

19.20 Pagán, Juan Bautista. LA DEMOCRACIA Y EL FUTURO. San Juan, Biblioteca de Autores Puertorriqueños, 1943. 142 p.

A philosophical interpretation of the true meaning of democracy.

19.21 Parrilla Bonilla, Antulio. PUERTO RICO: IGLESIA Y SOCIEDAD, 1967–1969, CONFERENCIAS, DISCURSOS, ENTREVISTAS. Cuernavaca, México, Centro Intercultural de Documentación, 1970. unp. (Sondeos, 66).

A compilation of speeches, interviews, lectures, and other statements by Bishop Parrilla divided into three major categories: church reform; Puerto Rico's political situation and other political issues; and cooperatives and other social action concerns.

19.22 Perea, Juan Augusto. EARLY ECCLESIASTICAL HISTORY OF PUERTO RICO. Caracas, Tip. Cosmos, 1929. 102 p.

Documented historical essay of the times of Alonso Manso, the first bishop in Puerto Rico and in the New World, 1513–1539.

19.23 Riestra, Miguel A. FUNDAMENTOS FILOSOFICOS DE LA EDUCACION. Río Piedras, Editorial Universitaria, Universidad de Puerto Rico, 1970. 317 p.

The first two parts deal with the fundamental principles of philosophy and the various concepts regarding the nature and the function of educational philosophy. The remaining four sections deal with idealism, realism, pragmatism, and existentialism.

19.24 Rosario Ramos, Tomás. LOS BAUTISTAS EN PUERTO RICO. APUNTES HISTORICOS. Prólogo de Rafael J. Rodríguez. Santo Domingo, Dominican Republic, Editorial Librería Dominicana, 1969. 176 p. illus., facsims., maps, ports., bibl.

A Baptist minister puts together the first history of the Baptist church in Puerto Rico, which was organized in 1899.

19.25 Saenz, Michael. Economic Aspects of Church Development in Puerto Rico: A Study of the Financial Policies and Procedures of the Major Protestant Church Groups in Puerto Rico, 1898–1957. Ph.D. dissertation, University of Pennsylvania, 1961. In DISSERTATION ABSTRACTS, v. 22, no. 4, p. 1035-A.

This study deals with two aspects of church growth—in numbers and in amount given—which lend themselves to objective inquiry and may also provide some indication of other, more subjective types of growth.

19.26 Soto, Juan B. LA TRAGEDIA DEL PENSAMIENTO. Río Piedras, Universidad de Puerto Rico, 1937. 225 p.

An exposition of philosophical thought. The author suggests that the solution to the tragedy of thought is to recognize that probabilism is the only justifiable criterion for judgment.

19.27 Soto, Juan Bautista. ESTUDIOS POLITICOS Y JURIDICOS. San Juan, Negociado de Materiales, Imprenta y Transporte, 1923. 155 p.

This study brings together five lectures delivered by the author in the law school of the University of Puerto Rico, which constitute a treatise on the philosophy of law. It covers law in philosophy, contemporary orientations of political and psychological problems, penal law and abnormal psychology, and the problem of delinquency from the biologic viewpoint.

20
SCIENCE AND TECHNOLOGY

20.1   Allen, Robert Porter. BIRDS OF THE CARIBBEAN. New York, Viking Press, 1961. 256 p. plates.

Ninety-eight color plates are accompanied by descriptions and an identification guide with the various names given to each species in the different countries of the region where they can be found.

20.2   Bagué y Ramírez, Jaime. GLOSARIO DE BIOLOGIA ANIMAL (ESPAÑOL-INGLES). GLOSSARY OF ANIMAL BIOLOGY. San Juan, Departamento de Agricultura y Comercio, 1952. Reprinted from *Almanaque Agricola de Puerto Rico, 1951-1952:* 193-373 p.

Alphabetical listing and definition of nearly three thousand Spanish terms used in animal biology with their English equivalents and definitions.

20.3   Beinroth, Friederich H. AN OUTLINE OF THE GEOLOGY OF PUERTO RICO. Río Piedras, Agricultural Experiment Station, University of Puerto Rico, Mayaguez Campus, 1969. 31 p. maps, diagrs., tables, bibl. (Bulletin 213).

Nontechnical, concise, up-to-date account of the island's geology.

20.4   Berryhill, Henry L., Jr. GEOLOGY OF THE CIALES QUADRANGLE, PUERTO RICO. Washington, Govt. Print. Off., 1965. 116 p. illus., maps, diagrs. tables, bibl. (U.S. Geological Survey. Bulletin 1184).

A geological study accompanied by a detailed map of an area covering approximately 184 square kilometers in north-central Puerto Rico. It describes the mineral resources and interprets the geological history and structural features of the area. The study is part of a continuing project for the geologic mapping of Puerto Rico carried out by the U.S. Geological Survey in cooperation with Puerto Rico's Economic Development Administration.

20.5   Biaggi, Virgilio. LAS AVES DE PUERTO RICO. Ilustraciones por Lucila Madruga de Piferrer y Christine Boyce. San Juan, Editorial Universitaria, Universidad de Puerto Rico, 1970. 371 p. illus, bibl.

After a brief history of ornithology in Puerto Rico the author embarks on the description of 239 species of birds found in the island. Chapters on bird classification, migration of wild life, and conservation are included. The book is enhanced by drawings of most of the birds, sixty-four of them in color.

20.6   Biaggi, Virgilio, Jr. THE PUERTO RICAN HONEYCREEPER (REINITA). Río Piedras, University of Puerto Rico, Agricultural Experiment Station, 1955. 61 p. illus., maps, tables, bibl. (Special Publication).

The first extensive life history study of a native Puerto Rican bird, the *reinita*, a member of the small family *coerebidae* that is confined to tropical and subtropical America.

20.7   Blanco, Enrique T. APUNTES PARA LA HISTORIA DE LA FAUNA ORNITOLOGICA DE PUERTO RICO. San Juan, Editorial Coquí, 1969. 114 p. ports., plates, bibl. (Ediciones Borinquen)

The author outlines some ideas for a history of the ornithological fauna of Puerto Rico, drawing on notes left by his late father, Tomás Blanco y González. He includes a catalog of the stuffed birds in his father's collection and plates of some of the species.

20.8   Bond, James. BIRDS OF THE WEST INDIES. Boston, Houghton Mifflin, 1961. 256 p.

Originally published in London in

1936, this book describes the various birds that inhabit the West Indies listed by their English names, followed by the Spanish and French equivalents.

20.9 Carnegie Institution of Washington. PAPERS FROM THE DEPARTMENT OF MARINE BIOLOGY. v. 12. Washington, 1918. 258 p. illus., bibl. (Carnegie Institution Publication no. 252).

Contents. Henry W. Fowler, "Some Amphibians and Reptiles from Porto Rico and the Virgin Islands"; Silvester, Charles F., "Fishes New to the Fauna of Porto Rico, with Descriptions of Eight New Species."

20.10 Chen, Ju-Chin. Petrological and Chemical Studies of Utuado Pluton, Puerto Rico. Ph.D. dissertation, Rice University, 1967. In DISSERTATION ABSTRACTS, v. 28, no. 5, 1987-B.

Studies of the Utuado Pluton and its associated rocks of volcanic and hydrothermal origins.

20.11 Dansereau, Pierre Mackay. Studies on the Vegetation of Puerto Rico. Mayagüez, University of Puerto Rico, Faculty of Arts and Sciences, 1966. 287 l. illus., diagr., tables, maps. (Institute of Caribbean Science, Special Publication no. 1). mimeographed.

Survey study which records and analyzes vegetation of Puerto Rico within six vegetation zones and their ecosystems. The first part is a description and integration of the plant communities; the second is an analysis and mapping of the Roosevelt Roads area.

20.12 Díaz-Piferrer, M., and Celeste Caballer de Pérez. TAXONOMIA, ECOLOGIA Y VALOR NUTRIMENTAL DE LAS ALGAS MARINAS DE PUERTO RICO: ALGAS PRODUCTORAS DE AGAR. Mayaguez, Instituto de Biología Marina, Colegio de Agricultura y Artes Mecánicas, 1964. 145 p. illus., tables, maps, bibl.

A study sponsored jointly by the Commonwealth Economic Development Administration and the Institute of Marine Biology of the Agricultural and Mechanical Arts College on the various kinds of agar-producing algae found in the littoral of Puerto Rico, the yields by species, their physical characteristics, and their industrial potential.

20.13 Engineering-Science Inc. CONTROL OF POTENTIAL SOURCES OF POLLUTION DUE TO PROPOSED COPPER MINING OPERATIONS IN PUERTO RICO. Arcadia, Calif., Engineering-Science, Inc., 1967. various pagings, illus., tables, diagrs.

Prepared under contract with the Mining Commission of the Commonwealth of Puerto Rico, the purpose of this study was to make a preliminary assessment of the potential air and water pollution that would be associated with the proposed development of the copper mining industry, and to explore and evaluate methods that would protect the air and water resources and still permit economically viable development of the industry.

20.14 Evermann, Barton Warren, and Millard Caleb Marsh. "Descriptions of New Genera and Species of Fishes from Puerto Rico." Extracted from U.S. Fish Commission, REPORT FOR 1899. Washington, Govt. Print. Off., 1899. p. 351-362.

Describes three genera and twenty species discovered during a two-month investigation of the aquatic life of the island conducted in the early months of 1899.

20.15 FLOWERS OF THE ISLANDS IN THE SUN. Paintings by Clarence E. Hall. Commentary by Graham Gooding. New York, A.S. Barnes, 1966. 143 p.

Full-color reproductions of paintings of thirty-two flowers. Although the specific islands where they grow are not mentioned, many of the flowers are found in Puerto Rico.

20.16 García-Martínez, Neftalí. PUERTO RICO Y LA MINERIA. San Juan, Ediciones Librería Internacional, n.d. 46 p. maps, tables, illus., bibl. refs. (Grupo de Evaluación Borinquen).

A discussion, by an opponent of the proposed mining operations for the Utuado-Adjuntas-Lares area, of some of the environmental, economic, and social implications of such operations. Even more important than those potential hazards, the author argues, would be the presence of big U.S. mining companies in Puerto Rico which "would constitute a force that would delay solving our problem of economic and political submission to the United States."

20.17   García Piquera, Carmen. GLOSARIO DE TERMINOLOGIA FORESTAL. San Juan, Depto. de Agricultura y Comercio, División de Información, 1955. 172 p. bibl. (Monografías, 5).
A glossary of English terms, and their Spanish equivalents, used in forestry.

20.18   Giusti, Ennio V. WATER RESOURCES OF THE COAMO AREA, PUERTO RICO. [Washington], U.S. Geological Survey, 1971. 31 p. illus. (Commonwealth of Puerto Rico. Water-Resources Bulletin, 9).
A report covering the hydrologic investigation conducted in 1967 in the Coamo area, on the south coast of Puerto Rico, with the purpose of making a preliminary, intensive reconnaissance of the water resources of the area.

20.19   Glover, Lynn, III. Geology of the Coamo Area, Puerto Rico: with Comments on Greater Antillean Volcanic Island Arc-Trench Phenomena. Ph.D. dissertation, Princeton University, 1967. In DISSERTATION ABSTRACTS, v. 28, no. 9, p. 3751-B.
Evidence from the Coamo district suggests that embryonic Puerto Rico was a topographically positive area of intermittently shoaling primary and reworked pyroclastics and minor lava and limestone.

20.20   Gonzalez-Pabón, José Felipe. Patterns of Psychopathology: Correspondences and Distinctions between Samples of American and Puerto Rican Mental Hospital Patients. In DISSERTATION ABSTRACTS INTERNATIONAL, v. 32, no. 9, p. 5439-B.
Investigation designed to verify the rationale that the clustering of symptoms among mental hospital patients is a relatively stable phenomenon and may justifiably be used as a basis for descriptive comparisons across cultures; and to explore the possibility

that the forms of behavior by which mental illness is manifested are somehow culturally determined. A portion of the text is in Spanish.

20.21   Gurnee, Russell H., Brother G. Nicholas, and John V. Thrailkill. "Discovery at the Río Camuy, Puerto Rico." In Oehser, Paul H., ed. NATIONAL GEOGRAPHIC RESEARCH REPORTS . . . DURING THE YEAR 1963. Washington, National Geographic Society, 1968. p. 115–126. map.
Results of a biological and geological exploration of a newly discovered cave in northwestern Puerto Rico.

20.22   Haydon, Rosa Navarro, and Mort D. Turner. ROAD LOG AND GUIDE FOR A GEOLOGIC FIELD TRIP THROUGH CENTRAL AND WESTERN PUERTO RICO. Mayagüez, P.R., Colegio de Agricultura y Artes Mecánicas, 1959. 89 p. illus., maps, bibl.
This guide, prepared for use by the participants in the Second Caribbean Geological Conference, outlines a trip from San Juan to Mayagüez by way of Camuy, San Sebastian, and Añasco with a return trip to San Juan through Ponce and Barranquitas. The itinerary offers some information on the geology, geologic history, flora, and fauna.

20.23   Herminda, Angel G., and Luis Morera. EXPLOTACION MINERA DEL COBRE EN PUERTO RICO: FACTORES LEGALES, ECONOMICOS Y DE CONTAMINACION. Río Piedras, Universidad de Puerto Rico, División de Impresos, 1969. 143 p.
An analysis of the legal, economic, and environmental factors of the proposed mining operations. The study was sponsored jointly by the Social Science Research Center and the Institute of Urban Law of the University of Puerto Rico.

20.24   Jolly, Wayne Travis. Petrologic Studies of the Robles Formation, South Central Puerto Rico. Ph.D. dissertation, State University of New York at Binghamton, 1970. In DISSERTATION ABSTRACTS INTERNATIONAL, v. 31, no. 12, p. 7370-B.
Study of the Robles formation of south central Puerto Rico, which is composed primarily of andesitic lavas and pyroclastic rocks.

20.25 Leopold, N.F. CHECKLIST OF BIRDS OF PUERTO RICO AND THE VIRGIN ISLANDS. Río Piedras, University of Puerto Rico, Agricultural Experiment Station, 1963. 119 p. illus. (Bulletin 168).

Analyzes "the confusing maze of local Spanish names in use for the birds of Puerto Rico." For each bird the checklist provides the following information: all the English names by which it is known, all the Spanish names used for it, the scientific name, and its status.

20.26 Little, Elbert L., Jr., Frank H. Wadsworth, and José Marrero. ARBOLES COMUNES DE PUERTO RICO Y LAS ISLAS VIRGENES. Acuarelas por Frances W. Horne. Puerto Rico, Editorial Universitaria, Universidad de Puerto Rico, 1967. 827 p. illus., maps, bibl.

Describes 250 of the most common or important species of trees, with drawings and useful information such as names, full-grown size, type, shape, flowers, woods and their uses, locality, and distribution. The book also includes an index of scientific and common names, and more than one hundred small maps. Also available in English: *Common Trees of Puerto Rico and the Virgin Islands*, (Agriculture Handbook Handbook 249), Washington, Govt. Print. Off.

20.27 Longwood, Franklin R. PUERTO RICAN WOODS: THEIR MACHINING, SEASONING, AND RELATED CHARACTERISTICS. Washington, U.S. Dept. of Agriculture, Forest Service, 1961. 98 p. tables, plates, bibl. (U.S. Dept. of Agriculture Handbook 205).

This study describes the characteristics and properties of sixty timbers of potential importance in the island, and the procedures used by the Tropical Forest Research Center in determining the properties of both indigenous and imported wood varieties.

20.28 Martínez, Isidro, ed. CANCER IN PUERTO RICO: INCIDENCE, PROBABILITY, MORTALITY AND SURVIVAL. INCIDENCIA, PROBABILIDAD, MORTALIDAD Y SUPERVIVENCIA, 1950-1964. San Juan, Central Cancer Registry, Division of Cancer Control, Dept. of Health, 1967. 550 p. tables, graphs. Text in English and Spanish; tables and figures in English.

A comprehensive statistical report on cancer in Puerto Rico, based on the island-wide Tumor Registry which began in 1950.

20.29 Matthews, Barbara M. AN ECOLOGICAL GUIDE TO THE LITTORAL FAUNA AND FLORA OF PUERTO RICO. Illustrated by Eric G. Matthews. San Juan, Dept. of Education Press, 1967. 72 p. bibl.

An introduction to the coastal marine environment of the island, which illustrates some 170 species. It is aimed at supplementing the ecological version of the Biological Sciences Curriculum Study with materials readily abundant in Puerto Rico.

20.30 Mayda, Jaro. ENVIRONMENT AND RESOURCES: FROM CONSERVATION TO ECOMANAGEMENT. Río Piedras, School of Law, University of Puerto Rico, 1968. 254 p. bibl.

An analysis of present problems, concepts, and practices, with a critique of the fractured approach to the resource problems and an outline of the elements that specialists should consider to develop a working model for resource management in the island.

20.31 Meyerhoff, Howard. GEOLOGY OF PUERTO RICO. Río Piedras, University of Puerto Rico, 1933. 306 p. illus., diagrs., maps. (Monographs of the University of Puerto Rico. Ser. B, Physical and Biological Sciences, no. 1).

This book is an outgrowth of some lectures delivered by the author at the University of Puerto Rico. It discusses salient features of Puerto Rico's physical development, as well as the geologic record and features which affect the activities of the people.

20.32 LA MINERIA DEL COBRE EN PUERTO RICO: ENTREVISTA A TRES CIENTIFICOS SOBRE SUS ASPECTOS ECOLOGICOS. San Juan, Misión Industrial de Puerto Rico, 1971. 43 p. illus.

In an introduction, the editors of this publication suggest that the Puerto Rican Government postpone all negotiations regarding the exploitation of the copper mines for at least five years until more is known about possible effects of mining on the ecology of the island. To back their appeal, they reproduce interviews with three experts: José F. Cadilla, geology professor at the University of Puerto Rico; Máximo Cerame-Vives, Director of the Department of Marine Biology of the university; and Richard Levins, former biology professor at the University of Puerto Rico, now teaching at the University of Chicago.

20.33 Mitchell, Raoul C. A SURVEY OF THE GEOLOGY OF PUERTO RICO. Río Piedras, University of Puerto Rico, Agriculture Experiment Station, 1954. 167 p. maps, tables, bibl. (Technical Paper no. 13)

The author states that "in comparison to other West Indian islands, it [Puerto Rico] is unique geologically, unique in the sense that whilst igneous events have played a dominant role in its geological development, Puerto Rico is not a volcanic island like Martinique or Dominica, it is not a predominantly plutonic island like Aruba or other islands off the South American Caribbean coast, nor yet is it a metavolcanic island like Tobago or a metavolcanic-metaplutonic island like Margarita."

20.34 Murphy, Louis S. FORESTS OF PORTO RICO: PAST, PRESENT AND FUTURE AND THEIR PHYSICAL AND ECONOMIC ENVIRONMENT. Washington, Govt. Print Off., 1916. 99 p. map, plates, bibl. (U.S. Department of Agriculture, Bulletin no. 354).

Describes the conditions, distribution, problems, and other aspects of the forests and includes descriptions of fifty-seven families of trees found in the island.

20.35 Nalwalk, Andrew Jerome. Geology of the North Wall of the Puerto Rico Trench. Ph.D. dissertation, University of Pittsburgh, 1967. In DISSERTATION ABSTRACTS, v. 28, no. 5, p. 1995-B.

The author states that, "combined with data from the Mid-Atlantic Ridge and the North American Basin, the analysis of samples from the North wall tends to support the permanency of ocean basis hypothesis."

20.36 National Academy of Sciences and National Academy of Engineering. SCIENCE AND TECHNOLOGY IN SUPPORT OF THE PUERTO RICAN ECONOMY. Washington, National Academy of Sciences-National Research Council, February 1967. 89 p. tables, diagrs., bibl.

Report prepared by the Committee on the Scientific and Technologic Base of Puerto Rico's Economy of the NAS-NRC under contract with the island's Economic Development Administration. The group analyzed the present situation of, and made recommendations concerning the technical requirements of industry and agriculture, the kinds and qualities of scientific and technological education required at all levels, the appropriate objectives and programming of Puerto Rican research and development activities, and the institutional structure that would best serve the purpose of such programs.

20.37 New York Academy of Sciences. SCIENTIFIC SURVEY OF PORTO RICO AND THE VIRGIN ISLANDS. New York, The Academy, 1919–1952. 19 v. illus., maps, tables, diagrs., bibls.

Contents. V. 1 (complete, with index): Part 1. History of the Survey, by N.L. Britton; Geological Introduction, by C.P. Berkey; Geology of the San Juan District, by D.R. Semmes; Part 2. Geology of the Coamo-Guayama District, by E.T. Hodge; Part 3. Geology of the Ponce District, by G.J. Mitchell; Part 4. The Physiography of Porto Rico, by A.K. Lobeck.

V. 2: Part 1. Geology of the Lares District, by B. Hubbard; Part 2. Geology of the Humacao District, by C.R. Fettke; Part 3. Geology of the Fajardo District, by H.A. Meyerhoff.

V. 3 (complete, with index): Part 1. Tertiary Mollusca from Porto Rico, by C.J. Maury; Part 2. Tertiary Mollusca from the Lares District, by B. Hubbard; Part 3. Fossil Corals of Porto Rico, by H.N. Coryell and V. Ohlsen; Part 4. Tertiary Foraminifera of Porto Rico, by J.J. Galloway and C.E. Heminway.

V. 4: Geology of the Virgin Islands,

Culebra and Vieques. Part 1. Introduction and review of the literature, by J.F. Kemp; Physiography, by H.A. Meyerhoff; Part 2. Physiography (concluded), by H.A. Meyerhoff.

V. 5 (complete, with generic index): Parts 1–4. Descriptive Flora—Spermatophyta (part), by N.L. Britton and Percy Wilson.

V. 6: Parts 1–2. Descriptive Flora—Spermatophyta (continued); Part 3. Descriptive Flora—Spermatophyta with Appendix (concluded) Pteridophyta, by W.R. Maxon; Part 4. Supplement to Descriptive Flora—Bibliography. Index to Volumes V and VI.

V. 7: Parts 1–2. Plant Ecology of Porto Rico, by H.A. Gleason and M.T. Cook; Part 3. Palaeobotany of Porto Rico, by A. Hollic.

V. 8: Part 1. Mycology, by F.J. Seaver and C.E. Chardon, with contributions by R.A. Toro, F.D. Kern and H.H. Whetzel, and L.O. Overholts; Part 2. Supplement to Mycology, by F.J. Seaver, C.E. Chardon, R.A. Toro, and F.D. Kern. Revision of the Myxomycetes, by R. Hagelstein, Myxophyceae, by N.L. Gardner; Part 3. The Diatomaceae of Porto Rico and the Virgin Islands, by R. Hagelstein.

V. 9 (complete, with index): Part 1. Mammals—Chiroptera and Insectivora, by H.E. Anthony; Part 2. Mammals—Rodentia and Edentata, by H.E. Anthony; Part 3. Birds—Colymbiformes to Columbiformes, by A. Wetmore; Part 4. Birds—Psittaciformes to Passeriformes, by A. Wetmore.

V. 10 (complete, with index): Part 1. Amphibians and Land Reptiles of Porto Rico, by K.P. Schmidt; Part 2. The Fishes of Porto Rico and the Virgin Islands—Brachiostomidae to Sciaenidae, by J.T. Nichols; Part 3. The Fishes of Porto Rico and the Virgin Islands—Pomacentridae to Ogocephalidae, by J.T. Nichols; Part 4. The Ascidians of Porto Rico and the Virgin Islands by W.G. Van Name.

V. 11: Part 1. Insects of Porto Rico and Virgin Islands—Diptera or Two-winged Flies, by C.H. Curran.

V. 12 (complete, with index): Part 1. Insects of Porto Rico and the Virgin Islands—Heterocera or Moths (excepting the Noctuidae, Geometridae and Pyralididae) by W.T.M. Forbes. Supplementary Report on the Heterocera of Porto Rico, by W.T.M. Forbes; Part 2. Insects of Porto Rico and the Virgin Islands—Moths of the Family Noctuidae, by W. Schaus; Part 3. Insects of Porto Rico and the Virgin Islands—Moths of the Families Geometridae and Pyralidae, by W. Schaus; Part 4. Insects of Porto Rico and the Virgin Islands—Rhopalocera or Butterflies, by W.P. Comstock.

V. 14: Part 1. Insects of Porto Rico and the Virgin Islands—Odonata or Dragon Flies, by E.B. Klots; Part 2. Insects of Porto Rico and the Virgin Islands—Homoptera (Excepting the Sternorhynchi) by H. Osborn; Part 3. Insects of Porto Rico and the Virgin Islands—Hemiptera—Heteroptera (excepting the Miridae and Corixidae) by H.G. Barber.

V. 15: Part 1. The Brachyuran Crabs of Porto Rico and the Virgin Islands, M.J. Rathbun; Part 2. Crustacea Macura of Porto Rico and the Virgin Islands, W.L. Schmitt, Amphipoda of Porto Rico and the Virgin Islands, by C.L. Shoemaker.

V. 16: Part 1. A Handbook of the Littoral Echinoderms of Porto Rico and the Other West Indian Islands, by H.L. Clark; Part 2. Polychaetous Annelids of Porto Rico and Vicinity, by A.L. Treadwell; Part 3. Bryozoa of Porto Rico with a Resume of the West Indian Bryozoan Fauna, by R.C. Osburn.

V. 17: Part 1. The Pelecypoda or Bivalve Mollusks of Porto Rico and the Virgin Islands, by R.A. McLean.

V. 18: Part 1. Porto Rican Archaeology, by F.G. Rainey; Part 2. A Large Archaeological Site at Capá, Utuado, with Notes on Other Porto Rico Sites Visited in 1914–15, by J.A. Mason, Appendix.—An Analysis of the Artifacts of the 1914–15 Porto Rican Survey, by I. Rouse; Part 3. Porto Rican Prehistory: Introduction; Excavations in the West and North, by I. Rouse; Part 4. Porto Rican Prehistory: Excavations in the Interior, South and East; Chronological Implications by I. Rouse.

V. 19: Part 1. Meteorology of the Virgin Islands, by R.G. Stone.

20.38 Núñez Meléndez, Esteban. PLANTAS MEDICINALES DE PUERTO RICO. Universidad de Puerto Rico. Estación Experimental Agrícola, 1964. 245 p. illus. (Boletín no. 176). Summary in Spanish and English.

Botanical descriptions with photographs of 112 medicinal plants of Puerto Rico and their therapeutic properties. It includes a glossary of scientific terms, methods of preparing infusions and a general index of scientific and common names in Spanish and English.

20.39   Otero, Jose L., Rafael A. Toro, and Lydia Pagán de Otero. CATALOGO DE LOS NOMBRES VULGARES Y CIENTIFICOS DE ALGUNAS PLANTAS PUERTORRIQUEÑAS. 2. ed. Mayagüez, Instituto de Agricultura Tropical, Universidad de Puerto Rico, 1946. 281 p. bibl. (Sobretiro del Boletín núm. 37, Estación Experimental Agrícola).

Compilation of all the common names given to the flora of Puerto Rico and their scientific equivalents. The work includes an index of common and scientific names, as well as the English equivalents of the common names of some of the plants mentioned in the catalog.

20.40   Pease, Maurice Henry. CRETACEOUS AND LOWER TERTIARY STRATIAGRAPHY OF THE NARANJITO AND AGUAS BUENAS QUADRANGLES AND ADJACENT AREAS. Washington, Govt. Print. Off., 1968. 57 p. illus., maps, bibl. (Geological Survey. Bulletin 1253).

A geologic investigation of an area in north-central Puerto Rico, immediately south of the capital city, done in cooperation with the Department of Industrial Research of the Puerto Rico Economic Development Commission. A geologic map of the area is enclosed.

20.41   Puerto Rico Nuclear Center. TENTH ANNIVERSARY SYMPOSIUM ON NUCLEAR ENERGY AND LATIN AMERICAN DEVELOPMENT. San Juan, 1967. 165 p. illus., bibl. refs. (PRNC-112).

Includes addresses on the Puerto Rico Nuclear Center and its potential development, and discusses the possible application of nuclear energy to help in the solution of some of Latin America's development problems.

20.42   Quevedo y Báez, Manuel. HISTORIA DE LA MEDICINA Y CIRUGIA DE PUERTO RICO. Santurce, Asociación Médica de Puerto Rico, 1946-1949. 2 v. (438, 889 p).

A history of medicine in Puerto Rico since the time of discovery through the first half of the twentieth century.

20.43   Rickher, James G., and others. WATER RECORDS OF PUERTO RICO, 1964-67. Ft. Buchanan, P.R., U.S. Geological Survey, 1970. 308 p. tables, bibl. refs.

Second of a series of reports on Puerto Rico water records, covering the period 1958-1967, done by the U.S. Geological Survey in cooperation with various agencies of the government of the Commonwealth of Puerto Rico. It provides data and rate of variation of streamflow, groundwater level and fluctuation, and the chemical and physical quality of water—all of which are pertinent to planning, developing, and managing water resources and water facilities.

20.44   Smith, Richard M., and Fernando Abruña. SOIL AND WATER CONSERVATION RESEARCH IN PUERTO RICO, 1938 TO 1947. Río Piedras, P.R., Agricultural Experiment Station, 1955. 51 p. illus., maps, bibl. (Bulletin no. 124).

20.45   Stahl, Agustín. ESTUDIOS SOBRE LA FLORA DE PUERTO RICO. Prólogo de Carlos E. Chardón. 2. ed. San Juan, Impr. Venezuela, 1936-1937. 3 v. (343, 373, 165 p.) bibl. refs. (Publicaciones de la Federal Emergency Relief Administration).

The foremost naturalist of Puerto Rico classifies and describes the island's flora. Originally published between 1883 and 1888 as a series of booklets, the work classified the thalamifloral, leguminous, chaliced, rubiaceous, and gamopetalous plant groups.

20.46   Wetmore, Alex. BIRDS OF PORTO RICO. Washington, Govt. Print. Off., 1916. 140 p. plates, map, bibl. (U.S. Department of Agriculture. Bulletin no. 326).

Results of a field study conducted in 1911-1912 by the U.S. Biological Survey and the government of the island with the purpose of obtaining accurate knowledge about the economic status and relative abundance of the birds found in the island. An annotated list of species forms the bulk of the work.

20.47 Warmke, Germaine L., and R. Tucker Abbott. CARIBBEAN SEASHELLS: A GUIDE TO THE MARINE MOLLUSKS OF PUERTO RICO AND OTHER WEST INDIAN ISLANDS, BERMUDA AND THE LOWER FLORIDA KEYS. Narberth, Livington Publ. Co., 1961. 346 p. plates, maps.

The authors indicate that "Puerto Rico's strategic position in the center of the Antillean Chain makes it one of the most interesting and certainly one of the richest islands for marine mollusks." They identify 858 Puerto Rican mollusks and estimate that there are another three or four hundred species to be added as diligent collecting continues over the years.

21
SOCIOLOGY

21.1 Back, Kurt W. SLUMS, PROJECTS AND PEOPLE: SOCIAL PSYCHOLOGICAL PROBLEMS OF RELOCATION IN PUERTO RICO. Durham, N.C., Duke University Press, 1962. 123 p. illus.

A study, based on 405 interviews in slums and housing projects in the metropolitan area of San Juan, which analyzes the attitudes and decisions of these people in connection with their relocation from slums to public housing. It also identifies the factors working in favor of and against such relocation.

21.2 Bourne, Dorothy D., and James R. Bourne. THIRTY YEARS OF CHANGE IN PUERTO RICO: A CASE STUDY OF TEN SELECTED RURAL AREAS. New York, Frederick A. Praeger, 1966. 411 p. maps, tables, bibl. (Praeger Special Studies in International Economics and Development).

A study of the changes that occured in ten rural areas where the Bournes had helped establish some public schools during the 1920s. It concludes that the improvement of material conditions is still the principal task for Puerto Ricans.

21.3 Blanco, Tomás. EL PREJUICIO RACIAL EN PUERTO RICO. 2. ed. San Juan, Editorial Biblioteca de Autores Puertorriqueños, 1948, c1942. 82 p.

An essay contrasting racial prejudice in Puerto Rico and in the south of the United States.

21.4 Brau, Salvador. DISQUISICIONES SOCIOLOGICAS Y OTROS ENSAYOS. Introducción por Eugenio Fernández Méndez. Río Piedras, Universidad de Puerto Rico, Instituto de Literatura Puertorriqueña, 1956. 409 p. illus.

Brau's essays on the Puerto Rican peasant, the press, the *danza*, coffee, and sugar help give a picture of social life and customs during and before the nineteenth century. An extensive essay on Brau by E. Fernández Méndez precedes the collection. (A selection of some of these essays has been published: *Ensayos: disquisiones sociológicas*, Río Piedras, P.R., Editorial Edil, 1972. 294 p.)

21.5 Buitrago Ortiz, Carlos. ESTRUCTURA SOCIAL Y ORIENTACIONES VALORATIVAS EN ESPERANZA, PUERTO RICO Y EL MEDITERRANEO. Río Piedras, P.R., Editorial Edil, 1970. 145 p. bibl.

The author examines social structure and value orientations at three levels: in a rural community on the Northeast of Puerto Rico, in the society and culture of the island as a whole, and in the Mediterranean area.

21.6 Caplow, Theodore, Sheldon Stryker, and Samuel E. Wallace. THE URBAN AMBIENCE: A STUDY OF SAN JUAN, PUERTO RICO. Totowa, N.J., Bedminster Press, 1964. 243 p. plates, diagrs., maps, tables, questionnaire. (A Social Science Research Center Study, College of Social Sciences, University of Puerto Rico).

A sociological study of the San Juan neighborhood—the characteristics of the city, its ecological history and zones, its relationship to Spanish and North American models, and the barrios into which the city is divided. It provides an analysis of various types of neighborhood data and discusses possible application of the findings to the problems of city planning in San Juan.

21.7 Center for New York City Affairs, New School for Social Research. Improving the Capability for Social Planning in Puerto Rico. New York, June 1969. 66 p. mimeographed.

This report, prepared for the Puerto Rican Planning Board, describes and assesses recent and current social planning efforts and makes recommendations for improving the Board's social planning capability. It identifies and describes a work program and the kind of organization and staff that would be needed for its proper functioning, and provides a design for inventorying existing social and related programs.

21.8 Cooney, Norma O'Neill. Control of Aggression in Child Rearing in Puerto Rico: A Study of Professed Practices Used with Boys and Girls in Two Socioeconomic Groups. Ph.D. dissertation, Columbia University, 1967. In DISSERTATION ABSTRACTS, v. 28, no. 2, p. 777-A.

The purpose of this study was to investigate control of aggression in child rearing in Puerto Rico as related to the socioeconomic status of the family and the sex of the child.

21.9 Fernández de Encinas, Serapio. SOCIOLOGIA RURAL DE CAYEY. Río Piedras, Editorial Universitaria, Universidad de Puerto Rico, 1971. 161 p. tables, bibl. refs.

First study of the rural sociology of the Cayey area: its agricultural economy and its limiting factors, the structure and distribution of the population, the rural culture, and the process of integration.

21.10 Fernández Méndez, Eugenio, ed. PORTRAIT OF A SOCIETY: READINGS ON PUERTO RICAN SOCIOLOGY. Río Piedras, University of Puerto Rico Press, 1972. 384 p. bibl.

A collection of writings on the island's culture, race relations, courtship and marriage, population, land tenure and reform, economy, migration, class structure, language, and religion by both Puerto Rican and foreign authors. A basic reference source.

21.11 Fernández Marina, Ramón, Ursula Von Eckardt, and Eduardo Maldonado Sierra. THE SOBER GENERATION: CHILDREN OF OPERATION BOOTSTRAP. Río Piedras, University of Puerto Rico Press, 1969. 798 p. illus.

A study that describes the attitudes, values, and positively functioning defenses with which competent adolescents belonging to the rising urban middle class confront the rapid changes occurring in Puerto Rico.

21.12 Fleagle, Fred K. SOCIAL PROBLEMS IN PORTO RICO. Boston, D.C. Heath, 1917. 139 p., tables.

A professor at the University of Puerto Rico looks at conditions in the island in the early part of this century.

21.13 Hansen, Millard, ed. SOCIAL CHANGE AND PUBLIC POLICY. Río Piedras, P.R., Social Science Research Center, 1968. 330 p., tables, bibl.

Papers presented during a seminar held at the University of Puerto Rico in February 1967 to explore the "disquiet about deviant conduct in the society, inefficient conduct and feelings of distress which were probably consequences of the extensive changes which had occurred so swiftly in the society of Puerto Rico."

21.14 Hernández Alvarez, Lila Inés de. MATRIMONIO EN PUERTO RICO: ESTUDIO SOCIO-DEMOGRAFICO, 1910–1968. Río Piedras, P.R., Editorial Edil, 1971. 177 p. graphs, tables, bibl.

A study on nuptiality in Puerto Rico conducted by the author while she was a researcher at the International Population and Urban Research program in the University of California at Berkeley. It analyzes not only the importance of nuptiality in determining population growth, but the disintegration of the family as well.

21.15 Kupperstein, Lenore R. JUVENILE DELINQUENCY IN PUERTO RICO: A SOCIO-CULTURAL AND SOCIO-LEGAL ANALYSIS. With the collaboration of Jaime Toro-Calder; foreword by Marvin E. Wolfgang. Río Piedras, University of Puerto Rico, Social Science Research Center, 1969. 261 p. tables, questionnaires, bibl.

The first publication of an international effort initiated by the United Nations in 1965 to examine juvenile court statistics and the legal machinery designed to deal with juvenile delinquency. After a review of the literature on juvenile delinquency in Puerto Rico for the past twenty years, the work studies the development and functioning of the juvenile court and related services; social change and its relation to juvenile delinquency and the administration of juvenile justice; and the nature of the offenses.

21.16 Landy, David. TROPICAL CHILDHOOD: CULTURAL TRANSMISSION AND LEARNING IN A RURAL PUERTO RICAN VILLAGE. Chapel Hill, University of North Carolina Press, 1959. 291 p. tables, bibl. Paperback: New York, Harper & Row, 1965. (A Social Science Research Center Study, University of Puerto Rico).

A study of the socialization process among families in a sugarcane area.

21.17 LaRuffa, Anthony L. SAN CIPRIANO: LIFE IN A PUERTO RICAN COMMUNITY. New York, Gordon and Breach Science Publishers, 1971. 149 p. plates, tables, maps, bibl. (Library of Anthropology).

An ethnographic account of community life and an interpretive discussion of some significant changes in San Cipriano, including the development of Pentecostalism in the community. The author, a professor at Herbert H. Lehman College, discusses the community "in terms of how it reflects what is happening in Puerto Rico, to what extent it is unique, and how the Puerto Rican reaction to the community reveals an overt racism in the island which is probably stronger than most people suspect."

21.18 López-Rey y Arrojo, Manuel. EXTENSION, CARACTERISTICAS Y TENDENCIAS DE LA CRIMINALIDAD EN PUERTO RICO, 1964-1970. Con Jaime Toro Calder y Ceferina Cedeño Zavala. Río Piedras, Programa de Investigación Criminológica, Universidad de Puerto Rico, 1971. tables, bibl. refs.

A study of criminality in Puerto Rico—its aspects, extension, juvenile offenses, characteristics, and trends—with recommendations for future policies in the field of crime control.

21.19 Lowenthal, David. WEST INDIAN SOCIETIES. Foreword by Philip Mason. Published for the Institute of Race Relations, London, in collaboration with the American Geographical Society, New York. New York, Oxford University Press, 1972. 385 p. map, bibl.

A scholarly study designed "to explain how the West Indies [defined as the archipelago from Florida to Venezuela, excluding Cuba, Puerto Rico and the Dominican Republic] and their people became what they are, to show what makes them unique or ordinary, and to describe how they get on with one another and with the world outside." It gives particular attention to the issue of race and colour. Although the book does not deal specifically with Puerto Rico, it does contain some material on the island.

21.20 Luciano, Wilson. A Comparative Analysis of the Occupational Values of Male High School Seniors in Urban and Rural Areas of Puerto Rico. Ph.D. dissertation, University of New Mexico, 1971. In DISSERTATION ABSTRACTS INTERNATIONAL, v. 32, no. 2, p. 741-A.

This study was designed to determine occupational and work values among seventeen-year-old urban and rural male high school seniors from six Puerto Rican public high schools.

21.21 Mintz, Sidney W. WORKER IN THE CANE: A PUERTO RICAN LIFE HISTORY. New Haven, Conn., Yale University Press, 1964. 288 p. Map, plates (Caribbean Series, 2).

The true story of Don Taso, a cane cutter in Barrio Jauca in the southern part of Puerto Rico, through which an anthropologist explains how economic, political, and ideological changes (and in the case of Don Taso, conversion to a religious faith) affect a rural community.

21.22   Morales Otero, Pablo, Manuel A. Pérez, and others. HEALTH AND SOCIO-ECONOMIC STUDIES IN PUERTO RICO. San Juan, 1937–1940, various pagings. tables, diagrs., bibl.
Reproduces a series of five monographs published in the *Puerto Rico Journal of Public Health and Tropical Medicine* which describe social and economic conditions in the rural areas of Puerto Rico during the 1930s.

21.23   Nieves Falcón, Luis. ACCION COMUNAL Y EDUCACION PRE-ESCOLAR EN ZONAS MARGINADAS. Prólogo de Wenceslao Serra Deliz. Río Piedras, Acción Social, 1970. 103 p. questionnaires
Describes the individual and collective actions of a newly organized public housing community, with special emphasis on a preschool education program, which had as its catalyst an organization known as Acción Social.

21.24   Nieves Falcón, Luis. DIAGNOSTICO DE PUERTO RICO. Río Piedras, Editorial Edil, 1971. 260 p. tables, bibl. refs.
Reproduces a series of articles and brief essays which the author groups in three sections. The first presents a global vision of the elements that constitute Puerto Rican society, the second presents a view of the students and teachers as objects of the social forces in operation in the country, and the third discusses some aspects of several important institutions, especially the university and the Popular Democratic party.

21.25   Nieves Falcón, Luis. LA OPINION PUBLICA Y LAS ASPIRACIONES DE LOS PUERTORRIQUEÑOS. 2. ed. Río Piedras, Editorial Universitaria, Universidad de Puerto Rico, 1972, c1970. 198 p. tables, questionnaire, bibl. refs.
A public opinion survey conducted by the Social Science Research Center of the university under the sponsorship of the Senate of Puerto Rico, with the purpose "of learning empirically the aspirations and opinions of the people of Puerto Rico."

21.26   PRIMER CICLO DE CONFERENCIAS PUBLICAS SOBRE TEMAS DE INVESTIGACION SOCIAL. Río Piedras, Centro de Investigaciones Sociales, Universidad de Puerto Rico, 1969. 192 p.
A series of nine public lectures sponsored by the Social Science Research Center of the University of Puerto Rico during the 1967–1968 academic year on the subjects of electoral conduct; rehabilitation of prisoners; incest; school dropouts; problems of the needy; penal reform; spiritualism as a religion; the adolescents of the urban middle class; and the teaching profession.

21.27   Ramírez, Rafael L., Carlos Buitrago Ortiz, and Barry B. Levine. PROBLEMAS DE DESIGUALDAD SOCIAL EN PUERTO RICO. San Juan, Ediciones Librería Internacional, 1972. 176 p.
n.a.

21.28   Reimer, Everett W., ed. SOCIAL PLANNING: COLLECTED PAPERS. Cuernavaca, México, Centro Intercultural de Documentación, 1968. various pagings. tables, diagrs., maps, (CIDOC Cuaderno no. 22).
A collection of papers written between 1957 and 1968 dealing with Puerto Rico's manpower needs and supply; unemployment, family income, and level of living; and the social problems associated with development.

21.29   Roberts, Lydia Jane, and Rosa Luisa Stefani. PATTERNS OF LIVING IN PUERTO RICAN FAMILIES. Río Piedras, University of Puerto Rico, 1949. 411 p. illus, tables.
A study of main aspects of family living in Puerto Rican families of all socioeconomic levels based on an island-wide representative sample of 1,000 families.

21.30   Rogler, Lloyd H., and August B. Hollingshead. TRAPPED: FAMILIES AND SCHIZOPHRENIA. New York, John

Wiley, 1965. 436 p. illus., tables, bibl. (A Social Science Research Center Study, University of Puerto Rico).

A study of a series of families who live in slums and public housing projects of San Juan, aimed at comparing the experiences of persons who are nonschizophrenic with those who are schizophrenic, determining the circumstances of the onset of the mental illness, and assessing the impact of mental illness on family life.

21.31 Rosario, José Colombán. THE DEVELOPMENT OF THE PUERTO RICAN JIBARO AND HIS PRESENT ATTITUDE TOWARDS SOCIETY. Río Piedras, University of Puerto Rico, 1935. 116 p. bibl. (Social Science Monographs, ser. C, no. 1).

A study of the Puerto Rican *jíbaro* or peasant—his ethnic, social, and cultural inheritance, religion, family patterns, and attitude toward work and leisure.

21.32 Rosario, José Colombán, and Justina Carrión. EL NEGRO: HAITI, ESTADOS UNIDOS, PUERTO RICO. Río Piedras, Universidad de Puerto Rico, Divisón de Impresos, 1951. 174 p. bibl.

Some sociological considerations on the Negro are followed by a discussion of the situation of the black man in Haiti, the United States, and Puerto Rico.

21.33 Safa, Helen Icken. AN ANALYSIS OF UPWARD MOBILITY IN LOW-INCOME FAMILIES: A COMPARISON OF FAMILY LIFE AMONG AMERICAN NEGRO AND PUERTO RICAN POOR. Syracuse, N.Y., Syracuse University, Youth Development Center, 1967. 141 p. tables, bibl.

Research report comparing low-income U.S. blacks with Puerto Rican poor in San Juan.

21.34 Seda Bonilla, Eduardo. INTERACCION SOCIAL Y PERSONALIDAD EN UNA COMUNIDAD DE PUERTO RICO. 2. ed. San Juan, Ediciones Juan Ponce de León, 1969. 190 p.

A follow-up look into Nocora, one of the communities included in J.H. Steward's *The People of Puerto Rico*, with the purpose of comparing the structure of social life in the community in 1948 and 1959.

21.35 Seda Bonilla, Eduardo. REQUIEM POR UNA CULTURA: ENSAYOS SOBRE LA SOCIALIZACION DEL PUERTORRIQUEÑO EN SU CULTURA Y EN EL AMBITO DE PODER NEOCOLONIAL. Río Piedras, Editorial Edil. 1970. 201 p. diagrs, bibl.

The author analyzes the problems of identity, racial prejudice, migration to the United States, cultural pluralism, and others, and concludes that Puerto Ricans are facing the danger of cultural extinction. He accuses both the Puerto Rican oligarchy and the U.S. neocolonial power as accomplices in an attempt at ethnocide against the Puerto Rican people.

21.36 Solá, Mercedes. FEMINISMO: ESTUDIO SOBRE SU ASPECTO SOCIAL, ECONOMICO Y POLITICO. San Juan, Cantero Fernández, 1922. 49 p.

A lecture delivered at the Ateneo Puertorriqueño on May 12, 1921, plus other writings by Ms. Solá in which she advocates equal rights for women in phrases that antedate and sound very much like those used fifty years later by the women's liberation movement.

21.37 Steward, Julian H., ed. THE PEOPLE OF PUERTO RICO: A STUDY IN SOCIAL ANTHROPOLOGY. With the cooperation of Robert A. Manners, Eric R. Wolf, Elena Padilla Seda, Sidney W. Mintz and Raymond R. Scheele. 2d ed. Indianapolis, Bobbs-Merrill, 1971, c1956. 540 p. illus., maps, bibl. (A Social Science Research Center Study, University of Puerto Rico.).

A landmark anthropological study of various segments and classes of Puerto Rican communities, with a chapter on the cultural background of contemporary Puerto Rico.

21.38 Tumin, Melvin M. SOCIAL CLASS AND SOCIAL CHANGE IN PUERTO RICO. With Arnold S. Feldman. 2d ed. Indianapolis, Bobbs-Merrill, 1971. 549 p. tables, bibl. refs. (A Social Science Research Center Study, University of Puerto Rico).

Based on interviews with 1,000 family heads from various social and economic strata and from different regions of the island, Tumin analyzes how the class structure influences social attitudes and conduct in the island.

21.39 Wolf, Eric Robert. CULTURE CHANGE AND CULTURE STABILITY IN A PUERTO RICAN COFFEE COMMU-NITY. Cambridge, Mass., Eagle Enterprises, 1951. 204 p. maps, bibl.

Doctoral dissertation aimed at determining what happens to a culture when people depend on a single cash crop, and what happens to this culture when the crop loses its former economic importance in the world market.

Part II

Government Documents (22-23)

22
PUERTO RICO

22.1 Agricultural Experiment Station. AN-NUAL REPORT. 1921/22–1938/39. Río Piedras, 1922–1939.

22.2 Board for Vocational Education. SOCIO-ECONOMIC CONDITIONS IN PUERTO RICO AFFECTING FAMILY LIFE. San Juan, Insular Procurement Office, Printing Division, 1945. 80 p. bibl. refs.

22.3 Bureau of Agricultural and Industrial Research. AVENUES OF APPROACH: AN INTRODUCTORY REVIEW OF PLANS AND PROJECTS WHICH HAVE BEEN SUBMITTED TO THE P.R.E.R.A. IN ORDER TO ESTABLISH INDUSTRIES AND TO DIVERSIFY FARMING IN PUERTO RICO ON A BALANCED ECONOMIC BASIS. San Juan, 1935.

22.4 Bureau of the Budget. INFORME ANUAL. 19 +   San Juan.

22.5 Bureau of the Budget. PRESUPUESTO MODELO DEL GOBIERNO DE PUERTO RICO. 19 +   San Juan. annual.

22.6 Bureau of Demographic Registry and Statistics. INFORME ANUAL DE ESTADISTICAS VITALES. ANNUAL REPORT ON VITAL STATISTICS. 1961+   San Juan.

22.7 Bureau of Economic and Social Analysis. MANPOWER REPORT TO THE GOVERNOR: A REPORT ON A SOCIETY IN TRANSITION. San Juan, [1967?]. 130 p. tables.

22.8 Bureau of Economic and Social Planning. ELEMENTOS DEL PLAN GENERAL DE DESARROLLO. San Juan, Area de Planificación, Oficina del Gobernador, Junta de Planificación, Negociado de Planificación Económica y Social, 1963

22.9 Bureau of Economic and Social Planning. INFORME ECONOMICO. San Juan, 1918.

22.10 Bureau of Economic and Social Planning. INGRESO Y PRODUCTO DE PUERTO RICO. PUERTO RICO INCOME AND PRODUCT. Annually 1940–1962. English and Spanish.

22.11 Bureau of Economics and Statistics. ANUARIO ESTADISTICO. STATISTICAL YEARBOOK. 1935+   San Juan. illus.

22.12 Bureau of Economics and Statistics. ESTADISTICAS HISTORICAS. HISTORICAL STATISTICS. 1959+   San Juan. illus. quinquennial.

22.13 Bureau of Economics and Statistics. EXTERNAL TRADE STATISTICS. San Juan. Report year ends June 30.

22.14 Bureau of Labor. ANNUAL REPORT. 1st–5th. San Juan, 1912–1917.

22.15 Bureau of Labor Statistics. EMPLEO Y DESEMPLEO EN PUERTO RICO. EMPLOYMENT AND UNEMPLOYMENT IN PUERTO RICO. San Juan, 1952–[1955?].

22.16   Bureau of Labor Statistics. INFORME ESPECIAL SOBRE MIGRACION. SPECIAL REPORT ON MIGRATION. San Juan.

22.17   Bureau of Labor Statistics. INGRESOS Y GASTOS DE LAS FAMILIAS EN PUERTO RICO, 1963: INFORME. INCOME AND EXPENDITURES OF THE FAMILIES, PUERTO RICO, 1963: REPORT. San Juan, Negociado de Estadísticas del Trabajo, División de Estudios Económicos Especiales, 1967–1968. 4 v. in 8.

22.18   Bureau of Labor Statistics. PATRONES OCUPACIONALES PARA 27 DE LAS PRINCIPALES INDUSTRIAS DE PUERTO RICO. Compilados y revisados por la Unidad de Investigaciones Ocupacionales de la Sección de Análisis de Salarios y Estudios Especiales. San Juan, 1949. 351 p.

22.19   Caribbean Economic Development Corporation. CARIBBEAN STATISTICAL YEARBOOK. San Juan, July 1967. 201 p.

22.20   Code Commission. REPORT OF THE CODE COMMISSION OF PORTO RICO. San Juan, 1902. 4 v. in 1. Published also in Spanish.

22.21   Collector of Customs. COMPARATIVE STATEMENT AND SUMMARY OF THE COMMERCE OF THE ISLAND OF PORTO RICO. Fiscal years . . . Bureau of Printing and Supplies.

22.22   Commission on Civil Rights. ANNUAL REPORT. no. 1+ 1966+ Report year ends June 30.

22.23   Commission on Civil Rights. LOS DERECHOS DE EXPRESION Y EL USO DE LAS VIAS PUBLICAS EN PUERTO RICO. San Juan, 1971. 79 l. bibl. refs. (Informes, 019).

22.24   Commission on Civil Rights. LA IGUALDAD DE LOS DERECHOS Y OPORTUNIDADES DE LA MUJER PUERTORRIQUEÑA. San Juan, 1972.

22.25   Commission on Civil Rights. INFORME ESPECIAL SOBRE EL DERECHO A LA VIDA, LA SEGURIDAD Y LA LIBERTAD PERSONAL FRENTE A LOS PROBLEMAS DE LA DELINCUENCIA, 20 DE MARZO DE 1968. 2. ed. rev. San Juan, 1972. 201 p. bibl. refs. (Informes, 012).

22.26   Commission on Civil Rights. INFORME ESPECIAL SOBRE LOS DERECHOS CIVILES Y LAS INTERVENCIONES DE LA POLICIA CON LOS CIUDADANOS, 27 DE DICIEMBRE DE 1967. 2. ed. rev. San Juan, 1970. 66 p. bibl. refs. (Informes, 009).

22.27   Commission on Civil Rights. LA VIGILANCIA E INVESTIGACION POLICIACA Y LOS DERECHOS CIVILES. San Juan, 1970. 83 p. bibl. refs. (Informes, 014).

22.28   Commission for Reorganization of the Executive Branch of the Government. INFORME SOBRE LA REORGANIZACION DE LA RAMA EJECUTIVA DEL GOBIERNO DE PUERTO RICO. Presentado al Gobernador por la Comisión de Reorganización. San Juan, 1949. 183 p. Issued also in English.

22.29   Commonwealth Board of Elections. ESTADISTICAS DE LAS ELECCIONES GENERALES. San Juan, Departamento de Hacienda.

22.30   Commonwealth Board of Elections. REPORT ON THE GENERAL ELECTIONS. San Juan.
        Summary of the straight ticket vote by parties, for governor of Puerto Rico and for resident commissioner to the United States.

22.31   Constitution. CONSTITUCION DEL ESTADO LIBRE ASOCIADO DE PUERTO RICO. San Juan, Cámara de Representantes, Secretaría, 1967. 120 p.

22.32   Constitution. LAS CONSTITUCIONES DE PUERTO RICO: HISTORIA Y TEXTO DE LAS CONSTITUCIONES DE PUERTO RICO. Recopilación y estudio preliminar de Manuel Fraga Iribarne. Madrid, Ediciones Cultura Hispánica, 1953. 553 p.

22.33 Constitution. CONSTITUTION ES-TABLISHING SELF-GOVERNMENT IN THE ISLANDS OF CUBA AND PORTO RICO. TRANSLATION. Promulgated by Royal Decree of November 25, 1897. Division of Customs and Insular Affairs, War Dept., August 1899. Washington, Govt. Print. Off., 1899. 24 p.

22.34 Constitutional Convention. DIARIO DE SESIONES. PROCEDIMIENTOS Y DEBATES DE LA CONVENCION CONSTITUYENTE DE PUERTO RICO, 1951–1952. San Juan, Departamento de Hacienda, Oficina de Servicios del Gobierno, División de Servicios del Gobierno, División de Imprenta, 1952. 922 p.

22.35 Crime Commission. COMPREHENSIVE CRIMINAL JUSTICE PLAN. San Juan, 1970. 255 p. illus., maps.

22.36 Dept. of Agriculture and Commerce. COFFEE FROM PUERTO RICO, U.S.A. New York, New York Service, 1942. 62 p. illus., tables.

22.37 Dept. of Agriculture and Commerce. IDEOLOGIA, PROGRAMAS Y ACTIVIDADES. Por Luis A. Izquierdo, Comisionado. San Juan, 1945. 148 p.

22.38 Dept. of Agriculture and Commerce. INFORME. San Juan. annual. Report year ends June 30.

22.39 Dept. of Agriculture and Commerce. PUERTO RICO, INDUSTRIAL AND COMMERCIAL: THE LOGICAL MANUFACTURING AND DISTRIBUTING CENTER FOR AMERICAN NATIONAL AND OVERSEAS MARKETS IN THE WESTERN HEMISPHERE. New York, New York Service, 1938. 64 p. illus., tables.

22.40 Dept. of Agriculture and Commerce. WHAT SUGAR MEANS TO PUERTO RICO IN EMPLOYMENT, IN TAX PAYMENTS, IN BUYING POWER AND IN LIVING STANDARDS. San Juan, 1940. 39 p.

22.41 Dept. of Education. INFORME ANUAL ESTADISTICO DEL SECRETARIO DE INSTRUCCION PUBLICA. STATISTICAL ANNUAL REPORT OF THE SECRETARY OF EDUCATION. Hato Rey.

22.42 Dept. of Education. RULES AND REGULATIONS OF THE DEPARTMENT OF EDUCATION OF PORTO RICO PROMULGATED BY THE COMMISSIONER OF EDUCATION UNDER AUTHORITY OF LAW. San Juan, 1911. 15 p.

22.43 Dept. of Health. Mental Retardation Program Planning Office. HELPING THEM TO HELP THEMSELVES: A COMPREHENSIVE PLAN FOR THE MENTALLY RETARDED IN PUERTO RICO. Report to the Governor and the Legislature. Santurce, 1966. 118 p.

22.44 Dept. of the Interior. ALBUM DE OBRAS MUNICIPALES: PUERTO RICO, 1919–1928. [San Juan, Negociado de materiales, imprenta y transporte, 1928.] 232 p. illus., tables.

22.45 Dept. of Justice. SUMARIO ESTADISTICO. STATISTICAL ABSTRACT. 1960+ San Juan.

22.46 Dept. of Labor. ANNUAL REPORT. 1st–7th. 1931/32–1937/38. San Juan, 1933–1938.

22.47 Dept. of Labor. CARACTERISTICAS DE LOS PASAJEROS QUE VIAJARON POR LA VIA AEREA ENTRE PUERTO RICO Y LOS ESTADOS UNIDOS. CHARACTERISTICS OF PASSENGERS WHO TRAVELLED BY AIR BETWEEN PUERTO RICO AND THE UNITED STATES. 19+ San Juan. annual.

22.48 Dept. of Labor. THE DEPARTMENT OF LABOR: 20 YEARS OF WORK, 1940 TO 1960. Edited by the Office of Industrial Labor and Public Relations. San Juan, 1960. [i.e. 1961]. 85 p.

22.49 Dept. of Labor. LEGISLACION SOCIAL DE PUERTO RICO. Compilada y anotada por Vicente Géigel-Polanco. San Juan, Negociado de Publicaciones y Educación Obrera, 1944. 928 p.

22.50 Dept. of Labor. LA SITUACION ECONOMICA DE PUERTO RICO COMO DETERMINANTE ESENCIAL DE LOS PROBLEMAS SOCIALES Y DE SALUBRIDAD. Por Manuel A. Pérez, comisionado. ECONOMIC BACKGROUND OF PUERTO RICO AS AN ESSENTIAL DETERMINANT IN

HEALTH AND SOCIAL PROB-LEMS . . . San Juan, Negociado de Materiales, Imprenta y Transporte, 1943. 19 p.

22.51 Department of Labor. Migration Division. A SUMMARY IN FACTS AND FIGURES: PROGRESS IN P.R.; PUERTO RICAN MIGRATION. New York, Migration Division, 1959. 21 p. illus.

22.52 Dept. of Public Works. REPORT. 1952/53+ San Juan. illus. annual. Report year ends June 30.

22.53 Dept. of State. ESTADO LIBRE ASOCIADO DE PUERTO RICO: SUS DOCUMENTOS CONSTITUCIONALES Y SIMBOLOS. San Juan, 1958. 79 p. illus.

22.54 Dept. of State. MEMORIA. 19 + San Juan. annual. Report year ends June 30.

22.55 Department of State. THE PLEBISCITE ON THE POLITICAL STATUS OF PUERTO RICO TO BE HELD ON JULY 23, 1967. San Juan, Department of State, Overseas Information Service, 1967. 50 p. illus., map.

22.56 Department of the Treasury. ANNUAL REPORT OF THE TREASURER OF PUERTO RICO. 1951/52 + San Juan.

22.57 Dept. of the Treasury. Office of Economic and Financial Research. PUERTO RICO ECONOMY & FINANCES, 1965. Prepared by Ting Chen Hsu, consultant. San Juan, 1966. 30 p. illus.

22.58 Dept. of the Treasury. Office of Economic and Financial Research. REPORT ON FINANCES AND ECONOMY. 19 + San Juan. illus.

22.59 Dept. of the Treasury. WHAT YOU SHOULD KNOW ABOUT TAXES IN PUERTO RICO. San Juan, Dept. of the Treasury, 1972. 101 p.

22.60 Division of Community Education. A Survey of Social Participation in a Puerto Rican Rural Community. [San Juan], 1952. 3 v. tables, questionnaire. mimeographed.

22.61 Division of Community Education. THE USE OF SOCIAL RESEARCH IN A COMMUNITY EDUCATION PROGRAMME. Prepared by the Analysis Unit of the Division of Community Education, Dept. of Education, San Juan, P.R., and the Survey Research Centre of the University of Michigan. Paris, Education Clearing House, UNESCO, 1954. 50 p. bibl. (Educational Studies and Documents, no. 10).

22.62 Economic Development Administration. ANNUAL BOOK OF STATISTICS OF PUERTO RICO. 1949/50 + San Juan.

22.63 Economic Development Administration. DIRECTORY OF FOMENTO PROMOTED AND ASSISTED MANUFACTURING PLANTS. 19 + San Juan, Economic Development Administration, General Economic Division. annual.

22.64 Economic Development Administration. INDUSTRIAL INCENTIVE ACT OF 1963. San Juan, Economic Development Administration, Office of Economic Research, 1970. 51 p.

22.65 Economic Development Administration. INFORME ANUAL AL GOBERNADOR. 19 + San Juan. illus. Report year ends June 30.

22.66 Economic Development Administration. LOCALLY AND NONLOCALLY OWNED ENTERPRISES IN PUERTO RICAN MANUFACTURING INDUSTRIES. Project director: Amadeo I.D. Francis. San Juan, 1963. 142 p. diagrs., tables. (Small Business Management Research Reports).

22.67 Economic Development Administration. PRODUCTION CAPABILITIES REPORTED BY COMMONWEALTH OF PUERTO RICO AREAS OF SUBSTANTIAL AND PERSISTENT LABOR SURPLUS: A DIRECTORY FOR FEDERAL PROCUREMENT AGENCIES. Prepared by the Industrial Action Committee in cooperation with the Economic Development Administration. [San Juan, 1961]. 81 p.

22.68 Economic Development Administration. STIMULATING GREATER LOCAL

INVESTMENT IN MANUFACTURING ENTERPRISES IN PUERTO RICO. Prepared by the Local Industries Research Section, Office of Economic Research, Economic Development Administration, Commonwealth of Puerto Rico under the management research grant program of the Small Business Administration. [Washington], 1960. 138 p. illus., bibl. (Small Business Management Research Report).

22.69 Emergency Relief Administration. FIRST ANNUAL REPORT OF THE PUERTO RICAN EMERGENCY RELIEF ADMINISTRATION FROM AUGUST 19, 1933, TO AUGUST 31, 1934. Prepared by the Bureau of Reports. San Juan, Bureau of Supplies, Printing and Transportation, 1935. 571 p. illus., maps, diagrs., ports., tables.
Second report, from September 1, 1934, to September 30, 1935, issued jointly with the Report of the Federal Emergency Relief Administration for Puerto Rico from October 1, 1935, to June 30, 1936. [Washington, Govt. Print. Off., 1939].

22.70 Environmental Quality Board. ENVIRONMENTAL REPORT. 1971 + Santurce. illus. annual.

22.71 Executive Secretary. FIRST ANNUAL REGISTER OF PORTO RICO. Prepared and compiled under the direction of the Hon. William H. Hunt, Secretary of Porto Rico, by James H. McLeary. San Juan, Press of the San Juan News, 1901. 319 p. tables, plates.
Also published in successive years.

22.72 Executive Secretary. REPORT. 1916/17 + Washington, Govt. Print. Off. Report year ends June 30.

22.73 General Court of Justice. RULES OF CIVIL PROCEDURE FOR THE GENERAL COURT OF JUSTICE OF PUERTO RICO. EFFECTIVE JULY 13, 1958. Orford, N.H., Equity Pub. Corp., 1958.

22.74 Government Development Bank for Puerto Rico. REPORT. 1948/49 + San Juan. illus. annual. Report year ends June 30.

22.75 Government Development Bank for Puerto Rico. A SPECIAL REPORT ON PUERTO RICO AQUEDUCT AND SEWER AUTHORITY. San Juan, 1966. 16 p. illus., map, ports.

22.76 Government Development Bank for Puerto Rico. A SPECIAL REPORT ON PUERTO RICO HIGHWAY AUTHORITY. San Juan, 1970. 16 p. illus., map.

22.77 Government Development Bank for Puerto Rico. A SPECIAL REPORT ON THE COMMONWEALTH OF PUERTO RICO. San Juan, 1970. 19 p. illus.

22.78 Government Development Bank for Puerto Rico. A SPECIAL REPORT ON PUERTO RICO INDUSTRIAL DEVELOPMENT COMPANY (PRIDCO). San Juan, 1967. 16 p. illus.

22.79 Government Development Bank for Puerto Rico. A SPECIAL REPORT ON PUERTO RICO URBAN RENEWAL AND HOUSING CORPORATION. San Juan, 1969. 16 p. illus., map.

22.80 Governor. ANNUAL REPORT. 1901+ Washington, Govt. Print. Off.

22.81 Governor's Committee for the Study of Civil Rights in Puerto Rico. INFORME AL HONORABLE GOBERNADOR DEL ESTADO LIBRE ASOCIADO DE PUERTO RICO. 3. ed. rev. San Juan, Comisión de Derechos Civiles, 1970. 212 p. (Informe, 001).

22.82 Governor. MESSAGE. [San Juan], Dept. of Education Press.

22.83 Governor (Allen, Charles H.). ADDRESS OF HIS EXCELLENCY CHARLES H. ALLEN TO THE TWO BRANCHES OF THE LEGISLATURE OF PUERTO RICO. DECEMBER 4, 1900. Puerto Rico, Tip. El País, [1901?]. 15 p.

22.84 Governor (Colton, George R.). ADDRESS OF HON. GEO. R. COLTON, GOVERNOR OF PORTO RICO, BEFORE THE FIRST GENERAL MEETING OF THE PORTO RICO ASSOCIATION AT SAN JUAN, FEBRUARY 8, 1910. [San Juan, 1910]. 21 p. Text in English and Spanish.

22.85   Governor (Colton, George R.). DIS-CURSO INAUGURAL DEL GO-BERNADOR GEORGE R. COLTON, PRONUNCIADO EN SAN JUAN, PUERTO RICO, NOVIEMBRE 6, 1909. San Juan, Bureau of Printing and Supplies, 1909. 11 p.

22.86   Governor (Davis, George W.). REPORT OF THE MILITARY GOVERNOR OF PORTO RICO ON CIVIL AFFAIRS. Washington, Govt. Print. Off., 1902. 834 p. plates, maps, plans.
        Includes "an account of the stewardship of the three military governors": Gen. John R. Brooke, Oct. 18–Dec. 9, 1898; Gen. Guy V. Henry, Dec. 9, 1898–May 9, 1898; Gen. George W. Davis, May 9, 1899–May 1, 1900.

22.87   Governor (Davis, George W.). REPORTS OF BRIG. GEN. GEORGE W. DAVIS ON INDUSTRIAL AND ECONOMIC CONDITIONS OF PUERTO RICO. War Department, Division of Insular Affairs, 1899. Washington, Govt. Print. Off., 1900. 47 p.

22.88   Governor (Muñoz Marín, Luis). DISCURSO ... CON MOTIVO DE SU INAUGURACION EL 2 DE ENERO DE 1953. San Juan, Departamento de Hacienda, Oficina de Servicios del Gobierno, División de Imprenta, 1953. 14 p.

22.89   Governor (Muñoz Marín, Luis). DISCURSO INAUGURAL DEL PRIMER GOBERNADOR [ELECTO] DE PUERTO RICO, 2 DE ENERO DE 1949. San Juan, Administración General de Suministros, Oficina de Servicios, División de Imprenta, 1949. unp.

22.90   Governor (Winship, Blanton). DISCURSOS ... SPEECHES MADE BY THE HON. GOVERNOR BLANTON WINSHIP, AND THE HON. EMILIO DEL TORO, CHIEF JUSTICE OF THE SUPREME COURT OF PUERTO RICO, IN CONNECTION WITH THE FESTIVITIES CELEBRATED AT SAN JUAN, P.R., ON JULY 4TH, 1936, COMMEMORATING THE ANNIVERSARY OF THE DECLARATION OF INDEPENDENCE OF THE UNITED STATES OF AMERICA. San Juan, Tip. San Juan, 1936. 37 p. Spanish and English.

22.91   Governor (Yager, Arthur). TWENTY YEARS OF PROGRESS IN PORTO RICO UNDER AMERICAN ADMINISTRATION. San Juan, Bureau of Supplies, Printing and Transportation, 1919. 11 p. English and Spanish.

22.92   Judicial Council. ANNUAL REPORT. 1939. San Juan. Also published in successive years.

22.93   Labor Relations Board. REPORT. 19 + San Juan.

22.94   Land Authority. ANNUAL REPORT. 19 + San Juan.

22.95   Laws, statutes, etc. ACTS OF THE LEGISLATURE. LEYES DE LA ASAMBLEA LEGISLATIVA. v. 1 +   1900/01 +   San Juan.
        Title varies slightly. Includes laws of the regular and special sessions of the legislature.

22.96   Laws, statutes, etc. ACTS AND RESOLUTIONS OF PUERTO RICO. 3d—legislature; 1957 +   Santurce, Equity de Puerto Rico; Orford, N.H., Equity Pub. Corp.

22.97   Laws, statutes, etc. CODE OF CRIMINAL PROCEDURE OF PUERTO RICO. San Juan, Bureau of Supplies, Printing, and Transportation, 1935. 430 p. English and Spanish on opposite pages.

22.98   Laws, statutes, etc. CODIGO CIVIL DE PUERTO RICO, ANOTADO BASADO EN EL TITULO 31, LEYES DE PUERTO RICO ANOTADAS. 2. ed. especial. Orford, N.H., Equity Pub. Corp., 1962. 1322 p.
        Kept up to date by cumulative supplements. First edition published in 1956 under title Leyes de Puerto Rico Anotadas (Stony Brook, N.Y., Equity House).

22.99   Laws, statutes, etc. CODIGO DE COMERCIO DE PUERTO RICO, ANOTADO. Edición especial, basada en el Título 10, Leyes de Puerto Rico, anotadas. Hato Rey, Equity de Puerto Rico, Orford, N.H., Equity Pub. Corp., 1971. 246 p.

22.100 Laws, statutes, etc. CODIGO DE ENJUICIAMIENTO CIVIL DE PUERTO

RICO. CODE OF CIVIL PROCEDURE OF PUERTO RICO. San Juan, Negociado de Materiales, Imprenta y Transporte, 1933. (Spanish and English on opposite pages.)

22.101 Laws, statutes, etc. CODIGO PENAL DE PUERTO RICO. PENAL CODE OF PUERTO RICO. San Juan, Bureau of Supplies, Printing and Transportation, 1937. 492 p.

22.102 Laws, statutes, etc. COMPILACION DE LAS ENMIENDAS INTRODUCIDAS A LOS CODIGOS DE PUERTO RICO DESDE 1912 A 1923. LEY MUNICIPAL ENMENDADA Y OTRAS LEYES APLICABLES A LOS MUNICIPIOS. Compiladas por Juan M. Herrero, subsecretario ejecutivo. San Juan, Negociado de Materiales, Imprenta y Transporte, 1924. 201 p.

22.103 Laws, statutes, etc. COMPILACION DE LEYES OBRERAS EXTRAIDAS DE LOS ESTATUTOS Y CODIGOS REVISADOS DE PUERTO RICO 1902-16. Compiladas y publicadas por el Negociado del Trabajo, Junio 15, 1916. San Juan, Negociado de Materiales, Imprenta y Transporte, 1916. 53 p.

22.104 Laws, statutes, etc. DECISIONES DE PUERTO RICO. Raúl Trujillo Santiago, compilador y publicista. San Juan, Departamento de Hacienda, 1964.

22.105 Laws, statutes, etc. LAWS OF PUERTO RICO ANNOTATED. Stony Brook, N.Y., Equity House, c1954–1955. v. illus.

22.106 Laws, statutes, etc. LEGISLACION AGRICOLA DE PUERTO RICO, 1944–1947. San Juan, Administración General de Suministros, 1947. 359 p.

22.107 Laws, statutes, etc. LEGISLACION COOPERATIVA DE PUERTO RICO. Río Piedras, Editorial Universitaria, Universidad de Puerto Rico, 1971. 314 p. bibl. refs.

22.108 Laws, statutes, etc. LEGISLACION SOCIAL DE PUERTO RICO. Compilada y anotada por Vicente Géigel-Polanco. San Juan, Negociado de Publicaciones y Educación Obrera, Departamento del Trabajo, 1944. 928 p.

22.109 Laws, statutes, etc. LEY DE AUTORIDADES SOBRE HOGARES Y LEY DE BARRIOS OBREROS DE PUERTO RICO. San Juan, 1950. 455 p.

22.110 Laws, statutes, etc. LEYES DEL TRABAJO ANOTADAS. BASADAS EN EL TITULO 29: LEYES DE PUERTO RICO ANOTADAS. Edición especial. Santurce, Equity de Puerto Rico; Orford, N.H., Equity Pub. Corp., 1966. 534 p. illus.

22.111 Laws, statutes, etc. PUERTO RICO ELECTION LAWS. Reprinted from Title 16, Laws of Puerto Rico Annotated. Edited and printed for the Commonwealth Board of Elections by Equity Pub. Corp., Orford, N H. San Juan, Commonwealth Board of Elections, 1965. 335 p.

22.112 Laws, statutes, etc. PUERTO RICO INSURANCE LAW (NO. 66, APPROVED JULY 16, 1921) CONTAINING ALL AMENDMENTS INCORPORATED UP TO MAY 1, 1939, AND APPENDIX ON LEGISLATION IN PUERTO RICO AFFECTING INSURANCE. 4th ed. San Juan, Bureau of Supplies, Printing, and Transportation, 1939. 208 p.

22.113 Laws, statutes, etc. PUERTO RICO (VOLUMENES 1-87) CASOS Y REGLAS. 2. ed. Compilados por Alberto Picó and Raúl Trujillo Santiago. Orford, N.H., Equity Pub. Corp., 1966. 262 p.

22.114 Laws, statutes, etc. REGLAS DE PRACTICA PARA PUERTO RICO: CIVILES. Orford, N.H., Equity Pub. Corp., 1959.

22.115 Laws, statutes, etc. RULES AND REGULATIONS OF PUERTO RICO. Orford, N.H., Equity Pub. Corp., [1958–59].

22.116 Laws, statutes, etc. THE SCHOOL LAWS OF PORTO RICO. San Juan, Bureau of Supplies, Printing and Transportation, 1928. 102 p.

22.117 Laws, statutes, etc. TAX LAWS OF PUERTO RICO. BASED ON TITLE 13, LAWS OF PUERTO RICO ANNOTATED. Orford, N.H., Equity Pub.

Corp., 1962. 857 p. illus. Kept up to date by pocket supplements.

22.118 Laws, statutes, etc. TRANSLATION. LAWS RELATING TO THE CIVIL ADMINISTRATION OF GOVERNMENT OF THE ISLAND OF PORTO RICO. Division of Customs and Insular Affairs, War Department, August 1899. Washington, Govt. Print. Off., 1899. 53 p.

22.119 Laws, statutes, etc. TRANSLATION OF COLLECTION OF LAWS REFERRING TO PUBLIC WORKS IN PUERTO RICO (1896). War Department, Division of Customs and Insular Affairs, 1899. Washington, Govt. Print. Off., 1899. 112 p.

22.120 Laws, statutes, etc. TRANSLATION OF THE LAW OF CIVIL PROCEDURE FOR CUBA AND PORTO RICO, WITH ANNOTATIONS, EXPLANATORY NOTES, AND AMENDMENTS MADE SINCE THE AMERICAN OCCUPATION. Washington, Govt. Print. Off., 1901. 544 p.

22.121 Laws, statutes, etc. TRANSLATION OF THE LAW OF CRIMINAL PROCEDURE FOR CUBA AND PORTO RICO WITH ANNOTATIONS, EXPLANATORY NOTES, AND AMENDMENTS MADE SINCE THE AMERICAN OCCUPATION. Washington, Govt. Print. Off., 1901. 393 p. English and Spanish on opposite pages.

22.122 Laws, statutes, etc. TRANSLATION OF THE PROVINCIAL AND MUNICIPAL LAWS OF PUERTO RICO. Division of Customs and Insular Affairs, War Department, August 1899. Washington, Govt. Print. Off., 1899. 58 p.

22.123 Legislature. CONCURRENT RESOLUTION SETTING FORTH TO THE PRESIDENT AND THE CONGRESS OF THE UNITED STATES OF AMERICA THE ECONOMIC AND SOCIAL EVILS CONFRONTING THE PEOPLE OF PUERTO RICO AND POINTING OUT SPECIFIC RECOMMENDATIONS FOR A COMPLETE ECONOMIC-SOCIAL REHABILITATION OF THE ISLAND. San Juan, Bureau of Supplies, Printing and Transportation, 1935. 126 p. maps, tables.

22.124 Legislature. CONCURRENT RESOLUTION TO DECLARE THAT THE FINAL STATUS OF PUERTO RICO SHOULD BE STATEHOOD AND THAT THE PEOPLE OF PUERTO RICO DESIRE THAT PUERTO RICO BECOME A STATE, FORMING A PART OF, AND ASSOCIATED WITH, THE FEDERATION OF THE UNITED STATES OF AMERICA . . . AND FOR OTHER PURPOSES. San Juan, Bureau of Supplies, Printing and Transportation, 1934. 13 p.

22.125 Legislature. CONCURRENT RESOLUTION TO REQUEST THE CONGRESS OF THE UNITED STATES TO AMEND, REENACT AND ADD CERTAIN SECTIONS TO THE ORGANIC ACT OF PORTO RICO. San Juan, Bureau of Supplies, Printing, and Transportation, 1925. 13 p.

22.126 Legislature. LETTER FROM THE SECRETARY OF PORTO RICO, TRANSMITTING A CERTIFIED COPY OF THE JOURNALS OF THE FIRST LEGISLATIVE ASSEMBLY. Washington, Govt. Print. Off., 1901. 334 p. (U.S. 57th Cong., 1st sess., House. Doc. 41).

22.127 Legislature. PUERTO RICO PLANTEA SU STATUS POLITICO PERMANENTE; RESOLUCION CONCURRENTE, APROBADA UNANIMEMENTE POR LA ASAMBLEA LEGISLATIVA DE PUERTO RICO, PARA PLANTEAR ANTE EL PRESIDENTE Y EL CONGRESO DE LOS ESTADOS UNIDOS DE AMERICA EL DERECHO DEL PUEBLO DE PUERTO RICO A QUE TERMINE EL SISTEMA COLONIAL DE GOBIERNO, Y A DECIDIR DEMOCRATICAMENTE EL STATUS POLITICO PERMANENTE A LA MAYOR BREVEDAD POSIBLE, SI FUERA FACTIBLE INMEDIATEMENTE. San Juan, Negociado de Materiales, Imprenta y Transporte, 1943. 8 p. Spanish and English.

22.128 Legislature. Committee on Unemployment. PRIMER/TERCER INFORME DE LA COMISION LEGISLATIVA PARA INVESTIGAR EL MALESTAR Y DESASOSIEGO INDUSTRIAL Y AGRICOLA Y QUE ORIGINA EL DESEMPLEO EN PUERTO RICO. FIRST REPORT OF THE LEGISLATIVE COMMITTEE

TO INVESTIGATE THE INDUSTRIAL AND AGRICULTURAL UNEASINESS AND RESTLESSNESS CAUSING UNEMPLOYMENT IN PORTO RICO. San Juan, 1930–1932. 3 v. plates, plans, tables, diagrs., forms. Spanish and English.

22.129 Legislature. House of Representatives. ACTAS DE LA CAMARA DE REPRESENTANTES DE PUERTO RICO. San Juan.

Supersedes *Journal*, House of Delegates, Legislative Assembly, 1900–1917.

22.130 Legislature. House of Representatives. HONRAS POSTUMAS; ERNESTO RAMOS ANTONINI, PRESIDENTE DE LA CAMARA DE REPRESENTANTES, ESTADO LIBRE ASOCIADO DE PUERTO RICO. San Juan, 1963. 315 p.

22.131 Legislature. House of Representatives. MIEMBROS Y FUNCIONARIOS DE LA ASAMBLEA LEGISLATIVA DEL ESTADO LIBRE ASOCIADO DE PUERTO RICO, DE 1900 A 1961. Preparado por Néstor Rigual. San Juan, 1962. 105 p.

22.132 Legislature. RESOLUTION TO REQUEST THE PRESIDENT OF THE UNITED STATES OF AMERICA TO APPOINT A NEW GOVERNOR OF PORTO RICO, AND FOR OTHER PURPOSES. San Juan, Insular Procurement Office, Printing Division, 1944. 7 p.

22.133 Legislature. Senate. ACTAS DEL SENADO DE PUERTO RICO. San Juan.

22.134 Legislature. Senate. REPORT ON THE SUGAR INDUSTRY IN RELATION TO THE SOCIAL AND ECONOMIC SYSTEM OF PUERTO RICO. By Esteban A. Bird. San Juan, Economic Research Section, Puerto Rico Reconstruction Administration, Jan. 23, 1937. (Senate Document no. 1).

22.135 Office of the Adjutant General. REPORT OF THE ADJUTANT GENERAL TO THE GOVERNOR OF PORTO RICO ON THE OPERATION OF THE MILITARY REGISTRATION AND SELECTIVE DRAFT IN PORTO RICO. San Juan, Bureau of Supplies, Printing and Transportation, 1924. 165 p. tables, forms, plates, ports.

22.136 Office of the Commonwealth of Puerto Rico, Washington, D.C. DOCUMENTS ON THE CONSTITUTIONAL HISTORY OF PUERTO RICO. 2d ed. Washington, 1964. 331 p.

22.137 Office of the Governor. THE PUERTO RICAN ECONOMY DURING THE WAR YEAR OF 1942; INFORMATION AFFECTING THE NATIONAL DEFENSE OF THE UNITED STATES WITHIN THE MEANING OF THE ESPIONAGE ACT, U.S.C. 31 AND 32, AS AMENDED. Prepared by the Office of Statistics, Office of the Governor, and Division of Territories and Island Possessions, Dept. of the Interior, Washington, 1943. 42 p. illus., bibl. refs.

22.138 Office of Information for Puerto Rico. PUERTO RICO'S FUTURE POLITICAL STATUS? WHAT THE RECORD SHOWS. [San Juan, 1945?] 42 p.

Brings together official statements and press comments regarding a bill introduced in May 1945 by Senator M. Tydings granting independence to Puerto Rico.

22.139 Office of Publicity and Promotion of Tourism. LAND AND LIBERTY; A BRIEF HISTORY OF PUERTO RICO'S LONG BATTLE TO OWN ITS OWN HOMES. By Raúl Gándara. San Juan, Bureau of Supplies, Printing and Transportation, 1943. 44 p. illus., maps., tables, diagr.

22.140 Office of Publicity and Promotion of Tourism. PUERTO RICO, THE STORY OF A WARBASE. San Juan, Bureau of Supplies, Printing & Transportation, 1943. 39 p. illus., maps, tables.

22.141 Office of Puerto Rico, Washington, D.C. PUERTO RICO'S POTENTIAL AS A SITE FOR TEXTILE, APPAREL AND OTHER INDUSTRIES. By Donald J. O'Connor, Chief Economist. Washington, 1948. 64 p.

Includes the Industrial Tax Exemption Act of Puerto Rico.

22.142 Planning Board. DIEZ AÑOS DE PLANIFICACION EN PUERTO RICO. By Rafael Picó, President of the Board. [San Juan], 1952. 184 p. ports., plates.

22.143 Planning Board. ECONOMIC DEVEL-
OPMENT OF PUERTO RICO, 1940–
1950, 1951–1960. San Juan, 1951. 179 p.
illus.

22.144 Planning Board. ECONOMIC REPORT
TO THE GOVERNOR. 1954+ [San
Juan]. annual.

22.145 Planning Board. A PROGRAM OF
TECHNICAL ASSISTANCE TO ECO-
NOMICALLY UNDERDEVELOPED
COUNTRIES; PUERTO RICO'S PAR-
TICIPATION Rev. [San Juan, 1950]. 48
p.

22.146 Planning Board. 29no (VIGESIMO
NOVENO) PROGRAMA ECONOMI-
CO DE CUATRO AÑOS: AÑOS FIS-
CALES 1973 A 1976. [San Juan], Oficina
del Gobernador, Junta de Planificación, 1972. 199 p. tables.
     Also available for the years 1972–
1975, 1971–1974, 1969–1972, 1967–1970,
1964–1967. Previously issued as a six-
year program under the agency's earlier name: Planning, Urbanizing and
Zoning Board, from 1944–1950 to
1949–1955.

22.147 Policy Commission. REPORT OF THE
PUERTO RICO POLICY COMMIS-
SION (CHARDON REPORT); JUNE 14,
1934. [San Juan, 1935?]. 146 p. tables.

22.148 Puerto Rico Development Company.
ANNUAL REPORT. 19 + San Juan.
illus., diagrs. English and Spanish.

22.149 State Guard. ANNUAL REPORT.
19 + San Juan. annual. Report ends
June 30.

22.150 Supreme Court. DECISIONES DE
PUERTO RICO; CASOS RESUELTOS
EN EL TRIBUNAL SUPREMO DE
PUERTO RICO. t. 1+ Sept. 25, 1899+
San Juan, Negociado de Materiales,
Imprenta y Transportación, 1906+.

22.151 Urban Renewal and Housing Corporation. ANNUAL REPORT. 19 +
San Juan. Report year ends June 30.

22.152 Urban Renewal and Housing Admin-
istration. Planning Office. INDUS-
TRIALIZED HOUSING SYSTEMS FOR
PUERTO RICO; A SURVEY OF CON-
STRUCTION METHODS FOR PRO-
GRAMS OF SOCIAL INTEREST. [San
Juan, 1971]. 75 p. illus., bibl. refs.

22.153 Vocational Education Division. AN-
NUAL DESCRIPTIVE REPORT TO THE
GOVERNOR OF PUERTO RICO AND
TO THE U.S. OFFICE OF EDUCATION.
San Juan, 1960–1964.

22.154 Vocational Rehabilitation Division.
REPORT. San Juan, 1950–1951.

22.155 War Emergency Program. ANNUAL
REPORT. San Juan, 1939–1945.

22.156 Water Resources Authority. ANNUAL
REPORT. 1941/42+ San Juan.
     Report year ends June 30.

22.157 Workman's Relief Commission. IN-
FORME ANUAL. San Juan, 19

23
UNITED STATES

23.1 Ad Hoc Advisory Group on the Presidential Vote for Puerto Rico. HEAR-
INGS. Washington, Govt. Print. Off.,
1971. 701 p. English and Spanish.

23.2 Ad Hoc Advisory Group on the Presidential Vote for Puerto Rico. THE
PRESIDENTIAL VOTE FOR PUERTO

RICO: REPORT. Washington, Govt.
Print. Off., 1971. 58 p. English and
Spanish.

23.3 Adjutant-General's Office. Military
Information Division. MILITARY
NOTES ON PUERTO RICO. Washing-
ton, Govt. Print. Off., 1898. 75 p. maps.

23.4 Army. Corps of Engineers. ROAD MAP, ISLAND OF PUERTO RICO. Washington, Army Map Service, U.S. Army, 1944. color map. 31-1/2 × 65-1/2 cm. (A.M.S. E431x)

23.5 Army. Dept. of Porto Rico. DIRECTORY OF THE MILITARY GOVERNMENT OF PORTO RICO. Headquarters, San Juan, April 30, 1900. Pub. by direction of the Commanding General. [San Juan, 1900]. 78 p.

23.6 Army. Dept. of Porto Rico. GENERAL ORDERS AND CIRCULARS; OCT. 18, 1898–DEC. 15, 1900. San Juan. 3 v. in 2. English and Spanish.

23.7 Army. Dept. of Puerto Rico. SPECIAL ORDERS. San Juan.

23.8 Army Map Service. PUERTO RICO 1:25,000. Washington, 1949. color maps, 56 × 54 cm. or smaller. (A.M.S. E835). Scale 1:25,000.

23.9 Atomic Energy Commission. AERO-RADIOACTIVITY SURVEY AND GEOLOGY OF PUERTO RICO. Washington, Govt. Print. Off., 1966. 24 p. illus., plate, bibl. refs.

23.10 Bureau of the Budget. Office of Statistical Standards. REPORT ON THE STATISTICAL SYSTEM OF PUERTO RICO TO THE DRIECTOR OF THE BUDGET, GOVERNMENT OF PUERTO RICO. By Donald C. Riley and James A. Lynn. Washington, 1948. 53 p.

23.11 Bureau of the Census. 1963 CENSUS OF BUSINESS: PUERTO RICO. Washington, Govt. Print. Off., 1965. 297 p. illus., forms, map. (BC63–PR).

23.12 Bureau of the Census. 1970 CENSUS OF POPULATION AND HOUSING; EMPLOYMENT PROFILES OF SELECTED LOW-INCOME AREAS. Washington, Govt. Print. Off., 1971. v. illus.

23.13 Bureau of the Census. 1963 CENSUS OF MANUFACTURES: PUERTO RICO. Prepared by the Bureau of the Census and Puerto Rico Bureau of Economic and Social Analysis. Washington, Govt. Print. Off., 1965. 193 p. forms, maps. (MC63–PR).

23.14 Bureau of the Census. FOURTEENTH CENSUS OF THE UNITED STATES; MANUFACTURES: 1919. PORTO RICO. Prepared under the supervision of Eugene S. Hartley, Chief Statistician for Manufactures, by Starke M. Grogan, Supervisor of the Census of Porto Rico. Washington, Govt. Print. Off., 1921. 14 p.

23.15 Bureau of the Census. INSULAR AND MUNICIPAL FINANCES IN PORTO RICO FOR THE FISCAL YEAR 1902–03. Washington, Govt. Print. Off., 1905. (Bulletin no. 24).

23.16 Bureau of the Census. OCCUPATION STATISTICS: 1910. ALASKA, HAWAII, AND PORTO RICO. Reprinted from Volume 4 of the thirteenth census reports. Washington, Govt. Print. Off., 1914. 292–300, 608–615 p. tables.

23.17 Bureau of the Census. PERSONS OF SPANISH ORIGIN IN THE UNITED STATES: NOVEMBER 1969. Washington, Govt. Print. Off., 1971. (Current Population Reports, ser. P–20, no. 213).

23.18 Bureau of the Census. PUERTO RICANS IN THE UNITED STATES. FINAL REPORT. 1963. 104 p. (PC(2)-1 D, U.S. Census of Population, 1960).

23.19 Bureau of the Census. PUERTO RICO. Washington, Govt. Print. Off., 1972. 106 p. (1970 Census of Housing: General Housing Characteristics. Ser. HC 1). English and Spanish.

23.20 Bureau of the Census. PUERTO RICO: MUNICIPIOS, BARRIOS, CITIES, ETC. MUNICIPIOS, BARRIOS, CIUDADES, ETC. 1960. Washington, Govt. Print. Off., 1961. map 41 × 97 cm. Scale ca. 1:200,000.

23.21 Bureau of the Census. PUERTO RICO: SENATORIAL DISTRICTS, MUNICIPALITIES, BARRIOS, CITIES, AND TOWNS. 1950. Washington, Govt. Print. Off., 1952. map 41 × 97 cm. Scale ca. 1:200,000.

23.22 Bureau of the Census. PUERTO RICO. UNITED STATES CENSUS OF AGRICULTURE, 1964. By Jules A. MacCallor. Washington, Govt. Print. Off., 1967. 321 p. illus.

23.23 Bureau of the Census. SELECTED CHARACTERISTICS OF PERSONS AND FAMILIES OF MEXICAN, PUERTO RICAN, AND OTHER SPANISH ORIGIN: MARCH 1971. Washington, Govt. Print. Off., 1971. 19 p. (Current Population Reports, ser. P-20, no. 224).

23.24 Bureau of the Census. U.S. TRADE WITH PUERTO RICO AND U.S. POSSESSIONS. 1942+ Washington, U.S. Govt. Print. Off. monthly, with calendar year summaries. (Report FT 800).
Title varies.

23.25 Bureau of the Census. Economic Statistics and Surveys Division. PUERTO RICO, AMERICAN SAMOA, GUAM, AND VIRGIN ISLANDS. Washington, Govt. Print. Off., 1972. 80 p. illus. (Country Business Patterns Series).

23.26 Bureau of Employment Security. PUERTO RICAN FARM WORKERS IN FLORIDA, HIGHLIGHTS OF A STUDY. Washington, U.S. Dept. of Labor, Bureau of Employment Security, prepared by Division of Reports and Analysis, 1955. 7 p. illus.

23.27 Bureau of Employment Security. PUERTO RICAN FARM WORKERS IN THE MIDDLE ATLANTIC STATES, HIGHLIGHTS OF A STUDY. Washington, U.S. Dept. of Labor, Bureau of Employment Security, Division of Reports and Analysis, 1954. 11 p. illus.

23.28 Bureau of Fisheries. INVESTIGATIONS OF THE AQUATIC RESOURCES AND FISHERIES OF PORTO RICO BY THE UNITED STATES FISH COMMISSION STEAMER FISH HAWK IN 1899. Extracted from U.S. Fish Commission Bulletin for 1900. Washington, Govt. Print. Off., 1900. 350 p. illus., plates, maps.

23.29 Bureau of Foreign and Domestic Commerce. PORTO RICO; WHAT IT PRODUCES AND WHAT IT BUYS. By Darwin De Golia, with foreword by Theodore Roosevelt, Governor of Porto Rico. Washington, Govt. Print. Off., 1932. 61 p. tables. (Dept. of Commerce. Trade information Bulletin no. 785).

23.30 Bureau of Foreign and Domestic Commerce. TRADE OF THE UNITED STATES WITH PUERTO RICO . . . 19 + Washington.

23.31 Bureau of Insular Affairs. MONTHLY SUMMARY OF COMMERCE OF THE ISLAND OF PORTO RICO; WITH COMPARATIVE TABLES OF IMPORTS AND EXPORTS, BY ARTICLES AND COUNTRIES. No. 1/2-10; July/August 1899-Apr. 1900. Washington, Govt. Print Off. 252 p.

23.32 Bureau of Labor Statistics. Dept. of Labor. POVERTY AREA PROFILES: NEW YORK PUERTO RICAN; PATTERNS OF WORK EXPERIENCE, BEDFORD-STUYVESANT, CENTRAL HARLEM, EAST HARLEM, SOUTH BRONX. Prepared by Horst Brand. Wash., Govt. Print. Off., May 1971. 62 p.

23.33 Bureau of Mines. Interior Department. MINERAL INDUSTRY OF PUERTO RICO, PANAMA CANAL ZONE, VIRGIN ISLANDS, PACIFIC ISLAND POSSESSIONS, AND TRUST TERRITORY OF PACIFIC ISLANDS. Washington, Govt. Print. Off., 1972. 7 p.

23.34 Bureau of Statistics. Dept. of Commerce and Labor. COMMERCIAL PORTO RICO IN 1906. Showing commerce, production, transportation, finances, area, population, and details of trade with the United States and foreign countries during a term of years. Washington, Govt. Print. Off., 1907. 69 p.

23.35 Bureau of Statistics. Treasury Department. Commerce of Porto Rico with Foreign Countries and the United States, and of the United States with Porto Rico, 1901. In ANNUAL REPORT ON COMMERCE AND NAVIGATION FOR 1901. Washington, Treasury Department, Bureau of Statistics, [1902?]. p. 1271–1408. tables.

23.36 Civil Service Commission. STUDY OF MINORITY GROUP EMPLOYMENT IN THE FEDERAL GOVERNMENT. Washington, Govt. Print. Off., 1969. 644 p. (SM 70–69B).

23.37 Committee on Revision of the Organic Act of Puerto Rico. REPORT ON PROGRESS OF PUERTO RICO. MESSAGE FROM THE PRESIDENT OF THE UNITED STATES, TRANSMITTING REPORT ON PROGRESS OF PUERTO RICO. Washington, Govt. Print. Off., 1943. 12 p. (78th Cong., 1st sess. House. Doc. 304).

23.38 Congress. Conference Committees, 1916–1917. CIVIL GOVERNMENT FOR PORTO RICO. Conference report to accompany H.R. 9533. Washington, Govt. Print. Off., 1917. 7 p. (64th Cong., 2d. sess. House. Report 1546).

23.39 Congress. House. Committee on Armed Services. Special Subcommittee on Real Estate. HEARINGS ON ACQUISITION REPORT NO. 102 AND DISPOSAL REPORT NO. 300. 91st Cong., 2d sess., June 10, 1970. Washington, Govt. Print. Off., 1970. 9305–9441 p.
Hearing on Culebra Island.

23.40 Congress. House. Committee on Armed Services. Special Subcommittee on Real Estate. NAVY ACQUISITION REPORT NO. 102 (NONHABITATION EASEMENTS), AND NAVY DISPOSAL REPORT NO. 102 (RELEASE OF 680 ACRES TO THE COMMONWEALTH OF PUERTO RICO). Report by the Real Estate Subcommittee of the Committee on Armed Services, House of Representatives, 91st Cong., 2d. sess. Washington, Govt. Print. Off., 1970. 9461–9468 p.
Report on Culebra Island.

23.41 Congress. House. Committee on Education. VOCATIONAL EDUCATION AND CIVILIAN REHABILITATION IN PORTO RICO. Hearing before the Committee on Education, 71st Cong., 3rd sess., on H.R. 12901, to extend the provisions of certain laws relating to vocational education and civilian rehabilitation to Porto Rico. December 8, 1930. Washington, Govt. Print. Off., 1930. 22 p.
Daniel A. Reed, chairman.

23.42 Congress. House. Committee on Education and Labor. INVESTIGATION OF MINIMUM WAGES AND EDUCATION IN PUERTO RICO AND THE VIRGIN ISLANDS. Hearings before a special investigating subcommittee of the Committee on Education and Labor, 81st Cong., 1st sess., pursuant to H. Res. 75. Washington, Govt. Print. Off., 1950. 210 p.
John Lensinski, chairman.

23.43 Congress. House. Committee on Foreign Affairs. ESTABLISHMENT OF THE CARIBBEAN ORGANIZATION. Hearing before the Subcommittee on International Organizations and Movements, 87th Cong., 1st sess., on H.J. Res. 384, providing for acceptance by the United States of America of the agreement for the establishment of the Caribbean Organization . . . April 20, 1961. Washington, Govt. Print. Off., 1961. 22 p.

23.44 Congress. House. Committee on Foreign Affairs. ESTABLISHMENT OF THE CARIBBEAN ORGANIZATION. Report to accompany H.J. Res. 384. Washington, Govt. Print. Off., 1961. 28 p. (87th Cong., 1st sess. House. Report 387).

23.45 Congress. House. Committee on Foreign Affairs. ESTABLISHMENT OF THE CARIBBEAN ORGANIZATION. Staff memorandum on the Caribbean Commission and the proposed Caribbean Organization. Washington, Govt. Print. Off., 1961. 45 p. (87th Cong., 1st. sess. House).

23.46 Congress. House. Committee on Insular Affairs. AFFAIRS IN PUERTO RICO. Hearing, January 8 and 10, 15–29, February 5, 1900. Washington, Govt. Print. Off., 1900. 261 p.

23.47 Congress. House. Committee on Insular Affairs. AMEND THE ORGANIC ACT OF PORTO RICO. Hearing, 68th Cong., 1st sess., on H.R. 6583. February 26, 1924. Washington, Govt. Print. Off., 1924. 22 p.
Louis W. Fairfield, chairman.

23.48 Congress. House. Committee on Insular Affairs. CHANGING THE NAME OF THE ISLAND OF PORTO RICO TO PUERTO RICO. . . . Report to accompany S.J. Res. 193. Washington, Govt. Print. Off., 1931. 2 p. (71st Cong., 3d sess. House. Report 2230).

23.49 Congress. House. Committee on Insular Affairs. A CIVIL GOVERNMENT FOR PORTO RICO. Hearings, 64th Cong., 1st sess., on H.R. 8501, a bill to provide a civil government for Porto Rico, and for other purposes. Washington, Govt. Print. Off., 1916. 3 v. in 1.
William A. Jones, chairman.

23.50 Congress. House. Committee on Insular Affairs. A CIVIL GOVERNMENT FOR PORTO RICO. Hearings, 63rd Cong., 2d sess., on H.R. 13818, a bill to provide a civil government for Porto Rico, and for other purposes; February 26, 28, and March 2. Washington, Govt. Print. Off., 1914. 74 p.
William A. Jones, chairman.

23.51 Congress. House. Committee on Insular Affairs. CIVIL GOVERNMENT FOR PORTO RICO. Report to accompany H.R. 9533. Washington, Govt. Print. Off., 1916. 3 p. (64th Cong., 1st sess. House. Report 77).

23.52 Congress. House. Committee on Insular Affairs. THE CIVIL GOVERNMENT OF PORTO RICO. Hearings, 68th Cong., 1st sess., on H.R. 4087, a bill to amend and re-enact sections 20, 22, and 50 of the act of March 2, 1917, entitled "An act to provide a civil government for Porto Rico, and for other purposes" and H.R. 6583, a bill to amend the Organic Act of Porto Rico approved March 2, 1917; February 13 and 14, 1924. Washington, Govt. Print. Off., 1924. 100 p.
Louis W. Fairfield, chairman.

23.53 Congress. House. Committee on Insular Affairs. EXTENSION OF THE PROVISIONS OF CERTAIN LAWS TO PORTO RICO. Hearing, 68th Cong., 1st sess., on H.R. 6294, a bill to extend the provisions of certain laws to Porto Rico; January 31, 1924. Washington, Govt. Print. Off., 1924. 29 p.
Louis W. Fairfield, chairman.

23.54 Congress. House. Committee on Insular Affairs. HEARINGS IN RELATION TO THE CONDITIONS IN PUERTO RICO AND ON A CABLE TO CUBA, PUERTO RICO, AND THE WEST INDIES. January 26, 1900. Washington, Govt. Print. Off., 1900. 64 p. tables.

23.55 Congress. House. Committee on Insular Affairs. HEARINGS ON FINANCE, COINAGE, CURRENCY, ETC. 57th Cong., 1st. sess. January 14–March 19, 1902. Washington, Govt. Print. Off., 1902. 7 v.

23.56 Congress. House. Committee on Insular Affairs. INVESTIGATION OF POLITICAL, ECONOMIC, AND SOCIAL CONDITIONS IN PUERTO RICO. Hearings before a subcommittee, 78th Cong., 1st sess., pursuant to H. Res. 159. Washington, Govt. Print. Off., 1943. tables, diagr.
C. Jasper Bell, chairman of subcommittee.

23.57 Congress. House. Committee on Insular Affairs. INVESTIGATION OF POLITICAL, ECONOMIC AND SOCIAL CONDITIONS IN PUERTO RICO. Report pursuant to H.R. 159. (78th Cong.) and H.R. 99 (79th Cong.) Washington, Govt. Print. Off., 1945. 50 p. diagrs. (79th Cong., 1st. sess. House. Report no. 497).

23.58 Congress. House. Committee on Insular Affairs. PORTO RICAN INTERESTS. Hearings, 68th Cong., 1st sess. September 10–11, 1919. Washington, Govt. Print. Off., 1919. 52 p.
Horace M. Towner, chairman.

23.59 Congress. House. Committee on Insular Affairs. PORTO RICAN LEGISLATION. Hearing. May 13, 1910. Washington, Govt. Print. Off., 1910. 25 p.
Marlin E. Olmsted, chairman.

23.60 Congress. House. Committee on Insular Affairs. PORTO RICO. Hearings, 69th Cong., 1st sess., on H.R. 4085, a bill to amend the Organic Act of Porto Rico; H.R. 11846, a bill to amend and reenact sections 20, 31, 33, and 38 of the act of March 2, 1917, entitled "An act to provide a civil government for Porto Rico, and for other purposes," as amended by an act approved June 7, 1924, and for the insertion of two new sections in said act between sections 5 and 6 and sections 41 and 42 of said act, May 4, 5, and 11, 1926. Washington, Govt. Print. Off., 1926. 65 p.
Edgar R. Kless, chairman.

23.61 Congress. House. Committee on Insular Affairs. TO AMEND THE ACT TO PROVIDE A CIVIL GOVERNMENT FOR PUERTO RICO. Hearings, 78th Cong., 2d sess., on S. 1407. August 26, 1944. Washington, Govt. Print. Off., 1944. 38 p.
C. Jasper Bell, chairman.

23.62 Congress. House. Committee on Interior and Insular Affairs. AMENDING THE ORGANIC ACT OF PUERTO RICO. Report to accompany H.R. 6502. Washington, Govt. Print. Off., 1948. 4 p. (80th Cong., 2d sess. House. Report no. 2035).

23.63 Congress. House. Committee on Interior and Insular Affairs. APPROVING THE CONSTITUTION OF THE COMMONWEALTH OF PUERTO RICO WHICH WAS ADOPTED BY THE PEOPLE OF PUERTO RICO ON MARCH 3, 1952. Report to accompany H.J. Res. 430. Washington, Govt. Print. Off., 1952. 31 p. (82d Cong., 2d sess. House. Report no. 1832).

23.64 Congress. House. Committee on Interior and Insular Affairs. THE NATIONALIST PARTY. A factual study of the Puerto Rican insurrectionists under Albizu Campos, the Blair House shooting, various assassination attempts, and of the Communist praise and support for these seditionists, prepared by William H. Hacket, staff consultant. Washington, Govt. Print. Off., 1951. 24 p.

23.65 Congress. House. Committee on Interior and Insular Affairs. PUERTO RICO CONSTITUTION. Hearings, 81st Cong., 2d sess., on H.R. 7674 and S. 3336, to provide for the organization of a constitutional government by the people, July 12, 1949–June 8, 1950. Washington, Govt. Print. Off., 1950. 190 p.
J. Hardin Peterson, chairman.

23.66 Congress. House. Committee on Interior and Insular Affairs. PUERTO RICO CONSTITUTION. Hearing, 82d Cong., 2d sess., on H.J. R. 430, a joint resolution approving the Constitution of the Commonwealth of Puerto Rico, which was adopted by the people of Puerto Rico on March 3, 1952; April 25, 1952. Washington, Govt. Print. Off., 1952. 40 p.
John R. Murdock, chairman.

23.67 Congress. House. Committee on Interior and Insular Affairs. PUERTO RICO, 1959. Hearings before a Special Subcommittee on Territorial and Insular Affairs, 86th Cong., 1st sess., on H.R. 9234, a bill to provide for amendments to the compact between the people of Puerto Rico and the United States, and related legislation. Washington, Govt. Print. Off., 1960. 815 p. tables.
Hearings held Dec. 3–10, 1959, in various cities of Puerto Rico.

23.68 Congress. House. Committee on Interior and Insular Affairs. PUERTO RICO, 1963. Hearings before the Subcommittee on Territorial and Insular Affairs, 88th Cong., 1st sess., on H.R. 5945 and other bills to establish a procedure for the prompt settlement, in a democratic manner, of the political status of Porto Rico. May 16 and 17, 1963. Washington, Govt. Print. Off., 1963. 314 p. diagrs. tables (Ser. no. 3).

23.69 Congress. House. Committee on Interior and Insular Affairs. PUERTO RICO: A SURVEY OF HISTORICAL, ECONOMIC, AND POLITICAL AFFAIRS, 1959. By Robert J. Hunter, Staff Consultant. Committee on Interior and Insular Affairs, House of Representatives. Washington, Govt. Print. Off., 1959. 115 p. tables. (86th Cong., 1st sess. Committee Print no. 15).

23.70 Congress. House. Committee on the Territories. TO ENABLE THE PEOPLE OF PUERTO RICO TO FORM A CONSTITUTION AND STATE GOVERNMENT. Hearings, 74th Cong., 1st sess., on H.R. 1394, a bill to enable the people of Puerto Rico to form a constitution and state government and be admitted into the Union on an equal footing with the states. May 22, June 4, 1935. Washington, Govt. Print. Off., 1935. 64 p. tables.
Robert A. Green, chairman.

23.71 Congress. House. Committee on Un-American Activities. COMMUNIST ACTIVITIES AMONG PUERTO RICANS IN NEW YORK CITY AND

PUERTO RICO. Hearings, 86th Cong., 1st sess. Washington, Govt. Print. Off., 1960. 2 pts.

Hearings held Nov. 16–20, 1959 (pt. 1 in New York City; pt. 2, San Juan).

23.72 Congress. House. Committee on Ways and Means. EXTENSION OF SOCIAL SECURITY TO PUERTO RICO AND THE VIRGIN ISLANDS. Hearings before a subcommittee of the Committee on Ways and Means, 81st Cong., 1st sess. November 15–22, 1949. Washington, Govt. Print. Off., 1950. 217 p.

A. Sidney Camp, chairman of subcommittee.

23.73 Congress. House. Committee on Ways and Means. GOVERNMENT OF PORTO RICO. Report to accompany H.R. 9541. Washington, Govt. Print. Off., 1909. 12 p. (61st Cong., 1st sess. House. Report 8).

23.74 Congress. Senate. Committee on Foreign Relations. CARIBBEAN ORGANIZATION. Hearing, 87th Cong., 1st sess., on S.J. Res. 75, providing for U.S. acceptance of the agreement for the establishment of the Caribbean Organization; May 2, 1961. Washington, Govt. Print. Off., 1961. 40 p.

23.75 Congress. Senate. Committee on Interior and Insular Affairs. AMENDING THE ORGANIC ACT OF PUERTO RICO. Report to accompany H.R. 3309. Washington, Govt. Print. Off., 1947. 5 p. (80th Cong., 1st sess., 1947. Senate. Report 422).

23.76 Congress. Senate. Committee on Interior and Insular Affairs. APPROVING PUERTO RICAN CONSTITUTION. Hearings, 82d Cong., 2d sess., on S.J. Res. 151, a joint resolution approving the Constitution of the Commonwealth of Puerto Rico, which was adopted by the people of Puerto Rico on March 3, 1952; April 29 and May 6, 1952. Washington, Govt. Print. Off., 1952. 126 p.

Joseph C. O'Mahoney, chairman.

23.77 Congress. Senate. Committee on Interior and Insular Affairs. PUERTO RICO CONSTITUTION. Hearing before a subcommittee, 81st Cong., 2d

sess., on S. 3336, a bill to provide for the organization of a constitutional government by the people of Puerto Rico; May 17, 1950. Washington, Govt. Print. Off., 1950, 66 p.

Joseph C. O'Mahoney, chairman.

23.78 Congress. Senate. Committee on Interior and Insular Affairs. PUERTO RICO CONSTITUTION. Hearing, 81st Cong., 2d sess. Statement of the Governor of Puerto Rico in support of his recommendation that Congress provide for the organization of a constitutional government by the people of Puerto Rico. Washington, Govt. Print. Off., 1950. 12 p.

Joseph C. O'Mahoney, chairman.

23.79 Congress. Senate. Committee on Interior and Insular Affairs. PUERTO RICO FEDERAL RELATIONS ACT. Hearing, 86th Cong., 1st sess., on S. 2023, a bill to provide for amendment to the compact between the people of Puerto Rico and the United States; together with memorandums of law and official agency views on a proposed substitute measure, S. 2708. Washington, U.S. Govt. Print. Off., 1960. 131 p.

23.80 Congress. Senate. Committee on Interior and Insular Affairs. PUERTO RICAN STUDY. Hearing before the Subcommittee on Territories and Insular Affairs, 88th Cong., 1st sess., on H.R. 5945, an act to establish a procedure for the prompt settlement, in a democratic manner, of the political status of Puerto Rico; November 7, 1963. Washington, Govt. Print. Off., 1964. 46 p.

23.81 Congress. Senate. Committee on Pacific Islands and Porto Rico. CIVIL GOVERNMENT FOR PORTO RICO. Hearings, 63d Cong., 2d sess., on S. 4604, a bill to provide a civil government for Porto Rico, and for other purposes. Washington, Govt. Print. Off., 1914. 56 p.

John F. Shafroth, chairman.

23.82 Congress. Senate. Committee on Pacific Islands and Porto Rico. CIVIL GOVERNMENT FOR PORTO RICO. Report to accompany H.R. 9533. Washington, Govt. Print. Off., 1916. 8

p. (64th Cong., 1st sess. Senate. Report 579).

23.83 Congress. Senate. Committee on Pacific Islands and Porto Rico. GOVERNMENT FOR PORTO RICO. Hearings, 64th Cong., 1st–2d sess., on S. 1217, a bill to provide a civil government for Porto Rico, and for other purposes. Washington, Govt. Print. Off., 1916. 3 v. in 2. tables.
John F. Shafroth, chairman.

23.84 Congress. Senate. Committee on Pacific Islands and Porto Rico. TO PROVIDE A CIVIL GOVERNMENT FOR PORTO RICO, AND FOR OTHER PURPOSES. Hearing, on H.R. 23000. Washington, Govt. Print. Off., 1911. 21 p.
Chauncy M. Depew, chairman.

23.85 Congress. Senate. Committee on Pacific Islands and Porto Rico. TO PROVIDE THAT THE INHABITANTS OF PORTO RICO SHOULD BE CITIZENS OF THE UNITED STATES. Hearing, on bill S. 2620. February 6, 1906. Washington, Govt. Print. Off., 1906. 16 p.

23.86 Congress. Senate. Committee on Small Business. TAX TREATMENT OF U.S. CONCERNS WITH PUERTO RICAN AFFILIATES. Hearings on the economic development program, 88th Cong., 2d sess. April 16 and 17, 1964. Washington, Govt. Print. Off., 1964. 395 p. illus., maps.

23.87 Congress. Senate. Committee on Territories and Insular Affairs. A BILL TO AMEND THE ORGANIC ACT OF PUERTO RICO. Hearings before a subcommittee, 78th Cong., 1st sess., on S. 1407, a bill to amend the act entitled "An act to provide a civil government for Puerto Rico and for other purposes," approved March 2, 1917, as amended, and known as the Organic Act of Puerto Rico; November 16, 17, 18, 24, 25, 26 and December 1, 1943. Washington, Govt. Print. Off., 1943. 605 p.
Dennis Chavez, chairman of subcommittee.

23.88 Congress. Senate. Committee on Territories and Insular Affairs. AMENDING THE ORGANIC ACT OF PUERTO RICO. Report to accompany S. 1407. Washington, Govt. Print. Off., 1944. 12 p. (78th Cong., 2d sess. Senate. Report 649A).

23.89 Congress. Senate. Committee on Territories and Insular Affairs. CHANGING THE NAME OF THE ISLAND OF PORTO RICO TO PUERTO RICO. . . . Report to accompany S.J. Res. 193. Washington, Govt. Print. Off., 1930. (71st Cong., 2d sess. Senate. Report 1116).

23.90 Congress. Senate. Committee on Territories and Insular Possessions. CIVIL GOVERNMENT FOR PORTO RICO. Report to accompany S. 4247. Washington, Govt. Print. Off., 1926. 3 p. (69th Cong., 1st sess. Senate. Report 1011).

23.91 Congress. Senate. Committee on Territories and Insular Possessions. THE CIVIL GOVERNMENT OF PORTO RICO. Hearings, 68th Cong., 1st sess., on S. 2448, a bill to amend the Organic Act of Porto Rico approved March 2, 1917, and for other purposes. Washington, Govt. Print. Off., 1924. 2 v.
Hiram W. Johnson, chairman.

23.92 Congress. Senate. Committee on Territories and Insular Affairs. ECONOMIC AND SOCIAL CONDITIONS IN PUERTO RICO. Hearings before a subcommittee, 78th Cong., 1st sess., pursuant to S. R. 309, a resolution authorizing an investigation of economic and social conditions in Puerto Rico; December 7, 8, 9, and 17, 1942. Washington, Govt. Print. Off., 1943. 178 p. tables.
Dennis Chavez, chairman of subcommittee.

23.93 Congress. Senate. Committee on Territories and Insular Affairs. ECONOMIC AND SOCIAL CONDITIONS IN PUERTO RICO. Hearings before a subcommittee, 78th Cong., 1st sess., pursuant to S. Res. 26, a resolution authorizing an investigation of economic and social conditions in Puerto Rico. Washington, Govt. Print. Off., 1943. 2 v. tables.
Dennis Chavez, chairman of subcommittee.

23.94   Congress. Senate. Committee on Territories and Insular Affairs. ECONOMIC AND SOCIAL CONDITIONS IN PUERTO RICO. Report pursuant to S. Res. 26, a resolution authorizing an investigation of economic and social conditions in Puerto Rico. Washington, Govt. Print. Off., 1944. 56 p. diagrs. (78th Cong., 1st sess. Senate. Report 628).

23.95   Congress. Senate. Committee on Territories and Insular Affairs. INDEPENDENCE FOR PUERTO RICO. Hearings, 79th Cong., 1st sess., on S. 227, a bill to provide for the withdrawal of the sovereignty of the United States over the island of Puerto Rico and for the recognition of its independence . . . and for other purposes. Washington, Govt. Print. Off., 1945.
Millard E. Tydings, chairman.

23.96   Congress. Senate. Committee on Territories and Insular Affairs. NOMINATION OF REXFORD G. TUGWELL. Hearings, 77th Cong., 1st sess., on the nomination of Rexford G. Tugwell as governor of Puerto Rico; August 6, 12, 13, and 18, 1941. Washington, Govt. Print. Off., 1941. 91 p. tables.
Millard E. Tydings, chairman.

23.97   Congress. Senate. Committee on Territories and Insular Affairs. PUERTO RICO. Hearings, 78th Cong., 1st sess., on S. 952, a bill to provide for the withdrawal of the sovereignty of the United States over the island of Puerto Rico and for the recognition of its independence, and so forth. May 3, 6, 10, 11, 1943. Washington, Govt. Print. Off., 1943. 335 p. tables, diagr.
Millard E. Tydings, chairman.

23.98   Congress. Senate. Committee on Territories and Insular Possessions. RELIEF OF PORTO RICO. Joint hearings before the Committee on Territories and Insular Possessions, U.S. Senate, and the Committee on Insular Affairs, House of Representatives, 70th Cong., 2d sess., on S.J. Res. 172 and H.J. Res. 333. December 10 and 11, 1928. Washington, Govt. Print. Off., 1929. 97 p. tables, form.
Hiram Bingham, chairman.

23.99   Congress. Senate. Committee on Territories and Insular Affairs. TO AMEND THE ORGANIC ACT OF PORTO RICO, APPROVED MARCH 2, 1917, AND TO EXTEND THE PROVISIONS OF CERTAIN LAWS TO PORTO RICO. Hearing, 71st Cong., 3d sess., on S. 5138. Washington, Govt. Print. Off., 1931. 33 p.
Hiram Bingham, chairman.

23.100   Congress. Senate. Select Committee on Equal Educational Opportunity. EQUAL EDUCATIONAL OPPORTUNITY. Hearings, 91st Cong., 2d sess. Washington, Govt. Print. Off., 1970. illus.
Pt. 8.—Equal educational opportunity for Puerto Rican children, November 23, 24 and 25, 1970: p. 3683–3973.
Walter F. Mondale, chairman.

23.101   Cuba and Porto Rico Special Commissioner. REPORT ON THE CURRENCY QUESTION OF PORTO RICO. By Robert P. Porter, January 3, 1899. Washington, Govt. Print. Off., 1899. 19 p. (Treasury Dept., Div. of Customs, Doc. no. 2082).

23.102   Dept. of Agriculture. NOTES ON THE FOREST CONDITIONS OF PORTO RICO. By Robert T. Hill. Washington, Govt. Print. Off., 1899. 48 p. illus. (U.S. Dept. of Agriculture. Division of Forestry. Bulletin no. 25).

23.103   Dept. of Agriculture. Soil Conservation Service. SOIL SURVEY LABORATORY DATA AND DESCRIPTIONS FOR SOME SOILS OF PUERTO RICO AND VIRGIN ISLANDS. Prepared in cooperation with Puerto Rico Agriculture Experiment Station. Washington, Govt. Print. Off., 1967. illus., map.

23.104   Dept. of Agriculture. TRADE OF PUERTO RICO. By Frank H. Hitchcock. Washington, Govt. Print. Off., 1898. 44 p. (U.S. Dept. of Agriculture. Section of Foreign Markets. Bulletin no. 13).

23.105   Department of Commerce. TRADING UNDER THE LAWS OF PORTO RICO. By Joaquín Servera, Chief, Section of Legal Information, Division of Commercial Law. Washington, Govt. Print. Off., 1927. 44 p. (Trade Promotion Series, no. 58).

23.106 Dept. of Commerce and Labor. COMMERCE AND INDUSTRIES OF ALASKA, HAWAII, PORTO RICO, AND THE PHILIPPINE ISLANDS. By A. G. Robinson, Commercial Agent of the Department of Commerce and Labor. Washington, Govt. Print. Off., 1913. 116 p. tables. (Special Agents Series, no. 67).

23.107 Dept. of Housing and Urban Development. PROGRAM REPORT: SELF-HELP HOUSING IN PUERTO RICO . . . Washington, Govt. Print. Off., June 1971. 8 p. illus. (HUD-228-SF).

23.108 Dept. of the Interior. PUERTO RICO. INFORMATION ON PUERTO RICO TRANSMITTED BY THE UNITED STATES TO THE SECRETARY-GENERAL OF THE UNITED NATIONS PURSUANT TO ARTICLE 73(e) OF THE CHARTER. Washington, June 1947. illus.

23.109 Dept. of Labor. Wage and Hour Division. AN ECONOMIC REPORT ON THE SUGARCANE FARMING INDUSTRY AND THE SUGAR MANUFACTURING INDUSTRY IN PUERTO RICO. Washington, 1972. 134 p.

23.110 Dept. of Labor. Wage and Hour Division. AN ECONOMIC REPORT ON THE GENERAL AGRICULTURE INDUSTRY IN PUERTO RICO. Washington, 1971. 131 p. bibl. (WH Publication 72-5).

23.111 Dept. of Labor. Wage and Hour Division. MINIMUM WAGE RATES FOR PUERTO RICO REQUIRED BY FAIR LABOR STANDARDS ACT. No. 2, May, 1970. Washington, U.S. Govt. Print. Off., 1971.

23.112 Department of State. CARIBBEAN ORGANIZATION. Washington, Govt. Print. Off., 1961. 53 p. (Treaties and Other International Acts Series, no. 4853).

"Agreement, with Annexed Statute, between the United States of America, France, the Netherlands, and the United Kingdom of Great Britain and Northern Ireland, signed at Washington, June 21, 1960, and the Joint Declaration, signed at San Juan, Sept. 6, 1961."

23.113 Dept. of State. Division of Historical Policy Research. DEVELOPMENT OF THE UNITED STATES POLICY TOWARD SELF-GOVERNMENT IN PUERTO RICO, 1898–1947. Washington, 1947. (Research Project no. 43).

23.114 Employment Service. LABOR CONDITIONS IN PORTO RICO. Report by Joseph Marcus, Special Agent, U.S. Employment Service. Washington, Govt. Print. Off., 1919. 67 p. plates.

23.115 Federal Maritime Commission. Bureau of Domestic Regulations. PUERTO RICAN-VIRGIN ISLANDS TRADE STUDY: A REGULATORY STAFF ANALYSIS. Washington, Govt. Print. Off., 1970. 251 p. illus., bibl.

23.116 Federal Works Agency. REPORT ON PUERTO RICO AND THE VIRGIN ISLANDS FOR THE FEDERAL WORKS ADMINISTRATOR. By George H. Field, Assistant to the Administrator. [Washington, 1943?] 123 p.

23.117 Forest Service. CARIBBEAN NATIONAL FOREST OF PUERTO RICO. Washington, Govt. Print. Off., 1936. 29 p. illus., maps.

23.118 Geological Survey. PUERTO RICO . . . QUADRANGLES. Washington, 19 col. maps 79 x 66 cm. or smaller. Scale 1:20,000 and 1:25,000.

23.119 Hydrologic Services Division. Cooperative Studies Section. GENERALIZED ESTIMATES OF PROBABLE MAXIMUM PRECIPITATION AND RAINFALL-FREQUENCY DATA FOR PUERTO RICO AND VIRGIN ISLANDS. Prepared for Engineering Division, Soil Conservation Service, U.S. Dept. of Agriculture. Washington, 1961. 94 p. charts, diagrs., bibl. (U.S. Weather Bureau. Technical Paper no. 42).

23.120 Insular Commission. REPORT OF THE UNITED STATES INSULAR COMMISSION TO THE SECRETARY OF WAR UPON INVESTIGATIONS MADE

INTO THE CIVIL AFFAIRS OF THE IS-
LAND OF PORTO RICO, WITH REC-
OMMENDATIONS. War Department,
Division of Customs and Insular Af-
fairs, June 9, 1899. Washington, Govt.
Print. Off., 1899. 76 p.

23.121 Laws, statutes, etc. LAWS RELATING
TO THE CIVIL ADMINISTRATION
AND GOVERNMENT OF THE ISLAND
OF PORTO RICO. Division of Customs and Insular Affairs, War Department. Washington, Govt. Print. Off.,
1899. 53 p.

23.122 Laws, statutes, etc. ORGANIC ACTS
FOR HAWAII AND PORTO RICO,
WITH AMENDMENTS THERETO AND
AN APPENDIX CONTAINING GEN-
ERAL LEGISLATION AFFECTING HA-
WAII, PORTO RICO, GUAM, AND
TUTUILA. Beginning with 56th Cong.,
1st sess., ending with 59th Cong., 2d
sess. Compiled and indexed for the
use of the Senate Committee on Pa-
cific islands and Porto Rico by C. E. Al-
den, clerk. Washington, Govt. Print.
Off., 1907. 107 p.

23.123 National Office of Vital Statistics. VI-
TAL STATISTICS SPECIAL REPORTS:
NATIONAL SUMMARIES. MORTAL-
ITY, U.S. AND EACH STATE, AND
ALASKA, HAWAII, PUERTO RICO
AND VIRGIN ISLANDS; 1958. Wash-
ington, Govt. Print. Off., 1960. 70 p. (v.
52, no. 3).

23.124 Porto Rico Special Commissioner. RE-
PORT ON THE ISLAND OF PORTO
RICO; ITS POPULATION, CIVIL
GOVERNMENT, COMMERCE, IN-
DUSTRIES, PRODUCTION, ROADS,
TARIFF, AND CURRENCY, WITH REC-
OMMENDATIONS. By Henry K. Car-
roll, Special Commissioner for the
United States to Porto Rico. Washing-
ton, Govt. Print. Off., 1899. 813 p. (U.S.
Treasury Dept. Doc. no. 2118).

23.125 President (Coolidge, Calvin). LETTER
OF ... TO GOVERNOR HORACE M.
TOWNER IN REPLY TO THE CON-
CURRENT RESOLUTION OF THE LEG-
ISLATURE OF PORTO RICO, COM-
MITTED TO COLONEL LINDBERGH,
AND ALSO TO A CABLEGRAM
SIGNED BY MESSRS. BARCELO AND
TOUS SOTO OF DATE JANUARY 19,

1928. San Juan, Bureau of Supplies,
Printing and Transportation, 1928. 32
p. English and Spanish texts.

23.126 President (Johnson, Lyndon Baines).
"Economic Status of Puerto Ricans:
United States and New York, New
York." *In* MANPOWER REPORT OF
THE PRESIDENT, 1964. Washington,
Govt. Print. Off., 1964. p. 115–118.

23.127 President (Kennedy, John F.). DOCU-
MENT NO. 198 ON THE PROPOSAL
TO PERFECT THE PUERTO RICAN
COMMONWEALTH ARRANGE-
MENT. May 20, 1963. Washington,
Govt. Print. Off., 1964. 416 p.

23.128 President (Roosevelt, Theodore R.).
MESSAGE FROM THE PRESIDENT OF
THE UNITED STATES RELATIVE TO
HIS RECENT VISIT TO THE ISLAND OF
PORTO RICO, TRANSMITTING THE
REPORT OF THE GOVERNOR OF
PORTO RICO. Washington, Govt.
Print. Off., 1906. 200 p. plates, map,
diagrs. (59th Cong., 2d sess. Senate.
Doc. 135).

23.129 President (Taft, William H.). AFFAIRS
IN PORTO RICO. MESSAGE FROM
THE PRESIDENT INVITING THE AT-
TENTION OF THE CONGRESS TO THE
LEGISLATIVE DIFFICULTIES IN
PUERTO RICO, WITH ACCOM-
PANYING PAPERS, AND RECOM-
MENDING AN AMENDMENT TO THE
FORAKER ACT. Washington, Govt.
Print. Off., 1909. 17 p. (61st Cong., 1st
sess. Senate. Doc. 40).

23.130 Puerto Rico Reconstruction Adminis-
tration. THE NEED FOR FEDERAL AID
IN PUERTO RICO. THE PURPOSES OF
THE PUERTO RICO RECONSTRUC-
TION ADMINISTRATION. Washing-
ton, Govt. Print. Off., 1936. 6 p.

23.131 Puerto Rico Reconstruction Adminis-
tration. PLANNING PROBLEMS AND
ACTIVITIES IN PUERTO RICO. PRE-
LIMINARY REPORT TO THE PUERTO
RICO RECONSTRUCTION ADMINIS-
TRATION AND THE NATIONAL RE-
SOURCES COMMITTEE. By Earl Han-
son, Planning Consultant. San Juan,
November 23, 1935 (amended as of
February 17, 1936). San Juan, 1936.
various pagings.

23.132 Puerto Rico Reconstruction Administration. REHABILITATION IN PUERTO RICO: BEING AN OUTLINE OF THE ORIGINS, OF THE FUNCTIONS AND THE ACCOMPLISHMENTS OF THE PUERTO RICO RECONSTRUCTION ADMINISTRATION. Harold Ickes, Administrator, Miles H. Fairbank, Assistant Administrator. San Juan, Impr. Venezuela, 1939. 48 p. port., map, tables, diagrs.

23.133 Tariff Commission. THE ECONOMY OF PUERTO RICO, WITH SPECIAL REFERENCE TO THE ECONOMIC IMPLICATIONS OF INDEPENDENCE AND OTHER PROPOSALS TO CHANGE ITS POLITICAL STATUS UNDER THE GENERAL PROVISIONS OF SECTION 332, PART II, TITLE III, TARIFF ACT OF 1930. Washington, 1946. 67 p. maps, tables.

23.134 Tariff Commission. PRELIMINARY REPORT: PUERTO RICO'S ECONOMY WITH SPECIAL REFERENCE TO UNITED STATES-PUERTO RICAN TRADE. Washington, 1943. 131 p. illus., map, tables.

23.135 Treaties, etc. TREATY BETWEEN THE UNITED STATES AND SPAIN. PEACE. SIGNED AT PARIS, DECEMBER 10, 1898. Washington, Govt. Print. Off., 1919. 14 p. (Treaty Series, no. 343) English and Spanish in parallel columns.

23.136 War Dept. CONDITIONS IN PORTO RICO. MESSAGE FROM THE PRESIDENT OF THE UNITED STATES, TRANSMITTING A REPORT MADE BY THE SECRETARY OF WAR UPON CONDITIONS EXISTING IN PORTO RICO. Washington, Govt. Print. Off., 1910. 25 p. (61st Cong., 2d sess. House. Doc. 615).

Includes "Memorandum of proposed changes in the Organic Act of Porto Rico," known as the Foraker Act.

23.137 War Dept. Dept. of Porto Rico. PUERTO RICO, EMBRACING THE REPORTS OF BRIG. GEN. GEO. W. DAVIS, MILITARY GOVERNOR, AND REPORTS ON THE DISTRICTS OF ARECIBO, AGUADILLA, CAYEY, HUMACAO, MAYAGÜEZ, PONCE, SAN JUAN, VIEQUES, AND THE SUBDISTRICT OF SAN GERMAN. Washington, Govt. Print. Off., 1900. 94 p.

Arranged by topics.

23.138 War Dept. SPANISH COLONIAL POSSESSIONS; REGULATIONS. Washington, Govt. Print. Off., 1898-1899. 4 v.

23.139 War Dept. Porto Rico Census Office. CENSUS OF PORTO RICO, TAKEN UNDER THE DIRECTION OF THE WAR DEPARTMENT, U.S.A., Bulletin nos. 1-3, June 11-August 29, 1900. Washington, Govt. Print. Off., 1900. 3 v. in 1.

23.140 War Dept. Porto Rico Census Office. REPORT ON THE CENSUS OF PORTO RICO, 1899. Washington, Govt. Print. Off., 1900. 417 p. plates, maps, diagrs.

Part III
Periodical Literature (24-25)

24
SELECTED PERIODICALS

24.1 Academia de Artes y Ciencias de Puerto Rico. BOLETIN. v. 1+ 1965+ San Juan. quarterly.

24.2 Academia Puertorriqueña de la Historia. BOLETIN. v. 1+ nov. 1968+ San Juan.

24.3 AGRICULTURA AL DIA. v. 1+ julio 1954+ San Juan, Departamento de Agricultura. illus. monthly.

24.4 ALMA LATINA. 1930–1965. San Juan, Imprenta Venezuela. illus., ports. monthly, 1930–1935; semimonthly, 1935–1965.

24.5 ASOMANTE. v. 1+ 1945+ San Juan, Asociación de Graduadas de la Universidad de Puerto Rico. quarterly. Index 1945–1959.

24.6 ATENEA. v. 1+ 19 + Mayagüez, P.R., Facultad de Artes y Ciencias del Colegio de Agricultura y Artes Mecánicas. quarterly.

24.7 Ateneo Puertorriqueño. REVISTA. v. 1–5; 1935–1940. San Juan.

24.8 AVANCE. v. 1 núm. 1+ julio 1972+ San Juan. weekly.

24.9 BOLETIN DE COMERCIO. año 1+ mayo 1943+ San Juan, Departamento de Agricultura y Comercio. irregular.
No more published?

24.10 BOLETIN MENSUAL DE ESTADISTICAS AGRICOLAS. v. 1+ 19 + Santurce, P.R., Oficina de Estadísticas Agrícolas.

24.11 BOLETIN DE ESTADISTICAS DEL COMERCIO. v. 1+ abr. 1968+ San Juan, Oficina de Economía y Planificación.

24.12 BOLETIN DE HISTORIA PUERTORRIQUEÑA. v. 1+ dic. 1948+ San Juan. illus. monthly.
No more published?

24.13 BOLETIN HISTORICO DE PUERTO RICO. año 1–14; feb. 1914–abr. 1927. San Juan, Tip. Cantero, Fernández, 1914–1927. bimonthly.
Supersedes *Repertorio histórico de Puerto Rico* (nov. 1896–dic. 1897), Cayetano Coll y Toste, editor.

24.14 BOLETIN MUNICIPAL. v. 1–11; 1958–1969. San Juan, Gobierno Municipal.

24.15 THE CARIBBEAN. 1961–1964. Hato Rey, P.R., Caribbean Commission. irregular.

24.16 THE CARIBBEAN FORESTER. 1939–1963. Río Piedras, P.R., Tropical Forest Experiment Station, United States Forest Service. quarterly.

24.17 THE CARIBBEAN JOURNAL OF SCIENCE. v. 1+ Feb. 1961+ Mayagüez, University of Puerto Rico, Institute of Caribbean Science. quarterly.

24.18 CARIBBEAN SENTINEL. v. 1+ April 25, 1942+ San Juan, Special Service

Office, Dept. of Puerto Rico, U.S. Armed Forces in the Caribbean. illus. weekly.

No more published?

24.19 CARIBBEAN STUDIES. v. 1+ April 1961+ Río Piedras, Institute of Caribbean Studies, University of Puerto Rico. quarterly.

24.20 CLARIDAD. v. 1+ junio 1959+ Río Piedras, P.R., Movimiento Pro Independencia-Partido Socialista Puertorriqueño. biweekly.

24.21 Colegio de Abogados de Puerto Rico. REVISTA. v. 1+ 19 + San Juan. quarterly.

24.22 CUADERNOS BIBLIOTECOLOGICOS v. 1+ 1970+ Humacao, P.R., Sociedad de Bibliotecarios de Puerto Rico. irregular.

24.23 CUADERNOS LINGUISTICOS. v. 1+ 19 + Río Piedras, Universidad de Puerto Rico, Biblioteca de Extramuros.

24.24 DIALOGOS. v. 1+ 1957 + Río Piedras, Departamento de Filosofía, Facultad de Humanidades, Universidad de Puerto Rico. semiannual.

24.25 EXCLUSIVO DE WASHINGTON. v. 1+ 1958+ Washington, Office of the Commonwealth of Puerto Rico. semimonthly.

24.26 EXTRAMUROS. 1962-1964. II Epoca: v. 1+ dic. 1967+ Río Piedras, División de Extensión, Universidad de Puerto Rico. quarterly.

24.27 GUAJANA. v. 1+ sept. 1962+ Río Piedras, P.R. irregular.

24.28 HISTORIA. 1. ser., v. 1-7, abr. 1951-dic. 1957. 2. ser., v. 1+ 1968+ Río Piedras, P.R. semiannual.

Publicación ... del Capítulo Beta de la sociedad nacional honoraria de historia Phi Alpha Theta.

24.29 LA HORA. v. 1+ sept. 1971+ San Juan, Partido Independentista Puertorriqueño. weekly.

24.30 HOY. v. 1 no. 1+ March 1972+ Washington, Cabinet Committee on Opportunities for Spanish-Speaking People. monthly.

24.31 HUMANIDAD. 1967-1969. Río Piedras, Escuela Graduada de Trabajo Social, Universidad de Puerto Rico. annual.

24.32 EL IMPARCIAL. v. 1 núm. 1+ 1919+ San Juan. daily.

24.33 Instituto de Cultura Puertorriqueña. REVISTA. v. 1+ 1958+ San Juan. illus. quarterly.

24.34 ISLA LITERARIA. año 1+ 1970+ San Juan. irregular.

24.35 JOURNAL OF AGRICULTURE OF THE UNIVERSITY OF PUERTO RICO. 1917-1931. Río Piedras, Agriculture Experiment Station, University of Puerto Rico. quarterly.

24.36 EL MUNDO. v. 1 núm. 1+ 17 feb. 1919+ San Juan, daily.

24.37 NOSOTROS. v. 1+ 1965+ San Juan, División de Educación de la Comunidad. quarterly.

24.38 EL NUEVO DIA. v. 1 núm. 1+ 19 + Ponce, P.R. daily. Supersedes EL DIA.

24.39 PEDAGOGIA. v. 1+ jun. 1953+ Río Piedras, Colegio de Pedagogía, Universidad de Puerto Rico. semiannual. English and Spanish.

24.40 THE PORTO RICO REVIEW. REVISTA DE PUERTO RICO. v. 1-6; 1906-1912. San Juan, W. Sweet. illus. weekly. English and Spanish.

24.41 PRO-REPUBLICA DE PUERTO RICO. año 1-3; en. 17, 1927-sept. 10, 1941. San Juan. illus., ports. irregular.

Boletín defensor de la independencia puertorriqueña. Redactores: juventud nacionalista.

24.42 PUERTO. v. 1+ 1967+ Río Piedras, Facultad de Estudios Generales, Universidad de Puerto Rico. semiannual.

24.43 PUERTO RICAN TRADE REVIEW. v. 1+ Oct. 1936+ Washington. illus., ports. monthly, 1936-1940; bimonthly, 1940.

No more published?

24.44 PUERTO RICO COMERCIAL. PORTO RICO COMMERCIAL. año 1–3; 1914–1917. San Juan. illus., ports. irregular.
Organo oficial de la Cámara de Comercio de Puerto Rico.

24.45 PUERTO RICO ILUSTRADO. 1886–1952. San Juan. weekly.

24.46 THE PUERTO RICO JOURNAL OF PUBLIC HEALTH AND TROPICAL MEDICINE. v. 1–26; 1925–1950. New York, Columbia University Press. frequency varies.

24.47 PUERTO RICO MONTHLY STATISTICAL REPORT. v. 1+ July 1943+ San Juan, Bureau of the Budget. Title varies.

24.48 QUARTERLY ECONOMIC REVIEW OF CUBA, DOMINICAN REPUBLIC, HAITI, PUERTO RICO. no. 1+ Mar. 1953+ London, Economist Intelligence Unit. illus. quarterly.
Title varies.

24.49 QUIMBAMBA. 1972+ New York, Los Amigos del Museo del Barrio. quarterly.

24.50 REBELION. v. 1+ 1965+ San Juan. Organo del Partido Nacionalista de Puerto Rico.

24.51 REVISTA DE ADMINISTRACION PUBLICA. v. 1+ ag. 1964+ Río Piedras, Universidad de Puerto Rico. irregular.

24.52 REVISTA DE CIENCIAS SOCIALES. v. 1+ mar. 1957+ Río Piedras, Colegio de Ciencias Sociales, Universidad de Puerto Rico. quarterly.

24.53 REVISTA DE DERECHO PUERTORRIQUEÑO. v. 1+ sept. 1961+ Ponce, Escuela de Derecho, Universidad Católica de Puerto Rico. quarterly.

24.54 REVISTA DE DERECHOS HUMANOS. v. 1+ sept. 1961+ San Juan, Comisión de Derechos Civiles.

24.55 REVISTA DE ECONOMIA Y ESTADISTICAS DE PUERTO RICO. 1960–1961. San Juan, Asociación Puertorriqueña de Economía y Estadística.

24.56 REVISTA DE ESTUDIOS HISPANICOS. v. 1+ feb. 1928+ Río Piedras, Departamento de Estudios Hispánicos, Universidad de Puerto Rico.

24.57 REVISTA DE HISTORIA DE PUERTO RICO. v. 1+ ag. 1942+ Mayagüez, P.R. irregular.

24.58 REVISTA GEOGRAFICA DE PUERTO RICO. año 1; mar.–dic. 1923. San Juan. illus., tables. monthly.
Merged into Revista de obras públicas de Puerto Rico.

24.59 REVISTA JURIDICA DE LA UNIVERSIDAD DE PUERTO RICO. v. 1+ mar. 1932+ Río Piedras, Escuela de Derecho, Universidad de Puerto Rico. monthly during academic year.

24.60 REVISTA DE OBRAS PUBLICAS DE PUERTO RICO. 1924–1936. San Juan. illus., plates, maps, diagrs. monthly.

24.61 REVISTA DEL COLEGIO DE COMERCIO. v. 1 núm. 1+ abr. 1966+ Río Piedras, Colegio de Comercio, Universidad de Puerto Rico. quarterly.

24.62 REVISTA/REVIEW INTERAMERICANA. v. 1+ Spring 1971+ Hato Rey, Editorial de la Universidad Interamericana de Puerto Rico. quarterly. Spanish and English.

24.63 THE RICAN. v. 1+ Fall 1971+ Chicago, The Rican Journal, Inc. quarterly.

24.64 SAN JUAN REVIEW. v. 1–3; 1964–1966. San Juan. monthly.

24.65 SAN JUAN STAR. v. 1 no. 1+ Nov. 2, 1959+ San Juan. daily.

24.66 SIN NOMBRE. v. 1+ 1970+ San Juan. quarterly.

24.67 STATUS OF ZOOLOGICAL RESEARCH IN THE CARIBBEAN. v. 1+ Jan. 1961+ Mayagüez, University of Puerto Rico, Institute of Caribbean Science. annual.

24.68 SUMMA. v. 1+ jul. 1950+ Río Piedras, Círculo de Estudios Filosóficos.

24.69 LA TORRE. v. 1+ 1953+ Río Piedras, Editorial Universitaria, Universidad de Puerto Rico. quarterly.

24.70 VERSIONES. v. 1+ sept. 1966+ San Juan. bimonthly.
Cuadernos de poesía y pintura.

24.71 LA VOZ DEL OBRERO. v. 1+ oct. 1937+ San Juan. irregular.
Revista independiente. Defensora del progreso político, social y económico de Puerto Rico.

25
JOURNAL AND MAGAZINE ARTICLES

Antiquities

25.1 Alegría, Ricardo E. On Puerto Rican Archaeology. illus., bibl. AMERICAN ANTIQUITY, v. 31, Oct. 1965: 246–249.

25.2 Coomans, H.E. Shells and Shell Objects from an Indian Site on Magueyes Island, Puerto Rico. illus. CARIBBEAN JOURNAL OF SCIENCE (Mayagüez, P.R.), v. 5, Mar./June 1965: 15–23.

25.3 Fagg, Bernard. Rock Gong and Rock Slides. illus. MAN (London), v. 57, Feb. 1957: 30–32.

25.4 Fernández Méndez, Eugenio. Los corrales de pesca indígenas de Puerto Rico. REVISTA DEL INSTITUTO DE CULTURA PUERTORRIQUEÑA, v. 9, oct./dic. 1960: 9–13.

25.5 Frassetto, Monica Flaherty. Preliminary Report on Petroglyphs in Puerto Rico. bibl., illus., map. AMERICAN ANTIQUITY, v. 25, Jan. 1960: 381–391.

Arts and Music

25.6 Alegría, R.E. La casa del Callejón de San Luis Rey. illus. INTERIORS, v. 127, June 1968: 80–83.

25.7 Alvarez Nazario, Manuel. Historia de las denominaciones de los bailes de bomba. REVISTA DE CIENCIAS SOCIALES (Río Piedras, P.R.), v. 4, mar. 1960: 59–74.

25.8 A. Nechodoma, Architect: Prairie School in Puerto Rico. illus. PROGRESSIVE ARCHITECTURE, v. 47, Sept. 1966: 166–169.

25.9 Art from Puerto Rico: Exhibition at the PAU. illus. AMERICAS, v. 18, July 1966: 40.

25.10 Balbuena de la Maza, Manuel. La Catedral de San Juan de Puerto Rico. ARTE EN AMERICA Y FILIPINAS (Sevilla), no. 2, 1936: 114–123.

25.11 Blanco, E.T. La Catedral de San Juan Bautista de Puerto Rico. illus., plan. ALMA LATINA (San Juan), v. 7, 1936: 43–61.

25.12 Cebollero, Pedro Angel. El cantar puertorriqueño. REVISTA DE LAS ANTILLAS (San Juan), v. 2, 1914: 141–143.

25.13 Contreras, Juan de. Vestigios de la "Edad Media" puertorriqueña. illus. REVISTA DEL INSTITUTO DE CULTURA PUERTORRIQUEÑA (San Juan), v. 2, en./mar. 1959: 1–7.

25.14 Habitat Lives. illus., plans, diagrs. ARCHITECTURAL FORUM, v. 130, Mar. 1969: 93.

25.15 Island Décor by D. and M. Rodríguez, for House in San Juan. illus. INTERIOR DESIGN, v. 37, June 1966: 114–117.

25.16 Klumb of Puerto Rico. illus. ARCHI-TECTURAL FORUM, v. 117, July 1962: 86–90.

25.17 Maloff, S. Climate for Art on an Island. illus. SATURDAY REVIEW, v. 44, Feb. 11, 1961: 58–59.

25.18 Marco Dorta, Enrique. La catedral de Puerto Rico: un plano de 1864. illus. ANALES DEL INSTITUTO DE ARTE AMERICANO E INVESTIGACIONES ESTETICAS (Buenos Aires), v. 13, 1960: 27–34.

25.19 Moskin, J.R. Renaissance in the Arts. LOOK, v. 25, Jan. 17, 1961: 28–29.

25.20 Ortiz, Juan E. El Hospital Militar de San Juan. illus. ALMA LATINA (San Juan), v. 11, sept. 1940: 30–31.

25.21 Preece, M. Puerto Rico Swallows the Hook. illus. LANDSCAPE ARCHI-TECTURE, v. 58, Jan. 1968: 112–113.

25.22 Rodríguez, Augusto A. Tanteando la cultura musical puertorriqueña. PRENSA (San Juan) v. 6, mar. 1959: 24.

25.23 Salas, Xavier de. Aportaciones a la obra de Luis Paret y Alcázar. illus. ARCHIVO ESPAÑOL DE ARTE (Madrid), v. 138, 1962: 132–133.

25.24 Schuyler, Montgomery. Our Acquired Architecture. illus. ARCHITECTURAL RECORD (New York), v. 9, Jan. 1900: 277–314.

25.25 Torre, J. de la, Architect: El Conquistador Hotel, Punta Gorda. illus., plans, diagr. ARCHITECTURAL RECORD, v. 146, Dec. 1969: 124–127.

Civilization

25.26 Agraít, Gustavo. Personalidad cultural y destino político de Puerto Rico. LA TORRE (Río Piedras, P.R.), v. 14, mayo/ag. 1966: 189–195.

25.27 Babín, María Teresa. 'Asomante' en la cultura puertorriqueña (1945–1965). ASOMANTE (San Juan), v. 21, jul./sept. 1965: 7–18.

25.28 Babín, María Teresa, and Nilita Vientós Gastón. La situación de Puerto Rico. SUR (Buenos Aires), no. 293, mar./abr. 1965: 113–122.

25.29 Benítez, Celeste, and Roberto F. Rexach. The Puerto Rican Identity Problem. SAN JUAN REVIEW, v. 1, 1964.

25.30 Benítez, Jaime. Discurso en el primer Centenario de Unamuno. LA TORRE (Río Piedras, P.R.), v. 13, mayo/ag. 1965: 11–16.

25.31 Cancel Negrón, Ramón. Un puertorriqueño en un mundo latinoamericano. PANORAMAS (Mexico D.F.), v. 2, en./feb. 1964: 139–146.

25.32 Figueroa Mercado, Loida. Puerto Rico—cultura y personalidad. RE-VISTA DE CIENCIAS SOCIALES (Río Piedras), v. 7, 1963.

25.33 Hostos, Adolfo de. ¿Quiénes somos los puertorriqueños? BOLETIN DE LA ACADEMIA DE ARTES Y CIENCIAS DE PUERTO RICO (Río Piedras, P.R.), v. 2, en./mar. 1966: 115–133.

25.34 Kazin, A. In Puerto Rico. COMMENTARY, v. 29, Feb. 1960: 108–14; Discussion, v. 29, May 1960: 430–434; v. 30, July 1960: 68.

25.35 Maldonado Denis, Manuel. Apuntes sobre la cuestión cultural en Puerto Rico. LA TORRE (Río Piedras, P.R.), v. 13, en./abr. 1965: 11–18.

25.36 Maldonado Denis, Manuel. Apuntes preliminares sobre la "inteligentsia" puertorriqueña y el Caribe hispánico. bibl. REVISTA DE CIENCIAS SOCIALES (Río Piedras, P.R.), v. 8, dic. 1964: 377–388.

25.37 Marrero Navarro, Domingo. Notas para organizar el estudio de la historia de las ideas en Puerto Rico. REVISTA DE HISTORIA DE LAS IDEAS (Quito), v. 1, 1959: 159–176.

25.38 Meléndez Muñoz, Miguel. La personalidad puertorriqueña. BOLETIN DE LA ACADEMIA DE ARTES Y CIENCIAS DE PUERTO RICO (Río Piedras, P.R.), v. 2, abr./jun. 1966: 301–308.

25.39 Patterson, W.D. Conversations between Two Cultures; Proposed North-South Center at the University of Puerto Rico. SATURDAY REVIEW, v. 44, May 20, 1961: 26.

25.40 Seda Bonilla, Eduardo. La cultura cívica de Puerto Rico. bibl., tables. REVISTA DE CIENCIAS SOCIALES (Río Piedras, P.R.), v. 13, abr./jun. 1969: 207–216.

25.41 Vientós Gastón, Nilita. The Identity Problem: Part Two. SAN JUAN REVIEW, v. 1, 1964.

Description and Travel

25.42 Abrahams, P. Puerto Ricans. illus. HOLIDAY, v. 29, Feb. 1961: 33–47.

25.43 Giovanni, N.T. di. Puerto Rico, a Farm in the Hills. illus. ATLANTIC, v. 210, Dec. 1962: 15.

25.44 Joseph, R. Presto Chango, P.R.! illus. ESQUIRE, v. 58, Nov. 1962: 114–117.

25.45 La Orden Miracle, Ernesto. Puerto Rico, hermano hispánico. REVISTA CONSERVADORA DEL PENSAMIENTO CENTROAMERICANO (Managua, Nic.), v. 20, oct. 1968: 5–9.

25.46 McDowell, B. Puerto Rico's Seven-League Bootstraps. illus. NATIONAL GEOGRAPHIC MAGAZINE, v. 122, Dec. 19, 1962: 755–793.

25.47 Moskin, J.R. Surprising Puerto Rico. LOOK, v. 25, Jan. 17, 1961: 21–27.

25.48 San Juan: The New Havana. illus. SATURDAY REVIEW, v. 48, Jan. 2, 1965: 41.

25.49 Sutton, H. Getting a Charge up San Juan Hill. illus. SATURDAY REVIEW, v. 46, Feb. 2, 1963: 24–26.

25.50 Sutton, H. Yes, We Have No Boiled Green Bananas. illus. SATURDAY REVIEW, v. 45, May 12, 1962: 52.

Economy

25.51 Andic, Fuat M. Income of Wage-Earner Families and Economic Development of Puerto Rico, 1941–1953. tables. CARIBBEAN STUDIES (Río Piedras, P.R.), v. 2, Jan. 1963: 14–27.

25.52 Andic, Fuat M. The Measurement of Inequality in the Distribution of Taxable Income in Puerto Rico, 1955–1958. tables. SOCIAL AND ECONOMIC STUDIES (Mona, Jamaica), v. 12, March 1963: 72–77.

25.53 Baer, W. Puerto Rico: An Evaluation of a Successful Development Program. bibl. refs., illus. QUARTERLY JOURNAL OF ECONOMICS, v. 73, Nov. 1959: 645–671.

25.54 Baquero, Jenaro. La importación de fondos externos y la capacidad absorbente de nuestra economía. REVISTA DE CIENCIAS SOCIALES (Río Piedras, P.R.), v. 7, mar./jun. 1963: 79–92.

25.55 Baquero, Jenaro. Magnitud y características de la inversión exterior en Puerto Rico. tables. REVISTA DE CIENCIAS SOCIALES (Río Piedras, P.R.), v. 8, mar. 1964: 5–13.

25.56 Beals, C. Password is Progress. illus. SATURDAY REVIEW, v. 43, Sept. 10, 1960: 40–41.

25.57 Berlin, Lawrence H. Puerto Rico as a Foreign Trade and Investment Center [foreign trade zone in Mayagüez]. INTER-AMERICAN ECONOMIC AFFAIRS, v. 14, Winter 1960: 45-58.

25.58 Bhatia, Mohinder S. Tax Exemption in a Developing Economy: A Case Study of Puerto Rico. NATIONAL TAX JOURNAL (National Tax Association, Boston), v. 13, Dec. 1960: 341-349.

25.59 Boomerang in Puerto Rico. illus. ARCHITECTURAL FORUM, v. 118, Apr. 1963: 91.

25.60 Carpenter, B. R. Puerto Rico's Tourist Industry [abstract]. ASSOCIATION OF AMERICAN GEOGRAPHERS. ANNALS, v. 52, Summer 1962: 323.

25.61 Castañeda, Rolando, and José A. Herrero. La distribución del ingreso en Puerto Rico: algunos comentarios en base a los años 1953-1963. REVISTA DE CIENCIAS SOCIALES (Río Piedras, P.R.), v. 9, dic. 1965: 345-362.

25.62 Castañeda, Rolando. Un modelo económico estático para Puerto Rico. REVISTA DE CIENCIAS SOCIALES (Río Piedras, P.R.), v. 11, mar. 1967: 95-109.

25.63 Chenyoung, Paul L. The Costs of Locating the Apparel Industry in Puerto Rico and Jamaica. bibl. CARIBBEAN STUDIES (Río Piedras, P.R.), v. 8, Apr. 1968: 3-29.

25.64 Curet, Eliezer. La formación interna de capital y el desarollo económico de Puerto Rico. REVISTA DE ADMINISTRACION PUBLICA (Río Piedras, P.R.), v. 3, dic. 1966: 21-38.

25.65 Dutta, M., and V. Su. Econometric Model of Puerto Rico. bibl. REVIEW OF ECONOMIC STUDIES (Edinburgh), v. 36, July 1969: 319-333.

25.66 Edel, Matthew O. Land Reform in Puerto Rico, 1940-1959. CARIBBEAN STUDIES (Río Piedras, P.R.), v. 2, Oct. 1962: 26-60; v. 2, Jan. 1963: 28-50.

25.67 Esteves, Vernon R. Desarrollo económico sin inflación; la experiencia de Puerto Rico. TRIMESTRE ECONOMICO (Mexico D.F.), v. 28, abr./jun. 1961: 229-246.

25.68 Esteves, Vernon R. Política de industrialización. REVISTA CONSERVADORA DEL PENSAMIENTO CENTROAMERICANO (Managua, P.R.), v. 20, jun. 1965: 8-15.

25.69 Freyre, Jorge. Análisis de los niveles de concentración en el sector manufacturero de Puerto Rico. TRIMESTRE ECONOMICO (Mexico D.F.), v. 29, oct./dic. 1962: 574-586.

25.70 Fried, Milton. Progreso económico de Puerto Rico. COMBATE (San José, Costa Rica), v. 3, sept./oct. 1961: 19-25.

25.71 González, Antonio Juan. La economía y el status político de Puerto Rico. REVISTA DE CIENCIAS SOCIALES (Río Piedras, P.R.), mar. 1966: 5-49.

25.72 Goodsell, C.T. Puerto Rico Moves Forward. illus. CURRENT HISTORY, v. 51, Dec. 1966: 321-326.

25.73 Haring, Joseph E. El comercio exterior como motor del crecimiento: el caso de Puerto Rico. TRIMESTRE ECONOMICO (Mexico, D.F.), v. 27, en./mar. 1960: 62-84.

25.74 Hayn, R. Puerto Rico's Economic Growth. bibl. footnotes, illus. INTER-AMERICAN ECONOMIC AFFAIRS, v. 12, Winter 1958: 51-58.

25.75 Lounsburg, John F. Economic Development in Latin America: Puerto Rico as a Case Study. REVISTA GEOGRAFICA, INSTITUTO DE GEOGRAFIA E HISTORIA (Río de Janeiro), v. 34, jan./jun. 1964: 27-32.

25.76 MacPhail, Donald D. Postwar Dairy development in Puerto Rico [abstract]. ASSOCIATION OF AMERICAN GEOGRAPHERS. ANNALS, v. 48, Summer 1958: 278.

25.77 MacPhail, Donald D. Puerto Rican Dairying: A Revolution in Tropical Agriculture. illus., maps. GEOGRAPHICAL REVIEW, v. 53, Apr. 1963: 222-246.

25.78 Mathews, Thomas G. The Agrarian Reform in Cuba and Puerto Rico. REVISTA DE CIENCIAS SOCIALES (Río Piedras, P.R.), v. 4, mar. 1960: 107–123.

25.79 Middrie, D.L. Food Problems in Puerto Rico's Development Program [abstract]. ASSOCIATION OF AMERICAN GEOGRAPHERS. ANNALS, v. 52, Summer 1962: 352.

25.80 Moskin, J.R. Energy and Brains Hammer out the Future. LOOK, v. 25, Jan. 17, 1961: 36.

25.81 Muñoz Marín, L. Our Progress in Puerto Rico. illus. AMERICAN FEDERATIONIST, v. 66, July 1959: 8–10.

25.82 O'Neal, B.B. White-Collar Salaries in Hawaii, Puerto Rico, and Alaska. bibl. footnotes, illus. MONTHLY LABOR REVIEW, v. 87, Mar. 1964: 301–304.

25.83 Packard, W.E. How to Win with Foreign Aid. NATION, v. 192, Apr. 8, 1961: 302–304.

25.84 Puerto Rico: Progress and Problems. bibl. WORLD TODAY (London), v. 14, May 1958: 216–226.

25.85 Puerto Rico's Example. THE ECONOMIST (London), v. 195, June 11, 1960: 1097–1098.

25.86 Puerto Rico: Island on its Way. illus. map. THE ECONOMIST (London), v. 231, Apr. 12, 1969: 48–50.

25.87 Reynolds, L.G. Wages and Employment in a Labor-Surplus Economy. bibl., illus. THE AMERICAN ECONOMIC REVIEW, v. 55, March 1965: 19–39.

25.88 Ramírez Pérez, Miguel A. Inferencias sobre economía gubernamental en el estudio de economía del Departamento de Salud de Puerto Rico. REVISTA DE CIENCIAS SOCIALES (Río Piedras, P.R.), v. 12, jun. 1968: 173–193.

25.89 Ramírez Pérez, Miguel A. El informe de economía en el gobierno y la ausencia del estudio sistemático de la economía gubernamental en Puerto Rico. REVISTA DE CIENCIAS SOCIALES (Río Piedras, P.R.), v. 11, jun. 1967: 146–160.

25.90 Ritter, N. Solid Win in Rich New Territory. illus. LIFE, v. 46, June 1, 1959: 110–113.

25.91 Rosen, Keith S. Puerto Rican Land Reform: The History of an Instructive Experiment. YALE LAW JOURNAL, v. 73, Dec. 1963: 334–356.

25.92 Ross, David F. The Costs and Benefits of Puerto Rico's Fomento Programmes. SOCIAL AND ECONOMIC STUDIES (Mona, Jamaica), v. 6, Sept. 1957: 329–362.

25.93 Ross, David F. Some Problems of Industrial Development in Puerto Rico. INTER-AMERICAN ECONOMIC AFFAIRS, v. 11, Fall 1957: 47–64.

25.94 Safa, H.I. Female-Based Household in Public Housing: a Case Study in Puerto Rico. illus. HUMAN ORGANIZATION, v. 24, Summer 1965: 135–139.

25.95 Segal, Aarón. La lección del desarrollo económico de Puerto Rico. COMERCIO EXTERIOR (Mexico, D.F.), v. 17, abr. 1967: 293–294.

25.96 Showcase of Progress Heads into Trouble. illus. U.S. NEWS & WORLD REPORT, v. 52, June 11, 1962: 68–70.

25.97 Slappey, S.G. How Puerto Rico's Future Affects U.S. Business. illus. NATIONS BUSINESS, v. 57, Dec. 1969: 50–54.

25.98 Smith, R.V. Distribution of Manufacturing and Population Change in Puerto Rico [abstract]. ASSOCIATION OF AMERICAN GEOGRAPHERS. ANNALS, v. 51, Dec. 1961: 422.

25.99 Solow, H. Forceful Ferré Family. illus. FORTUNE, v. 60, Oct. 1969: 144–147.

25.100 Steiner, S. Poor in Puerto Rico. NEW REPUBLIC, v. 165, Dec. 3, 1971: 8–9.

25.101 Stone, Leroy O. Population Redistribution and Economic Development in Puerto Rico, 1950–1960. SOCIAL AND ECONOMIC STUDIES (Mona, Jamaica), v. 14, Sept. 1965: 264–271.

25.102 Strassman, W.P. Is Puerto Rican Economic Development a Special Case?

INTER-AMERICAN ECONOMIC AFFAIRS, v. 18, Summer 1964: 61–76.

25.103 Wagenheim, K. Cracks in the Showcase. NEW REPUBLIC, v. 153, Oct. 16, 1965: 15–16. Reply, G. Laguardia, v. 153, Dec. 4, 1965: 36–37.

25.104 Weller, Robert H. A Historical Analysis of Female Labour Force Participation in Puerto Rico. SOCIAL AND ECONOMIC STUDIES (Mona, Jamaica), v. 17, Mar. 1968.

25.105 White, B. Puerto Rico—a Partial Developmental Model. AMERICAN JOURNAL OF ECONOMICS AND SOCIOLOGY, v. 22, Oct. 1963: 539–542.

25.106 Why Puerto Rico Thrives as Cuba Crumbles: with Interview with Governor Muñoz Marín. illus. U.S. NEWS & WORLD REPORT, v. 48, Mar. 28, 1960: 55–60.

Education

25.107 Benítez, Jaime. Actualidad de la educación en Puerto Rico. LA TORRE (Río Piedras, P.R.), v. 14, mayo/ag. 1966: 11–32.

25.108 Epstein, Erwin H. English and Politics in Puerto Rican Schools. EDUCATIONAL FORUM (West Lafayette, Ind.), v. 33, Jan 1969: 225–230.

25.109 Facio, Rodrigo, and Carlos Monge Alfaro. Informe al Consejo Universitario sobre la visita a Puerto Rico y su universidad. REVISTA DE LA UNIVERSIDAD DE COSTA RICA (San José), mayo 1962: 91–131.

25.110 Hernández, Miguelina N. de. Necesidades y problemas de los estudiantes

adolescentes de escuela superior en Puerto Rico. REVISTA DE CIENCIAS SOCIALES, v. 4, sept. 1960: 459–482.

25.111 Illich, Ivan. Commencement at the University of Puerto Rico. NEW YORK REVIEW OF BOOKS, v. 13, Oct. 9, 1969: 12–13.

25.112 Sussman, Leila. Democratization and Class Segregation in Puerto Rican Schooling: The U.S. Model Transplanted. tables, bibl. SOCIOLOGY OF EDUCATION, v. 41, Fall 1968: 321–341.

25.113 Walker, R. In Puerto Rico, a School for Dropouts Only. AMERICAN EDUCATION, v. 4, June 1968: 15–18.

Government and Politics

25.114 Albizu Campos, Laura de. Albizu Campos y la independencia de Puerto Rico: HUMANISMO (Habana), v. 8, mar./jun. 1960: 125–208.

25.115 Anderson, Robert W. The Puerto Rican Mainstream: The Spirit of Insular Politics. SAN JUAN REVIEW, v. 1, Oct. 1964.

25.116 Anderson, Robert W. Las elecciones de 1964 en Puerto Rico: una evaluación. REVISTA DE CIENCIAS SOCIALES (Río Piedras, P.R.), v. 9, sept. 1965: 263–271.

25.117 Beard, Belle Boone. Puerto Rico—the Forty-Ninth State? ATLANTA, v. 6, 1945: 105–117.

25.118 Bothwell, Reece B. Notas al margen de los partidos políticos en Puerto Rico. REVISTA DE LA ASOCIACION DE CIENCIAS POLITICAS DE PUERTO RICO, v. 2, 1964: 41–54.

25.119 Cabranes, José A. Self-Determination: What Puerto Rico Wants. CIVIL LIBERTIES. (New York), Oct. 1972: 2.

25.120   Canavan, F. Puerto Rico's Future. AMERICA, v. 115, July 30, 1966: 111–115.

25.121   Cancio, Hiram. The Power of the Congress to Enter into a Compact with the People of Puerto Rico—the Legal Status of the Compact. REVISTA DE DERECHO, LEGISLACION Y JURISPRUDENCIA DEL COLEGIO DE ABOGADOS DE PUERTO RICO, v. 22, mayo 1962: 341–392.

25.122   Cater, Douglas. Puerto Rico: The Best Answer to Castro. REPORTER, v. 24, Jan. 19, 1961: 32.

25.123   Cousins, Norman. Sin and Political Freedom. SATURDAY REVIEW, v. 43, Dec. 3, 1960: 34.

25.124   Dunne, E.J. Is Puerto Rico next? Statehood Pros and Cons. COMMONWEAL, v. 70, July 3, 1959: 348–350.

25.125   Ferrer Canales, José. Hora de Puerto Rico. CUADERNOS AMERICANOS (México, D.F.), v. 120, en./feb. 1962: 116–143.

25.126   Fischman, J. Church in Politics: The 1960 Election in Puerto Rico. WESTERN POLITICAL QUARTERLY, v. 18, Dec. 1965: 821–839.

25.127   García Passalacqua, Juan M. The Legality of the Associated Statehood of Puerto Rico. INTER-AMERICAN LAW REVIEW, v. 4, July/Dec. 1962: 287–315.

25.128   García Passalacqua, J.M. Puerto Rico: Whither Commonwealth. ORBIS, v. 15, Fall 1971: 923–942.

25.129   Gattell, Frank Otto. Independence Rejected: Puerto Rico and the Tydings Bill of 1936. bibl. footnotes. HISPANIC AMERICAN HISTORICAL REVIEW, v. 38, Feb. 1958: 25–44; Reply with rejoinder, by T.G. Mathews, Nov. 1958: 598–601.

25.130   Géigel Polanco, Vicente. La libertad política en Puerto Rico. CUADERNOS AMERICANOS (México, D.F.), v. 132, en./feb. 1964: 56–72.

25.131   Giménez de la Rosa, R. Tearing down Barriers. NATIONAL CIVIC REVIEW, v. 49, Sept. 1960: 172–173.

25.132   Gruber, Ruth. There are Few 'Independentistas' in Puerto Rico, But—. NEW YORK TIMES MAGAZINE, May 21, 1972: 30–31.

25.133   Heifetz, Robert. Manpower Planning: A Case Study from Puerto Rico. COMPARATIVE EDUCATION REVIEW, v. 8, June 1964: 28–36.

25.134   Helfeld, David M. Congressional Intent and Attitude toward Public Law 600 and the Constitution of the Commonwealth of Puerto Rico. REVISTA JURIDICA DE LA UNIVERSIDAD DE PUERTO RICO, v. 21, 1952: 255–320.

25.135   Here's where the Church Tried to Swing an Election: With Text of Pastoral Letter. illus. U.S. NEWS & WORLD REPORT, v. 49, Nov. 7, 1960: 59–61.

25.136   Hostos, Adolfo de. La Comisión del Status de Puerto Rico. BOLETIN DE LA ACADEMIA DE ARTES Y CIENCIAS DE PUERTO RICO (Río Piedras, P.R.), v. 4, abr./jun. 1968: 397–408.

25.137   Hostos, Adolfo de. De vuelta a Puerto Rico [1898]. BOLETIN DE LA ACADEMIA DE ARTES Y CIENCIAS DE PUERTO RICO (Río Piedras), v. 3, en./mar. 1967: 131–144.

25.138   Lewis, Gordon K. Puerto Rico: Case Study of Change in an Underdeveloped Area. JOURNAL OF POLITICS (Gainesville), v. 18, Nov. 1955: 614–650.

25.139   Lewis, Gordon K. Puerto Rico y la sociedad mundial. REVISTA DE CIENCIAS SOCIALES (Río Piedras, P.R.), v. 7, mar./jun. 1963: 7–33.

25.140   Liddin, H.J. Political Triangle in Puerto Rico. COMMONWEAL, v. 89, December 20, 1968: 394–395.

25.141   Liebman, Arthur. Powerlessness and Stability: Student Politics in Puerto Rico. INTERNATIONAL JOURNAL OF COMPARATIVE SOCIOLOGY (Leiden, Holland), v. 9, Sept./Dec. 1968: 208–222.

25.142   Liggett, T.J. End of a Clerical Venture: Christian Action Party. CHRISTIAN

CENTURY, v. 78, Aug. 9, 1961: 952–954. Trujillo alto accord. THE NATION, v. 196, Jan. 5, 1963: 2–4.

25.143 Magruder, Calvert. The Commonwealth Status of Puerto Rico. UNIVERSITY OF PITTSBURGH LAW REVIEW, v. 5, Fall 1963: 1–20.

25.144 Maldonado Denis, Manuel. ¿Declinar del movimiento independista puertorriqueño? REVISTA DE CIENCIAS SOCIALES (Río Piedras, P.R.), v. 9, sept. 1965: 285–302.

25.145 Maldonado-Denis, Manuel. El desarrollo constitucional de Puerto Rico. CIENCIAS POLITICAS Y SOCIALES (México, D.F.), v. 12, jul./dic. 1966: 179–192.

25.146 Maldonado-Denis, Manuel. El Estado Libre Asociado: una ficción. ECONOMIA Y CIENCIAS SOCIALES (Caracas), v. 11, en./mar. 1969: 94–110.

25.147 Maldonado-Denis, Manuel. Puerto Ricans: Protest or Submission? AMERICAN ACADEMY OF POLITICAL AND SOCIAL SCIENCE. ANNALS, v. 382, Mar. 1969: 26–31.

25.148 Maldonado-Denis, Manuel. Puerto Rico: libertad y poder en el Caribe. CASA DE LAS AMERICAS (Habana), v. 5, jul./ag. 1965: 35–46.

25.149 Maldonado-Denis, Manuel. Puerto Rico: problemas y perspectivas del momento político actual. CUADERNOS AMERICANOS (México, D.F.), v. 123, jul./ag. 1962: 42–66.

25.150 Maldonado-Denis, Manuel. Puerto Rico y la América Latina. CUADERNOS AMERICANOS (México, D.F.), v. 22, jul./ag. 1963: 7–22.

25.151 Maldonado-Denis, Manuel. Vigencia de Martí en el Puerto Rico de hoy. CUADERNOS AMERICANOS (México, D.F.), v. 152, mayo/jun. 1967: 131–146.

25.152 Mathews, Thomas G. La próxima década en la política puertorriqueña. REVISTA DE CIENCIAS SOCIALES, (Rio Piedras, P.R.), v. 9, sept. 1965: 273–284.

25.153 McWilliams, C. Puerto Rico: Plebiscite for Identity. illus. THE NATION, v. 195, Sept. 15, 1962: 123–128; Discussion, v. 195, Sept. 29, 1962: inside cover.

25.154 Meisler, S. Governor and the Bishops. THE NATION, v. 191, Dec. 3, 1960: 432–434. Reply, R. Nader, Dec. 31, 1960: inside cover.

25.155 Meyerson, M. Puerto Rico: Our Backyard Colony. illus. RAMPARTS MAGAZINE, v. 8, June 1970: 50–51.

25.156 Moskin, J. R. Muñoz, the Practical Revolutionist. LOOK, v. 25, Jan. 17, 1961: 30–33.

25.157 Moskin, J.R. Puerto Rico: Island at a Crossroads. illus. LOOK, v. 28, Mar. 24, 1964: 26–34.

25.158 Muñoz Marín, Luis. The Future of Puerto Rico. VITAL SPEECHES, v. 11, Aug. 1, 1945: 619–620.

25.159 Muñoz Marín, Luis. A New Idea in Statehood. UNITED NATIONS WORLD, v. 5, Feb. 1959: 57.

25.160 Muñoz Marín, Luis. Puerto Rico Refutes Charges of U.S. Colonialism by Cuba and U.S.S.R.: Letter and Message with Letter of Transmittal from Ambassador Wadsworth. U.S. DEPARTMENT OF STATE BULLETIN, v. 43, Oct. 24, 1960: 656–657.

25.161 Muñoz Marín, Luis. The Sad Case of Porto Rico. AMERICAN MERCURY, Feb. 1929.

25.162 Muñoz Marín, Luis. Vision for the Americas. STATE GOVERNMENT, v. 32, Fall 1959: 215–218.

25.163 Muñoz Marín, Luis. What Next in Porto Rico? THE NATION, v. 129, Nov. 20, 1929: 608–609.

25.164 Nieves Falcón, Luis. El futuro ideológico del Partido Popular Democrático. bibl. REVISTA DE CIENCIAS SOCIALES (Río Piedras, P.R.), v. 9, sept. 1965: 237–261.

25.165 Pabón, Milton. La Integración Política en Puerto Rico. bibl. REVISTA DE CIENCIAS SOCIALES (Río Piedras, P.R.), v. 10, jun. 1966: 131–144.

25.166 Puerto Rico: Will It Be the 51st State? Interview, L.A. Ferré. U.S. NEWS & WORLD REPORT, v. 66, Mar. 17, 1969: 104–105.

25.167 Un plebiscito colonial para Puerto Rico. REVISTA DE LA UNIVERSIDAD DE MEXICO (México, D.F.), v. 2, jun. 1967: 17–19.

25.168 Push, T. Puerto Rico's New Politics. THE NATION, v. 207, Nov. 25, 1968: 549.

25.169 REVISTA DE CIENCIAS SOCIALES. (Río Piedras, P.R.), v. 9, sept. 1965.
Issue devoted to political status question.

25.170 Rippy, M. Puerto Rico: The Next State? THE NATION, v. 189, Aug. 15, 1959: 63–65.

25.171 Rodríguez Ramón, Benjamin. The Puerto Rico Land Administration Act: Audacity in Land Planning. REVISTA DEL COLEGIO DE ABOGADOS DE PUERTO RICO, v. 24, ag. 1964.

25.172 Roig de Leuchsenring, Emilio. La libertad secuestrada. HUMANISMO (Habana), v. 8, nov. 1959/feb. 1960: 9–34.

25.173 Ross, D.F. Puerto Rico's New Administration. NEW REPUBLIC, v. 159, Nov. 23, 1968: 13–15.

25.174 Shereff, R. Fighting the Blood Tax in Puerto Rico. COMMONWEAL, v. 88, Sept. 27, 1968: 647–648.

25.175 Santiago, Carmen R. de. La revisión de los distritos territoriales, senatoriales y representativos de Puerto Rico. REVISTA DE CIENCIAS SOCIALES (Río Piedras, P.R.), v. 9, sept. 1965: 303–323.

25.176 Seda Bonilla, Eduardo. La función de la cultura en los procesos políticos [incl. English summary]. bibl. ANUARIO INDIGENISTA (México, D.F.), dic. 1969: 295–316.

25.177 Souza, José Ferreira de. Porto Rico: estado livre associado. REVISTA BRASILEIRA DE POLITICA INTERNACIONAL, Instituto Brasileiro de Relacoes Internacionais (Rio de Janeiro), v. 1, dez. 1958: 5–15.

25.178 Stern, David S. Notes on the History of Puerto Rico's Commonwealth Status. REVISTA JURIDICA DE LA UNIVERSIDAD DE PUERTO RICO, v. 30, 1961.

25.179 Still Popular in Puerto Rico. THE ECONOMIST, v. 213, Nov. 21, 1964: 834.

25.180 Trillin, C. U.S. Journal: Rights of Students to Engage in Political Activities. NEW YORKER, v. 45, Feb. 14, 1970: 120–126.

25.181 Tripped up in Puerto Rico [Eisenhower's goodwill tour], THE ECONOMIST, v. 194, Mar. 26, 1968: 1216.

25.182 Tugwell, Rexford Guy. View from Puerto Rico. THE NATION, v. 192, June 10, 1951: 496–497.

25.183 Wells, Henry. Administrative Reorganizations in Puerto Rico. WESTERN POLITICAL QUARTERLY, v. 9, June 1956: 470–490.

25.184 Wells, Henry. Paying for Elections. illus. NATIONAL CIVIC REVIEW, v. 53, Nov. 1964: 540–544.

25.185 Wells, Henry. Puerto Rico's Association with the United States. bibl. CARIBBEAN STUDIES (Río Piedras, P.R.), v. 5, Apr. 1965: 6–22.

History

25.186 Acevedo, Edberto Oscar. Puerto Rico, Nueva Granada y Perú a fines del siglo XVIII, según viajeros anónimos. BOLETIN DE LA ACADEMIA CHILENA DE LA HISTORIA (Santiago), v. 3, 1. semestre 1964: 197–251.

25.187 Alvarez Nazario, Manuel. El relato de Alonso Enríquez de Guzmán, el "caballero desbaratado," sobre su visita a Puerto Rico en 1534. REVISTA DEL INSTITUTO DE CULTURA PUERTORRIQUEÑA (San Juan), v. 3, 1960: 11–14.

25.188 Arana-Soto, Salvador. Los primeros hospitales de Puerto Rico. CUADERNOS HISPANOAMERICANOS (Madrid), v. 177, sept. 1964: 391–400.

25.189 Berbusse, E.J. Aspects in Church-State Relations in Puerto Rico, 1898–1900. THE AMERICAS, v. 19, 291–304.

25.190 Blanco, Tomás. El mito del jíbaro. REVISTA DEL INSTITUTO DE CULTURA PUERTORRIQUEÑA (San Juan), v. 2, 1959: 5–10.

25.191 Borges, Analola. El descubrimiento de Borinquén según las crónicas. BOLETIN DE LA ACADEMIA DE ARTES Y CIENCIAS DE PUERTO RICO (Río Piedras, P.R.), v. 5, oct./dic. 1969: 505–515.

25.192 Cabanillas de Rodríguez, Berta. Apuntes sobre la alimentación en Puerto Rico durante el siglo XVII. REVISTA DEL INSTITUTO DE CULTURA PUERTORRIQUEÑA (San Juan), v. 3, 1960: 24–26.

25.193 Campo Lacasa, María Cristina. Las iglesias y conventos de Puerto Rico en el siglo XVIII. REVISTA DEL INSTITUTO DE CULTURA PUERTORRIQUEÑA, v. 4, oct./dic. 1961: 14–19.

25.194 Campo Lacasa, María Cristina. Las obras de la catedral de San Juan en el siglo XVIII. REVISTA DEL INSTITUTO DE CULTURA PUERTORRIQUEÑA, v. 4, jul./sept. 1961: 45–48.

25.195 Caro de Delgado, Aida R. Alcaldes ordinarios como gobernadores de Puerto Rico en el siglo XVIII. REVISTA DEL INSTITUTO DE CULTURA PUERTORRIQUEÑA, v. 3, 1960: 17–19.

25.196 Cibes Viadé, Alberto. El gobernador Pezuela y la rebelión de los comerciantes. REVISTA DEL INSTITUTO DE CULTURA PUERTORRIQUEÑA, v. 4, oct./dic. 1961: 58–63.

25.197 Clark, Truman R. President Taft and the Puerto Rican Appropriation Crisis of 1909. THE AMERICAS, v. 26, Oct. 1969: 152–170.

25.198 Dávila, Arturo. Una acción naval de Ramón Power en Cabo Rojo. HISTORIA (Río Piedras, P.R.), nueva ser., v. 2, en. 1963: 23–31.

25.199 España. Archivo General de Indias. Visita Pastoral del Obispo don Pedro Martínez de Oneca [1753, documents]. REVISTA DE HISTORIA (Caracas), v. 4, mayo 1965: 59–76.

25.200 Díaz Soler, Luis M. Una evaluación de las teorías sobre el punto de desembarco de Cristóbal Colón en Puerto Rico. REVISTA DEL INSTITUTO DE CULTURA PUERTORRIQUEÑA, v. 4, oct./dic. 1961: 18.

25.201 Gattell, F.O. Art of the Possible: Luis Muñoz Rivera and the Puerto Rican Jones Bill. THE AMERICAS, v. 17, July 1960: 1–20.

25.202 Gattell, Frank Otto, ed. Puerto Rico through New England Eyes, 1831–1834. JOURNAL OF INTER-AMERICAN STUDIES, v. 1, July 1959: 281–292.

25.203 Gaudier, Martín. El descubrimiento de Puerto Rico. illus. BOLETIN DE LA ACADEMIA DE ARTES Y CIENCIAS DE PUERTO RICO (Río Piedras, P.R.), v. 4, abr./jun. 1968: 525–554.

25.204 Gómez, Labor. Proyecto para introducir colonos asiáticos en Puerto Rico. REVISTA DEL INSTITUTO DE CULTURA PUERTORRIQUEÑA (San Juan), v. 3, 1960: 41–44.

25.205 González García, Sebastián. Notas sobre el gobierno y los gobernadores de Puerto Rico en el siglo XVII. HISTORIA (Río Piedras, P.R.) nueva ser., v. 1, jun. 1962: 1–98.

25.206 Gutiérrez del Arroyo, Isabel. Un programa de gobierno en 1511. REVISTA DEL INSTITUTO DE CULTURA PUERTORRIQUEÑA (San Juan), v. 2, 1959: 39–41.

25.207 Lloréns, Washington. El descubrimiento de Puerto Rico. BOLETIN DE

LA ACADEMIA DE ARTES Y CIENCIAS DE PUERTO RICO (Río Piedras, P.R.), v. 5, oct./dic. 1969: 493-504.

25.208 Lluch Mora, Francisco. Algunos datos concernientes al origen y desarrollo de una comunidad puertorriqueña: Yauco. REVISTA DEL INSTITUTO DE CULTURA PUERTORRIQUEÑA, v. 4, abr./jun. 1961: 26-31.

25.209 María Teresa Gertrude, Sister. History of the Seminary in Puerto Rico. HORIZONTES (Ponce, P.R.), v. 5, abr. 1962: 66-78.

25.210 Méndez, Justo A. Recordando la Gesta de 1868. BOLETIN DE LA ACADEMIA DE ARTES Y CIENCIAS DE PUERTO RICO (Río Piedras, P.R.), v. 6, en./mar. 1970: 113-130.

25.211 Morales Padrón, Francisco. Primer intento de independencia puertorriqueña, 1811-1812. CARIBBEAN STUDIES (Río Piedras, P.R.), v. 1, Jan. 1962: 11-25.

25.212 Narváez, Ricardo A. From San Juan to Guadalajara. HISPANIA, v. 46. Dec. 1963: 802-803.

25.213 Negroni, H.A. Hostos y su pensamiento militar. ASOMANTE, v. 24, 1968: 21-35.

25.214 Perea Roselló, Pedro Luis. Nuevas páginas sobre la historia de Ponce. HORIZONTES (Universidad Católica de P.R., Ponce), v. 5, abr. 1962: 79-91.

25.215 Pérez Marchand, Monelisa Lina. El Grito de Lares (1868-1968). bibl. ASOMANTE (San Juan), v. 24, oct./dic. 1968: 7-20.

25.216 Rivera de Alvarez, Josefina. Diego de Torres Vargas, cronista puertorriqueño del siglo XVII. ATENEA (Mayagüez, P.R.), nueva ser., v. 2, 1965: 9-13.

25.217 Rodríguez Cruz, Juan, and George Ulibarri, eds. Informe final sobre la revolución de Lares, Puerto Rico. CARIBBEAN STUDIES (Río Piedras, P.R.), v. 8, Jan. 1969: 71-83.

25.218 Scott, Kenneth, ed. Charles Walker's Letters from Puerto Rico, 1835-1837. CARIBBEAN STUDIES (Río Piedras, P.R.), v. 5, Apr. 1965: 37-50.

25.219 Százdi, Adam. Credit without Banking in Early Nineteenth-Century Puerto Rico. THE AMERICAS, v. 19, Oct. 1962: 149-171.

25.220 Szászdi, Adam. Los registros del siglo XVIII en la Parroquia de San Germán. HISTORIA (Río Piedras, P.R.), v. 1, en. 1962: 51-63.

25.221 Tió, Aurelio. Carta anónima al Dr. Diego Alvarez Chanca. BOLETIN DE LA ACADEMIA DE ARTES Y CIENCIAS DE PUERTO RICO (Río Piedras, P.R.), v. 4, abr./jun. 1968: 555-584.

25.222 Tió, Aurelio. El despertar de un pueblo. BOLETIN DE LA ACADEMIA DE ARTES Y CIENCIAS DE PUERTO RICO (Río Piedras, P R.), v. 1, oct./dic. 1965: 111-128.

25.223 Whittaker, W.G. Santiago Iglesias Case, 1901-1902: Origins of American Trade Union Involvement in Puerto Rico. THE AMERICAS, v. 24, April 1968: 378-393.

Language

25.224 Academia Puertorriqueña. Puertorriqueñismos y americanismos que faltan en el diccionario de la Real Academia Española. BOLETIN DE LA ACADEMIA DE ARTES Y CIENCIAS DE PUERTO RICO (Río Piedras, P.R.), v. 3, abr./jun. 1967: 429-454.

25.225 Alegría, José S. Puerto Rico y la lengua española. AMBOS MUNDOS (México), v. 2, 1963.

25.226 Alonso, Martín. ¿Y usted qué Sr. Granda? BOLETIN DE LA ACADEMIA DE ARTES Y CIENCIAS DE PUERTO

RICO (Río Piedras, P.R.), v. 5, jul./sept. 1969: 317–320.

25.227 Alvarez Nazario, Manuel. Notas sobre el habla del negro en Puerto Rico durante el siglo XX. REVISTA DEL INSTITUTO DE CULTURA PUERTORRIQUEÑA (San Juan), v. 2, en./mar. 1959: 43–48.

25.228 Alvarez Nazario, Manuel. Principales deficiencias de lengua oral, lengua escrita y lectura, observadas en los estudiantes del Curso General de Español, (Español 1-2) en el Colegio de Agricultura y Artes Mecánicas. ATENEA (Mayagüez, P.R.), v. 1, oct. 1960: 79–85.

25.229 Arce de Vázquez, Margot. El español en Puerto Rico. ASOMANTE (San Juan), v. 5, 1949: 52–62.

25.230 Arce de Vázquez, Margot. José de Diego y la lengua. ASOMANTE (San Juan), v. 3, 1966: 33–52.

25.231 Cajigas, Teresa M. de. Phonemic Modifications of Anglicisms in Puerto Rican Spanish. ATENEA (Mayagüez, P.R.), v. 1, 1960.

25.232 Coll y Toste, Cayetano. El idioma castellano en Puerto Rico. BOLETIN HISTORICO DE PUERTO RICO (San Juan), v. 8, 1921: 43–47.

25.233 Coll y Toste, Cayetano. Vocabulario de palabras introducidas en el idioma español procedentes del lenguaje indoantillano. BOLETIN HISTORICO DE PUERTO RICO (San Juan), v. 8, 1921: 294–352.

25.234 Dillard, J.L. Sobre algunos fonemas puertorriqueños. NUEVA REVISTA DE FILOLOGIA HISPANICA (México, D.F.), v. 16, jul./dic. 1962: 422–424.

25.235 Dillard, J.L. Spanglish Store Names in San Juan, Puerto Rico. NAMES, v. 12, June 1964: 98–102.

25.236 Epstein, Erwin H. La enseñanza del idioma y el status político de Puerto Rico: una nueva evaluación. bibl. REVISTA DE CIENCIAS SOCIALES (Río Piedras, P.R.), v. 11, sept. 1967: 293–314.

25.237 Epstein, Erwin H. Linguistic Orientation and Changing Values in Puerto Rico. INTERNATIONAL JOURNAL OF COMPARATIVE SOCIOLOGY (Leiden, Holland), v. 9, Mar. 1968: 61–76.

25.238 Epstein, Erwin H. National Identity and the Language Issue in Puerto Rico. COMPARATIVE EDUCATION REVIEW, v. 11, June 1967: 133–143.

25.239 Fishman, J.A. Attitudes and Beliefs about Spanish and English among Puerto Ricans. VIEWPOINTS, v. 47, Mar. 1971: 51–72.

25.240 Fishman, J.A. and others. Bilingualism in the Barrio. bibl. MODERN LANGUAGE JOURNAL, v. 53, Mar.–Apr. 1969: 151–185, 227–258.

25.241 Fishman, J.A. Sociolinguistic Census of a Bilingual Neighborhood. AMERICAN JOURNAL OF SOCIOLOGY, v. 75, Nov. 1969: 323–339.

25.242 Fishman, J.A., and E. Herasimchuk. Multiple Prediction of Phonological Variables in a Bilingual Speech Community. AMERICAN ANTHROPOLOGIST, v. 71, Aug. 1969: 648–657.

25.243 Fishman, J.A. and C. Terry. Validity of Census Data on Bilingualism in a Puerto Rican Neighborhood. bibl. AMERICAN SOCIOLOGICAL REVIEW, v. 34, Oct. 1969: 636–650.

25.244 Fonfrías, Ernesto Juan. Geografía, voz y espíritu de Puerto Rico en el idioma español. CUADERNOS HISPANO-AMERICANOS, no. 181, 1965: 110–129.

25.245 Gili Gaya, Samuel. El hombre bilingüe. REVISTA DEL INSTITUTO DE CULTURA PUERTORRIQUEÑA (San Juan), v. 2, 1959: 1–3.

25.246 García Martínez, Alfonso. Idioma y derecho en Puerto Rico. REVISTA DEL COLEGIO DE ABOGADOS DE PUERTO RICO (San Juan), v. 20, 1960: 183–211.

25.247 García Passalacqua, Juan M. My Self! They Take Away My Self! BOLETIN DE LA ACADEMIA DE ARTES Y CIENCIAS DE PUERTO RICO (Río Piedras, P.R.), v. 5, jul./sept. 1969: 337–345.

25.248 Granda, Germán de. La desfonologización de /R/ /RR/ en el dominio lingüístico hispánico. THESAURUS, v. 24, 1969: 1–11.

25.249 Granda Germán de. La velarización de la "rr" en el español de Puerto Rico. REVISTA DE FILOLOGIA ESPAÑOLA,(Madrid), v. 49, 1966: 181–227.

25.250 Lloréns, Washington. Comentarios a refranes, modismos, locuciones de Conversao en el Batey [de Ernesto J. Fonfrías]. BOLETIN DE LA ACADEMIA DE ARTES Y CIENCIAS DE PUERTO RICO (Río Piedras, P.R.), v. 3, oct./dic. 1967: 937–966.

25.251 Lloréns, Washington. Lenguaje de germanía en Puerto Rico. REVISTA DEL INSTITUTO DE CULTURA PUERTORRIQUEÑA (San Juan), v. 2, abr./jun. 1959: 10–12.

25.252 Lloréns, Washington. Transculturación en Puerto Rico. BOLETIN DE LA ACADEMIA DE ARTES Y CIENCIAS DE PUERTO RICO (Río Piedras, P.R.), v. 5, jul./sept. 1969: 321–335.

25.253 Lloréns, Washington. Uso y abuso del gerundio en Puerto Rico. BOLETIN DE LA ACADEMIA DE ARTES Y CIENCIAS DE PUERTO RICO (Río Piedras, P.R.), v. 5, oct./dic. 1969: 531–545.

25.254 Lugo, Samuel. Localismos y frases corrientes. BOLETIN DE LA ACADEMIA DE ARTES Y CIENCIAS DE PUERTO RICO (Río Piedras, P.R.), v. 3, oct./dic. 1967: 871–883.

25.255 Matluck, Joseph H. Fonemas finales en el consonantismo puertorriqueño. NUEVA REVISTA DE FILOLOGIA HISPANICA (México, D.F.), v. 15, jul./dic. 1961: 332–343.

25.256 Morales Carrión, Arturo. Un libro del Sr. Granda. BOLETIN DE LA ACADEMIA DE ARTES Y CIENCIAS DE PUERTO RICO (Río Piedras, P.R.), v. 5, jul./sept. 1969: 321–335.

25.257 Narváez, Ricardo A. Algunos comentarios sobre la pronunciación del castellano en Puerto Rico. CULTURA (Tunja, Colombia), 2. época, en./sept. 1963: 213–218.

25.258 Olguín, L. Solutions in Communications: Language Blocks that Exist between Spanish and English. ELEMENTARY ENGLISH, v. 48, Mar. 1971: 352–356.

25.259 Real Academia Española. Palabras y acepciones puertorriqueñas aceptadas (mayo–agosto 1966). BOLETIN DE LA ACADEMIA DE ARTES Y CIENCIAS DE PUERTO RICO (Río Piedras, P.R.), v. 3, abr./jun. 1967: 421–428.

25.260 Rosa-Nieves, Cesáreo. El español de Puerto Rico en Nueva York. BOLETIN DE LA ACADEMIA DE ARTES Y CIENCIAS DE PUERTO RICO (Río Piedras, P.R.), v. 5, oct./dic. 1969: 519–529.

25.261 Rosa-Nieves, Cesáreo. El sentido poético en la lengua hablada del pueblo puertorriqueño. BOLETIN DE LA ACADEMIA DE ARTES Y CIENCIAS DE PUERTO RICO (Río Piedras, P.R.), v. 3, oct./dic 1967: 763–780.

25.262 Rosa-Nieves, Cesáreo. Ventana al texto. BOLETIN DE LA ACADEMIA DE ARTES Y CIENCIAS DE PUERTO RICO (Río Piedras, P.R.), v. 5, jul./sept. 1969: 347–351.

25.263 Schorer, C.E. English Loan Words in Puerto Rico. AMERICAN SPEECH, v. 28, 1953: 22–25.

25.264 Stahl, Agustín. El lenguaje de los indios borinqueños. BOLETIN DE LA ACADEMIA DE ARTES Y CIENCIAS DE PUERTO RICO (Río Piedras, P.R.), v. 3, oct./dic. 1967: 781–794.

25.265 Tollinchi, Esteban. La falacia del bilingüismo. REVISTA DE CIENCIAS SOCIALES (Río Piedras, P.R.), v. 11, jun. 1967: 183–203.

25.266 Torres Morales, José A. El español de las Antillas: algunas notas. REVISTA DEL INSTITUTO DE CULTURA PUERTORRIQUEÑA (San Juan), v. 2, oct./dic. 1959: 1–4.

25.267 Tovar, Antonio. Ni un día sin línea; lengua y literatura en Puerto Rico, II. BOLETÍN DE LA ACADEMIA DE ARTES Y CIENCIAS DE PUERTO RICO (Río Piedras, P.R.), v. 6, en./mar. 1970: 40-46.

25.268 Vientós Gastón, Nilita. Otra vez el bilingüismo. REVISTA DEL INSTITUTO DE CULTURA PUERTORRIQUEÑA, v. 5, jul./sept. 1962: 4-10.

Literary History and Criticism

25.269 Albornoz, Aurora de. El canto logrado. LA TORRE (Río Piedras, P.R.), v. 10, en./mar. 1962: 131-138.

25.270 Agraít, Gustavo. Una posible explicación del ciclo negro en la poesía de Palés. REVISTA DEL INSTITUTO DE CULTURA PUERTORRIQUEÑA, v. 2, abr./jun. 1959: 39-41.

25.271 Arce de Vázquez, Margot. Guayama en la poesía de Luis Palés Matos. REVISTA DEL INSTITUTO DE CULTURA PUERTORRIQUEÑA, v. 2, abr./jun. 1959: 36-38.

25.272 Babín, María Teresa. Literary Letter from Puerto Rico. BOOKS ABROAD, v. 32, Summer 1958: 255-256.

25.273 Babín, María Teresa. Landmarks in Contemporary Puerto Rican Letters. bibl. footnotes. THE AMERICAS: A QUARTERLY REVIEW OF INTER-AMERICAN CULTURAL HISTORY, v. 14, Jan 1958: 247-257.

25.274 Babín, María Teresa. Veinte años de teatro puertorriqueño, 1945-1955. ASOMANTE, v. 20, oct./dic. 1964: 20.

25.275 Belaval, Emilio S. Dramaturgia y realidad. BOLETÍN DE LA ACADEMIA DE ARTES Y CIENCIAS, v. 2, abr./jun. 1966: 191-202.

25.276 Callan, R. J. Puerto Rico's Angry Poets. COMMONWEAL, v. 75, Dec. 8, 1961: 276-278.

25.277 Campaña, Pedro. Figuración de la patria (Puerto Rico) en la poesía de Amelia Ceide. HORIZONTES. Revista de la Universidad Católica de Puerto Rico (Ponce, P.R.), v. 11, oct. 1967: 40-56.

25.278 Dauster, Frank. Drama and Theatre in Puerto Rico. MODERN DRAMA, v. 6, Sept. 1963: 177-186.

25.279 Dauster, Frank. Francisco Arriví: the Mask and the Garden. HISPANIA, v. 45, Dec. 1962: 637-643.

25.280 Dauster, Frank. The Theater of René Marqués. SYMPOSIUM (Syracuse, N.Y.), v. 1, Spring 1964: 35-45.

25.281 Enguídanos, Miguel. Poesía como vida: Luis Palés Matos. PAPELES DE SON ARMADANS (Palma de Mallorca), v. 12, mar. 1959: 241-278.

25.282 Ferrer-Canales, José. Temática de Géigel Polanco. REVISTA HISPANICA MODERNA, v. 34, 1968: 626-646.

25.283 González, José Emilio. Espiritualidad religiosa y arte en "El Semblante" de Evaristo Ribera Chevremont. LA TORRE, v. 16, abr./jun. 1968: 143-196.

25.284 González, José Emilio. La poesía puertorriqueña de 1945 a 1963. ASOMANTE (San Juan), v. 20, jul./sept. 1963: 52-79.

25.285 González, José Emilio. "Viaje" de Juan Martínez Capó. ASOMANTE (San Juan), v. 18, abr./jun. 1962: 27-43.

25.286 Guereña, Jacinto Luis. Circuito con Luis Palés Matos. LA TORRE (Río Piedras, P.R.), v. 11, oct./dic. 1963: 151-159.

25.287 Henríquez Ureña, Max. Méndez Ballester y su teatro de símbolos. LA NUEVA DEMOCRACIA, v. 42, abr. 1962: 32-41.

25.288 Homenaje a Luis Palés Matos. bibl. LA TORRE, v. 15, jul./sept. 1959; v. 8, en./jun. 1960: 13–336.

25.289 Laguerre, Enrique. Resumen histórico del relato en Puerto Rico. REVISTA DEL INSTITUTO DE CULTURA PUERTORRIQUEÑA, v. 1, oct./dic. 1958: 12–14.

25.290 Marqués, René. Pesimismo literario y optimismo político: su coexistencia en el Puerto Rico actual. CUADERNOS AMERICANOS (México, D.F.), v. 104, mayo/jun. 1959: 43–74.

25.291 Medwick, Lucille. Puerto Rican Poets. NEW YORK QUARTERLY, Summer 1970: 74–82.

25.292 Meléndez, Concha. Tristeza final en los poemas de amor de José de Diego. REVISTA DEL INSTITUTO DE CULTURA PUERTORRIQUEÑA, v. 2, en./mar. 1959: 19–21. Also v. 2, oct./dic. 1958: 3–7, "Poemas de amor de José de Diego."

25.293 Meléndez, Concha. Viaje primero de Juan Martínez Capó. LA TORRE (Río Piedras, P.R.), v. 10, abr./jun. 1962: 39–53.

25.294 Onís, Federico de. Autores cubanos y del Caribe: Luis Palés Matos. illus., ports. ISLAS (Santa Clara, Cuba), v. 1, mayo/ag. 1959: 393–664.

25.295 Pilditch, Charles. La escena puertorriqueña: los soles truncos. ASOMANTE, v. 17, abr./jun. 1961: 51–58.

25.296 Roggiano, Alfredo A. Los comienzos de la poesía en la América hispánica. HUMANITAS (México, D.F.), v. 5, 1964: 279–296.

25.297 Shaw, D.L. René Marqués' La muerte no entrará en palacio: An Analysis. LATIN AMERICAN THEATRE REVIEW, v. 2, 1968: 31–38.

25.298 Valdés-Cruz, R.E. Tres poemas representativos de la poesía afro-antillana. HISPANIA, v. 54, mar. 1971: 39–45.

25.299 Ward, J.H. 3d. Tentative Inventory of Young Puerto Rican Writers. HISPANIA, v. 54, dec. 1971: 924–930.

25.300 Wentersdorf, K.P. Spanish Analogue of the Peartree Episode in the Merchant's Tale. MODERN PHILOLOGY, v. 64, May 1967: 320–321.

25.301 Zapata Acosta, Ramón. La poesía de Francisco Lluch Mora. REVISTA HISPANICA MODERNA, v. 34, jul./oct. 1968: 810–815.

25.302 Zayas Micheli, Luis Osvaldo. Amelia Ceide en la poesía puertorriqueña. HORIZONTES. Revista de la Universidad Católica de Puerto Rico (Ponce, P.R.), v. 11, oct. 1967: 57–64.

Migration and Puerto Ricans in the U.S.

25.303 Acosta, M. Materials Developed by the Bilingual Project. NEW YORK SOCIETY FOR THE EXPERIMENTAL STUDY OF EDUCATION. YEARBOOK, 1967: 30–32.

25.304 Action Committee: Meeting of the Lower East Side Puerto Rican Action Committee. NEW YORKER, v. 44, Aug. 10, 1968: 20–23.

25.305 Adams, Velma A. Hostos Community College Mixes Dreams and Reality. illus. COLLEGE MANAGEMENT, v. 7, Mar. 1972: 15–22.

25.306 Anastasi, Anne, and Fernando A. Córdova. Some Effects of Bilingualism upon the Intelligence Test Performance of Puerto Rican Children in New York City. JOURNAL OF EDUCATIONAL PSYCHOLOGY, v. 44, 1953: 1–9.

25.307 Berger, L. University Programs for Urban Black and Puerto Rican Youth; SEEK Program. EDUCATIONAL RECORD, v. 49, Fall 1968: 382–388.

25.308 Berkowitz, E. Family Attitudes and Practices in Puerto Rican and Non-

Puerto Rican Pupils. HIGH POINTS, v. 43, Mar. 1961: 25–35.

25.309 Bocowik, F. Young Lords Take to the Streets. ATLAS, v. 19, Oct. 1970: 25–26.

25.310 Bosworth, Patricia. Look, Let's Have Justice around Here! NEW YORK TIMES, Sept. 12, 1971: D 5.

25.311 Bowman, Leroy. The Puerto Rican in America. HUMANIST, v. 22, Jan./Feb. 1962: 27–29.

25.312 Brooks, Tom. The Puerto Rican Story. INDUSTRIAL BULLETIN (New York), v. 39, June 1960: 6–12.

25.313 Brown, R. Mainlanders. ANTIOCH REVIEW, v. 31, Fall 1971: 325–332.

25.314 Budner, S., and others. Minority Retardate: a Paradox and a Problem in Definition. SOCIAL SCIENCE REVIEW, v. 43, June 1969: 174–183.

25.315 Burnharm, D., and S. Burnharm. El Barrio's Worst Block is Not All Bad. illus. NEW YORK TIMES MAGAZINE, Jan. 5, 1969: 24–25.

25.316 Carleton, R.O. New Aspects of Puerto Rican Migration. MONTHLY LABOR REVIEW, v. 83, Feb. 1960: 133–135.

25.317 Carrow, R.A. Comparative Study of the Family Relationships of Immigrant Chinese and Puerto Rican Children. GRADUATE RESEARCH IN EDUCATION AND RELATED DISCIPLINES, v. 4, Spring 1969: 85–87.

25.318 Casanova, Clara. Puerto Ricans. illus. INSTRUCTOR, v. 81, Jan. 1927: 43–46.

25.319 Cordasco, F.M. Puerto Rican Pupils and American Education. SCHOOL AND SOCIETY, v. 95, Feb. 18, 1967: 116–119.

25.320 Cordasco, Frank. Spanish Harlem: The Anatomy of Poverty. PHYLON, v. 26, Summer 1965: 195–196.

25.321 Cordasco, Francesco, and David Alloway. Spanish-Speaking People in the United States: Some Research Constructs and Postulates. INTERNATIONAL MIGRATION REVIEW, v. 4, Spring 1970: 76–79.

25.322 Cordasco, Francesco. Studies on the Disenfranchised: The Puerto Rican Child. PSYCHIATRIC SPECTATOR, v. 3, Nov. 1966: 3–4.

25.323 Castan, S. Victims of Welfare. illus. LOOK, v. 27, Mar. 26, 1963: 68–71.

25.324 Diaz, Eileen. A Puerto Rican in New York. DISSENT, v. 8, Summer 1961: 383–385.

25.325 Doob, C.B. Family Background and Peer-Group Development in a Puerto Rican District. bibl. SOCIOLOGICAL QUARTERLY, v. 11, Fall 1970: 523–532.

25.326 Elam, Sophia E. Acculturation and Learning Problems of Puerto Rican Children. TEACHERS COLLEGE RECORD, v. 61, Feb. 1960: 258–264.

25.327 Elam, Sophia E. Poverty and Acculturation in a Migrant Puerto Rican Family. bibl. THE RECORD, v. 70, Apr. 1969: 617–626.

25.328 Fitzpatrick, J.P. Intermarriage of Puerto Ricans in New York City. AMERICAN JOURNAL OF SOCIOLOGY, v. 71, Jan. 1966: 395–406.

25.329 Fleisher, B.M. Some Economic Aspects of Puerto Rican Migration to the United States. graphs, tables. THE REVIEW OF ECONOMICS AND STATISTICS (Harvard University) v. 45, Aug. 1963: 245–253.

25.330 Geismar, L.L., and U.C. Gerhart. Social Class, Ethnicity, and Family Functioning: Exploring Some Issues Raised by the Moynihan Report. JOURNAL OF MARRIAGE AND THE FAMILY, v. 30, Aug. 1968: 480–487.

25.331 Glazer, N. Puerto Ricans. COMMENTARY, v. 36, July 1963: 1–9. Reply, W.P. Gillotti, v. 37, Jan. 1964: 6.

25.332 Goldberg, Gertrude S. Puerto Rican Migrants on the Mainland of the United States. INFORMATION RETRIEVAL CENTER ON THE DISADVANTAGED (IRCD) BULLETIN, v. 4, Jan. 1968: 12 p.

25.333 Hamalian, L. and J.V. Hatch. City College Rebellion Revisited. illus.

CHANGING EDUCATION, v. 4, Winter: 1969: 15-21.

25.334 Hamilton, A. Here Come the Tutors: College Students Operate Their Own Education Corps. PTA MAGAZINE, v. 60, Dec. 1965: 7-9.

25.335 Hertzig, M.E., and H.G. Birch. Longitudinal Course of Measured Intelligence in Preschool Children of Different Social and Ethnic Backgrounds. bibl. AMERICAN JOURNAL OF ORTHOPSYCHIATRY, v. 41, April 1971: 51-72.

25.336 King, John. From Caguas to New York. SAN JUAN REVIEW, v. 2, June, 1965: 62-64.

25.337 Kuschman, W. Culturally Displaced and Project C.I.T.I.E.S. (Community Internship Training in an Educational Setting.) illus., EDUCATIONAL LEADERSHIP, v. 29, Oct. 1971: 71-73.

25.338 Hammer, Richard. Report from a Spanish Harlem "Fortress." NEW YORK TIMES MAGAZINE, Jan. 5, 1964: 22.

25.339 Hoffman, G., and J.A. Fishman. Life in the Neighborhood. INTERNATIONAL JOURNAL OF COMPARATIVE SOCIOLOGY (Leiden, Neth.), v. 12, June 1971: 85-100.

25.340 Lelyveld, J. Se habla español? illus. NEW YORK TIMES MAGAZINE, June 14, 1964: 65-66.

25.341 Lewis, C. Some Puerto Rican Viewpoints. CHILDHOOD EDUCATION, v. 43, Oct. 1966; 82-84.

25.342 Lewis, Oscar. In New York You Get Swallowed by a Horse. COMMENTARY, v. 38, Nov. 1964: 69-73.

25.343 Maldonado, Alex W. The Puerto Rican Tide Begins to Turn: Migrants Returning to Their Island Now Match the Numbers Moving to the Island of Manhattan. illus. NEW YORK TIMES MAGAZINE, Sept. 20, 1964: 84-85.

25.344 Maldonado, Alex W. Puerto Rico: The Migration Reverses. illus. NATION, v. 198, Mar. 16, 1964: 255-257.

25.345 Mattleman, M.S., and R.L. Emans. Language of the Inner City Child: a Comparison of Puerto Rican and Negro Third Grade Girls. bibl. THE JOURNAL OF NEGRO EDUCATION, v. 38, Spring 1969: 173-176.

25.346 Miller, B.S. Diffusing Tensions with Film: A Way away from Radical Polarizations; Hunter College High School. NATIONAL ASSOCIATION OF SECONDARY SCHOOL PRINCIPALS. BULLETIN, v. 54, Apr. 1970: 67-76.

25.347 Monserrat, Joseph. The Education of Puerto Rican Children in New York City. JOURNAL OF EDUCATIONAL PSYCHOLOGY, v. 28, Dec. 1944: 146-192.

25.348 Monserrat, Joseph. Literacy Tests: Puerto Rican Perspective. NEW YORK HERALD TRIBUNE MAGAZINE, Oct. 13, 1963: 9-10.

25.349 Morgan, T.B. Real West Side Story; Life of José Rivera. illus. LOOK, v. 24, Feb. 16, 1960: 22-27.

25.350 Mozer, R.J. Victims of Exploitation: New York's Puerto Ricans. CATHOLIC WORLD, v. 189, Sept. 1959: 441-446.

25.351 Murra, J.V. Up to the Slums. NATION, v. 188, May 2, 1959: 411-412.

25.352 Myers, George C. Migration and Modernization: The Case of Puerto Rico, 1950-1960. tables. SOCIAL AND ECONOMIC STUDIES (Mona, Jamaica), v. 16, Dec. 1967: 425-431.

25.353 Newfield, J. Harlem sí, Tammany no. COMMONWEAL, v. 75, Sept. 29, 1961: 10-12.

25.354 900,000 Puerto Ricans in the U.S. illus. U.S. NEWS AND WORLD REPORT, v. 47, Dec. 1959: 91-95.

25.355 No Hablo Inglés: Police Blamed for Puerto Rican Riots. NEW REPUBLIC, v. 154, June 25, 1966: 7.

25.356 O'Brien, Robert W. Hawaii's Puerto Ricans: Stereotype and Reality. SOCIAL PROCESS IN HAWAII, v. 23, 1959: 61-64.

25.357 O'Hara, M. We Heighten the Child's Self-Image through the School: a Selected Bibliography. HIGH POINTS, v. 48, June 1966: 71–79.

25.358 Ortiz, R. Culture and the People: Museo del Bario (sic). ART IN AMERICA, v. 59, May 1971: 27.

25.359 Out of the Melting Pot. THE ECONOMIST, v. 211, Apr. 18, 1964: 273.

25.360 Pagán de Colón, P. The Status of the Migrant: Address, Feb. 12, 1962. VITAL SPEECHES, v. 28, May 1, 1962: 445–448.

25.361 Palomares, V.H., and F. Negron, eds. Aspira Today, Accountability Tomorrow: Interview. THE PERSONNEL AND GUIDANCE JOURNAL, v. 50, Oct. 1971: 109–116.

25.362 Parket, E.C. Spanish-Speaking Churches. CHRISTIAN CENTURY, v. 78, Apr. 12, 1961: 466–468. Reply, A Cotto-Thurner, v. 78, June 28, 1961: 801.

25.363 Patterns Hamper Children: Cultural Differences and Consequences for Education. SCIENCE NEWS, v. 93, June 8, 1968: 555.

25.364 Puerto Rican Pupils. SENIOR SCHOLASTIC, v. 74, May 1959: 4T–5T.

25.365 Puerto Ricans Not Guilty. THE ECONOMIST (London), v. 193, Oct. 3, 1959: 44.

25.366 Puerto Ricans in New York City: Background Information for Teachers. CURRICULUM AND MATERIALS, v. 18, Spring 1964: 6–7.

25.367 Puerto Rico vs. New York. TRANSACTION, v. 5, Apr. 1968: 8.

25.368 From Puerto Rico to Pennsylvania: Culture Shock in the Classroom. PENNSYLVANIA EDUCATION, v. 2, May/June 1971: 22–29.

25.369 Puerto Rican Youth Speaks Out: Some Quotations. illus. THE PERSONNEL AND GUIDANCE JOURNAL, v. 50, Oct. 1971: 90–95.

25.370 Riots in a New Quarter [Chicago]. THE ECONOMIST (London), v. 219, June 1966: 1414.

25.371 Rodgers, Ron, with Diego Rangel. Learning for Two Worlds. AMERICAN EDUCATION, Nov. 1972: 28–31.

25.372 Rogler, Lloyd H. Growth of an Action Group: The Case of a Puerto Rican Migrant Voluntary Association. INTERNATIONAL JOURNAL OF COMPARATIVE SOCIOLOGY (Leiden, Netherlands), v. 9, Sept./Dec. 1968: 223–234.

25.373 Rosen, C.L., and P.D. Ortego, comps. Resources: Teaching Spanish-Speaking Children. THE READING TEACHER, v. 25, Oct. 1971: 11–13.

25.374 Samuels, G. I Don't Think the Cop is My Friend. illus. NEW YORK TIMES MAGAZINE, Mar. 29, 1964: 28.

25.375 Samuels, G. Walk along the Worst Block: East 100th Street. illus., NEW YORK TIMES MAGAZINE, Sept. 30, 1962: 18–19.

25.376 Sansis, Eva E. Characteristics of Puerto Rican Migrants to, and from, the United States. INTERNATIONAL MIGRATION REVIEW, v. 4, 1970: 22–43.

25.377 Schmitzler, W.F. Puerto Rican Workers get Labor's Help to the Better Life. AMERICAN FEDERATIONIST, v. 67, Fall 1960: 6–7.

25.378 Seda Bonilla, Edwin. Cultural Pluralism and the Education of Puerto Rican Youths. illus. PHI DELTA KAPPAN, v. 53, Jan. 1972: 294–296.

25.379 Seda Bonilla, Edwin. Patrones de acomodo del emigrante puertorriqueño a la estructura social norteamericana. REVISTA DE CIENCIAS SOCIALES, v. 2, jun. 1958: 189–200.

25.380 Seda Bonilla, Edwin. Social Structure and Race Relations. SOCIAL FORCES, v. 40, Dec. 1961: 141–148.

25.381 Senior, C. Puerto Ricans on the Mainland. illus. AMERICAS, v. 13, Aug. 1961: 36–43.

25.382 Silent Minority Starts to Speak Out. illus. U.S. NEWS AND WORLD REPORT, v. 69, July 30, 1970: 66–69.

25.383 Slaiman, Donald. Discrimination and Low Incomes [in New York State]. illus. AMERICAN FEDERATIONIST, v. 68, Jan. 1961: 17–19.

25.384 Sparks, Richard K. Coping with Culture Shock. INSTRUCTOR, v. 81, Dec. 1971: 71–72.

25.385 Stuart, Irving R. Intergroup Relations and Acceptance of Puerto Ricans and Negroes in an Immigrants' Industry. JOURNAL OF SOCIAL PSYCHOLOGY, v. 56, 1962: 89–96.

25.386 Stuart, Irving R. Minorities vs. Minorities: Cognitive, Affective, and Conative Components of Puerto Rican and Negro Acceptance and Rejection. JOURNAL OF SOCIAL PSYCHOLOGY, v. 59, Feb. 1963: 93–99.

25.387 Suchman, Edward A. Sociomedical Variations among Ethnic Groups. AMERICAN JOURNAL OF SOCIOLOGY, v. 70, Nov. 1964: 319–331.

25.388 Sumner, T. We Stand Tall: Intermediate School 52, Bronx, N.Y. illus. SENIOR SCHOLASTIC, SCHOLASTIC TEACHER, v. 93, Nov. 15, 1968: 16–17.

25.389 Taeuber, Irene B. Migration and Transformation: Spanish Surname Population and Puerto Ricans. POPULATION INDEX, Jan. 1966: 3–34.

25.390 Talerico, Marguerite, and Fred Brown. Intelligence Test Patterns of Puerto Rican Children Seen in Child Psychiatry. JOURNAL OF SOCIAL PSYCHOLOGY, v. 61, Oct. 1963: 57–66.

25.391 Thomas, A. and others. Examiner Effect in I.Q. Testing of Puerto Rican Working-Class Children. bibl. AMERICAN JOURNAL OF ORTHOPSYCHIATRY, v. 41, Oct. 1971: 809–821.

25.392 Thomas, P. Nightmare Night in "Mi Barrio." illus. NEW YORK TIMES MAGAZINE, Aug. 13, 1967: 16–17.

25.393 Trejo, A.D. Bicultural Americans with a Hispanic Tradition. illus. port. WILSON LIBRARY BULLETIN, v. 44, Mar. 1970: 757–760.

25.394 Valdéz, D.T. U.S. Hispano. SOCIAL EDUCATION, v. 33, Apr. 1969: 440–442.

25.395 Vasquez, H.I. Puerto Rican Americans. illus., bibl. NATIONAL ELEMENTARY PRINCIPAL, v. 50, Nov. 1970: 65–71.

25.396 Wakefield, Dan. Other Puerto Ricans. illus. NEW YORK TIMES MAGAZINE, Oct. 11, 1959: 24–25.

25.397 Wakefield, Dan. 200,000 New Yorkers Can't Vote. NATION, v. 188, Feb. 28, 1959: 183–185.

25.398 Walsh, J.F., and R. D'Angelo. I.Q.'s of Puerto Rican Head Start Children in the Vane Kindergarten Test. JOURNAL OF SCHOOL PSYCHOLOGY, v. 9 (2), 1971: 173–176.

25.399 Whitam, F.L. New York's Spanish Protestants. CHRISTIAN CENTURY, v. 79, Feb. 7, 1962: 62–64. Reply, J.E. Mercado, Mar. 28, 1962: 388.

25.400 Wilkerson, D.A. Programs and Practices in Compensatory Education for Disadvantaged Children. REVIEW OF EDUCATIONAL RESEARCH, v. 35, Dec. 1965: 426–440.

Population

25.401 Back, K.W. Model of Family Planning Experiments: The Lessons of the Puerto Rican and Jamaican Studies. MARRIAGE AND FAMILY LIVING, v. 25, Feb. 1963: 14–19.

25.402 Back, K.W., and others. Population Control in Puerto Rico: The Formal and Informal Framework. LAW AND CONTEMPORARY PROBLEMS, v. 25, Summer 1960: 558–576.

25.403 Cofresí, Emilio. El control de la natalidad en Puerto Rico. REVISTA DE CIENCIAS SOCIALES (Río Piedras, P.R.), v. 13, jul./sept. 1969: 379–385.

25.404 Cowgill, Ursula M. Recent Variations in the Season of Birth in Puerto Rico. PROCEEDINGS OF THE NATIONAL ACADEMY OF SCIENCES, v. 52, 1964: 149–151.

25.405 Godley, Frank H. La fecundidad y el nivel educacional: Puerto Rico, 1962. Includes English summary. ESTADISTICA, JOURNAL OF THE INTER-AMERICAN STATISTICAL INSTITUTE (Washington), v. 26, jun. 1968: 256–284.

25.406 Myers, George C., and Earl W. Morris. Migration and Fertility in Puerto Rico. tables. POPULATION STUDIES (London), v. 20, July 1966: 85–96.

25.407 Spencer, S.M. New Case History Facts on Birth-Control Pills. illus. SATUR-DAY EVENING POST, v. 235, June 30, 1962: 13–19.

25.408 Thimmesch, N. Puerto Rico and Birth Control. JOURNAL OF MARRIAGE AND THE FAMILY, v. 30, May 1968: 252–262.

25.409 Vázquez, José L. Fertility Decline in Puerto Rico: Extent and Causes. DEMOGRAPHY (Chicago), v. 5, 1968.

25.410 Vázquez, José L. Tendencias y patrones de la fecundidad en Puerto Rico. REVISTA DE CIENCIAS SOCIALES (Río Piedras, P.R.), v. 10, sept. 1966: 257–276.

25.411 Vázquez Calzada, José L. El crecimiento poblacional de Puerto Rico, 1493 al presente. bibl. REVISTA DE CIENCIAS SOCIALES (Río Piedras, P.R.), v. 12, mar. 1968: 5–22.

Religion and Philosophy

25.412 Clear, V. Breakthrough in Puerto Rico. CHRISTIAN CENTURY, v. 80, Oct. 2, 1963: 1216–1218.

25.413 Cook, Scott. The Prophets: A Revivalistic Folk Religious Movement in Puerto Rico. CARIBBEAN STUDIES (Río Piedras, P.R.), v. 4, Jan. 1965: 20–35.

25.414 Koss, Joan D. Terapéutica del sistema de una secta en Puerto Rico. bibl. REVISTA DE CIENCIAS SOCIALES (Río Piedras, P.R.), v. 14, abr./jun. 1970: 259–278.

25.415 Weigert, A. Machismo and the Priestly Vocation. illus. CATHOLIC WORLD, v. 199, June 1964: 152–158.

Science and Technology

25.416 Ashby, N. Our Smallest National Forest. illus. AMERICAN FORESTS, v. 69, Sept. 1963: 30–31.

25.417 Blanton, James H., and others. A Dietary Study of Men Residing in Urban and Rural Areas of Puerto Rico. AMERICAN JOURNAL OF CLINICAL NUTRITION, v. 18, 1966: 169–175.

25.418 Cambre Mariño, Jesús. Un problema actual en Puerto Rico: la creciente contaminación ambiental. RE-VISTA DE CIENCIAS SOCIALES (Río Piedras, P.R.), v. 13, abr./jun. 1969: 197–205.

25.419 Castellanos, Isidro. Los viajes del sabio naturalista alemán don Juan Gundlach a Puerto Rico [en 1873 y 1875]. ATENEA (Mayagüez, P.R.), nueva ser., v. 2, 1965: 45–60.

25.420 Distenfield, Ariel. Persisting Fetal Hemoglobin in a Puerto Rican Family.

NEW YORK STATE JOURNAL OF MEDICINE, v. 66, 1966: 981–984.

25.421 Fernández, Nelson A., et. al. Nutritional Status of People in Isolated Areas of Puerto Rico: Survey of Barrio Manilla, Vega Alta, Puerto Rico. AMERICAN JOURNAL OF CLINICAL NUTRITION, v. 17, 1965: 305–316.

25.422 Gordon, W.E. Arecibo Ionospheric Observatory. bibl., illus. SCIENCE, v. 146, Oct. 2, 1965: 26–30. Space Explorers Build Their Dream Telescope; Radio-Radar Telescope of Arecibo. illus. FORTUNE, v. 70, Aug. 1964: 127–129. Giant Radio Probe is Sizing Up Venus; Arecibo Ionospheric. illus. BUSINESS WEEK, Mar. 14, 1964: 48.

25.423 Rife, David C. Finger and Palmar Dermatoglyphics in Puerto Ricans. tables,

bibl. THE ANTHROPOLOGIST (Delhi, India), special vol. 1968: 133–143.

25.424 Siegel, M., and others. Racial Differences in Serum Gamma Globulin Levels: Comparative Data for Negroes, Puerto Ricans, and Other Caucasians. JOURNAL OF LABORATORY AND CLINICAL MEDICINE, v. 66, 1965: 715–720.

25.425 Van Peenen, H.J., and others. The Diego Factor in a Puerto Rican Family: A Case of Anti-Diego. BLOOD: THE JOURNAL OF HEMATOLOGY, v. 17, Apr. 1961: 457–461.

25.426 Weaver, John. The Nature of the "Nipe Clay" on Las Mesas, Western Puerto Rico. illus., plates, tables. ZEITSCHRIFT FUR WIRTSCHAFTS-GEOGRAPHIE (Hagen, Germany), neue Folge, v. 6, Aug. 1962: 218–232.

Sociology

25.427 Alvarez Nazario, Manuel. Procedencias africanas de los bozales traídos a Puerto Rico por la trata negrera. LA TORRE, v. 8, jul./sept. 1960: 107–135.

25.428 Back, K.W. Change-Prone Person in Puerto Rico. illus. PUBLIC OPINION QUARTERLY, v. 22, Fall 1958: 330–340.

25.429 Ball, John C., and Delia O. Pabón. Locating and Interviewing Narcotic Addicts in Puerto Rico. tables. SOCIOLOGY AND SOCIAL RESEARCH, v. 49, July 1965: 401–411.

25.430 Belcher, John C., and Pablo B. Vázquez Calcerrada. Factores que influyen en los niveles de vida en Puerto Rico. CARIBBEAN STUDIES (Río Piedras, P.R.), v. 9, Oct. 1969: 95–103.

25.431 Bodarsky, C.J. Chaperonage and the Puerto Rican Middle Class. JOURNAL OF MARRIAGE AND THE FAMILY, v. 26, Aug. 1964: 347–348.

25.432 Bryce-Laporte, Roy Simon. Family Adaptation of Relocated Slum Dwellers in Puerto Rico: Implications for Urban

Research and Development. JOURNAL OF DEVELOPING AREAS, Western Illinois University, v. 2, July 1968: 533–539.

25.433 Buitrago, Carlos. La investigación social y el problema de los investigadores puertorriqueños en las ciencias sociales y disciplinas relacionadas en Puerto Rico. bibl. REVISTA DE CIENCIAS SOCIALES (Río Piedras, P.R.), v. 10, mar. 1966: 93–103.

25.434 Buitrago Ortiz, Carlos. Los sectores medios en la sociedad puertorriqueña. bibl. REVISTA DE CIENCIAS SOCIALES (Río Piedras, P.R.), v. 12, dic. 1968: 541–567.

25.435 Caplow, Theodore, and Samuel Wallace. Ecología social de la zona de San Juan. REVISTA DE CIENCIAS SOCIALES, v. 5, sept. 1961: 327–338.

25.436 Cunningham, Ineke. Un inventario de investigaciones relacionadas con cambio social y política oficial en Puerto Rico. bibl. AMERICA INDIGENA (Mexico, D.F.), v. 30, en. 1970: 222–254.

25.437 Díaz de Concepción, Abigail. La carreta (comentarios de un psícologo social). bibl. REVISTA DE CIENCIAS SOCIALES (Río Piedras, P.R.), v. 9, mar. 1965: 77–81.

25.438 Fernández Marina, Ramón, and Ursula M. von Eckardt. Cultural Stresses and Schizophrenogenesis in the Mothering one in Puerto Rico. NEW YORK ACADEMY OF SCIENCES. ANNALS, v. 84, 1960: 864–877.

25.439 Gattell, F.O., ed. Puerto Rico in the 1830s: The Journal of Edward Bliss Emerson [excerpts]. THE AMERICAS, v. 16, July 1959: 63–75.

25.440 Hernández, Carlos. Algunas características del adolescente boricua. REVISTA DE CIENCIAS SOCIALES (Río Piedras, P.R.), v. 3, jun. 1959: 201–228.

25.441 Hollingshead, A.B., and L.H. Rogler. Lower Socio-economic Status and Mental Illness. bibl. illus. SOCIOLOGY AND SOCIAL RESEARCH, v. 46, July 1962: 387–396.

25.442 Jayawardena, Chandra. Ideology and Conflict in Lower Class Communities. bibl. COMPARATIVE STUDIES IN SOCIETY AND HISTORY, v. 10, July 1968: 413–446.

25.443 LaRuffa, Anthony L. Culture Change and Pentecostalism in Puerto Rico. SOCIAL AND ECONOMIC STUDIES (Mona, Jamaica), v. 18, Sept. 1969: 273–281.

25.444 Lauria, Anthony, Jr. "Respeto," "relajo," and Interpersonal Relations in Puerto Rico. ANTHROPOLOGICAL QUARTERLY, v. 37, 1964.

25.445 Lewis, Oscar. Children of Sánchez, Pedro Martínez, and La Vida [with discussion]. bibl. CURRENT ANTHROPOLOGY, v. 8, Dec. 1967: 480–500. Replies M.K. Opler, V. St. Erlich, v. 9, Dec. 1968: 451–452.

25.446 Lewis, Oscar. La muerte de Dolores. CASA DE LAS AMERICAS (Habana), v. 10, nov./dic. 1969: 60–70.

25.447 Liebman, A. Student Left in Puerto Rico. JOURNAL OF SOCIAL ISSUES, v. 27, no. 1, 1971: 167–181.

25.448 Lubshansky, Isaac, Gladys Egri, and Janet Stokes. Puerto Rican Spiritualists View Mental Illness: The Faith Healer as a Para-professional. tables. AMERICAN JOURNAL OF PSYCHIATRY, v. 27, Sept. 1970: 312–321.

25.449 Lugo Lugo, Herminio. Tradición, religión y ciencia. BOLETIN DE LA ACADEMIA DE ARTES Y CIENCIAS DE PUERTO RICO (Río Piedras, P.R.), v. 1, oct./dic. 1965: 55–66.

25.450 Mahney, S. To Puerto Rico with Love. NEW REPUBLIC, v. 143, July 25, 1960: 26–27.

25.451 Maldonado-Denis, Manuel. Hacia un esbozo de las oligarquías en el Caribe hispano-parlante. CARIBBEAN STUDIES (Río Piedras, P.R.), v. 7, Jan. 1968: 3–10. Same article published with bibliography in REVISTA MEXICANA DE SOCIOLOGIA (Mexico, D.F.), v. 30, en./mar. 1968: 79–86.

25.452 Maldonado-Denis, Manuel. Los problemas de la sociedad puertorriqueña y sus efectos en el estudiante universitario. ASOMANTE (San Juan), v. 25, en./mar. 1969: 43–54.

25.453 Mintz, Sidney W. The Caribbean as a socio-cultural area. CAHIERS D'HISTOIRE MONDIALE (Neuchatel, Switzerland), v. 9, 1966: 912–937.

25.454 Mintz, Sidney W. The Caribbean Islands and Latin America. VENTURES, Yale University Graduate School, v. 7, Fall 1967: 49–54.

25.455 Miranda de Jesús, Fredeswinda, and Ana A. Córdova. Características psico-sociales del estudiante de primer año de la Universidad de Puerto Rico, Río Piedras, 1960–61. REVISTA MEXICANA DE PSICOLOGIA (Guadalajara, Mexico), v. 1, nov. 1964: 368–380.

25.456 Montero Seplowin, Virginia. La aplicación de la escala de predicción Glueck a 50 menores en la cultura puertorriqueña. bibl. REVISTA DE

CIENCIAS SOCIALES (Río Piedras, P.R.), v. 10, mar. 1966: 105–116.

25.457 Mussen, Paul, and Luz Beytagh. La industrialización, la crianza del niño y la personalidad infantil. tables, bibl. REVISTA DE CIENCIAS SOCIALES (Río Piedras, P.R.), v. 12, jun. 1968: 195–219.

25.458 Myers, George C. Elusive Male: Some Methodological Notes on Survey Research Design. PUBLIC OPINION QUARTERLY, v. 33, Summer 1969: 255–259.

25.459 Oraku, I.O. Family Life-cycle and Residential Mobility in Puerto Rico. SOCIOLOGY AND SOCIAL RESEARCH, v. 55, Apr. 1971: 324–340.

25.460 Pabón, Milton. La intolerancia social hacia los grupos políticos minoritarios en Puerto Rico. bibl. REVISTA DE CIENCIAS SOCIALES (Río Piedras, P.R.), v. 14, abr./jun. 1970: 173–202.

25.461 Pérez de Jesús, Manuel. Desarrollo económico, crecimiento poblacional y bienestar social en Puerto Rico. bibl. REVISTA DE CIENCIAS SOCIALES (Río Piedras, P.R.), v. 12, mar. 1968: 23–51.

25.462 Picó, Rafael. El desarrollo de la comunidad: la experiencia en Puerto Rico. illus., map. BOLETIN DE LA ACADEMIA DE ARTES Y CIENCIAS DE PUERTO RICO (San Juan), v. 3, abr./jun. 1967: 383–420.

25.463 Preeble, Edward. Social and Cultural Factors Related to Narcotic Use among Puerto Ricans in New York City. THE INTERNATIONAL JOURNAL OF THE ADDICTIONS (New York), v. 1, Jan. 1966: 30–41.

25.464 Press, Irwin. The incidence of Compadrazgo among Puerto Ricans in Chicago. SOCIAL AND ECONOMIC STUDIES (Mona, Jamaica), v. 12, Dec. 1963: 475–480.

25.465 Prying into Poverty. TIMES LITERARY SUPPLEMENT (London), no. 3421, Sept. 21, 1967: 829–831.

25.466 Ramírez, Rafael L. Un nuevo enfoque para el análisis del cambio cultural en Puerto Rico. REVISTA DE CIENCIAS SOCIALES (Río Piedras, P.R.), v. 8, dic. 1964: 339–355.

25.467 Robinson, D. ed. How Latin America Can Save Itself from Castroism, by L. Muñoz Marín. READER'S DIGEST, v. 80, May 1962: 231–232.

25.468 Roca, Angelina Saavedra de. Algunos valores prevalecientes en la sociedad puertorriqueña. REVISTA DE CIENCIAS SOCIALES (Rio Piedras, P.R.), v. 7, mar./jun. 1963: 121–140.

25.469 Rodríguez Cruz, Juan. Las relaciones raciales en Puerto Rico. bibl. REVISTA DE CIENCIAS SOCIALES (Río Piedras, P.R.), v. 9, dic. 1965: 373–396.

25.470 Rogler, Lloyd H. A Better Life: Notes from Puerto Rico. illus. TRANSACTION, v. 2, Mar./Apr. 1965: 34–36.

25.471 Rogler, Lloyd, and August B. Hollingshead. Class and Disordered Speech in the Mentally Ill. JOURNAL OF HEALTH AND HUMAN BEHAVIOR, v. 2, Fall 1961: 178–185.

25.472 Rogler, Lloyd, and August B. Hollingshead. The Puerto Rican Spiritualist as a Psychiatrist. AMERICAN JOURNAL OF SOCIOLOGY, v. 67, July 1961: 17–21.

25.473 Safa, Helen Icken. The Female-based Household in Public Housing: a Case Study in Puerto Rico. tables. HUMAN ORGANIZATION, v. 24, Summer 1965: 135–139.

25.474 Scott, Joseph W. Sources of Social Change in Community, Family, and Fertility in a Puerto Rican Town. tables. AMERICAN JOURNAL OF SOCIOLOGY, v. 72, Mar. 1967: 520–530.

25.475 Seda Bonilla, Eduardo. Dos modelos de relaciones raciales: Estados Unidos y América Latina. tables. REVISTA DE CIENCIAS SOCIALES (Río Piedras, P.R.), v. 12, dic. 1968: 569–597.

25.476 Seda Bonilla, Eduardo. La educación y las elites en Puerto Rico. REVISTA DE CIENCIAS SOCIALES (Río Piedras, P.R.), v. 10, jun. 1966: 227–235.

25.477   Seda Bonilla, Eduardo. Social Structure and Race Relations. illus. SOCIAL FORCES, v. 40, Dec. 1961: 141–148.

25.478   Seda Bonilla, Eduardo. Toro Bravo: una comunidad tradicional de pequeños agricultores en el centro montañoso de Puerto Rico. REVISTA DE CIENCIAS SOCIALES (Río Piedras, P.R.), v. 12, jun. 1968: 239–253.

25.479   Steward, Julian H. Perspectives on Plantations. REVISTA GEOGRAFICA DO INSTITUTO PAN-AMERICANO DE GEOGRAFIA E HISTORIA (Río de Janeiro), v. 26, jan./jun. 1960: 77–85.

25.480   Straus, Murray A. Communication, Creativity, and Problem-Solving Ability of Middle-and Working-Class Families in Three Societies. tables. AMERICAN JOURNAL OF SOCIOLOGY, v. 73, Jan. 1968: 417–430.

25.481   Suchman, Edward A., and others. An Experiment in Innovation among Sugar Cane Cutters in Puerto Rico. table. HUMAN ORGANIZATION, v. 26, Winter 1967: 214–221.

25.482   Tió Nazario, Juan Angel. Costumbres tradicionales. BOLETIN DE LA ACADEMIA DE ARTES Y CIENCIAS DE PUERTO RICO (Río Piedras, P.R.), v. 3, oct./dic. 1967: 805–810.

25.483   Toro Calder, Jaime. El uso y abuso de bebidas alcohólicas y el problema del alcoholismo en nuestra sociedad: Estados Unidos y Puerto Rico. bibl., tables. REVISTA DE CIENCIAS SOCIALES (Río Piedras, P.R.), v. 13, abr./jun. 1969: 179–195.

25.484   Unbeatable Mayor of San Juan. illus. LIFE, v. 57, Sept. 26, 1964: 65–66.

25.485   Vientós Gastón, Nilita. Comentarios a un ensayo sobre Puerto Rico. CASA DE LAS AMERICAS (Habana), v. 6, mar./abr. 1966: 27–41.

25.486   Vientós Gastón, Nilita. Puerto Rico y la cultura de la pobreza. CUADERNOS AMERICANOS (Mexico, D.F.), v. 29, en./feb. 1970: 31–45.

25.487   Wallace, Samuel E. Patrones de violencia en San Juan. REVISTA DE CIENCIAS SOCIALES (Río Piedras, P.R.), v. 10, dic. 1966: 471–475.

25.488   Which Way for Puerto Rico? THE ECONOMIST (London), v. 224, July 22, 1967: 327.

Part IV
Audiovisual Materials (26–27)

26
MOTION PICTURES

26.1 ASSASSINS IN CONGRESS. Filmrite Associates. Released by Official Films, 1960. 3 min., sound, black and white, 16 mm. (Greatest Headlines of the Century).

Portrays events in Washington on March 1, 1954, when four Puerto Rican nationalists shot at and wounded several members of the U.S. House of Representatives in order to dramatize their belief in complete political independence for their country.

26.2 BEYOND THE VALLEY. Esso Standard Oil Co., 1958. Made by John Bransby Productions. 29 min., sound, color, 16 mm.

A young Puerto Rican father reviews, in terms of his own family, the changes brought about through increased industrialization. Shows how Puerto Rico was in the mid-fifties, changing from a three-crop agrarian society to a multi-industry economy. A longer version of this film was issued in Spanish in 1955.

26.3 EL BLOCKE. Cinepueblo Productions, 1972. 43 min., sound, black and white, 16 mm.

Chronicles the activities during one summer of a Puerto Rican community in New York City.

26.4 LA BUENA HERENCIA. Community Education Division, Commonwealth Department of Education, San Juan, n.d. Distributed by Quality Film Laboratories. 26 min., sound, color, 16 mm.

A documentary dealing with Puerto Rico's Indian heritage. An accompanying text, Isla y Pueblo (Pamphlet no. 29), is available.

26.5 CABO ROJO. Community Education Division, Commonwealth Department of Education, San Juan, n.d. 10 min., sound, black and white, 16 mm.

A short documentary on the way of life in Cabo Rojo, a small town of the western part of the island that was the birthplace of the pirate Cofresí.

26.6 CANTO A LA NATIVIDAD. Community Education Division, Commonwealth Department of Education, San Juan, n.d. 11 min., sound, black and white, 16 mm.

A typical Puerto Rican musical group interprets traditional Christmas carols. An accompanying two-volume text, Libros de Navidad, is available.

26.7 EL CONTEMPLADO. Community Education Division, Commonwealth Department of Education, San Juan, n.d. Distributed by Quality Film Laboratories. 13 min., sound, color, 16 mm.

This film, which takes its name from the poems of the Spanish poet Pedro Salinas in which he describes Puerto Rico, captures some of the beauty of the island scenery. Background music is provided by the chorus of the University of Puerto Rico. This film participated in the 1958 Venice Film Festival.

26.8 CONOZCA SUS PUEBLOS: ARECIBO. Community Education Division, Commonwealth Department of Education, San Juan, n.d. 12 min., sound, black and white, 16 mm.

A glimpse at the way of life in Arecibo, a city on the northern coast of Puerto Rico.

26.9 DANZAS PUERTORRIQUEÑAS. Community Education Division, Commonwealth Department of Education, San Juan, n.d. 13 min., sound, black and white, 16 mm.

A short film presenting a selection of Puerto Rican danzas interpreted by local artist José Raúl Ramírez.

26.10 DEMOCRACY AT WORK IN RURAL PUERTO RICO. U.S. Department of Agriculture, 1942. 21 min., sound, black and white, 16 mm. Another issue, 35 mm.

Outlines the history of Puerto Rico and discusses its agricultural resources and problems as of 1942.

26.11 DESDE LAS NUBES. Community Education Division, Commonwealth Department of Education, San Juan, n.d. 45 min., sound, black and white, 16 mm.

Documentary on the island's economic geography, showing its size, shape, and topography. It explains what the island does and does not produce.

26.12 ELISA TAVAREZ. Community Education Division, Commonwealth Department of Education, San Juan, n.d. 8 min., sound, black and white, 16 mm.

A short documentary of the life of Elisa Tavárez, a Puerto Rican pianist and noted interpreter of the danza.

26.13 FESTIVAL IN PUERTO RICO. National Film Board of Canada, 1961. Distributed by McGraw Hill Text Films. 28 min., sound, black and white, 16 mm.

Backstage view of the 1960 Casals Music Festival in Puerto Rico, featuring Maureen Forrester in a performance of Scarlatti's Salve Regina. It includes glimpses of the Puerto Rican scenery.

26.14 HARLEM CRUSADER. National Broadcasting Co. Made and released by Encyclopaedia Britannica Films, 1966. 29 min., sound, black and white, 16 mm. With teachers' guide.

Reports the story of tough-minded social worker Dean Murrow, who, working for the American Friends Service Committee, lived for five years among the people he was helping in Spanish Harlem in New York City.

26.15 EL HOMBRE ESPERADO. Community Education Division, Commonwealth Department of Education, San Juan, n.d. 43 min., sound, black and white, 16 mm.

Depicts the life and work of José Pablo Morales, politician and writer, who defended the rights of the Puerto Rican workers in the mid-nineteenth century.

26.16 HOLIDAY ISLAND. RKO-Pathe, 1953. 15 min., sound, color, 35 mm.

A travelogue including scenes of hotels, homes, historic buildings, monuments, etc.

26.17 AN ISLAND IN AMERICA. Antidefamation League of B'nai B'rith, 1972. Made by DMS Productions. 28 min., sound, color, 16 mm.

A profile of Puerto Rican communities on the mainland, including an account of social, cultural, and economic conditions set against a background of the history of the island. The film emphasizes new concepts in the education of Puerto Rican children, particularly the teaching of English as a second language.

26.18 JOSE MARTINEZ . . . AMERICAN. Audio Visual Department, Board of National Missions, United Presbyterian Church, 1964. 29 min., sound, color, 16 mm.

A view of the life of the major Spanish-American minority groups in the United States—Puerto Ricans, Mexicans, and residents of Spanish descent in New Mexico. Surveys the progress made by such groups, emphasizing their cultural heritage and their growing middle class.

26.19 JULIO ROSADO DEL VALLE. Organization of American States, n.d. 17 min., sound, color, 16 mm.

A visit to the studio of this Puerto Rican artist. The film, which has been recommended by Proyecto Leer in Washington, D.C., provides a look at one aspect of contemporary Puerto Rican cultural activity.

26.20 MAYO FLORIDO. Community Education Division, Commonwealth Department of Education, San Juan, n.d. Distributed by Quality Film Laboratories. 9 min., sound, color, 16 mm.

A brief artistic film highlighting Puerto Rico's flora. Folkloric music is used for the background.

26.21 MIGUEL: UP FROM PUERTO RICO. Bert Salzman Productions. Released by Learning Corp. of America, 1970. 15 min., sound, color, 16 mm. (Many Americans). With teacher's guide.

The story of how a boy born in Puerto Rico learns the advantages of biculturalism. Filmed on location in New York and Puerto Rico.

26.22 MILAGRO EN LA MONTAÑA. Community Education Division, Commonwealth Department of Education, San Juan, n.d. Distributed by Quality Film Laboratories. 31 min., sound, color, 16 mm.

Depicts the celebration of Christmas in a rural community in Puerto Rico. The Community Education Division has produced other short films on the observance of Christmas on the island: *Festival Navideño*, 9 min., *Nacimiento*, 8 min., and *Parranda Campesina*, 12 min.

26.23 LA MONTAÑA CANTA. Community Education Division, Commonwealth Department of Education, San Juan, n.d. 11 min., sound, black and white, 16 mm.

Some examples of Puerto Rican folkloric music.

26.24 NELSON ALBERT ROLON. Douglas Darnell, 1970. 11 min., sound, black and white, 16 mm.

A documentary study of a Puerto Rican boy living in East Harlem. The film explores his thoughts, feelings, and growing self-awareness.

26.25 NENEN DE LA RUTA MORA. Community Education Division, Commonwealth Department of Education, San Juan, n.d. Distributed by Quality Film Laboratories. 23 min., sound, color, 16 mm.

A documentary showing a child's fascination with the folkloric celebrations of the Fiestas de Santiago Apóstol in Loíza Aldea, a town of the north coast of the island, east of San Juan.

26.26 NINE ARTISTS OF PUERTO RICO. Organization of American States, n.d. 20 min., sound, color, 16 mm. English or Spanish narration.

Narrated by Puerto Rican actor José Ferrer, this film features a visit to the studios of nine of Puerto Rico's most important artists, among them, Lorenzo Homar, Julio Rosado del Valle, José Alicea, Rafael Ferrer, Olga Albizu and Rafael Villamil.

26.27 NOT BY BREAD ALONE. Administración de Fomento Económico, San Juan, n.d. 20 min., sound, color, 16 mm.

Describes Puerto Rico and its people, with emphasis on the island's achievements and goals.

26.28 OLAS Y ARENAS. Community Education Division, Commonwealth Department of Education, San Juan, n.d. 7 min., sound, color, 16 mm.

A short film inspired by "Olas y Arenas" ("Waves and Sands"), a song by the late Puerto Rican composer Sylvia Rexach.

26.29 ONE MAN: JOSE GONZALEZ. U.S. Information Agency, 1968. Made by Guggenheim Productions. 10 min., sound., color, 16 mm.

Tells the story of José González, a twelve-year-old Puerto Rican newspaper boy in Chicago, and shows him as he learns his route, delivers newspapers, and collects his first paycheck.

26.30 A PLEASURE TO BE HERE. Puerto Rico Tourism Development Co., 1972. 24 min., sound, color, 16 mm. Also edited into 10- and 15-minute lengths.

Narrated by Puerto Rican actor José Ferrer, this film describes the island's natural beauty, its rich Spanish heritage, and its growth as a modern society.

26.31 LA PLENA. Community Education Division, Commonwealth Department of Education, San Juan, n.d. Distributed by Quality Film Laboratories. 28 min., sound, color, 16 mm.

A documentary inspired by the *plena*, one of the most powerful musical expressions of the Puerto Rican culture.

26.32 PUERTO RICAN AMERICANS. Ealing Corp., 1970. 4 min., sound, color, super 8 mm. (Ethnic Groups).

Shows residential and cultural enclaves of Puerto Rican Americans in New York.

26.33 PUERTO RICAN PLAYLAND. Dudley Pictures Corp. Released by Universal Pictures Co., 1960. 5 min., sound, color, 35 mm. (Universal-International Color Parade).

A travelog of the tourist attractions of San Juan and vicinity. It includes a brief history of the island and points out ancient and modern points of interest.

26.34 PUERTO RICO. CBS Television. Released by McGraw-Hill, 1957. 55 min., sound, black and white, 16 mm. From the CBS television program *See It Now*.

A study of Puerto Rico, discussing migration, slums, prejudice, and the attempts of an underdeveloped area to pull itself up by its bootstraps. It explores some of the causes and effects of migration of Puerto Ricans to New York City and other metropolitan centers.

26.35 PUERTO RICO. Eastman Teaching Films, 1931. Released by Encyclopaedia Britannica Films. 11 min., silent, black and white, 16 mm. Also released under the title PORTO RICO.

Indicates development of Puerto Rico under U.S. control, and points out that location and climate make it a rich producer of agricultural raw materials. Describes San Juan, schools and colleges, rural life, and products.

26.36 PUERTO RICO. U.S. Department of the Army, 1950. Released for public educational use through U.S. Office of Education, 1951. 22 min., sound, black and white, 16 mm. Another issue, 35 mm.

Explains the struggle and growth of Puerto Rico with emphasis on its strategic value as a military, air, and naval base.

26.37 PUERTO RICO. WTTW. Released by NET Film Service, 1956. 29 min., sound, black and white, 16 mm. (America Looks Ahead).

A survey of the political and economic evolution of Puerto Rico. It explains Puerto Rico's then new political association with the United States and describes Puerto Rican efforts to realize economic benefits through that new status.

26.38 PUERTO RICO. Robert Davis Productions, 1957. 15 min., sound, color, 16 mm.

Depicts various aspects of Puerto Rico—its fifteenth-century streets and ancient forts, its tropical flora, industries, homes, beaches, and the San Juan Bautista Day celebration.

26.39 PUERTO RICO, CARIBBEAN COMMONWEALTH. Audio-Visual Materials Consultation Bureau, Wayne University, 1954. 34 frames, black and white, 35 mm. With teacher's guide.

Uses captioned photographs, maps, and charts to portray Puerto Rico today, its past struggles, and its progress in recent years. Stresses governmental affairs, and economic and political problems.

26.40 PUERTO RICO ISLA DEL PROGRESO. U.S. Industries, 1964. Made by GMP Productions. 12 min., sound, color, 16 mm. Spanish version also issued.

Uses a theme song entitled "This is Puerto Rico" as a background for contrasting the old and the new cultures and explaining the spirit of change in Puerto Rico. The film describes the island as a place in which to relax and points out its economic growth.

26.41 PUERTO RICO, ISLA DEL SOL. Puerto Rico Department of Tourism, 1968. Made by Tom Hollyman, Inc. 14 min., sound, color, 16 mm. Other versions issued in French and Spanish.

A tourist's view of Puerto Rico. Includes scenes of old San Juan, islands, water sports, and night life.

26.42 PUERTO RICO—ISLAND IN THE SUN. Dudley Pictures Corp. Made by Carl Dudley. Released by United World Films, 1961. 18 min., sound, color, 16 mm. (Your World Neighbors). With guide.

Describes the economic and social development of modern Puerto Rico. It discusses the island's industrialization program, education, housing, and better use of the land.

26.43 PUERTO RICO: ITS PAST, PRESENT, AND PROMISE. Encyclopaedia Britannica Films, 1965. 20 min., sound, color, 16 mm. With teachers' guide. Another issue, black and white.

Examines the improvements in the standard of living of Puerto Rico during recent years despite the overpopulation and limited resources of the island. It explains how the island has become a laboratory of study for underdeveloped nations in the world. The film has been recommended by Proyecto Leer in Washington, D.C.

26.44 PUERTO RICO MEANS BUSINESS. Economic Development Administration, Commonwealth of Puerto Rico, San Juan, 1967. Made by John J. Hennessey Motion Pictures. 19 min., sound, color, 16 mm.

Explains why Puerto Rico is an ideal place for new industrial plants as well as a pleasant place in which to live.

26.45 PUERTO RICO: THE CARIBBEAN AMERICANS. ABC Television Network. Made by Daniel Wilson. Released by International Film Bureau, 1970. 22 min., sound, color, 16 mm. (Discovery).

Presents the history and way of life of Puerto Rico as revealed in the experiences of a young man who goes to the United States to learn to make a better life for himself and then returns to the island.

It includes scenes of the sugar cane industry and a rat factory that breeds rats for research.

26.46 PUERTO RICO, THE NEW COMMONWEALTH. Popular Science Pub. Released by McGraw-Hill, 1955. 40 frames, color, 35 mm. (Middle America). With teaching guide.

Using captioned photographs, drawings and maps, this surveys the history and present status of Puerto Rico showing its progress from a colony to a democratic commonwealth. Shows how its industry and agriculture revolve around sugar, with pineapple and banana growing and native handicrafts to bolster the economy. Points out the problems resulting from over population.

26.47 PUERTO RICO—OPERATION BOOTSTRAP. Dudley Pictures Corp. Made by Carl Dudley. Released by United World Films, 1963. 17 min., sound, color, 16 mm. (Today's People in Our Changing World). With guide.

Tells the story of Operation Bootstrap, a far-reaching program to attract industry to Puerto Rico. It tells also of the introduction of low-cost modern housing, improvements in health and educational facilities, and increased employment.

26.48 PUERTO RICO: THE PEACEFUL REVOLUTION. CBS News, 1962. Made by Isaac Kleinerman. Released by McGraw-Hill. 27 min., sound, black and white, 16 mm. With guide.

Portrays the growth, development, and improvement of living standards in Puerto Rico under Governor Luis Muñoz Marín. The film, narrated in part by Governor Muñoz Marín, was telecast on the CBS-TV documentary show The Twentieth Century.

26.49 PUERTO RICO: SHOWCASE OF AMERICA. McGraw-Hill, 1962. 18 min., sound, color, 16 mm. With guide. Another issue, black and white.

Portrays the growth of the Puerto Rican economy. It describes Operation Bootstrap and the industrial revolution which has been accomplished peacefully in the island.

26.50 PUERTO RICO/U.S.A. William H. Murray Productions. Released by Classroom Film Distributors, 1964. 11 min., sound, color, 16 mm. With teacher's guide.

A film that traces the history of Puerto Rico, describing its discovery by Columbus and telling about the period when the Indian natives were exploited by Spanish explorers. It shows how Puerto Rico, through its

Operation Bootstrap program, has achieved a high degree of economic development.

26.51 PUERTO RICO AND THE VIRGIN IS-LANDS. Coronet Instructional Films, 1964. 11 min., sound, color, 16 mm. With teacher's guide. Another issue, black and white.

Presents a geographic, historical and cultural survey of the U.S. territories in the Caribbean. It describes the economic program by which the Commonwealth of Puerto Rico has attained the highest standard of living in Latin America.

26.52 QUE PUERTO RICO. Tibor Hirsch, 1963. Distributed by McGraw-Hill Text Films. 16 min., sound, color, 16 mm.

An impressionistic view of Puerto Rico, using native music and sound effects to give a picture of the island, and of the people at work, at prayer, and at fiestas.

26.53 RANK AND FILE. National Educational Television and Radio Center, 1971. Distributed by Indiana University Audio-Visual Center. 15 min., sound, color, 16 min.

Shows how in the New York local of the Transport Workers Union blacks and Puerto Ricans are fighting to form their own union in order to counter the discrimination they presently find.

26.54 A REPORT FROM SAN JUAN. Delta Films International. Released by Warner Bros., 1964. 17 min., sound, color, 35 mm. (Worldwide Adventure Special).

A travelogue of Puerto Rico, emphasizing the progress and modernization that has taken place in San Juan. Includes views of sports and recreational activities.

26.55 EL RESPLANDOR. Community Education Division, Commonwealth Department of Education, San Juan, n.d. 51 min., sound, black and white, 16 mm.

Depicts the history of slavery in Puerto Rico and its influence on the island's history. A historical summary, La Esclavitud, (Pamphlet no. 27), is available.

26.56 RICH HARBOR. Government Development Bank for Puerto Rico. Made by Norman Wright Productions. Released in the U.S. by Sterling Movies, 1959. 26 min., sound, color, 16 mm. Another issue, 35 mm.

Presents to American industry and the general public the advantages and opportunities available in Puerto Rican securities. Traces the history of the modern industrial movement known as Operation Bootstrap and shows what the country is accomplishing. Includes views of the island and its scenic attractions.

26.57 SANTERO. Produced by the Community Education Division of the Commonwealth Department of Education for the Museum of the University of Puerto Rico, n.d. Distributed by Quality Film Laboratories, 26 min., sound, color, 16 mm.

A documentary showing the work of Don Zoilo Cajigas, an old Puerto Rican santero or wood carver. This film was awarded a special mention in the 1956 Venice Film Festival, and participated in the Edinburgh Film Festival of the same year.

26.58 STRANGERS IN THEIR OWN LAND: THE PUERTO RICANS. ABC News. Released by ABC Media Concepts, 1971. 14 min., sound, color, 16 mm. With guide.

Shows the work in progress at the Puerto Rican Family Institute in New York City, which is run by and for Puerto Ricans. The film explains that the institute's main goal is to keep families together before abject living conditions split them.

26.59 TRABAJO PARA USTED. Produced by the U.S. Department of Labor and the Puerto Rican Farmers' Association, n.d. Distributed by the Community Education Division. 22 min., sound, color, 16 mm.

A film showing the problems encountered by Puerto Rican workers who migrate to farms in the United States. It discusses some actions which can help them face those problems.

26.60 TRIO VEGABAJEÑO. Community Education Division, Commonwealth Department of Education, San Juan, n.d. 10 min., sound, black and white, 16 mm.

A well-known local trio interprets some popular Puerto Rican songs.

26.61 TRULLA. Community Education Division, Commonwealth Department of Education, San Juan, n.d. 10 min., sound, black and white, 16 mm.

Three forms of country music—the *seis, the controversia* and the *mapeyé* —are interpreted by Puerto Rican musicians.

26.62 UPTOWN: PORTRAIT OF A N.Y.C. SLUM. Einstein College, 1966. Distributed by Danska Films. 29 min., sound, black and white, 16 mm.

A documentary study of a Puerto Rican and negro ghetto community. It focuses on the street life, activities, mores, tempo, and daily existence.

26.63 VECINOS. Community Education Division, Commonwealth Department of Education, San Juan, n.d. 28 min., sound, black and white, 16 mm.

A general introduction to the life styles in three areas of Puerto Rico: the mountains, the coastal valleys, and the city.

26.64 VISIT TO PUERTO RICO. International Film Bureau, 1962. 17 min., color, 46 mm. Available also in Spanish.

Surveys Puerto Rico's location, population, racial heritage, geography, topography, major cities, chief crops, and farming methods.

26.65 THE VOICE OF LA RAZA. Office of Economic Opportunity. Made and distributed by William Greaves, Inc., n.d. 53 1/2 min., sound, color, 16 mm.

An award-winning film on the problems facing the Spanish-speaking community of the United States in its effort to overcome job discrimination. The film features Anthony Quinn, around whose presence the action revolves. He moves about the country exploring the economic problems faced by Mexican-Americans and Puerto Ricans.

26.66 THE WORLD OF PIRI THOMAS. National Education Television and Radio Center. Released by Indiana University Audiovisual Center, 1968. 60 min., sound, color, 16 mm. Another issue, black and white.

Piri Thomas, author of *Down These Mean Streets* and *Savior, Savior, Hold My Hand*, describes Puerto Rican life in the Spanish Harlem ghetto in New York City.

26.67 YO, JUAN PONCE DE LEON. Community Education Division, Commonwealth Department of Education, San Juan, n.d. Distributed by Quality Film Laboratories. 20 min., sound, color, 16 mm.

A documentary about Juan Ponce de León, founder of the city of San Juan and first governor of Puerto Rico. The film uses scenes taken in San Juan and a series of paintings done specifically for the film by an artist of the Community Education Division. This film participated in the 1958 Venice Film Festival.

27
FILMSTRIPS

27.1 AMERICAN FAMILIES: THE GARCIAS. Coronet Instructional Films, 1971. 49 frames, color, 35 mm. and phonodisc: 1 side, 12 in., 33-1/3 rpm., 9 min. Also issued with phonotape in cassette. With study guide.

Introduces a family of Puerto Rican descent, showing father and grandfather at work and children at school and play.

27.2 THE COMMUNITY WORKER. Guidance Associates of Pleasantville, N.Y., 1970. 43 frames, color, 35 mm. and phonodisc: 1 side, 12 in., 33-1/3 rpm, 8 min., microgroove (Liking Your Job and Your Life). Also issued with phonotape in cassette. With discussion guide.

A spokesman for the non-English-speaking Puerto Ricans in the East Side of New York describes his personal and employment background, and conditions of work, and stresses his commitment to his people.

27.3 GEOGRAPHY OF PUERTO RICO. Imperial Film Co., 1966. 38 frames, color, 35 mm. (The Caribbean: Puerto Rico).

Describes the natural geography of Puerto Rico, which ranges from desert conditions to rain forest. Pictures the varied lives of the people in the interior of the island and in some of the smaller cities. With captions.

27.4 HISTORIC PUERTO RICO. Imperial Film Co., 1966. 38 frames, color, 35 mm. (The Caribbean: Puerto Rico).

Captioned views of relics of Spanish colonialism in old San Juan: El Morro, San Juan Water Gate, the Cathedral, La Fortaleza, El Convento, and several examples of Spanish architecture. Includes a brief history of the colonial period.

27.5 HOW MARIA AND RAMON LIVE IN PUERTO RICO. Warren Schloat Productions, 1967. 46 frames, color, 35 mm. (Children of foreign countries).

Based on the book María and Ramón, a Girl and Boy of Puerto Rico, by G. Warren Schloat, Jr., this filmstrip approaches the study of Puerto Rico through the experiences of teen-agers, with emphasis on national customs, geography, village life, arts and crafts, and religion.

27.6 IF YOU WERE BORN IN PUERTO RICO. Troll Associates, 1969. 42 frames, color, 35 mm. (Children around the World). For primary grades.

An account of life in Puerto Rico, depicting the land, customs and culture, food, clothing, and educational system. With captions.

27.7 THE ISLAND OF PUERTO RICO—CITIES. Urban Media Materials, 1972. 35 frames, color, 35 mm. With unit plan and student worksheets.

Introduces the names of the major cities on the island of Puerto Rico, including San Juan, Ponce, Mayaguez, and Caguas. Shows where the cities are located on the island and describes each place. With captions.

27.8 THE ISLAND OF PUERTO RICO—HOUSING. Urban Media Materials, 1972. 35 frames, color, 35 mm. With unit plan and student worksheets.

Presents pictures of the various housing styles found in Puerto Rico, in order to show the influence of geography and socioeconomic status on living standards. With captions.

27.9 THE ISLAND OF PUERTO RICO—INDUSTRY. Urban Media Materials, 1972. 35 frames, color, 35 mm. With unit plan and student worksheets.

An overview of the main industries of Puerto Rico. Shows workers in various occupations, and discusses government efforts to expand the economy of the island. With captions.

27.10 THE ISLAND OF PUERTO RICO—LOCATION AND LAND. Urban Media Materials, 1972. 35 frames, color, 35 mm. With unit plan and student worksheets.

An overview of the topography and location of Puerto Rico. It plots the location of the island in relation to the United States and other nations in the Western Hemisphere. Shows that although small in size, it has a varied topography and climate. With captions.

27.11 THE ISLAND OF PUERTO RICO—PEOPLE. Urban Media Materials, 1972. 35 frames, color, 35 mm. With unit plan and student worksheets.

Introduces people who live in Puerto Rico, and examines their customs and traditions. With captions.

27.12 JOSE, PUERTO RICAN BOY. Society for Visual Education, 1970. 69 frames, color, 35 mm. and phonodisc: 1 side, 12 in., 33-1/3 rpm., 16 min., microgroove. (Children of the Inner City). Also issued with phonotape in cassette. With teacher's guide.

Reveals the language, social, and economic problems of the inner-city Puerto Ricans through the home, community, and school experiences of José, his mother, and his sister after they arrive in the United States.

27.13 LAND, FEATURES, AND CITIES IN PUERTO RICO. Eye Gate House, 1972. 54 frames, color, 35 mm., with phonorecord or cassette. (Puerto Rico: A Regional Study Series, cat no. X313B).

Focuses on the contrast offered by the rugged mountains and coastal plains of the island.

27.14 LIFE IN PUERTO RICO. Eye Gate House, 1972. 51 frames, color, 35 mm., with phonorecord or cassette. (Puerto Rico: A Regional Study Series, cat. no. X313D).

Presents some of the contrasts between city life and life in the small towns and villages.

27.15 PROFILE OF PUERTO RICO. Teaching Aids Service, 1956. 50 frames, color, 35 mm. With manual.

Shows the land and people of Puerto Rico and describes their work, government, recreation, and religion. It stresses the progress made through Operation Bootstrap.

27.16 PUERTO RICAN AGRICULTURE AND INDUSTRY. Imperial Film Co., 1966. 38 frames, color, 35 mm. (The Caribbean: Puerto Rico).

Captioned views of some industrial and agricultural activities in Puerto Rico: tuna packing, sugar and pineapple growing and processing, power plants, petrochemical plants, tobacco culture, and other lesser industries.

27.17 PUERTO RICAN LEADERS OF 20TH CENTURY AMERICA. AVI Associates, 1970. Made by Joshua Tree Productions. 4 filmstrips, 55 frames each, color, 35 mm., and 2 phonodiscs, 2 sides each, 12 in., 33-1/3 rpm., 13 min. each side. With teachers' guide.

Contents.—Herman Badillo, Piri Thomas, Luis Quero Chiesa, José Feliciano.

27.18 PUERTO RICANS, PART 1. Warren Schloat Productions, 1968. 56 frames, color, 35 mm. and phonodisc. 1 side, 12 in., 33-1/3 rpm., 13 min., microgroove. (Minorities Have Made America Great, set 2). With teacher's guide and script.

Explains the social, psychological, and economic cycle that traps the United States' newest immigrants, the Puerto Ricans.

27.19 PUERTO RICANS, PART 2. Warren Schloat Productions, 1968. 74 frames, color, 35 mm. and phonodisc: 1 side, 12 in., 33-1/3 rpm., 19 min., microgroove. (Minorities Have Made America Great, set 2). With teacher's guide and script.

Discusses ways in which Puerto Ricans are dealing with their problems of becoming accepted American citizens.

27.20 PUERTO RICO. American Geographical Society, 1957. 40 frames, color, 35 mm.

A descriptive and explanatory treatment of Puerto Rico. Emphasizes the island's problems—overpopulation, extremes of poverty and wealth, reliance on a single commercial crop, and relative lack of industry—and shows how some of the problems are being tackled.

27.21 PUERTO RICO. Eye Gate House, 1965. 38 frames, color, 35 mm. (The West Indies, no. 7). With teacher's manual.

A film survey on Puerto Rico—its history, geography, acquisition by the United States, and accomplishments under a free enterprise system. Shows points of interest on the island.

27.22 PUERTO RICO. McGraw-Hill, 1964. Made by Centron Corp. 43 frames, color, 35 mm. (Middle America Series). With guide.

Views of Puerto Rico and its geographical features. Pictures sugar and pineapple plantations as well as small farms, modern highways, dams, factories, hospitals, schools, housing, shopping centers, resorts, and hotels.

27.23 PUERTO RICO AND THE PUERTO RICANS. Urban Media Materials, 1969. 2 filmstrips, color, 35 mm. and 2 phonodiscs: 2 sides each (1 side for manual projector, 1 side for automatic projector), 12 in., 33-1/3 rpm; pt. 1, 15 min., pt. 2, 16 min. English and Spanish narration. With teacher's guide and text in English and Spanish.

Examines aspects of Puerto Rico

and its people, including who they are, where they came from and why, and the contributions they are making to their newly adopted cities in the United States.

27.24 PUERTO RICO—THE CHIEF CITIES. Eye Gate House, 1960. 37 frames, color, 35 mm. (Alaska, Hawaiian Islands, and Puerto Rico, no. 9). With teacher's manual.

Describes some of the chief cities in Puerto Rico, including San Juan, Ponce, Mayaguez, and Caguas.

27.25 PUERTO RICO—HISTORIC AND GEOGRAPHIC BACKGROUNDS. Eye Gate House, 1960. 39 frames, color, 35 mm. (Alaska, Hawaiian Islands, and Puerto Rico, no. 7).

Describes the historical background and characteristics of Puerto Rico. Points out that Puerto Rico is a self-governing island commonwealth associated with the United States, and that Puerto Ricans are American citizens.

27.26 PUERTO RICO—HISTORY AND CULTURE. Urban Media Materials, 1969. 2 filmstrips, 58 frames each, color, 35 mm., and 2 phonodiscs: 2 sides each (1 side for manual projector, 1 side for automatic projector), 12 in., 33-1/3 rpm.; pt. 1, 22 min., pt. 2, 21 min. Recording with English and Spanish narration. With teacher's guide and text in Spanish and English.

Contents. 1. History. 2. Culture.

27.27 PUERTO RICO—THE PEOPLE AND INDUSTRIES. Eye Gate House, 1960. 42 frames, color, 35 mm. (Alaska, Hawaiian Islands, and Puerto Rico, no. 8). With teacher's guide.

Describes the dense population of Puerto Rico and explains that the island has free public schools but not enough to provide complete elementary school education for all children. Discusses various industries, including the growing of sugarcane, needlework, and the many new factories.

27.28 PUERTO RICO—A STUDY IN DEVELOPMENT. Current Affairs Films, 1962. 43 frames, black and white, 35 mm. (Current Affairs Filmstrip Series). With discussion guide.

Discusses the transition of Puerto Rico in the past twenty years from an underdeveloped country to one on the way to a diversified economy and a democratic government. It explains how Operation Bootstrap has contributed to the island's development.

27.29 PUERTO RICO TODAY. Visual Education Consultants, 1963. 41 frames, black and white, 35 mm. Revised version of the 1956 filmstrip of the same title. With guide.

Describes life in Puerto Rico, a self-governing commonwealth of the United States. It explains that before the 1940s the island was known as the "poorhouse of the Caribbean" but that today it is called a "showplace for democracy," and points out the reasons for this change.

27.30 PUERTO RICO, THE VIRGINS, AND MARTINIQUE. Herbert M. Elkins Co., 1962. 47 frames, color, 35 mm. (Our Neighbors to the South). With teacher's guide and vocabulary list.

Discusses the influence of the colonizing nations on the present-day West Indian islands of Puerto Rico, Martinique and the Virgin Islands. With captions.

27.31 PUERTO RICO'S PEOPLE. Imperial Film Co., 1966. 38 frames, color, 35 mm. (The Caribbean: Puerto Rico).

Captioned views of housing, recreation, and other living conditions of people of various cultural backgrounds and economic levels in Puerto Rico.

27.32 LOS PUERTORRIQUEÑOS. Schloat Productions, 1972. 100 frames, color, 35 mm. and phonodisc: 2 sides, 12 in. each side, 33-1/3 rpm., 12 min. With teacher's guide.

Presents interviews with Puerto Ricans to show the conflicts and problems of their orientation in the United States. A sociologist, a doctor, and an educator discuss the problems and possible solutions.

27.33 THE RED BALLOON. Department of Education, Commonwealth of Puerto Rico, 1966. Made by Vistapro. 34 frames, color, 35 mm. and phonotape: plastic, 1 reel (5 in.) 3-3/4 in. per sec.

An English language teaching film. Presents a dialogue about two boys who bought a big red balloon and then let it fly away. Includes a captioned and a noncaptioned version.

27.34 RESOURCES, AGRICULTURE AND INDUSTRY OF PUERTO RICO. Eye Gate House, N.Y., 1972. 47 frames, color, 35 mm., with phonorecord or cassette. (Puerto Rico: A Regional Study Series, cat. no. X313C).

A look at the island's agriculture, and a description of the construction and tourism industries.

27.35 U.S. COLONIALISM. Jones and Osmond. Released by Modern Learning Aids, 1968. 24 frames, color, 35 mm. (Critical Thinking Aids). With teacher's guide.

Part 1 presents the feelings of a landless Puerto Rican peasant soon after the Spanish-American War as he wonders whether it is better to be independent and poor or more prosperous and ruled by America. Part 2 shows a Cuban who must decide whether to accept or reject the Platt Amendment. With captions.

27.36 WHAT IS PUERTO RICO. Eye Gate House, N.Y. 1972. 51 frames, color, 35 mm., with phonorecord or cassette. (Puerto Rico: A Regional Study Series, cat. no. X313a).

A general introduction to the island including its geography, history, and government.

Publishers and Distributors

Academia de Artes y Ciencias de Puerto Rico
Apartado 22131
Estación Postal Universitaria
Río Piedras, Puerto Rico 00931

Asociación de Graduadas de la Universidad
  de Puerto Rico
Apartado 1142
San Juan, Puerto Rico

Ateneo Puertorriqueño
Apartado 1180
San Juan, Puerto Rico 00902

Batey Book Distributing Co.
69 Irving Place
New York, New York 10003

Biblioteca de Autores Puertorriqueños
Apartado 522
San Juan, Puerto Rico

Children's Music Center, Inc.
5373 W. Pico Blvd.
Los Angeles, California 90019

College Entrance Examination Board
Apartado 1275
Hato Rey, Puerto Rico 00919

Cuadernos de la Escalera
Apartado 22576, University Station
Río Piedras, Puerto Rico 00931

Ediciones Artísticas de Puerto Rico
Apartado 5451
San Juan, Puerto Rico 00906

Ediciones Librería Internacional
Apartado 23142, University Station
San Juan, Puerto Rico 00931

Editorial Club de la Prensa
Edificio González Padín
San Juan, Puerto Rico

Editorial Coquí
Apartado 21992, University Station
San Juan, Puerto Rico 00931

Editorial Cordillera
Avenida F. D. Roosevelt 237
Hato Rey, Puerto Rico 00919

Editorial Edil
Apartado 23088, University Station
Río Piedras, Puerto Rico 00931

Editorial Universitaria
Universidad de Puerto Rico—Apartado X
San Juan, Puerto Rico 00931

Editorial Xaguey
Apartado 22736
Río Piedras, Puerto Rico 00931

Francisco N. Castagnet, Inc.
Apartado 2506
Old San Juan Station
San Juan, Puerto Rico 00903

Heffernan Supply Co.
P. O. Box 5309
San Antonio, Texas 78201

Iaconi Book Imports
300 a Pennsylvania
San Francisco, California 94107

Instituto de Cultura Puertorriqueña
Apartado 4184
San Juan, Puerto Rico 00905

Inter American University of Puerto Rico
Apartado 1293
Hato Rey, Puerto Rico 00919

Las Americas Publishing Co.
40-22 Twentythird Street
Long Island, New York 11101

Librería Campos
San Francisco 266
San Juan, Puerto Rico

Librería Estrella Roja
Apartado Postal 2583
San Juan, Puerto Rico

Librería Internacional, Inc.
Saldaña 3
Río Piedras, Puerto Rico 00925

Puerto Rican Heritage Publications Inc.
802 Flushing Avenue
Brooklyn, New York 11206

Renaissance Editors
33 East 60 Street
New York, New York 10022

Spanish Book Corporation of America
Rockefeller Center Promenade
610 Fifth Avenue
New York, New York 10020

Spanish Music Center
319 West 48 Street
New York, New York 10030

Stechert-Hafner's Latin American Cooperative Acquisitions Program (LACAP)
31 East 10 Street
New York, New York 10003

The Rican Journal
P. O. Box 11039
Chicago, Illinois 60611

Troutman Press
Sharon, Connecticut 06069

Subject Index

Author Index

Title Index